Collin College Library
SPRING CREEK CAMPUS
Plano, Texas 75074

WITHDRAWN

HQ   Boles, Janet K.,
1115   1944-
B65
2004   Historical dictionary
        of feminism.
   $95.00

HISTORICAL DICTIONARIES OF RELIGIONS, PHILOSOPHIES, AND MOVEMENTS
Jon Woronoff, Series Editor

1. *Buddhism,* by Charles S. Prebish, 1993
2. *Mormonism,* by Davis Bitton, 1994. *Out of print. See No. 32.*
3. *Ecumenical Christianity,* by Ans Joachim van der Bent, 1994
4. *Terrorism,* by Sean Anderson and Stephen Sloan, 1995. *Out of print. See No. 41.*
5. *Sikhism,* by W. H. McLeod, 1995
6. *Feminism,* by Janet K. Boles and Diane Long Hoeveler, 1995. *Out of print. See No. 52.*
7. *Olympic Movement,* by Ian Buchanan and Bill Mallon, 1995. *Out of print. See No. 39.*
8. *Methodism,* by Charles Yrigoyen Jr. and Susan E. Warrick, 1996
9. *Orthodox Church,* by Michael Prokurat, Alexander Golitzin, and Michael D. Peterson, 1996
10. *Organized Labor,* by James C. Docherty, 1996. *Out of print. See No. 50.*
11. *Civil Rights Movement,* by Ralph E. Luker, 1997
12. *Catholicism,* by William J. Collinge, 1997
13. *Hinduism,* by Bruce M. Sullivan, 1997
14. *North American Environmentalism,* by Edward R. Wells and Alan M. Schwartz, 1997
15. *Welfare State,* by Bent Greve, 1998
16. *Socialism,* by James C. Docherty, 1997
17. *Bahá'í Faith,* by Hugh C. Adamson and Philip Hainsworth, 1998
18. *Taoism,* by Julian F. Pas in cooperation with Man Kam Leung, 1998
19. *Judaism,* by Norman Solomon, 1998
20. *Green Movement,* by Elim Papadakis, 1998
21. *Nietzscheanism,* by Carol Diethe, 1999
22. *Gay Liberation Movement,* by Ronald J. Hunt, 1999
23. *Islamic Fundamentalist Movements in the Arab World, Iran, and Turkey,* by Ahmad S. Moussalli, 1999
24. *Reformed Churches,* by Robert Benedetto, Darrell L. Guder, and Donald K. McKim, 1999
25. *Baptists,* by William H. Brackney, 1999
26. *Cooperative Movement,* by Jack Shaffer, 1999
27. *Reformation and Counter-Reformation,* by Hans J. Hillerbrand, 2000
28. *Shakers,* by Holley Gene Duffield, 2000

29. *United States Political Parties,* by Harold F. Bass Jr., 2000
30. *Heidegger's Philosophy,* by Alfred Denker, 2000
31. *Zionism,* by Rafael Medoff and Chaim I. Waxman, 2000
32. *Mormonism,* 2nd ed., by Davis Bitton, 2000
33. *Kierkegaard's Philosophy,* by Julia Watkin, 2001
34. *Hegelian Philosophy,* by John W. Burbidge, 2001
35. *Lutheranism,* by Günther Gassmann in cooperation with Duane H. Larson and Mark W. Oldenburg, 2001
36. *Holiness Movement,* by William Kostlevy, 2001
37. *Islam,* by Ludwig W. Adamec, 2001
38. *Shinto,* by Stuart D. B. Picken, 2002
39. *Olympic Movement,* 2nd ed., by Ian Buchanan and Bill Mallon, 2001
40. *Slavery and Abolition,* by Martin A. Klein, 2002
41. *Terrorism,* 2nd ed., by Sean Anderson and Stephen Sloan, 2002
42. *New Religious Movements,* by George D. Chryssides, 2001
43. *Prophets in Islam and Judaism,* by Scott B. Noegel and Brannon M. Wheeler, 2002
44. *The Friends (Quakers),* by Margery Post Abbott, Mary Ellen Chijioke, Pink Dandelion, and John William Oliver, Jr., 2003
45. *Lesbian Liberation Movement: Still the Rage,* JoAnne Myers, 2003
46. *Descartes and Cartesian Philosophy,* by Roger Ariew, Dennis Des Chene, Douglas M. Jesseph, Tad M. Schmaltz, and Theo Verbeek, 2003
47. *Witchcraft,* by Michael D. Bailey, 2003
48. *Unitarian Universalism,* by Mark W. Harris, 2004
49. *New Age Movements,* by Michael York, 2004
50. *Organized Labor,* 2nd Ed., by James C. Docherty, 2004
51. *Utopianism,* by James M. Morris and Andrea L. Kross, 2004
52. *Feminism,* 2nd Ed., by Janet K. Boles and Diane Long Hoeveler, 2004
53. *Jainism,* by Kristi L. Wiley, 2004.
54. *Wittgenstein's Philosophy,* by Duncan Richter, 2004.

Historical Dictionary of Feminism

Second Edition

Janet K. Boles
Diane Long Hoeveler

Historical Dictionaries of Religions, Philosophies, and Movements, No. 52

The Scarecrow Press, Inc.
Lanham, Maryland • Toronto • Oxford
2004

SCARECROW PRESS, INC.

Published in the United States of America
by Scarecrow Press, Inc.
A wholly owned subsidiary of
The Rowman & Littlefield Publishing Group, Inc.
4501 Forbes Boulevard, Suite 200, Lanham, Maryland 20706
www.scarecrowpress.com

PO Box 317
Oxford
OX2 9RU, UK

Copyright © 2004 by Janet K. Boles and Diane Long Hoeveler

All rights reserved. No part of this publication may be reproduced, stored in a retrieval system, or transmitted in any form or by any means, electronic, mechanical, photocopying, recording, or otherwise, without the prior permission of the publisher.

British Library Cataloguing in Publication Information Available

Library of Congress Cataloging-in-Publication Data

Boles, Janet K., 1944–
 Historical dictionary of feminism / Janet K. Boles, Diane Long Hoeveler. — 2nd ed.
  p. cm. — (Historical dictionaries of religions, philosophies, and movements ; no. 52)
 Includes bibliographical references.
 ISBN 0-8108-4946-1 (alk. paper)
 1. Feminism—Dictionaries. I. Hoeveler, Diane Long. II. Title. III. Series.

HQ1115.B65 2004
305.42'03—dc22
                    2004000060

♾™ The paper used in this publication meets the minimum requirements of American National Standard for Information Sciences—Permanence of Paper for Printed Library Materials, ANSI/NISO Z39.48-1992.
Manufactured in the United States of America.

Dedicated to our children

Christine and Nick
Emily and John

Contents

Editor's Foreword: Jon Woronoff	ix
Preface	xi
Acknowledgments	xiii
Reader's Note	xv
Acronyms and Abbreviations	xvii
Chronology	xxiv
Introduction	1
THE DICTIONARY	25
Bibliography	361
I. Reference Material (Bibliographies, Encyclopedias, Dictionaries, and Almanacs)	362
II. Feminist Journals	366
III. Feminist Web Sites	369
IV. Feminism—General	370
V. Women of Color Feminism	372
VI. Global Feminism	374
VII. Ecofeminism	375
VIII. Liberal Feminism	376
IX. Marxist Feminism	377
X. Postmodern Feminist Thought	378
XI. Radical Feminism	379
A. Reproduction	379
B. Mothering	379
C. Gender and Sexuality	380
D. Pornography	381
E. Lesbianism	382
XII. Socialist Feminism	383
XIII. Feminist/Women's Movement	383
A. Asia/Mideast/Africa	386

B. Australia/New Zealand 387
  C. Europe/Great Britain 388
  D. Latin America 391
  E. Russia/Soviet Union 392
  F. United States/Canada 393
  G. Men and Feminism/The Men's Movement 397
  H. AntiFeminism 398
  I. Third Wave Feminism 399
XIV. Anthropology and Sociology 400
XV. Arts, Architecture, and Aesthetics 402
XVI. Communication 405
XVII. Economics/Labor Movement 406
XVIII. History 407
XIX. Law/Feminist Jurisprudence 411
XX. Literature 414
XXI. Mythology 419
XXII. Pedagogy and Research 420
XXIII. Philosophy 423
XXIV. Psychoanalytic Feminism 425
XXV. Psychology 427
XXVI. Religion 428
XXVII. Science/Medicine 433
XXVIII. Social Work and Feminist Therapy 435

About the Authors 437

Editor's Foreword

Feminism has a very long history. Although the present-day activities and organizations are most familiar, they build on actions, pioneers, and role models that reach back through the centuries and even into antiquity and the biblical era. Over this time, the movement has undergone many changes and mutations, focusing on different goals at different times and adopting different tactics and strategies to attain them under different circumstances. Today it is broader and more varied than ever. It is also more global. Although much of the news still comes from the United States and Europe, there are activists and participants in every country on every continent, often working out their own solutions to their own problems but increasingly with the support of comrades around the world.

The length, depth, and breadth of the feminist movement is such that even those most deeply involved will not know some of what has gone before or has been done elsewhere. They may not even realize the extent and diversity of what is being achieved now. These are good reasons for publishing a revised and expanded edition of the *Historical Dictionary of Feminism*. Such a reference work can bring together, in a compact form, many of the strands. They include background on persons, organizations, campaigns and court cases, goals, and achievements. Despite some emphasis on the United States and Europe, where much of the action has been concentrated, there is considerably more material this time on other parts of the world and even on reactions among men and nonfeminist (even antifeminist) women. The movement is summed up in an introduction and traced in a chronology. Further sources of information are provided in an extensive bibliography.

This second edition grew out of a more collective first edition and was written by its lead authors, Janet K. Boles and Diane Long Hoeveler. Both of them are professors at Marquette University, one teaching political science, the other literature, in each case with an emphasis on the role and status of women. Both have also lectured and written extensively on feminism and feminist literary criticism. Meanwhile, they have greatly expanded their own understanding of the movement into other sectors, since this edition is substantially broader in its coverage of the many varied aspects and also the many different countries involved. This *Historical Dictionary of Feminism* includes numerous updated entries and entirely new ones as well as a thoroughly revised bibliography and more complete introduction and chronology. It is not quite a "new" book but it comes close to that, and it is certainly a very informative and insightful one.

Jon Woronoff
Series Editor

Preface

We are both committed feminists who chose to explore the then-newly emerging field of women's studies in our dissertations or early scholarship. One of us became active in the national feminist movement as a graduate student and later within the women's caucuses of her discipline, an engagement that has enriched her teaching, scholarship, and life for more than 25 years. The other has published extensively on feminist approaches to literature and served as coordinator of the Women's Studies Program at Marquette University for the past 10 years.

Although neither of us ever aspired to writing a dictionary of feminism, the response to the first edition was very encouraging. The small number of reviews that reference works receive were positive. But most satisfying was the adoption of the dictionary as a required textbook in at least one introductory course in women's studies, where students critiqued and debated our definitions. We are grateful to Jon Woronoff and to Scarecrow for a chance to revise this volume. In this new edition we were able to correct some of our errors and omissions, although no work of this size can ever do justice to feminism as philosophy and movement in all countries and in all periods. More substantively, we welcomed the opportunity to document the feminist movement of the 21st century. The globalization of the movement, the maturing of third wave feminism, and the increasing importance of electronic resources for organizing and communicating are addressed here. Revised editions often promise greater changes than are apparent to the reader. We hope that those familiar with the previous edition will note the many new and revised entries, a more internationally focused introduction, an expanded chronology, and an updated bibliography that is both more compact and more inclusive in its attention to feminist online resources and periodicals.

As in the first edition, we offer this *Historical Dictionary of Feminism* to our readers as a useful and succinct handbook of information about the history of the feminist movement. In doing so, we wish to pay tribute to the struggles of all those who have gone before us, individually or collectively, to change and improve the living conditions for women in the world.

Acknowledgments

The first edition of this dictionary involved a collaborative effort by the faculty of Marquette University. Although women's studies has traditionally been associated with the principle of collaboration, the other dictionaries on the subject then were not collaborative projects and did not attempt the same sort of interdisciplinary enterprise. By tapping the expertise of faculty in social work, management, engineering, law, nursing, education, communication, history, theology, languages, classics, English, philosophy, political science, anthropology, sociology, and psychology, we gained the many different voices that make up the contemporary feminist movement.

Although, as in the first edition, we as co-authors were not able to incorporate all of their submissions as written in this new edition (and in almost all cases have extensively edited or expanded the retained material), we wish to thank our present and past colleagues in all the above fields for their earlier contributions: Raquel Aguilú de Murphy, Rebecca Bardwell, Patricia Bradford, Lance Grahn, Carla Hay, Christine Firer Hinze, Susan Hopwood, Alice B. Kehoe, Christine L. Krueger, Courtney L. Marlaire, Patricia Marquardt, Kathleen McInnis-Dittrich, Sharon Pace, Georgia Pappanastos, Anne Pasero, John S. Pustejovsky, Belle Ragins, Krista Ratcliffe, Susan Riedel, Eufemia Sánchez de la Calle, Mary Anne Siderits, Gladys Simandl, Nancy Snow, Helen Sterk, Terry Tobin, Rose Trupiano, Lynn Turner, Carolyn Wells, Phoebe Williams, Holly Wilson, and Christine M. Wiseman.

We have also incurred debts to our graduate and undergraduate research assistants, supported by the Departments of English and Political Science as well as the Marquette University Women's Studies Program, for their work on this edition. Brooke Baenen, David Gilbert, John LeJeune, Sarah Stefenko, Jake Stratman, Carrie Wadman, Brandon Wilkening, and Nathanial Ziarek were untiring in fact-checking, document management, and all the other tasks we assigned to them.

The preparation of this edition has been facilitated by the electronic newsletters from the Feminist Majority, the National Organization for Women, the National Women's Political Caucus, the Wisconsin Women's Network, and Women's eNews. These were a vital supplement to the scholarship that appears in the bibliography.

Reader's Note

The *Historical Dictionary of Feminism* is organized so that entries are arranged alphabetically, and readers should know that 75 percent of the entries in this *Dictionary* have been newly written or revised for this second edition. The reader can also more fully explore a topic by using the cross-references provided in many entries, which are printed in **boldface** type within the entry. More information available on the same or related matters is provided at the end of an entry under See *also*. The reader is also directed to the term used here for an entry through the use of *See* references. We use a direct form of entry for discussing many feminist topics (e.g., see "feminist bookstores," not "bookstores, feminist").

As this book has been written for an English-speaking audience, we have provided foreign book titles in conjunction with their English translations. When the original title is available in English translation we have supplied that title in parenthesis and italics. If the book or periodical article has not been translated into English, then we provide a translation of the title in parentheses, no italics.

In the introduction, we have written an overview of the history and development of feminism as a movement and a philosophy. This should assist the reader in placing the entries of the dictionary within the larger context of the central concept.

We have also included an extensive bibliography at the end of the dictionary, organized in a way to maximize its usability. This bibliography also contains newly published sources, with an emphasis on global and third wave feminism, both new developments in the field. For further details, see the introductory essay that precedes the entries of the bibliography.

Acronyms and Abbreviations

AAUW	American Association of University Women
ABC	Act for Better Child Care
ACFODE	Action for Development
ACWF	All-China Women's Federation
ACLU-RFP	American Civil Liberties Union Reproductive Freedom Project
ACLU-WRP	American Civil Liberties Union Women's Rights Project
AERA	American Equal Rights Association
AFDC	Aid to Families with Dependent Children
AI	Artificial Insemination
AIDS	Acquired Immune Deficiency Syndrome
AIM	Action, Information, Motivation
AIWC	All-India Women's Conference
ALIMUPER	Acción para la Liberación de la Mujer Peruana (Action for the Liberation of Peruvian Women)
AMNLAE	Asociación de Mujeres Nicaragüenses "Luisa Amanda Espinoza" (Association of Nicaraguan Women)
ANC	African National Congress
AWARE	Association of Women for Action and Research
AWC	Afghanistan Women's Council
AWO	Arab Women's Organization
AWSA	American Woman Suffrage Association
AWSA	Arab Women's Solidarity Association
BFOQ	Bona Fide Occupational Qualification
BPW/USA	National Federation of Business and Professional Women's Clubs
BWTA	British Women's Temperance Association
BWU	Bulgarian Women's Union
CAC	Citizens' Advisory Council on the Status of Women
CAP	Contraceptive Action Programme
CAWP	Center for the American Woman and Politics
CCWI	Congressional Caucus for Women's Issues
CEDAW	Convention on the Elimination of All Forms of Discrimination Against Women
CEFEMINA	Centro Feminista de Información y Acción (Feminist

ACRONYMS AND ABBREVIATIONS

	Center for Information and Action)
CEW	Committee for the Equality of Women
CISW	Commission on Improving the Status of Women
CLUW	Coalition of Labor Union Women
CNM	Certified Nurse Midwife
COMADRES	Comité de Madres (Committee of Mothers)
COYOTE	Call Off Your Old Tired Ethics
CR	Consciousness-Raising
CRA	Civil Rights Act
CSM	Committee of Soldiers' Mothers of Russia
CSW	Committee of Soviet Women
CSWI	Committee on the Status of Women in India
CU	Congressional Union
CVS	Chorionic Villi Sampling
CWA	Concerned Women for America
CWGL	Center for Women's Global Leadership
CWLU	Chicago Women's Liberation Union
DAWN	Development Alternatives with Women for a New Era
DES	Diethylstilbestrol
DF	Deutscher Frauenrat (German Women's Council)
DOAW	Democratic Organization of Afghan Women
DSM	Diagnostic and Statistical Manual
EC	Emergency Contraception
ECOA	Equal Credit Opportunity Act
EEOC	Equal Employment Opportunity Commission
EF	Eagle Forum
EFU	Egyptian Feminist Union
EGE	Enosis Gynaikon Elladas (Union of Greek Women)
EMILY	Early Money Is Like Yeast
EOC	Equal Opportunities Commission
EPA	Equal Pay Act
ERA	Equal Rights Amendment
ERT	Estrogen Replacement Therapy
EWL	European Women's Lobby
FACE	Freedom of Access to Clinic Entrances
FACT	Feminist AntiCensorship Taskforce
FALTA	Feministskaia Al'ternativa (Feminist Alternative)
FAOW	Forum Against Oppression of Women
FFL	Feminists for Life
FFQ	Fédération des Femmes du Québec (Quebec Women's

	Federation)
FGM	Female Genital Mutilation
FKD	Fusen Kakutoku Domei (League for Woman's Suffrage)
FMC	Federación de Mujeres Cubanas (Federation of Cuban Women)
FMF	Feminist Majority Foundation
FMLA	Family and Medical Leave Act
FOMWAN	Federation of Muslim Women's Associations of Nigeria
FOS	Fear of Success
FR	Féministes Révolutionnaires (Revolutionary Feminists)
FRM	Fathers' Rights Movement
FWRM	Fiji Women's Rights Movement
GABRIELA	General Assembly Binding Women for Reforms, Integrity, Equality, Leadership, and Action
GAM	Grupo de Apoyo Mutuo (Mutual Support Group for the Appearance, Alive, of Our Children, Spouses, Parents, and Brothers and Sisters)
GFW	Global Fund for Women
GFWC	General Federation of Women's Clubs
GHB	Gamma Hydroxybutyric Acid
HRT	Hormone Replacement Therapy
IAW	International Alliance of Women
ICC	International Criminal Court
ICRW	International Center for Research on Women
ICW	International Council of Women
IUD	Intrauterine Device
IVF	In Vitro Fertilization
IWF	Independent Women's Forums
IWFL	Irish Women's Franchise League
IWLM	Irish Women's Liberation Movement
IWRAW	International Women's Rights Action Watch
IWU	Irishwomen United
IWY	International Women's Year
JFW	Justice for Women
JOBS	Job Opportunity and Basic Skills Program
KOWANI	Kongres Wanita Indonesia (Congress of Indonesian Women)
KWAU	Korean Women's Associations United
LDF	Ligue du Droit des Femmes (Women's Rights League)
LEAF	Women's Legal Education and Action Fund

LK	Liga Kobiet Polskich (Polish Women's League)
LWV	League of Women Voters
LYBD	Love Your Body Day
MCGS	Moscow Center for Gender Studies
MDF	Mouvement Démocratique Féminin (Democratic Feminist Movement)
MDM	Movimiento Democrático de Mujeres (Women's Democratic Movement)
MEMCH	Movimiento pro Emancipación de la Mujer Chilena (Movement for the Emancipation of Chilean Women)
MFPF	Mouvement Français pour le Planning Familial (French Movement for Family Planning)
MLD	Movimento di la Liberazione della Donna (Woman's Liberation Movement)
MLF	Mouvement pour la Libération des Femmes (Women's Liberation Movement)
MLM	Movimiento para la Liberación de la Mujer (Women's Liberation Movement)
MLWS	Men's League for Women's Suffrage
MM	Moral Majority
MOMUPO	Movimiento de Mujeres Pobladoras (Movement of Shantytown Women)
MPU	Men's Political Union for Women's Enfranchisement
MUDE	Mujeres por la Democracia (Women for Democracy)
MVM	Man-Vrouw-Maatschappij (Man-Woman-Society)
MWR	All-Russian Sociopolitical Movement of Women of Russia
NAC	National Abortion Campaign
NAC	National Action Committee on the Status of Women
NACW	National Association of Colored Women
NACW	National Association of Commissions for Women
NARAL	National Abortion and Reproductive Rights Action League
NAWSA	National American Woman Suffrage Association
NBFO	National Black Feminist Organization
NCL	National Consumers League
NCNW	National Council of Negro Women
NCWK	National Council of Women of Kenya
NCWO	National Council of Women's Organizations
NCWS	National Council of Women's Societies

ACRONYMS AND ABBREVIATIONS • xxi

NEA	National Endowment for the Arts
NEWW	Network of East-West Women
NFIW	National Federation of Indian Women
NIH	National Institutes of Health
NOMAS	National Organization for Men Against Sexism
NOW	National Organization for Women
NRLC	National Right to Life Committee
NSWS	National Society for Women's Suffrage
NUSEC	National Union of Societies for Equal Citizenship
NUWSS	National Union of Women's Suffrage Societies
NWAF	National Women's Aid Federation
NWCI	National Women's Council of Ireland
NWHN	National Women's Health Network
NWP	National Woman's Party
NWPC	National Women's Political Caucus
NWRO	National Welfare Rights Organization
NWSA	National Woman Suffrage Association
NYRF	New York Radical Feminists
NYRW	New York Radical Women
OSA	Operation Save America
OWAAD	Organization of Women of African and Asian Descent
OWL	Older Women's League
PAC	Political Action Committee
PAG	Pluralistic Action Groups for Equal Rights of Men and Women
PASS	Post-Abortion Stress Syndrome
PBA	Partial-Birth Abortions
PC	Politically Correct
PCSW	President's Commission on the Status of Women
PDA	Pregnancy Discrimination Act
PFA	Platform for Action
PK	Promise Keepers
PMDD	Premenstrual Dysphoric Disorder
PMS	Premenstrual Syndrome
PPD	Postpartum Depression
PPFA	Planned Parenthood Federation of America
PPP	Postpartum Psychosis
PRWORA	Personal Responsibility and Work Opportunity Reconciliation Act
RAWA	Revolutionary Association of the Women of Afghanistan

RCRC	Religious Coalition for Reproductive Choice
RCSW	Royal Commission on the Status of Women in Canada
REAL	Realistic, Equal, Active, for Life
RICO	Racketeer Influenced and Corrupt Organizations Act
RT	Reproductive Technologies
SAFO	Svobodnaia Assotsiatsiia Feministskikh Organizatzii (Free Association of Feminist Organizations)
SBS	Southall Black Sisters
SCSW	State Commissions on the Status of Women
SIGI	Sisterhood Is Global Institute
SinC	Sisters in Crime
SIS	Sisters in Islam
SOFA	Solidarite Fanm Ayisyen (Haitian Women in Solidarity)
SPUC	Society for the Protection of the Unborn Child
SRZh	Soiuz Ravnopraviia Zhenshchin (All-Russian Union of Equal Rights for Women)
SVF	Schweizerischer Verband für Frauenrechte (Swiss Association for Women's Rights)
SWC	Status of Women Canada
TANF	Temporary Assistance to Needy Families
TLW	True Love Waits
TSS	Toxic Shock Syndrome
TWLM	Toronto Women's Liberation Movement
UDI	Unione delle Donne Italiane (Italian Women's Union)
UFCS	Union Féminine Civique et Sociale (Women's Civic and Social Union)
UFSF	Union Française pour le Suffrage des Femmes (French Union for Women's Suffrage)
UFV	Unabhängiger Frauenverband (Independent Women's Association)
UNIFEM	United Nations Development Fund for Women
VAWA	Violence Against Women Act
VFA	Veteran Feminists of America
WAC	Women's Action Coalition
WAC	Women's Action Committee
WAG	Women's Action Group
WAP	Women Against Pornography
WCF	Women's Campaign Fund
WCTU	Woman's Christian Temperance Union
WDU	Women's Democratic Union

WEAL	Women's Equity Action League
WEDO	Women's Environmental and Development Organization
WEEA	Women's Educational Equity Act
WEL	Women's Electoral Lobby
WFL	Women's Freedom League
WFN	Women's Freedom Network
WIN	Women in Nigeria
WISH	Women in the Senate and House
WITCH	Women's International Terrorist Conspiracy from Hell
WJCC	Women's Joint Congressional Committee
WLM	Women's Liberation Movement
WLUML	Women Living Under Muslim Laws
WNC	Women's National Coalition
WNC	Women's National Commission
WOI	Women's Organization of Iran
WOR	Women of Russia
WOW	Women on Waves
WRC	White Ribbon Campaign
WSPU	Women's Social and Political Union
WTUL	Women's Trade Union League
WUR	Women's Union of Russia
WWC	Women Workers' Council
WWCTU	World's Woman's Christian Temperance Union

Chronology

1405   Christine de Pizan completes *The Book of the City of Women.*

1501   *The Book of Margery Kempe* appears.

1549   Marguerite de Navarre publishes *L'Heptaméron,* a series of 72 short stories in which gender issues are explored.

1589   Jane Anger publishes a pamphlet that advances the idea of female superiority.

1611   Aemilia Bassano Lanyer's *Salve Deus Rex Judaeorum,* 11 short dedications to women (Eve, Pilate's wife), is published.

1621   Lady Mary Wroth publishes her *Urania,* provoking scandal in England.

1622   Frenchwoman Marie de Gournay publishes *The Equality of Men and Women.*

1637-1647   Maria de Zayas y Sotomajoy publishes *Novelas Amorosas* and its sequel, *Parte Segunda,* an examination of the lives of women in Spain.

1648   Margaret Brent appears before the Maryland State Assembly to request the right to vote twice, first as a landowner and again as Lord Baltimore's attorney.

1653   Margaret of Cavendish, Duchess of Newcastle, begins publishing her 14 different works on women in England.

1660   **1 June:** Quaker preacher Mary Dyer is hanged on Boston Common for subversion of male authority in church and state.

1670   Aphra Behn's dramas begin appearing on British stage, depicting women in active social roles.

1692 **10 June:** Bridget Bishop is hanged, the first official execution of the Salem, Massachusetts, witch trials.

1694 Mary Astell calls for an institution for female education similar to that for men in her *Serious Proposal to the Ladies*.

1776 **31 March:** Abigail Adams writes her husband John, asking that women's rights be included in the new code of laws about to be drafted for American independence.

1791 Olympe de Gouges's *The Declaration of the Rights of Woman and the Female Citizen* is published. **Summer:** Etta Palm d'Aelders of the Netherlands asks for equal rights for women and equal education for girls in her address to the National Assembly of France.

1792 *A Vindication of the Rights of Woman* by Mary Wollstonecraft is published.

1793 **30 October:** Women are barred from political activity in France.

1810 Women in Sweden are given access to trade and sales occupations.

1825 William Thompson and Anna Wheeler in *Appeal of One Half of the Human Race against the Pretensions of the Other Half* advocate woman suffrage.

1829 Suttee is prohibited in the Bengal presidency by the British.

1832 **21 September:** Maria Stewart becomes the first American woman to speak (on women's rights) before an audience of both men and women.

1840 **12 June:** Conflict about women's public role emerges at the World AntiSlavery Convention in London.

1845 *Women in the Nineteenth Century* by Margaret Fuller is published.

1848 **19-20 July:** A women's rights convention is held at Seneca Falls, New York.

1851 A Prussian law forbids women from joining political parties or attending meetings where political subjects are discussed. **28-29 May:** Sojourner Truth delivers her "Ain't I a Woman?" speech at an Ohio abolition convention.

1867 **20 May:** John Stuart Mill offers a motion to grant woman suffrage in the House of Commons.

1868 King Mongkut of Thailand gives women the right to choose their marriage partners and prohibits a husband from selling his wife without her consent. **30 October:** The National Society for Women's Suffrage is founded in England.

1869 *The Subjection of Women* by John Stuart Mill (England) and *The Rights of Women* by Léon Richier (France) are published. **May:** The National Woman Suffrage Association is formed in the United States. **24-25 November:** The American Woman Suffrage Association is formed in the United States.

1871 **11 January:** Victoria Chaflin Woodhull addresses a committee of Congress (on woman suffrage). **18 January:** Paragraph 218 of the German Penal Code makes abortion punishable by up to five years' imprisonment and prohibits the sale and use of contraceptives.

1873 The US Supreme Court (in *Bradwell v. Illinois*) upholds the exclusion of women from the practice of law, using "separate spheres" ideology. **18 June:** Susan B. Anthony is fined $100 for attempting to vote for president.

1874 **18 November:** Frances Willard founds the Woman's Christian Temperance Union.

1877 **July:** The trial of Annie Besant and Charles Bradlaugh for distribution of a birth control pamphlet opens in London.

1878 **July:** An International Women's Rights Congress is held in France.

1879 *Woman and Socialism* by August Bebel is published.

1882 Dr. Aletta Jacobs opens the world's first birth control clinic in Amsterdam. **16 August:** The Married Women's Property Act is passed in England.

1884 Friedrich Engels's *The Origin of the Family, Private Property and the State* is published.

1886 *The High Caste Hindu Woman* by Pandita Ramabai analyzes the oppression of women in India.

1893 **19 September:** New Zealand becomes the first nation to enfranchise women.

1895 The second volume of *The Woman's Bible* is published. **27 April:** the word "feminist" appears for the first time in a book review in the *Athenaeum*.

1897 In Japan, Yukichi Fukuzawa in *The New Greater Learning for Women* challenges Confucian teaching about women.

1898 Charlotte Perkins Gilman publishes *Women and Economics*.

1899 Qasim Amin publishes *Tahrir al-mar'a* (The Emancipation of Women) in Egypt.

1900 *The Woman Worker* is published by Nadezhda Krupskaya in Russia.

1902 Marguerite Souley-Darqué teaches the first women's studies course in Paris. **2 February:** The Empress of China issues a decree against foot-binding.

1904 **June:** The International Woman Suffrage Alliance is formed.

1906 **7 March:** Finland becomes the first European nation to adopt woman suffrage.

1908 Norway passes an equal pay law. **December:** The All-Russian Conference of Feminists attracts 1,045 delegates.

1911 **18 March:** The first celebration of International Women's Day is held in Europe.

1913 **4 June:** English suffragist Emily Davison is killed when she throws herself under the horse of King George V.

1916 **13-16 January:** The first Mexican Feminist Congress is held. **June:** The National Woman's Party is founded in the United States.

1918 **February:** English women over 30 receive the vote. **24 May:** Canadian women of English and French extraction are enfranchised in federal elections.

1919 Pope Benedict XV endorses woman suffrage. **19 March:** Huda Sha'rawi leads demonstrations of veiled Egyptian women in support of the nationalist cause. **28 June:** The Versailles Peace Treaty promises French women equal pay for equal work. **28 November:** Lady Nancy Astor is elected to the British House of Commons as its first woman member. **23 December:** The Sex Disqualification (Removal) Act allows Englishwomen to be lawyers, jurors, judges, and members of Parliament.

1920 **12-18 February:** The League of Women Voters is established in the United States. **26 May:** France gives a medal to women having at least five children. **31 July:** France bars contraceptive devices and abortions. **26 August:** The Nineteenth Amendment grants US women suffrage. **November:** The Union of Soviet Socialist Republics becomes the first European nation to legalize abortion.

1923 **16 March:** Huda Sha'rawi founds the Egyptian Feminist Union. **December:** The Equal Rights Amendment is introduced in the US Congress.

CHRONOLOGY • xxix

1924 December: María Jesús Alvarado Rivero of Peru is imprisoned and later exiled because of her campaign for married women's rights.

1925 September: Elvira Carrillo Puerto is elected to the Mexican Chamber of Deputies but is denied the seat on the basis of sex.

1929 *A Room of One's Own* by Virginia Woolf in England and *The Women's Question* by Phan Boi Chau in Vietnam are published. **18 October:** The Privy Council rules that women are persons in the Canadian Persons case.

1930 20 October: Vietnam Women's Union is formed to advocate for participation in national defense and development.

1931 February: German women begin an "I have aborted" campaign against Paragraph 218. **15 May:** Pope Pius XI calls for a ban on the employment of married women to protect women and the family.

1936 8 January: Iran becomes the first Muslim country to ban the veil.

1937 30 April: Filipino women approve woman suffrage in an all-female plebiscite.

1944 April: France enfranchises women. **September:** The Italian Women's Union is founded.

1946 21 June: The United Nations Commission on the Status of Women is established.

1947 Princess Aicha of Morocco unveils and reads a feminist speech. Marynia Farnham and Ferdinand Lundberg in *Modern Women: The Lost Sex* argue that working women have lost their femininity and increased male alcoholism and juvenile delinquency.

1948 1 January: The new Italian Constitution grants women equality and the right to work.

1949 Simone de Beauvoir publishes *The Second Sex*, in which the phrase "women's liberation" is first used.

1951 **January:** Members of Bint al-Nil (Daughters of the Nile), an Egyptian women's political party, briefly occupy parliament demanding representation for women.

1952 **20 December:** The UN General Assembly adopts the Convention on the Political Rights of Women.

1954 **15 April:** Margaret Sanger, in a speech urging Japanese women to use contraception, becomes the first woman to address the Diet.

1955 **2 August:** Judaism accepts its first female cantor.

1958 **1 January:** The Treaty of Rome, which established the European Economic Community and endorsed equal pay, goes into effect.

1960 **January:** *Izvestia* reports that women comprise 45 percent of the workforce but are a majority of the Soviet Union's professionals. **24 January:** A Roman synod decrees that women with bare arms or wearing male attire will be denied the sacrements. **26 July:** Mrs. Sirimavo Bandaranaike of Ceylon becomes the first female prime minister of a modern parliamentary government.

1961 **9 May:** India outlaws the practices of brideprice and dowry. **14 December:** John F. Kennedy establishes the President's Commission on the Status of Women.

1963 **February:** *The Feminine Mystique* by Betty Friedan is published. **10 June:** The US Equal Pay Act is passed.

1964 **2 July:** Title VII of the Civil Rights Act prohibits sex discrimination in US employment. **November:** Casey Hayden and Mary King write a paper critical of the status of women in the Student Nonviolent Coordinating Committee.

1965 **March:** Two Australian women chain themselves to a footrail at a Brisbane hotel, demanding the right of women to drink in the public bar.

1966 **28-29 June:** The National Organization for Women is formed.

1967 **16 February:** The Royal Commission on the Status of Women in Canada is established. **14 July:** The Abortion Act is passed by the British Parliament. **31 August-4 September and 31 October:** The first local radical feminist groups form in Chicago and New York.

1968 Psych et Po is organized in France. **June:** Anne Koedt challenges Freudian concepts of female sexuality in her essay "The Myth of the Vaginal Orgasm." The Zurich Manifesto, issued by the Women's Liberation Movement (*Frauenbefreiungsbewegung*), denounces Swiss institutions. **7 September:** A protest of the Miss America Pageant is held. **28-30 November:** The first national women's liberation conference is held in Chicago and draws women from 37 states and Canada.

1969 **February:** The National Association for Repeal of Abortion Laws is founded in the United States. **March:** Cornell offers the first course in women's studies at a US university. **21 March:** The Redstockings hold the first speak-out (on abortion) in New York City. **October:** Zelda D'Aprano chains herself to the front doors of the Commonwealth Offices in Melbourne, protesting the Arbitration Commission's failure to award equal pay to women.

1970 These classics of new feminism are published: *Sexual Politics* by Kate Millett; *The Female Eunuch* by Germaine Greer; *Sisterhood Is Powerful* by Robin Morgan; *Our Bodies, Ourselves* by the Boston Women's Health Collective; and *The Dialectic of Sex* by Shulamith Firestone. **27 February-1 March:** The first national women's liberation conference in Great Britain is held at Ruskin College (Oxford). **March:** Dutch feminists demonstrate at a medical convention by displaying slogans written across their stomachs. **9 May:** Canadian feminists' abortion caravan arrives in Ottawa. **29 May:** The British Equal Pay Act receives the Royal Assent. **26 August:** The Women's Strike for Equality brings demonstrations in most major US cities. French feminists dedicate a wreath to the wife of the unknown soldier honored at the Arc de Triomphe. **3 December:** The first women's professional tennis tour is formed after women are suspended by the US Lawn Tennis Association for challenging gender inequality in prize money.

1971 Erin Pizzey establishes the first shelter for battered women (in Chiswick, England). **6 March:** The Irish Women's Liberation Movement releases a manifesto, "Chains or Change: The Civil Wrongs of Irish Women." **April:** A manifesto is signed by 343 prominent Frenchwomen who acknowledge having had one or more illegal abortions. **7 April:** Woman suffrage is adopted in Switzerland. **6 July:** In West Germany, 374 women sign a letter similar to the French manifesto on abortion, published in *Der Stern*. **10 July:** The National Women's Political Caucus is formed in Washington, D.C. **22 November:** The US Supreme Court (in *Reed v. Reed*) invalidates a law on the basis of sex discrimination.

1972 **22 March:** The Equal Rights Amendment is passed by the US Congress and sent to the states for ratification. **7-9 April:** The National Action Committee on the Status of Women is formed in Canada and holds its first national convention. **20-22 April:** Women protesting the exclusion of women from major art gallery exhibits hold the first National Conference for Women in the Visual Arts. **23 June:** Title IX of the Education Amendments of 1972 bans sex discrimination in all federally assisted education programs in the United States. **15 July:** *Ms.* (United States) begins publication. **October:** The trial in Bobigny, France, of a teenage girl builds public support for reform of abortion laws. **15 November:** Jeanne Martin Cissé of Guinea becomes the first woman to chair the UN Security Council.

1973 **22 January:** The US Supreme Court (in *Roe v. Wade*) establishes a woman's right to an abortion. **3 July:** The up-coming trial of "the three Marias" in Portugal stirs protests in Europe and the United States. **10 September:** Conservative Judaism allows women to be counted as part of the quorum for congregational worship. **20 September:** Billie Jean King beats Bobby Riggs in a tennis match. **24 October:** Betty Friedan meets with Pope Paul VI, who thanks her for all she has done for the women of the world. **19 December:** The Irish Supreme Court, ruling in the McGee Case, establishes the right of a woman to import contraceptives for her personal use.

1974 **2 February:** Pope Paul VI issues the *Marialis Cultus* that calls Mary a feminist. **13 May:** Italy defeats a referendum to abolish divorce. **June:** The first National Women's Music Festival is held at the University of Illinois. **12 June:** Girls are allowed to play Little League Baseball in the United States. **October:** The Royal Canadian Mounted Police admit women.

1975 The British Parliament passes the Sex Discrimination Act. *Signs* begins publication in Chicago. These groups are formed: the Eagle Forum (United States); the National Women's Aid Federation (Great Britain); and the National Abortion Campaign (Great Britain). **19 June:** The British Parliament passes the Sex Discrimination Act. **23 June-4 July:** The United Nations' first Conference on the Decade for Women is held in Mexico City. **24 October:** Ninety percent of all Icelandic women go on strike against sex discrimination. **December:** The National Women's Health Network stages its first demonstration at the US Food and Drug Administration.

1976 South Australia becomes the first government to criminalize marital rape. **January:** An article in an American Medical Association journal declares male chauvinism a certifiable psychiatric illness. **31 January:** Pope Paul VI warns women of movements for equality that can depersonalize and masculinize them. **8 March:** The International Tribunal on Crimes Against Women opens in Brussels. **8 April:** Bangladesh targets 10 percent of government jobs to women. **June:** Feminists protest "snuff films" that portray the torture and murder of women as pornographic entertainment. **Fall:** "Take Back the Night" marches are held in the major cities of Italy. **November:** *Harper's Magazine* publishes "Requiem for the Women's Movement."

1977 Princess Misha of the royal family of Saudi Arabia is publicly executed for wedding a man of her choice. **January:** The National Women's Studies Association is founded in the United States. **28 January:** Pope Paul VI approves the exclusion of women from the priesthood because they lack a natural resemblance to Christ. **25 April:** Australian Women Against Rape stage their first Anzac Day Parade action. **31 May:** Janet Guthrie becomes the first woman driver in the Indianapolis 500. **18-**

21 November: The National Women's Conference in Houston sets an agenda for women in the National Plan.

1978 **8 March:** The first Women's History Week is celebrated in Sonoma County, California. **March-September:** Five women employees at American Cyanamid are sterilized as a condition of employment under a fetal protection policy. **17 May:** The Italian Parliament adopts the most liberal abortion law in Europe after a national referendum. **7 June:** Pope Paul VI supports the use of excommunication to oppose Italy's new abortion law. **November:** The first national feminist conference on pornography is held in San Francisco.

1979 **March:** Judy Chicago's The *Dinner Party* opens at the San Francisco Museum of Art. **10 March:** Fifteen thousand Iranian women seize the Palace of Justice and demand the restoration of rights lost after the overthrow of the Shah. **2 July:** The US Mint releases the Susan B. Anthony dollar coin. **21 July:** The Women's Rights National Historic Park is dedicated in Seneca Falls, New York. **Fall:** The first feminist samizdat *Woman and Russia* appears. **September:** The Mathura Rape Case decision is announced by the Supreme Court of India. **5 December:** Sonia Johnson is excommunicated by the Mormon Church for her support of the Equal Rights Amendment. **18 December:** The UN General Assembly adopts the Convention on the Elimination of All Forms of Discrimination Against Women.

1980 **6 March:** Novelist Marguerite Yourcenar is the first woman to be elected to the French Academy since its foundation in 1635.

1981 Portugal passes a law prohibiting the use of a female image as an advertising device. **March:** Almost 25 percent of the UN's women employees report having been sexually harassed in the workplace. **22 May:** The Ministry of Women's Rights is created in France. **25 September:** Sandra Day O'Connor is appointed to the US Supreme Court. **11 December:** Twenty thousand women form a human chain around the women's peace camp at the Greenham (England) missile base.

1982 Sicilian women, widowed by the Mafia, form a group to oppose the culture of male violence and female submissiveness. Carol Gilligan publishes *In a Different Voice*. **January:** Women in Algeria present a petition with 10,000 signatures to the National Assembly and demonstrate against a proposed Family Code that would weaken women's rights. **30 June:** The deadline for ratifying the Equal Rights Amendment expires. **November:** Pakistani women protest the exclusion of women athletes from the Asian Games.

1983 **April:** The chador is made compulsory in Iran. **23 April:** Iceland's Women's Alliance becomes the first women's party to win seats in a national legislature. **30 December:** The Minneapolis City Council passes a feminist anti pornography ordinance, which is vetoed by the mayor.

1984 **13 January:** Former local television anchor Christine Craft wins $325,000 in damages for her demotion on the grounds of age, appearance, and lack of deference to men. **19 April:** Australia officially adopts a national anthem with new nonsexist language. **31 May:** Romanian President Nicolae Ceausescu requires married women to have monthly pregnancy tests in the workplace and obtain a medical explanation of their failure to bear at least four children. **1 July:** Liechtenstein becomes the last European nation to adopt woman suffrage. **19 July:** Geraldine Ferraro receives the Democratic Party's nomination for vice-president of the United States.

1985 The world's first feminist university (the Kvinneuniversitetet) is established in Loten, Norway. **17 May:** The Japanese Diet passes a bill that urges employers to adopt nondiscriminatory employment practices. **25 June:** Tracey Thurman of Connecticut is awarded $2.3 million in the first civil suit won by a battered wife. **14 December:** Wilma Mankiller becomes the first woman to lead a major American Indian tribe, the Cherokee Nation of Oklahoma.

1986 **1 April:** The first pay equity raises from the state of Washington are mailed to employees. **19 June:** The US Supreme Court rules (in *Meritor v. Vinson*) that workplace sexual harassment is illegal. *The New York Times* accepts "Ms." as a courtesy title. **30 June:** The last of the Playboy clubs closes. **4 November:** Voters in San Francisco approve a charter amendment that requires pay equity for the city workforce.

1987 **Spring:** The National Museum of Women in the Arts, the world's only museum dedicated to female artists, opens. **16 August:** In a union poll, 84 percent of Spanish woman workers report being sexually harassed. **25 November:** Queen Elizabeth II opens membership in the Most Noble Orders of the Garter and Thistle to nonroyal women.

1988 **3 February:** The New Jersey Supreme Court invalidates the surrogacy contract in the "Baby M" case. **September:** RU 486 is approved for use in France. Pope John Paul II issues an apostolic letter "On the Dignity of Women" defining women's vocations as virginity and motherhood. **October:** Wang Xingjuan establishes China's first crisis line for women. **2 December:** Benazir Bhutto becomes the first female head of an Islamic state and announces an ambitious women's rights agenda for Pakistan.

1989 **February:** Canada abolishes laws excluding women from combat. **July:** The National Organization for Women announces its interest in forming a new US political party. **2 July:** Japanese women force the resignation of the prime minister, who was accused of an affair with a geisha. **6 December:** Fourteen women engineering students at the University of Montréal are killed by a man who resented feminists in the school.

1990 **February:** The Des Moines (Iowa) *Register* fights the stigma of rape by publishing the survivor's name (with her permission). **9 February:** Namibia's new gender-neutral constitution bans sex discrimination and endorses affirmative action. **April:** The Women's Library and Information Center, devoted to feminist scholarship and activism, opens in Istanbul. **6 November:** Forty-seven Saudi Arabian women drive a few blocks in Riyadh to protest the ban on women drivers.

1991 **11 March:** Brazil's Superior Justice Tribunal rules that men may no longer use defense of honor to justify the murder of unfaithful wives or lovers. **20 March:** The US Supreme Court (in *International UAW v. Johnson Controls*) rules that employers cannot exclude fertile women from jobs to protect potential fetuses. **April:** The Women's National Coalition forms for the inclusion of women's rights in the new South African constitution. **15 May:** The Random House Webster's *College Dictionary* is published after eliminating sexist language in its definitions. **June:** Four hundred thousand Swiss women strike for equal pay. **11 October:** Before a Senate hearing, Anita Hill charges US Supreme Court nominee Clarence Thomas with sexual harassment. **31 October:** The Navy investigates charges that drunken Marine Corps pilots assaulted 26 women in a hotel hallway at the

Tailhook Association Convention. **25 November-10 December:** The first "16 Days of Activism Against Gender Violence" campaign is held.

1992   January: The "Miss Canada" beauty pageant is abolished in response to a lobbying campaign by women's groups. **27 February:** The Canadian Supreme Court (in *Regina v. Butler*) rules that pornography is defined by the harm it does to women's pursuit of equality. **13 March:** Petitions signed by more than 200,000 women from 100 countries demand that the UN make women's rights and violence against women a priority at the 1993 World Conference on Human Rights. **3 April:** China approves the "Law for the Protection of Women's Rights and Interests" that guarantees sex equality in political, economic, cultural, social, and family affairs. **5 April:** Over 750,000 participate in the pro-choice "March for Women's Lives," the largest demonstration in Washington, D.C. history. **16 April:** A district court in Japan issues that nation's first decision against sexual harassment. **May:** An Egyptian court upholds the government's dissolution of the Arab Women's Solidarity Association and the seizure of its assets after the group opposed the Gulf War. **18 July:** A mob in Zinder, Niger, attacks bars and bordellos after Muslim clerics charge that the indecent dress and immoral behavior of women are causing a drought. **8 August:** Hassiba Boulmerka of Algeria wins the Olympic gold medal for the 1,500-meter run, despite Islamic complaints about her immodest dress. **29 October:** Irish women gain the right to free access to abortion information and the right to travel abroad for an abortion.

1993   Female heads of government are chosen in Burundi, Canada, Pakistan, Poland, Rwanda, and Turkey; a woman speaker is elected in the parliament of Japan. New Zealand women begin a petition drive for equal representation in parliament on the 100th anniversary of woman suffrage. **5 February:** The US Family and Medical Leave Act is signed into law. **25 February:** Vietnam establishes the National Committee for the Advancement of Women. **28 April:** More than one million girls around the world participate in the first Take Our Daughters to Work Day. **15 June:** The United Nations' Conference on Human Development defines violence against women as a human rights violation. **August:** Pope John Paul II issues an encyclical that continues the Catholic Church ban on artificial birth control, divorce, abortion, and homosexuality. **November:** Women's rights activist Toujan Faisal becomes the first woman to be elected to the Jordanian parliament.

1994 **21 January:** A Virginia jury acquits Lorena Bobbitt, charged with cutting off her husband's penis in retaliation for earlier sexual assaults. **24 January:** Opening arguments in the murder trial of former football star O. J. Simpson are heard; alleged batterer Simpson is charged with the fatal stabbing of his ex-wife and her friend. **12 March:** The Church of England ordains its first women priests. **15 March:** The Vatican permits girls to become altar "boys." **21 March:** The US Academy Award for Best Short Documentary is won by *Defending Our Lives*, a film about women imprisoned for killing their batterers. **26 May:** The US Freedom of Access to Clinic Entrances Act becomes law. **9 June:** The Organization of American States adopts the Convention on the Prevention, Punishment and Eradication of Violence Against Women. **20 July:** Canada grants refugee status to a Somali woman based partially on her fears of female genital mutilation. **27 July:** A Michigan judge revokes the child custody of a single mother who was attending college and had placed her daughter in a day-care center; he awards custody to the biological father whose homemaker mother could care for the child. **10 August:** Feminist author Taslima Nasreen flees Bangladesh under charges of blasphemy against the Koran. **5-13 September:** Delegates to the Cairo international population conference support women's reproductive rights and safe abortions in nations where the procedure is legal. **18 September:** The victorious Social Democratic Party of Sweden offers an equal number of male and female parliamentary candidates and later appoints women to half of the cabinet positions. **December:** The first sexual harassment suit against the UN is settled for $210,000.

1995 **6-12 March:** The UN World Summit on Social Development states that the empowerment of women is essential to solving social, economic, and environmental problems. **26 May:** The US Immigration and Naturalization Service recognizes sexual violence, including rape and domestic violence, as grounds for political asylum. **14 June:** The Japanese government establishes a fund to compensate "comfort women" forced into prostitution for Japanese occupation forces during World War II. **Summer:** The first radio station solely devoted to women's issues begins broadcasting in the United Kingdom. **5 July:** An Armenian women's party receives 17 percent of the vote in the country's first post-Soviet national election and wins eight seats in parliament. **10 July:** Pope John Paul II apologizes for the church's past discrimination against women and congratulates feminists for their accomplishments. **4-15 September:** The UN's Fourth World Conference on Women is held in Beijing, China. **7 September:** US Senator Robert Packwood resigns after the Senate Ethics Committee unanimously recommends his expulsion for sexual harassment of his female staff. **November:** The US Glass Ceiling Commission reports that women and minorities are extremely underrepresented in senior management posts.

1996 **10 April:** US President Bill Clinton veteos a bill banning partial-birth abortions. **June:** The International Criminal Tribunal prosecuting war crimes in the former Yugoslavia defines sexual assault as a crime against humanity. **13 June:** Fauzinga Kasinga, who fled Togo to escape genital mutilation, is granted political asylum by the US Board of Immigration Appeals. **28 September:** The US Congress agrees to move a statue of Lucretia Mott, Susan B. Anthony, and Elizabeth Cady Stanton from the Capitol Crypt, where it sat for over 75 years, to the Rotunda. **12 October:** The US Congress outlaws the possession of Rohypnol, the date rape drug. **5 November:** California voters approve a law that prohibits race and gender considerations in public employment, contracting, and college admissions. **21 December:** Thailand's law imposing higher penalties for pimps, brothel owners, and consumers of prostitution becomes effective.

1997 **January:** Harpist Anna Lelkes becomes the first female member of the 155-year-old Vienna Philharmonic Orchestra. **27 February:** A constitutional amendment permitting divorce goes into effect in Ireland, leaving Malta the only European nation where divorce is illegal. **March:** Malaysia's National Museum opens an exhibition on infidelity that features tools used in various societies to torture female offenders. **4 April:** Peru repeals a 1924 law that allowed rapists to avoid criminal prosecution if they marry their victims. **July:** The Moscow Center for Gender Studies conducts its first summer school to teach a new women's studies college curriculum. The Women's Caucus of Cameroon is formed and later receives support from the nation's president for its feminist policy agenda. **18 October:** A memorial to the nearly two million US women who have served or are serving in the armed forces is dedicated.

1998 **14 February:** The first V-Day is held to protest violence against women and to celebrate the vagina. **13 April:** San Francisco becomes the first US city to adopt a local ordinance modeled on the UN Convention on the Elimination of All Discrimination Against Women. **9 June:** The Southern Baptist Convention (United States) calls for wives to willingly and joyfully submit to their husbands' leadership. **29 June:** The *Time* magazine cover story asks, "Is Feminism Dead?" **August:** Senegal's first domestic violence shelter opens.

1999 **April:** The Zimbabwean Supreme Court rules that in cases where social norms conflict with constitutional guarantees of equal rights for women, customs prevail. **16 May:** The Emir of Kuwait grants women the right to vote and hold office. **June:** Using EMILY's List as a model, Japanese women form Women in New World, International Network (WIN WIN) to elect more women to the Diet. **9 October:** Margaret MacGregor is the first woman to officially box—and beat—a man. **23 October:** A conference commemorating the centennial of Arab women's emancipation is held. **23 November:** The National Assembly of Kuwait rejects the emir's grant of political rights to women by a two-thirds vote.

2000 **8 March:** The first Global Women's Strike is held. Kuwaiti women activists file a suit against the interior minister and the parliament speaker, demanding full political rights. **16 March:** Female members of the Social Democratic Party create an all-female shadow cabinet after the prime minister of the Czech Republic refuses to appoint women to his cabinet. **31 March-2 April:** The Feminist Majority Foundation's Expo 2000 features over 250 international speakers. **17 October:** Over 10,000 women from more than 100 countries demonstrate outside the UN for the end of poverty and violence against women. **19 October:** Former US President Jimmy Carter resigns from the Southern Baptist Convention because of its ban on women pastors. **22 December:** For the first time women can complain directly to the UN about discrimination, sexual exploitation, and other violations of women's rights under international treaties.

2001 **22 January:** US President George W. Bush reinstates the "global gag rule." **March:** Twenty-five thousand Indian sex workers meet in Calcutta to demand government recognition and eventual unionization to combat harassment. **15 June:** The Women's eNews begins delivering an

Internet report on US and international feminist issues. **Summer:** A German court takes into account the monetary value of a wife's housework and child care in awarding spousal support. **August:** Brazilian women are granted equal legal rights by the legislature. **September:** Urban Outfitters, a US retailer, removes a men's t-shirt that depicts a naked kneeling cowgirl labeled like cuts of beef. **13 September:** US Baptist minister Jerry Falwell charges that God allowed terrorists to attack the United States on September 11 because of the work of feminists, abortionists, pagans, and homosexuals. **December:** For the first time in its 600-year history, Britain's House of Commons sets aside 10 minutes each week for a cabinet minister to answer questions about women's issues. Kenya becomes the 10th African nation to outlaw female genital mutilation. **5 December:** An interim government for Afghanistan, including a new ministry for women's affairs and two female ministers, is announced.

2002 **1 January:** Turkish women receive legal equality. **4 February:** The International Bible Society announces a forthcoming revision of the Old and New Testaments that will retain a male God but replace gender specific terms with androgynous ones. **26 February:** Turkey rescinds a law that authorized virginity tests for high school girls suspected of having premarital sex after several girls had attempted suicide to avoid the test. **25 March:** The sentence of a Nigerian woman, sentenced to be buried up to her waist and stoned to death for adultery, is overturned. **9 May:** Thirty-four women appear on the local ballot in Bahrain in the first election in which women are allowed to vote. **June:** The American Medical Association supports state legislation to permit breastfeeding in public. **6 June:** A Pakistani court frees a rape victim, who had been charged with adultery for having relations with someone not her husband and sentenced to death. **9 June:** Swiss voters approve early-term abortions by a margin of almost 3 to 1. **11 July:** Chang Sang, an ordained Presbyterian minister, is appointed as Korea's first female prime minister. **22 July:** The Vatican excommunicates seven Roman Catholic women who failed to repent their ordinations in Austria. **31 July:** The Korean parliament rejects the appointment of Chang Sang because of ethical questions. **18 August:** The *New York Times* announces that it will begin printing announcements of same-sex unions. **2 September:** The Supreme Court of Afghanistan upholds a ban on radio broadcasts of women singers in Kabul. **4 September:** The World Summit on Sustainable Development in Johannesburg adopts a final plan that guarantees access for women to health care and reproductive services. **19 September:** The Washington State Supreme Court rules that taking upskirt photographs or videos in a public place without a woman's permission is not prohibited under the state's voyeurism law. **10 October:** A Northern Territory (Australia) judge rules that a 50-year-old Aboriginal man's rape of a teenage girl is traditional culture, not a crime. **30 October:** Argentina's Congress passes a law providing free birth contol and advice. **2-3 November:** The Arab Women's Organization forms to research the legal status of women in the 20 Arab nations. **18 November:** An editorial in the *New York Times* asks that golfer Tiger Woods not participate in the Masters Tournament at the all-male Augusta National Golf Club. **10 December:** Nine Swedish women writers and academics issue a critical statement, noting that this year only men received Nobel prizes and that since the awards were begun in 1901 only 3 percent of the recipients have been women. **12 December:** A New York appellate court agrees that a woman should be awarded all marital assets ($17 million) in a divorce settlement after her husband attacked her with a barbell. **13 December:** The 11 female members of the Iranian Parliament demand an end to death by stoning as a punishment for adultery.

2003 **16 January:** The Vatican announces that it has compiled a dictionary of phrases and words, including "gender" and "reproductive rights," that reflect antiChurch views. **20 January:** A pro-Pakistani militant group orders all Muslim women in Kashmir to quit their government jobs by 25 January or face death; they also demand that all girls over 14 marry immediately. **25 January:** Women in Kabul take driving tests for the first time since 1992. **5 February:** The first International Day Against Female Genital Mutilation and Other Harmful Traditional Practices is observed. **8 March:** Zimbabwe lowers custom duties on tampons and sanitary napkins. **12 March:** The Sudanese Medical Council prohibits the involvement of medical staff in female genital mutilation. **3 April:** Harvard University appoints its first female law school dean. **13 April:** The Supreme Court of Israel denies women equal access to Jerusalem's Western Wall and directs them to a separate area for silent prayer. **15 April:** Finland becomes the first European country to have women serving together as prime minister and president. **28 April:** Students at women-only Smith College vote to replace female pronouns in the student constitution with gender-neutral terms. **11 May:** A bride in India cancels her wedding and has her groom and members of his family arrested after a dowry of

$25,000 is demanded minutes before the ceremony. **29 May:** King Mswati of Swaziland blames "women who wear pants" for the world's problems. **11 June:** A US federal district court judge dismisses a lawsuit by the National Wrestling Coaches Association, which charged that Title IX threatened men's collegiate sports teams. **20 June:** Women on Waves performs its first abortion with RU-486 in international waters off the coast of Poland. **12 August 2003:** Iran's Guardian Council vetoes the parliament's earlier ratification of the UN Convention on the Elimination of All Forms of Discrimination Against Women. **26 September:** An Alabama county circuit court judge upholds a $115 million judgment against a man who maimed an abortion clinic nurse in a 1998 bombing. **1 October:** New York becomes the 4th state to require that hospitals offer rape victims emergency contraception. **10 October:** Shirin Ebadi of Iran becomes the first Muslim woman to win a Nobel Peace Prize, in recognition of her work promoting the rights of women and children. **18 November:** The Massachusetts Supreme Court rules that, under the state constitution, gay and lesbian couples have the right to marry. **7 December:** A group of women in Chicago announce plans to raise money to have the backlog of Illinois rape evidence kits tested at private labs. **25 December:** Iran's best-known dancer and 24 of her students are arrested on charges of dancing in public before an all-female audience.

Introduction

Feminism as a social, political, economic, and intellectual movement has been defined variously over the past 200 years. The current consensus is that there is no one feminism but, in fact, many traditions within a larger movement dedicated to securing equity for women. The overview below of the history of feminism, with some emphasis on the United States and British contexts, is intended to explain the causes for these different feminisms within the larger movement.

Origins of the Movement

The feminist movement is sometimes said to have originated in the writings of the Greek poet Sappho, but this seems a pedantic claim given the thousands of years between Sappho's life and any active organized effort to improve living conditions for women. Other scholars claim that the modern feminist consciousness began during the Renaissance, when writers like the Frenchwoman Christine de Pizan wrote for the first time for women and about women. Pizan's *The Book of the City of Women* (1405) argues that women need to build their own city, apart from men, where they will not be attacked and slandered by men. Although Pizan, like a very few other exceptional women, managed to publish her writings, she was very distinctly a singular voice. Another early feminist manifesto was the broadside published in 1589 by one Jane Anger, either an actual historical woman or an "agent provocateur." This piece of prefeminism is typical of the litany of grievances published by women against men at this time: "We are the grief of man, in that we take all the grief from man: we languish when they laugh, we sit sighing when they sit singing, and sit sobbing when they lie slugging and sleeping" (Jane Anger, *Her Protection for Women*, 1589).

The modern feminist movement, although it may recognize a kindred spirit in these early women writers, actually grew out of the intellectual, social, and political milieu that produced the French and American Revolutions. The word "feminism" is of even more recent vintage, having been coined in 1882 by Hubertine Auclert, the organizer of the first female suffrage society in France. The term has a literal meaning of "woman's social movement/political ideology." By the 1890s these terms—*féminisme* and *féministe*—appeared throughout Europe and in their anglicized forms in England. By 1910 they had migrated to North and South America. Women in the 19th century framed their movement not as "feminist," but in terms of "woman suffrage," "the woman movement," and "woman's rights." The popular convention, however, has been to apply "feminism" retroactively to include these earlier struggles for women's advancement.

The Individual Rights Tradition

A seminal document in the development of the individual rights movement was John Locke's *Two Treatises of Government* (1690), which argued that all individuals have a natural right to the freedom of life, liberty, and possessions that no government can suppress. His ideas were seized by a number of writers over the next century to agitate for political and social change, particularly in France and America, and they were finally adapted and modified by Mary Wollstonecraft in her *Vindication of the Rights of Woman* (1792). Wollstonecraft had begun her writing career by publishing a book on the education of women, and this concern recurs in her *Vindication*. She also wrote two novels in the sentimental and gothic traditions, both of which provided her with the ideology of woman as the innocent victim of oppressive forces beyond her control. For Wollstonecraft women were human beings and individuals in the same way that men were human beings and individuals. She did not believe that women should be defined by their sexual identities nor that their sexuality should be used to deny them access to full personhood with all of the individualist rights that men possessed. Wollstonecraft was very much a product of the Enlightenment, however, and her highest values were Reason and Rationality. She argued that if women were educated to develop fully their faculty of reason then they would have the same qualities that men have. In other words, she condemned the enfeebling and trivial educations that women received as producing physically weak, vacuous, and sensual creatures not fit for any serious work or responsibility. Although she believed that women must escape the gilded cage of marriage and sexual parasitism, she also recognized that only the exceptional woman also would be able to have a career as a governess or midwife perhaps. For most women, she admitted, the problem was how to make the roles of wife and mother more palatable. Wollstonecraft recommended that women be recognized by the law as equals to their husbands, both in owning property and in the right to earn their own livings. A properly educated woman will make a superior wife and mother, one who will approach her responsibilities with reason and rationality as her guiding forces.

John Stuart Mill was the other leading spokesman for the early British feminist tradition of equal rights. His treatise *The Subjection of Women* (1869) condemns the legal subordination of women to men, and advocates the position that women and men are equal in "privileges and power." He too condemns the existing educational system that produces women who are encouraged to cultivate artificial natures in order to ensnare men as a means of financial support. But like Wollstonecraft, Mill also concludes his treatise by saying that educated women will best serve society by working in their homes as reasonable and companionate wives and mothers.

Other early British leaders in the feminist equal rights movement were Unitarian women such as Barbara Leigh Smith Bodichon and her friend Bessie Parkes, Harriet Martineau, author of *On Female Education* (1823), and William Fox, editor of the *Monthly Repository*, which published articles written by Fox advocating reform of the divorce laws and female suffrage. Bodichon and Parkes were instrumental in getting the Married Women's Property Bill before Parliament in 1856, and they later founded the *Englishwoman's Journal* and the Society for Promoting the Employment of Women. These women, along with Emily Davies, Elizabeth Garrett Anderson, and Anna Jameson, formed the nucleus of woman suffrage activists in Britain around 1860.

In the United States the equal rights tradition of feminism formally began with the "Declaration of Sentiments," a document produced by the Women's Rights Convention held at Seneca Falls, New York, in 1848. This document paraphrases the United States Declaration of Independence by asserting that "all men and women are created equal." It then condemns the socially sanctioned forms of discrimination against women that occurred throughout America: no property rights, no access to divorce, no guaranteed child custody, no access to education or the professions, no right to serve as a religious or political leader, no code of morality that applied to men and women equally.

Prominent leaders in the US wing of equal rights feminism include Lucretia Mott, Susan B. Anthony, Victoria Woodhull, Lucy Stone, the Grimke sisters, and Elizabeth Cady Stanton; all are women who were originally galvanized by their work in the antislavery movement. Bitterly stung in the post-Civil War era by black leader Frederick Douglass, who they felt rejected women in order to ensure the vote for black men, Stanton and Anthony formed in 1869 an organization for women only, the National Woman Suffrage Association, a then-radical group that advocated the inclusion of women in the fifteenth Amendment to the US Constitution. Six months later, the American Woman Suffrage Association (AWSA), open to both sexes, was formed by Lucy Stone and her husband, Henry Blackwell. The AWSA was a more moderate group that drew its members from civic and professional ranks and adopted the gradualist strategy of state referenda for women's suffrage.

The equal rights feminist tradition of the Enlightenment era believes that the so-called differences between men and women are caused by the social environment, and that if social, educational, and financial opportunities were identical the sexes would also be identical. It emphasizes freedom of rights and responsibilities, self-determination, autonomy, and control over one's fate. This tradition sparked the fight for suffrage and now spearheads the abortion rights campaign.

The Evangelical Tradition

Another major influence on the feminist movement has been the Protestant and, specifically, the Evangelical tradition. It is no coincidence that the vast majority of women involved in the early feminist movement were either Unitarians or Quakers. Both are religions that advocate strong individualist positions in regard to every believer's personal relationship to God. Both religions also fostered the belief that women were human individuals before they were sexual creatures, and as such were deserving of the same political rights as men. Also not coincidentally, the feminist movement flourished in countries that were primarily Protestant and highly industrialized. In countries with no strong middle class, no tradition of education, and no professional opportunities for women, feminism did not develop or thrive.

Organizations like the New York Female Reform Society, founded in 1834 to convert prostitutes, formed the nucleus of the female purity crusade that was to culminate in the temperance movement in America (and now undergirds the antifeminist movements in the United States). In England the feminist purity campaign crystallized around the Contagious Diseases Acts in the 1870s. This campaign, largely led by Josephine Butler, sought to repeal a law that required prostitutes to have regular medical examinations for venereal diseases. Designed to protect males and military personnel, feminists believed that it encouraged, indeed that it promoted, a double sexual standard for men and women.

Temperance was the other major goal of reform efforts in the 19th and early 20th centuries for women in both England and the United States. The British Women's Temperance Association and the Woman's Christian Temperance Union (WCTU) both held that women would continue to be victimized as long as men drank. Both organizations believed that there was a direct connection between alcohol and deviant sexual practices, and both groups claimed that men corrupted by alcohol were abusive of their wives and children and wasteful of the family's earnings.

The Evangelical tradition of feminism believes that women are essentially different from men, physically, spiritually, and emotionally. Because of these differences between the sexes, women are seen, paradoxically, as physically inferior and spiritually superior. Their physical weakness requires that they be "protected," and thus the Evangelical tradition has often been in the forefront of pushing for protective legislation for women. They have also been involved in institutionalizing what became known in the 19th century as the doctrine of "separate spheres" and the "cult of domesticity." The "separate spheres" doctrine maintained that women were naturally suited to the family and private realm of the hearth and home, while men were naturally suited to the working world and the public domain. The two sexes were then naturally complementary in their roles and functions, rather than in competition with each other. The "cult of domesticity" was the literary and artistic expression of the separate spheres doctrine. In innumerable poems, paintings, and novels women were encouraged and lauded for their angelic ministrations as devoted wives and mothers of triumphant capitalists.

The Socialistic Tradition

The third major influence on the development of the early feminist movement was socialism, or a variety of intellectual movements that we now recognize as socialistic. Early socialist theorists such as Robert Owen, founder of the Owenite community at New Harmony, Indiana, was an advocate of radical change in the family. Owen, like John Humphrey Noyes,

Charles Fourier, and the Saint-Simonians, advocated a communal style of living, with women to be shared among the men of the group. Childraising was to be done by the community at large, and women and men were not to assume individual parental ownership of children. Group marriage, equal sexual freedom for women and men, and the rejection of traditional marriage as a type of property ownership made socialistic theories attractive to a number of feminists, particularly Frances Wright, Victoria Woodhull, and Anna Wheeler.

The writings of Karl Marx and Friedrich Engels on the family, the role of women under capitalism, and equality for women under socialism have also had a major impact on feminism. Engels's *Origin of the Family, Private Property and the State* (1884) states that women are the true bearers of the world's moral future. It was thought that women already embodied the values that men would possess only when they lived under the conditions of socialism.

The most influential socialist work of the period was August Bebel's *Woman and Socialism* (1879), which included a long discussion of the oppression of women under capitalism. Bebel claimed that the sex/cash nexus corrupted bourgeois marriage, led to the prevalence of prostitution, and created the factory system that devoured so many proletariat women. The only solutions according to Bebel were equal rights for women, including the vote, equal training for the professions, and equal legal protection against financial exploitation.

The socialistic tradition within feminism can also be seen in the writings of Charlotte Perkins Gilman, who advocated group living in cooperatives where all housework and childrearing would be done through a collective group effort. The socialistic tradition can also be seen, in somewhat muted form, in the work of Jane Addams of Hull House, Chicago, and the larger social work movement, which sought to bring humane living conditions to the rapidly increasing urban neighborhoods in both England and the United States. In England the Fabian Movement, and specifically the Fabian Woman's Group, saw itself as leading the reform movement. The Fabian Mabel Atkinson wrote in 1914, "it becomes clear that the only path to the ultimate and most deep lying ends of the feminist movement is through socialism, and every wise feminist will find herself more and more compelled to adopt the principles of Socialism" ("Economic Foundations of the Women's Movement," *Fabian Tract* #175, June 1914). Other British women involved in the social movement were: Mary Carpenter, who sought to reform the Ragged Schools; Louisa Twining, of the Workhouse Visiting Societies; Mary Ann Baines, of the Ladies National

Association for the Diffusion of Sanitary Knowledge; and Florence Nightingale, who worked for the construction of hospitals.

Socialist feminism continued throughout the 19th and 20th centuries in the formation of "welfare socialism." This movement seeks free abortions for poor women and other government-supported services that help to equalize living and working conditions for working-class women and their children. Welfare feminism, with its roots in a strong labor union movement and an organized socialist tradition, is much more prevalent in Britain than it is in America, where the middle-class origins of feminism are still a dominant influence on the character of the movement.

Zenith of the Movement, 1870-1928

Generally considered the heyday of the modern feminist movement, the period of 1870-1928 is characterized by extremely active suffrage activity and parallel educational and social reform movements. Women from all walks of life, but particularly those involved in the antislavery and temperance movements, combined forces to push for votes for women in England and the United States. In England the suffragists were opposed by the ruling Liberal Party, largely because the Liberals believed that votes for women would increase the Conservative voter base. Ironically, the Conservative Party itself offered a good deal of opposition, largely because it was suspicious of any movement that aimed to broaden the voter base. The suffragists were also opposed by prominent women themselves, most notably those writing in the *Nineteenth Century* magazine (1889). One famous article was signed by women like the Fabian Beatrice Webb and the writer Mrs. Humphrey Ward, among others, who claimed that they had no need for the vote because they were already represented by their husbands or fathers. For such women the idea of female suffrage was simply a form of plural voting, redundant, because women would always vote as their men instructed. Suffragists were accused of advocating free love, overthrowing traditional female roles as wives and mothers, and wanting to impose strict moral codes of behavior and temperance on men.

Two factors turned the tide for the suffrage movement in the late 19th century. The first was the growth of the settlement movement led by women like Eleanor Rathbone, Alice Crompton, and Emmeline Pethick-Lawrence, all of whom turned their energies to the suffrage issue after realizing its importance in changing social conditions for women. The other factor was the growing labor movement, which linked women's suffrage with work and pay concerns. The catalysts for the successful passage of universal women's suffrage in Britain were the Pankhurst family, Richard, Emmeline, and their daughter Christabel. The English suffragists faced innumerable obstacles before they won full and universal suffrage in 1928, not the least of which came from brewing interests that feared the association between feminism and temperance.

Although the situation in the United States was somewhat different, the issue was resolved in an almost identical fashion. The US suffrage movement was complicated not just by the class issue, but also by the race issue. In America, also, the vote had to be won state by state before a federal amendment could be passed, as was the case for the amendment that had given African American men the vote earlier. A major victory was won when Frances Willard, head of the Woman's Christian Temperance Union (WCTU), brought the group into support of female suffrage in 1883. But by breaking down the churches' opposition to suffrage, the WCTU mobilized the brewery interests against votes for women. Another complicating factor was the large number of immigrant women who also wanted the vote. Feminists like Elizabeth Cady Stanton supported suffrage for "educated" women only, and by 1903 this was a common view held by a number of women's organizations. In the South support for suffrage was complicated further by the large numbers of African American men enfranchised by the fifteenth Amendment. Factions within a number of women's groups advocated votes for white women only, as an attempt to retain the vestiges of white supremacy as long as possible. Carrie Chapman Catt took control of the mainstream and unified National American Woman Suffrage Association in 1915. But two years later the movement again split over tactics when the more radical National Woman's Party, led by Alice Paul, organized picketing around the White House. Although not as militant as the most extreme activists in Britain, the pickets were effective in frightening the government, which saw in them the threat of large-scale social disorder. Suffrage for women in the United States was finally secured in 1920.

There were also well-developed women's movements in almost every other nation during the late 19th and early 20th centuries. Several of these were initially led by male intellectual reformers (e.g., Qasim Amin in Egypt, Yukichi Fukuzawa in Japan, and K'ang Yu-wei in China) as part of a larger quest for modernity and/or national independence. But in all parts of the world, including the Middle East, Japan, and Latin America, elite women founded suffrage societies, literary clubs, and girls' schools. They worked for many social reforms and legal rights. Some adopted militant tactics: violence, demonstrations, and hunger strikes.

In Western Europe the women's movements were often small, elite-based groups led by well-educated, middle-class women residing in the largest cities. Because Protestantism places a greater emphasis on universal education than other religions, the strongest women's movements during this period were in the Protestant nations of Western Europe. And even in Asia, many feminist leaders were Christian converts.

First wave feminism worldwide was rooted in moral reform; both abolition (in Brazil) and the World Woman's Christian Temperance Union (in many nations, including the anglophone democracies of Canada, New Zealand, and Australia plus Norway, China, Japan, and Egypt) played major roles in movement building. The trafficking of women in prostitution was denounced. The first issue to emerge in almost all countries was women's education (access to higher education in Western Europe, Canada, and the United States and literacy elsewhere). Often feminist demands were channelled through a traditional-sounding women's club (e.g., the Bluestocking Society of Japan, the Club Femenino de Cuba, and the Women's Reading Circle of Chile). Next followed demands for legal reform in the status of women (e.g., property rights, divorce reform, and employment rights). European trade union women demanded improvements in working conditions for women. In non-European nations the focus was often on cultural or religious issues such as purdah, suttee, footbinding, veiling, child marriage, polygamy, and concubinage.

Woman suffrage eventually was adopted as a goal in almost all nations as a means to these social and legal ends. The concept of the modern nation-state at that time legitimized the extension of formal legal equality to women and undercut the power of religious rulers. In some societies (e.g., Cuba) nationalism played a role in defining suffrage as a feminine movement that accepted women's traditional role as essential for progre- but rejected gender equality. In nondemocratic nations the vote assumed a different meaning.

The Lull, 1928-1960

There was not a universal doldrums period for the feminist movement. Although almost 40 nations had extended full or partial suffrage to women by 1928, most of the world's women were not enfranchised until after 1940. Woman suffrage came to most Latin American countries in the

1940s and 1950s. Women in France and Japan received the vote only after the end of World War II. Notable latecomers were Switzerland (1971), Liechtenstein (1984), South Africa (1994), and, most recently, Bahrain (2002). Women in Saudi Arabia and Kuwait still are not permitted to vote.

A major transformation (and fragmentation) of the women's movements in both England and the United States, however, occurred shortly after the vote was won. Attention clearly shifted to improving women's educational opportunities, and women began to enter the professions in record numbers during these years. Women like Mary Harris, widely known as "Mother" Jones, were involved in labor unions and in improving the working conditions and pay scales for women workers. Another major concern during this period was the development and distribution of birth control information and devices. Marie Stopes in Britain and Margaret Sanger in the United States were the major forces here. Women also began political careers; Edith Summerskill in England entered Parliament in 1938 and founded the Married Women's Association, a group designed to improve the economic position of the wife in the home.

One major issue that confronted feminism during this period was protective legislation, laws that enacted different treatment for women because they were generally recognized to be weaker. A number of professional women's groups, including the American Medical Woman's Association, realized that such legislation worked to protect some women while it hampered others. The Business and Professional Women's Clubs opposed protective legislation that hurt the interests of white-collar women. In 1927 in California the group successfully blocked the imposition of an eight-hour day on all female workers except nurses, maids, and cannery workers. But for women in low-paid, unskilled fields, protective legislation continued to be the best hope they had for improving their working and living conditions.

Another major concern during this period was the fight to end the practice whereby women lost their teaching and civil service jobs once they married. White-collar unions within Britain fought throughout this period for equal pay and against the marriage bar, as well as an end to the "family wage," which gave married men with children preferential pay and employment opportunities.

There is no doubt, however, that women's status was tied to the economic and military conditions of this period. During the Depression working women were viewed with contempt and suspicion, largely because they were seen as taking away employment from men who needed it to support a family. World War II saw women working outside the home in large numbers, primarily because of the extreme manpower shortage. Once the war ended and the soldiers returned, however, women were quickly relegated to domesticity again, this time in the newly constructed suburbs, the dumping ground for middle-class women and the ever-increasing number of children they were encouraged to bear. Powerful social forces and the new medium of television encouraged women to quietly accept their new homes, identities, and roles as wives and mothers. "The problem that had no name," as Betty Friedan called it, began to emerge as women, once active and contributing to their societies, gradually named their boredom. Many emerged from the 1950s with only the vaguest memory of work outside the home, equal pay, educational opportunities, and professional careers.

Modern Feminism, 1961 to the Present

The US contemporary women's movement, 1961 to the present, is characterized by a number of historical events that have largely been mythologized as media happenings: the failure of the Equal Rights Amendment (ERA); the marches on Washington, D.C.; the so-called "bra burnings"; the high visibility of such prominent feminists as Betty Friedan, Gloria Steinem, Kate Millett, and Germaine Greer. For all the media hoopla, however, the basic issues facing women have remained remarkably constant and unchanged. In many ways the contemporary struggles the feminist movement faced mirrored the legacy from the 1890s. The struggle to pass the ERA and secure abortion rights were based in the concerns of the individual rights tradition; the fight against the ERA, also led by women, recalled the Evangelical tradition within the feminist movement; and the social critique, the consciousness-raising activities, and the concern with child care facilities reflected the socialistic tradition that has been such a dominant part of the movement.

One branch of this contemporary feminist movement, popularly known as the Women's Liberation Movement, grew out of the radical political protest activities of the 1960s. Women who committed themselves to opposing the war in Vietnam and the racism in the American South found themselves also treated like second-class citizens. They realized that they had much in common with colonized people or people of color vis-à-vis their white, middle-class male comrades. Many leaders in the women's movement recalled their own experiences in these earlier movements. Radical male students, occupying deans' offices on college campuses, sent dispatches to the press while the women among them brought in food (inspiring the later slogan: "Women make policy, not coffee"). Stokely Carmichael, leader of the Student Nonviolent Coordinating Committee (SNCC) and the larger "black power" movement, made it known that "the only position for women in SNCC is prone" (quoted in Winifred D. Wandersee, *On the Move: American Women in the 1970s* [1988], 2).

Beginning in 1967, numerous independent women's liberation groups began to emerge in US cities. The groups were small, informally organized, and committed to exploring women's common experiences through consciousness-raising (C-R). Because of internal organizational problems, most of these groups had disbanded by 1975 and their participants had either joined the parallel women's rights movement or had become involved in providing alternative services to women, such as health care, rape crisis counseling, and shelter from domestic violence.

The second branch, the liberal women's rights movement, began with the founding of the National Organization for Women (NOW) in 1966. This branch is deeply rooted in earlier government policies to study the status of US women (through a 1961 president's commission on that topic) and to ensure racial equality under the law. The expectation arose that gender equality would also be addressed. Building on the inspiration of Betty Friedan's classic manifesto, *The Feminist Mystique* (1963), and with Friedan as its first president, NOW would prove to be the most visible, largest, and most durable of the US feminist political groups. NOW quickly gained an impressive membership and had formed some 600 affiliate chapters by 1973. It also organized more than two dozen national task forces, addressing issues from poverty, to education, to sports, to day care and other matters judged to be critical to improving the quality of women's lives.

NOW and the many other women's rights groups that subsequently have been organized focus on political and legal improvements for women, in accordance with an adherence to the individual rights tradition. But it could not escape political problems of its own, the price of any successful organization. Friedan herself, it must be admitted, pursued an agenda less radical than most of NOW's membership. She never admitted to a patriarchal system in American society or asserted that women, as a class, were oppressed by men. In fact, she did not oppose "the system" as such, and wanted mostly to bring more American women into it. She did not want to join NOW to the militant leftist critique that had become so pronounced by the end of the 1960s. In 1968, however, Ti-Grace Atkinson proclaimed "feminism is the theory; lesbianism is the practice" (*Amazon

Odyssey [1974]) and led a splinter group out of the organization. Friedan denounced the dangers of this militancy and the "infantile deviants" who advocated abolition of marriage and the family. She warned: "We cannot have these, our brightest and most spirited young women, turning their backs on society. This is an awfully old-fashioned hang-up" (quoted in Wandersee, op. cit., 42).

The abortion issue also produced tensions. At its second meeting in 1967, NOW formulated a very strongly libertarian statement on the repeal of laws governing abortion, echoing the feelings of its membership that complete discretion of women in matters of abortion must have a standing in law. But although it was most certainly true that at that time, and since, a clear majority of American women supported such freedom of choice, it was also a fact that within NOW many women considered the issue too radical a demand for a fledgling movement. When the strong pro-choice resolution passed, some conservative women broke from the organization and formed the Women's Equity Action League (which, ironically, soon came to support reproductive rights).

An even more thorny controversy had emerged by the end of the 1960s—lesbianism. Betty Friedan, ever the political strategist, feared that any embracing of this cause would identify the woman's movement, and the NOW organization itself, as radical and far removed from public sentiments and norms of conduct. She did, however, give a cautious and token support for lesbian rights. And at its 1971 convention NOW declared its support of a woman's right to her own sexuality. Lesbian spokeswomen by the middle 1970s had convinced some doubtful feminists that female same-sex love belonged to a historical continuum dating back at least to the Victorian era and that it held a viable place in any movement that stressed the unity of women against the dominating structures of patriarchal power. Adrienne Rich, poet and critic, offered her own celebration in her *Of Woman Born* (1976), praising motherhood, creativity, female bonding, and the lesbian experience collectively as the ingredients of the common female self.

NOW's growth accompanied significant changes for women in American life during the 1970s. By the end of the decade a record 51 percent of women were holding jobs outside the home. But one had to read the statistics cautiously. Most women said they worked because of financial necessity, an unwelcome fact of a more uncertain economy. And only one in seven women held employment in the professions; over half of these women were nurses or teachers. On the other side of the ledger, by the early 1980s women held half the seats in the nation's law schools. By the middle 1980s they constituted more than half the nation's college students.

Demographics redefined the "normal" pattern of American life in the 1970s and 1980s, and although it was not clear to what extent the feminist movement influenced the changes, none should dismiss it as a negligible contributor. Greater independence for women caused many to think skeptically about following traditional life patterns. Women were now choosing to marry later in their lives than previously. And they were less anxious to have children. Outstanding among the statistical data was the dramatic drop in fertility rates in the United States, from 3.7 births per woman in 1955-1959 to 1.8 births in 1975-1980. "The Cult of True Womanhood" had clearly lost its mystique.

More disturbing yet was the growing phenomenon of single-parent families. The end of the 1970s counted 7.7 million of them. They owed something to the increase of the divorce rate at the same time, for by 1975 there was almost one divorce in the United States for every two marriages. Divorce lowered the income for women while it increased it for men. Now sociologists began to talk about the "feminization of poverty." One of three single-parent families (and they were overwhelmingly female-headed) lived below the poverty line as opposed to only one of 18 among two-parent families. By the end of the 1980s single-parent families constituted about 20 percent of all, but the ratio for black families had grown to more than half.

One divisive issue within the women's movements of the industrial democracies is a concern that the feminist movement is producing gains primarily for middle- and upper-class white women. NOW itself appeared to many, including some of its own members, as insufficiently attentive to minority and blue-collar women. Karen DeCrow led an effort to address this problem in 1974, hoping also to involve more men in the organization. Some of the charges of feminist elitism came from black women. Novelist Alice Walker expressed the frustrations of this group when she addressed a convocation at Sarah Lawrence College in 1972. But black feminism confronted problems, too, as it addressed black females' grievances against black males, as in the novels of Toni Morrison and in the highly controversial book by Michelle Wallace, *Black Macho and the Myth of the Superwoman* (1979).

Another branch of contemporary feminist theory known as radical feminism believes that the source of women's oppression can be found in the "patriarchy," the systemic control and domination by males of all

INTRODUCTION • 15

power and capital in society. While most contemporary feminists will agree with that statement, they differ on strategies for addressing the problems that plague women. Marxist feminism, as this school is called, is much more prevalent in Great Britain, where feminists like Michelle Barrett have published on women as a class, not simply a gender.

Another radical group of feminists, led by Shulamith Firestone, took the position that biology is destiny and that as long as women gave birth to children they would always be discriminated against economically and sexually. Firestone advocated that technology take over the role of childbearing, thereby freeing women from the indignities of pregnancy and lactation, and making them economically independent and as free as men from the consequences of their sexual activities. Firestone's theories served as the catalyst for the fiction of Marge Piercy (*Woman on the Edge of Time*, 1976), in which babies are developed in test tubes and breastfed by their fathers, and Joanna Russ (*The Female Man*, 1975), who envisions a future all-female utopia in which all men have been exterminated. Examples of this position can also be found among contemporary radical feminists who have also condemned marriage, romantic love, and the sexual games that are played between men and women, advocating instead a communal arrangement of free love relationships (à la the Oneida community or New Harmony), celibacy, or all-female communities based on a lesbian separatist ethos.

Another avenue of escape from gender polarities has been the movement toward andrógyny. Here men and women both recognize that gender is a limiting and constricting force that pushes them into sex-typed roles and behaviors. Both sexes renounce the artificiality of these roles and agree to a shared sexual identity based on the "best" that either gender offers. Thus men are both strong and emotional; women are both intuitive and rational. Both sexes assume equal responsibility for child care and household obligations, regardless of their employment responsibilities or status. The popularity of this ethos can be seen in the number of novels and art works celebrating androgyny that proliferated throughout the 1970s, particularly Ursula Le Guin's *Left Hand of Darkness* (1969).

Another aspect of the contemporary feminist movement is an extreme exaltation of the mother and a fixation on the mother-child relationship. Paradoxically, while some feminists would seek to release women from their biological tie to maternity, others try to find a lost period of history known as the matriarchy, ruled over by mother-queens. Feminist historical revisionism led to the claim that the patriarchy was created only after the overthrow of the reign of the great mother (for an early prefeminist account of this theory, see Robert Graves's study *The White Goddess* [1948; rpt. 1966]). Such feminists see a radical form of separatism, a rejection of all men as colleagues and friends, as the only way out of the current sexual warfare.

Yet another form of contemporary feminism is concerned with the "second stage" of feminism, as Betty Friedan called it. This second stage began when women, mostly middle-class and well-educated, tried to combine marriage and children with the demands of a full-time professional career. The result for these "superwomen" was exhaustion and depression that most could not accept. For many women the agenda for the feminist movement now is how to make society more hospitable for women with children. This has led to a challenge to the individual rights preference for policies that focus on gender equality under law. Now it is argued that women can only be treated equally through policies that recognize gender differences and the special needs of women for child care and family leave.

Despite the inner dilemmas of feminism in the 1970s and early 1980s, the movement was able to congeal around one dominant cause—the proposed Equal Rights Amendment to the United States Constitution. A simple statement to prevent sexual discrimination in law and social practice, the amendment seemed to be so much aligned with American values that it was irresistible. Both the Democratic and Republican Parties officially endorsed it at their presidential convention, the House of Representatives passed it 354-23, in October 1971, the Senate approved it, 84-8, on March 22, 1972. From there, the measure passed easily through state legislatures across the country and was nearing two-thirds majority of these endorsements by the end of the decade.

But few had counted on the opposition of a remarkably effective opponent of the ERA—the indomitable Phyllis Schlafly. She might have been the perfect example of the 1970s liberated woman—articulate, intelligent, self-confident, and in her own way, courageous. She was a devout Roman Catholic and long-time Republican Party activist, on the far right side of the party's constituency. As early as February 1972 Schlafly had established the National Committee to Stop ERA. It began to sign on a series of allies—the National Council of Catholic Women, the Daughters of the American Revolution, the Ku Klux Klan, and, yes, the Communist Party of the United States. Furthermore, the National Right to Life Committee, especially after the Supreme Court decision of *Roe v. Wade* in 1973, also fueled the countermovement. So did Jerry Falwell's religious organization, the Moral Majority, help to make antiERA seem a profamily issue.

Schlafly did succeed in making the feminist cause in ERA seem elitist and privileged. She charged that victims of ERA would be divorced mothers who would lose their privileges under the law, while women in all classes would be susceptible to the military draft. In a dramatic reversal, states now voted against endorsing the ERA. Some attempted to reverse their earlier approvals. Despite Congress' extension of an earlier deadline, the ERA could not muster the needed state approvals in order to find its way into the Constitution.

These events, however much they helped make the feminist movement a major political story of the 1970s and 1980s, probably had little effect. What many see as a "backlash" against feminism (e.g., the June 29, 1998, *Time* cover story that asked, "Is Feminism Dead?") is due in large part to the accomplishments of women in all aspects of American life. Women's gains under the law continue to grow, from the educational and credit equity policies of the 1970s to the violence against women and family leave legislation of the 1990s. The threat to abortion rights after the unfavorable *Webster* decision in 1989 brought growth (and younger women) to NOW, which had suffered a drop in membership after the defeat of the ERA. These younger feminists, the so-called third wave, came to the movement with their own literature, their own music, and a challenge to veteran feminists to reach out to women of color, immigrants, and the poor (i.e., women who are economically marginal and most vulnerable to exploitation and violence). This set the stage for the next era of the movement, global feminism.

The British feminist movement, like those in the United States, became visible in the late 1960s and was led by young women formerly active in student, international peace, and Marxist politics. Although British feminism shares the dual origins—women's rights and liberation—of the US movement and the same liberal, socialist, and radical feminist traditions, its subsequent development has been distinctive. Britain has no overarching national organization comparable to NOW. Instead, the proliferating local Marxist feminist groups moved directly into instrumental projects such as the world's first shelters for battered women, rape crisis centers, health clinics, and the Greenham Common peace encampment. A feminist culture is supported by women's studies, bookstores, presses, and the emergence of a "girl power" movement among young women. Mass protests are an additional tactic. In 1979 over 100,000 participants demon-

strated against restrictions proposed to the Abortion Act of 1967. The context of British politics has facilitated effective feminist participation inside labor unions and the Labour Party, which in 1990 established women-only short lists for winnable parliamentary seats and formed a Women's Unit to influence policy when it came to power in 1997. British feminists participate in the European Women's Lobby and within the 300 Group that promotes the movement of women into elective and appointive public office on all levels. British feminists have also been successful in constructing national coalitions around a single issue such as abortion and in forming cooperative relationships between groups such as the Southall Black Sisters and Justice for Women around domestic violence. Its many legislative victories have given birth to opposition groups such as the pro-life Society for the Protection of the Unborn Child and the antifeminist UK Men's Movement.

Although contemporary feminism has been strongest in the Western industrial democracies with their tradition of liberal civic rights, virtually every nation now has some type of national women's movement. Many of these movements date from the late 1960s, but by the 1980s most countries had at least one women's center, a hotline or shelter against violence, and a campaign to reform discriminatory laws. As in the United States and Great Britain, Western feminist movements emerged from other movements for international peace, racial equality, student power, and socialist politics. In the 1960s and 1970s small radical feminist groups were formed and had to compete with women's rights groups within unions and political parties and with other types of women's organizations.

By the mid-1990s only the feminist movements of the United States, Canada, the Netherlands, and Italy had a genuine national mass base. Although women in Scandinavia have served as a vanguard in achieving almost complete formal legal equality, autonomous women's movements have been limited there. Several of these are first wave groups that did not disband after woman suffrage. Western feminist projects and strategies strikingly parallel those in the United States: consciousness-raising, women's centers and shelters, collectives, cultural groups, and magazines such as *Emma*. Feminist protests have been especially pervasive (e.g., Canada's abortion caravan, Australia's Anzac Day Parade, the Dolle Mina of the Netherlands and Belgium, and Féministes Révolutionnaires of France). Women's gains under the law continue to grow although the past 40 years have not brought uniform success. Neoconservatism in Canada and the United Kingdom in the 1980s presented a new resistance to feminist change.

For many non-Western women, feminism is associated with racism and imperialism; those on the ideological left also view feminism as Western and bourgeois. In Latin America and Russia in particular women have organized in feminine movements that honor women's traditional role as wife and mother and do not challenge sex roles as do feminists. Communist nations have traditionally authorized a single group to represent women's quest for equality, a practice termed "state feminism." With the fall of communism in Eastern Europe in 1989, preservation of access to contraception, abortion, maternity leave, jobs, and education became issues for women in these countries. Service projects sponsored by new independent feminist groups are valued as sources of jobs for women.

In Latin America women's movements grew out of opposition to authoritarian leaders of the left and right. Women, however, discovered that democracy also requires a challenge to *machismo* and sex discrimination. Here women form neighborhood-based groups that combine human rights and traditional gender interests (e.g., El Salvador's Comité de Madres, Argentina's Mothers of the Plaza de Mayo, and the work of Nobel laureate Rigoberta Menchu of Guatemala). In some Latin American guerrilla movements, male leaders have allowed women to participate in combat and have placed feminist issues on the revolutionary agenda in order to gain international financial and political support.

In Africa, Asia, and the Middle East, women have mobilized around nationalism in a postcolonial era. No broad-based feminist movement exists in an Islamic society today or in Asia, outside Japan and China. Governments in Turkey and Iran emancipated women in advance of a feminist movement. In most non-Western nations "women's movement" is less precise than "women's committee/caucus/network." Second wave feminist activity is often confined to an advantaged sector of middle-class, well-educated professional women or young leftists residing in one to four large cities and operating through many small, local groups rather than a large national organization. Even so, most nations have one or more coalition groups that seek to enroll all women's organizations as affiliates. Universal feminist issues include education, employment, equal pay, legal equality, reproductive freedom, child care, health care, protection from violence and sexual harassment, homemaker rights, and political power.

Autonomous women's movements have faced great difficulties in authoritarian communist, religious, and military regimes. Reversals in the legal and social status of women in Chile, Egypt, and Iran followed the rise of repressive regimes; the Women's Organization of Iran and the Arab

Women's Solidarity Association have been particular targets of Islamic fundamentalists who view the preservation of women's traditional role as a barrier against Westernization, imperialism, and secular society. Weaker fundamentalist movements against feminism are also found in the Jewish, Catholic, Protestant, and Hindu faiths (e.g., the move to permit the heavily Catholic Republic of Ireland to retain a more restrictive abortion policy than allowed by the European Union). It is also not uncommon for a nation's women's movement to be closely linked with or sponsored by a ruling political party (e.g., the Peronist Women's Party of Argentina, the Union of Greek Women, the All-India Women's Conference, the former Committee of Soviet Women, and the All-China Women's Federation). This allows male-dominated regimes to co-opt potential women's leaders and channel feminist activity through the public bureaucracy.

International Feminism, 1830 to the Present

Robin Morgan entitled her collection of radical feminist essays *Sisterhood Is Powerful* (1970). This term has passed into general usage to mean that the united actions of women can effect powerful changes in society. Her *Sisterhood Is Global* (1984) was one of the earliest attempts to document the contemporary international women's movement. Although this effort may have been premature, during the past two decades a global feminist movement has genuinely moved from brave slogan to reality.

As described by Bonnie Anderson in *Joyous Greetings* (2000), the first international women's movement was built, 1830-1860, by a small group of elite women in the United States, the United Kingdom, Germany, and France. These women worked through a network based on letters, personal visits, a common body of published writings, and shared tactics and issues. Their goals were civil and political equality, suffrage and office-holding, and social justice in wages, education, and health care. They discussed divorce, domestic violence, prostitution, rape, employment, and nonsexist parenting. They also questioned male-centered religion and sexist language.

The national campaigns for women's rights dating from the mid-19th century were accompanied by the birth of a more inclusive international movement. Conferences and organizations that drew participants from all parts of the world typify this period of international feminism. A temperance movement had appeared in Europe by the 1830s and was international by 1851. The World WCTU was formed in 1884 and by 1920 was organized in over 40 nations. In 1878 the first International Women's

Rights Congress was held in France, and many others followed. In 1888 the International Council of Women (ICW) was organized and by 1913 had three million members from 23 nations. Still in existence today, the ICW has affiliates in 70 nations; in many countries the national council of women serves as an important lobbying coalition. In 1904 the International Woman Suffrage Alliance (IWSA) was formed and by 1929 had 51 national members. After roughly half of all nations had enacted woman suffrage, the name International Alliance of Women (IAW) was adopted in 1946. The group currently has 60 affiliates. The other major international women's group of this period was the Socialist Women's International, organized in 1907 to work for the vote, equal pay, and maternity insurance. After World War I it had almost one million members.

Because the World WCTU, the ICW, and the IWSA were of US origin, the white, middle-class, often racist and ethnocentric women from wealthy, developed nations that dominated the international suffrage movement connoted imperialism in some parts of the world. These suffragists traveled abroad, particularly to the anglophone democracies, Japan, and South America. In colonial countries women's movements were strengthened by exposure to Western dress, education, and ideas such as monogomy and individualism. The IWSA sought to take the suffrage movement to non-Western women, but Carrie Chapman Catt found in 1911 that the movement in Asia was already strong and had been organized since the 19th century. The involvement of the international socialist movement provided some social class balance. In 1911 the first international women's day was celebrated after a campaign conducted by the Socialist Women's International as a way to support woman suffrage.

The triennial conventions of the ICW and IAW helped to maintain the international feminist network after the end of World War II. The studies of the UN's Commission on the Status of Women, established in 1946, made clear that in no country were women politically or legally equal to men. The UN International Women's Year (1975), its Decade for Women (1976-1985), and its world conferences for women served as important catalysts and resources for national women's movements, particularly in poor, newly independent nations where women's rights were viewed as a measure of modernity. And the adoption of the UN's Convention on the Elimination of All Forms of Discrimination Against Women in 1979 created the expectation that change for women would occur.

Two events in the late 1980s brought a major shift in the development of international feminism. The third UN world conference on women, held in Nairobi in 1985, was the first not dominated by North America and Europe. The fall of communism in Eastern Europe in 1989 (accompanied by economic reforms in China to facilitate world trade and Beijing's designation as the site for the fourth UN women's conference in 1995) allowed the formation of many new independent women's organizations with ties to feminists in the industrial democracies. Western foundations have responded by funding these nongovernmental women's groups throughout the developing world and Eastern Europe. Western feminists were also open to the adoption of a new global agenda to maintain relevance. This was facilitated by advances in electronic communications and the increasing involvement of national governments, regional organizations, and, in particular, the United Nations.

Where once the international feminist movement was coordinated through postal service letters, telephone calls, travel, and print publications, the Internet and e-mail are now favored options. Virtually every feminist group, including those in nations such as Afghanistan, has a well-developed web page with links to an international network. International feminist actions are publicized and organized over the Internet; virtual demonstrations take place as women throughout the world petition through e-mail.

By 1992, 153 nations had at least one (and often several) bureaucracy for women. Thirty-six had a ministry of women's affairs (a cabinet position) and 123 had a Commission on the Status of Women. The European Union has adopted binding directives or strong recommendations on equal pay, equal employment opportunity, pension equity, maternity and parental leave, child care, women in political leadership, and sexual harassment. The Organization of American States has adopted a policy on violence against women.

But most central to the globalization of the women's movement is the United Nations, which has taken the lead in collecting statistics, drafting conventions, holding conferences, and developing international laws that relate to the rights of women. Beginning in 1993 women's issues have been addressed at UN conferences on a variety of topics. Violence against women has been defined as a human rights violation. Women's access to health care and reproductive services has been guaranteed. Rape is treated as a crime against humanity in cases coming before the International Criminal Court. Women's empowerment has been officially linked to solving social, economic, and environmental problems. Since 2000 women have been allowed to complain directly to the UN about any violation of women's rights under international treaties.

A number of new global feminist organizations have been formed to promote women's rights and political leadership, to finance women's development and service projects, and to influence UN policy. Some of the best known are the Center for Women's Global Leadership (1989), the Global Fund for Women (1987), the International Women's Rights Action Watch (1985), and the Women's Environmental and Development Organization (1990). Although all of these groups are based in the United States, the Sisterhood Is Global Institute (1984) rotates its headquarters, and Development Alternatives with Women for a New Era (1984) is a Southern-hemisphere network for feminist research.

Coordinated feminist demonstrations take place in many cities of the world, often to commemorate a day recognized by the UN against, for example, female genital mutilation or violence against women. The participation in many of these actions is extensive. The World March of Women in 2001 presented a petition to the UN secretary-general with over five million signatures from 5,200 women's groups in 161 nations. A recent Sixteen Days of Activism Against Gender Violence featured locally planned arts events, vigils, demonstrations, and lectures in more than 90 nations.

The current international feminist agenda parallels the second wave agenda of the 1960s and 1970s, but with a more inclusive and global thrust. The US global gag rule is viewed as a threat to women's reproductive freedom in the less-developed world. Similarly, AIDS in women is linked with child marriage, female genital mutilation, incest, rape, and trafficking in women. Women in development and the impact of globalization on women in both developed and developing nations are of great concern. Religious or cultural practices involving, among others, suttee, honor killings, and dowry or stove deaths have been denounced. Most recently the Campaign to Stop Gender Apartheid in Afghanistan succeeded in gaining the attention of the world during Taliban rule. Feminist publicity surrounding cases of women being sentenced to beheading or stoning for having been raped or having sex outside marriage have brought reversals. Trafficking in women, including sex tours and the purchase of mail-order brides, has achieved a priority status.

But despite this new global feminism with its considerable unity of purpose, the contemporary feminist movement has many different voices. The movement is composed not of any one group with one clear agenda, but of a number of different groups, each with their own ideologies and concerns. Basic questions focus on whether women and men are inherently and intrinsically different from each other and whether those differences justify different treatment in employment and before the law. Those questions have been answered variously and contradictorily over the past 200 years. Feminism has sought to shape and reflect how women have viewed themselves, as wives, mothers, or workers. It has considered how and why women have accepted or rejected their roles within society and their own individual families. And it has tried to improve and reform society to fit its own best imaginings of what a just society for all people should, and would, be.

THE DICTIONARY

-A-

ABC BILL, ACT FOR BETTER CHILD CARE. An omnibus bill, popularly called the ABC bill, passed by the US Congress in 1990 in response to a widely perceived crisis in **day-care** services for children. The law provided for tax credits for the child care expenses of low-income working parents, grants to provide child care for families on **welfare**, funds to the states to increase the quality and quantity of child care services, health and safety standards for programs receiving federal support, and authorization for vouchers that could be used at centers run by religious organizations. Feminists had strongly supported federal funding for child care since the early 1970s. They were concerned, however, that the bill threatened the legal doctrine of separation of church and state and could lead to greater influence for the **antifeminist** religious right.

ABOLITIONIST MOVEMENT. A 19th century political movement to abolish slavery in the United States and Great Britain. Historians of the US women's movement have noted strong links between this drive and **woman suffrage**. Early American feminists were active in both organizations, and although **racism** and **sexism** within the ranks of both movements led to their eventual split, the abolitionist movement provided invaluable experience in political organizing. For example, in 1840, at the World AntiSlavery Convention in London, women were permitted to sit in the galleries but not allowed to speak. Among them were **Lucretia Mott** and **Elizabeth Cady Stanton**. In Britain, some female abolitionists eventually became involved in woman suffrage but the two movements were not similarly joined.

ABORTIFACIENT. *See* RU 486.

ABORTION. The termination or loss of pregnancy before the fetus is viable or able to live outside the uterus. Feminist movements throughout history have viewed a woman's control over her own **reproduction**

as a core issue. The **new feminist movement** views safe and legal abortion as a central goal, just as earlier movements embraced **family planning**. At a minimum, an elective abortion should be a choice for women for personal or therapeutic (medical/health) reasons and the incidence of septic abortions, in which an infection occurs, should be extremely low. With the exception of Portugal, Malta, and Ireland, abortions are legal in Western Europe and the United States. However, access is a problem in the United States, where 86 percent of US counties have no abortion providers. The strong **pro-life movement** there also makes aid to international family planning agencies politically difficult. See also BACK-ALLEY ABORTION; HYDE AMENDMENT; ROE V. WADE.

ABORTION CARAVAN. A 1970 DIRECT ACTION BY CANADIAN FEMINISTS who drove from Vancouver to Ottawa to focus public attention on the issue. **Speak-outs** on **back-alley abortions** and the need for legalization were held at each stop. Once in Ottawa, some women chained themselves to seats in the House of Commons. The action followed a 1969 amendment to the federal Criminal Code that legalized the distribution of **birth control** information and **abortions**, if approved by a therapeutic abortion committee (TAC). In 1988, the Supreme Court declared TACs unconstitutional and established the right to abortion on demand.

ABORTION CLINIC VIOLENCE. See CLINIC PROTECTION.

ABZUG, BELLA SAVITSKY (1920-1998). An American lawyer and feminist politician. She was a co-founder of Women Strike for Peace (1961-70), the **National Women's Political Caucus**, and the **Women's Environmental and Development Organization**. Abzug served in the US House of Representatives from New York City, 1971-77. In Congress she was an outspoken exponent of feminism and was criticized for her aggressive style, one that might have been viewed as an asset in a man. She was noted both for her large hats and the amendment barring **sex discrimination** that she commonly attached to every possible piece of legislation during debate. After electoral defeats for the US Senate and mayor of New York City and a brief term as co-chair of President Jimmy Carter's National Advisory Committee on Women, Abzug became active in the international feminist and environmental movements. She wrote *Gender Gap: Bella Abzug's Guide to Political Power for Women* (1984).

ACID ATTACKS. A practice in which sulfuric acid is directed against young women, often by rejected suitors or husbands dissatisfied with the **dowry** or wishing to take a second wife in conservative Islamic nations such as Bangladesh, India, and Nigeria. With a disfigured face, the victim often has to leave school and work and is made unmarriageable. Although illegal the crime is only rarely prosecuted. Women's groups and the United Nations Children's Fund have established services for acid **survivors**. Feminists note that facial slashing of models and actresses occurs in the United States and Europe, suggesting a universal belief that a woman's value lies in her beauty. *See also* DOWRY DEATHS.

ACQUAINTANCE RAPE. *See* DATE RAPE.

ACQUIRED IMMUNE DEFICIENCY SYNDROME. *See* AIDS.

ACTION COUNCIL FOR WOMEN'S LIBERATION/ AKTIONSRAT FÜR DIE BEFREIUNG DER FRAUEN. One of the first organizations of the new German women's movement, founded in Berlin in 1968 to challenge the "comfortable path of dependence" articulated by men of the New Left as an option for women. Its politics aimed to end the exploitation of women in the family and in society. Its programs were based on the needs of mothers; it established alternative children's and mothers' support centers in Berlin. Ultimately the programs failed because of opposition and indifference within the Left itself, and the group disbanded after two years.

ACTION FOR DEVELOPMENT (ACFODE). The most active Ugandan women's rights organization, founded in 1985. ACFODE is a nonsectarian, nonpartisan group that has supported the right of women to run for local office and the establishment of a ministry for women and a women's desk in every ministry. It has been active on **violence against women, female genital mutilation**, education, and the rights of domestic workers.

ACTION FOR THE LIBERATION OF PERUVIAN WOMEN/ACCIÓN PARA LA LIBERACIÓN DE LA MUJER

PERUANA (ALIMUPER). A Peruvian feminist **collective**, organized in 1973 to defend women's rights and engage in **consciousness-raising** on human rights violations. ALIMUPER has been active on many issues of **reproductive freedom** and works with women in trade unions and the slums. Described as combining a mixture of North American feminism and Latin American liberation theology, the group has marched against **beauty pageants** and has allied with the **Mothers of the Plaza de Mayo**.

ACTION, INFORMATION, MOTIVATION (AIM). An Irish lobby group established in 1972 by **liberal feminists** who noted an absence of a political focus in the **women's liberation movement**. AIM led the campaign for reforms in family law and **domestic violence** policy and provided information and legal advice to women on their rights to protection and welfare. The group was very effective and, although still active into the 1990s, much of its agenda had already been achieved. AIM is notable for having entered into mainstream politics in advance of many other feminist groups.

ACUÑA, ANGELA (1888-1983). Costa Rica's first female lawyer and the founder in 1923 and long-time leader of La **Liga Feminista**. Acuña brought the Pan American Round Table Movement, devoted to improving regional understanding and conditions for women and children, to San Jose in 1936. Although she had moved to Los Angeles before Costa Rican women received suffrage in 1949, she became the first female ambassador (from Costa Rica) to the Organization of American States in 1957 and published a history of Costa Rican women in 1969.

AD HOC COMMITTEE OF WOMEN ON THE CONSTITUTION. *See* CANADIAN CHARTER OF RIGHTS AND FREEDOMS, SECTION 28.

ADAM, JULIETTE LAMBER LA MESSINE (1836-1936). A French author, educated by her feminist father. Adam was a firm believer in female autonomy. She responded to Pierre-Joseph Proudhon's theory of women's inferior social value with *Idées antiproudhoniennes sur l'amour, la femme et le mariage (AntiProudhonian Ideas of Love, Women, and Marriage* [1858]). She argued that employment frees adults of both sexes, that the distinction between "masculine" and "feminine" virtues is not significant, and that women have their own intrinsic value not based on their associations with men.

ADAMS, ABIGAIL SMITH (1744-1818). The wife of the second US president, John Adams. She was a spokesperson for women's rights and education in the new democracy and expressed her views in famed letters like her 1776 admonition to her husband to "remember the ladies." She demonstrated political insight about the value and inclusion of women in democracy, and advised her husband and her son John Quincy Adams, the 6th president.

ADDAMS, JANE (1860-1935). The co-founder of Hull House of Chicago (1889), one of the earliest **settlement houses** in the United States. She was elected vice president of the **Women's Trade Union League** in 1903 and of the **National American Woman Suffrage Association** in 1911. Addams also helped organize the National Progressive Party and the Women's Peace Party. She presided at the International Congress of Women in 1915 and served as president of the Women's International League for Peace and Freedom, 1919-1929. She was awarded the Nobel Peace Prize in 1931. Addams was one of the leading exponents of **social feminism** in the United States and lent her considerable prestige to the cause of women's rights.

ADOLESCENT GIRLS. A recent focus of feminist educators on the phenomenon of the "mean girl" in middle school and high schools. In an attempt to understand adolescent female culture in the United States, feminist researchers have identified a variety of teen subcultures dominated by the mean girl (also called the alphas or the **queen bees**), followed by floaters (girls who move from clique to clique), bankers (who use information to cause trouble inside and outside the clique), targets (loners, humiliated and excluded by others because of appearance or class), **sluts** (girls who get demonized as sexually aggressive and experienced, mostly when they are not), and wanna-bes (pleasers or messengers). Rachel Simmons's *Odd Girl Out* (2002); Emily White's *Fast Girls: Teenage Tribes and the Myth of the Slut* (2002); and Rosalind Wiseman's *Queen Bees and Wannabees* (2002) are recent key texts in understanding these trends.

ADVERTISING, IMAGE OF FEMINISTS IN. A caricature of American feminists as all white, middle-class, **lesbian "Feminazis"** in the popular press and culture. In an attempt to change this negative and dismissive stereotype, the **National Organization for Women (NOW)** has produced a series of advertising images that present feminists as construction workers, chefs, CEOs, mothers, daughters, wives and partners. According to former NOW president Patricia Ireland, the advertisements "will shape the way women in the movement are viewed by the public. For many years, advertising has been used to sell, degrade and demean women. Now we're using advertising to do just the opposite—to uplift and honor women" (*NOW National Times*, Fall 1999).

ADVISORY COUNCIL ON THE STATUS OF WOMEN (CANADA). *See* ROYAL COMMISSION ON THE STATUS OF WOMEN IN CANADA (RCSW).

AFFIRMATIVE ACTION. The organizational policies and practices involved in the selection, retention, and promotion of qualified women and minorities in the United States. Affirmative action is concerned with numerical balance in the workforce and uses hiring goals and timetables. In 1965 President Lyndon Johnson signed Executive Order 11246, which required federal contractors to take affirmative action on behalf of racial and ethnic minorities. In 1968 Executive Order 11375 also included sex. In the 1980s and 1990s the policy came to be viewed by some as a denial of the rule of merit. In 1996 California voters adopted an initiative referendum to dismantle affirmative action in that state. Other states and the US Congress have introduced similar legislation. Not until 2003 did the US Supreme Court act to affirm the policy in two challenges of lower court rulings on racial admissions policies at the University of Michigan. *See also* REVERSE DISCRIMINATION.

AFGHANISTAN WOMEN'S COUNCIL (AWC). A nongovernmental organization, formed by Fatana Gailani in 1993 to provide health care and education to women and children in the refugee areas of Pakistan and to teach women their rights within the Afghan cultural and religious tradition. Composed of well-educated Afghan women, the AWC runs a school, clinic, and hospital in Peshawar and Kabul and publishes a monthly feminist newspaper *Zan-e-Afghan* (*Afghan Women*). The group was represented at meetings to form the new post-war national government in 2001. This group should not be confused with the old pro-Soviet group, the **Democratic Organization of Afghan Women**, that became the Afghan Women Council in 1987.

AFRICAN NATIONAL CONGRESS (ANC) WOMEN'S LEAGUE. *See* WOMEN'S NATIONAL COALITION.

AFRICAN AMERICAN FEMINISM. A viewpoint that relies on an interpretive strategy called **womanist** theory, popularized by **Alice Walker**. African American feminism stresses the interactive effects of sex, **gender**, class, race, and sexuality and the error of analyzing the oppression of women in isolation from their race. African American women have historically been activists for women's rights, and have understood the lived experiences of slavery and enforced domesticity in a way that white women have not, but they have been hesitant to embrace a movement that defines the experience of white, middle-class women as universal. Black feminists focus on racial self-affirmation and the building of black community and institutions (particularly the black church), but they have also been active in support of many feminist movement goals. *See also* BELL HOOKS, NATIONAL ASSOCIATION OF COLORED WOMEN; NATIONAL BLACK FEMINIST ORGANIZATION; NATIONAL COUNCIL OF NEGRO WOMEN.

AFRICAN AMERICAN FEMINIST CRITICISM. The effort to illuminate the unique qualities of the African American female experience in American life and culture as they are reflected in literature. Typical approaches to the genre include the attempt to discover lost works by early slave women writers (such as Phyllis Wheatley or Harriet Jacobs) in order to prove that African American women, although denied a formal education, could produce important and significant literary works on their condition. Another critical focus of the field has been to separate the literary works of African American women from white women, thereby arguing for a separate literary tradition for African Americans. Perhaps the most important articulation of an **African American feminist** critique has been posed by Barbara Christian, who has outlined three principles for a black feminist literary criticism: it would "work from the assumption that Black women writers constitute an identifiable literary tradition"; it would be "highly innovative, embodying the daring spirit of the works themselves"; and it would trace the "**lesbian**" subtext in black women's novels (see her "Toward a Black Feminist Criticism," 174-5)

AGEISM. The negative and prejudiced attitudes directed toward the elderly. Feminists note that older women are subject to both ageism and **sexism** in a society that values women for their sexual, **reproductive**, and nurturing capacities, all of which peak during one's youth or middle years. Older feminists are forming groups such as the **Older Women's League** and creating "croning" rituals to celebrate aging.

AGORAPHOBIA. A condition defined as a fear of being in public places. Due to this fear an individual often restricts personal activities severely, rarely or never leaving home or doing so only with a companion. It is one of the most commonly diagnosed phobias seen clinically in females. It typically begins in early adulthood in women who have been married about five years and have chosen a traditional lifestyle. They also have typically been overprotected by their parents. **Feminist therapists** link agoraphobia with traditional **sex role socialization** behaviors such as dependency, unassertiveness, fear of being alone, and fear of functioning autonomously.

AGRARIAN FEMINISM. A version of **social feminism** found among Canadian and US farm women, driven by household agricultural production and the sexual division of farm labor. The family farm has traditionally been viewed as the husband's property; land was often passed on to sons, bypassing the wife and daughters. In the **first wave** agrarian feminists supported "home economics" as a confirmation of their coequal role in production. During the **second wave** farm women demanded recognition as a full partner in the family enterprise and a legal claim to family assets through **marital property** laws.

AID TO FAMILIES WITH DEPENDENT CHILDREN (AFDC). *See* TEMPORARY ASSISTANCE TO NEEDY FAMILIES (TANF).

AIDS (ACQUIRED IMMUNE DEFICIENCY SYNDROME). An often fatal viral infection caused by the retrovirus human immunodeficiency virus (HIV). It is transmitted through the blood or other bodily fluids and thus is often contracted through sexual contact. While the incidence of the disease in the United States was initially highest in gay men, AIDS is now recognized as a worldwide pandemic in which 75 percent of HIV infections take place through heterosexual sex. A majority of HIV cases are in the developing world. It is projected that by 2005 more than 100 million people will have become HIV positive, and by 2010 more than 40 million children will have been orphaned by the disease in Africa alone. In 2000, 50 percent of all adults living with HIV were women. The figure for women was 55 percent in North Africa and the Middle East and 58 percent in sub-Saharan Africa. The HIV virus is transmitted to the fetus in approximately 30 percent of pregnancies of infected women, but women often fail to see their vulnerability to the disease and fail to protect themselves from it. The **global feminist** movement is concerned that world leaders and medical researchers have largely ignored women with AIDS. In 2003 the International AIDS Trust formed a Women's Leadership Initiative to extend prevention programs and care to women. Composed of prominent female leaders such as **Mary Robinson**, the Initiative's primary program to curb HIV infections among women is improving women's rights. On average, women are infected 10 years earlier than men due to early marriages, women's inequality within marriage, **female genital mutilation**, incest, forced **prostitution**, and **rape** among women in developing nations.

"AIN'T I A WOMAN?" The title of the most famous speech given by the African American slave and **abolitionist Sojourner Truth**. In the speech, Truth confronts her white audience with the black woman's claims to humanity. Like the white woman, she too has borne children, worked for their survival, and, unlike the white woman, seen them sold into slavery. She then asks her audience why they do not give blacks and women equal rights, when, as she points out, Christ himself was born of a woman. Although Truth was illiterate and left no written records of her speeches, we have them reconstructed and reprinted in *History of Woman Suffrage* (1881-1902). The term is now used in general parlance to suggest that all women, regardless of race or class, share a common experience of discrimination.

ALIBERTY, SOTERIA (1847-1929). A Greek teacher and feminist, who formed the first Greek women's association, Ergani Athena. Aliberty founded a school for girls in Romania to serve the Greek community and wrote biographical studies of notable Greek women for the *Women's Newspaper* of Athens.

ALIMONY. An amount paid to one spouse by the other for financial maintenance upon **divorce** or separation. With the ruling of the US Supreme Court in *Orr v. Orr* (1979), all state laws on alimony must be **gender-neutral**. The court rejected a view of women as economically dependent in marriage. Rehabilitative, or temporary, alimony may be awarded to the dependent spouse for education and training. Although feminists once viewed permanent alimony as "blood money" and supported this shift, they now recognize the problems faced by older **displaced homemakers** in earning wages sufficient to approximate their former lifestyles. This has become particularly evident in Eastern and Central Europe. With the turmoil of economic transition in the postcommunist era, alimony payments have not been enforced by the legal system and women, themselves unemployed, must continue to live with their former husbands following divorce.

ALL-CHINA WOMEN'S FEDERATION (ACWF). The official women's organization within the Chinese Communist Party (CCP), formed at a national congress of representatives of local women's associations on April 3, 1949. Thereafter, all other women's groups in China were absorbed into the organization. The goals were to unite women, advance their status, and implement the new legal rights of women after national liberation. By 1952 branches of the federation were active in 80 percent of local government units. During the Cultural Revolution (1966-1969), the CCP suspended the federation. In 1979 the ACWF was reestablished and has become active in a government campaign for women's and children's rights. It has attracted more young and well-educated activists and is more independent in representing women's interests. The ACWF has been particularly responsive to **wife abuse** and infanticide stemming from the policy of limiting a couple to **one child**. Since the reforms of the 1980s, the ACWF is no longer the only women's group; many groups based on occupation, profession, and age have formed. However, because of its resources, including three women's newspapers and magazines, the ACWF has the potential to develop into a strong feminist organization.

ALLENDE, ISABEL (1942-). A Chilean novelist and the first female practitioner of the Latin American literary style of magic realism with the publication of *The House of Spirits* (1985). Allende self-identifies as a feminist, although her own views of Latin American **sexual politics** and love sometimes depart from North American feminist thought.

ALLIANCE OF COSTA RICAN WOMEN/ALIANZA DE MUJERES COSTARRICENSES. A women's rights group formed in 1952 to advance equality and combat **violence against women**. The alliance runs training programs for women and is allied with the Afro-Carribbean and Afro-Latin American Women's Networks in litigation against racism and discrimination. Its current project focuses on landownership for women housed in low-income areas.

ALL-INDIA WOMEN'S CONFERENCE (AIWC). A group formed in 1927 that was active in the independence movement and spearheaded the Indian women's movement of the 1930s and 1940s for education, legal equality, and abolition of child marriage. The organization originally attracted members from many ideologies, classes, and religions. Later the AIWC, with its connections to the Congress Party of Gandhi and Nehru, became more elite-based. By the 1970s the group had become primarily a reformist social service and lobbying agency. However, its extensive network of local branches made it a valuable participant in **new feminist** coalitions against **rape** and **dowry deaths**.

ALL-RUSSIAN SOCIOPOLITICAL MOVEMENT OF WOMEN OF RUSSIA (MWR). A group created in 1996 to consolidate the efforts of women's organizations to advance a feminist agenda. A goal was to create a women's voting bloc in national elections. MWR was instrumental in the signing of the **Charter of Women's Solidarity** and has monitored the implementation of the **Convention on the Elimination of All Forms of Discrimination Against Women**.

ALL-RUSSIAN UNION OF EQUAL RIGHTS FOR WOMEN/SOIUZ RAVNOPRAVIIA ZHENSHCHIN (SRZh). The largest feminist organization in Russian history, with 80 branches and over 12,000 members by 1907. It was the primary advocate for **woman suffrage** and women's rights, 1905-1908, and organized an All-Russian Women's Congress in 1908. The SRZh declined under Tsarist repression of radical political movements and disbanded in 1909. Most members joined the government-sponsored Russian League for Equal Rights as an outlet for continued suffrage work.

ALPERT, JANE. *See* "MOTHER RIGHT."

ALTERNATIVE BIRTH MOVEMENT. An alliance growing out of the feminist critique of the **medicalization of childbirth**, consisting of loosely coordinated efforts to inform patients about the benefits and availability of **home births, midwifery, birthing centers** and **birthing rooms, natural childbirth,** and other family-centered birth techniques. Those involved are particularly critical of obstetrical interventions such as fetal monitoring, caesarean sections, induced labor, and routine use of drugs and episiotomies. US feminists have been concerned with returning decision-making power to women in childbirth and lowering the high rate of infant mortality and birth injury in the United States, in comparison with other industrial nations.

ALTERNATIVE INSTITUTIONS. *See* COUNTER-CULTURE.

ALTERNATIVE WORK SCHEDULES. *See* FLEXITIME.

ALVARADO RIVERO, MARÍA JESÚS. The first modern champion of women's rights in Peru and founder in 1914 of Evolución Femenina (Feminine Evolution), Peru's first women's organization. In 1923 she helped organize the National Council of Women, an affiliate of the **International Woman Suffrage Alliance**, and served as its first secretary. In 1924 she was jailed as a political prisoner and later exiled to Argentina for 12 years for printing political pamphlets that supported Indians' and women's rights and for her attempt to involve the National Council in a project to give **married women** certain legal rights.

AMAZONS. A race of warrior women in Greek mythology who lived in Asia Minor and, according to legend, cut off their right breasts in order to use their bows more easily. They practiced a radical gynocracy, fought men in battle, and permitted neighboring men only a brief annual visit to impregnate them. They killed all sons and trained their daughters in the art of war. Some scholars have suggested that Greek traders' encounters with distant nations where men were customarily absent for months on hunting or trading expeditions, leaving women to manage villages, may have lent credence to the myth of the Amazons. The Amazons are seen as a projection of the male fear of female dominance and militancy. Feminists have embraced the idea of a strong group of women who are the military equal of men.

AMERICAN ASSOCIATION OF UNIVERSITY WOMEN (AAUW). A US organization of female college graduates, established in 1881 as the Association of Collegiate Alumnae, to advance educational and employment opportunities for women. A supporter of **social feminism** in the post-suffrage era, the AAUW shifted to a **women's rights** position in the 1960s and has played a major role in lobbying for feminist issues. The group has been a strong advocate of sex equity in education; their 1992 report on this topic, *How Schools Shortchange Girls*, refocused national attention to **gender** bias in the classroom, **sexual harassment**, and the increasing gender gap in science.

AMERICAN CIVIL LIBERTIES UNION WOMEN'S RIGHTS PROJECT (ACLU-WRP) AND REPRODUCTIVE FREEDOM PROJECT (ACLU-RFP). Two feminist litigation groups within the ACLU. The ACLU-WRP was formed under the leadership of **Ruth Bader Ginsburg** as a result of *Reed v. Reed* **(1971)** to use the **equal protection** clause to expand women's rights. The ACLU-RFP was created in 1974 to defend the decision in *Roe v. Wade* **(1973)** against the **pro-life movement** and has become a center of legal and litigation expertise on the subject of **abortion** rights. Janet Benshoof led the ACLU-RFP for 15 years, before resigning to form the Center for Reproductive Law and Policy. Both projects have been parties to many of the major court cases in their respective areas.

AMERICAN EQUAL RIGHTS ASSOCIATION (AERA). A group founded in 1865 to promote the interests of both blacks and women. Under the leadership of Wendell Phillips and Horace Greeley, it shifted to a focus on passage of the **Fourteenth Amendment**, with its introduction of the word "male" into the Constitution. In 1869 the AERA split on the issue of including the word "sex" in the fifteenth Amendment (and thus enfranchising both black males and women); this led to the formation of the **National Woman Suffrage Association** by AERA members **Elizabeth Cady Stanton** and **Susan B. Anthony**.

AMERICAN INDIAN FEMINISM. A tribal model of feminism found among the Native Americans of North America. In many tribal cultures women and men are viewed as equally sacred. **Liberal feminism** is seen as a white concept that conflicts with the precedence given community. Although some Native women living in urban areas are active in national feminist organizations, feminist groups such as Women of

All Red Nations and the Indigenous Women's Network represent Native women living on tribal lands. American Indian women have labored under the stereotype of Pocahontas, princess and squaw, and point to the example of Sacagawea, who may have initiated **woman suffrage** and feminism in the far West during her explorations with Lewis and Clark, 1804-1806.

AMERICAN WOMAN SUFFRAGE ASSOCIATION (AWSA). An organization founded in 1869 by **Lucy Stone** to focus exclusively on the **woman suffrage** issue in contrast to the **National Woman Suffrage Association (NWSA)**, which was concerned with a broad-based women's rights agenda. The AWSA was a more conservative organization, open to both men and women, and accepted the state-by-state enfranchisement of women through state referenda, as opposed to passage of a national constitutional amendment. This split between the AWSA and the NWSA continued until their merger in 1890.

AMIN, QASIM (1863-1908). A French-educated Egyptian lawyer and judge, recognized as the first Arab feminist and called "the Liberator of Egyptian Women." His *Tahrir al-mar'a* (*The Emancipation of Women*, 1899) called for liberalizing usage of the veil, primary-school education for girls, and reform of polygamy and **divorce** laws. The book was the center of the first major controversy in the Arab press and sparked the formation of an Arab feminist movement. Scholars today criticize Amin's eurocentric bias in that he accepted the superiority of Western civilization and expressed contempt for Muslim society and Egyptian women in particular. At root, Amin supported a **patriarchal** Western-style system of **male dominance**. His second book *Al-Mar' a al-jadida* (*The New Woman*, 1900) was written as a rebuttal to his critics and included support for women's rights to higher education and professional careers.

AMNIOCENTESIS. A procedure commonly performed on pregnant women to obtain a sample of amniotic fluid from the uterus to assess fetal health, genetic abnormalities, and maturity. Chorionic villi sampling (CVS) is another prenatal test to detect genetic birth defects and can be performed during the first trimester, as early as the 8th week of pregnancy. This permits prompt diagnosis, earlier fetal treatment, and earlier and safer **abortions**. Since sex can also be determined, female infanticide is a potential problem in cultures where male babies have greater value. One United Nations study found that of approximately 8,000 abortions performed in Bombay after amniocentesis, only one involved a male fetus. Tests that allow families to determine the sex of a fetus have been banned in India since 1994. Feminists support these curbs. An additional problem for feminists is that the pictures accompanying the procedure ("baby's first photographs") give "personhood" to the fetus.

ANARCHIST FEMINISM. A theory, derived from **Emma Goldman**, that argues that the state and man-made law, based on violence and coercion, are responsible for **gender** inequality. Legal equality for women in such a system cannot advance the status of women. Anarchist feminists envision a society without hierarchical structures of domination, one that respects the individual and maximizes cooperative social relations. Anarchist support for personal autonomy has greatly influenced the debate on **reproductive freedom**.

ANATOMY IS DESTINY. *See* BIOLOGICAL DETERMINISM.

ANDROCENTRISM. *See* PHALLOGOCENTRIC.

ANDROGYNOUS. A balance of stereotypically feminine and stereotypically masculine characteristics. Some feminists (**Virginia Woolf** and **Hélène Cixous**) have seen androgyny as a new ideal of psychological functioning because it undercuts or erases the rigid binaries of masculine and feminine. Others, however, like Elaine Showalter, firmly reject the notion, claiming that by eliminating **gender** differences it also fails to recognize the specificity of women's experience and oppression. Other contemporary feminists (**Judith Butler**) are uncomfortable about the use of the term insofar as it is predicated on **sex role** stereotypes.

ANGELOU, MAYA (1928-). An African American poet, screenwriter, actress, and novelist. Angelou has had a checkered career, working as a Creole cook, streetcar conductor, waitress, dancer, madam, singer, and an editor for an English-language magazine in Egypt. She is best known among feminists as a civil rights activist and as the author of the autobiographical series: *I Know Why the Caged Bird Sings, The Heart of a Woman, All God's Children Need Traveling Shoes,* and *A Song Flung Up to Heaven* (1970-2002). In addition, she has published four collections of poetry and read her poem "A Rock, a River, a Tree" for former President Bill Clinton's inauguration in 1993. She teaches American Studies at Wake Forest University and in 2001 agreed to develop a line of greeting cards and gifts for Hallmark.

ANGER, JANE (ca. late 16th century). An English pamphleteer who argued, in the pamphlet *Jane Anger, Her Protection for Women. To defend them against the Scandalous Reports of a late Surfeiting Lover, and all other Venetians that complain so to be overcloyed with women kindnesse* [sic] (1589), that the biblical story of creation offered proof that **Eve** was superior to Adam, as she was created from flesh and given the ability to procreate, while he came from dust. Therefore, by extension, all women were superior to men. Jane Anger may have been a pseudonym used by a man, though this point remains unclear.

ANNEKE, MATHILDE FRANZISKA (1817-1884). A German social activist, writer, and founder of the first German feminist newspaper *Frauen-Zeitung* in 1848. Her **radical feminist** essay "Woman in Conflict with Social Conditions" (1847) attracted much attention. After her emigration to the United States in 1849, she founded the *Deutsche Frauen-Zeitung*, the first US feminist newspaper, and represented Wisconsin at a national women's rights convention in Washington, D.C. in 1869.

ANOREXIA NERVOSA. *See* EATING DISORDERS.

ANTHONY, SUSAN BROWNELL (1820-1906). The best known of the early US women's rights and **woman suffrage** leaders and present at the first women's rights convention at **Seneca Falls** (1848). Anthony was active in the **temperance** and **abolitionist movements**, but during the 1850s she also worked for **equal pay** for women in the New York State Teachers' Association and organized canvassing and petitions for suffrage and for the passage of the New York **Married Women's Property Act** (1860). After the Civil War she concentrated on women's rights. From 1868 to 1870 she edited *The Revolution*, a radical journal demanding suffrage, equal education, equal employment opportunities, and trade unions for women. In 1869, with **Elizabeth Cady Stanton**, she formed the **National Woman Suffrage Association**, and in 1888 she convened the meeting which founded the **International Council of Women**. In 1892 she became the president of the **National American Woman Suffrage Association**; in 1904, with

Carrie Chapman Catt, she founded the **International Woman Suffrage Alliance** in Berlin. She was also the co-editor of *History of Woman Suffrage*, four volumes (1881-1902). She appeared in 1936 on a US postage stamp. In 1979 a dollar coin honoring her was minted; because of its confusing similarity to the quarter coin, it was replaced in 2000 with a new coin in the image of American Indian Sacajawea. *See also* UNITED STATES V. ANTHONY.

ANTIABORTION MOVEMENT. *See* PRO-LIFE MOVEMENT.

ANTIFEMINISM. A philosophical opposition to female equality because of its perceived threat to the model of the traditional family composed of a male wage earner supporting a homemaker wife and children. The antifeminist position, based on a natural law of **biological determinism** and religious principles, dictates separate, but complementary, spheres for the sexes. Women are to be confined to the **domestic sphere** of homemaking and **child care**, while men work outside the home and act as head of the household. Stable family life requires that women have limited choices regarding **divorce**, **abortion**, and a demanding profession within the paid labor force. During the 1980s the New Right **pro-family** movement was the leading proponent of antifeminism in the United States.

ANTIFEMINIST MOVEMENTS. The organized opposition to feminist goals, in particular those of the **Equal Rights Amendment** and legalized **abortion**. These countermovements have a largely female constituency and seek to defend the traditional family and the full-time homemaker. Antifeminists believe that **gender-neutral laws** will deny women long-established protection under the law: exemption from combat, domestic support in marriage, and special benefits in the workplace. *See also* ANTIFEMINISM; CONCERNED WOMEN FOR AMERICA; EAGLE FORUM; INDEPENDENT WOMEN'S FORUM.

ANTIOCH COLLEGE SEXUAL CONSENT CODE. A part of the student conduct code adopted in 1991 by this Yellow Springs, Ohio, institution. The male is required to ask explicit permission from his potential partner at every stage of the sex act (including asking to hold hands). Antioch was motivated by a series of **sexual assaults** on campus in 1990. Even though the language was drafted by students, the code attracted widespread ridicule in the US media for both the document and feminist concern about **date rape**. Many US colleges have subsequently adopted less rigid versions of the code.

ANTIPORNOGRAPHY MOVEMENT. *See* MINNEAPOLIS PORNOGRAPHY ORDINANCE.

ANTISUFFRAGISM. The organized opposition to the **woman suffrage movement**. Antisuffragist ideas were expressed by public officials, political parties, journalists, and ordinary citizens. Groups such as the National Association Opposed to Woman Suffrage and the National League for Opposing Woman's Suffrage led the movement in the United States and Great Britain, respectively. Common objections involved woman's traditional domestic role, which would be threatened by the franchise. Some also argued that women lacked the qualities essential for citizenship. Both liberal and conservative political parties feared an unknown women's vote. Authoritarian and non-Western governments viewed the female vote as a dangerous democratic or foreign idea. Although antisuffragism never attracted a membership comparable to that of supporters, its existence delayed the success of the suffrage movement in every nation.

ANZAC DAY PARADE MOVEMENT. An action by Australian feminists to protest **rape** in war, staged for several years during or before the traditional ceremony for the nation's veterans (originally of the Australia and New Zealand Army Corps [ANZAC]). The demonstrations began in 1977 and participation steadily increased until, in 1981, 61 women were arrested. The marches were well publicized, effectively raised the issue of rape, and provoked the government to repress the protests.

APPROPRIATION. A term used in feminist literary criticism to refer to either women's use of traditionally **masculist** forms of discourse, or to male writers' use of female voices, as in the "ventriloquizing" effect of a female narrator.

ARAB FEMINISM. A Pan-Arab women's movement combining feminism, nationalism, and a concern for the Palestinian cause. It emerged from the formation of the **Egyptian Feminist Union** in 1923. The first Arab Women's Conference was held in 1929 in Jerusalem, and Lebanon, Syria, and Palestine also formed Arab Women's Union groups that year. The **International Alliance of Women** (IAW) was asked in 1939 to intervene on behalf of Palestine, but the IAW was allied with Western imperialism. The Arab Feminist Union was organized in 1944 with six nation-members. The coalition supported **woman suffrage**, marital law reform, and access to education, employment, political office, and health care within independent Arab nations. The new regimes could not accept independent women's groups, however, and appropriated them for nonfeminist purposes during the 1950s and 1960s.

ARAB WOMEN'S ORGANIZATION (AWO). A women's rights group formed in 2001 under the auspices of the Arab League but with financial and administrative independence. The AWO will research the legal status of women in the 22-nation region and make recommendations for uniform laws modeled on the more progressive governments of Egypt and Tunisia.

ARAB WOMEN'S SOLIDARITY ASSOCIATION (AWSA). A Pan-Arab feminist organization (Jam'iyya Taddamun lil-Mar'a al-Arabiyya) formed in 1985 in Cairo with **Nawal el-Saadawi** as president. The AWSA has chapters in several Arab countries and in some ethnic communities outside the Middle East. As a consequence of its challenge to fundamentalist Islamic teaching on women, in 1989 the group was ordered by the Egyptian government to cease publication of its journal *Nun*. In 1990 the AWSA itself was dissolved by the government and its assets were seized and given to the government-sponsored Women of Islam. This abolition was upheld in May 1992 by an administrative court that noted the group "threatens the peace and political and social order."

ARBATOVA, MARIIA IVANOVNA (1957-). A Russian journalist, playwright, and television personality and the nation's most prominent feminist of the 1990s. Her first play caused a sensation because it was about **abortion** and the heroine was a gynecologist. Beginning in the late 1980s, Arbatova wrote about the women's movement, with an emphasis upon the poor health system and the secondary status of women in society. Unlike other notable Russian feminists, she does not work closely with Western feminists. Because of her positive attitude toward love, motherhood, and men, she is credited with legitimizing feminism in Russia.

ARMAND, INESSA FYODOROVA (1875-1920). A Russian and international communist, born in Paris of an English father and French mother and brought up in Moscow. In 1904 she joined the Bolshevik Party. Later she met Lenin in Paris and in 1917 she returned with him to Russia and settled in Moscow. From 1918 to 1920 she was in charge of implementing women's rights in the Soviet Union and was the first head of the **Zhenotdel** (Women's Department). She organized the first school for the wives of workers in Petrograd and Moscow, wrote several articles on women's role in politics, and was in charge of organizing the participation of women in the Bolshevik Party.

ARTIFICIAL INSEMINATION (AI). *See* REPRODUCTIVE TECHNOLOGIES.

ASIAN AMERICAN FEMINISM. A movement that combines a struggle against US **racism** and Asian **sexism**. Asian American women object to their media image as an erotic and submissive female. The writings of feminist authors such as **Maxine Hong Kingston** provide a different definition of Asian womanhood, as does the comedy of Margaret Cho. Women such as Filipino-American Irene Natividad, head of the **National Women's Political Caucus**, 1985-1989, have been important leaders in the feminist movement. Because of the linkage with their native cultures, Asian American feminists have been very active on issues such as **violence against women, international traffic in women, sweatshops**, and female infanticide. Asian American feminist groups include the National Asian Pacific American Women's Forum, National Network of Asian and Pacific Women, and Asian Immigrant Women Advocates.

ASKING THE WOMAN QUESTION. A feminist legal methodology that poses a set of questions formulated to uncover the **gender** implications of rules and practices, which might otherwise appear neutral or objective. It was first referenced by **Simone de Beauvoir** in *The Second Sex* (trans. 1953).

ASSERTIVENESS TRAINING. A course designed to teach people, especially women, how to communicate their wants, needs, and feelings directly rather than indirectly. The purpose is to help habitual nurturers of others to meet their own needs through appropriate verbal and nonverbal expression. Assertiveness training took hold in the 1960s and 1970s as modern feminism was gaining ground. Often assertiveness training classes were a first step for a woman to break out of the traditional roles she had been in and begin to redefine her life in more personally satisfying ways.

ASSOCIATION OF NICARAGUAN WOMEN/ASOCIACIÓN DE MUJERES NICARAGUENSES "LUISA AMANDA ESPINOZA" (AMNLAE). The Sandinista women's organization was established in 1977 as the Association of Nicaraguan Women Confronting the National Problem to resist Samoza and demand human rights and economic reforms. After the revolution in 1979 it assumed its current name, honoring the first female party member to die in combat. The new name reflected an alternative to traditional **gender roles:** childless and a revolutionary. AMNLAE succeeded in advancing gender equality in a nonthreatening way, but lost much of its effectiveness when the ruling party kept **reproductive** health issues off the agenda. An independent women's movement, including an autonomous AMNLAE, returned with the election of Violeta Chamorro in 1990.

ASSOCIATION OF WOMEN FOR ACTION AND RESEARCH (AWARE). The first women's group in Singapore to identify itself as feminist. AWARE, formed in 1985, is a hierarchical, nonconfrontational organization that prefers to engage in closed-door negotiations rather than public lobbying. It supports full equality and equal opportunities for women and offers free legal aid, family and personal counseling, financial training, and a hotline for women in crisis. Current priorities are **violence against women**, education, and **media images of women**.

ASTELL, MARY (1666-1731). An Englishwoman of letters, called the "Philosophical Lady." Astell was a strong defender of women's rights. In *A Serious Proposal to the Ladies* (1692), she condemns the stifling of women's intelligence and proposes a school for women with a similar curriculum to men's schools. In *Christian Religion* (1704), she argues that if God had not wanted women to use their reason, He wouldn't have given them any. And in her work, *Some Reflections upon Marriage* (1700), Astell argues that marriage should be between equals, not a man oppressing his wife into slavery. She supported education for women and outlined controlling facets of **patriarchal** society in works such as *A Letter to a Lady Written by a Lady* (1696) and *An Essay in Defence of the Female Sex* (1696).

ASTON, LOUISE (1814-1871). A **radical feminist** German writer and activist. Aston wore her hair short, dressed in male clothing, and smoked cigars, causing traditional feminists to distance themselves from her defiance of **gender roles** and femininity. She was exiled from Berlin, 1846-1848, because of her beliefs in sexual freedom and emancipation from **patriarchal** institutions such as church, monarchy, and marriage. She published a weekly newspaper recognized as the first German women's movement periodical. Her leaflet *Meine Emanzipation* (1846) and an autobiographical novel *Aus dem Leben einer Frau* (*From a Woman's Life*, 1847) reflect her views.

ATALANTA. According to Greek mythology, the legendary huntress and runner who rejected (and, in some accounts, killed) her suitors after defeating them in a footrace. A modern-day version for children appearing in *Free to Be . . . You and Me* has her outrunning all suitors except one, who is her equal. They tie, become friends, and then each sets out alone to explore the world. After returning home, they may or may not marry.

ATKINSON, TI-GRACE (1939-). A founding member of the New York chapter of the **National Organization for Women (NOW)** and **The Feminists**. Atkinson left NOW in 1968 in protest against its hierarchical structures. In 1970 she left The Feminists after being **trashed** by the group for her prominence in the media and prohibited from contact with the press. A collection of her writings, *Amazon Odyssey*, was published in 1974.

ATWOOD, MARGARET (1939-). A Canadian woman poet and novelist who has published a series of novels that have meditated on the role and identity of contemporary Canadian women: *The Edible Woman* (1969), *Surfacing* (1972), *Lady Oracle* (1976), *Life before Man* (1979), *Bodily Harm* (1982), and *The Handmaid's Tale* (1985). The latter book is best known among feminists as a fictional recreation of the theories of the **radical feminist Andrea Dworkin**. *The Handmaid's Tale* presents itself as science fiction, but it is actually a feminist critique of the reproductive system in place now under the **patriarchy**. Her most recent novel, *Oryx and Crake* (2003), is another vision of a dystopian future in which women are sexually victimized, and the heroine, Oryx, is forced into child pornography. In her poetry Atwood has explored the myths and stereotypes that have confined and dehumanized women throughout history. Her thesis can be summed up in the words of one of her heroines, in *Surfacing*: "That above all, to refuse to be a victim."

AUCLERT, HUBERTINE (1848-1914). A French writer and socialist feminist, called "the French **suffragette**" because of her militant tactics. Auclert founded Droit de la Femme (Women's Rights) in 1878; the group, renamed the Société de Suffrage des Femmes (Women's Suffrage Society) in 1883, supported **woman suffrage**, **equal pay**, **divorce** reform, and equal access to the professions for women. She wrote several books on women's rights, including *Le Droit politique des femmes* (*The Political Rights of Women*, 1878). In her weekly **suffragist** newspaper *La Citoyenne* (*The Citizeness*, 1881-1891), Auclert may have been the first to use the term "feminist" in a 1882 article.

AUGSPURG, ANITA (1857-1943). A German leader, along with her companion Lida Gustava Heymann, of the radical wing of the **woman suffrage movement**. Concerned with women's rights, Augspurg became Germany's first female lawyer. Heymann, a teacher, was active in **dress reform** and the trade union movement. After their meeting in 1896, they worked together through the moderate Federation of German Women's Associations, the German Union for Women's Suffrage, which they co-founded in 1902, and finally the German Women's Suffrage League, a militant group they formed in 1913 on the model of the English movement. Both helped to found the **International Woman Suffrage Alliance** and the Women's International League for Peace and Freedom. Their memoirs *Erlebtes-Erschautes* (*Deeply-Felt*) were published in 1972.

AURORA LEIGH. A book-length verse-novel published in 1856 and generally considered to be one of the most influential protofeminist documents published in England before the rise of an organized feminist movement. The heroine, an orphaned poet, becomes the vehicle for her author **Elizabeth Barrett Browning's** expression of her own social, literary, and ethical beliefs. Aurora, who bears a number of similarities to that other extremely popular Victorian heroine Jane Eyre, also voices a creed that Jane shared: "I too have a vocation—work to do . . . most serious work." The poem attacks the inferior education most women receive, and it goes on to defend the right of women to intellectual self-determination.

AWAKENING, THE. A novel by Kate Chopin, published in 1899, that was violently denounced in the press as "an essentially vulgar story" about a married woman's decision to leave her husband and children, have an adulterous affair, and kill herself. The action of the novel, set in New Orleans, explored the gilded cage of marriage, the stifling effects of marriage and maternity on a woman's creativity, and the essentially deadening social conventions that kept a woman tied to a loveless marriage. Although the novel was vilified at its publication and then "lost" for almost 75 years, it was rediscovered by **feminist literary critics** in the 1970s and has been widely reprinted and taught during the past 30 years.

AWAKENING FOUNDATION/FU NU SHIN CHIH. Taiwan's first feminist organization, formed in 1987 by professional women in Taipei. The women had founded a monthly feminist magazine in 1982 to raise women's consciousness at a time when feminist organizations were prohibited under martial law as too radical. The foundation publishes books, sponsors exhibits and lectures, and provides legal advice to women on **domestic violence, sexual harassment,** and family law. In 1994 it opened Taiwan's first **feminist bookstore,** FemBooks.

-B-

BABY M. *See* IN RE BABY M.

BACK-ALLEY ABORTION. An illegal, unsafe, and expensive **abortion** performed outside the traditional medical system by (often) unlicensed personnel. By keeping abortions in "back alleys," feminists argue that the social problem can be ignored and the woman held responsible. Although such procedures were most common before the modern era of legalized abortion, feminists today point to evidence that women are again resorting to these alternatives in the belief that legal abortions are no longer available in their area because of governmental regulations.

BACKLASH. A counterassault on women's rights that attempts to reverse the achievements of the feminist movement. The current movement is portrayed as having seriously harmed women through its advocacy of **gender-neutral** child custody and **alimony** laws, **no-fault divorce**, and the interests of career women rather than the needs of **pink-collar** mothers. Feminists have also been accused of encouraging women to postpone marriage and motherhood until the opportunities for either become remote. These reactions against women's rights historically have been triggered by the perception that the status of women is rapidly improving. The term is currently used in Canada, the United States, Great Britain, and other European nations.

BACKLASH, MEXICAN. A backlash against feminists led by Mexican radio shock-jock Oscar Muzquiz. Muzquiz announced his search for "*La Fodonga del Ano*," or "The Female Slob of the Year" by inviting husbands to nominate their wives if those women do not shave their legs, serve only packaged food, and watch television all day. Muzquiz began a crusade against "shameless" women who live independently, marry late, and work outside the home. Feminism is presented as the "Americanization" of Mexico, as a new high of 33 percent of all Mexican women work outside the home.

BAJER, MATILDE (1840-1934). A Danish feminist and co-founder of the Danish Women's Association in 1871. She also organized a feminist library and discussion group (1871), a women's trade school (1872), and the Danish Women's Progress Association (1886), which was the forerunner of the Danish **woman suffrage movement**. She worked for **married women's** rights, abolition of **prostitution**, and economic opportunities for women as well as the vote.

BAMBARA, TONI CADE (1939-1995). An African American novelist and leading voice of black literary feminism. She was born Toni Cade, but she took the name "Bambara" from a name she found in her great-grandmother's trunk. Bambara edited the anthology *The Black Woman* (1970) and published the short story collections *Tales and Stories for Black Folks* (1971), *Gorilla, My Love* (1972), and *The Sea Birds Are Still Alive* (1977). Her last novel, *Those Bones Are Not My Child* (1999), was edited for publication by **Toni Morrison**. All of her works deconstruct the stereotypes about black women and generally focus on the struggle between the generations in black culture. Specifically, she is concerned with depicting the clash between the accommodationist generation of blacks and the more militant African centrist blacks.

BARBIE DOLL. A very popular US fashion doll that first appeared in 1959 with a large wardrobe and many accessories. Feminists have criticized the doll's large breasts and tiny waist for creating unrealistic body image standards for girls. However, when a speaking Barbie complained that "math class is hard," feminist protests resulted in the removal of that phrase from the doll's chip. Despite attempts to market alternative toys, including a Dara doll in traditional Islamic dress issued by the Iranian government, Barbie sales remain high. More generally, it serves as a feminist term for a shallow woman excessively concerned with physical appearance, reflected by her use of heavy makeup.

"BAREFOOT AND PREGNANT." A shorthand expression for the subjugation of women, restricted to a domestic role with limited mobility. In the early history of the **National Organization for Women**, local chapters frequently gave "Barefoot and Pregnant Awards" to men for acts of egregious **sexism**. *See also* KINDER-KÜCHE-KIRCHE.

BARRETT, MICHELE (1949-). The author of *Woman's Oppression Today* (1980), a seminal document in the contemporary **Marxist feminist** movement in Britain. Barrett argues that capitalism uses processes of stereotyping, compensation, collusion, and recuperation in order to culturally produce women as commodities for a market economy. Barrett's more recent publications are *The AntiSocial Family* (1982), *The Politics of Diversity: Feminism, Marxism, and Nationalism* (1986), and *The Politics of Truth: From Marx to Foucault* (1991).

BARRY, KATHLEEN. *See* INTERNATIONAL TRAFFIC IN WOMEN.

BATTERED HUSBAND SYNDROME. A **backlash** term that suggests that abuse of men in intimate relationships is more frequent than wife abuse. Feminists note that such studies fail to distinguish between offensive and defensive violence or the severity of the injury. Because men are less likely to be persistently and seriously injured, there is no clinical evidence of a trauma syndrome that describes **domestic violence** against men.

BATTERED WOMAN SYNDROME. A pattern of behaviors of women suffering from repeated abuse by a significant other, usually a husband or boyfriend but sometimes an older child. The batterer is usually, but not always, male. It consists of three phases: tension, followed by minor abuse; more serious violence, followed by the woman's "learned helplessness" to remedy the situation; a temporary lull in abuse, during which the woman forgives her assailant. In some states, testimony on this pattern is admissible as a defense in cases where women have injured or murdered their abusers. It is argued that a consistent pattern of abuse inflicts damage that prevents a woman from protecting herself according to the usual self-defense standards of reasonable force only when death or serious injury is an imminent danger. Feminists argue that battered women fear for their lives from an unarmed man and may legitimately use a weapon against his fists and kicks or wait until he is asleep or otherwise vulnerable to retaliate.

BATTERED WORD SYNDROME. A laconic reference to the demonizing of certain terms associated with the contemporary women's movement. Public opinion polls taken in the 1970s found a sharp decline in support for the goals of the movement when they were presented in terms of **women's liberation**. Similarly in the 1990s the ideals of feminism were supported as the label was rejected. The **National Organization for Women** began an "F" Word Campaign to restore the term to respectability.

BEARD, MARY RITTER (1876-1958). An American historian, author, feminist, and political activist. She helped form the **Women's Trade Union League** in New York and edited *The Woman Voter* for the New York Women's Suffrage League. She was a member of the **National Woman's Party** but left it in 1920 because she supported **protective labor laws** rather than an **Equal Rights Amendment**. Her *Woman as a Force in History* (1946) is viewed as a pathbreaking work in women's history.

BEAUTY PAGEANTS. Stylized contests based on exaggerated physical displays of women's and girls' bodies. Feminists have condemned such contests because they exacerbate the cultural obsession with thinness for women, while at the same time reinforcing the notion of women as passive objects of the **male gaze**. The **Miss America** competition is the culmination of 1,200 state and local pageants, while there are currently countless international, national, regional, state, and local pageants in which young girls, teens, and young women compete in bathing suits and evening gowns. Compared to dog shows by feminists, the beauty pageant encourages the notion that there is an ideal female body type, one that is extremely tall and thin. As such, contestants are prone to **eating disorders**, while pageant organizers have taken to obscuring their demands behind the guise of requiring "physical fitness." Another ruse perpetrated by the organizers is the more recent attempt to align the pageants with social causes, such as "world peace." The proliferation of the beauty pageant subculture has also infiltrated the entire female market, so that girls as young as one year old are being entered in beauty pageants. The recent murder of Jon Benet Ramsay is often cited by feminists as the logical end result of the early sexualization of girls forced to perform in a beauty pageant culture. *See also* MISS WORLD PROTEST.

BEAUVOIR, SIMONE DE (1908-1986). A French existential philosopher and author of the influential *The Second Sex* (first translated into English in 1953), a seminal document in the history of feminist thought. At one time the student and lover of Jean-Paul Sartre, de Beauvoir's book has been seen as a response to his existential masterpiece *Being and Nothingness* (1943). De Beauvoir seeks in her work to understand why women have been constructed as the **"other"** by men. She notes that traditionally the sources for this oppression have been seen in biology, psychoanalysis, and history. But de Beauvoir reviews these three areas and says instead that the reason for women's relegation to "otherness" can be found in her being: "It is not in giving life but in risking life that man is raised above the animal; that is why superiority has been accorded in humanity not to the sex that brings forth but to that which kills." Because men were free from the **reproductive** burdens that women faced, they were free to become subjects capable of shaping their own futures and going to war. This has raised their status above women, who are defined by the limitations of their bodies.

BECKER, LYDIA (1827-1890). An English **suffragist** leader of the Manchester Women's Suffrage Committee and the **National Society for Women's Suffrage**. Convinced that women should study science, she spoke at Liverpool girls' schools and published *Botany for Novices* (1864) and *Elementary Astronomy* (1866). Strongly influenced by the writings of **Barbara Bodichon** and **Richard Pankhurst**, she published her own article "Female Suffrage" in the *Contemporary Review* in 1867. In 1868 she became the first Englishwoman to speak publicly on **woman suffrage**. In 1868, with Richard Pankhurst, she prepared the test case, *Chorlton v. Lings*, which argued that women had the right to vote under older English law because they were included under the generic term "men." It was ruled that custom outweighed the letter of the law, and that new legislation would be required. During the last 20 years of her life Becker edited the *Women's Suffrage Journal*, reporting on all Parliamentary speeches and events related to the cause.

BEECHER, CATHERINE ESTHER (1800-1878). An American writer and educator. Beecher's best-known text, *A Treatise on Domestic Economy, for the Use of Young Ladies at Home and at School* (1856), demonstrates her interest in elevating the character of women's service in the **domestic sphere**. The Christian virtues of service and self-denial were the foundation for Beecher's appraisal of the sacred nature of women's labor in the home. In order to instruct women in their holy mission, Beecher established several colleges and wrote extensively on the need and practical means for educating women. She was a strong advocate of **republican motherhood** and, therefore, an **antisuffragist**.

BELLY-CASTING. A new trend among late-stage pregnant women who make plaster molds of their distended stomachs or whole torsos and turn them into bowls, sculptures, and other decorative items. This public celebration of the pregnant belly is in sharp contrast to earlier days when expectant mothers stayed out of public view and wore shapeless tent-dresses. Today maternity clothes are featured in fashion magazines, and covers of nude pregnant celebrities reflect the pride that women take in their bodies. *See also* LOVE YOUR BODY DAY.

BELMONT, ALVA ERSKINE SMITH VANDERBILT (1853-1933). An American **woman suffrage** leader, speaker, and author who donated the **National Woman's Party (NWP)** mansion in Washington, D.C., where she served as NWP president from 1921 to 1933. She was the US representative to the **International Woman Suffrage Alliance** conventions in 1926 and 1930. After divorcing William Kissam Vanderbilt, she used her wealth to support women's causes.

BENNETT, LOUIE (1870-1956). An Irish trade unionist and **woman suffrage** leader. She and her companion Helen Chenevix founded the

Irish Women's Reform League (1911) to link woman suffrage with improved working conditions for women and the Irishwomen's Suffrage Federation (1913) to coordinate local suffrage society activities.

BESANT, ANNIE (1847-1933). An English feminist challenger, with Charles Bradlaugh, of legal barriers to the promulgation of **birth control** information. In 1877 they reissued Charles Knowlton's contraceptive manual, *Fruits of Philosophy*. Besant's action cost her the custody of her daughter. Also in 1877 Besant helped found the British Malthusian League to disseminate **contraceptive** information.

BETANCOURT DE MORA, ANA (1832-1901). The first Cubana to speak for women's emancipation. At the 1869 Constitutional Congress at Guáimaro she charged that "everything is enslaved in Cuba, the cradle, the color, sex." She was exiled to Spain for her beliefs and remained there until her death.

BHUTTO, BENAZIR (1953-). Pakistani prime minister, 1988-1990 and 1993-1996, and the first woman to lead an Islamic nation. Educated at Harvard and Oxford, Bhutto supported women's rights and democracy and opposed the influence of religious fundamentalists even while wearing the traditional tunic and shawl. She was twice removed from office on corruption charges and now lives in exile.

BIBLE, FEMINIST EXEGESIS. The 19th century use of biblical texts which were supportive of women to counter the passages used by those who wished to keep women in the **domestic sphere**, especially in the **woman suffrage** debate. Also, specific biblical women were held up as models for women. By the end of the 19th century, feminists such as **Elizabeth Cady Stanton** began to view the biblical text as **sexist** and thoroughly **androcentric**. In the 20th century a second stage of feminist exegesis recognized that women in the Bible cannot serve unambiguously as **role models** for women seeking **empowerment** and social change. Feminist biblical exegetes of the late 20th century, while not necessarily completely rejecting the authority of biblical texts, do not recognize sexist texts as authoritative. Many acknowledge ways the Bible has been used as a source of empowerment for women. Using methods developed by feminist historians, many feminist exegetes argue that women and their stories need to be written back into the biblical texts. *See also* FEMINIST LIBERATION THEOLOGY; FEMINIST SPIRITUALITY; WOMAN'S BIBLE.

BILL OF RIGHTS FOR WOMEN. A list of eight public policy demands adopted by the **National Organization for Women** at their 1967 national conference. The most controversial involved passage of the **Equal Rights Amendment** and legalization of **abortion**. Others dealt with **equal employment opportunity, day care, maternity leave**, discrimination in education, and **welfare** reform. By 1996 all had been enacted into law.

BILLINGTON-GRIEG, TERESA (1877-1964). An English **suffragette**, who helped to found the **Women's Social and Political Union**. She later organized the **Women's Freedom League** and was an important leader of the Scottish **woman suffrage movement**. She subsequently broke with the entire movement and denounced it in her *The Militant Suffrage Movement* (1911).

BIOLOGICAL CLOCK. A term that suggests that women who delay childbirth until after age 30 to concentrate on careers face a "now or never" choice complicated by greater infertility. The feminist movement has been criticized for encouraging women to pursue career fulfillment as their chances for motherhood expire. The publication of **Sylvia Ann Hewlett's** *Creating a Life: Professional Women and the Quest for Children* (2002) reignited the debate with her suggestion that young professional women refocus their career paths or begin dating men of lower education or earning capacity. Actually, high-achieving women by ages 36-40 are slightly more likely to be married and mothers than other employed women.

BIOLOGICAL DETERMINISM. An explanation of women's subordinate status based on physiological differences, in particular women's unique **reproductive** role and lesser physical strength. **Antifeminists** thus see **male dominance** as natural. Most feminists believe that women's oppression is not rooted in biology per se but in **gender roles** based on these biological differences. However, some **radical feminists** such as **Shulamith Firestone** espouse a version of biological determinism.

BIRTH CONTROL. *See* FAMILY PLANNING.

BIRTH CONTROL PILL. A daily oral form of estrogen and progesterone that inhibits ovulation and thereby prevents conception. In 1953 **Margaret Sanger** asked Yale biologist Gregory Pincus to investigate a contraceptive pill and persuaded philanthropist Katherine McCormick to support the project. Birth control pills have been available since 1960 in a variety of forms and are intended for long-term use. Although feminists initially welcomed a medical innovation that was convenient and effective, by the late 1960s usage had been linked with fatal blood clots, strokes, cancer, and other less serious sideeffects. The high-dose estrogen pills were removed from the European market in the early 1970s, and, under prodding from the **women's health movement**, they were banned in the US market in 1988. *See also* MALE PILL.

BIRTH PROJECT, THE. A 1985 work by **Judy Chicago** that uses the birth process as a metaphor for creation. The project consists of over 80 needlework units, which range from very small petit point to 20-foot crochetwork. Between 1980 and 1985 Chicago traveled to meet and work with over 130 craftswomen in the United States, Canada, and New Zealand who executed the pieces. *The Birth Project* toured, 1985-1987, and was seen by a quarter of a million people. The pieces were later given to **birthing centers**, hospitals, universities, and museums. Previously, few images of birth existed in Western art despite the universal nature of the experience.

BIRTHING CENTER. A freestanding primary care center providing homelike birthing experiences and access to acute care hospital services and specialist consultation as needed. These centers emphasize a family-centered approach with minimal use of technology. Advantages include cost savings and reduced cesarean delivery rates. Birthing centers are a part of the **alternative birth movement** supported by many feminists.

BIRTHING ROOM. A room in a hospital or **birthing center** in which the mother experiences labor, delivery, and recovery. It may also be used for the entire postpartum stay. The atmosphere is homelike in furnishings and decor. Ideally, there is greater decision-making power for the woman experiencing an uncomplicated birth, and support persons and siblings may be present. *See also* ALTERNATIVE BIRTH MOVEMENT.

BIRTHNAME. See LUCY STONE LEAGUE; NAMING CONVENTIONS.

BISEXUALITY. An orientation or condition that is explained by three dominant theories: biological, suggesting hermaphroditism, or the presence of both sexual organs in one person; psychological or Jungian, as in the presence of "masculine" and "feminine" traits or qualities in one person; and sexual, or the attraction to both men and women as sexual partners by one person, who cannot identify as either purely heterosexual or homosexual. **Freudian** psychological theory argues that "normal" development moves from bisexuality to heterosexuality, but French feminists such as **Hélène Cixous** argue that bisexuality is a type of resistance to "monosexuality," or sexuality focused on the phallus. A current variation of the bisexuality phenomenon is the Bi-Curious Female. This is a woman who wants the advantage of being gay (female comradery) while retaining straight privileges (being associated with a powerful man). Such a woman need not come out of the closet, but **lesbian feminists** see these women as "undecided," responding to **lesbian** chic and invading lesbian spaces with their boyfriends.

"BITCH MANIFESTO." An essay, written by **Chicago Women's Liberation Union** founder Joreen (political scientist Jo Freeman), to redefine the common pejorative used against "unfeminine" women to that of a feminist ideal: an assertive, ambitious, and self-determined woman. The article was reprinted in the **New York Radical Women's** *Notes from the Second Year* (1970). The tradition was continued when the **third wave feminist** magazine *Bitch* was founded in 1996 for outspoken and opinionated young women and Elizabeth Wurtzel published the popular *Bitch: In Praise of Difficult Women* (1998).

BLACK FEMINISM. See AFRICAN AMERICAN FEMINISM.

BLACK MATRIARCHY. A stereotypical image cultivated by social scientists to characterize, and thus denigrate, the role of black women in relationship to their children and black men. The myth has perpetuated the belief that domineering and aggressive women have weakened men, thus leading to the general deterioration of black family life.

BLACKWELL, ALICE STONE (1857-1950). An American feminist and a supporter of **woman suffrage, abolition,** peace, and the women's trade union movement. In 1887 she began editing the "Women's Column," a collection of woman suffrage items sent to newspapers around the country. She assisted in establishing the bond between the **American Woman Suffrage Association** and **Susan B. Anthony's** rival organization, the **National Woman Suffrage Association.** Blackwell became the recording secretary of the new **National American Woman Suffrage Association** in 1890 when the two groups merged. She was the author of *Lucy Stone: Pioneer in Women's Rights* (1930), the biography of her mother. She was also the niece of Elizabeth Blackwell, the first woman physician, and **Antoinette Blackwell,** the first woman minister ordained in America.

BLACKWELL, ANTOINETTE BROWN (1825-1921). The first woman minister to be ordained in America and an active speaker for **woman suffrage.** She supported the right of women to be paid for work outside the home and called for the equality of women in a harmonious universe. She reinterpreted the Bible to reconcile feminism with Christianity and argued against Charles Darwin and Herbert Spencer, who claimed that males were mentally and physically superior.

"BLAMING THE VICTIM." A phrase coined by William Ryan in 1976 to describe the process of attributing personal fault for social problems to those persons who are the victims of socioeconomic and political forces beyond their control or, in other words, placing the responsibility of an event on the person who was the recipient of the damage. For example, women are often blamed for irresponsible childbearing yet simultaneously are denied access to comprehensive **reproductive** health care. Another example is blaming women for being **raped.**

BLATCH, HARRIET EATON STANTON (1856-1940). The daughter of **Elizabeth Cady Stanton** and a leader of the American **woman suffrage movement,** especially in New York. In 1907 she organized the Equality League of Self-Supporting Women, a suffrage group that was the first to include working-class members and to utilize parades and outdoor rallies as tactics. Blatch was also a member of the **National Woman's Party** and a supporter of the **Equal Rights Amendment.**

BLOOMER, AMELIA JENKS (1818-1894). The publisher and editor of the first prominent women's rights newspaper, *The Lily*, in 1849. A **suffragist** and **temperance** leader, she introduced and popularized a new garment, the Bloomer costume, a tunic belted at the waist and a short skirt about knee length over Turkish pantaloons which took the weight of long skirts off women's backs. Intended to give women greater freedom of movement than their restrictive, corseted dress, the "Bloomer" became an object of derision. Advocates of equal rights for women were often ridiculed as "bloomers."

BLUE-COLLAR WOMEN. *See* NONTRADITIONAL OCCUPATIONS, WOMEN IN.

BLUESTOCKING. A term originally applied in 1756 to Benjamin Stillingfleet by Elizabeth Montagu (1720-1800), when he wore blue, not white, stockings to public meetings in order to show his solidarity with the working class. Later the term was used by Montagu and her allies to describe male scholars who were supportive of the writings of females. Both men and women, liberal and dedicated to advancing the work of women and the lower classes, called themselves "Bluestockings," but by the end of the century the term had taken on derogatory connotations and was used only to describe female writers who were meddling in the public sphere instead of staying within the private, **domestic sphere**. The original female members of the Bluestocking circle included, in addition to Montagu, Elizabeth Carter (1717-1806) and Hester Chapone (1727-1801). They rejected the work of **Lady Mary Wortley Montagu** because they believed that she did not combine feminine virtue with learning and education. Instead, they embraced male writers, particularly **Shakespeare**, as the subjects of their scholarship.

BLUESTOCKING SOCIETY/SEITOSCHA. A Japanese women's literary group founded in 1911 by Hiratsuka Raicho. Its journal, *Seito*, addressed such issues as **abortion**, motherhood, **prostitution**, and **woman suffrage** and published Western feminists, including **Emma Goldman** and **Olive Schreiner**. It was on occasion censored by a government concerned with corruption of traditional feminine virtues and stopped publication in 1916. The Bluestocking group gradually disbanded after having raised **feminist consciousness** and presented a model for the **"new woman"** in Japan.

BOBIGNY TRIAL, THE. A 1972 trial held in a Paris suburb, where a poor 17-year-old girl, raped by a schoolboy, received an **abortion**. Her mother and two of her mother's friends were charged under a 1920 law that prohibited obtaining or aiding in abortion. The defense argued that, in arranging for her daughter's abortion, the mother was performing a maternal duty. As a result of the national dialogue arising from the case, abortion was made legal in France in 1975.

BODICHON, BARBARA LEIGH-SMITH (1827-1891). An English aristocrat who argued in the pamphlet *A Brief Summary in Plain Language of the Most Important Laws Concerning Women, Together with a Few Observations Thereon* (1854) that **married women** had precious few legal rights. In 1855 she, along with others, organized a committee to petition Parliament to increase married women's control over their property and earnings. In 1865 Bodichon delivered a paper to the Kensington Society calling for **woman suffrage**; this led to a committee to work for suffrage, a petition drive to Parliament, and the beginning of the British suffrage movement.

BODY POLITICS. A term used to suggest that the human body is a social and ideological product constructed to conform to or reinforce prevailing attitudes toward "women's appropriate place" in society. Building on the theories of **Michel Foucault**, this concept sees the human body as perceived, interpreted, and represented differently in different historical periods because of differing material cultures, technologies, and means of control. What Foucault has called "the discourse of the body" emerged in the late 18th and early 19th centuries as a response to a new set of social, political, and cultural meanings that gave new significance to both male and female bodies. The obsessive biologization of femininity can be seen in the 19th century's need to equate women's bodies with **reproduction** and the forces of nature, and to claim that women were uniquely prone to various new diseases, like hysteria, that originated in their bodies.

BOGUS CLINICS. *See* FAKE CLINICS.

BONA FIDE OCCUPATIONAL QUALIFICATION (BFOQ). A term referring to a justification of what would otherwise constitute unlawful **sex discrimination**. Section 703 (e)(1) of Title VII of the US **Civil**

Rights Act of 1964 allows individuals to be hired on the basis of sex when that characteristic is reasonably necessary to the normal operation of a particular business or enterprise. Even while upholding mandatory **maternity leave** for flight attendants for reasons of passenger safety, the Supreme Court indicated that the BFOQ exception is subject to an "extremely narrow" interpretation. In *Phillips v. Martin Marietta Corporation* (1971), for example, the Court concluded that an employer's policy which denied employment to women but not men with preschool-age children was unlawful. The Court suggested that the BFOQ exception might be applied if an employer could prove that family obligations are more relevant to the job performance of a woman than a man; to date, this "sex plus" test has not been met.

BOSTON WOMEN'S HEALTH BOOK COLLECTIVE. A nonprofit group founded in 1969 as an advocate for accessible information about women and health. In 1970 the New England Free Press published a newsprint edition of what would become the best-selling commercial book entitled *Our Bodies, Ourselves* (1973). The collective has continued to operate and has published other editions and books. *Our Bodies, Ourselves for the New Century* (1998) reflects their more diverse membership in terms of class, race and ethnicity, age, sexual identity, and disabilities. Another revision is planned in 2005 for the 35th anniversary. Profits are used to fund other women's health projects such as the Our Bodies, Ourselves Global Network, which helps women's groups outside the United States to translate and adapt the text.

"BOTTLE BABY DISEASE." A health crisis among children stemming from the practices of infant formula manufacturers to encourage use of their product in developing countries. In using the free samples, new mothers become dependent on formula as their breast milk dries up from disuse. Because of the cost of the product (between $900 and $1,200 annually), women in developing nations dilute it and also use unsafe water or unsterilized containers. In 1984 a seven-year international boycott of Nestlé, widely publicized by women's groups, forced some reforms, and in 1993 all infant food manufacturers agreed to stop providing free samples in developing countries that prohibited this practice. Although women's groups note that the companies are not in compliance with these new rules, the rise of the **AIDS** epidemic has altered feminist strategies. Because **breastfeeding** accounts for one-third of all HIV-infected babies, the provision of free formula to HIV-positive mothers is supported.

BOURGEOIS FEMINISM. A term used by **Marxist feminists** to describe those who support equal rights for women but deny or ignore the need for system-transforming change in society. According to this critique, these middle-class reformers are counterrevolutionary dilettantes, who dabble in politics as an avocation.

BOYER, ELIZABETH. See WOMEN'S EQUITY ACTION LEAGUE.

"BOY-TOY." A derisive and disapproving term that refers to an intimate relationship between a woman and a younger man. Feminists note that this is an example of a **double standard** that ignores that the sexual drives of older women and younger men may be more similar than the conventional "May-to-December" relationships between older men and younger women. See also TROPHY WIFE.

BRA-BURNERS. See MISS AMERICA PAGEANT PROTEST.

BRADLAUGH, CHARLES. See BESANT, ANNIE.

BRADWELL V. ILLINOIS, 83 US 130 (1873). A decision of the US Supreme Court that upheld the exclusion of women from the practice of law. It is perhaps best known for Justice Joseph P. Bradley's expression of the **"separate spheres"** ideology, in which the male spouse was the breadwinner and the couple's representative for public purposes, while the woman's role dominated the family and the home. The separate spheres ideology became the basis for upholding many laws limiting women's rights, including *Hoyt v. Florida* (1961), which upheld a state law that automatically exempted women from serving on juries unless they volunteered their names. The Court agreed that women should be free to decide if jury duty would be compatible with their special domestic responsibilities. This policy was rejected by the Court in *Taylor v. Louisiana* (1975) on the grounds that restricting jury service to only special groups or systematically excluding identifiable segments that played major roles in the community was a violation of a criminal defendant's right to be tried by a jury comprised of a fair cross section of the community.

BRAUN, LILY (1865-1916). A German writer and member of the Social Democratic Party. Her strong feminist views, expressed in *Die Frauenfrage* (*The Women's Question,* 1901), alienated party leaders who believed that women's issues should be subordinated to those of the working class as a whole. Braun was forced to leave the party, but she continued to work for the radical, militant wing of German feminism.

BREAD AND ROSES. A Boston **women's liberation** network formed in 1969 by Meredith Tax and Linda Gordon to link through weekly meetings small local **feminist collectives** engaged in their own projects. Women were involved in **women's studies**, antiwar efforts, arts groups, **zap actions**, and **consciousness-raising**. The group was **politico** in approach and lasted until 1973.

BREAST CANCER. A form of cancer that occurs in breast tissue. It can be treated by surgical removal of the breast and all adjoining lymph tissue (radical mastectomy), removal of just the breast tissue (mastectomy), or removal of just the cancerous tumor (lumpectomy). Surgery is usually followed by radiation and chemotherapy. Feminists have questioned the use of radical mastectomy, despite evidence that in the early stages a lumpectomy has similar survival rates. They have also challenged the overselling of mammograms in detection and the overuse of dangerous drugs such as tamoxifen in treatment. Feminists have become increasingly vocal about prevention and support more research into possible environmental causes. US feminists have succeeded in greatly increasing the amount of money allocated for research, including revenues from a special postage stamp. The **women's rights movement** has also moved to protect breast cancer **survivors** against discrimination in **employment** and **insurance**.

BREAST IMPLANTS. Elective cosmetic surgery to augment (increase) the size of women's breasts or for reconstruction following mastectomy. The procedure has become controversial due to complications resulting from the use of silicone gel implants. Dow Corning, the primary supplier of these implants, was forced into bankruptcy after a US court in 1995 awarded $4.2 billion to women with implants suffering from autoimmune and neurological diseases. In 1999 a National Academy of Sciences study concluded that implants had no linkage to these diseases. Women's health advocates continue to be concerned about the safety of implants. The feminist movement has also been critical of the importance placed on the female breast that causes women to be dissatisfied with their bodies. *See also* BREAST CANCER.

BREASTFEEDING. The use of milk produced by a woman's mammary gland to feed an infant. The modern **women's rights movement** has encouraged the practice because of health benefits to both mother and child, particularly in developing countries where formula is expensive and water is often unsafe. The right of women to nurse in public and to pump milk in the workplace for later use is also supported. *See also* "BOTTLE BABY DISEASE."

BREMER, FREDRIKA (1801-1865). A Swedish novelist and social reformer. She is credited with introducing the "domestic" novel in 1831, including *Hertha* (1856), which greatly influenced the status of women in Sweden, as did her classic work written after traveling in America, *The Homes of the New World* (1853). She actively supported women's legal rights and founded a school to train female teachers. She also opposed the church's political conservatism and theological rigidity, while pressuring the government to change its laws in regard to women. The first national Swedish women's group, the **Fredrika Bremer Association** honors her work.

BRIDEGIFT/BRIDEWEALTH/BRIDESERVICE. A practice whereby a bridegroom demonstrates respect for his bride (bridegift) and her family (bridewealth) by presenting them with gifts or assisting them with his labor (brideservice). These established the groom's ability to support a wife and do not involve purchasing a woman from her family. Bridewealth continues to be a common practice among many societies in Africa, Asia, and the Pacific, as well as some American Indian tribal nations. The alternative custom is **dowry** in most European and South Asian countries. *See also* DOWRY DEATHS.

BRITISH WOMEN'S TEMPERANCE ASSOCIATION (BWTA). A group formed in 1876 to eliminate drunkenness in England by both political means, through pressure on Parliament to eliminate grocers' liquor licenses, and evangelical means, through the use of missionaries among the poor. By 1892 the BWTA had some 577 branches with approximately 45,000 members. Under the leadership of Lady Henry Somerset, the BWTA became actively involved in **woman suffrage**.

BROWN, RITA MAE (1944-). A contemporary American **lesbian** novelist and poet. She joined the **National Organization for Women** in 1968 and insisted that the group confront the issue of lesbian rights. As one of the **Radicalesbians**, she wrote *The Woman-Identified Woman* (1970) and has been active as a lecturer on feminism and gay liberation. She has published widely, from collections of poetry—*The Hand that Cradles the Rock* (1971), *Songs to a Handsome Woman* (1973)— to collections of essays—*A Plain Brown Rapper* (1976)—to *Rubyfruit Jungle* (1973), one of the first works to present the lesbian "coming-out" experience, and *Rita Will: Memoir of a Literary Rabble-Rouser* (1997). In the 1990s she began writing a mystery series with her cat as co-author and is now a full-time novelist rather than an activist-writer.

BROWNING, ELIZABETH BARRETT (1806-1861). England's first major female poet. She was also a translator, **abolitionist**, feminist, and political activist for Italian unification. Browning's importance for feminism, despite her avoidance of women's groups, lies in her publication of a number of poems that plead for women's rights, the need for an equal education, and intellectually rewarding employment. *See also* AURORA LEIGH.

BRUNDTLAND, GRO HARLEM (1939-). The prime minister of Norway in 1981, 1986-1989, and 1990-1996. She was active in the **new feminist movement** and advocated for feminist issues such as liberal **abortion** laws and the political participation of women. In 1986 she named eight women to her 18-member cabinet and established a tradition of a 40 percent female quota in cabinet formation. In 1998 Brundtland, a medical doctor, became the head of the UN's World Health Organization, where she worked on women's health issues until her term concluded in 2003. She also sought a worldwide ban on tobacco advertisements and urged drug companies to lower the price of their **AIDS** drugs in poorer nations. She continues to lecture on global health issues.

BULGARIAN WOMEN, THE COMMITTEE OF. An organization within the Communist Party, in operation 1944-1990 as the sole women's group in Bulgaria. Although lacking influence within a totalitarian one-party regime, the group's journal *Zhenata dnes* (*Woman Today*) was a popular and liberal journal. Official goals included improving the status of women, public education, and lobbying for needed policy changes. In 1990 a splinter group, the Women's Democratic Union, emerged to assist in women's transition to a postcommunist economy. It has embraced both feminist and traditional roles for women and works with the European Parliament on legal projects.

BULGARIAN WOMEN'S UNION (BWU). An organization formed in 1901 by professional women and the wives of politicians. The BWU supported **woman suffrage**, education for girls and women, and women's access to elected office and the professions. It was disbanded in 1946 with the communist takeover and was reestablished in 1993. The BWU has over 6,000 members in over 100 chapters throughout the nation. It focuses on traditional charity work, **family planning**, and **violence against women**.

BULIMIA NERVOSA. See EATING DISORDERS.

BUNINA, ANNA (1774-1829). An early 19th century poet generally credited with originating women's poetry in Russia. The author of both poems and essays, Bunina constructed a female poetic persona, rejected conventional **gender roles** and engaged in professional rivalry with the more popular male poets of her day.

BURNS, LUCY (1879-1966). An American feminist, participant in the English **woman suffrage movement**, and leader of the militant wing of the American suffrage movement. The **Women's Social and Political Union** (WSPU), led by the **Pankhursts**, bestowed a special medal for valor on Burns, who was arrested numerous times and joined in the prison **hunger strikes** in 1909. In 1912 Burns returned to the United States and organized the immense suffrage parade the day before Woodrow Wilson's inaugural. That same year she helped form the Congressional Union for Woman Suffrage (CU). With **Alice Paul**, Burns shaped the major policies of the CU and of its successor organization, the **National Woman's Party (NWP)**. Imprisoned in 1917 for picketing the White House, she was sentenced to prison in the notorious Occoquan Workhouse, where she joined hunger strikers and was force-fed, which brought the suffrage cause to national attention.

BURQA. The required veil worn by Afghan women under the Taliban, 1996-2001. This head-to-toe, heavy garment only allows a mesh opening for the eyes and is far more restrictive than other Islamic veils. The **Campaign to Stop Gender Apartheid in Afghanistan** sold swatches of a burqa to be worn as a sign of solidarity with the women there. The garment poses hearing and vision hazards and has been linked with asthma, depression, vitamin D deficiency, and headaches. The burqa is expensive, and poor women under the Taliban either shared the garment or stayed inside to avoid a beating for revealing skin in public. The burqa was made optional in 2002, but Afghan women continue to wear it for safety and security. *See also* MCSALLY, MARTHA.

BUTLER, JOSEPHINE GREY (1828-1906). An English moral reformer and feminist. Butler was one of the leaders of the Ladies' National Association for the Repeal of the **Contagious Diseases Acts** and the founder of the first international **moral reform** society, the English, Continental and General Federation for the Abolition of Government Regulation of **Prostitution.** She viewed **woman suffrage** as an instrument for social reform.

BUTLER, JUDITH (1956-). A contemporary feminist philosopher who publishes on sexual difference, language theory, and queer epistemologies. Professor of comparative literature and rhetoric at the University of California-Berkeley, Butler gained attention with the 1990 publication of her book *Gender Trouble* in which she argued that feminists had erred in seeing "women" as a group with similar interests, characteristics, and values. Instead, she argues that by accepting "male" and "female" bodies as the bedrock of culture, feminists have placed themselves in the same position they were trying initially to escape. Her position on **gender** is that there is no "natural" sexual predisposition, as all sexual positions are equally culturally constructed and produced by language. Influenced by the theories of **Michel Foucault,** Butler sees gender and desire as free-floating and discursive: "There is no gender identity behind the expressions of gender; identity is performatively constituted by the very 'expressions' that are said to be its results" (GT, 25). By "gender trouble," she means mobilizing subversively to create a confusion and proliferation around the category of gender. Recent books by Butler include *Excitable Speech: A Politics of the Performative* (1997), *The Psychic Life of Power* (1997), and *Bodies that Matter: On the Discoursive Limits of 'Sex'* (1993).

-C-

CALIFORNIA FEDERAL SAVINGS AND LOAN ASSOCIATION V. GUERRA, 479 US 272 (1987). A US Supreme Court decision that determined whether a California fair employment law, which created for pregnant employees a qualified right to reinstatement after **maternity leave**, was valid. The petitioners argued that Title VII of the **Civil Rights Act of 1964** forbids the state of California from legislating practices that favor pregnant women. The Court concluded that Congress did not intend to prohibit preferential treatment of pregnant women in the **Pregnancy Discrimination Act.** Feminists were split on the importance of this case. Those committed to the equal treatment of women feared the revival of **protective labor laws** that could make employers less willing to hire women. Others argued that preferential treatment of pregnancy simply recognized the differential burden of childbearing. The passage of the **Family and Medical Leave Act of 1993** rendered the dispute moot by providing a leave for both fathers and mothers after the birth of a child.

CALL OFF YOUR OLD TIRED ETHICS (COYOTE). The first **prostitutes'** union, founded in San Francisco on Mother's Day 1973 by Margo St. James, a former prostitute. COYOTE seeks to decriminalize prostitution in the United States, end the stigma attached to sex work, and promote safe sex. It also helps those choosing to leave the occupation. Feminist response is mixed. Most feminists support decriminalization, but some view prostitution as a form of economic and social exploitation of women.

CAMPAIGN TO STOP GENDER APARTHEID IN AFGHANISTAN. A movement begun in 1997 by the **Feminist Majority Foundation** to build public awareness of the plight of women under the Taliban. More than 200 women's and human rights groups joined the effort that adopted many of the strategies of the South African anti-apartheid campaign. With the fall of the Taliban in 2001, the group became the Campaign to Help Afghan Women and Girls and now works for women's rights and participation within the new government and for development and peacekeeping assistance. Some feminists have shifted their attention to gender apartheid policies in Saudi Arabia. *See also* BURQA.

CAMPBELL, KARLYN KOHRS (1937-). A contemporary American feminist rhetorical historian, theorist, and author of a two-volume critical work on women's public address, called *Man Cannot Speak for Her*. Campbell is known for her thorough reconstruction of women's historical situations and their unique strategic responses to the situations. Her work, which critiques women in terms appropriate to them, has helped to establish the field of feminist rhetorical criticism.

CAMPOAMOR RODRÍGUEZ, CLARA (1888-1972). A Spanish feminist, lawyer, and suffrage leader. As one of the first two women to serve in the national legislature in 1931, Campoamor is credited with the passage of the **woman suffrage** act that same year. Ironically, she was forced to defeat a weakening amendment offered by her female colleague. Her role in winning the vote for women alienated her Radical Party, which refused to renominate her in 1933. Her efforts to get her own group, the Women's Republican Union, on the ballot were unsuccessful, and she left Spain.

CANADIAN CHARTER OF RIGHTS AND FREEDOMS, SECTION 28. A provision of the federal Constitution adopted in April 1982 which guarantees the equal rights and freedom of males and females. The provision was the product of a two-year campaign primarily by anglophone feminists, including the **National Action Committee on the Status of Women (NAC)**. This coalition of women's groups, the Ad Hoc Committee of Women on the Constitution, was also successful in gaining an exemption of Section 28 from a provision allowing provinces to ignore charter guarantees in special limited circumstances. The **Fédération des Femmes du Québec**, unable to support the federal charter because of issues of provincial autonomy, withdrew from the NAC over this issue. Feminist litigation using this section and the equality provisions of Section 15 has brought important changes in laws on **abortion, child support, rape, sexual harassment**, and pregnancy discrimination.

CAPETILLO, LUISA (1879-1922). A Puerto Rican feminist, working-class leader, and author. Capetillo is believed to be the first woman in Puerto Rico to wear pants in public. In 1910 she founded *La Mujer*, a women's rights paper, and wrote the first women's rights manifesto. She was an advocate of free love and a sharp critic of the power of marriage to enslave women and the exploitation of female manual workers.

CAREER FEMINISM. A tradition based on individual self-determination and achievement in the labor force, assertive resistance to male-imposed barriers, and a willingness to help other women through **networking** and **mentoring**.

CARRASCO, PANCHA (FRANCISCA) (1826-1890). A Costa Rican war heroine who has become a symbol of the **new feminist movement**. During the Battle of Rivas (1856) she grabbed a rifle, joined the front, and helped to secure the San Juan River. She was able to serve President Juan Rafael Mora after the war because she was literate, unlike most women of her time. The Pancha Carrasco Collective was founded in 1986 as a **consciousness-raising** support group for women.

CARRILLO PUERTO, ELVIA (1878-1967). A Mexican socialist politician who, with her brother Felipe, formed feminist leagues in Yucatan to combat immorality and illiteracy and to advocate **birth control**. She was elected to the Yucatan legislature in 1923 and to the national Chamber of Deputies from San Luis Potosi in 1925, a seat she was denied on the grounds that suffrage and office-holding were restricted to males. Returning to Yucatan, she organized the Liga Orientadora de Acción Femenina (Orienting League of Feminine Action) to lobby for **woman suffrage**.

CARTER, ANGELA (1940-1992). A British novelist and essayist, best known in the United States as a feminist reteller of traditional fairy tales. In *The Bloody Chamber* (1979) she presents a **postmodern** version of Red Riding Hood and the Bluebeard story in order to reverse the power in the texts. In "The Company of Wolves" she presents Red Riding Hood as calmly seducing the wolf, while eating the lice off his body. A profound interest in the Marquis de Sade motivates much of her vision, as does her conviction that the mysterious permutations of desire control most of human behavior.

CASA DELLA DONNA. A house for women founded in Rome by the **Movimento di la Liberazione della Donna**, which simply occupied a vacant church on October 2, 1976. At various times the house was a **birth-control** clinic, a day-care center, and an office coordinating antiviolence and **reproductive freedom** activities. The house also functioned as a **women's center** for other feminist groups and projects.

CASGRAIN, THÉRÈSE (1896-1981). A Quebec **woman suffrage** leader and feminist, radio hostess, and politician. In 1922 Casgrain was a founder of the Provincial Franchise Committee, later the League for Women's Rights. Her influencial radio program *Femina*, broadcast during the 1930s in both French and English, was directed at giving rural women more social awareness. Quebec women won the right to vote in 1940. Casgrain became the first woman to head a Canadian political party in 1946, was a co-founder of the **Fédération des Femmes du Québec** in 1966, and was appointed to the Senate in 1970.

CAT AND MOUSE ACT. The popular name for the Prisoner's Temporary Discharge for Ill Health Act passed by the British Parliament in 1913 to deal with **hunger strikes** staged by the **Women's Social and Political Union**. Women imprisoned for militant suffrage actions were permitted to refuse food but were released when they became ill to prevent their martyrdom. When recovered, the women were arrested and reimprisoned as many times as needed to complete their sentences. The technique was successful but also controversial because it could prolong a short sentence over a very long period. *See also* WOMAN SUFFRAGE MOVEMENT.

CATHOLIC FEMINISM. A belief that the Roman Catholic Church must adjust its religious tradition on women within today's more egalitarian society. There are three main approaches. The most conservative, **holistic feminism**, embraces the movement without challenging the church's traditional teaching on women. A moderate approach is to challenge **patriarchal** organization and espouse **liberal feminism** by accepting church social teaching and ignoring its sexual teaching. The most radical tradition seeks to reshape church doctrine on **reproduction** by noting the primacy of conscience within Catholic social teaching. This is the approach of Catholics for a Free Choice, a US group founded in 1973.

CATHOLICS FOR A FREE CHOICE. *See* CATHOLIC FEMINISM.

CATT, CARRIE CHAPMAN (1859-1947). An American **woman suffrage** leader and founder of the **League of Women Voters**. She is credited with bringing a strong organization to the **National American Woman Suffrage Association** as its president, 1900-1904 and 1915-1920. She also served as president of the **International Woman Suffrage Alliance**, 1904-1923. In 1912 Catt took control of the New York suffrage movement, organizing two major campaigns which eventually won the state vote for women in 1917. After national suffrage was won in 1920, Catt became active in the peace movement.

CELIBACY. A conscious decision by some feminists to conserve energy that otherwise would be spent on men and sex. The **Feminists** advocated celibacy as an alternative lifestyle choice. Such abstinence could be permanent or for a limited period to permit women to discover themselves. Most feminists do not regard celibacy as a realistic solution to inegalitarian relations between the sexes but do recognize it as a form of sexuality.

CELL 16. An early Boston **radical feminist** group formed by Roxanne Dunbar in 1968. Originally known as the Female Liberation Front, the group pioneered **self-defense** by studying karate, advocated **celibacy** and **separatism**, and published *No More Fun and Games*. In 1970 the group and its journal were the targets of an attempted takeover by the Socialist Workers Party, a conflict that weakened the group and led to its demise in 1973.

CENTER FOR THE AMERICAN WOMAN AND POLITICS (CAWP). A research center founded in 1972 as part of the Eagleton Institute of Politics, Rutgers University, to examine the status and impact of women in public office in the United States. Through its publications and conferences, the CAWP has been central to the formation of a network of female officials and in introducing many of these women to the feminist agenda.

CENTER FOR WOMEN'S GLOBAL LEADERSHIP (CWGL). A US research center founded in 1989 at Rutgers University as part of its Institute for Women's Leadership. CWGL promotes feminist principles in policy-making in local, national, and international settings, with an emphasis on human rights. It coordinates the **Sixteen Days of Activism Against Gender Violence Campaign** and annually holds an international conference to promote women's leadership.

CERETA, LAURA (1469-1499). An Italian Renaissance feminist whose letters, published in 1488, were widely read in Europe. Cereta was a well-educated intellectual and ardent feminist. She wrote of the oppression of women in marriage, supported a woman's right to an education, and decried the lack of information on the contributions of women to society and history.

CERTIFIED NURSE MIDWIFE (CNM). *See* MIDWIFERY.

CHARTER OF WOMEN'S SOLIDARITY. A 1997 declaration signed by 39 Russian women's organizations and 10 female politicians or public figures, supporting the advancement of women in society. Its broad agenda reflected the diversity of the signatories, which included feminist, peace, and charitable organizations. By 1999 more than 300 groups had signed the charter. *See also* ALL-RUSSIAN SOCIOPOLITICAL MOVEMENT OF WOMEN OF RUSSIA (MWR).

CHASTITY BELT. Any locking device that prevents sexual intercourse, especially by women. Associated with the Middle Ages, the belts were first mentioned and pictured in a book published in 1405 and were endorsed by 19th century Western physicians for both boys and girls to prevent masturbation. Erotic versions are currently available, and in the United States and Western Europe the male model accounts for 75 percent of sales. Elsewhere the majority are sold for women, who may be forced to wear them. In Western nations, many female customers are abuse **survivors** who feel safer in this restraint.

CHICAGO, JUDY (JUDY COHEN, 1939-). *See* BIRTH PROJECT; THE; DINNER PARTY, THE.

CHICAGO WOMEN'S LIBERATION UNION (CWLU). The first, largest, and most enduring of the **socialist feminist** unions, formed in 1969. In the early 1970s the CWLU had around 500 dues-paying members, more than the local chapter of the **National Organization for Women**, and a number of projects, including the **Jane Collective**. It disbanded around 1977, a victim of leftist sectarian disputes.

CHICANA. A term referring to a woman of Mexican origin residing in the United States who has had to fight oppression both within her own culture and from outside. The struggle is threefold: to overcome repression by colonialism, by the Anglos, and by men. She has sought to forge her own identity on **gender**, race, and culture issues simultaneously. This effort is manifested not only in political action but also in artistic endeavors such as literary, theatrical, and other diverse cultural presentations.

CHICANA FEMINISM. The awareness by women within the Chicano movement of issues especially related to them and needing to be viewed from a feminist perspective. During the 1970s **Chicanas** began to examine their role not only as Mexican-Americans within US society, but also their position in the Chicano movement itself. They confronted *machismo* from within and without; they looked anew at racial and **gender** stereotyping of Chicanas; they studied the role of the Chicana in the family and the workplace; and they attempted to define the nature of Chicana feminism and its relevance to the general feminist movement. During the past few decades, numerous national conferences have dealt with issues of general concern to Chicanas: education, employment, gender and race discrimination, health care. Chicana feminist writings have proliferated. Chicana feminists emphasize the interstructuring of race, class, and gender **oppressions**. Only when these issues are viewed together and as interconnected can the experience of the Chicana be adequately understood and appreciated. *See also* LATINA FEMINISM.

CHILD CARE. *See* DAY CARE.

CHILD SUPPORT ENFORCEMENT. A commitment from government and the courts to award and collect financial support from a child's noncustodial parent, usually the father, regardless of the legal relationship of the parents. The United States has a poor record of awarding and enforcing child support (compared with Germany, where there is a compliance level of 75 percent). Beginning with the Child Support Enforcement Amendment of 1984, the US Congress has greatly strengthened the laws. Although feminists see enforcement as helpful in terms of providing economic support, such efforts also reinforce a woman's economic dependency on the father of her children and may force a mother to continue contact with an abusive partner.

CHIPKO MOVEMENT. An effort to combat deforestation in northern India. The movement, composed mostly of women and their children, began in the 1970s when British industrial log-cutting became critical. Indian village women must travel widely to gather firewood and fodder because of deforestation. In 1973 hundreds of protesters literally hugged the trees ("chipko" in Hindi) and succeeded in preventing their removal. Chipko originally was not viewed as a part of the women's movement, but since the 1980s it has become a symbol of feminism and **ecofeminism**.

CHISHOLM, SHIRLEY (1924-). The first African American woman to serve in the US Congress (1969-1983, from New York) and a candidate for the Democratic nomination for president in 1972. She has documented her experiences in *Unbought and Unbossed* (1970) and *The Good Fight* (1973). One of her major accomplishments was coverage of (mostly female) domestic workers in the minimum wage law. She also worked for the rights of women and racial minorities, for the improvement of employment and educational opportunities, and for reforms in inner-city living conditions. After retiring from Congress, she held the Purington Chair at Mount Holyoke College until 1987.

CHODOROW, NANCY (1944-). An American sociologist whose publications have challenged the traditional view that females are biologically predisposed toward nurturing infants. Mothering, she has argued, fulfills a woman's psychological need for reciprocal intimacy that originates during her own babyhood when she and her own mother perceived each other as extensions of each other. Mothers are also close to their infant sons, but they view their male children as different and do not share with them the same sense of "oneness" that they experience with their daughters. Mature males, unaccustomed to a psychologically intimate relationship, are, therefore, content to leave mothering to women. This theory, developed in *The Reproduction of Mothering* (1978) and *Feminism and Psychoanalytic Theory* (1989), argues for a change in traditional parental roles. Chodorow's most recent book, *The Power of Feelings* (2003), argues that psychoanalysis offers a theory of subjectivity—or individual experience—that is not found elsewhere in feminist or social thought. Emotions allow us to make sense of our experiences, and she stresses the importance of unconscious fantasies to "help us construct our inner world as well as our sense of the external world." Further, she argues that **gender** is "an individual creation." One's sense of gender is "animated" by one's own selective synthesis of bodily experience, cultural beliefs and practices, and personal relational history.

CHOISIR/TO CHOOSE. A liberal **feminist** group especially prominent in the French **abortion** and **rape** reform movements, led by lawyer and Parliament member Gisèle Halimi and organized in 1971 to defend the signers of the *Manifeste des 343 femmes*. In 1974 the group helped to form a feminist political party, the Parti Féministe Unifié Français, which was not successful in national elections. Choisir used litigation, lobbying, and electioneering as main strategies and in 1978 issued its platform for legal and social change, the Common Program for Women.

CHORIONIC VILLI SAMPLING (CVS). *See* AMNIOCENTESIS.

CHORLTON V. LINGS (1868). *See* BECKER, LYDIA.

CHUPIREN/PINK PANTHERS. A Japanese **women's liberation** organization founded by Misako Enoki in 1972. The pink-helmeted group received much media attention for their direct actions against male adulterers and batterers and for legalization of **abortion** and **birth control pills** in Japan. Enoki retired from public life and Chupiren was disbanded after her Japan Woman's Party failed to win a seat in the legislative elections of 1977.

CINDERELLA COMPLEX, THE. The pattern of pathological female dependence on men described by Colette Dowling in her 1981 popular book with the same name. While feminists join Dowling in her concern about those women who look to men to rescue them, they have objected to the book's implication that, as a whole, women are more dependent than men.

CIRCUMCISION, FEMALE. *See* FEMALE GENITAL MUTILATION.

CITADEL. *See* UNITED STATES V. VIRGINIA.

CITIZENS' ADVISORY COUNCIL ON THE STATUS OF WOMEN (CAC). A body established in 1963 by US President John F. Kennedy to continue the work of the **President's Commission on the Status of Women**. The council continued to operate until 1977, when President

Jimmy Carter appointed a similar body that was disbanded under President Ronald Reagan. Composed of private citizens, the CAC played an important role in implementation of subsequent antidiscrimination policies through its research and publication program and its sponsorship of national conferences of **State Commissions on the Status of Women. Antifeminists** charged that the council's private citizen membership allowed it to publish feminist propaganda and lobby for feminist causes at government expense. CAC support for the **Equal Rights Amendment** and the **International Women's Year** was especially criticized.

CIVIL RIGHTS ACT OF 1964, TITLE VII (CRA). A US law making it unlawful to discriminate against individuals in **employment** because of sex, race, color, religion, or national origin. The law covers private employers with more than 15 employees, unions, employment agencies and federal, state, and local government. Although the CRA was primarily directed toward racial equality and was passed before the revival of a feminist movement, **sex discrimination** was included because of the interest of many members of Congress and women's groups.

CIVIL RIGHTS MOVEMENT, THE. The movement begun by African Americans in the US south in the 1950s to challenge racial prejudice and segregation. Its importance with respect to the women's movement is similar to the 19th century **abolitionist movement**. Even though the leadership was male dominated, for the black and white women who took part in numerous sit-ins and demonstrations during the 1960s, it fostered **consciousness-raising** on issues of inequality, injustice, and oppression, while at the same time providing experience in political mobilization. However, sexual and racial politics within the movement eventually led to exclusion of whites from some civil rights groups in the mid-1960s. According to feminists, the resulting separation along racial lines (e.g., the "black power" movement and the "white" antiwar movement) culminated in the formation of groups that were typically male dominated. However, the leadership for the **new feminist movement** eventually emerged from the ranks of these other activist groups.

CIXOUS, HÉLÈNE (1937-). A leading French **postmodern** feminist and author of a number of feminist works that explore the relation between language and culture. Cixous's theories are not easy to summarize, but she is basically concerned with the distinction between women as biological and social and "female," "feminine" or "other," where these terms refer metaphorically to the condition of being other in a relation of difference rather than in opposition. Cixous has tried to create a feminine language and female society outside of and apart from male language and society, and has been criticized for doing so by other French feminists like **Julia Kristéva**. Generally speaking, Cixous is concerned with how the politics of language controls the social roles assigned to women. Most of her early writings have been translated into English and published in this country as *The Newly-Born Woman* (1986) and *Inside* (1986). Cixous is most accessible through her much-reprinted essays, "The Laugh of the Medusa" and "Castration or Decapitation?"

CLAFLIN, TENNESSEE CELESTE. See WOODHULL, VICTORIA CLAFLIN.

CLASSISM AND FEMINISM. The critique that feminist discourse, historically the domain of white middle-class women, has often occluded or ignored the systematic harms of class segregation, disparity, and exploitation. Some feminists now explore the complex interactions of classism, defined by **Audre Lorde** as "the belief in the inherent superiority of one class over the other and thereby the right to **dominance**," with **sexism** and **racism**. Both the compounded sufferings of women caused by class and the feminists' own unacknowledged classism are exposed, and transformative responses are sought. *See also* OPPRESSIONS, INTERSTRUCTURING OF; RACISM AND FEMINISM.

CLICK! A term referring to a moment of feminist insight triggered by a personal experience (e.g., a woman suddenly conscious of having repeatedly thanked her husband for cleaning a common living area). These experiences lead some women to develop a **feminist consciousness** that exposure to abstract **feminist political theory** would not produce.

CLINIC PROTECTION. The protection from **harassment** of women who enter clinics where **abortions** are performed. People are trained in nonviolent tactics, such as escorting women or forming human barriers to prevent **pro-life** activists from blocking access to the clinic. US and

Canadian clinic protectors have also had to deal with bombings, arson, and other attacks upon abortion facilities and death threats (and eight murders since 1991) directed against clinic personnel. Antiabortion groups in other nations such as France have adopted some of these tactics. In 1994 the Freedom of Access to Clinic Entrances Act (FACE) was passed. This law makes it a federal crime to injure, intimidate, or interfere with someone trying to enter or leave an abortion clinic. FACE has led to a decline in clinic violence and has been upheld by the federal courts. *See also* NOW, ET AL. V. SCHEIDLER, ET AL.; OPERATION SAVE AMERICA.

CLINTON, HILLARY RODHAM (1947-). A US senator from New York, elected in 2000, and the wife of former US president Bill Clinton. As a nationally acclaimed Yale-educated attorney who had always been her husband's policy partner, she has been a feminist **role model** for the nation and a sympathetic figure following the disclosure of her husband's relations with **Monica Lewinsky** and **Paula Jones**. Some of her comments during the 1992 presidential election campaign ("I suppose I could have stayed home and baked cookies," and "I'm not some little woman standing by her man") raised controversy as did her direction of the president's national health care proposal, 1993-1994. Clinton also focused on women's and children's issues such as mammography and TV violence and on a book about children. She has assumed a high profile in the Senate and is frequently mentioned as a possible presidential candidate. Her memoir *Living History* (2003) received an advance of $8 million.

CLITORIDECTOMY. *See* FEMALE GENITAL MUTILATION.

CLONING. *See* STEM CELL RESEARCH.

CLOTHESLINE PROJECT. A feminist campaign focusing on **violence against women** modeled on the **AIDS** quilt. The action began on Cape Cod, Massachusetts, in 1990 as part of a **Take Back the Night** demonstration. T-shirts, each decorated by an abuse **survivor** (or her friend, in cases of death) to reflect her story and feelings, are hung on a clothesline. Dozens of projects nationally and internationally have collected as many as 50,000 garments.

CLUB FEMENINO DE CUBA. A Cuban women's club, formed in 1917, to advance social issues such as children's courts, **prostitution,** women's prisons, and women's rights. In 1923 the club formed an association of women's groups that organized the First National Women's Congress in Havana (1923) to discuss a broad range of social reform and women's issues. In 1925 the club held a second congress, where a split developed between the **radical feminists** of the club and conservative and religious feminists, who supported **woman suffrage** but also the traditional family and a class-based society. In 1928 the club was supplanted by the newly formed Alianza Nacional Feminista (National Feminist Alliance) as the leading feminist group. Suffrage was granted in 1934.

CLUB WOMAN'S MOVEMENT. The involvement of middle-class American women during the last two decades of the 19th century in voluntary associations. These early groups were committed to literary study and self-improvement but also social, economic, and political reforms such as **temperance, woman suffrage,** child labor, conservation, and health care. This period marked the first widespread public role for women in their communities. In 1890 the club movement formed the **General Federation of Women's Clubs.** Black women's clubs, excluded from this federation, formed the **National Association of Colored Women.**

COALITION AGAINST TRAFFICKING WOMEN. *See* INTERNATIONAL TRAFFIC IN WOMEN.

COALITION FOR WOMEN'S APPOINTMENTS. An effort by US women's groups to encourage new presidents to appoint qualified women to policy-making positions. The first "talent bank" was organized in 1969 by the **National Federation of Business and Professional Women's Clubs.** In 1976 the **National Women's Political Caucus** established the present coalition, which is reformed at the beginning of each new administration.

COALITION OF LABOR UNION WOMEN (CLUW). A women's caucus within the American Federation of Labor-Congress of Industrial Organizations (AFL-CIO), established in 1974 to seek equality for women within the union movement and in the larger society. The CLUW has urged greater union efforts to organize women in service occupations, inclusion of women in union leadership, and more active support of women's issues by the AFL-CIO. In 1980 CLUW president Joyce Miller became the first woman elected to the AFL-CIO Executive Council. Under pressure from the CLUW, the AFL-CIO has vigorously lobbied on feminist issues such as **child care, comparable worth,** the **Equal Rights Amendment, family leave,** and **pregnancy discrimination.** Its 18,000 members constitute approximately 1 percent of female union members, primarily those already within the leadership ranks of union committees and local office. Despite this upper-status bias, the CLUW effectively serves as a network for female union members and a liaison with other women's groups and the AFL-CIO.

CODE NAPOLÉON DE 1804. The civil code of France establishing the family, not the individual, as the basic unit of society and giving the husband as "head" control over all family property. It stated that the wife owed obedience to her husband and was barred from public life unless her husband permitted or required such involvement. The code was amended during the late 19th and early 20th centuries to extend certain rights to **married women,** and between 1965 and 1975 the Napoleonic family code was almost completely rewritten to give married women equal rights in the family. The code, however, was adopted throughout Europe in the early 19th century and its influence is also found in the family codes of Japan, Egypt, parts of Central and South America, Canada, and Louisiana.

CODEPENDENCY. A relationship between two people that includes excessive dependency upon one another, so that each is expected to meet unhealthy emotional needs of the other. This term is often used to describe the relationship between an alcoholic and his or her partner, where not only is the partner's life consumed in meeting the needs of the alcoholic, but the alcoholic also meets the needs of the partner to be needed. As codependency became increasingly defined as a female neurosis, some feminists became wary of a possible cult of the **victimization of women.**

COLLADO, MARÍA (1899-?). An upper-class Cuban **suffragist** who founded and led the Partido Demócrata Sufragista. In 1929 she began and edited *La Mujer,* the party's journal that ran until 1942. She was both a radical and a conservative who supported **gender** equality and rejected **patriarchy.** Collado was committed to improving working conditions for women but betrayed her **elitism** by arguing that the wealthy should lead the movement and could represent lower-class women. Further she believed that **Marxist** and **socialist feminists** hurt the movement by taking the focus off gender issues.

COLLECTIVE. An organization based on principles of radical participatory democracy and equality characterized by lack of hierarchy and consensual decision-making. These communities operate with only minimal specialization of labor and rules and an equal sharing of profits and rewards. Many **women's liberation movement** groups were organized as collectives, as were the first feminist **counter-culture** institutions.

COLLETT, CAMILLA (1813-1895). A Norwegian novelist who was the first to write in *Amtmannens dötre* (*The Sheriff's Daughter*, 1855) on women's subordinate position in Norwegian society. The furor that greeted its publication only strengthened her feminism, as reflected in her later writings. She remained aloof, however, from the organized women's movement in Norway.

COLONIZATION, EFFECT UPON WOMEN. An area of research that originally focused on the effects of imperialism on "third world" countries. More recently feminists have performed a critique of the negative effects of imperialist colonization upon women. Colonization disrupts the political-economic structure of the colonized nation and imposes a regime often based on conscripted male labor. Families must accommodate the loss of able-bodied men who may be furloughed only long enough to impregnate their wives again (reproducing the labor force). The women are left in rural areas to raise crops and maintain homes alone for most of the year. Market enterprises are restricted by the colonial agents, curtailing women's independent incomes. Traditional political and religious structures that may have provided women with status or power are usually ignored or replaced with a hierarchical **patriarchal** government. Colonial policies encourage the treatment of **woman as other**, while racist practices encourage colonial agents to co-habit with local women (whom they were often forbidden to marry) and sometimes encourage them to bring wives from the home country and establish homes in government compounds where local women serve as domestics and nannies. The imposition of the colonial government's culture denigrates colonial peoples and frequently devalues their arts, especially those practiced by women. Independence movements have encouraged revivals or development of indigenous arts, but global economics have prevented restoration of preconquest political-economic patterns. Further information is available in Gayatri Spivak, *In Other Worlds* (1987). See also DEVELOPMENT, WOMEN IN.

"**COLONIZATION OF THE FEMALE.**" A phrase used in **feminist literary criticism** to refer to a male author's **appropriation** of female subjectivities or experiences, such as the equation of masculine literary production with giving birth. Feminist literary critiques of "**androgyny**" in male authored texts frequently rely on the charge of colonization of the female, or the notion that males absorb the female in order to present themselves as self-propagating, in a denial of their reliance on the mother's body.

COLOR, WOMEN OF. A phrase used in the United States to describe women who are of African, Asian-Pacific, Hispanic, or American Indian heritage. This umbrella term recognizes that common experiences of **racism** and **sexism** unite these women across vast differences of culture and language. The **intersectionality** of race, class, and **gender** in their daily lives is the principal framework for discussing racial-ethnic women. See also OPPRESSION, INTERSTRUCTURING OF.

"**COMFORT WOMEN.**" A term used to describe Asian women forced into **prostitution** by the Japanese Army during World War II. As many as 200,000 women from six Asian nations were sent to military bases, where they were daily raped and beaten by soldiers. Although many women died in captivity, some by murder, **survivors** began to speak out in the early 1990s and three Korean women filed a compensation suit in Japan in 1991. After demonstrations by Korean women, Japanese Prime Minister Kiichi Miyazawa publicly apologized for the episode. Of the $1.3 billion paid by Japan in war reparations, none was paid to these women and no one was tried for these crimes. In 1995 the government established a compensation fund for them.

COMMISSION ON IMPROVING THE STATUS OF WOMEN (CISW). A Russian bureaucracy, created in 1997 to coordinate governmental and civic group efforts to advance women's rights. It is also responsible for making recommendations that would bring Russia into compliance with international treaties on women. Although the

Women's Union of Russia has representation, the independent feminist movement has not been included and the CISW maintains a very low public profile.

COMMITTEE FOR THE EQUALITY OF WOMEN. See ROYAL COMMISSION ON THE STATUS OF WOMEN IN CANADA (RCSW).

COMMITTEE OF MOTHERS/COMITÉ DE MADRES (COMADRES). A Salvadoran human rights organization established in 1977 by 12 mothers with the support of Archbishop Oscar Romero. Its purpose was to protest against political violence and death squad activity in El Salvador. In 1978 its members staged their first public demonstration. By the mid-1980s, as the violence grew, its membership increased to 400. Like other mothers' organizations in Latin America, COMADRES initially utilized the traditional **gender roles** of mother and wife as the basis for national and international political and human rights activism. It has gradually adopted a feminist stance that includes women's rights within the human rights framework. Since the 1990s COMADRES has focused on both state and **domestic violence**, women's participation in elections, and **self-help** projects to make women independent.

COMMITTEE OF SOLDIERS' MOTHERS OF RUSSIA (CSM). An organization created in 1989 to protect the human rights of draftees, soldiers, and their parents. The group became visible internationally during the war in the separatist republic of Chechnya as Russian mothers walked onto bases and pulled their sons from the frontlines. This challenge to authority brought the group a Nobel Peace Prize nomination in 1995. Although the CSM is admired by **global feminists** for their message of peace and nonviolence, the group has preferred to invoke traditional Russian ideas of motherhood and womanhood rather than identify with feminism.

COMMITTEE OF SOVIET WOMEN (CSW). The official women's group of the Communist Party of the Soviet Union. It was a successor of the sponsored women's movement active in the postrevolutionary period but disbanded in 1930 when female equality had, in theory, been achieved. With the resurgence of feminism in the West, members of the CSW, chaired by the first woman astronaut, Valentina Tereshkova, represented the nation at international women's conferences where they reported that Soviet women were world leaders in equality and happiness. The CSW was transformed into the **Women's Union of Russia** in the 1990s.

COMMITTEE ON THE STATUS OF WOMEN IN INDIA (CSWI). A body established by the Indian government in 1971. In 1975 it released its influencial report *Towards Equality.* Its data on women's status in religion and the family, in health care, and under law were new to many well-educated citizens and led to pressures for new public policies and heightened interest in **empowering** women through community organization and cultural change.

COMMUNES. *See* SEPARATISM.

COMMUNITY PROPERTY. *See* MARITAL PROPERTY LEGISLATION.

COMMUTER MARRIAGE. A union in which both husband and wife are employed in different locales, thus requiring the maintenance of two residences and co-habitation only during work holidays. Such arrangements have become increasingly common as women have attained professional and managerial positions that are not easily coordinated with a spouse in a similarly demanding career.

COMPARABLE WORTH. The principle that men and women should receive equal compensation when employed in positions that require comparable, rather than identical, skill, responsibility, and effort. The concept evolved from the **equal pay for equal work** doctrine in response to the fact that traditionally female occupations receive lower compensation than traditionally male occupations. This results in positions such as mechanics, janitors, and bus drivers receiving higher wages than primary school educators, nurses, and child care workers. In the mid-1970s US feminists adopted pay equity as a goal and were successful in gaining comparable worth policies in several state and local governments. The opposition of the Reagan administration, the loss of a federal appeals court case in 1985, and a perceived conflict with market-set wages prevented further adoption of the policy in the United States. In 1999, however, the Canadian Human Rights Tribunal awarded C$3.5 billion dollars to more than 200,000 female civil servants in a pay equity lawsuit, and in Ontario all companies with more than nine employees must implement pay equity. A 2002 study of the **wage gap** in Minnesota, where comparable worth for state employees is required, found a gap of 73 percent for all women workers and a gap of only 97 percent for women who work for the state. *See also* OCCUPATIONAL SEGREGATION.

COMPULSORY STERILIZATION. *See* STERILIZATION ABUSE.

CONCERNED WOMEN FOR AMERICA (CWA). A religious fundamentalist **antifeminist** women's organization founded in 1979 by **Beverly LaHaye.** The group, with its 500 local chapters and 500,000 members, claims to be the largest women's public policy organization in the United States. Its daily radio program and monthly *Family Voice* promote opposition to **abortion,** secular humanism and sex education in the schools, and **homosexuality.** The CWA uses litigation and grassroots lobbying as tactics.

CONGRESS TO UNITE WOMEN. A regional conference of **women's liberation** groups held in New York City, November 21-23, 1969. The Congress was the first large meeting of local feminist groups and over 500 women attended. A press conference held at the conclusion announced the movement to the nation. Later congresses were held in other cities and parts of the country.

CONGRESSIONAL CAUCUS FOR WOMEN'S ISSUES (CCWI). A group formed in 1977 as the Congresswomen's Caucus within the US House of Representatives. Its purpose was to facilitate the exchange of information on women's policy issues between female members of Congress, the bureaucracy, and feminist organizations and to organize support for pending legislation and monitor implementation after enactment. In 1981 the name was changed and membership was opened to congressmen. Only congresswomen, however, could serve on the executive committee that set policy. In 1995, when public funds were cut off to all legislative caucuses, the CCWI became an informal all-female group, and Women's Policy, Inc. was formed to track federal legislation affecting women and families as a separately incorporated but associated policy center.

CONGRESSIONAL UNION. *See* PAUL, ALICE.

CONGRESSWOMEN'S CAUCUS. *See* **CONGRESSIONAL CAUCUS FOR WOMEN'S ISSUES.**

CONSCIOUSNESS-RAISING (CR). A feminist strategy of small-group discussions concerned with increasing a victim's awareness of discrimination, oppression, and **sexual harassment**. A key component of **feminist therapy** and the early **women's liberation** groups, CR is tied to the notion that many of the stumbling blocks for women are social in origin. CR has been most often associated with groups in which women could share their experiences. Today CR is most likely to occur on the internet.

CONSORCIO PARA EL DIÁLOGO PARLAMENTARIO Y LA COMUNICACIÓN HACIA LA EQUIDAD/CONSORTIUM FOR PARLIAMENTARY DIALOGUE AND COMMUNICATION TOWARD EQUALITY. Mexico's feminist lobby in the federal Congress. The consortium, formed in 1999, is a coalition of local activists and organizations that proposes and advocates for legislative reform, with an emphasis on ending legal forms of discrimination.

CONSORTIUM OF WOMEN'S NONGOVERNMENTAL ASSOCIATIONS. A US-funded coalition of Russian women's groups, formed in 1994 to build the Russian women's movement and expand programming for women. Ninety-nine groups from 37 regions have joined the consortium. These groups have received many grants for training, travel, Internet communication, conferences, and publications. After an initial period of US leadership, the consortium is now run by Russian women.

CONTAGIOUS DISEASES ACTS. English legislation of 1864, 1866, and 1869 that authorized the police to detain and subject to a medical examination any woman suspected of being a **prostitute** in order to guard the health of military personnel. Earlier attempts to subject male soldiers to such examinations had been rejected; instead, the policy sought to ensure that male sexual needs could be safely met. Under strong opposition from a Victorian feminist group led by **Josephine Butler**, the acts were suspended in 1883 and repealed in 1886. From their participation in this and other **moral reform** movements, English women and women in other parts of the British Empire and Europe, began to demand the vote. **Antisuffragists** saw the linkages between the two issues as further proof that a female vote would end **male domination.**

CONTEMPORARY FEMINIST MOVEMENT. See NEW FEMINIST MOVEMENT.

CONTRACEPTIVE ACTION PROGRAMME (CAP). See MCGEE CASE.

CONTRACEPTIVE EQUITY. The requirement that if an employee health **insurance** plan covers prescription drugs and devices, it must cover prescription **contraceptives.** Feminists point out that when **Viagra**, a drug for male impotence, is included in coverage, the exclusion of contraceptives, used almost exclusively by women, represents **gender discrimination.** In 2000 a ruling by the US **Equal Employment Opportunity Commission** agreed, as did a decision in 2001 by a US district court in Washington, D.C.. By 2003 20 US states required contraceptive equity.

CONTRACEPTIVE TRAIN. See MCGEE CASE.

CONTRACEPTIVES. See BIRTH CONTROL PILL; FAMILY PLANNING.

CONVENTION ON THE ELIMINATION OF ALL FORMS OF DISCRIMINATION AGAINST WOMEN (CEDAW). An international treaty adopted by the United Nations General Assembly on December 18, 1979, and ratified or acceded to by 170 nations. The United States signed it in 1980, but the US Senate has failed to ratify it. The women's convention is a statement of women's human rights and a framework for women's participation in the **development** process. Ratifying governments are obligated to eliminate **sex discrimination** and to file periodic reports on that effort with the Committee on the Elimination of Discrimination Against Women, an independent group of experts established under the convention. Ignored by the US Senate for decades, the treaty has been accused of being a blueprint for foisting the West's feminism on a global community. CEDAW bans "any distinction, exclusion, or restriction made on the basis of sex."

COSMETIC GENITAL SURGERY. A procedure performed on infants born with sexually ambiguous genitals and increasingly on adult women. In most cases the female child will receive a **clitoridectomy** and the male will be treated surgically and with hormones to live as a female. Feminists object to these definitions of "normal" and suggest that the operation be delayed until the child can make the decision. As women show more of their bodies in swim attire and in men's magazines, requests to reduce enlarged, asymmetrical labia, reconstruct vaginas stretched by childbirth, and remove excess skin from the pubis are becoming more common. Feminists warn that this surgery can result in sexual dysfunction, chronic pain, and disfigurement.

COUNTER-CULTURE. The alternative women-owned institutions that provide services to other women and help to create a women's community. The myriad of such enterprises include bookstores and publishing houses, restaurants and coffee houses, churches, record companies and music festivals, theater groups, **day-care** centers, credit unions and banks, art galleries, and professional and business services such as health care, legal aid, and car repair. These institutions offer a refuge from a **male-dominated** world, a challenge to the legitimacy of this system, and a promise of a women's culture based on female values. *See also* CULTURAL FEMINISM.

COUNTERFEIT CLINICS. *See* FAKE CLINICS.

COURTESY TITLES. *See* MS.

COUSINS, MARGARET (1878-1954). A co-founder of the **Irish Women's Franchise League** and of the Indian Women's Association and the **All-India Women's Conference** after her emigration in 1915. She was the first non-Indian member of the Indian Women's University at Poona, the founder and first head of the National Girls School in Mangalore, and the first woman magistrate in India.

COVERTURE. The common law doctrine that, with marriage, a woman's separate status disappeared and she became the legal responsibility of her husband. She had no right to own property, control her own wages, sue or be sued, or sign contracts. The first break with this doctrine came in England and the United States with the adoption of **Married Women's Property Acts**.

CRAIG V. BOREN, 429 US 190 (1976). A decision of the US Supreme Court that established a new standard for evaluating laws that make distinctions on the basis of sex. At issue in this case was the constitutionality of an Oklahoma statute prohibiting the sale of low-alcohol beer to males under the age of 21 and females under the age of 18. The Court concluded that Oklahoma's scheme failed to satisfy the new intermediate standard: that it be "substantially related" to "important" governmental objectives. The issue before the Court was whether the differential treatment of males and females violated the **Equal Protection** clause in the **Fourteenth Amendment**. The intermediate standard recognizes the legitimacy of some **gender** classifications without a theory about which are legitimate and why. In a 1981 case dealing with **statutory rape**, for example, sex-based classifications were permitted. Women's rights advocates had hoped to get the Court to rule sex a suspect classification, which would require a "compelling" governmental purpose for discrimination. The proposed **Equal Rights Amendment** would have done this, and this new standard served to undermine the ratification effort by implying it was now unnecessary.

CROSS-DRESSING. The habit of assuming the clothing of the opposite sex in order to experience a sexual identification with that other sex. Cross-dressing challenges the binary categories of male and female. The term is generally applied to men who assume the undergarments of women for sexual satisfaction. Some have suggested that this may be the flip side of feminism in that these men want to feel soft and glamorous. In earlier times the habit was recognized and condemned when women (such as George Sand) assumed the dress of a man. Feminists of the **dress reform** movement, however, viewed male attire as liberating. Another possible manifestation of this phenomenon can be discerned in the tradition of the "sworn virgin" of northern Albania. Such women, who desire to avoid an arranged marriage, swear an irreversible oath to remain **celibate** and live as men for the rest of their lives. Dressing as men, these women carry guns, smoke, assume male labor, and become heads of households. Although the communist government attempted to eliminate the custom, recent research (by René Gremaux and Antonia Young) has documented that the custom still exists in Albania.

CULT OF DOMESTICITY OR TRUE WOMANHOOD. A concept that emerged in the 19th century, particularly in England and the United States, extolling motherhood and the **domestic sphere** as a woman's appropriate and important areas of activity. Advocates often talked about the moral superiority of women and frequently argued that the "hand that rocks the cradle rules the world." This bourgeois movement idealized the domestic femininity of women, glorified women's role as homemaker, and elevated thinking from religion to science. Coinciding with the shift to extradomestic production, this view also described women as physically and cognitively "weaker" and less fit for the world of work. Feminists claim that these ideas contributed to the devaluation of women's labor and economic dependence on men and that they ignored the need (and reality) of women who performed wage labor (especially **women of color** and of the working class). Conversely, these images **empowered** women to lead a **moral reform feminist** movement.

CULT OF VICTIMIZATION. *See* VICTIMIZATION OF WOMEN.

CULTURAL FEMINISM. A later branch and transformation of **radical feminism** that celebrates female differences and advocates the creation of a **separatist** feminist **counter-culture** in which women's superior nurturing and pacific values can transform society. In contrast to **difference feminism**, this tradition is nonpolitical and focuses instead on individual change. The theory is rooted in the writings of **Margaret Fuller** and **Charlotte Perkins Gilman** and is partly responsible for the renewed interest in **matriarchy** and the **goddess**.

CYBERSEX. Graphic and violent on-line role-playing or "virtual sex" on a computer. Some feminists argue that fantasy and reality are blurred in a world where men are sexually dominant and women are passive, willing victims. Other feminists suggest that women can act out their desires in safety here and note that government attempts to control the Internet can stifle adult communication. For example, "filters" to control minors' access to **pornography** have blocked discussions of **breast cancer**.

CYCLE OF ABUSE. A term used by theorists who study **domestic violence** to describe a pattern in which a batterer commits violence, repents, and is forgiven. A peaceful honeymoon phase ensues, followed by a period of escalating tension. Finally, tension increases to the point where battery occurs again and the cycle starts over. The term "cycle of abuse" is also used to describe a behavior pattern in which those who have been battered as children batter their own children in turn, establishing a generational cycle of abuse. *See also* BATTERED WOMAN SYNDROME.

-D-

DALKON SHIELD. An intrauterine **birth control** device (IUD) marketed by A. H. Robins, 1970-74, and linked with perforated uteri, miscarriages, stillbirths, infections causing permanent sterility, and several deaths. Although the product was taken off the market in 1974, a worldwide recall of the shields still being worn was not begun until 1984 after a 10-year campaign by the **National Women's Health Network**. In 1985 Robins declared bankruptcy after losing several lawsuits brought by injured women. As a part of a reorganization plan, the Dalkon Shield Claimants Trust was established in 1989 and had paid out almost $3 billion to nearly 400,000 women when it closed in 2000.

DALTRO, LEOLINDA DE FIGUEREIDO (1860-1935). A Brazilian founder of the feminist Partido Republicano Feminino in 1910. Daltro was one of the first to support suffrage and the advancement of women in Brazil. She lobbied the legislature, organized demonstrations, and frequently ran for public office. She was unable to build an effective suffrage movement despite her continued activism through the 1920s. In 1932, when the vote was won, she ran unsuccessfully for Congress as the pioneer of **woman suffrage**.

DALY, MARY (1928-). An American theologian and self-described **radical feminist** "Nag-Gnostic philosopher." Daly writes and lectures to expose what she sees as lies of the patriarchal "foreground" and to replace them with truths of her radical feminist "background." Her many books explore issues in ethics, religion, and the place of women in Christianity and the church. Daly's critiques of **patriarchy's** myths and languages have become progressively more radical as her language play becomes more "outrageous." *The Church and the Second Sex* (1968) argues for equality of the sexes within the Catholic Church, while *Beyond God the Father* (1973) envisions a new definition of God that will create a space of "human becoming." *Gyn/Ecology* (1978) calls for a radical feminist meta-ethics with which any woman can begin "re-fusing" patriarchal history and "dis-covering" her own history as well as its connections with other women's histories. *Pure Lust* (1984) suggests an alternative to "phallic lust" that will capture the humor, hope, and harmony of women who challenge patriarchy. Her other books include *Wickedary* (1987), *Outercourse: The Be-Dazzling Voyage* (1992), and *Quintesssence* (1998). For 25 years Daly restricted her course in feminist ethics at Boston College to female students in order to create a safe environment for open discussion and taught the same course to men as a tutorial. In 1998, fearing a lawsuit under **Title IX**, the college told her to either admit men to that class or resign. In 1999 she was removed from the faculty, despite tenure, and in 2001 Daly's lawsuit was settled out of court with her retirement.

DATE RAPE. Sexual intercourse forced by an acquaintance. Often the incident occurs during a regular social engagement such as a "date," in which the victim is coerced or manipulated into sexual intercourse. The perpetrator ignores protests or interprets them as encouragement. The victim may not interpret such an event as a "real rape" and tends not to report it. Because of feminist **consciousness-raising** about date rape and efforts to reduce miscommunication between women and men, many US colleges now hold student orientations on the topic. *See also* VICTIMIZATION OF WOMEN.

DATE RAPE DRUG. A powerful tranquilizer such as Rohypnol or gamma hydroxybutyric acid (GHB) that is slipped into drinks by men to make women groggy or unconsciousness so that **rape** is not resisted. Possession of both drugs is illegal in the United States. They have also been reformulated to turn drinks or coasters blue or murky so that detection is easier for women.

DAUGHTERS OF BILITIS. *See* MARTIN, DEL.

DAVIES, (SARAH) EMILY (1830-1921). An English feminist and educational reformer with the Society for Promoting the Employment of Women. In 1861 she became editor of the feminist *English Woman's Journal*. She was active in the **woman suffrage** cause and helped to organize the first suffrage petition presented to Parliament by **John Stuart Mill** in 1866. Her opinions were published in *Thoughts on Some Questions Relating to Women 1860-1908* (1910).

DAVIS, PAULINA KELLOGG WRIGHT (1813-1876). The founder and editor of *Una* (1853-1855), the first feminist publication in the United States. Davis, a wealthy widow after 1845, toured the US East Coast with a mannequin to teach women about their bodies and hygiene and published the monthly *Una* at her own expense. She was active in a variety of women's rights causes, including the **National Woman Suffrage Association.**

DAVISON, EMILY WILDING (1872-1913). An English **Women's Social and Political Union** activist who threw herself in front of the king's horse on Derby Day, June 4, 1913, and was trampled to death. This event has come to epitomize the extremism and escalating violence of the militant wing of the English **woman suffrage movement** led by the **Pankhursts.**

DAY CARE. Child care facilities for preschool and primary school-age children. The current shortage of day-care facilities is due to the increase in women's **labor force participation** and the lack of social policy and planning. Many organizations provide day-care services or offer day-care vouchers as part of employee benefit packages. In countries such as the United States, without an extensive system for out-of-home child care, **new feminists** made government-subsidized day care a core goal as a right of every woman. **Antifeminists** see day care as undermining the traditional role of women. *See also* ABC BILL; WORK-FAMILY CONFLICT.

DEAD WHITE EUROPEAN MALE. A term used to denigrate the university's traditional curricular focus on what is known as the "canon" or "canonical" literary writers, philosophers, musicians, artists, and historians. In the "culture wars" that took place on university and college campuses during the 1980s and 1990s, feminists insisted that the traditional course of study privileged authors such as **Shakespeare** over his female contemporary dramatists, or Milton over women poets writing during the same period. The same argument has been extended to the study of male philosophers, artists, etc. By attempting to open up the curriculum to previously ignored or denigrated female writers, as well as people of color, feminists argued that all students would receive a more well-balanced and historically accurate view of the broad picture of culture and cultural productions.

DECADE FOR WOMEN. See INTERNATIONAL WOMEN'S YEAR.

DECLARATION OF SENTIMENTS. See SENECA FALLS CONVENTION.

DECLARATION OF THE RIGHTS OF WOMAN. See GOUGES, MARIE OLYMPE DE.

DECLARATION OF THE RIGHTS OF WOMEN. A statement written by **Matilda Joslyn Gage** and **Elizabeth Cady Stanton** for the US centennial in 1876. Read by **Susan B. Anthony** on behalf of the **National Woman Suffrage Association**, the declaration described the inferior legal status of women and demanded equality. Its most controversial assertion was that the United States could not claim to be a democracy because of its treatment of women and therefore was illegitimate.

DECONSTRUCTION. A theory of meaning in philosophy, literary criticism, or other disciplines in the humanities that attempts to describe the limits of understanding. Deconstruction tests the assumptions underlying intellectual arguments in order to question the supposedly "self-evident" claims on which they are based. Instead of trying to find a way of understanding new phenomena and placing them into a "bounded" context, deconstruction seeks to expose the unexamined premises that define the supposedly new phenomena, their paradigms, and boundaries. Deconstruction typically critiques unexamined notions of meaning, such as "God," "the center," "origins," "time," "the self," "Nature," the "subject." Feminism has had a stake in deconstruction insofar as the methodology has exploded long-held tenets that have provided the undergirding of the **patriarchy**. Once the subject is decentered and viewed as a social construction, **gender** itself can be viewed as an artificial construct, a play of signifiers. See also DERRIDA, JACQUES.

DEFICIT PERSPECTIVE. An argument, developed by Fern Johnson, that this view permeates much of the research done on women's and men's language. Those who adopt the deficit approach posit that women's language is inherently inferior to men's. In other words, women's speech is deficient in comparison to men's. A variant of this perspective, the new deficit approach, takes the position that while women's speech is deficient, it can be remedied and women can learn to speak like men. Johnson and other feminists argue that both these perspectives cause negative interpretations to be applied to women's speech.

DEITIES, FEMALE. The expression of divinity in female form. Scholars debate how communities' perception of female strength and power in the divine realm has reflected and/or influenced the actual historical status of women. Many scholars assert that **goddesses** were invented by men for the purpose of exerting control over women. This is challenged by a second century A.D. invocation to **Isis** that proclaims: "for all time; thou didst make the power of women equal to that of men."

DE LA CRUZ, MARÍA (1912-?). An advocate of **woman suffrage** and emancipation in Chile and founder of the Partido Femenino Chileno (Chilean Women's Party) in 1946. In 1950 de la Cruz was the first Chilean woman to run (unsuccessfully) for national political office. She helped to build a women's movement that was a key to the presidential election of 1952. After her election in 1953 as Chile's first female senator, however, the feminist movement lost momentum and the party disbanded in 1954.

DE LA CRUZ, SOR JUANA INÉS (1648-1695). A Mexican nun and the first woman to voice the "feminist protest" in Latin America. Sor Juana defended and affirmed women and thus affirmed herself. Her poetry is an expression of her revolutionary sensibility. She spoke out against traditions and myths that enslave women, such as the cult of virginity and the **double standard**. In her time Sor Juana gained wide recognition, but it was mainly due to attempts to silence her and make her conform. In 1693 she wrote a letter to the Bishop of Puebla that constituted a powerful declaration of the rights of women based on the equality of their souls.

DEL-EM. A simple menstrual-extraction suction device, invented by Californian Lorraine Rothman in 1971, to allow women to perform early **abortions** for each other. Although never widely used in the United States for **self-help** abortions after legalization in 1973, the device is used for therapeutic reasons and convenience and has been introduced in Latin America as a self-help abortion technique.

DEMOCRATIC ORGANIZATION OF AFGHAN WOMEN (DOAW). A women's rights group, formed in 1965, to combat female illiteracy, forced marriage, and **brideprice** and to support **woman suffrage**. In the 1970s four of its members were elected to parliament. DOAW also won the right for women to study abroad, to work outside the home, and, in 1988, to have constitutional equality. It was the only women's group to support the Soviet invasion, and in 1987 it assumed a new name, the Afghan Women Council.

DEPENDENT PERSONALITY DISORDER. A diagnosis often given to an individual, usually a woman, who is generally passive in relationships, has low **self-esteem**, and tends to tolerate abusiveness. Feminists object to this behavior pattern being labeled a "personality disorder" because such a diagnostic label further stigmatizes what many women experience as learned female **gender role** behavior.

DERANIYAGALA, EZLYNN (1908-1973). The first Sri Lankan woman barrister and long-time president of the All-Ceylon Women's Conference (1944), the core national organization for women's rights. She twice served as president of the **International Alliance of Women**.

DEROIN, JEANNE (1805-1894). An early French feminist who retained her birth name after marriage in 1832. In the 1840s she edited a socialist women's paper *L'Opinion des femmes* and wrote a pamphlet decrying women's enslavement. She was the first woman to run for the National Assembly in 1849 on the platform that an all-male assembly could not legislate for women. After her exile to London in 1852, she continued to write feminist tracts.

DERRIDA, JACQUES (1930-). One of the most influential of living philosophers, generally considered one of the founders of **deconstruction**, a major theoretical movement that has had enormous effects on philosophy, literary criticism, psychoanalysis, theology, linguistics, and art. Born in Algiers and educated in France, Derrida is not a feminist nor is he sympathetic to advancing the feminist agenda, but several of his terms and philosophical strategies have been **appropriated** by feminist critics—specifically his attack on the notion of a "center" of meaning, the "logos." Derrida denounced this desire for a center as "logocentrism" (in his *On Grammatology*, 1976), and it was this notion that was adapted and modified by the **French feminists** as **phallogocentrism**. Derrida also coined the term "différance" to explain the divided nature of the sign, while feminist theorists have adapted it to explain the undecidable nature of **gender** constructions. Characteristic applications of Derrida's theories to feminism include a denunciation of all binary oppositions (culture/nature, male/female), an assault on the notion that there are any determinate bounds, limits, or margins to a text (or a gender), and the idea that supposedly literal terms are themselves metaphors whose metaphoric meanings have been forgotten.

DES (DIETHYLSTILBESTROL). A synthetic progesterone prescribed to as many as 4.8 million pregnant American women, 1941-71, to prevent miscarriage, despite evidence that DES was ineffective. A link was established in 1971 to unusual vaginal and cervical cancer in young women exposed in utero to DES and its use in pregnancy was banned. Feminist groups mounted an outreach program to warn DES daughters about the need for early cancer screening. Cases of vaginal and cervical cancer due to DES exposure declined in the 1990s, but DES continues to be marketed to treat advanced prostate and **breast cancer** in the United States and to prevent miscarriage and suppress lactation in less-developed nations.

DE SILVA, AGNES. Sri Lanka's most prominent **woman suffrage** leader. In 1925 she petitioned for the vote on behalf of the Women's Society. Later she was active in the Women's Franchise Union. In 1931, when the vote was extended to women, she unsuccessfully ran for Congress in an election that brought the first women to the legislature.

DESPARD, CHARLOTTE FRENCH (1844-1939). An English **suffragist** who stood apart from the mainstream movement because of her claim that even a partial franchise would be of benefit to both the wealthy class of women and the working classes. Strongly attached to the Labour Party, Despard broke with the **Women's Social and Political Union** (WSPU) in 1907 and formed the **Women's Freedom League**. Her views on feminism were colored by her primary concern, the problems of women and children. Her approach to feminism was spiritual rather than materialist; she argued in one of her speeches that spiritual love was at the core of the women's movement because she saw the movement as an expression of women's spiritual nature.

DEVELOPMENT, WOMEN IN. A feminist critique of modernization in the Third World that suggests a decrease in the status of women. Although women there produce most domestically consumed food, development funds for agricultural equipment and training are targeted to men. With the widespread destruction of forests and tillable land, men must migrate to cities, leaving women to engage in even more difficult subsistence farming. Those women who also migrate must accept the lowest paying of urban jobs. Women's groups such as the **Global Fund for Women** and the **International Center for Research on Women** assist women with microloans for businesses and community development. *See also* COLONIZATION, EFFECT UPON WOMEN.

DEVELOPMENT ALTERNATIVES WITH WOMEN FOR A NEW ERA (DAWN). A network of scholars and activists from the Southern Hemisphere that engages in feminist research and analysis of the global environment. DAWN was established in 1984 and works throughout Africa, Asia, Latin America, the Caribbean, and the Pacific for **gender** and economic justice. Priorities are sustainable livelihoods, sexual and **reproductive** health rights, and the political economy of globalization.

D'HERICOURT, JENNY (1809-1875). A French physician who began publishing feminist articles in 1855. Some of these denounce Pierre-Joseph Proudhon's argument of the "exceptional woman" who does not fit **misogynist** conceptions. In her work *A Woman's Philosophy of Woman* (1864), she used her medical knowledge to argue areas of morality and social and political philosophy. She refuted Jules Michelet who said that **menstruation** is proof that women are weak and inferior. She moved to the United States later and worked with the leaders of the women's movement.

DIALECTIC OF SEX, THE. A 1970 feminist work by Shulamith Firestone that argues that the power of the **patriarchy** is located in the biological inequality of the sexes. For Firestone, the only way for women to escape their subjugation is to use technology to divorce themselves and their bodies from the tyranny of **reproduction**. Once the biological family is destroyed as a reproductive unit, it will also be destroyed as an economic unit, thereby freeing women from unpaid labor in the home. Firestone advocated an **androgynous** culture that would abolish the categories associated with marriage. *See also* ECTOGENESIS.

DIETHYLSTILBESTROL. *See* DES.

DIFFERENCE FEMINISM. A belief that the sexes differ in significant ways and that some women's values are superior and should be celebrated. The writings of **Carol Gilligan** and **Mary Daly** have been especially important in this reexamination of women's traditional role. Some feminists fear that any retreat from **equality feminism** will only reinforce **gender stereotypes** and derail the movement for change. Many feminist legal scholars, however, argue for differential treatment of women; without policy accommodations for childbirth and **child care**, they feel that women can never be equal in society.

DIGITAL DIVIDE. A term describing differential access to computers and the Internet. Those with lower incomes and education levels are disadvantaged, as are women and persons of color. Feminists complain that computer culture is dominated by **patriarchal** values. The technical professions continue to have very low numbers of women; computer rooms in educational institutions may be hostile as males try to deny females access to machines or intimidate them with **pornography**. Some also warn that telecommunicating work from home could become a new **sweatshop** for women instead of a solution to the **work-family conflict**. For those women with Internet access, there is a huge array of female-oriented on-line resources. *See also* FEMINIST WEB ZINES.

Dilation and extraction (D AND X). *See* PARTIAL-BIRTH ABORTION.

DINNER PARTY, THE. An artwork unveiled by Judy Chicago in 1979. It traces the history of Western women through 39 carved or sculptured place settings grouped around a triangular banquet table. A tile floor lists 999 other women of achievement. Because of Chicago's symbolic usage of the vulva and the vagina, the installation has been controversial since its first exhibition. It has been seen by almost one million people at 15 sites in six countries and three continents, but until 2002 it had no institutional home. It is now permanently housed at the Brooklyn Museum of Art's Elizabeth A. Sackler Center for Feminist Art.

DINNERSTEIN, DOROTHY (1923-1992). The author of *The Mermaid and the Minotaur: Sexual Arrangements and Human Malaise* (1977). Dinnerstein argued that the oppression of women is caused by their monopoly of and obsession with the act of mothering. Because women remember their own mothers as so powerful, they themselves spend most of their adult lives trying to reject their own mothers and all things feminine. But because of her sexual similarity to her mother, a girl can never fully escape her mother and thus never achieves the autonomy and power that a male achieves. The only way out of this malaise, according to Dinnerstein, is dual parenting, which will have the effect of breaking down the sexual divisions that now are so rigid and confining to both sexes.

DISADVANTAGES APPROACH. A feminist legal approach which asserts that less attention should be paid to differences and more attention should be given to disadvantages stemming from them in order to further the goal of eliminating disadvantages experienced by oppressed members of society. *See also* DIFFERENCE FEMINISM.

DISPLACED HOMEMAKER. A woman who, after spending many years as an unpaid family caretaker, has been abandoned, **divorced**, or widowed. Ineligible for a family support **pension** because her children are no longer minors, she usually will be qualified only for low-wage work, with few or no benefits. In 1974 Tish Sommers and Laurie Shields formed the Alliance for Displaced Homemakers, which sensitized the US feminist movement to the special problems of full-time homemakers. By the 1990s over 1,000 government-funded programs were providing job training and counseling for displaced homemakers.

DIVORCE. *See* NO-FAULT DIVORCE.

DIVORCE AND MATRIMONIAL CAUSES ACT (1857). An English law that made civil **divorce** available, apart from religious courts, and established some property rights for **married women**, the first break with **coverture**. The **separate spheres** doctrine was maintained, however, and women could be divorced for a single act of adultery, whereas men had to commit some other offense in addition to adultery to give a wife grounds for divorce.

DODSON, BETTY. See FEMALE SEXUALITY.

DOHM, HEDWIG (1833-1919). A German feminist and writer who rejected the contemporary **bourgeois feminist** view that women were destined for motherhood. Personally acquainted with the major literary figures of her age, she wrote about housework, motherhood, childrearing, and sexuality in works that are both highly insightful and viciously witty, demonstrating the need for economic, intellectual, and political independence of women. Her works include *Jesuitry in the Household* (1873), *The Nature and Rights of Women* (1874), and *The Antifeminist* (1902).

DOLLE MINA/MAD MINA. A direct action **radical feminist** group founded in the Netherlands in 1969 and in Belgium in 1970. It was named for the earlier feminist leader **Wilhelmina Drucker**. Its widely publicized protests on **abortion**, education, **child care**, and public toilets led to its name becoming a generic term for any Dutch feminist. Dolle Mina members walked topless in the streets and wrote "boss of my own body" on their stomachs when they disrupted a doctors' convention in support of **abortion** and **contraceptives**. All local groups had disbanded by the end of the 1970s.

DO-ME FEMINISM. A label given to the new generation of feminists by *Esquire* in a February 1994 article. These young women are portrayed as openly female and lacking sexual inhibitions so as to refute the stereotype of feminists as man-hating **lesbians**. Many feminists view "do-me feminism" as a male invention that seeks to portray women as sex-crazed objects of lust.

DOMESTIC LABOR. See HIDDEN WORK.

DOMESTIC PARTNERSHIPS. Long-term nonmarital companion relationships particularly involving, although not limited to, gay and **lesbian** couples. By 2002 more than 50 US cities and counties, five US states, and several cities in Western Europe and Australia had enacted ordinances affording domestic partners certain rights traditionally reserved for legally married couples if they register for licenses. The rights are usually limited to visiting privileges at city hospitals and jails, access to school records of partners' children, and qualifying for dependent health care coverage on one partner's employer-sponsored insurance program. To obtain a license, generally domestic partners must have lived together for at least six months, not be closely related by blood, and intend to remain in "a relationship of mutual support, caring, and commitment."

DOMESTIC SPHERE. The conventional dichotomy between a public sphere inhabited by men who engage in social, cultural, and political activities and a private sphere in which women are concerned with domestic and personal issues. This separate spheres doctrine long justified women's legal and political inequality. Feminist theorists today note that the distinction between "public" and "domestic" is neither universal nor necessary to human societies. Its dominance in industrial capitalist nations is linked to the practice of maximizing profits by eliminating homemaking from the category of waged labor.

DOMESTIC VIOLENCE. The abuse that occurs in the home inflicted by family or other household members. The term encompasses incest and sexual abuse as well as physical battering. Weaker persons such as women, children, and the elderly are most likely to be victims. Perpetrators are likely to be those household members who are physically strongest. With the opening of the first **women's battery shelter**, feminists have worked to provide services for victims and to reform the criminal justice system's response to these offenses. *See also* BATTERED WOMAN SYNDROME; CYCLE OF ABUSE.

DOMINANCE. *See* MALE DOMINANCE.

DOMINANCE APPROACH. A feminist legal theory advanced by **Catharine MacKinnon** and founded on the premise that it is impossible to know whether there are important differences between the sexes that have not been created by **male dominance.** Advocates assert that any law, practice, or policy that perpetuates the subordination of women should be repealed.

DOUBLE JEOPARDY. *See* RACISM AND FEMINISM.

DOUBLE SHIFT. A sardonic feminist reference to the longer workday of a woman who is employed full-time in the paid labor force and continues to perform the bulk of **domestic labor.** After completing a full day's work outside the home, the woman begins the second shift as a wife and/or mother. In marriages between two full-time employees, the fact that most women earn less than men often means that the women will get no more than minimal assistance with housework from their spouses. Feminists support "symmetrical marriages" in which partners share housework and **child care** while both participate in the paid labor force.

DOUBLE STANDARD. A term referring to the two different sets of behaviors proscribed for men and women. **Gender** expectations for women include maintenance of virginity, marital fidelity, and other restrictions on sexual behavior. Feminists object to these different standards, particularly when legal codes hold women liable for the same behaviors for which men are either not punished or treated less harshly.

DOUCHING. The rinsing and cleaning of the vagina to remove menstrual blood, semen, or odor. When commercial solutions were marketed to young women as a route to sexual desirability, feminists denounced the suggestion that women were unclean. Although medical evidence indicates that douching increases the risk of infection, ectopic pregnancy, and cervical cancer, up to 28 percent of women, 20-24, engage in this practice.

DOW, UNITY (1959-). The first female high court judge in Botswana and advocate for women's rights. She was the plaintiff in a successful suit in 1990 to allow Botswanan women to pass citizenship to their children. While in private practice, she established the nation's first legal aid center for women, the Metlhaetsile ("The Time Has Come") Women's Information Center.

DOWRY. The wealth a woman brings to a marriage, provided by her family so she can have some means of support should she be widowed or deserted. These gifts are controlled by the husband during the marriage but are considered to be the woman's property to be returned to her upon desertion, **divorce,** or death of the husband or passed on to her children upon her death. Dowries have been universally provided and continue to be widely practiced in India despite the Dowry Prohibition Act of 1961 (and later amendments). Because of the incidence of **dowry deaths,** women's groups work for the enforcement of these laws and for better property rights for **married women.** *See also* BRIDEGIFT/BRIDEWEALTH/BRIDESERVICE.

DOWRY DEATHS. A practice prevalent in India, whereby young married women are abused and then set on fire, poisoned, drowned, or strangled by their husbands or in-laws because their **dowry** is viewed as inadequate. Burning young brides if they have not given birth to a male heir within one year of marriage is so common in India that it is also called "oven death." These deaths are usually classified by police as suicides or accidents. The husband is then free to remarry and collect a new dowry. India prohibits a demand for dowry, but the law is poorly enforced. Since the Indian women's movement began to publicize dowry deaths in the late 1970s, local police have established special AntiDowry and Crimes Against Women units to investigate **domestic violence**.

DRESS FOR SUCCESS. A clothing style for businesswomen featuring well-tailored suits that allow women to be taken seriously in the workplace. The originator of the term was male fashion consultant John T. Molloy, whose bestseller *The Women's Dress for Success Book* (1977) argued that clothing that emphasizes sexual attractiveness is a deterrent to business success. For the next decade, annual sales of suits rose and dresses declined. Feminists welcomed this trend in that suits were often better made and remained fashionable for a longer period of time. By the late 1980s, however, female executive dressing was criticized by fashion writers as boring and masculine.

DRESS REFORM. A 19th century movement to destroy the **sexual division of labor** by freeing women from restrictive fashions that tied them to the home. US feminist advocates of this new practical attire included **Amelia Bloomer, Lucy Stone,** and **Elizabeth Cady Stanton,** who believed that since men and women had a common nature their dress should also be similar.

DRIVE-BY DELIVERIES AND MASTECTOMIES. A term referring to the very short hospital stays permitted US women. Following the passage of the Health Care Reform Act of 1992—which eliminated the state hospital rate-setting system—insurers were free to negotiate price discounts with hospitals, including per diem contracts. Research has found that the percentage of one-day stays increased 18 times by 1994, regardless of the payer. Health maintenance organizations (HMOs) were suspected of forcing women into one-day stays, but in fact hospital regulations and legislation used to force women out of the hospital early. Most childbirths are routine vaginal deliveries and women are able to leave the hospital within 24 hours. Twenty percent are Cesarean sections, that leave women prone to complications and infections, which are increased with an early departure from the hospital. In 1996 federal legislation required a minimum two-day stay for uncomplicated vaginal deliveries and a four-day stay for a Cesarean section. As for mastectomies, most physicians agree that women require at least four to five days recovery time in the hospital after such surgery. Congressional bills to assure women of at least 48 hours hospital recovery time after a mastectomy have failed to pass as of 2003.

DRUCKER, WILHELMINA (MINA) ELISABETH (1847-1925). The leading Dutch feminist of the 19th century and founder of De Vrije Vrouwenbeweging (Association of Free Women) in 1889. She edited the group's journal, *Evolution*. Her nickname was **Dolle Mina** (Mad Mina) due to her fervent support of women's rights.

DUAL CAREER COUPLES. The partners in a relationship in which both pursue work and career roles while simultaneously maintaining a family life. It was originally viewed as a nontraditional relationship, but with the increase of women in the labor force, the relationship is now commonplace. *See also* MOMMY TRACK; WORK-FAMILY CONFLICT.

DUAL LABOR MARKET. The division of the labor market into the primary sector, which has high-paying jobs (usually held by men), and the secondary sector (dominated by women and minorities), which has lower-paying jobs. Women and minorities are trapped in secondary labor markets by discrimination, **sexism**, and the inflexibility of the primary labor market to accommodate special employment considerations.

DUAL ROLE. *See* DOUBLE SHIFT.

DUGDALE, HENRIETTA (1826-1918). A leader, along with her friend Annie Lowe (1834-1910), in the **woman suffrage movement** in Victoria, Australia. Dugdale began working for the vote in 1869, 16 years before she and Lowe formed the first suffrage society. Both viewed the vote as a way to protect women against violent crimes. Dugdale's *A*

Few Hours in a Far-Off Age (1883) presented a utopian post-suffrage future.

DURAND, MARGUARITE (1865-1936). A French journalist, actress, and feminist. She founded the world's first women's daily newspaper, *La fronde*, a **social feminist** publication that supported **temperance, woman suffrage,** and economic and legal rights for women, 1897-1905. She donated her feminist archives to Paris in 1931.

DWORKIN, ANDREA (1946-). An American **radical feminist** whose writings are concerned with questions of sexuality, sexual roles, and sexual deviations. She is the author of *Intercourse* (1987), which considers the psychology of sex and sexual roles; *Letters from a War Zone* (1988), which considers sexual discrimination, **pornography,** and feminism; and the autobiographical *Heartbreak: The Political Memoir of a Feminist Militant* (2002). Her *Our Blood* (1976) calls for the abandonment of the quest for sexual equality. Dworkin now believes that more radical solutions are required to achieve a complete social realignment of the sexes. She is also noted for her co-authorship of the **Minneapolis Pornography Ordinance.**

-E-

EAGLE FORUM (EF). An American **antifeminist** organization formed by **Phyllis Schlafly** in 1972 to continue the work of her Stop ERA movement, which was instrumental in preventing the ratification of the **Equal Rights Amendment.** The group is active in 37 states and has a membership of 80,000, primarily women, that is heavily drawn from the Republican Party's political right and conservative Catholics. The group has opposed **abortion, day care, comparable worth, family leave,** and **women's battery shelters.** In recent years the EF has broadened its agenda to include issues such as national defense and has established groups for college students and teenagers.

EARNINGS GAP. *See* WAGE GAP.

EARTH MOTHER. The use, in early theology, of female fertility to view the earth as the source of divine life. In contemporary feminism, the term is applied to women committed to naturalistic processes, such as **natural childbirth** or nutrition. They are frequently involved in raising children and affirming kindness in motherhood. Many are also concerned about the earth. *See also* ECOFEMINISM.

EAST MEETS WEST FEMINIST TRANSLATION GROUP. A Beijing-based women's group, organized in 1993 to plan for the 1995 UN Women's Conference in China. The group initially translated English language materials on Western and **international women's movements** into Chinese in hopes of bridging the gap in communications born of different terms and concepts. These were published in Chinese women's media. Beginning in 1995 Chinese women's writings were translated into English, and the group began to shift its focus from translation to a discussion forum on feminism. The group now works with other Chinese feminist groups on women's issues.

EASTMAN, CRYSTAL (1881-1928). A US journalist, peace worker, feminist, and labor lawyer. A **suffragist**, Eastman joined the Political Equality League in 1912 in Milwaukee and led the drive for **woman suffrage** in Wisconsin. In 1913 she joined with **Alice Paul** and **Lucy Burns** to found the Congressional Union for Woman Suffrage.

EATING DISORDERS. A term referring to eating problems, including anorexia nervosa and bulimia, that are most commonly found in young women. Anorexia involves a refusal to eat that leads to severe weight loss, malnutrition, and sometimes cessation of menstruation. A bulimic binges or gorges on food and may then, in an effort to avoid gaining weight, purge herself by inducing vomiting or taking laxatives, diet pills, and diuretics. The disorders involve distortion of body image such that an emaciated person may view herself as fat, a misperception that can lead to death. The increase in these disorders has been credited to the media's representation of feminine beauty as being thin and the association of happiness with beauty. Feminists also note that as many women gain power in society, the ideal woman is increasingly defined in childlike dimensions.

EBADI, SHIRIN (1947-). An Iranian lawyer and human rights activist who in 2003 became the first Islamic woman to receive the Nobel Peace Prize. Ebadi was one of the first female judges in Iran, serving as the president of the city court of Tehran, 1975-1979. After the 1979 revolution, she was forced to resign and was frequently imprisoned. Ebadi is an activist for the rights of women, children, and refugees. She is the founder of the Association for Support of Children's Rights and the Center for the Defense of Human Rights. Even though she does not call herself a feminist, Ebadi supports legal equality for women and argues that Islam does not require the denial of women's rights. In a recent court case, she has argued against a "blood money law" that requires that the parents of a raped and murdered girl pay for the execution of the male killer whose life is valued twice that of their daughter.

ECCLESIAZUSAE, THE, OR WOMEN IN COUNCIL. A play written by Aristophanes and first produced in 412 B.C. It is yet another satire of women's role in Athenian society. In this play, Artistophanes depicts what would happen if women gained political control of the state. They adopt male clothing, take seats in the assembly on the Pnyx, command a majority of votes, and enact a series of revolutionary proposals—including one that all property and all women be held in common. The play's humor supposedly lies in the need of the women to safeguard the rights of the old and ugly among them, so that these women will also have access to the young and handsome men. A sex farce in some ways similar to his **Lysistrata**, the play mocks women's political aspirations and reveals the levity with which the male Athenian population viewed women. See also THESMOPHORIAZUSAE, OR A WOMEN'S FESTIVAL.

ECOFEMINISM. A feminist tradition that emerged in the 1980s to explore relations between environmental issues and women's issues. Born of the global environmental crisis, the ecofeminist movement has spawned many groups such as the WomanEarth Institute and has succeeded in gaining leadership positions for women in mainstream environmental organizations. Ecofeminists view domination—of women, minority groups, animals, the earth—as the basic problem, rather than **patriarchy.** Ecofeminists speak of an interconnected web of life that encompasses all of the earth's residents.

ECTOGENESIS. The gestation of human beings outside the uterus. This would involve a technology that frees women from the burden of childbearing by moving the process into an artificial placenta within a laboratory from conception to birth. Scientists disagree on the feasibility of the process despite advances in the treatment of preterm infants. Both the **pro-life movement** and most feminists oppose ectogenesis (but see *The Dialectic of Sex*), despite its potential as an alternative to **surrogacy**. *See also* REPRODUCTIVE TECHNOLOGIES.

EDUCATION AMENDMENTS OF 1972. *See* TITLE IX, EDUCATION AMENDMENTS of 1972.

EGALITARIAN FEMINISM. *See* EQUALITY FEMINISM.

EGYPTIAN FEMINIST UNION (EFU). A group founded by **Huda Sha'rawi** in 1923 after the ruling Wafd Party and the new national constitution restricted suffrage to men. The goals of the group were: political, social, and legal equality for women; access to education at all levels; and **divorce** law reform. The EFU provided scholarships to women for foreign study, primary school and vocational training for girls, aid to widows, and health care. Composed of upper- and middle-class women, the EFU remained vital for a quarter century and published two journals, *L'Egyptienne* and *Al-Misriyya*. It was disbanded as an independent political organization in 1956, the year that the ruling regime granted **woman suffrage**, and reformed as the Huda Sha'rawi Association, a social service group under government control.

ELECTORAL FEMINISM. A **second wave** strategy to put more feminist women into elected office and to encourage women's political participation. Studies showed that women in public office were more supportive of women's issues than were their male colleagues and that women voters slightly favored female candidates. "When women run and women vote, women win" became a popular slogan. *See also* CENTER FOR THE AMERICAN WOMAN AND POLITICS; EMILY'S LIST; GENDER GAP; GENDER PARITY; WOMEN'S CAMPAIGN FUND.

ELITISM. A charge leveled against a feminist by other feminists due to perceived violation of the antileadership ethic and power-seeking behavior. More recently concern about elitism has involved the upper-status bias of participation in the feminist movement. This, it is feared, may lead the movement to place the needs of **women of color** and **pink-collar** women below those of women in careers and the professions. *See also* TRASHING.

EMERGENCY CONTRACEPTION (EC). *See* MORNING-AFTER PILL.

EMILY'S (EARLY MONEY IS LIKE YEAST) LIST. A US political action committee (PAC) founded in 1984 by IBM heir Ellen Malcolm to provide campaign funding and technical assistance to **pro-choice** Democratic women running for high political office and to mobilize the women's vote. In every national election since 1992 except one, the group has raised more money than any other congressional PAC, giving rise to state laws to prevent their directly receiving donations earmarked for their endorsed candidates from their network of 73,000 members. EMILY's List has become the model for women's PACs, including the WISH (Women in the Senate and House) List that supports pro-choice Republican women.

EMMA. A German monthly feminist magazine and the first in Europe. Founded in 1977 by **Alice Schwarzer,** *EMMA's* circulation is 80,000. *EMMA* has campaigned against *Frauenhass* (woman-hating) in an attempt to get the German government to collect statistics on **hate crimes** against women and has received a commitment from the German chancellor to consider the marketing of **RU 486**. **Andrea Dworkin** wrote *Letters from a War Zone* at the invitation of *EMMA*, where it was published in 1986, two years before it appeared in English.

EMPLOYMENT, SEX DISCRIMINATION IN. The **gender**-based bias in employment decisions relating to compensation, terms, conditions, or privileges of employment. Discrimination may occur in hiring, promotion, transfers, and training. It may be direct and deliberate or may entail unnecessary policies or procedures that have an unintended adverse impact on women (e.g., height and weight requirements for police officers). *See also* CIVIL RIGHTS ACT OF 1964 TITLE VII; EQUAL EMPLOYMENT OPPORTUNITY COMMISSION V. SEARS, ROEBUCK & CO.

EMPOWERMENT. The process of helping individuals, usually women, minorities, and others who have been politically impotent, to increase their personal and sociopolitical influence in improving their own circumstances. Empowerment for women requires that women identify their own experiences, feelings, and values and that women decide for themselves what is deserving of private and public communication. Many feminist projects involve empowerment, which must be initiated by women.

EMPTY NEST SYNDROME. The negative feelings experienced by some parents when grown children have left the home and the caretaking aspects of the parental role are accordingly diminished. Women are thought to be especially vulnerable to such feelings if they have perceived motherhood to be the central component of their identity. Feminists argue that these emotions are comparatively rare; most women with young adult children experience increased happiness.

ENGELS, FRIEDRICH (1820-1895). The author of *Origins of the Family, Private Property and the State* (1884), an influential **Marxist** analysis of women and the family. Engels joined with other 19th century scholars in suggesting that society was not always **patriarchal**. Earlier there had been some form of **matriarchy** with a **sexual division of labor** based on biology. Within these **separate spheres**, each sex held equal power. With the development of private property and a market economy controlled by men came patriarchy, monogamy, and a subordinate role for women in **reproduction**. Engels argued that women would be liberated only when class oppression is ended and urged women to become full-time waged workers as a route to that goal. This analysis forms the basis of much **second wave socialist** and **radical feminist** theory. Feminists break with Engels on several points, including his subordinating women's oppression to class oppression, his **essentialism**, and his failure to foresee the stress of the **double shift**.

ENGLISH WOMAN'S JOURNAL. A magazine founded in 1858 by **Barbara Leigh-Smith Bodichon** and Bessie Rayner Parkes, sometimes known as the "Ladies of Langham Place," and **Anna Jameson**. This magazine quickly became the major forum for discussing women's issues and problems in Victorian England.

ENOKI, MISAKO. *See* CHUPIREN.

ENSLER, EVE. *See* VAGINA MONOLOGUES.

EQUAL CREDIT OPPORTUNITY ACT OF 1974 (ECOA). A US law that outlaws discrimination on the basis of sex or marital status in any aspect of a credit transaction (such as getting a credit card, a mortgage, a consumer or business loan). Before the ECOA was passed, single women were often required to have a male relative as a co-signer, the incomes of wives of childbearing age were not fully counted in home mortgage applications, and women had difficulty establishing credit in their own names after **divorce** or death of a spouse. The Federal Reserve Board now requires that credit records be maintained in the names of both spouses and that no questions be asked of applicants regarding childbearing intentions. The percentage of woman-owned small businesses has risen from 4.6 percent in 1972 to almost 40 percent.

EQUAL EMPLOYMENT OPPORTUNITY COMMISSION (EEOC). A US bureaucracy established by the **Civil Rights Act of 1964.** It is charged with investigating complaints of **employment discrimination** and providing interpretation of court cases and legislation. The EEOC can act as the employee's attorney or issue the right to sue. It also publishes guidelines on discrimination, **sexual harassment** and other related topics that are used by employers, legislators and the courts. Feminists charged that the EEOC initially ignored its mandate to investigate charges of **sex discrimination** in employment, a situation that led to the formation of the **National Organization for Women.**

EQUAL EMPLOYMENT OPPORTUNITY COMMISSION V. SEARS, ROEBUCK & CO., 628 F. SUPP. 1264 (N.D. ILL. 1986) AFF'D, 839 F.2D 302 (7TH CIR. 1988). The opinions of the US district and appeals courts that involved allegations that a department store employer discriminated against female employees when filling the higher-paying commission sales positions. The commission presented statistics that reflected substantial underrepresentation of women in these positions. Nevertheless, the courts accepted Sears' explanation that female employees preferred lower-paying noncommission positions. The case received unusual notoriety when two noted feminist historians testified on opposing sides. Rosalind Rosenberg noted that women are socialized to be less competitive and that the easier but more secure and congenial sales jobs might be preferred as more compatible with the demands of the home. Alice Kessler-Harris argued that, given the opportunity as during both world wars, women have quickly moved into higher-paying, traditionally male jobs.

EQUAL OPPORTUNITIES COMMISSION (EOC). A British bureaucracy created in 1975 to enforce the Equal Pay Act of 1970 and the Sex Discrimination Act of 1975 in all areas of **gender discrimination**. The EOC is independent from government but is sponsored by the Equality Minister of the Women and Equality Unit of the Department for Trade and Industry. Although the EOC continues to maintain a low profile in its advocacy for women and does not have representation from the women's movement on its 15-member board, it has raised public awareness of the issues and has provided grants for many feminist projects and conferences.

EQUAL PAY ACT OF 1963 (EPA). A US law that forbids wage discrimination on the basis of sex. It requires organizations to pay men and women the same wages for substantially equal work. Equal work is defined by skill, effort, responsibility, and working conditions. **Gender** differences in wages are permitted when there are differences in merit, seniority, or the quality or quantity of work. As originally introduced, the law would have provided equal pay for **comparable worth**, but this language was rejected as too far-reaching. Retailer Wal-Mart currently faces a class-action suit, filed in 2001 by over 1.5 million of its past and present workers, who charge **sex discrimination** in pay. It is potentially the largest civil rights class-action settlement in US history.

EQUAL PAY FOR EQUAL WORK. The equal compensation of men and women who occupy essentially the same position. This concept was one of the first raised to remedy **sex discrimination** in the workplace. Feminists have since enlarged their demands to encompass **comparable worth** or paying men and women equal wages when occupying comparable positions.

EQUAL PROTECTION. A US constitutional protection that mandates equal treatment under state, local, and federal laws for all citizens except in those circumstances where distinctions among citizens are justifiable. The **Fourteenth Amendment** specifically states that "no State shall deny to any person within its jurisdiction the equal protection of the laws." The US Supreme Court first applied the principle to **sex discrimination** in *Reed v. Reed* (1971), when the Court invalidated an

Idaho state law that required that a man be chosen as the administrator of an estate in cases where an equally qualified man and woman sought the post. *Frontiero v. Richardson* (1973) is also notable because four justices agreed that the most stringent test, "strict scrutiny," should be applied to laws based on sex. Other justices declined to join that opinion because the **Equal Rights Amendment**, which would have imposed that standard, was still before the states. *See also* CRAIG V. BOREN; PERSONNEL ADMINISTRATOR OF MASSACHUSETTS V. FEENEY.

EQUAL RIGHTS AMENDMENT (ERA). A proposed US constitutional amendment, first introduced by the **National Woman's Party** in 1923, that provided, in its final wording, that "equality of rights shall not be denied or abridged by the United States or by any State on account of sex." In 1972, as a result of the mobilization of the **new feminist movement**, the amendment was approved by the US Congress and submitted to the states for ratification. By 1982, the new extended deadline set by Congress, the amendment had only been ratified by 35 of the needed 38 states and it died. During its decade before the states, the ERA assumed an importance to feminists comparable to that of **woman suffrage** during the **first wave** of feminism. It also played a central role in building the **antifeminist movement**. It continues to be reintroduced in each session of Congress, this time with no time limitations and a new name, "the constitutional equality amendment." A second approach, the three-state strategy, claims that the 35 original ratifications are still valid and seeks an additional three ratifications. The ERA Summit, a coalition of 30 women's groups formed in 1991, coordinates this effort.

EQUAL RIGHTS FEMINISM. *See* EQUALITY FEMINISM.

EQUALITY DAY. A Canadian holiday celebrated on April 17, the day when one of the women's equality provisions (Section 15) of the **Canadian Charter of Rights and Freedoms** came into effect.

EQUALITY FEMINISM. The belief that, despite biological and social role differences, men and women should be treated exactly the same under the law. During the period 1920-1960 egalitarian feminists supported the **Equal Rights Amendment** and opposed **protective labor laws** in conflict with **social feminists**. By the late 1960s most **liberal**

feminists held an equality perspective and denied that there were any important differences between the sexes. With the rise of a **feminist counter-culture** in the 1980s, however, some feminists argued that women could be treated equally only by recognizing differences. *See also* DIFFERENCE FEMINISM.

ESCORT SERVICES. *See* CLINIC PROTECTION.

ESPIN, VILMA (1930-). A Cuban feminist and Communist Party leader. Espin has led delegations to international women's conferences. In 1960 she helped form and became the head of the **Federation of Cuban Women**, which works to advance the status of women in all areas of society. She is married to Fidel Castro's brother, Raul.

ESSENTIALISM. A term used to imply that there is some a priori essence or quality in men and women that is as inherent as their genes. This essential "femininity" or "masculinity" buttresses politically conservative arguments about what can and cannot occur for men and women in our society. Believing that women must assume full responsibility for childbearing because they are naturally nurturing is an example of an argument made on essentialist grounds.

ESTES, CLARISSA PINKOLA. *See* WILD WOMAN MOVEMENT.

ESTROGEN REPLACEMENT THERAPY (ERT). A prescription drug of estrogens for menopausal and post-menopausal women intended to replace the loss of estrogen production by the body as women age. Some feminists expressed concerns about health risks as well as the possibly underlying motivation, that of maintaining youthful body images for **sexist** reasons. Aging naturally is offered as an alternative. An ERT study by the **Women's Health Initiative** was suspended in 2002 when it concluded that the regimen does more harm than good by increasing **breast cancer**, heart attacks, strokes, and blood clots.

ETATS-GÉNÉRAUX DE LA FEMME. A conference of French **equality** and **reform feminists** held in 1970 under the sponsorship of the women's magazine *Elle* to consider the status of women. **Radical feminists** interrupted the conference to protest the high status of those invited to participate. Even so, resolutions were passed on a number of issues and many preexisting women's organizations shifted their attention to women's rights as a result of the meeting.

ETHIC OF CARE. *See IN A DIFFERENT VOICE.*

EUROPEAN WOMEN'S LOBBY (EWL). A coalition of over 3,000 women's groups in the 15 states of the European Union. Based in Brussels, the EWL seeks sexual equality and links political decision makers with women's organizations.

EVALUATION BIAS. The presence of **gender discrimination** in judging an individual's ability. A female is viewed as less competent than a male despite having identical or equal qualifications. This may occur in the review of writing, art, or job applications, particularly in fields traditionally dominated by men. Although antifemale bias is most common, men in female-dominated activities may also experience bias.

EVANGELICAL FEMINISM. A movement of US women in the late 18th and 19th centuries to spread Christianity and improve the conditions of **prostitutes**, working-class immigrants, children, and the poor. In attacking male drunkenness and the sexual **double standard**, the movement adopted a feminist perspective. *See also* MORAL REFORM FEMINISM; SOCIAL GOSPEL MOVEMENT, WOMEN AND.

EVE. The first woman whose history is described in *Genesis*, the first book of the Bible. Although Eve has been portrayed as a temptress who disobeyed God, caused the fall of man, and inflicted the pain of childbirth and **male dominance** upon all women, a feminist reading of her story is that of an equal in the Garden of Eden. Rather than Eve being created from a spare rib of Adam, the first person is viewed as having neither **gender** nor sex and Eve is seen as an equal helper. *See also* LILITH.

EVE'S GARDEN. A New York store for women that sells books, videos, vibrators, dildos, massage oils, and other sex-oriented products in a pleasant environment. It was the first of its kind in 1974 when Dell Williams opened the shop as a feminist tribute to **female sexuality**. Other sex boutiques that cater to women now exist.

EXISTENTIAL FEMINISM. A reference to the work of **Simone de Beauvoir** and her book *The Second Sex* (1953). This analysis uses existential categories (immanence-transcendence, subject-object, and self-other) to explain the oppression of women. De Beauvoir maintains that women have become the "other" to men, seen as inherently different from and inferior to men. According to de Beauvoir, this occurs primarily because of women's biology and her ability to give birth. Women's oppression consists of being viewed and then treated as an object who is closer to the natural, material, corruptible world in contrast to men, who are viewed as primarily rational, spiritual, and above the taint of the physical world.

-F-

FAKE CLINICS. The antiabortion counseling services that place advertisements in telephone book Yellow Pages that promise **abortion** information and **problem pregnancy counseling**, but instead only provide **pro-life** information. In the United States and Canada, it is estimated that around 3,000 bogus clinics exist, in contrast to approximately 2,500 **family planning** clinics and abortion providers. Because of their nonprofit, noncommercial nature, neither national laws against false advertising nor state consumer fraud statutes are always applicable. However, charges of practicing medicine without a license have led some to convert to medical clinics with ultrasound and part-time medical personnel composed of Catholic and evangelical volunteers.

FALCÓN, LIDIA (1935-). One of Spain's best-known and most controversial feminist theorists. A writer and lawyer, she began to publish a series of texts on women's rights in 1964, and in 1976 she started *Vindicación feminista* as an homage to **Mary Wollstonecraft**. Falcón hoped to use this journal to build a national feminist movement, but publication ceased after three years due to lack of financial and reader support. She was one of the founders of Spain's Feminist Party in 1979. Falcón is Spain's most polemical feminist and is viewed as too radical and strident by many.

FALWELL, JERRY. *See* MORAL MAJORITY.

FAMILY AND MEDICAL LEAVE ACT OF 1993 (FMLA). A US law that allows workers to take up to 12 weeks of unpaid leave with benefits during any 12-month period for birth, adoption, or placement of a foster child, a serious personal illness, or the care of a child, spouse, or parent with a serious health condition. Workers are guaranteed their old job or an equivalent position upon return. The act only applies to private employers with more than 50 workers and full-time workers who have been with the same employer for over a year. Although US feminists wanted paid leave and broader coverage of employers (only 5 percent of employers are included), two earlier vetoes of this bill by President George Bush had made the movement more pragmatic and they contented themselves with a **gender-neutral law**.

FAMILY LEAVE. A national policy of unpaid or paid leave, with job security, for men and women for personal disability, childbirth, adoption, or to care for ill dependents. By 1990 every Western European nation required paid, job-protected **maternity leave**. In 1993 the US Congress passed the (unpaid) **Family and Medical Leave Act**. Because family leave can be taken by fathers as well as mothers, it was hoped that employers would not view women workers as more expensive and thus less desirable employees and that men would assume a larger role in **child care**. In countries where parental leave is public policy, however, it is primarily mothers who take the leave because of traditional **gender roles** and the greater earning power of men.

FAMILY PLANNING. The conscious planning of the number and spacing of one's own children for the physical health of the mother and the emotional and financial security of the family as a whole. Family planning requires both education about human **reproduction** and access to **birth control** information and **contraceptive** practices. The US Supreme Court in *Griswold v. Connecticut* (1965) ruled that a state law that prohibited the use of contraceptives by married couples violated constitutional rights of **privacy**. This decision not only ensured access to birth control but laid the foundation for **Roe v. Wade** and legalized **abortion**. Family planning has been universally supported by feminist movements because it allows women to take control of the reproductive process and permits them to decide to have fewer children and focus on other parts of their life such as a career. *See also* REPRODUCTIVE FREEDOM.

FAMILY POLICY. A national philosophical and legislative commitment to comprehensive social and financial services that support the family such as **child care, reproductive** health, employment and training, and family social services. Feminists often note that the United States is the only industrialized Western nation which does not have a comprehensive family policy, in part due to the lack of political power of women and children, the primary beneficiaries of a family policy.

FAMILY VIOLENCE. See DOMESTIC VIOLENCE.

FAMILY WAGE. A rate of pay that is adequate to support an entire family. That one wage earner is assumed to be the male head of household. A belief in this "just" wage has also led to hiring and salary preferences for married men on the assumption that they provide the sole economic support for a family.

FARRELL, WARREN (1940-). A lecturer and author of the male feminist book *The Liberated Man* (1974) and the **backlash** books *Why Men Are the Way They Are* (1986), *The Myth of Male Power* (1993), *Women Can't Hear What Men Don't Say* (1999), and *Father and Child Reunion* (2001). Once active in the early (feminist) men's "liberation" movement and head of the Masculine Mystique Task Force of the **National Organization for Women**, Farrell now argues that feminism has made women too independent and left men powerless. He has been active in the **men's movement** for **fathers' rights** and in his most recent book argues that after an intact two-parent family and joint custody, a child does best with a single custodial father.

FAT OPPRESSION. The discrimination faced by overweight women in a society that values **physical attractiveness**. The common bumper sticker "no fat chicks" is evidence that "fat is a feminist issue." A variety of feminist comedians, organizations, and zines such as *Fat!So?* have focused on the issue and have strongly criticized the diet and fashion industries.

FATHERS' RIGHTS MOVEMENT (FRM). A **backlash** group of **men's movement** organizations centered around the injustices faced by men who are excluded from the household except as provider and, after **divorce**, as visitor. The movement began in the 1950s and 1960s with the formation of Parents and Children for Equality (PACE) and the Divorce Racket Busters of California. By the 1980s there were several fathers' rights associations in every state. Core issues are divorce, **child support** and custody, and **alimony**, but the movement has expanded to include issues of **sex discrimination** beyond family law. The movement is composed of many groups but has no unified national organization that provides coordination. This may be due to a cleavage between conservatives who support the **patriarchy** and a return to traditional **gender roles** and liberals who seek formal equality in **gender-neutral law**.

FAULKNER, SHANNON. *See* UNITED STATES V. VIRGINIA.

FAUX FEMINIST. A woman who calls herself a feminist but really is an **antifeminist**. Such women, often writers and college professors, are frequently quoted in the media and espouse a nonfeminist approach to issues such as **women's studies, date rape,** and **sexual harassment**. Even though these women have no background of participation in the movement, they are presented as the new voices of feminism and their organizations as representative of average women. Prominent pseudofeminists are **Camille Paglia, Wendy Shalit,** Katie Roiphe, and Christina Hoff Sommers, a leader of the **Independent Women's Forum** and the **Women's Freedom Network**.

FAWCETT, MILLICENT GARRETT (1847-1929). An English proponent of **married women's property** rights and **woman suffrage**. When previously contentious factions united in 1897 to form the **National Union of Women's Suffrage Societies** (NUWSS), Fawcett was chosen as its leader. She served as president until 1918 when women received the vote and her group became the National Union for Equal Citizenship. Fawcett eschewed the militant tactics endorsed by the **Pankhursts**.

FEAR OF SUCCESS (FOS). A term associated with the work of Matina Horner suggesting that some persons are strongly motivated to avoid occupational or other achievement because of the perceived negative consequences. Horner argued that such motivation was especially prominent in high-ability achievement-oriented women, but subsequent research has revealed it in a significant number of men as well. Feminists view FOS as a conceptually flawed measure that offers a facile explanation of why all women don't achieve.

FÉDÉRATION DES FEMMES DU QUÉBEC (FFQ). A coalition founded in 1966 to promote women's rights through the media, governmental lobbying, and public education in francophone Canada. In 2002 FFQ had 160 group affiliates and many individual members. It is the coordinator of the **World March of Women.**

FEDERATION OF CUBAN WOMEN (FMC). Also known as the FEDERACIÓN DE MUJERES CUBANAS. The sole women's group permitted in Cuba after the Castro takeover in 1960. Led by the nonfeminist **Vilma Espín,** the FMC by 1990 had enrolled 80 percent of Cuban women. Although women's rights are not a priority, the group has been involved in retraining women to participate in all sectors of the economy, not just as domestic workers and **prostitutes,** in developing new programs in health, education, and **child care,** and in changing family law.

FEDERATION OF MUSLIM WOMEN'S ASSOCIATIONS OF NIGERIA (FOMWAN). A feminist federation of over 150 groups, founded in 1985. The FOMWAN, relying upon a liberal interpretation of Islamic teaching, asserts that women have been emancipated for over a thousand years under the **Shari'a**. The group focuses on inheritance rights, child custody with **divorce,** equal access to education, and equity in marriage agreements. It also supports **family planning** for spacing but not limiting the number of children. In 2002 the FOMWAN toured West Africa to encourage the creation of similar organizations in those nations.

FELIX, CONCEPCION. A Filipina **woman suffrage** leader and founder in 1905 of the Asociacion Feminista Filipina, a suffrage and social service organization. Until suffrage was extended in 1937, Felix was active in many other groups and often spoke to the legislature on suffrage bills. In 1937, when a plebiscite was called among women on the suffrage issue, she toured the country registering over 500,000 women, of whom 447,725 approved woman suffrage.

FEMALE CHAUVINISM. The assumption that traditional female values are superior and that **patriarchal** and male values are responsible for women's oppression, war, racism, and environmental problems. *See also* CULTURAL FEMINISM; DIFFERENCE FEMINISM.

FEMALE CIRCUMCISION. *See* FEMALE GENITAL MUTILATION.

FEMALE CONDOM. A woman-controlled **contraceptive** device that lines the entire vagina during sex to prevent pregnancy and disease. More than 18 million have been sold since 1992. Although cumbersome and more expensive than the male version, the product has been used by the UN in developing countries to prevent **AIDS**.

FEMALE DETECTIVE FICTION. A type of mystery with a woman protagonist. This genre has been dominated by women writers since its inception in the 1840s. Mysteries with female detectives usually have feminist undertones; not only do women solve the crime, they also prove cleverer than men. Women authors traditionally use less violence and stress women's independence and resourcefulness. However, some of the most popular contemporary female private investigators are skilled in **self-defense.** *See also* SISTERS IN CRIME.

FEMALE EUNUCH, THE (1972). A major document in the **contemporary feminist movement.** This book by Germaine Greer, an Australian woman educated in England, elaborated on **Simone de Beauvoir's** *The Second Sex* (1953). Like Beauvoir, Greer criticized women for being inner directed, defined by their otherness as "female eunuchs." Greer saw women as allowing themselves to become "deformed and debilitated" by the destructive effects of **sexism** on their lives. Deprived of scope and meaningful work, they lose their energy to purpose activity and never develop as full human beings. As Greer writes, "this [lack of authenthic personhood] is the condition which is meant by the *female eunuch.*"

FEMALE GAZE. A recent feminist modification of Laura Mulvey's definition of **"male gaze,"** or the notion that classic cinema positions the male as voyeur and the woman as static, passive, subject-less object of his gaze. Noting that women also view films, recent **feminist film critics** have proposed that women take pleasure in viewing similar scenes of men as **sex objects** or objects of violence and beating. Mary Ann Doane (in "Film and the Masquerade: Theorizing the Female Spectator," *Screen* 23 [1982]) has, for instance, attempted to use Joan Riviere's theory of "feminine masquerade" to explain the female gaze: "what might it mean [for a woman] to masquerade as spectator?. . . to assume the mask in order to see in a different way?" (82). She goes on to note that the female spectator of film is given two options: "the masochism of over-identification and the narcissism of becoming one's own object of desire, in assuming the image in the most radical way. The effectivity of the masquerade lies precisely in its potential to manufacture a distance from the image, to generate a problematic within which the image is manipulable, producible and readable by the woman" (87).

FEMALE GENITAL CUTTING. *See* FEMALE GENITAL MUTILATION.

FEMALE GENITAL MUTILATION (FGM). The removal of all or part of a young girl's external genitalia (the clitoris and the labia minora), followed by the closing of the vulva with thread or thorns (infibulation) to guarantee virginity, decrease sexual pleasure, and make the future woman marriageable. This Muslim practice (primarily in Africa, but also the Middle East and Southeast Asia) is viewed by Western feminists as torture and a human rights violation. **Alice Walker**, in her novel *Possessing the Secret of Joy* (1992) and the co-authored *Warrior Marks: Female Genital Mutilation and the Sexual Blinding of Women* (1993), has been active in opposition. The practice appears to be in decline as an alternative coming-of-age ceremony emerges. The "Cutting through Word" ritual involves a week of seclusion and lessons about adult life (e.g., health, **reproduction**, peer pressure, and **self-esteem**) for a group of girls. Ten African nations have banned FGM, and it is considered a human rights violation under UN conventions. The World Health Organization, however, estimates that up to 140 million women and girls have undergone FGM. This practice is also called female circumcision, female genital cutting, and clitoridectomy.

FEMALE MAN, THE. A novel published by the American **lesbian feminist** author **Joanna Russ** in 1975. This fabulation, considered a work of **feminist science fiction**, depicts a variety of women living in the past, present, and future. Perhaps the most shocking aspect of the book is its vision of the future—an all-female utopia that has exterminated all men and reproduces through the merging of two ova, always producing more women. It was one of the most controversial novels of the 1970s due to its **radical feminist** anger over male attitudes toward women.

FEMALE SEXUAL SLAVERY. *See* INTERNATIONAL TRAFFIC IN WOMEN.

FEMALE SEXUALITY. A contested term, suggesting both anatomical differences between men and women (biological identity), as well as activity (to perform sexual acts). Feminists have traditionally distinguished sex from **gender**, arguing that women are not characterized by specific or particular qualities that they possess because they are female. Instead, they have argued against such an **essentialist** position, claiming instead that sexuality is culturally and socially constructed, as are sexual desires. Prominent proponents against essentialism include **Judith Butler**, Diana Fuss, and **Monique Wittig**. In addition to theorists of heterosexuality (**Julia Kristéva**) and **lesbianism** (Terry Castle, Teresa de Lauretis), there are also advocates of masturbation as the ultimate form of "safe sex" for women. A contemporary pioneer in liberating women from **heterosexism** has been **Betty Dodson**, author of *Sex for One* (1974) as well as *Celebrating Orgasm* (video documentary). Dodson has been a controversial advocate for masturbation as safe and liberating. *See also* EVE'S GARDEN.

FEMALE/FEMININE PRINCIPLE (RELIGION). A symbolic projection growing out of the social importance of recognizing the role of the female in the perpetuation of the community. Although believed by some devotees of **feminist spirituality** or Jungian psychoanalysis to be immanent, such a principle is a human cognitive construct, not empirically based. Archaeological data cannot determine how ancient or widespread the concept of a cosmic female principle may have been. Similarly, ethnographic or historic art or practices cannot be assumed to embody such a concept unless this is specifically verified in text. Where such a principle is found, it is usually complementary to a male (or masculine) principle in a dualistic cosmology.

FEMALE-HEADED HOUSEHOLD. *See* SINGLE-PARENT FAMILY.

FEM/CRITS. A term used to describe those feminists who draw upon the critical legal studies movement as a foundation for their theories. They reject the premise of law's neutrality, oppose the hierarchy in democracy, and note how dichotomies such as public/private and form/substance reinforce **male dominance**. Such feminists also reject equality discourse.

FEMICIDE. A term coined to describe the most extreme form of **sexist** terrorism, the murder of women by men, who use as their justification **misogyny**, a sense of entitlement, or frustration at women's perceived "advantages" in the marketplace. Research on the topic began in earnest after the 1989 murder of 14 young women at the University of Montreál. Recognizing that the act was very effective as social control, feminists have seen the act as a **hate crime** and not been willing to excuse it as the act of a demented individual. The goal of such violence against women is to preserve male supremacy. Varieties of femicide include **honor killings, rape** murder, immolation of **witches** in Western Europe, and wife murder. Femicidal mayhem has been featured in **pornography**, "slasher films," "splatterpunk" horror novels, as well as super-hero comic books. A central source for the topic is Jane Caputi and Diana Russell, *Femicide: The Politics of Women Killing* (1992).

FEMINAZI. A term coined by conservative radio talk host Rush Limbaugh to describe feminists who oppose all restrictions on **abortion**. It is now used to refer to feminists who enforce **political correctness** similar to the German National Socialists' insistence on socially correct thought. The term is probably just a striking interposition of words in that Nazis saw women's role as **reproduction**.

FEMININE MYSTIQUE, THE. A seminal document in the American feminist movement, published by **Betty Friedan** in 1963. Based on an article she had published originally in 1960 in *Good Housekeeping*, "Women Are People Too!" Friedan went on to amass personal interviews and data from popular culture, sociology, and psychology in order to construct her argument about the malaise striking middle-class, largely suburban wives and mothers. Friedan's book is the first easily accessible work to attribute women's problems to a sex-based society rather than to any personal failures of women themselves.

FEMINISM/FEMINIST. *See* BATTERED WORD SYNDROME.

FEMINIST ALTERNATIVE/FEMINISTSKAIA AL'TERNATIVA (FALTA). A Russian group formed in 1990 as the Free Association of Feminist Organizations/Svobodnaia Assotsiatsiia Feministskikh Organizatzii (SAFO); it assumed its present name in 1993. SAFO was notable as one of the first registered organizations that used the term "feminist" in its name and for its support of the first **Independent Women's Forum**. FALTA's activities include peer counseling, a journal, **women's studies** lectures and workshops, and advocacy for victims of violence.

FEMINIST ANTICENSORSHIP TASKFORCE (FACT). See PORNOGRAPHY, FEMINIST DEBATE ON.

FEMINIST ARCHETYPAL CRITICISM/THEORY. One of the first waves of feminist approaches to literature and culture. This methodology tended to focus on images of women in literature written by men, arguing that men could only depict women in essentially Jungian categories: mother, sister, wife, beloved, femme fatale, and muse. According to Jungian theory, which undergirds archetypal criticism, women were always complements to men, anima to the more dominant, culturally aggressive animus. Thus, early feminist critics tended to recognize ways in which women were passive and compliant, prone to irrationality or instability. Another tactic of archetypal criticism is to recognize the ways in which females are coded as aberrant or castrated, "**female eunuchs**," according to Germaine Greer.

FEMINIST ART AND AESTHETIC THEORY. A recent academic attempt to rediscover and evaluate the artistic productions of lost or marginalized women painters and photographers. Feminist art history is predicated on exposing women's absence from creating dominant art forms. It seeks to build a **counter-cultural** tradition, frequently avant-garde, that opposes the dominance of **patriarchal** ideology in the visual arts. It poses the question, What would art that did not oppress or exploit women look like? It seeks to oppose **sexism** in culture and it frequently seeks to use art for propagandistic purposes. Beginning in the 1960s, vaginal imagery, **goddess** lore, and traditional craft techiques challenged **male-dominated** art and used the female body as a site for feminist theory. Institutions such as all-female galleries, arts magazines and journals, and protest groups were founded and artists such as **Judy Chicago**, Miriam Shapiro, Faith Ringgold, and Bettye Saar emerged as feminist icons. *See also* GUERRILLA GIRLS; PERFORMANCE ART.

FEMINIST BOOKSTORES. A group of commercial enterprises in North America that sell pamphlets, newspapers, magazines, and books about women, feminism, and the women's movement. These stores are typically community resources that offer many of the same services as **women's centers** and, in the early years, were often owned by feminist **collectives.** Today the stock of feminist bookstores reflects the interest of mainstream publishers in feminist topics. They remain a major sales outlet for feminist publishing houses and for **lesbian** fiction, antiracist and **nonsexist children's literature,** and books by and about **women of color.** The number of feminist bookstores in the United States and Canada has declined from more than 120 in 1997 to 74 in summer 2001 because of competition from online and chain bookstores. *Feminist Bookstore News* ceased publication in 2000 after 24 years. Even so, Amazon Bookstore, which opened in 1970 in Minneapolis, filed an unsuccessful lawsuit in 1999 against the Internet retailer of the same name, charging copyright infringement.

FEMINIST CARTOONISTS. The female practitioners of the genre who primarily appear in the independent underground comic book press and speak to women's interests. In 1972 the Wimmen's Comix Collective was formed to publish all-female artists. In 1994 Friends of Lulu was founded to promote women's participation in the comics business. Topics such as surviving adolescence and the workplace, **female sexuality,** and **self-esteem** are addressed in a sometimes violent or erotic manner. Syndicated cartoonists such as Lynda Barry (*Ernie Pook's Comeek*). Cathy Guisewite (*Cathy*), and Nicole Hollander (*Sylvia*) are also within this tradition.

FEMINIST CENTER FOR INFORMATION AND ACTION/CENTRO FEMINISTA DE INFORMACIÓN Y ACCIÓN (CEFEMINA). The oldest feminist group in Costa Rica. The CEFEMINA grew out of the Movimiento para la Liberación de la Mujer (Women's Liberation Movement, MLM), which was founded in 1974 by wealthy European-educated women exposed to Western feminism. The MLM focused on **reproductive freedom.** With the name change in 1981, The CEFEMINA has shifted its attention to poor women and programs on housing, health, unionization, microloans, and **domestic violence.**

FEMINIST CONSCIOUSNESS. A set of attitudes held by women that includes: a recognition of membership in and shared interests with a group called "women"; awareness and rejection of women's unequal status in society; and support for collective action by the group to change their status. Most feminist movement participants have this sense of group consciousness, which is a prerequisite for social change.

FEMINIST ECONOMICS. An approach to the study of economics that rejects the model of rational and self-interested "economic man" and the wisdom of a free market system. Critics argue that this traditional model ignores social and cooperative aspects of economic behavior. They also note that the market neither corrects for inequities such as **gender discrimination** nor does it result in pay commensurate with the social value of labor. Feminist economics is a method of analysis that focuses on **gender** and views both gender and economics as socially constructed. The International Association for Feminist Economics was established in 1992.

FEMINIST EPISTEMOLOGY. A body of knowledge acquired through the unique ways women know the world and the way they understand the multiplicity of experiences that all women have undergone. Current feminist thinking emphasizes that there is no one female experience or female nature, but many different ways of knowing that one is a woman. Whereas each school of feminism emphasizes only one aspect of the female condition—class, psychology, otherness—contemporary feminist epistemology tries to grasp the entire picture of race, sexual orientation, class, and age in order to appreciate the differences and validities of how all women know the experiences of femaleness.

FEMINIST EXPO. The conferences organized in 1996 and 2000 in Washington, D.C. by the **Feminist Majority Foundation** to bring together women and women's groups to work for change. The exhibitions, performances, symposia, roundtables, career fair, and training sessions attracted 7,000 persons from 45 nations in 2000.

FEMINIST FILM THEORY. A recent conjunction between the women's movement and the film industry. The first stage in **feminist consciousness** about film resulted in a campaign against **sexism** within the film industry, including discrimination against female directors and producers. The second stage resulted in analyses of sexism in filmic representation of women as **bitch**, whore, or femme fatale. And the third stage was the use of film for propaganda purposes such as documentary cinema about the living conditions of women in various countries. These issues have been explored in *Women and Film*, the first journal of feminist film criticism, founded in 1972 and published in California. The first feminist film festivals took place in New York and Edinburgh and began the task of rediscovering the work of lost female directors: Dorothy Arzner, Leni Riefenstahl, Maya Deren, Sally Potter, Marguerite Duras, Laura Mulvey, Michelle Citron, Chantal Akerman, and Yvonne Rainer. A useful summary of the history of feminist film can be found in Ann Kaplan's *Women and Film* (1983). *See also* FEMALE GAZE.

FEMINIST GEOGRAPHY. An academic subfield dating from the 1970s that examines how **gender** relations are reinforced or reflected in the built environment. Men and women experience spaces and places differently and this contributes to the social construction of place and a gendered environment.

FEMINIST HUMOR. A type of comedy that focuses on **gender** inequity and **sexist** assumptions. Oppression on the basis of race, class, and sexual orientation are also common themes of this change-oriented approach. **Antifeminists** counter with humor that rejects this challenge to the **patriarchy**, as is reflected in the number of jokes featuring a powerful or **lesbian** Hillary Clinton. Feminist comedy generally does not rely on put-downs, one-liners, and lengthy "jokes." Among the best-known feminist comedians are: Elayne Boosler, Margaret Cho, Kate Clinton, Whoopi Goldberg, and Lily Tomlin.

FEMINIST JURISPRUDENCE. An examination of the principles underlying **patriarchal** laws and the adjustment of these principles to include the experiences of women. One goal is to expose legal principles which operate to constrain or limit women.

FEMINIST LEGAL THEORY. An examination of the functions of law by women in which emphasis is placed on the methods the legal system uses to define the female's subordinate role and to advance the power and control of males.

FEMINIST LIBERATION THEOLOGY. A contemporary religious scholarship guided by theoretical and practical commitments to emancipation and justice for women. Reflecting liberation theology's starting point in concrete crises of oppressed peoples, feminist liberation theologians are rooted in the **standpoints** and experiences of particular communities of women. **Patriarchal** dimensions of religious traditions and texts are critiqued, and their liberative features interpreted, from vantage points intentionally informed by justice seeking and solidarity with women. See also FEMINIST SPIRITUALITY.

FEMINIST LITERARY CRITICISM, MATERIALIST. An adaptation of the **Marxist** assumption that subjectivity is socially constructed that focuses attention on literary structures which produce **gender** ideology. It considers how society causes men and women to identify themselves as "masculine" or "feminine." A materialist feminist literary critic also looks at the material (e.g., economic, racial) circumstances in which texts by and about women and/or **gender** are produced and read.

FEMINIST LITERARY CRITICISM, NEW HISTORICIST. An examination of literature as a site of the production and enforcement of, as well as opposition to, hierarchical power relations. As in the work of **Michel Foucault**, new historicist feminist literary criticism considers historically specific power struggles, but focuses on **gender** relations ignored by Focauldian critique.

FEMINIST MAGAZINES. Those periodicals exclusively devoted to the principles of women's rights. The **woman suffrage movement** published journals of their proceedings, activities, and general discussions of other reform issues. The **new feminist movement** produced many local newsletters and literary magazines. *Ms.*, begun in 1972, was the first popular, mainstream feminist periodical. *Off our backs*, founded in 1970, is the longest surviving feminist newspaper in the United States. In recent years print publications have been struggling, as online **feminist web zines**, journals, and blogs (Web logs) proliferate. The English *Spare Rib*, for example, folded in 1993 after a 21-year run. The growth of **women's studies** has been accompanied by the appearance of numerous scholarly journals, both print and online, in all regions of the world.

FEMINIST MAJORITY FOUNDATION (FMF). A nonprofit organization founded in 1987 by **Eleanor Smeal** and Peg Yorkin to increase the number of feminist women in leadership positions in the United States. At that time a majority of US women self-labeled as "feminists." The FMF engages in public education, research, policy development, organizing, and training. Its political arm, the Feminist Majority, lobbies and engages in direct action. The group has been a leader on **RU 486** and in the **Campaign to Stop Gender Apartheid in Afghanistan**. It is the sponsor of the **Feminist Expo** and the owner of *Ms.* Its "four choices" campaign focuses on **reproductive freedom**, careers, leadership, and fighting the **backlash**. Its Feminist Majority Leadership Alliance is a national network of feminist groups at more than 130 universities.

FEMINIST MORAL THEORY. A newly developing field of inquiry that draws upon women's experiences as a way of refashioning traditional Western approaches to moral theory. Feminist moral theory is both critical and constructive. It seeks to expose and critique the male biases inherent in the concepts and methods of traditional ethical theory, and to reconceive and rearticulate those concepts and methods in ways representative of and congenial to the distinctive features of women's experiences. Although contributions to feminist moral theory are rich and diverse, a central development in this area has been an **ethic of care**.

FEMINIST MUSIC AND MUSICOLOGY. A cultural movement that developed during the late 1960s and is best represented within the folk tradition, at the National Women's Music Festivals held annually since 1974, at the **lesbian**-oriented Michigan Womyn's Music Festival held annually since 1976, and at the more recent **Lilith Fairs** and **Ladyfests**. A feminist musicology has documented **sex discrimination** in conservatory admissions and the bias against women composers, instrumentalists, and conductors and has attempted to gain some recognition for these early female musicians. Feminists have also protested against the violent and **sexist** lyrics of popular music and pornographic album art and have founded performance groups, record and promotion companies, festivals, and publications for a new women's music. Prominent feminist musicians include: Meg Christian, Holly Near, Cris Williamson, the **Indigo Girls**, and k.d. lang. Olivia Records and the

Ladyslipper Catalog of women's music are also important parts of this network.

FEMINIST NETWORK/FEMINSTA HÁLÓZAT. A Hungarian group founded in 1990 to promote women's equality and political participation and to combat **gender discrimination**. The group has lobbied government and demonstrated for **abortion** rights. Its major strategy, however, is public education through lectures, seminars, research, and translation and publication of feminist literature and its own magazine.

FEMINIST PEDAGOGY. A recent instructional strategy that fosters resistance to "masterful meaning" and "reductive **appropriations**" of women to dominant **patriarchal** discourses. Feminist pedagogy stresses personal engagement of students with materials (through self-reflective journals and group reports) as well as the oppositional (debates, forums to explore differing perspectives on an issue). The goal of feminist pedagogy is to challenge authority and **deconstruct** the false universality of patriarchally institutionalized meanings. It also seeks to overthrow the objectifying, hegemonic reduction/appropriation of the "other" in favor of an oppositional practice, one which does not reduce the personal into the universal (always male, middle-class, and heterosexual).

FEMINIST PERSPECTIVES IN HEALTH EDUCATION. An attempt to address and integrate feminist concerns specific to the health-related professions. It encompasses curricular inclusion of feminist ideologies to inform students and raise consciousness about the **androcentric** biases and social behaviors embedded in the **male-dominated** medical field.

FEMINIST PHENOMENOLOGY. The work of contemporary **postmodern** feminists, who make use of phenomenological method, that is, giving precise descriptions of women's lived experiences and providing etymological analysis of linguistic terms that have been used to oppress women. The purpose is not to explain women's oppression but instead to **empower** women by validating their experience. Some common topics are women's eroticism, bodily comportment, **essentialism**, and capacities for subversive language use.

FEMINIST POLITICAL THEORY. A variety of traditions and movements that seek to articulate political theories based on women's experiences, especially that of oppression. **Liberal feminism** seeks to extend the values and ideals of traditional political liberalism to women. **Radical feminism** seeks to overthrow the system of **male domination** and to articulate political values and ideals that grow out of women's experiences of **gender** oppression. **Socialist feminism** tries to combine the central insights of radical feminism and **Marxism.**

FEMINIST PRACTICAL REASONING. A feminist approach that combines practical deliberation with an emphasis on identifying and accounting for the perspectives of the excluded by reasoning from contextual frameworks. It focuses on individual fact-finding as opposed to the application of universal rules.

FEMINIST PRESS. A publishing house, established in 1970 in New York by English professor Florence Howe and specializing in **nonsexist children's literature** and reissued books by women that attracted little attention on first publication. The press also publishes the *Women's Studies Quarterly.*

FEMINIST READING GROUPS. Reading groups for support, **mentoring**, and intellectual exchange specifically organized and focused on literary works of interest to feminists. As there are so many varieties of feminism, the reading groups are as varied as are the women involved in them. Many groups are focused exclusively on **feminist science fiction**, fantasy, and utopian literature. Other groups focus exclusively on GayTrek for gay Star Trek fans. Others are more traditional, focusing on the novels of Jane Austen or following one of the popular television book club selections. A number of feminist reading groups "meet" only online, at a variety of listservs for members.

FEMINIST SCIENCE. The pursuit of scientific knowledge shaped and broadened by feminist ideology. Feminist science may differ from "status quo" science in the types of scientific questions posed, the methods of experimental subject selection, the processes used to acquire data, and the bases for generating results and conclusions.

FEMINIST SCIENCE FICTION. A genre that permits authors to envision an advanced technological future where **gender** equality exists. Science fiction was long viewed as a **male-dominated** form in which women were either rescued or conquered. Beginning with Ursula LeGuin's *The Left Hand of Darkness* (1969), more women began writing science fiction that introduced feminist themes of **androgyny** and empathy. Since 1977 an annual international feminist science fiction convention has been held in Wisconsin. Broad Universe, a group formed in 2000, promotes the genre through their website. And since 1991 the James Tiptree Jr. Award has been conferred for science fiction that expands or explores our understanding of gender.

FEMINIST SOCIAL WORK. The practice of social work using a feminist orientation that acknowledges societal discrimination against women and specifically attempts to help women overcome problems related to this discrimination (e.g., unpaid labor in the home, low-wage work, and prescribed **sex-role** behaviors such as dependency).

FEMINIST SPIRITUALITY. The critical reflection upon religious matters, usually from the perspective of a particular faith community, which has its starting point and goal in a concern for the voices, the experiences, and the flourishing of women. In its Christian and Jewish forms, feminist spirituality unmasks, critiques, and denounces elements of scripture, tradition, and practice that have wreaked or legitimated harm against women. Prominent feminist practitioners include Elizabeth Schüssler Fiorenza, *But She Said* (1992), which argues that the Western cultural "frame of meaning" is not just androcentric but that it is kyriocentric (master centered). Gender asymmetry forces us to read Jesus as "Man" and therefore perpetuates the position of woman in the Bible as victim, weak, and inferior. Another manifestation of feminist spirituality is the attempt to retrieve and reinterpret elements of tradition and scripture that offer liberative paradigms. In its post-Christian, pagan, or **goddess** centered forms, feminist spirituality deliberately leaves behind dominant historical religious traditions to seek uniquely female-centered forms of religious interpretation and practice. Sometimes called "the new paganism," this form of feminist spirituality focuses on goddess worship or "Green Religion." Meeting in groups to enact ancient ceremonies of worship, called **wiccas** or covens, green feminists pay homage to a variety of Celtic female **deities**. Their original connection with nature and the powers of earth and fertility are also growing in popularity among this sect of feminist spiritualists. *See also* FEMINIST LIBERATION THEOLOGY.

FEMINIST THERAPY. An approach that emerged in the mid-1970s as a part of the feminist critique of psychiatry and psychotherapy. New insights into the psychology of women are incorporated and an attempt is made to transform the hierarchical relationship between therapist and client. The client, usually a woman, is assisted to identify and deal with problems that relate to **sex discrimination** and **sex role stereotyping** in the family and wider society. Techniques include **consciousness-raising**, education, and **assertiveness training**.

FEMINIST WEB ZINES. The electronic magazines created by writers, editors, students, artists, and homemakers as an alternative to traditional women's magazines that are dominated by fashion and cosmetics advertising. There are thousands of these e-zines on a variety of topics. Readers can give feedback and see their comments instantly posted. Currently two-thirds of **feminist magazines** only appear online.

FÉMINISTES RÉVOLUTIONNAIRES (FR). A French **radical feminist** group, organized in 1970, with a membership that included **Simone de Beauvoir** and **Monique Wittig**. The strongly **separatist** group staged dramatic protests such as the *Manifeste des 343 Femmes* and the dedication of a wreath to the wife of the unknown soldier honored by a tomb at the Arc de Triomphe.

FEMINISTS FOR LIFE (FFL). A **pro-life** organization for feminists who oppose **abortion**, organized in 1972 by two Ohio members of the **National Organization for Women** who left or were expelled for their dissenting views. Most feminists view the FFL's agenda as solely abortion, but the group supports the **Equal Rights Amendment** and **family leave**. Its consistent opposition to all forms of violence makes it an ally against **domestic violence** and clinic violence as well. The FFL notes that many early feminists such as **Mary Wollstonecraft** and **Susan B. Anthony** were critics of abortion. The group has over 4,000 members and publishes *The American Feminist*.

FEMINISTS, THE. A **radical feminist** group formed in 1968 by **Ti-Grace Atkinson** and other members of the **National Organization for Women** and **New York Radical Women** as "The October 17th

Movement." In keeping with their commitment to nonhierarchical organization, the Feminists developed the lot system for random rotation of creative and boring tasks within the group and an equitable system for allotting discussion time in meetings. A restrictive set of rules mandating compulsory work and attendance and limiting the percentage of members co-habiting with men led to many resignations in 1969. The group formally disbanded in 1973.

"**FEMINIZATION OF POVERTY.**" A phrase identified by social scientist Diana Pearce in 1978 to describe the growing proportion of the US poor comprised of women and their children. This increase in poverty is due to marital instability and women's inability to successfully participate in the labor market while fulfilling the responsibilities of raising children. Although feminists denounce this trend, they also object to the assumption that poverty would not exist if these women developed and sustained an economic relationship with a man. The 2000 census showed a sharp decline in poverty among single-mother households due to a strong economy, greater acceptance of **single mothers** in the workforce, and better **child support enforcement.**

FEMINOLOGY. The science of women and used to refer to **women's studies** programs in other countries, most notably in Scandinavia and Russia. It was originally used in 1902 as the title of a course taught by **Marguerite Souley-Darqué** that resembled contemporary women's studies courses in content. At contemporary centers of feminology there is an **essentialist** emphasis on the development of women's historic roles and an avoidance of Western feminist frameworks of **patriarchy** and inequality.

FEMMES NOUVELLES/NEW WOMEN. A French working-class feminist **collective** of the 1830s. A splinter from the Saint-Simonian socialists, this group may have been the first **separatist** women's movement. The women writing for their newspaper *La femme libre* (The Free Woman, 1832-34) used only their first names to symbolize independence from men. They tried to appeal to all women on the basis of a common bond as mothers, but the movement collapsed under the pressure of wage earning.

FEMOCRAT. A feminist who is employed in a powerful position within a public bureaucracy and works on women's issues. The term is primarily associated with Australian feminists who consciously sought public jobs after the defeat of the supportive Labor Party government in 1975. Elizabeth Reid, Prime Minister Gough Whitlam's advisor on women's affairs, was the first femocrat. The femocrat strategy uses public administration as an alternative to female elected officials to advance **gender** sensitivity and represent women in policy-making.

FERN, FANNY. *See* PARTON, SARA PAYSON WILLIS.

FERRARO, GERALDINE (1935-). The Democratic nominee for vice president of the United States in 1984 and the first woman to appear on a major political party's ticket in that country. She was selected by presidential candidate Walter Mondale after strong lobbying from feminists. Although she and Mondale were defeated, Ferraro was an outspoken advocate for women's issues during the campaign and a very effective fund-raiser among women. Ferraro, a lawyer, served in the US House of Representatives, 1979-85. In 1992 and 1998 she lost the New York Democratic primary for the Senate. Since then she has been active in international women's and human rights activities and briefly co-hosted a cable television political talkshow.

FETAL PROTECTION POLICIES. The employment policies that prohibited women of childbearing years from working in (generally higher paying) positions that may expose them to substances that are harmful to a fetus unless women provide proof of sterility. These policies were defined as illegal **sex discrimination** in the United States in *International Union, UAW v. Johnson Controls* (1991) because fertile women were able to perform the battery manufacturing jobs in question as well as anyone else. Feminists generally hailed the decision as one that gave women the right to weigh the risks and choose high-paying, dangerous jobs, but they also urged that the workplace be made safe for all workers.

FETAL RIGHTS. An emerging area of legal discourse in which a woman and her fetus are viewed as two separate entities with potentially conflicting interests and each with legal rights. This doctrine originates in the **pro-life movement** that portrays the fetus as a preborn baby and stresses the ability of medical science to treat the fetus in utero and to link infant health problems with a woman's consumption of tobacco, drugs, and alcohol and exposure to toxic chemicals during pregnancy.

Some US women, prosecuted for using alcohol or drugs while pregnant, have been jailed or denied custody of their children; others, seriously ill, have been forced to have a cesarean section. Although feminists are concerned that the rights of women are being compromised here, many also urge that rehabilitation programs begin to accept pregnant women. To date, the courts have not upheld involuntary Cesareans or **fetal protection policies.** However, in *Whitner v. South Carolina* (1996) the South Carolina Supreme Court upheld a child abuse conviction of a woman who had smoked cocaine during pregnancy by ruling that a viable fetus is covered under state child abuse law.

FETAL TISSUE RESEARCH AND TRANSPLANTS. *See* STEM CELL RESEARCH.

FIGUERO, ANA (1908-1970). A Chilean feminist and UN leader. Figuero was the president of the committee that won **woman suffrage** in 1948. After serving as the head of the Women's Bureau in the Ministry of Foreign Affairs, she was sent as an envoy to the United Nations, where she became the first woman to chair a committee of the General Assembly in 1951.

FIJI WOMEN'S RIGHTS MOVEMENT (FWRM). A **radical feminist** group, formed in 1986 out of concern with **rape, violence against women,** and the exploitation of women in the garment industry. The group uses a variety of strategies—public educaton, lobbying, media campaigns, and demonstrations—to advance its broad agenda. In 1996 it achieved the repeal of a law prohibiting night work by women.

FIRESTONE, SHULAMITH (1944-). *See* DIALECTIC OF SEX, THE.

FIRST WAVE FEMINISM. The worldwide campaign for women's rights waged in the 19th and early 20th centuries. Key demands centered on education, **married women's** legal rights, employment opportunities, and suffrage. By the late 1930s **woman suffrage** had been adopted in most nations and a woman's right to equal treatment had been validated. *See also* SECOND WAVE FEMINISM; THIRD WAVE FEMINISM.

FLAPPER VOTE. A popular phrase used in Britain during the 1920s to describe the anticipated voting behavior of women, 21-29, who had not been enfranchised by the franchise act of 1918. The Conservatives feared that these young women would vote for the Labour Party. Because of male deaths during World War I, there were two million more female voters in the electorate with the passage of the **Representation of the People (Equal Franchise) Act of 1928.**

FLEXITIME. An organizational practice that involves alternatives to the 9 a.m. to 5 p.m. work schedule. Flexitime allows employees to choose different hours, such as 7 a.m. to 3 p.m. or 11 a.m. to 7 p.m. This policy is particularly useful for parents in that a child's daily activities can be coordinated with a parent's hours of work. The practice is widespread in Europe and is becoming more available in the United States. *See also* WORK-FAMILY CONFLICT.

FLORA TRISTÁN CENTER FOR THE PERUVIAN WOMAN. The largest women's group and one of the most active feminist organizations in Peru. The Flora Tristán Center was organized in 1979 and is active on issues of health, **reproductive freedom,** and **violence against women.** It makes videos, issues reports, offers workshops, and provides legal services in fulfilling its mission of improving the status of women.

FORMS OF ADDRESS. *See* NAMING CONVENTIONS.

FORUM AGAINST OPPRESSION OF WOMEN (FAOW). A Bombay-based public education group established in 1979 as the Forum Against Rape in response to the **Mathura rape case.** Its agenda has expanded to include **dowry, domestic violence,** and **sexual harassment.** The FAOW is a volunteer-run membership group that meets weekly. It has been very active recently in cases of violence against Islamic women in the Indian state of Gujarat.

FOUCAULT, MICHEL (1926-1984). The leading French theorist of discourse, or of how language is formed by social institutions in accordance with institutional rules that make certain kinds of knowledge possible. Foucault's major works focus on how madness and modern medicine were invented through the invention of asylums and clinics. After the failure of the Paris uprising in May 1968, Foucault turned his attention to the exercise of power through social practices, including language, or what he called "discursive practices." His *Discipline and*

Punish (1975) examined the evolution of the prison system and its exercise of power over the human body. His final work, the three-volume *History of Sexuality* (1976-1986), traced the invention of the construction of the "**homosexual**." Feminist interest in Foucault centers on how he enunciated issues of power in relation to social institutions and their locus in the human body.

FOUQUÉ, ANTOINETTE. *See* POLITIQUE ET PSYCHANALYSE.

FOURTEENTH AMENDMENT. *See* EQUAL PROTECTION.

FREDRIKA BREMER ASSOCIATION. A Swedish **liberal feminist** group, formed in 1884 as a **woman suffrage** organization. Since the mid-1970s it has concentrated on **networking** and increasing the role of women in political life.

FREE ASSOCIATION OF FEMINIST ORGANIZATIONS (SAFO). *See* FEMINIST ALTERNATIVE (FALTA).

FREE MARKET FEMINISM. A tradition that assumes that women have equal access to the economy and can compete successfully in a **gender-neutral** marketplace. This term is associated with **Margaret Thatcher** who felt that women should not seek special treatment such as **family leave** or **affirmative action**.

FREE TO BE . . . YOU AND ME. A 1972 children's record album by US actress Marlo Thomas that sold over 500,000 copies. It became a book, a television special and home video, and a stage play. It is considered the model for **nonsexist children's literature** with its songs and stories about William's doll, crying, and **Atalanta**. Each issue of *Ms.* for many years contained "stories for free children."

FREEDMAN, MARCIA (1938-). A US immigrant to Israel, philosophy professor at the University of Haifa, and member of the Israel Knesset, 1973-1977. Freedman was one of the founders of the **new feminist movement** in Israel. During her years in the national legislature, Freedman, as its only feminist, raised many women's issues, including **abortion** reform and **domestic violence**. After leaving the Knesset and returning to the United States in 1981, Freedman established Israel's first **women's battery shelter**, **women's centers**, and the Community

School for Women, an institution without walls that brings courses in **women's studies** and women's economic **empowerment** to low-income women in Israel.

FREEDOM OF ACCESS TO CLINIC ENTRANCES ACT (FACE). See CLINIC PROTECTION.

FRENCH, MARILYN (1929-). The author of *Beyond Power: On Women, Men and Morals* (1985) and the feminist potboiler *The Women's Room* (1976). French's serious analysis, *Beyond Power*, sees **sexism** as the root cause of all oppression in society. She condemns the **patriarchy** for instituting "stratification of men above women [which] leads in time to stratification of classes: an elite rules over people perceived as 'closer to nature,' savage, bestial, animalistic." Because women were identified with nature, men grew to fear and desire to control them. She sees the only solution to this impasse as the cultivation of values such as "love and compassion and sharing and nurturance, as well as control, structure, possessiveness, and status." She has continued to publish works of fiction and nonfiction, including *Women's History of the World* (2000), after a successful treatment for cancer.

FRENTE ÚNICO PRO-DERECHOS DE LA MUJER/SOLE FRONT FOR WOMEN'S RIGHTS. A feminist coalition formed in Mexico in 1935 after three congresses for women had been held, 1931-1934. Founder Maria del Refugio Garcia saw **woman suffrage** as a unifying issue for all, and she built an organization of 800 women's groups around a broad program of political, social, and economic demands. Although Mexican women were not enfranchised until 1958, they almost achieved that goal in the late 1930s with their meetings, marches, and **hunger strikes**.

FREUD, SIGMUND (1856-1939). An Austrian physician and founder of psychoanalysis, noted for his theory of **sexual politics** and the concept of "penis envy." According to Freud, girls react to their lack of a phallus by rejecting their clitoris (deficient penis) and their mothers (other women). They gravitate toward their fathers and, later, other men and compensate by giving birth, preferably to a son through whom they then live. Heterosexuality is thus ensured, but a struggle between husband and wife continues as she seeks to infantilize her husband in her retreat to the **domestic sphere**. Feminists have viewed Freud as **misogynistic** and **patriarchal** and reject the idea of a woman's body as incomplete. Contemporaries like **Karen Horney** suggested that "womb envy" may be more powerful than "penis envy." Feminists have also pointed out that Freud's thinking was based on his work with emotionally disturbed patients and that there is no evidence that these developments occur inevitably in the lives of normal females. Efforts to validate "penis envy" through nonclinical methods have been unsuccessful. Other feminist theorists like **Juliet Mitchell** and **Nancy Chodorow** have used Freudian theory to explain women's condition in a patriarchal society.

FRIEDAN, BETTY (1921-). The woman viewed as the catalyst of the **new feminist movement** in the United States. Her description of **"the problem that has no name"** in *The Feminine Mystique* (1963) brought a critical discussion of women's domestic life to the widespread attention of the public. She was one of the founders of the **National Organization for Women (NOW)** and served as its first president. She was also one of the convenors of the **National Women's Political Caucus**. Friedan lectures and writes widely on the women's movement and public policy. She has been associated with a number of American universities since founding NOW and has published five additional books: *It Changed My Life* (1976), *The Second Stage* (1981), *The Fountain of Age* (1993), *Beyond Gender: The New Politics of Work and Family* (1997), and *Life So Far: A Memoir* (2000). Although political conservatives continue to view Friedan as a radical, many feminists see her as reactionary because of her charge that the women's movement has replaced the feminine mystique with a feminist mystique that has brought the two sexes and work and family into further conflict and split women.

FRIGIDITY. An obsolete term to describe women who do not experience sexual desire. Feminists believe that this term is often used as a put-down for women who are well within the normal range of sexual desire and experience but who are perceived by the user of the label as unavailable.

FRINGE FEMINISM. A term that has two meanings within the feminist movement. For feminists, fringe feminism is associated with the **third wave** culture of independent "outsider" feminist music, art, and writing that appear and are celebrated in **feminist web zines**. **Antifeminists** use the term to describe the current stage of feminism in which men face inequities and the "lunatic fringe" dominates the movement.

FUKUZAWA, YUKICHI (1834-1901). A Meiji period reformer who opposed the traditional Confucian views of women. His *Essay on Japanese Women* (1879) and *The New Greater Learning for Women* (1897) criticized the status of women in Japan and advocated equal rights and education for women.

FULLER, MARGARET (1810-1850). An American journalist and reformer. After brief stints as a teacher, translator, and an editor of *The Dial*, a transcendentalist magazine, she began a career as America's first self-supporting woman journalist. She used transcendentalist philosophy and Kantian epistemology in her *Woman in the Nineteenth Century* (1845), the first major feminist manifesto in America, and applied them to women. She called for complete freedom and equality for women and urged the forging of a self-reliant **sisterhood**. This book is credited with inspiring the Declaration of Sentiments of the **Seneca Falls Convention** and serving as the intellectual basis of US **first wave feminism**. Fuller advocated an **androgynous** consciousness, claiming that there was "no wholly masculine man," just as there was "no purely feminine woman." She believed in the primacy of the spirit and urged women to turn inward to find their true natures and strength.

FURIES, THE. The most prominent of the early **lesbian feminist collectives**, founded in 1971 in Washington, D.C., by a dozen women, including **Rita Mae Brown** and Charlotte Bunch. The group disbanded within a year but not before providing analyses of **heterosexism**, lesbian feminist **separatism**, and **political lesbianism**. The name is adapted from Aeschylus's ancient Greek play in which "The Furies," angry female spirits, refuse to avenge Oerestes's murder of his mother Clytemnestra.

FUSEN KAKUTÔKU DÔMEI (FKD) / LEAGUE FOR WOMAN'S SUFFRAGE. A Japanese group formed in 1924 by Fusae Ichikawa. Although it remained small and elite, the FKD actively lobbied for a suffrage bill as well as other political rights for women after the extension of universal manhood suffrage in 1925. The suffrage movement peaked in 1931 with the defeat of a very limited women's civil rights bill that was opposed by the FKD. In 1933 the group shifted its attention to community politics and dissolved in 1949, four years after **woman suffrage** was imposed by the occupation forces.

-G-

GAGE, MATILDA JOSLYN (1826-1898). A US women's rights activist and compiler, with **Susan B. Anthony** and **Elizabeth Cady Stanton**, of the *History of Woman Suffrage* (1881-1906). Her **radical feminist** perspective on **prostitution**, marriage customs, **rape**, and child custody may have resulted in a less prominent role for her in **woman suffrage** history. She was president of the **National Woman Suffrage Association** in 1869. She founded the Women's National Liberal Union in 1890 to work for the separation of church and state. Her *Women, Church and State: The Original Exposé of Male Collaboration Against the Female Sex* (1893) argued that a prehistorical **matriarchy** was overthrown by a **patriarchal** union between church and state.

GALINDO, HERMILA (1896-1954). A Mexican feminist and early supporter of **woman suffrage**. As editor of *Mujer Moderna*, 1915-1919, Galindo promoted her radical views on women and the role played by the Catholic Church in obstructing the advancement of women. Moderate feminists rejected many of her positions, and in 1919 she was removed from her position in the government and withdrew from feminist activity.

GAMMA HYDROXYBUTYRIC ACID (GHB). *See* DATE RAPE DRUG.

GAY AND LESBIAN CRITICISM. An effort to make visible that which has been made invisible in heterosexual culture. This tradition presents itself as a form of rebellion against the sexual norms of the **patriarchy** and **heterosexism**. Prominent theorists in the attempt to discuss the power issues implicit in same-sex relationships in literature and culture include **Monique Wittig**, *The Lesbian Body* (1976); Eve Kosofsky, *Between Men: English Literature and Male Homosocial Desire* (1985) and *Epistemology of the Closet* (1990); **Adrienne Rich**, *Of Woman Born* (1979); and Lillian Faderman, *Surpassing the Love of Men: Ro-*

mantic Friendship and Love Between Women from the Renaissance to the Present (1981).

GAY/STRAIGHT SPLIT. A cleavage within the US **women's liberation movement**, primarily occurring during the period 1970-72. The conflict centered on the role of **lesbians** as lesbians within the movement and the priority of lesbian issues on the feminist agenda. Underlying the split was much mutual misunderstanding and distrust as lesbians perceived **heterosexism** within the movement and straight women believed their feminist credentials were being questioned. See also LAVENDER MENACE; POLITICAL LESBIANISM; "WOMAN-IDENTIFIED WOMAN, THE."

GENDER. A term variously used to denote: the equivalent of sex; those qualities of femaleness and maleness that develop as a result of socialization rather than biological predisposition; and any qualities associated with femaleness or maleness, regardless of their roots in biology or socialization. Some feminists prefer a definition of gender as socially constructed and distinct from the biological term "sex." Other feminists are less certain due to disagreement on the future of gender. Some prefer **androgyny**, while others want to retain a distinctively female set of bahaviors and values. Usage of the terms is interchangeable, however, in popular discourse.

GENDER AND COMMUNICATION. An area of research that focuses on the role that **gender** socialization and **male dominance** play in the verbal and nonverbal communication of men and women. Scholars seek to identify and explain male- and female-specific patterns of communication that are unique to each sex and the differences between men and women in these patterns and styles of speech. University of California linguist Robin Tolmach Lakoff was a pioneer in the development of this field with her examination of the linkage between language and the status of women in the United States (see her *Language and Woman's Place* [1975]). Women's more polite and deferential style has been linked with their subordinate position in society born of dominance and with their different gender subculture. The publication of Georgetown University linguist Deborah Tannen's *You Just Don't Understand: Men and Women in Conversation* (1990), brought gender differences in communication style to public awareness. The impact of these differences on intimate relationships, family, marriage, and the workplace (see Tannen's *Talking From 9 to 5: How Women's and Men's Conversational Styles Affect Who Gets Heard, Who Gets Credit, and What Gets Done at Work* [1994]) has been of particular interest to feminists. *See also* DEFICIT PERSPECTIVE; GENDER DISPLAYS; REFRAMING.

GENDER CONSCIOUSNESS. *See* FEMINIST CONSCIOUSNESS.

GENDER DISCRIMINATION. The differential treatment of those distinguished as male or female. When US courts have interpreted the prohibition against "sex" discrimination in Title VII of the **Civil Rights Act of 1964**, they have adopted a narrow definition of sex, which basically corresponds to gender discrimination. A broader definition of discrimination is available to the courts. This more expansive construction of sex discrimination includes not only discrimination based on **gender** but also discrimination based on sexuality, sexual preferences, or sexual practices.

GENDER DISPLAYS. The act of marking one's **gender** through engaging in sex-specific behavior. Gender displays are a product of culture, not nature. Both women and men engage in gender displays—for example, women by preening their hair, crossing their legs at the knees, dressing in skirts and hose and men by dressing in pants and low-heeled shoes, sitting with legs open, and growing mustaches. Insofar as a woman consciously resists engaging in gender displays, she increases her ability to define herself rather than being defined by her gender.

GENDER GAP. The difference in the proportion of women and men who vote for a candidate. First noted in the United States in the early 1980s, this divergence is based in attitudinal differences between the sexes on a variety of policy issues, including international peace, civil rights, social **welfare**, and the environment. These differences in voting behavior are important because women are a larger proportion of the eligible electorate and are somewhat more likely to vote than are men in some political systems.

GENDER PARITY. A requirement, also known as *parité*, within as many as 25 parliamentary systems that a minimum percentage of elected officials or party candidates must be women. This policy is found throughout the world. For example, in both Argentina and Mexico women must receive at least 30 percent of the positions on party lists in elections. In French local elections 50 percent of the candidates must be women and in national elections public subsidies to the parties are reduced if women receive fewer than half of the nominations. In India, one-third of the seats on local governing councils are reserved for women. The immediate impact of these laws is to increase the number of women in elected office, although passage is controversial and in France the wealthier major parties accept lower public subsidies and only nominate women for about 20 percent of available national positions.

GENDER ROLE. A term that refers to stereotyped behavior prescribed on the basis of apparent or assigned male or female sex. "**Gender**" is preferred to "sex" because an individual's genetic sex is seldom determined. Instead, the individual's appearance is the basis for prescribing role. This means that infants are assigned to male or female gender on the basis of external genitalia, and children and adults are assigned on the basis of costume and mannerisms, both of which are learned social behaviors. Society demands ascription of all individuals to one or the other gender category, man/boy or woman/girl.

GENDER STRATIFICATION. A condition usually discussed in relation to issues of inequality between men and women and the (stratified) distribution of social and economic resources of society along **gender** lines. Although men have more access to these resources in most societies, there is variation historically and cross-culturally. Central determinants are the division of labor along gender lines and the degree to which women's labor is more or less socially valued. As power and status relates to the production of goods in any society, women's status is related to their contribution to the production of valued goods. It is high where women produce most of the food supply (as in **hunter/gatherer** societies) and low where production of valued goods occurs outside the household (as in industrialized societies).

GENDER STUDIES. A recent trend toward converting university and college **women's studies** programs, focused primarily on the experiences of women in societies, to broader-based programs that examine the impact of socially constructed **gender** identifications on both men and women. Opponents of gender studies programs, primarily women, have argued that the curriculum already privileges the academic study of males and their experiences as men in society. Proponents of gender studies argue that both men and women are forced into narrow, socially constructed gender categories that need to be examined and eliminated before both sexes can achieve equality and understanding of each other.

GENDERED CITY. A feminist critique of an urban environment that privileges men's needs and creates a gendered division of public and private space. Housing, transit, and other public services are designed from a male perspective. Women who are both workers and caregivers do not benefit from traditional zoning for separate commercial, residential, and workplace land use. Other scholars note that women have made a contribution to the built environment in the construction of boarding houses, playgrounds, public baths, and **settlement houses**.

GENDER-NEUTRAL LAW. A law that does not use masculine or feminine references and does not have a differential effect on men and women. Although feminists support the removal of clearly discriminatory statutes based on **sex role stereotypes** and **domestic sphere** ideology, many also question the wisdom of uniform gender neutrality in areas where men and women are biologically and socially different. Here equality may result in greater burdens on women who experience a **work-family conflict**.

GENERAL ASSEMBLY BINDING WOMEN FOR REFORMS, INTEGRITY, EQUALITY, LEADERSHIP, AND ACTION (GABRIELA). A Filipina feminist political party and broad coalition, formed in 1984 and honoring resistance leader Gabriela Silang. Priority issues include **traffic in women**, women's human rights, **prostitution**, and **media images of women**. GABRIELA has linkages with over 200 women's organizations, making it the largest feminist group in the Philippines.

GENERAL FEDERATION OF WOMEN'S CLUBS (GFWC). An international organization linking women's clubs in over 20 countries, 6,500 clubs in the United States, and over one million members worldwide. Founded in 1890 in the United States to encourage literary and social activities, the GFWC quickly became active in Progressive reforms such as **protective labor laws** and abolition of child labor and in 1914 endorsed **woman suffrage**. Although in the 1920s it again became more social and apolitical, the GFWC did endorse the **Equal**

Rights Amendment in 1944 and was active in the campaign for ratification. State federations have also been supportive of contemporary feminist issues such as **rape** and **domestic violence**.

GENERIC PRONOUNS. *See* NONSEXIST LANGUAGE.

GERMAN WOMEN'S COUNCIL/DEUTSCHER FRAUENRAT (DF). A coalition of organizations founded in 1952. It encompasses 57 women's groups and 11 million members, including women trade unionists, women in the political parties, and members of women's occupational groups and sports federations. The DF is a member of the **European Women's Lobby** and **United Nations Development Fund for Women (UNIFEM)**. In pursuit of its goal of women's equality, it has called for a ban on all low-paying ("580-mark") jobs, which are primarily held by women.

GHEZALI, SALIMA (1958-). An Algerian journalist and feminist activist. In 1989 she founded the Association for Women's Emancipation to counter the adoption of an oppressive Family Code, and in 1991 she began the feminist journal *Nyssa*, which ceased publication after 18 issues because of lack of funds. Since 1994 when Ghezali became the editor of *La Nation*, Algeria's most widely read French language weekly, the government has regularly closed it down. She currently serves as vice-president of the group Women of Europe and of the Maghreb, which she co-founded, and writes for the Algerian newspaper *Libre Algérie*.

GILBERT, SANDRA (1936-) AND SUSAN GUBAR (1944-). The co-authors of *Madwoman in the Attic* (1979) and *No Man's Land*, 2 vols. (1988 and 1989), co-editors of *The Norton Anthology of Literature by Women: The Tradition in English* (1985) and prominent American literary historians and critics. As co-authors and co-editors, they have produced some of the most important texts in the American feminist literary revival. They are credited with exploring the psychodynamics of Anglo-American women in the 19th and 20th centuries, specifically that the "anxiety of authorship" that plagues women authors resulted from the stereotyped notion that literary creativity is exclusively male. This anxiety produced in women writers a tendency to create female characters who are monstrous or dangerous, "usually in some sense the author's double, an image of her own anxiety and rage."

GILLIGAN, CAROL (1936-). A professor of law and education at New York University and the founder of **difference feminism**. Her research centers on adolescence, moral reasoning and conflict resolution, identity development, and the contribution of women's thinking to psychological theory. Her best-known work, *In a Different Voice* (1982), concerns her revisions of Lawrence Kohlberg's theories of moral development in males. Her other books include *Making Connections: The Relational Worlds of Adolescent Girls at Emma Willard School* (co-edited with Nona P. Lyons and Trudy J. Hanmer, 1989) and *Meeting at the Crossroads: Women's Psychology and Girls' Development* (with Lyn M. Brown [1992]). Her *Birth of Pleasure* (2002) explores the psychology and possibility of love in **patriarchy**. In 2001 actress Jane Fonda gave Harvard University a major donation for a Center on Gender and Education and an endowed professorship named for Gilligan, on the eve of her departure from Harvard.

GILMAN, CHARLOTTE PERKINS (1860-1935). A prominent American feminist writer and theorist, author of one of the most famous Gothic short stories ever published, "The Yellow Wallpaper" (1892). Based on her own experience, the story depicts the disastrous consequences on a young mother of a treatment for **postpartum depression** prescribed by the well-respected nerve specialist, Dr. S. Weir Mitchell. After her own breakdown and **divorce**, Gilman remarried and gained custody of her daughter. She spent the rest of her life lecturing, writing, and editing a feminist newspaper, *The Forerunner* (1909-16). Her major feminist works include *Women and Economics* (1898) and *The Home: Its Work and Influence* (1903); both were denunciations of what she called "**androcentrism,**" and both advocated communal cooperation over masculine aggression and possessiveness. Although a supporter of **woman suffrage**, Gilman did not believe that housework made women their husband's equal. She instead argued that a woman's economic dependence ensured her subordinate role.

GINSBURG, RUTH BADER (1933-). A member of the US Supreme Court since 1993 and pioneering litigator of women's rights cases during the 1970s as a founder of the **American Civil Liberties Union's Women's Rights Project.** Most notably, she argued and won the landmark **equal protection** cases *Reed v. Reed* (1971) and *Frontiero v. Richardson* (1973). Before being appointed to the Supreme Court, she was a law professor at Rutgers University and Columbia University and a widely acclaimed legal scholar. She served on the US Court of Appeals, 1980-1993. She is a moderate voice on the Court, but one who is strongly committed to the legal doctrine of equal rights.

GIRL POWER. A term, along with "girlie culture," that celebrates the growing self-confidence of young women in managing their lives. It is associated with the movie *Buffy the Vampire Slayer*, the Spice Girls, an all-woman musical group popular with preteenage girls, and the **riot grrrls movement**. These feminist "girlies" are reclaiming those symbols of traditional femininity that were rejected by the **second wave**. Older feminists feel that linking lipstick with **empowerment** demeans unachieved equality for women. They worry that this youth culture may focus too much on the personal and cultural and neglect politics.

GLASS CEILING. The discriminatory barriers affecting women in mid-management positions that prevent their advancement to higher ranks. Although women are advancing to middle-level managerial positions, they are infrequently found in top-level positions and directorships. Among top earners in the US Fortune 500, only 5.2 percent are women. The government of Sweden has announced plans to impose gender quotas for corporate boards unless 25 percent of board members are female by 2004. The International Labour Organisation has suggested that "glass walls" keep mid-level women from being trained for these top positions. Feminists, sensitive to charges of an upper-status bias in their agenda, also note that most women workers are embedded in a "sticky floor" of low-paying jobs.

GLOBAL FEMINISM. An international women's movement that emerged in the mid-1970s as an outgrowth of the **International Women's Year** and is rooted in the commonalities of women's lives: low economic status and the burden of the **double shift**. Broadly defining all issues as women's issues, this international network has critically examined the impact of **development**, **patriarchal** religions, **international traffic in women**, and the Westernization of the Third World. Some see a Western bias toward liberal individualism and modernization in the term and use "transnational feminism" to describe this movement.

GLOBAL FUND FOR WOMEN (GFW). A US foundation that provides small grants to women's groups working on economic **development**, education, health care, and **violence against women**. Since its formation in 1987, the GFW has given $24.5 million to 2,000 groups in 159 countries. The organization grew out of a concern that governments and international development programs rarely funded women's advocacy groups, particularly in very poor countries.

GLOBAL GAG RULE. A pejorative term for a regulation that bars US aid to international **family planning** programs that use their own separate funds to perform legal **abortions** or provide information about this procedure. The policy, begun in 1984 under Ronald Reagan, rescinded by Bill Clinton, and reinstated by George W. Bush in 2001, is targeted against forced **sterilization** and abortion but opponents charge that these abuses are not substantiated and place poor women at jeopardy. The Bush version does not affect the international **pro-life movement**. A domestic gag rule on federally funded clinics was also issued in 1988, but was rarely enforced while under court challenge and was repealed by Clinton in 1993.

GLOBAL WOMEN'S STRIKE. An annual action held since 2000 on March 8 (**International Women's Day**) to protest the inequality of women workers. The idea originated with Irish women's groups and is now coordinated by the London-based International Wages for Housework Campaign. Women and girls in over 60 nations go on strike to demand more social and less defense spending, pay for caretakers, and **comparable worth**. The campaign represents women's globalization.

GODDESS (RELIGION). The recognition within most religions of one or more manifestations or embodiments of "female" qualities associated with **reproduction** and nurturance. Projection of "feminine" qualities upon a cosmic symbol is a projection and legitimation of social qualities important to the survival and well-being of a social group. Veneration of a goddess does not indicate **matriarchal** rule or even particular respect for women, as is illustrated by **Mary of Nazareth** in European societies. Contemporary belief and feminist interest in a Goddess religion are 20th century creations reflecting the increased opportunities for women to live independently and work in a variety of fields. It also indicates a dissatisfaction with religions that symbolize **deities** only as males. Goddess religion legitimates and reinforces contemporary women by projecting a cosmic dimension to their lives. Claims are made for great antiquity of this religion, to legitimate it through a myth of a primordial origin. Goddess religion in America and Europe is a real contemporary religion but not a survival of ancient religion.

GOLDMAN, EMMA (1869-1940). A Russian immigrant to the United States, **anarchist, feminist,** and pioneer advocate of **birth control.** She introduced the concept of the **"New Woman,"** a woman who attacked conventional marriage and advocated "free love." In 1916 she was arrested and jailed for 15 days for distributing birth control information. She worked as a nurse and midwife in New York City when not involved in writing or cross-country lecture tours advocating voluntary motherhood and family limitation. Despite the fact that "Red Emma" opposed **woman suffrage** as a "fetish," **radical feminists** embraced her as a **role model** for challenging convention.

GOLDSTEIN, VIDA (1869-1949). An Australian leader of the United Council for Women's Suffrage and owner and editor of the feminist paper *The Australian Woman's Sphere* beginning in 1899. In 1903 she was one of the founders of the Women's Federal Political Association. She was the first (and unsuccessful) woman candidate for the Australian Parliament after the federal vote was achieved in 1902. In 1909 she began the periodical *The Woman Voter.*

GOUGES, MARIE OLYMPE DE (1748-1793). A French playwright and pamphleteer who wrote *Les Droits de la Femme (Declaration of the Rights of Woman,* 1791) in Paris in response to the "Declaration of the Rights of Man" written for the French Revolution. An activist in the time of the revolution, she attempted to establish women's clubs for intellectual and political discussion, but they were outlawed. In her *Declaration* she argues, based on natural law assumptions, for full equal rights for women and equal opportunity of employment, education, and public office. Part of the treatise includes a social contract to serve as a replacement for marriage vows and calls for **married women** to be able to own property. In *Le Cri du Sage par une Femme (The Call of the Wise by a Woman,* 1789) she urges people not to assume that the interests of women are included in those of their male relatives. She was sentenced to death by Robespierre and guillotined.

GOURD, EMILIE (1879-1946). A Swiss feminist and journalist. She founded *Le mouvement féministe*, a paper she edited until her death and in which she campaigned for a broad range of women's rights. She served as president of the Swiss Women's Association, 1914-1928, and organized many plebiscites on **woman suffrage**.

GOURNAY, MARIE LE JARS DE (1565-1645). A French author of poetry, essays, political works, and translations of classics. Her mentor was Michel de Montaigne and she was known as his spiritual daughter. Gournay was a staunch supporter of the rights of women to be educated and, in *Grief des Dames* (*Women's Complaint*, 1641) she expresses anger that men would not converse seriously with a woman. In *Égalité des Hommes et des Femmes* (*The Equality of Men and Women*, 1641) she argues that women are equal to men and that the essence of a human being is the soul, not his or her sex.

GRASS-ROOTS FEMINISM. The branch of the movement based in local communities and focused on organizing, **consciousness-raising**, and services to women. Generally **radical** and **socialist feminists** are involved. In nations with well-developed women's movements (e.g., Canada, Europe, India, the United States), both grass-roots and **institutionalized feminists** are active.

GREEN PARTY. *See* KELLY, PETRA.

GREENHAM COMMON WOMEN'S PEACE CAMP. A British feminist **collective** of, at its height, over 30,000 women. It was established in 1981 to protest the installation of Cruise missiles at a US airbase outside Newbury, England. The encampment attracted an extensive support network in the United Kingdom and from all over the world and provided the model for the Seneca Women's Peace Encampment in Romules, New York. Both camps combined **feminist spirituality** with nonviolent direct action and civil disobedience against militarism. The Cruise was withdrawn in 1991 and the camp closed in 1994.

GREER, GERMAINE (1939-). *See* FEMALE EUNUCH, THE.

GRIMKÉ, SARAH (1792-1873) AND ANGELINA (1805-1879). The two sisters known as **abolitionists** and women's rights advocates in the United States. Born into a wealthy family in the US South, they were among the first women to lecture in public in the United States. They viewed women's rights and antislavery as related human rights issues. In 1838 Sarah wrote *Letters on the Equality of the Sexes and the Condition of Woman*, one of the first essays on women's equality by an American. It is most notable for providing a biblical justification for the equality of women. The *Letters* also offered a critical analysis of women's subjection within marriage and introduced the concept of **comparable worth** in paying a laundress and woodsman for equally long and arduous labor.

GRIPENBERG, ALEXANDRA (1859-1913). A Finnish feminist, writer, and politician. She led the moderate feminist group the Finnish Women's Association (FWA), established in 1884. The FWA supported a broad agenda, including **woman suffrage**. In 1906, when the suffrage was extended, Gripenberg left the group to join the Finnish Party's Women's Association and was elected to the Diet in 1907.

GROUP CONSCIOUSNESS. See FEMINIST CONSCIOUSNESS.

GUBAR, SUSAN. See GILBERT, SANDRA.

GUERRILLA GIRLS. A New York-based **collective** of anonymous women artists and gallery professionals who challenge white **male dominance** of the art world. The group was formed in 1985, in response to the underrepresentation of women artists (19 out of 165 artists) in an international show at New York's Museum of Modern Art. The women wear gorilla masks and fishnet stockings when staging their **zap actions** and plastering the city with witty posters. Their agenda now includes **sexism** and racism in politics and all areas of culture, which brought an action at the 1997 Academy Awards to protest the lack of female directors. They present workshops and lectures around the world and sell their posters over the Internet. In 1995 they published *Confessions of the Guerrilla Girls* to advise other women on organizing similar actions and have written other books on female stereotypes and art history. *See also* FEMINIST ART AND AESTHETIC THEORY; PERFORMANCE ART.

GYNOCRITICISM. A term coined by the literary critic Elaine Showalter in her seminal essay "Feminist Criticism in the Wilderness." Showalter defines "gynocriticism" as the study of women's writing and the processes and manifestations of female creativity. She distinguishes it from the early emphasis in **feminist literary criticism**, which examined the stereotyped images and representations of women in literature primarily written by male authors. Gynocriticism is a criticism which concerns itself with developing a specifically female framework for analyzing works written by women, from their production to their motivation and interpretation.

-H-

HAINISCH, MARIANNE (1839-1936). An Austrian writer, feminist and early supporter of women's higher education. She founded the General Austrian Women's Association in 1899. As its president, she worked for marriage reform, **woman suffrage**, and the abolition of legalized **prostitution**. Hainisch published several books on women's role in the economy and contributed to **feminist magazines**.

HAITIAN WOMEN IN SOLIDARITY/SOLÏDARITE FANM AYISYEN (SOFA). A network of urban and rural women that supports **grass-roots** projects in 19 Haitian communities. Formed in 1986, SOFA draws more than 60 percent of its members from expatriates during the Francois and Jean-Claude Duvalier regimes. The group defends women's rights and works on issues of health care, political participation, and employment.

HALE, SARAH JOSEPHA (1788-1879). A US opponent of enfranchisment for women and editor of the first major magazine for women, the *Ladies Magazine*, later the *Godey's Lady's Book*. Although she never endorsed the women's movement, Hale was an advocate of higher education for women, admission to the medical professions for women, and **dress reform**.

HALIMI, GISELE (1927-). *See* CHOISIR.

HAMILTON, CICELY (1872-1952). A British feminist writer and founder of the Women Writers' Suffrage League in 1908. Hamilton advocated women's psychological and financial independence from men in her *Marriage as a Trade* (1909), an analysis of women's economic oppression within marriage. Her pamphlet and later play *How the Vote Was Won* (1909) was one of the British **woman suffrage movement**'s greatest public relations successes. In a humorous way it presented a women's strike in which their male relatives march on Parliament, demanding female suffrage.

HANIM, FATMA ALIYE (1864-1924). A Turkish writer and the first Ottoman woman to support women's rights and to oppose polygamy on the grounds that the Koran did not require it. Hanim frequently wrote for women's magazines and published *Nisvan-i Islam* (*Muslim Women*) in 1891. Born into a wealthy family, Hanim encouraged Turkey to adopt Western traditions and freedoms and was a frequent translator of Western works into Turkish.

HARASSMENT. *See* SEXUAL HARASSMENT; STREET HARASSMENT.

HARPER, FRANCES ELLEN WATKINS (1825-1911). An African American lecturer, author, and reformer. She delivered her first antislavery speech, "Education and the Elevation of the Colored Race," in 1854 in New Bedford, Massachusetts. She traveled throughout the country for the next six years, varying her lectures with recitations from her *Poems on Miscellaneous Subjects* (1854), her volume of antislavery poetry. She stressed the need for education, **temperance**, and a higher standard of domestic morality among African Americans. She also denounced **racism** within the **woman suffrage movement**. In 1896 she helped to organize the **National Association of Colored Women** and in 1897 became its president.

HATE CRIMES. A term encompassing illegal speech or behavior directed toward others on the basis of their race, color, creed, religion, sex, or sexual orientation. In 1993 the US Supreme Court upheld in *Wisconsin v. Mitchell* a state law that assessed longer sentences for violent crimes motivated by bias. Although the United States and 49 states have some type of hate crimes law, most do not include sex. Some state and local legislatures have criminalized biased verbal or written insults, but in 1992 the Court struck down in *R.A.V. v. St. Paul* a local ordinance of this type on the grounds that constitutionally protected free speech was being prohibited. Critics charge that this legal approach requires **politically correct** speech and behavior. Supporters argue that hate speech is a violation of **equal protection** if it creates a **hostile environment** for women and minorities.

HAYS, MARY (1760-1843). An English feminist and author of the anonymously published *Appeal to the Men of Great Britain on Behalf of the Women* (1798). A close friend of **Mary Wollstonecraft**, Hays also advocated greater freedom for women in marriage and ownership of property. Also a novelist, Hays published *The Memoirs of Emma Courtney* (1796), the story of an independent and educated woman; *The Victim of Prejudice* (1799), about an illegitimate orphan girl; and the *Dictionary of Female Biography*, six volumes (1803).

HEALTH MOVEMENT. *See* WOMEN'S HEALTH MOVEMENT.

HERETICAL RELIGIOUS SECTS, WOMEN IN. The movements, such as the Gnostics and Montanists in the Patristic era, Cathars and Albigensians in the Middle Ages, and the followers of Anne Hutchinson in 17th century America, that are viewed as departing from established religious doctrines. These groups have also often allowed women to play significant roles. Although differences in doctrinal matters were decisive in assessing the orthodoxy of a given sect, feminists suggest that many of these groups were declared heretical expressly because of the high status and responsible positions of the women within them.

HERLAND. An early feminist novel written by **Charlotte Perkins Gilman** in 1915 depicting an all-woman utopia. Reprinted in 1979, it has become a standard text taught in women's literature classes. The sequel, *With Her in Ourland* (1916), continues the story and takes the protagonists back into civilization.

"HERSTORY." A term used by some feminists to distinguish **women's history** from "his story" by telling the past from a woman's perspective. Critics have noted that this term is rarely used, even by feminist historians, because the root of "history" is a Greek word meaning "inquiry." The word is meaningless in languages other than English and cannot be translated. Many of the words of women's rights and feminism do originate in English, but use of this particular term may constitute cultural imperialism.

HETERODOXY. A club consisting of about 100 self-styled "**radical**" **feminists**, including **Charlotte Perkins Gilman**, Mabel Dodge Luhan, Agnes DeMille, and **Elsie Clews Parsons** and based in New York City's Greenwich Village (137 MacDougal Street). Founded in 1912, the group was committed to radical social, political, sexual, and economic change, frequently inviting **Margaret Sanger** to lecture on **birth control** methods. Further information can be found in Judith Schwartz, *The Radical Feminists of Heterodoxy, Greenwich Village, 1912-1940* (1982).

HETEROSEXISM. A term used by feminists to describe the tendency to regard heterosexuality more positively—more "normal" than other sexual orientations—because religious, legal, medical, and scientific discourses have privileged heterosexuality as the norm. The term is sometimes used as the equivalent of "homophobia." Although the term does not imply that heterosexuality is wrong, it is linked with attempts to control all women who are perceived to be either in search of or a part of an emotional and economic relationship with men. Discussions of heterosexism within the women's movement in the 1970s led to a broad acceptance of **lesbian** rights.

HEWLETT, SYLVIA ANN (1946-). An economist and author of *A Lesser Life: The Myth of Women's Liberation in America* (1986), a revisionist view that charges that feminism is an elite-dominated movement that has ignored the needs of working mothers for **child care, maternity leave,** and **protective labor laws.** She also attacks the movement for championing **no-fault divorce** and **gender-neutral** domestic support laws. Her later books have dealt with parenting, children, and the problems women face in leading a balanced life. Feminists have sympathized with her history of being denied tenure at Columbia University after being told that she had allowed childbearing to dilute her focus on career. However, her *Creating a Life* (2002) has revived the debate concerning women's **biological clock** and has drawn criticism from feminists.

HIDDEN WORK. A term used to describe women's work. To the extent that much of women's contributions are not (have not been) in the paid labor force and because our concept of work is tied to paid employment, women's work remains "hidden." Some suggest that the development of paid labor has resulted in the devaluation of women generally. Feminist scholars have emphasized women's essential and distinctive contributions: within the household (e.g., the provision of food, shelter, and clothing); in maintaining ties to the extended family and community (e.g., family and social networking, volunteer work, and ties to school and community activities); and in support of employers (e.g., by caring for workers in the paid labor force and providing an available pool of cheap labor). For these reasons, feminists stress that every mother is a working mother.

HILL, ANITA (1956-). An African American law professor and former government attorney who accused African American Supreme Court Justice nominee Clarence Thomas of **sexual harassment** in a case that received national publicity during televised confirmation hearings. Professor Hill's credibility was sharply questioned, but no conclusion was reached about whether her charges were true. The Senate voted, 52-48, to confirm Thomas. In the aftermath, Hill became a powerful symbol for the feminist movement of the treatment of women who speak out against harassment. She told her story in *Speaking Truth to Power* (1997) and is a professor of social policy, law, and **women's studies** at Brandeis University.

HO HSIANG-NING (1879-1972). A Chinese revolutionary and feminist. In 1923 she became a member of the Kuomintang Congress and head of the Women's Department. She was also one of the first women to bob her hair as an expression of independence in the 1920s. She went into exile in Hong Kong after the assassination of her husband in 1925, but returned to Beijing in 1949 and assumed a government post. In 1960, she was named the honorary chair of the **All-China Women's Federation**.

HOLISTIC FEMINISM. A conservative version of **Catholic feminism** that uses traditional church theology to honor women as primarily wife and mother. This tradition is associated with Harvard law professor Mary Ann Glendon, who has served as a Vatican delegate to United Nations women's conferences and believes that feminism is an inclusive movement permitting many viewpoints. Holistic feminism rejects a feminism that is critical of family life and supports gay rights and **abortion**. It supports feminist concern with violence, poverty, oppression, exploitation, and objectification. Women should be free to exercise their abilities free of discrimination, but without undermining their role within the family. Critics suggest that holistic feminists are redefining feminism in order to include traditional Catholic women within a powerful and influencial movement.

HOLYOAKE, GEORGE JACOB (1817-1906). An English male feminist who is known as the "father" of feminism. He published his own newspaper, *The Oracle of Reason*, where he advocated his secularist, liberal, and feminist beliefs. He recorded his support of women's equality in *The Workman and the Suffrage* (1858) and *Sixty Years of an Agitator's Life* (1893). A vigorous supporter of socialist society, education for women, and atheism, he called for a women's movement in the United States as well as in England.

HOME BIRTH. The delivery of an infant within the home. The birth may be attended by a physician, certified nurse **midwife**, lay midwife, or no one except family or friends. In reaction against the **medicalization of childbirth**, US feminists have expressed interest in and support for the home birth movement even though about 99 percent of births there occur in hospitals. A majority of the world's women continue to give birth in nonhospital settings, but the Netherlands, where 30 percent of births take place in the home, is an exception among advanced industrial nations. *See also* ALTERNATIVE BIRTH MOVEMENT.

HOMOSEXUALITY. *See* LESBIANISM.

HONOR KILLINGS. The practice of male relatives killing a female member accused of bringing shame upon the family, often because of adultery, **divorce**, or **rape**. Although most common in the Middle East and parts of South Asia, the murders also occur in any culture that believes a woman is the property of her family. The UN Population Fund estimates that 5,000 killings occur annually, including in Western Europe, the United States, and Latin America. Islam does not sanction the practice, but some clerics support it on the grounds of protecting national traditions from Western values, a position also reflected in the laws of Syria, Jordan, and Morocco that provide lenient sentences for male relatives.

HOOKS, BELL [PSEUDONYM OF GLORIA WATKINS] (1952-). An **African American feminist** writer and cultural critic. hooks uses only lowercase letters in a pseudonym in order to have her own voice and to focus attention away from herself and on her work and its contents. hooks is a prolific writer and has produced, 1981-2002, 20 books of **feminist political theory**, autobiography, and poetry. Her books include *Feminist Theory: From Margin to Center* (1984) and *Talking Back: Thinking Feminist, Thinking Black* (1989). She is most concerned with black women and changing the interconnected "white supremist capitalist **patriarchy**." hooks teaches English and **women's studies** at the City University of New York.

HORMONE REPLACEMENT THERAPY (HRT). *See* ESTROGEN REPLACEMENT THERAPY (ERT).

HORNEY, KAREN (1885-1952). A German-American psychoanalyst trained in Freudian analysis, but who went on to question **Sigmund Freud's** assumptions about **female sexuality** and **biological determinism**. Horney believed that women's behavior is often rooted in socialization, not biology. Most notably Horney claimed that rather than women experiencing "**penis envy**," men envied women's ability to give birth. Further, Horney understood "penis envy" as women's envy for man's superior status in society. She published extensively on the reasons for the distrust between the sexes, the development pattern of young girls, and the roots of conflict with the mother. After she published *New Ways in Psychoanalysis* (1930), she was forced to resign from the New York Psychoanalytic Society because she so threatened traditional Freudian truisms. Along with Marie Bonaparte, Helene Deutsch, and Anna Freud, she is generally recognized as one of the first feminist psychoanalysts.

HOSTILE ENVIRONMENT. A working or educational environment filled with unwelcome sexual attention. It is created by communication practices which demean women through objectifying and sexualizing them. Such practices include invasion of personal space, touching, comments on appearance, sexual propositions, and sexual expletives. These practices reinforce **male dominance** through overt and covert intimidation. A hostile environment is the product of one type of illegal **sexual harassment**.

HOUSEWIFE FEMINISM. A term coined by Shiota Sakiko to describe the impact of the Japanese feminist movement on public policy. When **sex discrimination** in employment was addressed in Japan in 1986, the laws were revised to favor housewives by establishing a **mommy track**. Working women fell into two groups, career/managerial and general clerical assistants. Tax codes and welfare policies were also changed to accommodate housewives. Few women are permitted to enter the management track, and no other policies have been enacted to lessen the **work-family conflict**. Because housewife feminism accepts that role for women as a norm and does not challenge the **patriarchy**, it provides no basis for addressing issues of **traffic in women** and **domestic violence**.

HOW THE VOTE WAS WON. See HAMILTON, CICELY.

HOWE, JULIA WARD (1819-1910). An American author and lecturer best known for the "Battle Hymn of the Republic," first published in the *Atlantic Monthly* in February 1862. Howe was also a **woman suffrage** leader who helped found the New England Woman Suffrage Association and was active in the **American Woman Suffrage Association**. A frequent speaker at conventions and legislative hearings, she was a founder of the *Women's Journal* (1870) and edited *Sex and Education* (1874). In 1873 she joined in founding the Association for the Advancement of Women, an organization that tried to advance the cause of equal education and professional and business opportunities for women. Howe was one of the founders of the **General Federation of Women's Clubs** as well as the first president of the Massachusetts Federation.

HUERTA, DOLORES (1930-). **Chicana** co-founder and first vice-president of the United Farm Workers' Union (UFW) in 1962. Huerta has become more active in the feminist movement, particularly on **sexual harassment** as a workers' rights issue and the role of **Latinas** in public life and in the UFW. She was a co-founder and vice-president of the **Feminist Majority Foundation**. In 1992 she was chosen as the first head of the 21st Century Party, the Nation's Equality Party, an abortive attempt by the **National Organization for Women** to form a new US political party.

HUMAN LIFE AMENDMENT. See PRO-LIFE MOVEMENT.

HUNGER STRIKES. A tactic used in the **woman suffrage movement** in several countries. It originated in 1909 with Scotswoman Marion

Wallace Dunlop of the **Women's Social and Political Union**. Imprisoned for stenciling a slogan on a wall in Parliament, she refused food for 91 hours. Initially hunger strikers were released; later use of forcible feeding led to injury, at least one death, and increased sympathy and media coverage for these **suffragettes**. *See also* CAT AND MOUSE ACT.

HUNT, HARRIOT KEZIA (1805-1875). An American physician, feminist reformer, and the first woman to practice medicine in the United States. She set up a medical clinic for women and children in Boston after studying privately with a physician. Harvard Medical School accepted her in 1850, the same year black men were admitted, but men students protested and she was forced to withdraw. The Female Medical College of Philadelphia awarded her an honorary degree of Doctor of Medicine in 1853. Hunt's medical theories were based on physiology, natural laws, and the science of disease prevention. She advocated attention to diet, bathing, rest, exercise, and sanitation, and in 1843 founded the Ladies Physiological Society in Charlestown, Massachusetts, a center for medical reform for working-class women and children.

HUNTER/GATHERER DEBATE. A challenge to the view of women's role in early cultures as restricted to the home, raising children, and tending crops while men went into the wilderness to hunt and fight. Feminist scholars suggest that because women brought in over 70 percent of the food the term should be "gatherer-hunter." Mary Zeiss Stange in *Woman the Hunter* (1997) argues that Paleolithic women hunted with hard-edged weapons of their own making and women continue to do so in surviving hunter-gatherer cultures. It should be noted, however, that a break with man-the-hunter/killer would rob some feminists of their explanation of male **violence against women**.

HYDE AMENDMENT. A provision, named for its sponsor US Representative Henry Hyde of Illinois, passed in several sessions of Congress since 1976 to restrict the use of federal funding for **abortions**. These bans affect Medicaid and disabled Medicare recipients, military personnel, Peace Corps volunteers, federal workers, federal prison inmates, American Indians, and residents of the District of Columbia. Although the exceptions have varied, federal money usually can be used when pregnancies are life-threatening or result from **rape** or incest that is promptly reported to the police. The US Supreme Court in *Harris v. McRae* (1980) upheld the amendment as reflecting a "legitimate congressional interest in protecting potential life." The renewal of the provision is highly contested by **pro-life** and **pro-choice** forces. It is an important symbol for both movements, even though its impact on reducing abortion has proven negligible.

HYPATIA (ca. 370-415 A.D.). Born and died in Alexandria, Egypt, and the first woman to make a substantial contribution to the study of mathematics. Daughter of the philosopher and mathematician Theon, Hypatia studied mathematics under the tutelage of her father. She was so highly regarded that she became the head of the Alexandria Platonist School in 400 A.D., where she lectured on mathematics and the Neoplatonism of Plotinus and Iamblichus. Hypatia's success as a teacher, along with her mastery of science, came to represent the threatening power that early Christianity associated with paganism. She was murdered in 415, although it is uncertain whether she was murdered by a fanatical Christian sect, the Nitrian monks, or by an Alexandrian mob. Her death began the decline of Alexandria as a major center of ancient learning. There is considerable controversy over her writings, with some arguing that she did original research and writing while others argue that she only assisted her father in his researches and publications. The Victorian novelist Charles Kingsley made her the heroine of his novel *Hypatia, or New Foes with an Old Face* (1852), thereby perpetuating the legend that she was beautiful as well as brilliant. In 1983 members of the Society for Women in Philosophy founded a journal named for Hypatia to provide a forum for the discussion of philosophical issues raised by the **new feminist movement**.

HYPHENATED NAMES. *See* NAMING CONVENTIONS.

-I-

"I AM WOMAN." A popular song of 1972, co-written and performed by Australian Helen Reddy, that became the unofficial anthem of the **new feminist movement**. The lyrics state: "I am woman, hear me roar in numbers too big to ignore, and I know too much to go back to pretend." The song appeared on the soundtrack of a movie about the **women's**

liberation movement, *Stand Up and Be Counted*, and won a 1973 Grammy Award for Reddy as the best female pop vocal.

ICHIKAWA, FUSAE (1893-1981). The organizer, with Hiratsuka Raicho and others, of the feminist Association of New Women (1919) and the League for Women's Suffrage (1924) in Japan. In 1945 she was instrumental in gaining General Douglas MacArthur's support for the women's vote; that same year, she founded the Women's Suffrage Center. After being purged in 1947 for her wartime activities, Ichikawa returned to politics and served almost continuously in the Diet's House of Councillors, 1953-1974. During the **United Nations's Decade for Women**, Ichikawa formed a coalition of 48 women's groups that gained parliamentary approval of the UN **Convention on the Elimination of All Forms of Discrimination Against Women.** *See also* WOMAN SUFFRAGE MOVEMENT.

IDENTITY POLITICS. An attempt to make **feminist political theory** and action coherent with one's personal life and to develop a group culture. This may involve forming separate organizations, such as caucuses, in order to assert culture and identity. This presents a dilemma for the feminist movement because differences between women are emphasized rather than commonalities. This may involve viewing **lesbianism** as a political definition, not a clinical sexual identity, and addressing questions of class, race, and sexual practices such as sadomasochism and their legitimacy within the feminist community. These disputes contributed to the decline of the **radical feminist** branch of the movement in the 1960s and 1970s. But specialized organizations may also make it easier to develop shared feminist agendas across diverse groups that often have conflicting interests.

"I'M NOT A FEMINIST BUT" SYNDROME. A set of beliefs that includes support for an equal role in society for women but rejects the efforts of the feminist movement. Even among many who support **gender** equality, the term "feminist" evokes negative connotations from which they seek to disassociate themselves. *See also* BATTERED WORD SYNDROME.

IN A DIFFERENT VOICE. A book, published by **Carol Gilligan** in 1982, that suggests that women's moral development and moral reasoning are distinctively different from those of men and introduces the notion that women's moral experience gives rise to an "ethic of care" and value on community that men do not possess. She presents a new conception of women's moral development as consisting of three stages: self-oriented, other-oriented, and, at the highest stage, an appropriate balance between the concerns for self and others. Gilligan argues that care is the distinguishing hallmark of women's moral experiences. The ethic of care provides an alternative to traditional Western conceptions of ethics that are based on such notions as virtue, rights, duty, justice, and respect. Gilligan has been criticized for using anecdotal evidence, small samples, and not sharing her data with other scholars who have not been able to duplicate her findings. Even so, the book established her as a pioneer in **gender studies**.

IN RE BABY M, 537 A. 2D 1227 N.J., 1988. A New Jersey Supreme Court case that ruled that **surrogacy** is illegal in that it constitutes baby selling. The parties to the suit were William and Elizabeth Stern, a married couple, and Mary Beth Whitehead, who for a fee of $10,000 agreed to be inseminated with Stern's sperm and to turn over that child to the Sterns for adoption. Whitehead refused to surrender Baby M after birth. The court upheld a lower court's custody award to William Stern but restored Whitehead's parental rights, including visitation privileges. Feminists were deeply divided on the case. **Equality feminists** believed that women are competent to enter into contracts involving their bodies; **difference feminists** viewed surrogacy as victimization of both infertile women and those who, in reality, signed over control of their bodies in entering these contracts. The issue of class exploitation was also an underlying concern in a case involving two affluent well-educated scientists and a high school dropout with a history of **domestic violence** and **welfare** dependency. Outside New Jersey surrogacy contracts have been upheld as legal.

IN VITRO FERTILIZATION (IVF). See REPRODUCTIVE TECHNOLOGIES.

INCLUSIVE LANGUAGE. See NONSEXIST LANGUAGE.

INDEPENDENT WOMEN'S ASSOCIATION/UNABHÄNGIGER FRAUENVERBAND (UFV). A group formed in 1989 by women from the German Democratic Republic (East Germany) as a feminist group committed to the emancipation of women in the new Germany.

In adopting the title "Independent," the founders differentiated themselves from the Communist Party's official women's group, the Democratic League of Germany. The UFV established **women's centers** and services for women in the larger cities. In 1991 membership was opened to all German women, and the UFV coordinated the women's strike action in 1994 and worked against further restrictions in **paragraph 218**. Its origins in the East, however, was a barrier to growth, and it disbanded in 1998.

INDEPENDENT WOMEN'S FORUM (IWF). A US **antifeminist** group formed in 1992 by successful, politically prominent women angered by **Anita Hill's** testimony and the role of feminist organizations. The group has around 1,600 members, publishes *The Women's Quarterly*, and its leaders regularly appear before Congress and in the media to oppose the goals of the feminist movement. The IWF presents itself as an alternative to the **National Organization for Women** and has become the primary spokesperson for the antifeminist movement since the defeat of the **Equal Rights Amendment**. Many of its past and present board members received appointments in the administration of George W. Bush.

INDEPENDENT WOMEN'S FORUMS (IWF). The two meetings held in Dubna, Russia, in 1991 and 1992 to discuss women's issues and women's participation in elections for the federal Duma following the breakup of the Soviet Union. These forums mark the birth of an independent women's movement in post-Soviet Russia. The development of a communications network between various nongovernmental women's groups was one accomplishment of these conferences.

INDIGO GIRLS. An Atlanta-based feminist rock group composed of Amy Ray and Emily Saliers, along with a three-woman touring band (Carol Isaacs, Clare Kenny, and Brady Blade). Founded in 1987, the group has performed in Cuba and is committed to social justice and peace issues. Recent titles include "Nuevas Señoritas," written in honor of the women who have fought for change in the Chiapas region of Mexico. Other songs, like "Become You," concern Ray's struggle to reconcile her Southern identity with the historical heritage of racism in the South. The Indigo Girls maintain an "Activism" link on their website, documenting their recent feminist activities.

INDIVIDUALIST FEMINISM. See LIBERAL FEMINISM.

INDONESIAN INDEPENDENT WOMAN ORGANIZATION. The first modern women's organization in that country, formed in Jakarta in 1912. The members were elite women who were primarily concerned with social issues such as modern education for girls and ending forced marriage and polygamy. The women also published articles on the **international women's movement** and the role of Indonesian women in it.

INFIBULATION. See FEMALE GENITAL MUTILATION.

INSANITY PLEAS (DEFENSE). A successful criminal defense that results in the commitment of the defendant to a mental institution until sanity has been restored. Acceptance of such a defense in a jury trial is usually noted by a jury finding of "not guilty by reason of insanity." In recent years, a substantial minority of US states has adopted the Model Penal Code approach, which allows that a defendant is not responsible for the crime if, at the time, because of mental disease or defect, that person lacked substantial capacity either to appreciate the criminality (wrongfulness) of that conduct or to conform to the requirements of the law. Victims of **domestic violence** who have killed or mutilated their batterers in self-defense have been acquitted on the grounds of temporary insanity, a defense strategy that feminists usually support. Another successful defense argument is that of "necessity," that the victim's crime prevented a greater crime by the batterer. ("Necessity" has also been unsuccessfully used to defend **pro-life** activists accused of murder and arson in **abortion clinic violence**.) The United States, unlike Western Europe, has only rarely extended the insanity defense to women committing infanticide while suffering a severe form of **postpartum depression** termed postpartum psychosis (PPP), possibly because the American Psychiatric Association has not yet termed PPP a mental disorder. Use of this defense in cases of **premenstrual syndrome (PMS)** is more controversial in that there is an implication that all menstruating women are irrational and victims of biology.

INSTITUTIONALIZED FEMINISM. The branch of the movement based within traditional political institutions such as legislatures, political parties, and public bureaucracies and focused on the legal rights of women. Generally **liberal feminism** is of this type. In nations with well-developed women's movements (e.g., Canada, Europe, India, the United States), both **institutionalized** and **grass-roots feminism** are active.

INSURANCE, SEX DISCRIMINATION IN. *See* PENSION AND INSURANCE EQUITY.

INTERMEDIATE STANDARD OF CONSTITUTION SCRUTINY. *See* CRAIG V. BOREN.

INTERNATIONAL ALLIANCE OF WOMEN (IAW). A group founded in 1904 as the International Woman Suffrage Alliance, under the leadership of **Carrie Chapman Catt**, to press for the female vote in all countries with representative forms of government. By 1929 around 51 national **woman suffrage** societies had become members. The group had a more radical and activist perspective than the **International Council of Women**. In 1946, with suffrage won in many nations, it adopted its present name and a broader agenda of women's rights, peace, and support for the United Nations. It currently has 60 group affiliates and meets triennially in conference.

INTERNATIONAL CENTER FOR RESEARCH ON WOMEN (ICRW). An organization founded in 1976 to promote the full participation of **women in development** and to advocate for women's issues. Based in Washington, D.C., with an office in India, the ICRW has a fellowship program to bring development researchers and women activists from developing nations to Washington to learn more about sustainable development.

INTERNATIONAL COUNCIL OF WOMEN (ICW). An organization founded by the **Elizabeth Cady Stanton** and **Susan B. Anthony** branch of the American **woman suffrage movement** in 1888, at a conference to celebrate the 40th anniversary of the **Seneca Falls Convention**. Only national women's councils can be affiliates, and by 1914 more than 20 nations, including Australia, South Africa, and Argentina, had established these councils. The ICW is moderately feminist and its congresses, now held at three-year intervals, provide for the exchange of ideas across national boundaries. Its agenda includes most women's rights issues of the time, except, for a long period, suffrage on which unanimity did not exist. In many European countries, these national councils of women remain as important lobbying groups and the ICW now has 70 council members.

INTERNATIONAL CRIMINAL COURT (ICC). A permanent institution to prosecute acts of genocide, crimes against humanity, and war crimes. The ICC was created under the auspices of the United Nations in The Hague through a treaty that became effective in 2002. It was approved by 89 nations, but not the United States. More than 300 women's groups worldwide formed the Women's Caucus for Gender Justice to successfully lobby the UN to include gender-based crimes such as **rape**, involuntary pregnancy and **sterilization**, and **sexual slavery** as crimes against humanity.

INTERNATIONAL DAY AGAINST VIOLENCE TOWARD WOMEN. A day (November 25) established by a resolution of the UN General Assembly in 1999. The day was declared at the first Latin American and Caribbean Feminist Meeting in Bogota in 1981 to coincide with the murder of the three Mirabel sisters by the Trujillo dictatorship in the Dominican Republic in 1960. A **white ribbon** has been adopted as the global symbol of opposition to **violence against women**.

INTERNATIONAL FEMINIST NETWORK AGAINST FEMALE SEXUAL SLAVERY. *See* INTERNATIONAL TRAFFIC IN WOMEN.

INTERNATIONAL TRAFFIC IN WOMEN. The sexual exploitation of women through **sex tours** and **prostitution** on a global scale. Women from poorer countries in Eastern Europe, Asia, and Latin America are promised service jobs in richer nations like Canada, the United States, and Japan and in the Middle East and Western Europe but are instead forced into prostitution. Other women are sold by their own poor families. Sexual trafficking ranks only below arms smuggling and narcotics as the most lucrative criminal activity in the world. Annual victimization estimates range between 700,000 and three million women and children, the largest slave trade in history. In 1983 Kathleen Barry formed the International Feminist Network Against Female Sexual Slavery to combat these practices. Currently the Coalition Against Trafficking Women, with affiliates in 24 countries, is working for an inclusive definition of trafficking for a UN Convention Against Transnational Organized Crime and for a UN Convention Against Sexual Exploitation.

INTERNATIONAL WOMAN SUFFRAGE ALLIANCE. *See* INTERNATIONAL ALLIANCE OF WOMEN.

INTERNATIONAL WOMEN'S DAY. An event celebrated annually on March 8, particularly in countries with a strong socialist movement. In 1910 **Clara Zetkin** and Luise Zietz of the **Socialist Women's International** led the drive to designate a day for a celebration of women as a recruitment device for the socialist movement and as a way to support **woman suffrage**. The first event was held on March 18, 1911, and continued on that date until 1922 when Lenin adopted March 8 to coincide with the anniversary of the 1917 Russian Revolution. With the rise of the **new feminist movement** in the late 1960s, nonsocialist nations have joined this feminist celebration.

INTERNATIONAL WOMEN'S MOVEMENT. *See* GLOBAL FEMINISM.

INTERNATIONAL WOMEN'S RIGHTS ACTION WATCH (IWRAW). A global network of several thousand individuals and organizations, begun in 1985 to monitor implementation of the **Convention on the Elimination of All Forms of Discrimination Against Women** and other United Nations treaties and conventions on women. The program, based at the Humphrey Institute of Public Affairs, University of Minnesota, serves as an international resource and communications center for women's human rights. The IWRAW publishes a quarterly newsletter, *Women's Watch*.

INTERNATIONAL WOMEN'S YEAR (IWY) (1975). An event proclaimed in 1970 by the United Nations, which sponsored a world conference that year in Mexico City. Conferees adopted a World Plan of Action for the improvement of the status of women within the legal, economic, political, social, and cultural system of each country. The International Women's Year was extended to a Decade for Women (1976-85) by the United Nations and three more world conferences were held in Copenhagen (1980), Nairobi (1985), and Beijing (1995). Although delegations to all conferences were selected on the basis of official position or personal connections, rather than feminist ideology or policy expertise, these events helped to establish an international feminist network. Moreover, they were also attended by numerous women's nongovernmental organizations and received extensive coverage in the media. *See also* PLATFORM FOR ACTION.

INTERSECTIONALITY. The legal requirements noted by law professor Kimberle Crenshaw that **minority women** base their discrimination claims on either evidence of **sex discrimination** or race discrimination, but not both. These requirements permit employers to invidiously discriminate against minority women as long as they do not discriminate against minority men or white women.

INTRAUTERINE DEVICE (IUD). *See* DALKON SHIELD.

INVOLUNTARY STERILIZATION. *See* STERILIZATION ABUSE.

IRIGARAY, LUCE (1930-). A contemporary French feminist and theorist, best known as the author of *The Sex Which Is Not One* and *The Speculum of the Other Woman* (both 1985). The latter is a study of the **phallocentric** bias in **Sigmund Freud** and cost Irigaray her teaching position at the University of Paris (Vincennes). Irigaray argues that women are distinctively different from men and that this difference is biologically based. Only when women assert their *jouissance* can they subvert phallocentric oppression and speak in their own voices. Irigaray proposes a "woman's writing" which defies male monopoly and the risk of **appropriation** into the existing **patriarchal** system by establishing as its originating principle the diversity and fluidity of the female sexual organs. Irigaray argues that woman's problematic relationship to masculine language is caused by her sexuality: "Woman has sex organs just about everywhere. She is infinitely other in herself. That is undoubtedly the reason she is called temperamental, incomprehensible, perturbed, capricious—not to mention her language in which she goes off in all directions and in which he is unable to discern the coherence of any meaning. Contradictory words seem a little crazy to the logic of reason, and inaudible for him who listens with ready-made grids, a code prepared in advance. In her statements—at least when she dares to speak out—woman retouches herself constantly" (see her *Speculum of the Other Woman*). *See also* L'ÉCRITURE FÉMININE.

IRISH WOMEN'S FRANCHISE LEAGUE (IWFL). The most prominent and militant of the **woman suffrage** groups in Ireland. Founded in 1908 by **Hanna Sheehy Skeffington** and Constance Markiewicj, the IWFL presented an alternative to the more traditional Irish Women's Suffrage and Local Government Association. Composed of Irish nationalists, the group was an Irish-run movement rather than a branch of the **Women's Social and Political Union.**

IRISH WOMEN'S LIBERATION MOVEMENT (IWLM). A radical **feminist** group formed in 1970. In 1971 it published its manifesto "Chains or Change," picketed the Archbishop's Dublin residence, staged a well-attended meeting in Mansion House, organized the **contraceptive train**, and produced the entire *Late, Late Show* for Irish television. But by 1972 the IWLM had ceased to exist, torn apart by disputes over **lesbianism, elitism**, and Northern Ireland between **separatists, politicos**, and "careerists" who shunned the feminist label. Activists joined other groups and projects, but not until the emergence of **Irishwomen United** in 1975 was there a comparably visible feminist group in Ireland.

IRISHWOMEN UNITED (IWU). A feminist group, established in 1975 and lasting until 1977. During that time the IWU held the first public meeting of the **new feminist movement** in Liberty Hall, began the **Contraceptive Action Programme** in 1976, and served as the catalyst for many **grass-roots self-help** and service groups such as hotlines and **rape crisis centers**. Its protests against **male-only clubs** and for **contraception** and **equal pay** attracted media attention but little support from other feminists. Internal cleavages between **lesbian, socialist**, and **radical feminists** led to its demise.

ISIS. An ancient Egytian goddess, worshipped as a "great mother," the embodiment of fertility and the cycle of nature. Married to her brother Osiris, she had the power to restore his life after his murder, and hence was worshipped throughout the early Mediterranean world well into the Roman era. She had her own priests and many temples dedicated to her worship, with the largest temple situated on the island of Philae in the Nile delta. As Christianity spread, early believers in Jesus' divinity were particularly concerned to wipe out Isis worship, and a systematic desecration of her statues and temples began. In addition, her role and identity was collapsed with the **Virgin Mary's**, so that worship of a "great mother" would continue, but would be identified with the mother of Jesus rather than an ancient Egyptian fertility cult.

ISLAMIC FEMINISM. A contemporary movement to change and improve the status of Islamic women by reinterpreting and reforming religious teaching and scripture. Primarily elite urban women within Islamic societies lead this challenge to the male monopoly on interpreting the Koran, but do not question the **sexual division of labor**. Instead they seek to recognize women's role in the family and weaken male control over women. These changes could lead to a greater role for women in education, politics, and the economy, but within a still-segregated educational system and labor force. Control over **female sexuality** and moral standards within an Islamic republic is also compatible with this conservative feminist tradition.

ITALIAN WOMEN'S UNION/UNIONE DELLE DONNE ITALIANE (UDI). A group formed in liberated areas in 1944 to work for the political and economic rights of women. After the end of World War II, the UDI became associated with the Communist Party, which caused Catholic women to withdraw. The large (upwards of 250,000 members) organization now represents the **reform** branch of the movement and has successfully worked for **day care**, **divorce** and **abortion** law reform, **equal pay**, **maternity leave**, and spousal benefits. In 1982 the UDI ended its formal links with the Communist Party.

-J-

JACOBS, ALETTA (1854-1929). The first female doctor in the Netherlands, credited with opening the world's first **birth control** clinic in 1882 in Amsterdam. She advocated shorter working hours, **protective labor laws**, venereal disease education, the abolition of regulated **prostitution**, and reform of the marriage laws. She was a prominent **suffragist** as well. In 1883 her attempts to register to vote led the government to formally restrict the voting rolls to men. She was a founder and president of the Dutch Suffrage Association and active in the **International Alliance of Women**. In 1911 she toured the world for suffrage with **Carrie Chapman Catt**. During World War I she led the peace movement with **Jane Addams**.

JAMESON, ANNA (1794-1860). An Irish feminist and writer whose travel books, art books, and literary criticism included protests against women's position in society. Among her most successful works are *Characteristics of Shakespeare's Women* (1832), essays on the women characters in **Shakespeare's** dramas as if they were actual historical women, and *Sacred and Legendary Art* (1848-1860).

JANE COLLECTIVE. A **Chicago Women's Liberation Union** project that performed around 11,000 illegal **abortions**, 1969-1973. After 1970 the women of the collective began to perform abortions themselves and had a safety record for first-trimester procedures comparable to clinics in states with legalized abortions. Counseling, **birth control** information, and a Pap smear were part of the abortion services provided for an average cost of $45.

JAPANESE FEMINISM. *See* HOUSEWIFE FEMINISM.

JEWISH FEMINISM. A type of feminism in which ethnicity and religion intersect with **gender**. Religious Jewish women seek greater participation for women in religious and community life and the inclusion of feminist ideals (and the exclusion of **sexist** practices) within Judaism. Since 1999 Jewish Women Watching has staged guerrilla actions in New York that take on Jewish institutions with humor. The survival of Jews and Israel is a major goal but a feminist commitment to peace and democracy is also reflected in concern for the rights and humanity of the Palestinians and Middle East peace.

JINNAH, FATIMA (1893-1967). A Pakistani advocate for women's emancipation in Islamic society. An active member of the Muslim League, Jinnah led the All-India Muslim Women's Committee after its foundation in 1938. She was the sister of the Quaid-e-Azam Mohammad Al Jinnah, the founder of Pakistan and its first governor general. Fatima was his companion during the struggle for Pakistan's independence and is known as "Madar-e-Millat" (mother of country). She ran for president in the 1965 election as the candidate of the opposition to the totalitarian military regime. The government declared 2003 the "year of Fatima Jinnah," and her residence after her brother's death was turned into a museum, the Fatima Jinnah House. She established many institutions for women's education and training, including the

Fatima Jinnah Women's Medical College. The Fatima Jinnah Women University was founded in 1998 to honor her contributions to the cause of women's emancipation.

JIU JIN (QUIU JIN) (1875-1907). A nationalist and feminist who revolted against the Manchu dynasty and supported the emancipation of Chinese women. Born into the gentry and classically educated, Jiu Jin left her husband and children to study in Japan for two years. She challenged the traditional Confucian role for women by riding horseback, fencing, drinking wine, and adopting Western male dress. In 1906 she published the *Chinese Women's Journal* and formed a women's army. She was executed in 1907 for her role in a plot to overthrow the government.

JOAN OF ARC, SAINT (1412-1431). A French national heroine and Catholic saint who led the French army to several victories against the English. She was tried as a witch and **cross-dressing** heretic by the English and burned at the stake. Some feminist scholars have viewed her as admirably **androgynous**, but also regretably militaristic and "mad." Others suggest that her life is a cautionary tale that women should ignore their inner voices and submit to male authority.

JOB SHARING. The division of job responsibilities of one full-time position between two employees, typically to permit them to fulfill child-rearing responsibilities. Ideally both employees will be eligible for fringe benefits and promotions. In practice, both supervisors and colleagues may view these workers as less committed to the organization. About 1 percent of US employees participate in this program; 90 percent are women, most with children at home. Under a 2003 law in the United Kingdom, parents with young or disabled children have the right to request job sharing or telecommuting (work performed at home by computer link).

JOINT CUSTODY. A legal arrangement between a child's parents, who no longer have (or never had) a legal relationship with each other. Joint custody stipulates that both parents be involved in the physical care and/or major decisions about the child's well-being rather than granting specific legal custody to one or the other of the parents. In most of these arrangements, the child remains under the primary care of the mother. For this reason, some feminists have expressed concern that fathers may threaten to ask for joint custody as a way of receiving a more favorable division of **marital property** and lower **child support** awards.

JONES, "MOTHER" MARY HARRIS (1837-1930). A teacher and dynamic labor activist who was an official organizer for the United Mine Workers and co-founder of the Industrial Workers of the World. Jones' first association with a labor organization was with the **Knights of Labor** in 1871. Thereafter she traveled throughout the United States working on behalf of various labor groups. She was actively involved in Socialist Party politics and was arrested on numerous occasions for her support of striking miners. Jones was critical of her feminist contemporaries whom she felt were too removed from the realities of poor women. **New feminists**, however, have embraced her feisty spirit that urged women to raise more hell and fewer daisies.

JONES, PAULA CORBIN (1967-). The plaintiff in a **sexual harassment** lawsuit against US President Bill Clinton. She alleged that he had propositioned her for sex in an Arkansas hotel room at a time (1991) when she was an employee of the state where he served as governor. In 1998 *Jones v. Clinton* was dismissed for lack of evidence that she had suffered any tangible workplace damages. Feminists were criticized for not supporting Jones as they had **Anita Hill**. The movement saw the case as too politically charged and too removed from the conventional legal definition of sexual harassment to advance women. They were also concerned about the very conservative individuals and groups that were aligned with Jones, who had rebuffed offers from the **National Organization for Women** for a conference call. *See also* LEWINSKY, MONICA (1973-).

JUSTICE FOR WOMEN (JFW). *See* SOUTHALL BLACK SISTERS (SBS).

-K-

KAHLO, FRIDA (1910-1954). A Mexican-born artist who began to paint in 1925 following a near-fatal streetcar accident that caused her lifelong pain, disability, and infertility. Undergoing more than 30 operations during her lifetime, Kahlo also produced over 200 paintings, several of which dealt with her physical pain and its effects on her life. A communist and a passionate supporter of Mexican indigenous culture, Kahlo was married to the Mexican muralist Diego Rivera in 1929 and, apart from a brief divorce (1939-1940), she remained married to him until her death. Of Hungarian-Jewish descent on her father's side, she was also of Indian descent on her mother's side, and she accentuated her "Mexicanismo"—the passionate embrace of preColonial Mexican history and cultures a way to separate her art work from those of other women artists of the time. Her art works have increased tremendously in value over the past 30 years, and feminists have celebrated her as an early feminist artistic icon who had the strength and courage to embrace her own artistic individuality and idiosyncracies.

K'ANG YU-WEI (1858-1927). A prominent Chinese leader of the reformist movement of the 1890s to expand women's rights. His *Book of the Great Community* (1903) described the inferior status of women and an egalitarian society where marriage is a renewable contract and men and women wear **unisex** clothing. In 1892 he formed the first "Unbound-Feet Society" in Canton.

KARTINI, RADEN AJENG (1879-1904). A founder of the women's movement in Indonesia. Both a product of and a party to polygynous marriages, she opposed the practice and forced marriage generally. Denied the right to study beyond age 12, she supported women's education by forming a girls' school. After her death in childbirth at age 25, her letters, *Through Darkness Into Light*, were published in Holland and translated into Indonesian in 1923. Kartini later became a cult figure who is recognized as a national heroine.

KATO, SHIDZUE (1897-2001). An aristocratic Japanese women, who, at her husband's urging, became a **new woman**. She worked for **woman suffrage**, reform of feudal family law, social and political equality for women, and especially for **family planning**. She helped to establish the Women's Research Institute in 1925 to study women's problems. Beginning in 1932 she helped to form several birth control groups and in 1934 opened a small clinic in Tokyo, where she distributed **contraceptives** that she made in her kitchen. Kato was elected to the lower house of the Diet in 1946 and moved in 1950 to the upper house, where she served until 1974. She was president of the Family Planning Federation of Japan from 1974 until her death.

KAUFFMANN, CAROLINE (ca. 1840s-1924). A French **suffragette** and leader of the feminist group Women's Solidarity. She led protests at the 1904 centenary celebrations of the **Code Napoléon** and in 1906 at the National Assembly, where deputies were showered with **woman suffrage** leaflets. Her arrests and the dominant view in France that even marches were too radical diluted her influence, and she drifted into spiritualism and obscurity.

KEHAJIA, KALLIOPI (1839-1905). A Greek educator and feminist. In 1872 she founded The Society for Promoting Women's Education, which provided education and training in the crafts. In her work as headmistress in several girls' schools and in her travel abroad, Kehajia was alert to ways to improve the status of Greek women. After returning from the United States in 1888, she wrote a newspaper series on the achievements of US women in hopes of motivating Greek women to organize.

KELLY, PETRA (1947-1992). A founder of the Green Party and activist in the peace, ecology, and feminist movements in West Germany. She brought one of the first suits against a pornographer for slander, libel, and **hate crimes**. Kelly served in the German Parliament (Bundestag), 1983-90. The circumstances surrounding her gun-related death at the hands of her lover-companion, a former NATO general, continue to be controversial. She correctly predicted that the reunification of Germany would diminish the legal rights of women in both East and West Germany.

KENNEDY, FLORYNCE (FLO) (1916-2000). An African American lawyer, civil rights activist, feminist lecturer and writer, and founder of the Feminist Party and the Coalition Against Racism and Sexism. Kennedy led one of the first legal challenges (in 1971) to the use of tax-exempt funds by the US Catholic Church in its antiabortion activities. Kennedy was among the relatively few **women of color** who participated in the **women's liberation movement** and was among the founders of the **National Organization for Women**.

KESSLER-HARRIS, ALICE. See EQUAL EMPLOYMENT OPPORTUNITY COMMISSION V. SEARS, ROEBUCK AND CO.

KINDER-KÜCHE-KIRCHE (CHILDREN, KITCHEN, CHURCH). A phrase used in the same way as the English "**barefoot and pregnant.**" The National Socialist Party in Germany during the 1930s and 1940s attempted to link national economic problems and working women. The Nazis largely succeeded in reviving the traditional role of German women as the ideal. In the first volume of *EMMA*, editor **Alice Schwarzer** suggested that the materialist thinking of the postwar period had in fact replaced "church" with "consuming" (*Konsum*).

KINGSTON, MAXINE HONG (1940-). A contemporary Asian-American fiction writer who established her prominence with the publication of *The Woman Warrior: Memories of a Childhood among Ghosts* (1976), an autobiographical narrative, one of the most frequently assigned books on college campuses. Fiercely feminist, Kingston positions her writings within a **matriarchal** tradition, taking inspiration from her own mother, a physician in China who was forced to work as a maid after she emigrated to America. Her basic argument is that identity is defined in relation to one's own community and the stories that the community passes on about values and struggles.

KISHIDA, TOSHIKO (1863-1901). A Liberal Party lecturer for women's issues and **woman suffrage** and the first woman speaker to travel widely in Japan. In 1883 she was arrested and jailed after a speech ("Daughters Confined in Boxes") that attacked the Japanese family system and the isolation of upper-status women in the home. Kishida supported education and job training for women, legal equality, and identical sexual codes for men and women. She founded the Kyoto Women's Lecture Society and was a frequent contributor to women's magazines. Her 1884 editorials were the first publications on women's rights by a Japanese woman.

KNIGHT, ANNE (1786-1862). An English **abolitionist** with the Women's AntiSlavery Society in the 1830s. She is credited with publishing the first leaflet on **woman suffrage** in 1847 and with establishing a suffrage association in 1851. Knight invented brightly colored labels with feminist messages to paste on her envelopes; her demand for women's political equality based on global examples first appeared on a pink label.

KNIGHTS OF LABOR, WOMEN. A US Catholic labor organization, founded in 1869, that achieved national recognition under the leadership of Terrence V. Powderly and Leonora Barry, who was appointed to the Knights' executive board as general investigator for women's labor. In 1886 women members received approval to set up a women's association, the Lady Knights of Labor. Chartered "ladies locals" brought women together from every sphere of labor (including domestic) for cooperative organizing. Comprising up to 10 percent of the union's membership by the late 1880s, the Lady Knights worked for **equal pay, woman suffrage,** and the **temperance movement.**

KOEDT, ANNE. *See* "MYTH OF THE VAGINAL ORGASM."

KOLLONTAI, ALEXANDRA (1872-1952). The foremost feminist socialist in the Russian Social Democratic Party, with responsibility after 1905 for organizing working-class women. The only female commissar (of charities and public welfare) in Lenin's government, she subsequently headed the Women's Department, the **Zhenotdel.** Through influential essays, such as "The Social Basis of the Woman's Question" (1908), she promoted communal housework, free maternity care, the legalization of **abortion,** and egalitarian marriage easily terminated by **divorce.** Her advocacy of a woman's right to control and enjoy her own sexuality and her personal sexual behavior ultimately cost her Lenin's support. She was removed from office in 1922 and exiled to minor diplomatic posts.

KONGRES WANITA INDONESIA (KOWANI)/CONGRESS OF INDONESIAN WOMEN. A coalition of more than 70 national women's groups, formed at the first All-Indonesian Women's Congress on December 22, 1928. Beginning in 1959 that date is celebrated as Indonesia Woman's Day. KOWANI participated in the war for independence and then worked to ensure that women's equal legal rights, including **woman suffrage,** were included in the new constitution of 1945. The group has also successfully lobbied for the formation of a commission on the status of women and marriage reform.

KOREAN WOMEN'S ASSOCIATIONS UNITED (KWAU). An autonomous coalition formed in 1987 by over 30 feminist groups in the wake of the **rape** and torture of a female labor organizer and other sex torture cases. It is now composed of worker, peasant, religious, research, environmental, housewife and antiviolence groups in addition to the original **radical feminist** members.

KRAMERS, MARTINA (1863-1934). A Dutch journalist and activist in Holland's Woman Suffrage Association. In 1895 she helped form the Association to Promote Women's Interests and later began to participate in the international **woman suffrage movement** through the **International Council of Women** and the **International Woman Suffrage Alliance**, whose newspaper she edited, 1904-1913. Kramers was forced out as editor by **Carrie Chapman Catt**, who threatened to expose Kramers' life with a married man.

KRISTÉVA, JULIA (1941-). A contemporary French feminist, novelist, theorist, and essayist, best known for her semiotic and psychoanalytic writings: *Revolution in Poetic Language* (1984), *Tales of Love* (1987), *Powers of Horror* (1982), *Black Sun* (1989), and *About Chinese Women* (1977). Born in Bulgaria, Kristéva has conducted a critique of structuralism and advocated instead what she calls "semanalysis," a poststructuralist approach to literature that sees the text as a dynamic "working" of language through the desires of the speaking subject as she reacts to the social and economic forces we know as history. In literature writers take the ideologies of their culture and displace or decenter them by using linguistic signifiers in unusual or shocking ways. The result is polyvalence, or multiple meanings that undermine or suspend all oppositional meanings. Kristéva posits a "chora," or prelinguistic, preoedipal signifying process centered on the mother that she calls the "semiotic." This original voice is repressed when we gain **patriarchal** language, which she labels the "symbolic." The semiotic can always break out in revolutionary ways—particularly in avant-garde poetry—as a "heterogeneous destructive causality" that assaults the stable "subject." This assault undermines the rationality of phallic discourse and the power of the "law of the Father," the patriarchal system that keeps women in a marginal status. Kristéva sees women as "hysterics," outsiders to **male-dominated** discourse, largely because of their ability to bear children and their marginality in relation to masculine culture: "If women have a role to play it is only in assuming a negative function: reject everything finite, definite, structured, loaded with meaning, in the existing state of society. Such an attitude places women on the side of the explosion of social codes: with revolutionary movements" (see her *Polylogue* [1977]).

KROG, GINA (1847-1916). The leader of the Norwegian suffrage movement and editor of the **feminist magazine** *Nylaende* (New Frontiers), 1887-1916. Rebuffed in 1885 by the Norwegian Feminist Society when she sought to organize the group around **woman suffrage**, Krog formed the Female Suffrage Union to work for the vote in local elections. In 1895, buoyed by the Radical Liberal Party's interest in woman suffrage bills, she assumed leadership of the National Female Suffrage Union. For pragmatic reasons, she supported a property-based franchise for women and was successful in 1901, when the municipal vote was extended to propertied females.

KRUPSKAYA, NADEZHDA (1869-1939). The wife of V. I. Lenin and editor of *The Working Woman* (1913). Krupskaya's *The Woman Worker* (1900) was only a small brochure but was extremely popular and influential in the socialist women's movement. It was both an accessible Russian **Marxist** analysis on women and the first revolutionary statement to women written by a Russian since the 1870s (and the first by a Russian woman).

KVINNEUNIVERSITETET. The first feminist university, founded in 1985 in Loten, Norway. A bylaw states its goal as "building a center for education based on feminist values and feminist methods of instruction." The university is small, offers degrees recognized by the ministry of education, and emphasizes off-campus and adult education.

-L-

LABARCA HUBERTSON, AMANDA (1886-1975). A feminist leader in Chile and founder in 1915 of the Círculo de Lectura (Women's Reading Circle) that in 1919 helped to form a National Council of Women to work for **woman suffrage**. In 1944 Amanda Labarca was chosen to lead the newly formed Federation of Women's Organizations and in 1949 Chilean women received the vote.

LABOR FORCE PARTICIPATION. A reference to paid employment in the labor force. Women's labor force participation in the United States has been steadily increasing. In 1949 less than 25 percent of married women held jobs; by 2000 it was 62 percent. More significantly, 59 percent of married women with children under the age of six were in the labor force in 1997. This trend is also reflected internationally where women's employment increased from 33 percent in 1960 to 54 percent in 1995. The growth in labor force participation among women, particularly in developed nations, has led to an increase in **dual-career couples** and the need for more **day care** and family-friendly organizational policies and practices such as **flexitime** and **job sharing**. *See also* FAMILY LEAVE; WORK-FAMILY CONFLICT.

LACAN, JACQUES (1901-1981). A French psychoanalyst whose writings have been collected in the large volume *Ecrits* (1977), best known among feminists for his revision of traditional Freudian theory. According to Lacan, the true subject of psychoanalysis and language was the unconscious mind, rather than the ego. Lacan claimed that the unconscious was structured like a language and could only reveal its meanings through the connection of its signifiers. Lacan reformulated **Sigmund Freud's** theories about psychosexual development by seeing them as stages in the use of language. The prelinguistic stage he called the "imaginary" and the stage after the acquisition of language he called the "symbolic." In the first stage he claimed that there was no clear distinction between the subject and the object, or between self and others. But in the second stage the child assimilates the inherited system of linguistic differences, and then learns to accept its predetermined "position" in such linguistic oppositions as male/female, father/son, mother/daughter. Lacan saw the symbolic realm of language as the realm of the law of the father, in which the "phallus" (the symbol of the father's power) was the "privileged signifier" for all discourse. Lacan further claimed that all discourse was driven by a "desire" for a lost and unachievable object, as if moving incessantly along a chain of unstable signifiers without any possibility of coming to any final point of meaning of fixed significance.

LADUKE, WINONA (1959-). An Ojibwe activist, writer, and vice-presidential candidate of the US Green Party in 1996 and 2000. The Greens endorsed the platform of the **National Organization for**

Women, but LaDuke is primarily known for her **ecofeminism** and her leadership of the Indigenous Women's Network. Many noted that LaDuke was almost invisible in the 2000 campaign during which she had a baby, worked full-time, and honored her earlier commitments to the indigenous movement. Both feminists and American Indian activists urged her to withdraw lest she attract votes from Democratic candidate Al Gore and help to elect the less supportive George W. Bush.

LADY KNIGHTS OF LABOR. *See* KNIGHTS OF LABOR, WOMEN.

LADYFESTS. A group of locally run events celebrating women in the arts, modeled on **Lilith Fair**. The festivals feature live music, films, readings, art exhibits, and workshops and classes on issues relevant to young feminists. Beginning with the first Ladyfest in Olympia, Washington, in 2000, more then 20 have been held in North American and Western European cities. The Ladyfests share a name but are otherwise unrelated; each gives its proceeds to a local women's group.

LA FEMME. The first automobile designed exclusively for the female driver by Dodge, 1955-1956. It was available in pink or lavender, had floral upholstery with a matching raincoat, umbrella, boots, and handbag, and came with a pink comb, compact, and lipstick as standard equipment. Only 300-1,100 of these models were made. Although US women make 80 percent of all car-buying decisions, only certain models like minivans for transporting children are marketed to women today. *See also* ADVERTISING, IMAGE OF FEMINISM.

LAHAYE, BEVERLY (1930?-). A US **antifeminist** spokesperson, author, founder, and chairwoman of **Concerned Women for America** (CWA). LaHaye is the wife of Baptist minister Tim LaHaye, a cofounder of the **Moral Majority**. LaHaye is well-known in religious circles for her book *The Spirit-Controlled Woman* (1976) and a sex manual for evangelicals, *The Act of Marriage* (1976), co-written with her husband. She hosts a daily radio program *"Beverly LaHaye Today"* and has lent her name to the Beverly LaHaye Institute: A Center for Studies in Women's Issues of the CWA.

LAKOFF, ROBIN TOLMACH (1942-). *See* GENDER AND COMMUNICATION.

LANGE, HELENE (1848-1930). An activist in the first German women's movement. Lange overcame strong resistance to earn a teaching license and then became an advocate of education for women. In 1894 she founded the Federation of German Women's Associations. As its leader until 1930, she resisted the influence of more **radical feminists**, even to the point of refusing admission of Social Democrat groups. She did, however, support the easing of Germany's **abortion** laws.

LANTERI, JULIETA (1873-1932). A pioneering Argentine feminist, **suffragist**, and politician. Long associated with the *librepensadores* (freethinker) movement that endorsed **woman suffrage** in 1908, Lanteri co-founded the National League of Women Freethinkers in 1909 and in 1910 began publishing *La Nueva Mujer*. Her radical anticlerical stances and personal flair brought her national prominance. She was successful in establishing the legal basis of women's citizenship when, as a naturalized citizen, she voted in elections 1911-1916. After being disqualified, she received a court ruling that there were no constitutional differences between the political rights of men and women. In 1920 she founded the National Feminist Party and joined other feminists in a mock women's election in which 4,000 women participated.

LATE TERM ABORTIONS. *See* PARTIAL-BIRTH ABORTIONS.

LATINA FEMINISM. The gender consciousness of women of Latin American origin living in the United States. Latinas are drawn from many races, ethnicities, cultures, and nationalities and identify as **women of color**. Many Latino cultures emphasize rigid **gender roles** and the values of **patriarchal** society. Latina feminism addresses both racism and the sexual oppression within their own culture. A seminal event was the **sexual assault** on 56 women in New York's Central Park after the Puerto Rican Day Parade in 2000. The next year Puerto Rican and other Latina groups joined with other feminists in the Central Park Rally Against Sexism.

LAVENDER MENACE. A term used in 1969 by members of the **National Organization for Women** to describe the threat that some feared **lesbians** presented to the legitimacy of the **new feminist movement** as opponents attempted to equate feminism with lesbianism. In response, at the second Congress to Unite Women, held in New York City in May 1970, about 20 lesbians wearing T-shirts bearing the words "Lavender Menace" read a position paper presenting lesbianism as a political choice. As a group, the Lavender Menace later changed its name to Radicalesbians. *See also* POLITICAL LESBIANISM.

LAWSON, LOUISA (1848-1920). An Australian journalist and feminist. From 1888-1905, she published *Dawn*, the first Australian journal edited, printed, and published solely by women. It had a broad feminist agenda, but emphasized suffrage. Lawson was active in several **woman suffrage** groups and is considered "the mother of suffrage in New South Wales." Although she did not support the franchise for aboriginal women, she was concerned with their status. A **feminist magazine** *The Dawn*, begun in 1993, is dedicated to her.

LEAGUE OF WOMEN VOTERS (LWV). A group formally organized in 1920 as the US post-suffrage successor of the **National American Woman Suffrage Association** in order to integrate women into the political system. The league was a participant within the early **social feminist** coalition, the **Women's Joint Congressional Committee**, but withdrew in the 1950s and ignored feminist issues until its endorsement of the **Equal Rights Amendment** in 1972. The group has since become a major force within state and national women's rights lobbies. Despite its preference during much of its history to be classified as a "public interest" group rather than a "women's" group and its strict policy of nonpartisanship, the league has trained and motivated many women to seek elective office.

L'ÉCRITURE FÉMININE. A term coined by the leading French contemporary theorists, **Julia Kristéva, Luce Irigaray, Hélène Cixous,** and **Monique Wittig** to mean writing that is based on female objectivity and the physiology and bodily instincts of women as distinct from men. This writing seeks to resist the **patriarchal** system by which man has sought to objectify the external world in relation to his power. *L'Écriture féminine* takes as its source the mother, or the mother-child relationship before the child gains **male-dominated** verbal language. It is this prelinguistic potentiality in the unconscious that reveals itself in women's writings that seek to undermine fixed meaning, and defy the "closure" of **phallocentric** language. The **new French feminists** emphasize as a form of rebellion a quality that they term *jouissance*.

LEILA KHALED COLLECTIVE. *See* TORONTO WOMEN'S LIBERATION MOVEMENT.

LERNER, GERDA (1920-). An American historian instrumental during the 1960s and 1970s in legitimizing **women's history** and **women's studies** in the academic curriculum. An author who examines American women, African American women, and feminists in history as well as the effect of **patriarchy** on civilization, her works include *Black Women in White America* (1972), *The Majority Finds Its Past: Placing Women in History* (1979), *The Creation of Patriarchy* (1986), and *The Creation of Feminist Consciousness* (1993). She published her autobiography *Fireweed* in 2002.

LESBIAN FEMINISM. A tradition that links institutionalized heterosexuality to women's subordinate status and stresses the social, rather than the biological, construction of sexuality. Lesbian feminists have variously presented lesbianism as a viable option and as a political imperative for feminists. Rejecting the idea of a universal female experience, lesbian feminists focus on the differences between gay and straight women. *See also* GAY/STRAIGHT SPLIT; LAVENDER MENACE; POLITICAL LESBIANISM; SEPARATISM; "WOMAN-IDENTIFIED WOMAN, THE."

LESBIAN MORAL THEORY. A reflection on the unique ethical experiences and ethical needs of **"the woman-identified woman"** and all women. This often means a critique of the traditional philosophical emphasis on ethical rules and principles, in addition to a valorization of what enables women to develop individual integrity and agency in relation to others. In general, this tradition believes that father-centered ethics diminish women's capacity for moral action while women-centered ethics **empower** women as moral agents.

LESBIAN MOTHERHOOD. The condition of being both a **lesbian** and a mother, whether within a heterosexual marriage or through adoption, **artificial insemination,** or heterosexual intercourse outside marriage. These women often face legal challenges to child custody, difficulties in obtaining artificial insemination services, and disqualification as an adoptive parent despite support since 2002 of the American Academy of Pediatrics for the adoption of children by gay and lesbian couples.

The feminist movement has become increasingly supportive of the rights of lesbian mothers.

LESBIANS. A term for female homosexuals who relate to other women as sexual partners, either as a biologically determined response or a consciously chosen political statement as a "woman-identified woman." In the United States and most of Western Europe, lesbian couples are denied the right to marry, lack survivor's benefits, group **insurance** coverage for partners, and rights of guardianship. In some US cities and states, **domestic partnership** policies extend these benefits. Lesbians are not covered under most laws barring **domestic violence** and discrimination in housing, **employment**, and public accommodations. Lesbian sexual activity was protected under the right to **privacy** by the US Supreme Court in *Lawrence v. Texas* (2003). Lesbians have played major roles as leaders and participants in feminist movements and in the modern gay liberation movement. Despite early tensions between feminists of different sexual orientations, the feminist movement currently supports the gay political agenda. Lesbians have been especially active in building cultural institutions such as **feminist bookstores**, **women's centers**, and music groups. In other countries, however, homosexuality is viewed as a sign of Western decadence, and lesbians there are far more oppressed. One term for "homosexual" in Chinese, for example, has a literal meaning of "the foreigner's disease."

LÉVI-STRAUSS, CLAUDE (1908-). A French anthropologist who did fieldwork in Brazil among Amazonian Indians during the 1930s. From his analysis of their social structures and from extensive surveys of American Indian mythologies, Lévi-Strauss concluded that the statuses of men and women form a central problem in human thought. In an early monograph on marriage relationships in small lineage-structured societies, he presented women as a form of communication passed between lineages; this excessively **androcentric** viewpoint was abandoned in his later works. Lévi-Strauss has asserted what appears to be a vulgar formula—man:woman/culture:nature—but, in fact, he reflects on the theme "To what larger realms do men, and women, belong?"

LEWINSKY, MONICA (1973 -). A White House intern who conducted a sexual affair with then-President Bill Clinton, provoking his impeachment during the summer of 1999. Lewinsky has been viewed by feminists as a scheming manipulator who exposed the president to humiliation or as a victim of the president's lust brought on by a midlife crisis. Lewinsky's co-worker, Linda Tripp, taped her conversations with Lewinsky and then turned them over to Special Prosecutor Ken Starr, already investigating the president for a real-estate transaction. Feminists see Tripp as the classic careerist and politically motivated manipulator using the younger woman for her own Republican agenda. **Third wave feminists** have supported Lewinsky's freedom to make her own choices, even if they were not the wisest. They have also supported Lewinsky, not as a victim of a rapacious man but as a young woman with a libido of her own. *See also* JONES, PAULA CORBIN.

LIBERAL FEMINISM. The strand of the movement (also termed "mainstream feminism") that is based on traditional political liberalism, which accepts a positive view of human nature and the ideals of liberty, equality, justice, dignity, and individual rights. There is also confidence that society, properly reformed, can maximize individual autonomy and ensure equality of opportunity. Liberal feminists believe that women should enjoy the same rights and treatment as men. Prominent liberal feminists include **Mary Wollstonecraft, John Stuart Mill, Elizabeth Cady Stanton,** and **Susan B. Anthony.** In the contemporary US feminist movement, groups such as the **National Organization for Women** and the **National Women's Political Caucus** are primarily composed of liberal feminists, in contrast with those of the **women's liberation** branch, and pursue their goals through conventional political activities of lobbying, litigation, and legislation. Feminist critics of liberal feminism see a **patriarchal** bias in values such as individualism, freedom, rationality, and equality. They argue that each reflects the experiences of men and not of all humanity.

LIGA FEMINISTA/FEMINIST LEAGUE. A Costa Rican group, founded in 1923 by **Angela Acuña** to promote women's rights, including **woman suffrage**. During Acuña's residence in Europe, 1927-1931, the league became less feminist and changed its name to La Sociedad Cultural (The Cultural Society). Upon her return, Acuña revitalized the league, which led the **woman suffrage movement** until the mid-1940s.

LIGUE DU DROIT DES FEMMES (LDF)/WOMEN'S RIGHTS LEAGUE. A group formed in 1974 by members of the **Féministes**

Révolutionnaires to seek changes in French laws that oppress women. The group is registered as a formal association and serves as a link between **radical** and **egalitarian feminists**. It has recently focused on equal opportunities for older women.

LILITH. The mythological first wife, a predecessor of **Eve**, to the biblical Adam. According to this tale that first appeared in the Middle Ages, Lilith was created from dust by God at the same time as Adam. She refused to submit to her husband sexually and demanded equality. Leaving the Garden of Eden, she was cursed by God for her open sexuality and independence. In response Lilith threatened to prey upon newborn babies, and amulets against her were worn in the Middle Ages. She is a **goddess** to neopagans and a **role model** to **Jewish feminists**, who publish a magazine named for her. She remains a demon, the feminine dark side of the divine, to Orthodox Jews.

LILITH FAIR. A traveling North American and European rock festival of female musicians and woman-led groups, founded by Canadian singer and guitarist Sarah McLachlan as a response to the exclusion of female artists from music festivals such as Lollapolooza. For three years, 1997-1999, both well-known and unknown artists performed and female artisans and women's groups set up tables to sell products and distribute information on women's issues. Named for the mythical character **Lilith**, the tour was criticized by conservatives who objected to children attending a festival that celebrates a pagen figure. *See also* LADYFESTS.

LINTON, ELIZA LYNN (1822-1898). An English novelist and US **antifeminist** journalist. After emigrating to the United States, Linton began writing for *The Saturday Review*, a strong opponent of women's rights. In 1868 she published "The Girl of the Period," in which she attacked the modern woman as a hard, unhealthy, ambitious national disaster. She quickly became the spokesperson for reactionary sentiment on women's role, even though she personally supported **divorce** reform and **protective labor laws**.

LIPOVSKAIA, OLGA (1954-). The founder and director of the St. Petersburg Center for Gender Issues, which promotes **gender** equality in Russia. Lipovskaia came to feminism in 1985 when she read a book on feminist issues, dedicated to the English women's movement. In 1987 she began writing for a samizdat feminist journal *Zhenskoe chtenie* (*Women's Reading*). She was one of the founders of the **Feminist Alternative**.

LOCKWOOD, BELVA (1830-1917). The first woman lawyer to practice before the US Supreme Court. She was a founder of the Universal Franchise Association in 1867, an active member of the **National Woman Suffrage Association**, and a successful lobbyist for laws to improve the legal status of women. As the candidate of the National Equal Rights Party in 1884 and 1888, she was one of the first women to run for president of the United States.

LONDON WORLD ANTISLAVERY CONVENTION (1840). The catalyst for the 1848 **Seneca Falls Convention**. The conference's refusal to seat American women delegates on the convention floor, relegating them instead to the visitor's gallery as observers, focused the attention of delegates **Lucretia Mott** and **Elizabeth Cady Stanton** on the inequitable treatment of women.

LORDE, AUDRE (1934-1992). An **African American lesbian feminist** poet and founder, with Barbara Smith, of Kitchen Table: Women of Color Press. The author of 13 books of poetry and essays, Lorde served as poet laureate of New York State and helped form Sisterhood in Support of Sisters in South Africa. Her works include *I Am Your Sister: Black Women Organizing across Sexualities* (1985), *Sister Outsider* (1984), and *Our Dead behind Us* (1986). Her legacy is celebrated in the film *A Litany for Survival: The Life and Work of Audre Lorde* (1995).

LOVE YOUR BODY DAY (LYBD). A national day to speak out against **advertising** and **media images of women** that are offensive, harmful, dangerous, and disrespectful and to celebrate women's bodies in all their diversities. First sponsored by the **National Organization for Women** Foundation's Women's Health Project in 1998, the annual event is observed with art exhibits, **speak-outs**, and pickets across the United States.

LOWE, ANNIE. *See* DUGDALE, HENRIETTA.

LUCY STONE LEAGUE. A movement to encourage women to retain their birthname after marriage. The group is named for **woman suffrage** and **abolition** leader **Lucy Stone**, who kept her own name rather than assume her husband's name at the time of her marriage. The first league was formed in 1921 as a multi-issue feminist organization. It disbanded and then was reborn in 1950, only to falter again. It was revived in 1997 as a group for those who wish to retain, modify, or create their names. Today's Lucy Stoners hope that equal numbers of men and women will do each and that the names of children will also be evenly distributed. *See also* NAMING CONVENTIONS.

LUISI, PAULINA (1875-1950). The leader of the women's movement in Uraguay in the early 20th century. She was the first Uraguayan woman to receive a medical degree in 1909 and is credited with dramatically improving conditions for women in the health professions. In 1916 she founded the Uruguayan National Council of Women and in 1919 the Uruguay Alliance of Women for Suffrage. Both groups pursued a broad feminist agenda as a means of achieving **woman suffrage**. Luisi continued to represent both groups at international conferences, but focused on the alliance at home due to some personality conflicts with other women in the national council. The vote was won in 1932.

LUTZ, BERTHA MARIA JULIA (1899-1976). A Sorbonne-educated biologist and lawyer who helped to organize the **woman suffrage movement** in Brazil. In 1918, in reponse to a newspaper columnist's attack on US and English feminists, Lutz wrote an article calling for the establishment of a Brazilian women's rights league. In 1922 she founded the Brazilian Federation for the Advancement of Women, an affiliate of the **International Woman Suffrage Alliance.** After the vote was won in 1932, Lutz remained active in the **international women's movement** and attended the **International Women's Year** conference in Mexico City in 1975.

LUXEMBURG, ROSA (1871-1919). A revolutionary socialist born in Russian Poland, where she helped found the Polish Social Democratic Party. After moving to Berlin in 1899, she became a leader of the German Socialist Party. She typified those socialists who supported working women's movements but distanced themselves from the feminist agenda advocated by other socialists like **Clara Zetkin**. A founder with Karl Liebknecht of the Spartakus League, which promoted a working-class revolution, "Red Rosa" was executed in 1919 for her role in the abortive Spartacist Revolt in Berlin.

LYSISTRATA. A Greek fictional heroine of Aristophanes' antiwar comedy of the same name (the name Lysistrata means "releaser of war"). She successfully masterminds a sex-strike among the women of Greece to force a truce between the Athenians and Spartans during the Peloponnesian War. Her activism and militancy are uncharacteristic of real Greek women, who lived in virtual seclusion in the home and were politically powerless. Even attendance at the theater was denied to them, and all the actors would have been male. Lysistrata's feminist actions were the product of wishful thinking and pure comic fantasy—the absurdity of women dictating political policy through sexual bribery. *See also* ECCLESIAZUSAE, THE, OR WOMEN IN COUNCIL; THESMOPHORIAZUSAE, OR A WOMEN'S FESTIVAL.

LYSISTRATA PROJECT. A **global feminist** action occurring on March 3, 2003. Thousands of actresses from all over the world took part in a reading of the ancient Greek play as part of a protest against the US and British-led war against Iraq. Sponsored in 56 countries, the Lysistrata Project also sought to raise money for charities working for peace and humanitarian projects in the Middle East and elsewhere. The organizers said that the Lysistrata Project has a simple message, "no peace, no sex."

LYTTON, LADY CONSTANCE (1869-1923). An English aristocrat and member of the **Women's Suffrage and Political Union.** Lady Lytton was imprisoned several times for her suffrage protests but was always released on health grounds when on **hunger strike.** Disguising herself as a working-class woman in 1911, she was arrested and force fed. Her subsequent stroke and partial paralysis attracted much publicity and sympathy for the **woman suffrage** cause. As an invalid, she wrote suffrage articles and organized petition drives.

-M-

MACAULAY-GRAHAM, CATHARINE SAWBRIDGE (1731-1791). An English historian and political pamphleteer who together with her brother, John Sawbridge, was an influential figure in the late 18th century English parliamentary reform movement. She criticized the political philosophy of David Hume, Edmund Burke, and Thomas Hobbes, and in her *Letters on Education* (1790), refuted Jean Jacques Rousseau's arguments on the complementary roles of men and women and his claims that women are inferior. She recommended that boys and girls be educated together in similar subjects.

MACHO. A word of Spanish origin meaning "male" and having come to represent exaggerated displays of maleness or *machismo*, with emphasis on excessive virility and **dominance** of and superiority over women, physically, psychologically, and emotionally. *Machismo* carries with it a set of attitudes that automatically relegate woman to an inferior position and justify an abuse of power, force, and position. A *macho* is by association considered a **sexist**. A positive characteristic is that such men support their families out of a sense of duty. *See also* MARIANISMO.

MACKINNON, CATHARINE (1946-). A prominent US law professor, legal theorist, and advocate against **violence against women**. In her writings on **feminist jurisprudence**, she has cautioned that the law should not be viewed as an effective agent for social change; instead, she argues in *Only Words* (1993) that lawyers and judges have redefined **pornography** as "political speech." She is known for co-authoring the **Minneapolis Pornography Ordinance**, for developing the distinction between *quid pro quo* and **"hostile environment" sexual harassment** (in *Sexual Harassment of Working Women*, 1979), and for her statement that **"radical feminism** is feminism" (in *Feminism Unmodified*, 1987). According to MacKinnon, all other feminisms are only modified attempts to integrate women into a man-made system. Since 1985 the Supreme Court of Canada has adopted many of her views on equality, hate speech, and pornography. Her definition of **rape** as genocide has been accepted by the **International Criminal Court**.

MAIL-ORDER BRIDES. The marketing of women from developing nations in Asia, Latin America, and Eastern Europe to men in the industrial democracies of North America, Western Europe, Australia, and Japan. The men select wives from mail-order catalogs, videos, pictures on the Internet, or **sex tours** provided by commercial agencies. Feminists see these arrangements as both **sexist** and **classist** as older men, unhappy with changing **gender roles**, seek more compliant poor women. These immigrant brides are often subject to abuse and, fearing deportation, remain silent. Under President Corazon Aquino, the Philippines became the first nation to prohibit the practice as a human rights violation. These marriages should not be confused with Asian "picture brides" of the early 20th century. Many Japanese and Korean women immigrated to the United States, chosen on the basis of photographs, to enter into a marriage arranged by families of the same ethnic origin.

MAINSTREAM FEMINISM. *See* LIBERAL FEMINISM; WOMEN'S RIGHTS MOVEMENT.

MALAKHOVSKAIA, NATALIA (1947-). A Russian feminist who became involved in the underground movement and founded the **Mariia Club**, an illegal women's organization. She was a contributor to *Woman and Russia*, which led to her exile to Vienna in 1980.

"MALE BASHING." A perjorative term used to accuse feminists of engaging in character assassination against all males, regardless of their sympathies or beliefs. A **backlash** phenomenon, feminists are frequently accused of engaging in "male bashing" in order to segregate men and women. **Mary Daly**, for instance, was accused of "male bashing" in her female-only theology classes. In its extreme form, any criticism of the **patriarchy**, hegemony, or institutionalized **sexism** is accused of being a form of "male bashing" and is simply dismissed as prejudiced, irrational criticism of victimized males. Websites maintained by men to document incidents of "male bashing" are filled with quotations by **Robin Morgan**.

MALE CHAUVINIST. A widely used **new feminist movement** term denoting a man who believes in the natural superiority of his sex and in the restriction of women to a traditional role. Viewed as a "man-hating" expression by its critics, the term is seen by feminists as a neutral shorthand concept that identifies the target and facilitates movement unity.

MALE DOMINANCE. The tendency for men to be allotted social roles giving them ascendancy over women. This is not universal in human or primate groups and has been linked to situations where men are frequently called upon to defend the community. Because most historic and ethnographic accounts deal with societies at war, our data are biased toward heavy representation of male dominance. When this possible bias has been considered, the finding is that social relations are complex even in simply structured small societies. Men may assert dominance in hopes of persuading others, while women ignore these overtures and quietly proceed with their tasks. Or one sex may be allowed a more decisive voice according to the activity involved.

"MALE GAZE, THE." A phrase that describes the dominant **feminist film theory**. According to Laura Mulvey (in "Visual Pleasure and Narrative Cinema"), the male gaze defines and dominates women as erotic objects in films, rendering them absent, silent, or marginal or omnipowerful in the discourse of the film. The voyeuristic pleasure of looking at someone lies at the heart of film, and women have functioned for the male gaze as perfect objects onto which the male has projected his own fantasies about women—by seeing them either as mothers, whores, **bitches**, or castrating femme fatales. *See also* FEMALE GAZE.

MALE MENOPAUSE. A subject of debate among biologists and psychologists, who now recognize it as separate from the male "mid-life" crisis, a problem of psychosocial adjustment. Not completely identified with sexual dysfunction or hormonal decreases, the male menopause appears to vary greatly among men, with approximately 40 percent of men between 40 and 60 experiencing some degree of lethargy, decreased libido, weakness, loss of lean body mass and bone mass, and increased impotence. As feminists have encouraged the recognition of female menopause, they have paved the way for a similar syndrome to be recognized in aging men. **Hormone replacement therapy**, once championed by women but now discouraged for its health risks, is currently being tested on men who are undergoing testosterone replacement therapy.

MALE-ONLY CLUBS. Those organizations that restrict their membership to men. In the 1980s the US Supreme Court began to reject the argument that nondiscrimination laws should not apply to some of these private associations. In *Roberts v. United States* (1984) and *Board of Directors of Rotary International v. Rotary Club of Duarte* (1987), the Court ruled that service organizations such as the Rotary Club and the

Jaycees were large, nonselective groups that were not "distinctly private" and thus could not claim a right to private association. Feminists also argue that men's clubs, where many business contacts are made, restrict the professional opportunities of excluded women. Both the United States and Great Britain permit some private clubs to discriminate in their membership policies, but these policies at the famed golf clubs of Scotland and the Augusta National Golf Club, where the US Masters Tournament is held, are also being challenged by activists who threaten boycotts of products sold during television broadcasts of tournaments.

MALE PILL. A version of the **birth control pill** for men. This feminist goal came closer to reality when researchers in Scotland (2000) and Australia (2002) announced that a 100 percent effective pill with no dangerous side effects had been developed and could be available in a few years. Drug companies have not seen such a pill as profitable because they would lose female customers. There are also concerns that men will still define oral **contraception** as women's responsibility and women may not trust men to be truthful about taking the pill. However, the popularity of **Viagra** may have broken the taboo against controlling the male **reproductive** system.

MALINCHE, LA (1504-1529). A woman known as the "Mexican Eve," the Indian noblewoman offered to Cortez upon his arrival in Veracruz in 1519. She served him as guide, interpreter, and lover. She has been perceived negatively for supposedly "selling out" both herself and her country and is often referred to pejoratively as *la chingada* or the "fucked one." Her legend helps men to rationalize their **dominance** over women who cannot be trusted. Her name also implies sexual passivity and exploitation by men and by a white society. Recent feminist revisionism is attempting to reverse this perception.

MAMONOVA, TATIANA VALENTINOVNA (1943-). A Russian poet, writer, and painter who is considered the founder of the contemporary Russian women's movement. She was the driving force behind *Woman and Russia* and after her exile in 1980 has continued her work in the United States and Europe. She has served on the international advisory board for *Ms.* and lectured and published widely. In 1993 she founded the **ecofeminist** *Woman and Earth Almanac*, which is distributed free to women's groups in Russia and Eastern

Europe and engages in a variety of activities such as video production, film festivals, and international tours.

MANIFESTE DES 343 FEMMES. A public acknowledgment published in the weekly newsmagazine *Le Nouvel Observateur* on April 5, 1971, and signed by 343 Frenchwomen, including **Simone de Beauvoir**, actress Catherine Deneuve, writer Françoise Sagen, **Gisèle Halimi**, and **Yvette Roudy**, that they had had at least one **abortion**. In 1973 a number of French doctors issued a letter acknowledging their own participation in abortions. These actions are credited with placing abortion on the public agenda in France.

MANN ACT. The popular name for the White Slave Traffic Act passed by the US Congress in 1910. It prohibited interstate transportation of women for any "immoral purpose" despite a lack of evidence of any international or national organized syndicate. Under expansive Supreme Court interpretations, it became a vehicle for prosecuting women for extramarital or premarital sex as well as **prostitution**. Feminist scholars view this "white slave ideology" as a reaction against women's increasing independence and movement outside the **domestic sphere**.

MAN-WOMAN-SOCIETY. ALSO KNOWN AS MAN VROUW MAATSCHAPPIJ (MVM). The first **second wave feminist** group in the Netherlands, formed in 1968. Modeled on the **liberal feminist National Organization for Women**, MVM became more radical with its later competition with **Dolle Mina**.

MAQUILADORA. A term of Spanish origin referring to "runaway US companies" that have relocated to Mexico to take advantage of low wages and lax safety, environmental, and union regulations. The concept is now generally applied to factories owned by multinational corporations that employ many young unmarried Third World women at wages and under working conditions that local men and Western workers would not tolerate. Feminists argue that this exploitation of young women in the global factory affects the economies of both the Third World nations and the older industrial nations from which the factories moved in their owners' search for cheaper labor. On the other hand, it provides much-needed earnings for huge numbers of women who would otherwise be unemployed. It also enhances their status and leverage. See also DEVELOPMENT, WOMEN IN.

MARIANISMO. A reference to the Christian cult of the powers of **Mary of Nazareth** (the Virgin Mary), similar to other **goddess** traditions. The importance of Mary has declined in most Catholic countries but maintains considerable strength in the Iberian peninsula and Latin America. From a feminist perspective, rather than being a sign of the repression of women, *Marianismo* lends credence to the notion of female supremacy as a counterbalance to *machismo*. See also MACHO.

MARIIA. A club of religious Russian feminists formed in 1980 out of a dispute with the **Woman and Russia** collective. Mariia's exiled founders published six issues of their almanac from Paris and Frankfort, 1980-1983, and then disbanded. The group attempted to develop a distinctively Russian feminism, based on the role of **Mary of Nazareth** in the Orthodox Church. In contrast to the Western emphasis on equality, Mariia focused on the emotional, not the intellectual, strengths of women and the church as women's sanctuary.

MARITAL PROPERTY. A legal principle that gives both spouses vested rights (such as ownership, management, and control) in all property acquired during marriage by the personal efforts of either spouse. This recognizes that marriage is an economic partnership to which both spouses contribute, with household or wage labor or both, and in which each has an equal share. This affects the division of property upon the death of one spouse and/or dissolution of the marriage. US feminists have strongly supported adoption of the model Uniform Marital Property Act (1983) in the states because of the protections extended to traditional housewives and women who have taken low-paying jobs in order to support their husbands in graduate and professional training.

MARITAL RAPE. Sexual intercourse forced on one spouse by the other, generally involving the assault of the wife. Many men incorrectly believe that intercourse is their right in marriage and refuse to honor their wife's communication that she does not desire it at a particular time. Marital rape is now against the law in all US states as a result of a feminist campaign to reform state laws on **rape**. However, in 33 states there are some exemptions from rape prosecution given to husbands, usually involving a situation where a woman has temporary or permanent mental or physical disabilities that prevent her consent and force is not used. By 2000 only 26 countries had laws to prosecute marital rape, and in all marital rape continues to be treated as less serious than other forms of rape. In many systems, under the "doctrine of presumed consent," a woman is viewed as having agreed to everything, including sex, that her husband asks of her in their marriage.

MARRIAGE MOVEMENT. A group of programs associated with the Coalition for Marriage, Family, and Couples' Education, based at the Institute for American Values in New York. Their goal is to reduce **divorce** and **single parenthood** and childbearing by repealing **no-fault divorce** and establishing public policy incentives to encourage marriage. Feminists fear that such policies could lead poor women into abusive relationships; marriage should not be viewed as the solution to poverty. Since 1998 the Alternatives to Marriage Project has worked for fairness for unmarried people, including those who choose not to marry, cannot marry, or live together before marriage.

MARRIED WOMEN'S PROPERTY ACTS. The statutes enacted in the 19th century in the United States and England to "emancipate" wives from **coverture**, which prevented wives from owning property free from their husband's control. The acts also gave women control over the choice of their domicile and the right to enter into contracts and to sue and be sued. Additional laws were passed in the 20th century as both countries moved to **no-fault divorce** and the concept of **marital property** to recognize the value of women's unpaid labor in the home.

MARTIN, DEL (1921-). The co-founder in 1955 of Daughters of Bilitus, a support and social group for **lesbians**, and its first president. An advocate of homosexual rights, she and her partner Phyllis Lyon joined the **National Organization for Women** in 1968 at the special rate for couples and Martin later served as an officer of her local chapter. Her books include *Lesbian/Woman* (with Lyon, 1972), *Battered Wives* (1976), *The Male Batterer: A Treatment Approach* (co-authored, 1985), and *When Violence Begins at Home* (co-authored, 1997). She currently works on issues of interest to older women.

MARTINEAU, HARRIET (1802-1876). An English writer, best known for a series of articles that agitated for the improvement of women's lives. She supported the feminist position on education, work, and marriage at least 30 years before the emergence of an organized women's movement in England. Her article "On Female Education" (1823) denied the inferiority of the female mind and demanded a formal system of education for women that would allow them to reach their potentials as wives and mothers. She signed a petition to Parliament on **woman suffrage** in 1855. One of her 1859 articles inspired a group of feminists to found the Society for Promoting the Employment of Women. Even as an invalid, she aided in the campaign against the **Contagious Diseases Acts**, 1869-1871.

MARVIN V. MARVIN, 18 CAL.3D 660, 134 CAL.RPTR. 815, 557 P.2D 106 (1966). A celebrated decision from which the term "palimony" arises. It involved Michele Triola, a nightclub singer, who gave up her career for six years to become a full-time homemaker for actor Lee Marvin. Although she had changed her last name to Marvin, she did so without benefit of marriage. When Lee Marvin left her for another woman and discontinued voluntary support payments for which he had no obligation under applicable **divorce** statutes, Michele Marvin sued him for half of the $3.6 million in property accumulated during their relationship. According to a majority of the California Supreme Court, courts could promote equity in such circumstances through various legal doctrines. Although Marvin could not prove that the property was acquired through "mutual effort," she was awarded $104,000 for reeducation. Feminists, although sympathetic to her plight, urge that women protect themselves in such relationships through a written contract.

MARX, KARL (1818-1883). The founder of communism and a socialist reformer. Both Marx and **Friedrich Engels** believed that socialism would bring about a profound change in **gender** relations and the relief of women's economic repression. Although Marx rarely discussed feminist issues at length or in specific terms, he appointed English schoolteacher Harriet Law to the General Council of the International Workingmen's Association, or First International.

MARXIST FEMINISM. A branch of feminism that examines the connection between **gender** status and production methods, applies Marxist theories to the role of families in society, and asserts that the burdens of physical and social **reproduction** in the home operate to reinforce a **male-dominated** economic and political order. This tradition also notes that since women work in the home, unlike men they have no place to escape from material alienation. Marxist feminists support **wages for housework** and have recently begun to examine the impact of the **welfare** state upon women. *See also* ENGELS, FRIEDRICH.

MARY MAGDALENE, FEMINIST INTERPRETATIONS. A New Testament figure traditionally portrayed as a converted prostitute who was the first witness to the resurrection of Jesus. Feminist scholars of early Christianity now suggest that she was never a whore but instead an important disciple who was present at the Last Supper. She was the only apostle that Christ kissed on the lips and named as his companion, raising the possibility that they were married and that she was a mother of Jesus's child (his "holy grail"). Some scholars, however, have estimated that she was at least approaching 50 when Jesus died at 33. Her lack of submissiveness and her importance as a leader made her dangerous to a **male-dominated** Church that distorted her identity in the late 6th century. The Vatican formally repudiated her false image in 1969.

MARY OF NAZARETH, FEMINIST INTERPRETATIONS. The examination of scripture, doctrine, and popular piety concerning Mary, the mother of Jesus, to expose the degree to which, especially in the Catholic West, Mary came to be a symbol for maternal or feminine features of divinity, operating alongside dominant masculine imagery for God to, in turn, support or indirectly subvert patriarchal symbolism and practice. The highpoint of Mariology occurred in 1854 when Pope Pius IX declared the Virgin Mary to have been the only woman born without original sin, to have been the product of an "immaculate conception" herself. By disentangling the poor Jewish villager, Miriam of Nazareth, from the near-divine "Queen of Heaven and Earth," feminist theologians seek to reinstate the former as a genuinely inspiring woman of faith and courage, and the latter as revealing feminine dimensions of deity that **patriarchy** had obscured. In 1974 Pope Paul VI issued a document describing Mary as a feminist, an activist, and a woman who, while obedient to God, was neither timid nor submissive. *See also* DEITIES, FEMALE; FEMINIST SPIRITUALITY; MARIANISMO; VIRGIN OF GUADALUPE.

MASARYK, TOMAS (1850-1937). The founder of the modern Czechoslovakia and its president, 1918-1935. As a legislator and college professor, Masaryk supported women's rights and helped to develop a Czech women's movement. His journal *Our Era* ran a column on women's issues, 1905-1915, and his advocacy ensured **woman suffrage** soon after an independent republic was established under his presidency.

MASCULIST/MASCULINIST. The tendency to assign all value and meaning in male-defined terms. The masculinist impulse reads history as a series of wars, political events, and **male-dominated** episodes and reads literature as a series of texts written by male authors.

MAŠOTENE, ONA (1883-1949). A Lithuanian feminist and founder of the Alliance of Lithuanian Women in 1905. She was active in a variety of local and national women's groups, including the Russian National Women's Congress, before World War I. She later worked for national independence and founded the Council of Lithuanian Women in 1929.

MATERNAL FEMINISM. *See* SOCIAL FEMINISM.

MATERNAL INSTINCT. The presumption that women have a biological readiness, ability, and desire to be mothers. This "instinct" has been linked to other characteristics with which women have been credited such as their emotionality, their preference to work communally, and their care taking. While researchers have failed to find concrete evidence of such an instinct in humans, the concept continues to have consequences for women. Feminists believe that it creates pressure on women to have children, feelings of inadequacy regarding mothering, and often elicits guilt in women who do not wish to have children. It also suggests that women should have a greater role in the raising of children. And, because of the subordinate role of women, there is often little social and economic support for **child care**.

MATERNAL THINKING. A perspective from **difference feminism** and **social feminism** presented by philosopher Sara Ruddick. She suggests that an **ethic of care** and concern is developed by the act of mothering and that this way of thinking must not be restricted to the **domestic sphere** in that maternal thinking challenges the prevailing impersonal and amoral public order. Emphasis is on the positive achievements of maternal practices, not the **victimization of women.**

MATERNITY LEAVE. The release time from work for a pregnant woman. In the United States, the time allowed is usually only the period directly surrounding birth and a short period for physical recovery. This results in distress for many women and children and inadequate time for bonding. In some European countries, especially in Scandinavia, the period is larger while in most third-world countries it is considerably less, if granted at all. *See also* CALIFORNIA FEDERAL SAVINGS AND LOAN ASSOCIATION V. GUERRA; FAMILY LEAVE; PREGNANCY DISCRIMINATION ACT.

MATH ANXIETY. A term coined by science writer Sheila Tobias to explain the lack of mathematical competence exhibited by a disproportionately large percentage of women. The use of the term "anxiety" refers to the observation that the lack of mathematical competence is usually not due to lack of ability, but rather is due to a societally imposed lack of expectation of mathematical ability based on **gender.** Mathematician Lyn Olson has called this the "feminine mathtique." This became relevant as the feminist movement began to encourage women to enter nontraditional fields such as engineering and the physical sciences that required mathematical training. Girls are now receiving more encouragement from parents, teachers, and counselors to study math and "math avoidance" is declining.

MATHURA RAPE CASE. A decision of the Supreme Court of India, issued in September 1979, that is linked with the rapid growth of the women's movement in India. The case involved the alleged **rape** of a young untouchable orphan in 1972 while in police custody after her brother had reported her kidnapping by her boyfriend. In reversing a decision of guilty by an intermediate appeals court, the supreme court interpreted her lack of physical injury as denoting consent, not submission. An outraged "Open Letter to the Chief Justice of India" from four (two male and two female) law professors was widely circulated as women demonstrated and formed new women's groups throughout the nation.

MATRIARCHY. The rule by women. Despite the concept's importance in the current feminist revival and as an element within female utopian writing and philosophy, there is not one soundly documented instance, in history, ethnography, or archaeological recovery, of a society truly ruled by women as a class. Those classical societies that elevated **goddesses** to highest status in their pantheons were **patriarchal** (like Western societies idealizing **Mary of Nazareth**). PreClassical Western societies and non-Western societies with female images prominent in their art or pantheons may similarly be masking patriarchy through manipulating images of the subordinated class or may reflect an egalitarian society with more complementary roles for men and women. The idea of matriarchy, even if imaginative, does provide a new way of thinking about power and **gender**.

MATRIFOCAL. Those families headed by women, in which men are marginal. Matrifocal families are common in impoverished areas where there is little employment for men but women can subsist on government **welfare** or have somewhat better opportunities for employment. Matrifocal families appear to be a strategy for dealing with endemic poverty, not a cultural tradition.

MATRILINEAL. The practice of tracing descent or inheriting through female links. Matrilineal societies may claim that the bond between mother and child is the strongest or least equivocal bond, but anthropological theory suggests that matrilineality is most often correlated with a political-economic structure built upon corporate (as opposed to individual) landowning units. Women and their brothers are the basic workgroup in these societies; men either live during marriages in their wives' homes or maintain principal residence in their matrilineal house. It is not unusual for societies to designate certain rights and privileges as being inherited through the mother and others through the father. In such cases, residence and farmland may be obtained through the mother's lineage, religious roles through the father's. Contemporary matrilineal societies are found in Africa, the Pacific, and North America. They are most common in the Pacific Islands (e.g., the Trobrianders) and among American Indians in the Southwest (e.g., the Hopis).

MCCLUNG, NETTIE LETITIA (1873-1951). The most prominent Canadian proponent of **social feminism** as a member of the Alberta Assembly, 1921-26, where she sponsored bills on children's health care, mothers' **pensions**, and **married women's property** rights. McClung was an early advocate of **birth control**, a **temperance** leader, and one of the litigants in the **Persons** case. She was also a best-selling novelist and with other members of the Canadian Women's Press Club formed the Political Equality League in 1912 to work for **woman suffrage**.

MCCORVEY, NORMA (1947-). The anonymous plaintiff in *Roe v. Wade*, which established the precedent of legal **abortion** in the United States in 1973. For many years McCorvey was active in the **pro-choice movement** and was employed as the marketing director of a Texas abortion clinic. In 1995 she announced her support of the **pro-life** position and founded the "Roe No More Ministry" to promote a Christian antiabortion message. McCorvey, an uneducated drug and alcohol abuser at the time of her famous lawsuit, charged pro-choice activists with **classism** in their treatment of her. She revealed that she never had an abortion and also lied about being **raped**. She had given birth to the child of her boyfriend. She was angered when she learned that her lawyer had once had an illegal abortion and could presumably have helped her to do the same had she not been seeking a person to challenge a legal principle.

MCGEE CASE. A 1973 ruling by the Irish Supreme Court that established the right of women to import **contraceptives** for personal use under a constitutional right to marital privacy. The case grew out of the Contraceptive Train action by members of the **Irish Women's Liberation** Movement who traveled to Belfast in 1971, bought condoms and other contraceptives, and returned to Dublin where customs officials let them pass even though these were illegal imports. Mary McGee, a mother of four with a heart condition, had ordered a contraceptive jelly from England some years earlier upon her doctor's advice only to have it confiscated. She filed a lawsuit in 1972. Despite her victory in 1973, the Irish Parliament only passed **family planning** legislation in 1979 under pressure from the Contraceptive Action Programme, a large group coalition effort for the general legalization of contraception.

MCSALLY, MARTHA (1966-). A US Air Force pilot who challenged the requirement that she and other US servicewomen wear the full-body Islamic *abaya* while off-base when stationed in Saudi Arabia. She noted that the State Department had no similar requirement for their female employees, and servicemen were prohibited from adopting local dress. Feminists rallied around her suit charging **sex discrimination**

and violation of her religious rights by forcing her to adopt the practices of another religion. The Department of Defense, under a legislative order from Congress, rescinded the veiling rule. Servicewomen in Saudi Arabia still may not drive, sit in the front seat, or leave the base without a male escort.

MEAD, MARGARET (1901-1978). The best-known American anthropologist of the 20th century. Mead aimed most of her publications, including a monthly column in the women's magazine *Redbook*, at a general readership. Mead is best known for her work on personality and culture, based on fieldwork in Samoa, New Guinea, and Bali. Mead championed women, especially encouraging mature women to return to college and prepare for professional careers. She was particularly interested in the interaction of women with their children, a topic generally ignored by male fieldworkers. Mead saw herself not as a feminist but as an advocate for the general liberalization of American society. She endorsed the **Equal Rights Amendment** in the 1940s, at the request of **Alice Paul**, and in 1965 she edited a commercial version of the report of the **President's Commission on the Status of Women**. She viewed feminism, however, as "antimale" and did not formally join the movement.

MEDIA IMAGES OF WOMEN. *See* ADVERTISING, IMAGE OF FEMINISTS IN; TELEVISION, IMAGE OF WOMEN IN.

MEDIA STARS. *See* TRASHING.

MEDICALIZATION OF CHILDBIRTH. A feminist critique of how the birthing process has been removed from women, both physically and emotionally, since the advent of modern medicine and hospital births. Specific objections involve the definition of pregnancy as abnormal, the overuse of technology and drugs, and the use of overt professional power to exert control over women's birthing decisions. *See also* ALTERNATIVE BIRTH MOVEMENT.

MEDICALIZATION OF MENOPAUSE. A feminist critique of how menopausal women's bodies have been and are being used for medical experimentation. It rejects the view that menopause and its related symptoms are abnormal and thus require rigorous drug and other treatment. Feminist studies have revealed a range of medical responses from denial that women's symptoms exist to excessive treatment with bone scans, **estrogen replacement therapy**, and other drugs such as antidepressants.

MEDICALIZATION OF WOMEN'S BODIES. A feminist critique of the ways in which women's bodies have been used historically and presently for medical experimentation. Included are explorations of the **misogynist** contributions of **Sigmund Freud** and certain medical diagnoses and procedures such as schizophrenia, hysteria, depression, **breast cancer**, birthing, uterine cancer, **contraception**, infertility treatments, and menopausal treatments. *See also* WOMEN'S HEALTH MOVEMENT.

MEIR, GOLDA (1898-1978). The prime minister of Israel, 1969-1974, and a female **role model** despite her militaristic stances against the Arab nations and her sometimes hostile remarks ("Women's liberation is just a lot of foolishness"). Her photograph was featured on a feminist poster in the 1970s with the caption, "But can she type?" Because she never explicitly supported women's rights, she is dismissed as a **token woman** by Israeli feminists. Operating within a man's world, she chose to ignore her sex and her chance to advance the status of women in Israeli society and politics.

MENCHU, RIGOBERTA (1959-). A Quiché Mayan political activist from Guatemala and recipient of the 1992 Nobel Peace Prize. She was active in the women's movement while still a teenager. Propelled into a position of human rights and indigenous leadership, including a prominent role in the Committee of Peasant Unity (Comité de Unidad Campesina) in the early 1980s by the murder of her parents and brother, she became a leading spokesperson for Guatemalan Indians. Her outspoken criticism of government policies and vivid accounts of the Indians' plight in the country's civil war prompted her exile in 1981. Life abroad led to publication of her memoir *I Rigoberta Menchu* (1984) and the international recognition of her feminist, indigenist, and Christian critique of social injustice. She remains a leading proponent of rights for women, native peoples, and peasants. In 1999 she addressed the International Confederation of Free Trade Unions' World Women's Conference in Brazil, calling for women to oppose globalization while fighting for peace and democracy.

MEN'S LEAGUE FOR WOMEN'S SUFFRAGE (MLWS). An English group of prominent men, founded by Herbert Jacobs in 1907. As voters, the members ran as and endorsed parliamentary candidates. Lawyers defended **suffragettes;** writers and academics published supportive books, pamphlets, and newspapers. Its moderate tactics allied it most closely with the **Women's Freedom League.**

MEN'S MOVEMENTS. A term encompassing a variety of responses to the feminist movement, ranging from support for **gender** equality and changing men's roles to the "men's rights," "**fathers' rights,**" and New Age **masculist** movements that are in direct opposition to the feminist movement and seek to regain men's power and entitlement. In the 1970s the **National Organization for Women** sponsored **consciousness-raising** groups for feminist men who believed that the male role imposed costs on men and on male-female relationships and contributed to **rape** and **domestic violence. Warren Farrell** and Marc Feigen Fasteau (*The Male Machine*, 1974) were prominent spokespersons for this movement. The spiritualist/cultural movement associated with Robert Bly encourages men to get in touch with the "wild man within." This separatist movement arose in reaction to the prominence of sensitive men in the entertainment industry like Alan Alda and Phil Donohue and the fear that men have lost their identities in a female-dominated world. The **backlash** men's rights movement originated in changes in domestic relations law involving **marital property,** child custody, and **child support enforcement** that were perceived as denying equal rights to men and fathers. More recent issues have involved complaints concerning **reverse discrimination** in **employment** and false charges of **sexual harassment,** child abuse, and incest. *See also* MILLION MAN MARCH; MONTRÉAL MASSACRE; NATIONAL ORGANIZATION FOR MEN AGAINST SEXISM; PROMISE KEEPERS; UK MEN'S MOVEMENT.

MEN'S POLITICAL UNION FOR WOMEN'S ENFRANCHISEMENT (MPU). The most militant and violent of the Englishmen's suffrage groups, founded in 1910 by dissatisfied members of the **Men's League for Women's Suffrage.** The MPU was initially allied with the **Women's Social and Political Union (WSPU),** although after 1912 the WSPU stopped working with men out of fear that male violence was hurting their cause.

THE DICTIONARY • 213

MEN'S RIGHTS MOVEMENT. *See* FATHERS' RIGHTS MOVEMENT.

MEN'S STUDIES. An area of teaching and research coordinated by the American Men's Studies Association (AMSA), an academic component of the National Organization for Men (NOM), a group that later renamed itself the National Organization for Changing Men (NOCM) and finally the **National Organization for Men Against Sexism (NOMAS)**. Its Men's Studies Task Group (MSTG) has organized conferences, instituted a newsletter and journal, *Men's Studies*, and supported antisexist political agendas. Men's studies classes have been taught at a handful of colleges since the mid-1970s, and some universities and colleges currently offer programs with undergraduate certificates in men's studies. Typical issues in men's studies courses are the need to evaluate the impact of dominant forms of masculinity on society and to articulate alternative nondominating masculinities. In general, the field is supportive of both feminism and **women's studies**.

MENSTRUAL CYCLES AND BEHAVIOR. The research linkages between the menstrual cycle and behaviors such as violence, suicide, admission to psychiatric hospitals, accidents, and eating patterns. Even though much of this research contains methodological flaws, it has given rise to well-known **sexist** stereotypes and has led women to believe that they are impaired each month. These findings have also given rise to the argument that women are not reliable and should not hold responsible positions in business and government. *See also* PREMENSTRUAL SYNDROME.

MENSTRUAL EXTRACTION. *See* DEL-EM.

MENSTRUATION AND CULTURAL ASPECTS. A topic of interest to feminists because of the negative connotations of menstruation and menopause in Western societies. Western cultural tradition has considered menstruation a "curse" linked, after the establishment of Christianity, to **Eve's sin**. **Premenstrual syndrome** has been considered evidence of the debilitating effect of this female "handicap." Other cultural traditions see menstruation as a boon to women that regularly cleanses their bodies. The "hag" or crone image of the menopausal woman in Western culture is foreign to many societies who respect such women. Anthropologists have found that the supposed physical symptoms of menopause (hot flashes, depression) are not recognized in many societies, and, in fact, only a minority of Western women report the symptoms. Since the emergence of the **new feminist movement**, there is an unprecedented openness about menstruation in books, advertising, and entertainment programs. Women writers and artists have embraced it as a uniquely female and creative experience, a symbol of women's productivity and renewal.

MENTAL ILLNESS AND GENDER. A feminist critique of the linkage of women with a higher incidence of psychological problems. Definitions of what constitutes "normal" female behavior have been used to label, punish, and control women. Aspects of women's bodies, such as **menstrual cycles**, and women's efforts to adapt to traditional cultural roles have been viewed as factors in the development of mental illness. Feminism has been accused of making women unwell because it encourages them to assume male roles. **Feminist therapy** developed as a response to **Sigmund Freud's gender**-based explanations of mental illness. *Women and Madness* (1972) by Phyllis Chesler is a feminist classic on this topic.

MENTORING. A developmental relationship between senior mentors and junior protégés. The relationship may be informally developed or formally assigned. Mentors are usually senior, higher-ranking organizational members with advanced experience and knowledge who take an active interest in the career and well-being of the protégé, who is usually younger and at an earlier career stage. The establishment of such a relationship is related to the protégés' mobility, career satisfaction, and compensation and to the mentors' sense of life satisfaction and fulfillment. Feminists have been concerned that women are less involved in mentoring relationships than men because men in organizations are less likely to mentor women and women are excluded from informal workplace **networks**. Special mentoring programs for women have been developed and high-ranking women have been encouraged to participate in these programs.

MIDWIFERY. The practice of a person, usually a woman, trained to assist women through pregnancy, childbirth, and the postpartum period and to provide care of the newborn infant as well as general care for all women. Historically, women have had **home births**, with a midwife in attendance. In industrialized nations outside the United States, certified nurse-midwives continue to manage most normal deliveries in hospitals. US feminists have strongly supported the greater reliance on midwives and view access to midwifery care as a **reproductive freedom** issue. *See also* ALTERNATIVE BIRTH MOVEMENT; MEDICALIZATION OF CHILDBIRTH.

MIFEPRISTONE. *See* RU 486.

MILL, HARRIET HARDY TAYLOR (1807-1858). An English feminist, libertarian philosopher, and author of "The Enfranchisement of Women," an article published in 1851 in the *Westminster Review*. As the wife of **John Stuart Mill**, she influenced him to write his classic feminist treatise, *The Subjection of Women* (1869), in accordance with her own views on the subject, and she very likely co-authored *On Liberty* (1859). Her 1832 essay on marriage and **divorce** calls for equal access of women to education and employment while married and states that divorce should be available with no grounds required (i.e., "**no-fault divorce**").

MILL, JOHN STUART (1806-1873). An English philosopher, best known among feminists for his *The Subjection of Women* (1869), generally considered to be a classic example of the individualist school in 19th century feminist thought. Mill was concerned with the legal barriers to women's equality, arguing that female subordination was a type of slavery imposed on the weaker by the stronger. He goes on, like **Mary Wollstonecraft**, to claim that we cannot know the true nature of women because they have been corrupted and further weakened by an inferior system of education. Mill wanted women to enter marriage as equal partners and to have the right to earn their own support after marriage. As a member of Parliament, 1865-1869, Mill spoke for **woman suffrage**, presented a petition, and introduced a suffrage amendment in 1867.

MILLETT, KATE (1934-). A US feminist sculptor, activist, and author, best known for *Sexual Politics* (1970), an early text in the contemporary **radical feminist** movement and in **feminist literary criticism**. Millett argued that all sex is political because male-female relationships are rooted in power sited in a caste system. Millett based a number of arguments on a literary critique of male authors like D. H. Lawrence and Henry Miller, but she finally recommended the elimination of **gen-**

der as the only means of improving women's condition in the **patriarchy**. Many of Millett's publications after *Sexual Politics* were out-of-print until the University of Illinois Press began to reissue them in 2000. Millett founded the Women's Art Colony Farm that supports itself through the sale of Christmas trees. She has also survived the suicide of her lover and residence in mental institutions, as related in her *Sita* (1977) and *The Loony-Bin Trap* (1990).

MILLION MAN MARCH. A 1995 Washington D.C. event organized by Nation of Islam leader Louis Farrakhan for black male atonement to black women for failure to be strong **patriarchal** figures in the family. Although women were not invited to the rally and most **African American feminists** attacked the gathering, a few notable black women such as Betty Shabazz, the widow of Malcolm X, and **Maya Angelou** spoke. A Million Woman March was held in Philadelphia in 1997 for black women; the demonstration matched the crowds of the 1995 march, but not the personal impact on participants.

MINISTÈRE DES DROITS DE LA FEMME. The French ministry of women's rights, created in 1981 by President François Mitterrand to help eliminate discrimination against women and broaden support for women's rights. **Yvette Roudy**, the first minister of women's rights, 1981-1986, became a full minister with cabinet status in 1985, making France the first modern nation to create a large-scale executive agency dealing with women's rights.

MINNEAPOLIS PORNOGRAPHY ORDINANCE. An ordinance written by **Andrea Dworkin** and **Catharine MacKinnon** and twice vetoed by the mayor after passage by the Minneapolis city council in 1983. It would have allowed women, harmed by **pornography**, to sue the makers and distributors for **sex discrimination**. It was adopted in 1984 in Indianapolis and overturned by a federal court as an unconstitutional abridgement of free speech. The ordinance defined pornography as the "sexually explicit subordination of women, graphically depicted in words or pictures" that debased women. Among the contexts specified were women "enjoying" pain, **rape**, or humiliation; serving as **sex objects** for domination, conquest, exploitation, and possession; or appearing in positions of servility or submission or display. The ordinance was criticized by some feminists; others suggested that legislatures prohibit sexually explicit visual portrayals of force or violence that lack redeeming literary, artistic, political, or scientific value.

MINOR V. HAPPERSETT, 88 US (21 WALL.) 627 (1875). A decision of the US Supreme Court that concluded that the **Fourteenth Amendment** to the Constitution did not enfranchise women. The suit involved a woman who had unsuccessfully attempted to register to vote in Missouri, which restricted the suffrage to men. The Court ruled that suffrage was not a right of national citizenship protected by the **Fourteenth Amendment**. Nor did that amendment add the right of suffrage to the privileges and immunities of citizenship. Since the Constitution did not confer the right of suffrage upon anyone, the constitutions and laws of the various states which reserved the right of suffrage to men alone were not void.

MINORITY WOMEN. See COLOR, WOMEN OF.

MISOGYNY. A term meaning, literally, hatred of women. Feminists have argued that social institutions such as **patriarchal** religions, educational systems, governments, and legal and medical practices are all constructed on misogynistic principles of exclusion and demonization of women. Misogyny takes various forms—physical (such as **female genital mutilation** (in Africa), **burqas** (in Afghanistan and the Middle East), scapegoating (such as blaming women for rising cases of **domestic violence** in which they themselves are the victims), demonization (rabid fear of women who meddle in political affairs), ostracism, discrimination, and silencing. **Feminist literary critic Kate Millet** perceived misogyny as at the root of the literary works of D. H. Lawrence, Norman Mailer, Henry Miller, and Jean Genet. Millett observed: "however muted its present appearance may be, sexual dominion obtains nevertheless as perhaps the most pervasive ideology of our culture and provides its most fundamental concepts of power" (*Sexual Politics* [1970], 25).

MISS AMERICA PAGEANT PROTEST. A demonstration staged in 1968 against the annual **beauty pageant** in Atlantic City to dramatize the impact of male-imposed standards of personal appearance upon women. Organized by **New York Radical Women**, the action involved around 200 women who crowned a live sheep Miss America and tossed symbols of women's status as **sex objects** into a trash can. Although the items—brassieres, high-heeled shoes, fashion magazines, hair curlers—were never ignited, the press reported a fire, and feminists thereafter were termed "bra-burners."

MISS WORLD PROTEST. A **women's liberation movement** action held at the international **beauty pageant** in London in 1970. With the contestants on stage with US entertainer Bob Hope, a group of ill-groomed women entered blowing whistles, mooing like cows, and waving signs stating "Miss-conception" or "Miss-judged." Their smokebombs and stinkbombs forced all to flee the stage and resulted in the arrest of five demonstrators and widespread media attention to the new movement.

MITCHELL, JULIET (1940-). A prominent contemporary British feminist, best known as the author of *Woman's Estate* (1971), *Psychoanalysis and Feminism* (1974), and *Women, the Longest Revolution: Essays on Feminism, Literature and Psychoanalysis* (1984). Her *Mad Men and Medusas: Reclaiming Hysteria* was published in 2000. Mitchell's first book argues that women's condition has been "overdetermined" by the structures of production, the socialization of children, and the realities of **reproduction** and **female sexuality**. Before women can improve their condition they must radically reform all three areas of their lives. In shaping such a theory, she seeks to combine the perspectives of **Marxist, liberal,** and **radical feminists**. In her later books Mitchell argues that women must finally radically reshape their interior lives, their psyches, before they can be fully free from **patriarchal** thought patterns.

MOMMY TRACK. A controversial term that refers to the differential treatment and tracking of women with children in organizations. The term did not appear in, but grew out of, a 1989 article by Felice N. Schwartz in *Harvard Business Review*. The practice can result in positive outcomes, such as providing women with the option of taking low-pressure positions while raising a family. However, it can also lead to women being relegated against their will to positions with low power, authority, and responsibility. *See also* EMPLOYMENT, SEX DISCRIMINATION IN; FLEXITIME; HOUSEWIFE FEMINISM.

MONTAGU, LADY MARY WORTLEY (1689-1762). A prominent English letter writer and poet in an age when learned women were treated with ridicule and contempt. Her almost 900 letters present a vivid picture of a number of issues that concerned upper-class women in the 18th century: the importance of gaining an education, access to medical care, and the **sexual politics** of love and marriage.

MONTRÉAL MASSACRE. The murder of 14 women at the École Polytechnique of Montréal University in 1989 by an armed man shouting "you're all fucking feminists." Since 1991 profeminist Canadian men have annually marked the anniversary of these shootings by pinning **white ribbons** to their lapels as a symbol of their opposition to male **violence against women**. The White Ribbon Campaign (WRC) has spread to the United States, Europe, and Japan and now involves continuous educational work in schools. In the early years the WRC was criticized by Canadian feminists for waging an expensive annual male-controlled direct-mail campaign to distribute 1.5 million ribbons. The white ribbon has been adopted as a global symbol and is now worn from November 25 to December 6 and on **International Day Against Violence Toward Women**. *See also* FEMICIDE.

MORAL MAJORITY (MM). A conservative political organization cofounded by US Baptist minister Jerry Falwell in 1979 to combat the decline of public morality. The group was strongly **antifeminist** in its opposition to **abortion** and the **Equal Rights Amendment** and had close ties to **Concerned Women for America**. The group disbanded in 1989, but not before registering millions of new voters. The MM had a broad agenda and faltered as its members left for single-issue abortion or **pro-family** groups that used MM's own direct-mail tactics to further drain money and members.

MORAL REFORM FEMINISM. A tradition based on religious beliefs in social justice, world peace, and nonviolence. Nineteenth-century US feminists within this tradition fought urban vice and slavery and participated in the **settlement house** and **temperance movements**. The movement believed that women were sexually and morally pure and that men should be sexually restrained. Contemporary feminist critiques of **violence against women, sexual harassment, international traffic in women,** and **sweatshops** also stem from this tradition.

MORGAN, ROBIN (1941-). A **radical feminist** author, editor, and poet. Morgan was a founding member of **New York Radical Women,**

Women Against Pornography, and **Women's International Terrorist Conspiracy from Hell (WITCH)**, and a long-time contributing editor and editor of *Ms*. She is also the founder of the **Sisterhood Is Global Institute**. Her best-known works include *Sisterhood Is Powerful* (1970), an anthology of **new feminist** writings, *Going Too Far* (1977), a collection of her essays, including the influential "Goodbye to All That," *Sisterhood Is Global* (1984), one of the earliest attempts to document the **international women's movement**, and *Sisterhood Is Forever* (2003). Morgan is also noted for her evolution from "**politico**" to **cultural feminist** and for her role in the **Miss America Pageant protest** and in shaping Jane Alpert's "**Mother Right**." Her *Saturday's Child: A Memoir* (2000) recounts her experience as one of radio's Quiz-Kids.

MORNING-AFTER PILL. A prescription drug used to prevent conception after **rape**, **contraceptive** failure, or unprotected intercourse. This concentrated dose of **birth control** hormones is highly effective if taken within five days after intercourse. The drug is safer than over-the-counter painkillers, but only 68 percent of US women are aware of it, and doctors and druggists may refuse to prescribe or dispense it. In 2002 the **Feminist Majority Foundation** sponsored an action to collect petitions to make emergency contraception (EC) available nationally without a prescription, as it is in five US states and more than a dozen other nations. EC is sometimes confused with **RU 486**, which can cause an **abortion** up to 12 weeeks after conception and has been opposed by the **pro-life movement**.

MORRISON, TONI (1931-). A contemporary African American novelist, recipient of the 1993 Nobel Prize for Literature, and theorist, best known as the author of a series of novels about African American women: *The Bluest Eye* (1970), *Sula* (1973), *Song of Solomon* (1977), *Tar Baby* (1981), *Beloved* (1987), *Jazz* (1992), and *Paradise* (1998). The first two novels stress the destructive effects that dysfunctional families have on forming a young woman's self-identity and **self-esteem**. The third novel also concerns the maturation process, but in this book Morrison sketches its development over four generations of one family. The more recent novels stress the influence that the heritage of slavery has had on African American families and their self-definition. Morrison has also published theoretical works that attempt to understand the role that African Americans have played in mainstream American culture: *Playing in the Dark: Whiteness and the Literary Imagination* (1992) and *Race-ing Justice: En-gendering Power: Essays on Anita Hill, Clarence Thomas, and the Construction of Social Reality* (1992). Morrison has rejected the idea that *Paradise* is a feminist novel, but notes that she personally has always merged "black" and "feminist" in forming her identity and that *Sula* is written about female friendships.

MOSCOW CENTER FOR GENDER STUDIES (MCGS). Russia's first feminist research center, established in 1990. It promotes **women's studies**, lobbies for **gender** equality within government and the media, and helps to coordinate the independent Russian feminist movement. It has an active publications program and sponsors workshops, conferences, and seminars.

MOTHER EARTH. The belief that earth is an ecosystem and gives life. It is sometimes argued that many cultures, such as American Indians, have adopted this notion as is exemplified in their worship of Mother Earth and the accompanying belief in harmony, egalitarian relationships, reverence for life, and pervasive spirituality. It also has been used as a metaphor for the **goddess** by some feminist theologians to replace or supplant the white male in most Western **patriarchal** religions. The metaphor has given many women hope and a deeper sense of their spirituality and connectedness to earth and to others. But anthropologists argue that the Mother Earth imagery is either fiction by Euro-American writers or a reference to a female generative principle poorly understood by European observers. The concept of Mother Earth is actually Classical European. *See also* ECOFEMINISM.

"MOTHER RIGHT." An early **cultural feminist** essay written in 1973 by Weather Underground fugitive Jane Alpert in which she uses women's **reproductive** capacity to explain **gender** differences. She argues that biology is the basis of women's powers and that all women are united by maternal and pacific qualities which **empower**, not disadvantage. *See also* MATERNAL THINKING.

MOTHERHOOD ENVY/WOMB ENVY. The envy by males of activities unique in motherhood (e.g., pregnancy, childbirth, and nursing). **Karen Horney** countered **Sigmund Freud's** notion of "**penis envy**" with this possible analogue in males.

MOTHERS' MOVEMENTS. A term encompassing movements that are based in the authority of women's traditional role as wife and mother. The formation of these groups is often sparked by issues of war, human rights, or restoring democracy to a nation. Initially these groups are "feminine" and not "feminist," but many have come to identify with the feminist movement as the conditions driving their origins improve and participants experience oppression as women within their marriages and in contact with government authorities. *See also* COMMITTEE OF SOLDIERS' MOTHERS OF RUSSIA; MOTHERS OF THE PLAZA DE MAYO; MOVEMENT OF SHANTYTOWN WOMEN; MUTUAL SUPPORT GROUP FOR THE APPEARANCE, ALIVE, OF OUR CHILDREN, SPOUSES, PARENTS, AND BROTHERS AND SISTERS; WOMEN IN BLACK.

MOTHERS OF THE PLAZA DE MAYO/MADRES DE LA PLAZA DE MAYO. An Argentine human rights organization established in 1976 by middle-class women to protest the murder and disappearance of family members in political violence that became known as the "Dirty War." Although not the first political organization of mothers in Latin America, it is largely responsible for defining the **mothers' movement** in the region. The group held its first weekly public assembly at the Plaza de Mayo, site of the Government House and the national monument to Argentine independence, in Buenos Aires on April 30, 1977. These mothers established the recognized ritual forms of women's protest: public marches, the wearing of white head scarves on which are written the names of disappeared family members, and posters bearing the names and photographs of missing or dead husbands and children. The mothers numbered only 14 in 1977, but by 1983 they had grown into one of the largest and most vigorous popular movements in Latin America. This group significantly contributed to the fall of the Argentine military government in 1983. The group, now the Mothers and Grandmothers of the Plaza de Mayo, continue to demonstrate every Thursday at the Plaza.

MOTT, LUCRETIA (1793-1880). An American Quaker who founded the first Female AntiSlavery Society in Philadelphia in 1833. Denied her seat as a delegate to the 1840 **London World Antislavery Convention,** she concluded with her fellow delegate, **Elizabeth Cady Stanton,** that the "woman question" required political action. The two women, together with Martha Wright (Mott's sister), Mary Ann McClintock, and Jane Hunt organized the 1848 Women's Rights Convention at **Seneca Falls**. Because of the Quaker boycott of electoral politics, Mott initially opposed **woman suffrage**, but later became active and spent her last two years working on the merger that led to the **National American Woman Suffrage Association**.

MOUVEMENT DÉMOCRATIQUE FÉMININ (MDF). A group of women's rights activists, including **Yvette Roudy**, that was established in 1961 as a women's political club associated with the noncommunist left. MDF members played a key role in the development of French feminism in both the pre1968 **women's rights** and post-1968 **women's liberation movements**. The group remained small and Paris based, but were successful in using their contacts within political parties and government to achieve their legal reforms. When François Mitterand formed his new Socialist Party in 1971, many MDF members joined, and the group lost momentum.

MOUVEMENT FRANÇAIS POUR LE PLANNING FAMILIAL (MFPF). The French branch of **Planned Parenthood**, founded in 1956. The movement rapidly expanded nationwide in membership and clinics. Although it opposed a 1920 law prohibiting the availability of contraceptive information and devices, the group long denied any conflict with Catholic teaching on that topic. The Neuwirth law of 1967 authorized the sale of contraceptives. In 1968 less than 4 percent of French women of childbearing age used **birth control pills**, but by 1995 the use of contraceptives had climbed to 67 percent. The MFPF identifies as a feminist organization and currently works to improve sex education, parent-child communication about sex, and teen awareness of **contraception**.

MOUVEMENT POUR LA LIBÉRATION DES FEMMES (MLF). The generic media-created name for the **new feminist movement** in France. In 1979 **Psych et Po** registered MLF as their trademark for operating a chain of **feminist bookstores**, magazines, and a publishing house (all called *des femmes*). The resulting lawsuits over the use of the MLF name, initials, and logo ended the MLF as a national movement.

MOVEMENT FOR THE EMANCIPATION OF CHILEAN WOMEN/MOVIMIENTO PRO EMANCIPACIÓN DE LA

MUJER CHILENA (MEMCH). A broad coalition for women's rights, formed in 1935 as a **woman suffrage** organization and active until the vote was won in 1949. In 1983 the group was revived as a feminist organization; this link with the earlier Chilean movement served to refute charges that feminism is a foreign ideology. MEMCH-83 initially served to bring together antigovernment women's groups that sought a return to democracy with women's equality ("Democracy in the country and in the home"). Currently it is a leftist movement of lower-class women that coordinates women's social groups and organizes support for UN charters on women.

MOVEMENT OF SHANTYTOWN WOMEN/MOVIMIENTO DE MUJERES POBLADORAS (MOMUPO). A Chilean group formed in 1980 to mobilize working-class women in the slums outside Santiago. MOMUPO members engaged in the March of Empty Pots from their homes and then organized the Marches of the Empty Shopping Bags at local farmers' markets where women protested high prices and shortages and announced their boycott of goods to protest the dictatorship. The group at first rejected the feminist label but now brings in middle-class feminists for workshops on human rights, sexuality, and **domestic violence**. The MOMUPO, however, remains a **mothers' movement** that is less interested in women's access to the labor force and professions.

MOVIMENTO DI LA LIBERAZIONE DELLA DONNA (MLD)/ WOMAN'S LIBERATION MOVEMENT. A loose network of Roman feminist **collectives**, formed in 1970 and leader of the referendum drive in 1971 to repeal the **abortion** law and to defeat the anti**divorce** referendum in 1974. In 1976 it founded the **women's center** in Rome, the **Casa della Donna.** The MLD has been associated with the Radical Party, the Socialist Party, and the workers' movement in Italy, but withdrew from all party alliances in 1978.

MOVIMIENTO DEMOCRÁTICO DE MUJERES (MDM)/ WOMEN'S DEMOCRATIC MOVEMENT. A Spanish group organized in 1965 by communist and Catalan socialist women. The MDM had feminist goals, but only became openly feminist in 1974 when it changed its name to the Movimiento para la Liberación de la Mujer (Women's Liberation Movement).

MOZZONI, ANNA MARIA (1837-1920). An author and the most important early **liberal feminist** in Italy. She came to prominance with her *La Donna e i suoi rapporti sociali* (*Woman and Her Social Relationships*, 1864), which urged middle-class women to look beyond the home. A frequent contributor to *La Donna*, a feminist newspaper published 1868-88, Mozzoni supported **divorce** and **woman suffrage**. In 1881 she founded the League for the Promotion of the Interests of Women, a forerunner of the **Italian Women's Union**.

MS. The established term of address when a woman's marital status is unknown, dating from (at a minimum) the 18th century. A combination of the courtesy titles "Miss" and "Mrs.," "Ms." has been popularized by feminists who argue that women should be recognized as individuals rather than being identified by their relationship with a man. **Antifeminists** have ridiculed and resisted the term as a challenge to the **patriarchy**. This response may be realistic in light of studies that show women who adopt that title are perceived like a man in terms of leadership and greater competence. *See also* NAMING CONVENTIONS.

MS. A glossy popular monthly periodical founded in 1972 by a group of New York women, including **Gloria Steinem**, to accurately cover the **new feminist movement**. In 1980 it became a nonprofit publication, and in 1990 it became a bimonthly without advertisements. *Ms.* underwent several changes of ownership and two breaks in publication, 1987-1998. In 1999 a group of women investors, including Steinem, purchased the magazine, and in 2001 they transferred ownership to the **Feminist Majority Foundation**. From a peak circulation of 500,000 in 1976, the magazine's subscription and newsstand sales have fallen to 110,000. Nonprofit advertising is accepted in this now-quarterly publication.

MS. FOUNDATION FOR WOMEN. A US organization founded in 1972 by **Gloria Steinem** and other editors of *Ms.* to distribute the expected profits from the magazine to the women's movement. Although co-founder Marlo Thomas gave profits from *Free To Be . . . You and Me*, the foundation has had to raise funds for the grants that it gives to local and national women's groups as seed money for innovative programs. The Ms. Foundation is the nation's only national, multi-issue public women's fund and has won an award as one of the best 100 charities in the United States. It originated and continues to coordinate the annual **Take Our Daughters to Work Day.**

MUD MARCH. The first major outdoor rally for English **woman suffrage**, held in London on February 9, 1907. It was sponsored by the **National Union of Women's Suffrage Societies** and attracted over 40 women's groups and 3,000 individuals, who marched in a pouring rain. This assembly of respectable (and some titled) women provided the model for other large suffrage processions.

MULLER, MARY (1820-1902). A New Zealand feminist and leader of the women's movement. Because of her husband's disapproval, Muller advocated in secret for women as "Femina" in articles that were reprinted nationally. In 1869 her *An Appeal to the Men of New Zealand* attracted the attention of **John Stuart Mill.** She felt validated when New Zealand became the first nation to adopt **woman suffrage** in 1893.

MULTICULTURALISM. Another manifestation of the "culture wars" and the attempt to displace the emphasis on the "**dead white European male**" from the center of the university curriculum. Just as the works of women have been ignored or denigrated as not speaking to the "universal" human condition, so have works by Hispanic, Asian, Native American, and African Americans. These four recognized ethnic groups have entered the college and university curriculum through the study of their literary works, as well as their histories in the United States. In addition to the academic study of multicultural writers, feminists have embraced the writings of multicultural women in an attempt to redefine feminism as a movement that extends beyond white, middle-class, professional women. Multicultural feminists include **bell hooks, Audre Lorde,** Gloria Anzaldúa, and Trinh T. Minh-ha.

MURARO, ROSE MARIE. A Brazilian leftist author among the first to speak of **women's liberation** in her best-selling books such as *A mulher na construção do mundo futuro* (*Women in the Building of a Future World*, 1967) and *Libertação sexual da mulher* (*Women's Sexual Liberation*, 1971). As director of a publishing house, she invited **Betty Friedan** to Rio de Janeiro in 1971 to mark the publication of the Brazilian edition of *The Feminist Mystique* even though Muraro viewed Friedan as part of a system-supporting bourgeois movement against men. In 1986 she unsuccessfully ran for the Constituent Assembly as an avowed feminist.

MURRAY, PAULI (1910-1985). An African American lawyer who was active in the **civil rights movement** for women and blacks. She was a member of the **President's Commission on the Status of Women**, one of the founders of the **National Organization for Women**, and the first black woman ordained in the Episcopal Church in 1977. She is credited with working behind the scenes to retain **sex discrimination** in **Title VII** of the **Civil Rights Act of 1964**. Her *Autobiography of a Black Activist, Feminist, Lawyer, Priest, and Poet* (1987) recounts her multifaceted life.

MUTTIPOLITIK (MOMMY POLITICS). An East German feminist critique of public policy that, according to feminists in the former West Germany, addressed only one role of women, that of motherhood, and thus reinforced traditional **gender roles**, limited women's professional options, and maintained gender inequity. This internal conflict with unification reflected East German women's strong identification with the pronatalist policies of their former country and a feeling that West German feminists were arrogant and authoritarian.

MUTUAL SUPPORT GROUP FOR THE APPEARANCE, ALIVE, OF OUR CHILDREN, SPOUSES, PARENTS, AND BROTHERS AND SISTERS/GRUPO DE APOYO MUTUO (GAM). A Guatemalan human rights organization formed by women to protest abuses and state-sponsored terrorism. This group was established in June 1984 by about 25 women who met while searching Guatemala City morgues for disappeared and dead family members. Despite the brutal murder of two of its leaders in March 1985, its membership grew to about 1,000 by 1986. The GAM was the most prominent human rights organization in the country in the mid-1980s. Like that of similar groups in Latin America, the GAM's political activism emerged out of women's traditional family roles of nurture and protection and was sustained by feminist solidarity and mutual support. Since 1998 it has been affiliated with Pax Christi International.

"MYTH OF THE VAGINAL ORGASM." A feminist classic published by Anne Koedt in 1968. The essay challenges the linkage between **frigidity** and vaginal eroticism. According to Koedt, the center of **female**

sexuality (and orgasm) is the clitoris and the vaginal orgasm does not exist. Instead, women have been defined sexually in terms of the male orgasm that requires the friction of penetration. This critique became the center of feminist demands that women define their own sexuality and demand sexual techniques that pleasure them, whether obtained from a man, another woman, or themselves.

-N-

NA'AMAT/PIONEER WOMEN. The first **Jewish feminist** organization in Palestine. It was formed in 1921 as Moetzet Hapoalot (Women Workers Council) as a part of the Histadrut labor coalition. The new women settlers protested a movement where men worked the land and built the country, and women were relegated to the **domestic sphere**. Na'amat provided agricultural and vocational training for women and built a network of **day-care** centers, kindergartens, and children's village dormitories for the children of working mothers. It continues many of these projects in Israel, as well as immigrant settlement and **domestic violence** work. Na'amet has become an international movement, with chapters in 12 nations, and is the largest Jewish women's organization in the world. **Golda Meir** served as its general-secretary, 1927-1930.

NAIDU, SAROJINI (1879-1949). An Indian poet, nationalist politician, and feminist. In 1917 she began her long campaign for **woman suffrage** under British rule. During the 1920s a limited female franchise was adopted in some provinces and incrementally expanded later. Full woman suffrage was finally established in 1949 under the new constitution of an independent India. Naidu was the first woman governor of an Indian state, Uttar Pradesh, where she served, 1947-1949, until her death.

NAMING CONVENTIONS. The system for naming people that historically has meant that women use the name of a man, whether father or husband, as a last name. Feminists, in protest against this male-oriented system, have suggested that women: choose a surname that is not related to any male relative; retain their birthname, both before and after marriage; or, with marriage, create a new name or hyphenate the two partners' birthnames. Under common law, a person has the right to use any name she or he likes so long as there is no intent to defraud. Women have adopted their husbands' names as a matter of social custom and not because the law requires it. A second aspect to naming conventions concerns courtesy titles (i.e., Miss, **Ms.**, Mr., Mrs., etc.). Although "Ms." was introduced to parallel "Mr.," one survey showed few respondents understood the term, and many believed "Ms." should be used only for **divorced** or widowed women. *See also* LUCY STONE LEAGUE.

NANCY DREW. The heroine of a series of mysteries designed for **adolescent girls**, published 1930-1953. This girl detective is now recognized as a young feminist **role model** who is smart, strong, and independent in a man's job. Although author Carolyn Keene was a pseudonym for a variety of ghostwriters, the first and best was Mildred Wirt Benson, who created the spunky character. In the 1950s some of the earlier versions were rewritten to remove racially offensive language. Critics charge that Nancy also became more traditional. In the 1990s a new series, The Nancy Drew Files, introduced a sexually active main character.

NARAL PRO CHOICE AMERICA. A US single-issue **pro-choice** group formed in 1969 as the National Association for Repeal of Abortion Laws. After the legalization of **abortion** in 1973, the group became the National Abortion Rights Action League (NARAL) and added "and Reproductive" in 1994 to signal a broader focus. In 2003 it assumed its present name in order to place a greater emphasis on choice, rather than abortion, and to ensure the use of "pro-choice" in a news story in situations where editorial policy prevents its use by reporters to describe the movement. NARAL (no longer an acronym) has over 500,000 individual and organizational members, with affiliates in 26 states and Canada. The group has a well-staffed Washington, D.C. headquarters, a political action committee, and a foundation. President Kate Michelman emerged in the 1980s as the leading spokesperson for women's **reproductive freedom**.

NARIPOKKHO. A Bangladeshi feminist group that formed in 1983. It has become a leading organization against **acid attacks**, in working with sex workers, and on issues of health, **reproductive freedom, development**, and human rights. Naripokkho has an active research and publication program and also engages in lobbying and public education.

NASRIN, TASLIMA (1962-). A Bangladeshi physician and writer, forced into exile by Islamic fundamentalists for her feminist, secular views. She has lived in Europe since 1994, when a reward for her assassination was offered. Although the publication of her *Lajja* (Shame) caused the furor, her newspaper columns, beginning in 1989, on **domestic violence**, the education of girls, and the oppressiveness of the Islamic female dress code also offended clerics. Her decision to go into exile has been criticized by some **grass-roots feminists** in Bangladesh. In her own defense, Nasrin points to her scholarship fund for girls in grades 7 through 10 as evidence that she is still engaged in her home country.

NATIONAL ABORTION AND REPRODUCTIVE RIGHTS ACTION LEAGUE (NARAL). *See* NARAL PRO CHOICE AMERICA.

NATIONAL ABORTION CAMPAIGN (NAC). A group formed in Great Britain in 1975 to coordinate the **abortion** rights movement and to defend the 1967 Abortion Act. This nonhierarchical organization loosely links local groups, many of which are a part of trade unions. The NAC focuses on public education through demonstrations as well as lobbying Parliament. According to its critics, the NAC is pro-abortion rather than **pro-choice** in that it supports abortion on demand for any reason up to the time of birth without legal or medical restrictions.

NATIONAL ACTION COMMITTEE ON THE STATUS OF WOMEN (NAC). A coalition of over 700 Canadian women's groups, formed in 1972. Representing over five million women, the NAC is the nation's largest feminist lobby group and is notable for its inclusion of **women of color**, aboriginal women, and women with disabilities within its leadership. Despite its heavy reliance on the federal government as a source of operating funds, the NAC successfully opposed the proposed national constitution of 1992 on the grounds that it would weaken women's established rights. It prepares voters' guides and in 1997 published *The Shocking Pink Paper* about women's lives in Canada.

NATIONAL AMERICAN WOMAN SUFFRAGE ASSOCIATION (NAWSA). An organization formed in 1890 when the **National Woman Suffrage Association** and the **American Woman Suffrage Association** merged. The first three presidents were **Elizabeth Cady Stanton** (1890-1892), **Susan B. Anthony** (1892-1900), and **Carrie Chapman Catt** (1900-1904, and later 1915-1920). The NAWSA attracted over 200,000 members, and **woman suffrage** became a well-funded and prestigious cause. After suffrage was won in 1920, the NAWSA became the **League of Women Voters**.

NATIONAL ASSOCIATION OF COLORED WOMEN (NACW). The African American counterpart of the **General Federation of Women's Clubs**, formed in 1896 as a feminist, **suffragist**, and civil rights organization linking local black women's clubs. Under the leadership of its first president, **Mary Church Terrell**, a wealthy suffragist and **National Woman's Party** member, the NACW also supported the **Equal Rights Amendment**. With the formation of the **National Council of Negro Women** in 1935, the NACW declined in prominance but continues to represent over 1,000 local clubs that are engaged in community service projects. **Equal pay** and **child care** are top priorities.

NATIONAL ASSOCIATION OF COMMISSIONS FOR WOMEN (NACW). *See* STATE COMMISSIONS ON THE STATUS OF WOMEN (SCSW).

NATIONAL BLACK FEMINIST ORGANIZATION (NBFO). A group founded in 1973 to advance the rights of African American women within the feminist and civil rights movements and to confront **sexism** and racism through a single organization. Eleanor Holmes Norton and Margaret Sloan were among its founders and early leaders. Within a year of its formation, the NBFO had more than 2,000 members in 10 chapters but by 1975 the national structure had disbanded and only the local chapters continued to operate for at least four, and possibly, eight more years.

NATIONAL COMMISSION ON THE OBSERVANCE OF INTERNATIONAL WOMEN'S YEAR. A body established by US President Gerald Ford in 1975 to coordinate US participation in the **International Women's Year**. Congress extended the life of the commission to March 1978, and provided funding for meetings in every state and territory and for a National Women's Conference. At this conference, held in Houston, Texas, November 18-21, 1977, delegates adopted the National Plan of Action, a 26-plank program addressing major issues affecting women.

NATIONAL CONSUMERS LEAGUE (NCL). A **social feminist** group founded in 1899 to reform the workplace for women in industrial America. Under the leadership of Florence Kelley, the league argued for child labor laws and **protective labor laws** before legislatures and the courts. The group supported **woman suffrage** in order to enfranchise a more humanistic, reform-oriented constituency but strongly opposed the **Equal Rights Amendment**. Although the organization still exists, it has not been active on women's rights issues since the 1930s.

NATIONAL COUNCIL OF NEGRO WOMEN (NCNW). An African American coalition organization, founded by Mary McLeod Bethune in 1935 to advance racial equality and the particular interests of black women. As a part of the **Women's Bureau Coalition**, the NCNW long opposed the **Equal Rights Amendment** but worked on many other women's issues: appointments of black women to federal office, **equal pay**, equal employment opportunity, and **sterilization abuse**. Since 1986 the NCNW has sponsored Black Family Reunions to counteract negative images and has also become active in Africa through its five partner organizations there. The NCNW provides outreach to 4 million women through its 38 US affiliated organizations and over 250 local sections.

NATIONAL COUNCIL OF WOMEN OF CANADA. A women's rights organization formed in 1893 by Lady Aberdeen, the wife of the governor-general of Canada. With its elite membership, the national council was the most influencial Canadian women's group in the **woman suffrage** campaign after it officially endorsed suffrage in 1910. The national council continues to operate through a network of Local Councils of Women in 20 Canadian cities and Provincial Councils of Women in five of the provinces.

NATIONAL COUNCIL OF WOMEN OF KENYA (NCWK). A broad coalition formed in 1964 to coordinate the activities of all women's groups. Many of its programs in sewing, crafts, and home economics are traditional, but the NCWK also works for women's **empowerment**. It formed the National Committee on the Status of Women in the early 1990s for public education on democracy and women's political rights. It also sponsors scholarships and training for women and girls. The NCWK is best known for its Greenbelt Movement, a program to combat desertification and to provide a forum for women's leadership on the environment.

NATIONAL COUNCIL OF WOMEN'S ORGANIZATIONS (NCWO). A coalition of over 100 US women's groups that together have more than six million members. The NCWO, originally the Council of Presidents, coordinates advocacy for women's issues. It was formed in 1985 after a series of meetings of the heads of the groups. The coalition members support the **National Plan of Action** and regularly adopt a comprehensive Women's Agenda. The NCWO became more visible in 2002 when it assumed leadership of the effort to get the **male-only club** where the Masters' Golf Tournament is held to admit women.

NATIONAL COUNCIL OF WOMEN'S SOCIETIES (NCWS). An important coalition of traditional women's service groups in Nigeria, formed in 1958 by elite women. Although the NCWS originally sought to create a federation of nonpolitical women's groups, in 2003 it organized the "Women Arise Rally" against the systematic exclusion of women from public office.

NATIONAL FEDERATION OF BUSINESS AND PROFESSIONAL WOMEN'S CLUBS (BPW/USA). An organization founded in 1919 to advance the status of employed women and to support legal equality for women. An early (1937) supporter of the **Equal Rights Amendment**, the BPW has also been active on behalf of **affirmative action**, **equal pay**, national and **state commissions on the status of women**, and women in elected and appointed public office. Although the BPW has now become primarily a women's rights organization, rather than a service club, the membership long resisted the feminist label and in 1966 rejected suggestions that it become a civil rights group for women. The BPW has 30,000 members in over 1,600 local chapters and is the lead organization on workplace equity issues such as the **wage gap**.

NATIONAL FEDERATION OF INDIAN WOMEN (NFIW). A group formed in 1954 as the women's wing of the Communist Party of India. It operates as both a lobby group for women's rights in New Delhi and a provider of services to poor and working-class women. Although the NFIW has joined feminist coalitions opposing **rape** and **dowry** and participates in the **Global March of Women**, it remains aloof from the feminist label, in keeping with its belief in state socialism as the key to women's emancipation. It was designed to be the radical alternative to existing women's groups and one that would reach beyond the middle class by attracting members from different castes, classes, and religions.

NATIONAL LIBERATION CONFERENCE. A meeting held at Ruskin College, Oxford, in February 1970, and viewed as the beginning of the **new feminist movement** in Great Britain. The conference agreed upon four national goals: **equal pay**; equal education and opportunity; 24-hour **day-care** centers; and free **contraception** and **abortion** on demand. The conference grew out of the omission of **women's history** from an earlier history workshop at the college. National conferences were held through 1978, when a split developed between the radical and socialist strands of the movement.

NATIONAL ORGANIZATION FOR MEN AGAINST SEXISM (NOMAS). The oldest pro-feminist men's group in the United States, formed in 1975 at the first annual National Conference on Men and Masculinity. Its agenda is **gender** equality, social justice, gay rights, and antiracism. It currently has chapters in seven states and two divisions: the **Men's Studies** Association and the Ending Men's Violence Network. Until 1981, when it became a national membership organization with by-laws and a council, it was only a loose network for holding the conference. It became the National Organization for Changing Men in 1983. NOMAS seeks to differentiate itself from **antifeminist men's movement** groups.

NATIONAL ORGANIZATION FOR WOMEN (NOW). The largest and oldest **new feminist** organization in the United States, founded by **Betty Friedan**, among others, in 1966. NOW has a dues-paying membership of around 280,000 in over 400 local chapters in all 50 states. NOW supports a legal defense and education fund and a political action committee and publishes a newsletter, *National NOW Times*. NOW was established by those active in **state commissions on the status of women** as a civil rights group on the model of the National Association for the Advancement of Colored People. As additional **liberal feminist** groups have formed, NOW has increasingly taken more radical positions on issues such as **abortion**, **lesbian** rights, and the need for a feminist party in US politics.

NATIONAL PLAN OF ACTION. *See* **NATIONAL COMMISSION ON THE OBSERVANCE OF INTERNATIONAL WOMEN'S YEAR.**

NATIONAL RIGHT TO LIFE COMMITTEE (NRLC). The largest of the US **pro-life** groups, established as a separate organization by the Catholic Church in 1973 to coordinate the anti**abortion** campaign for a human life bill and/or constitutional amendment that would extend full legal rights to an embryo upon conception. The NRLC has attempted to distance itself from the Catholic Church and has succeeded in building a broader-based organization of around 3,000 local chapters in all 50 states, with a claimed membership of over 12 million. The NRLC has not taken a public position on **contraception** but threatened a boycott of any drug company marketing **RU 486**.

NATIONAL SOCIETY FOR WOMEN'S SUFFRAGE (NSWS). A coalition of local English **woman suffrage** societies, formed in 1868. Beginning in 1870 the monthly *Women's Suffrage Journal*, edited by society president **Lydia Becker**, chronicled their activities. The NSWS used home, ward, and district meetings to educate the public. It organized demonstrations and published letters, articles, and pamphlets. An internal disagreement over accepting political parties as affiliates led to the formation of the **National Union of Women's Suffrage Societies**.

NATIONAL UNION OF WOMEN'S SUFFRAGE SOCIETIES (NUWSS). The largest of the British **woman suffrage** groups. Formed in 1887 by 17 women's groups, the NUWSS, under the leadership of **Millicent Garrett Fawcett**, brought unity to the movement and expanded to include almost 500 local societies by 1914. The group used legal methods but became more activist in competition with the **Women's Social and Political Union**. They organized the famous **Mud March**, other large demonstrations, and a pilgrimage that brought women walking from all over the country to London. After the passage of a limited woman suffrage act in 1918, the NUWSS became the National Union of Societies for Equal Citizenship. Under its new president **Eleanor Rathbone**, the group continued to work for full suffrage as well as **equal pay**, **divorce** reform, widow's **pensions**, and employment opportunities for women.

NATIONAL WELFARE RIGHTS ORGANIZATION (NWRO). A US organization of public assistance recipients formed in 1967 to **empower** poor (mostly African American) women to act as their own advocates within the **welfare** system and to seek improvements in public assistance programs. Johnnie Tillmon, a welfare mother, was its well-known chairperson, but the group was dominated by paid male staff and financed by middle-class Euro-Americans who agreed that "every woman is just one man away from welfare." The NWRO peaked in 1969 with 22,000 members and 500 local chapters. In 1972 poor black women took over the group and aligned it with the feminist movement. When funding dried up in 1975 in the backlash against welfare, the NWRO disbanded. It has served, however, as a model for the many local and state welfare rights groups formed since 1975.

NATIONAL WOMAN SUFFRAGE ASSOCIATION (NWSA). An exclusively female organization, founded in 1869 by **Elizabeth Cady Stanton** and **Susan B. Anthony** to secure a **woman suffrage** amendment to the US Constitution. The group formed in the wake of the split in the **American Equal Rights Association** over the suffrage issue, a circumstance Stanton and Anthony attributed to the preponderance of men in that organization. The NWSA was considered the radical wing of the suffrage movement in its insistence on a constitutional amendment and its commitment to other women's rights issues. In 1890 the group merged with the **American Woman Suffrage Association** to form the **National American Woman Suffrage Association**.

NATIONAL WOMAN'S PARTY (NWP). A US group founded by **Alice Paul** in 1913 (under the name "Congressional Union") to promote **woman suffrage** and, after suffrage, to advance **equality feminism**. The NWP was the militant wing of the US suffrage movement and staged parades, pickets, and **hunger strikes**. In 1923 the NWP proposed the **Equal Rights Amendment**, which became its sole domestic issue for many years. The NWP maintained a feminist presence, 1920-60, in Washington, D.C., at a time when the movement was largely in abeyance. It also worked for the inclusion of "sex" in Title VII of the

Civil Rights Act of 1964 and for a provision on sex equality in the United Nations Charter. The NWP headquarters is in their historic Sewell-Belmont House on Capitol Hill. The house was the home and office of Alice Paul, 1927-1972, and now the NWP devotes itself to its preservation as a museum.

NATIONAL WOMEN'S AID FEDERATION (NWAF). A nonhierarchical coalition, established in 1975, to link local antiviolence groups and shelters in Great Britain. In addition to supporting over 250 member organizations and a national **domestic violence** hotline, the NWAF works on national and local reforms for **battered women** services and treatment under the law. One achievement is the Domestic Violence Act of 1976 giving a battered woman the right to a restraining order. In the 1990s provisions in family law, housing policy, and police procedures included services for the victims of domestic violence.

NATIONAL WOMEN'S ASSOCIATION OF BHUTAN. A group formed by the government in 1981 to improve the status of women, especially those in rural areas. The group initially did not adopt women's equality as a goal on the grounds that Bhutanese women were already equal. The association has encouraged traditional arts and culture, sponsored health training, distributed yarn and vegetable seeds, and introduced smokeless stoves in villages. It also developed a program of nonformal education for women that has been implemented by government in all parts of the nation. The group is currently one of only two nongovernmental organizations officially registered in Bhutan and is heavily funded by the government.

NATIONAL WOMEN'S CONFERENCE. *See* NATIONAL COMMISSION ON THE OBSERVANCE OF INTERNATIONAL WOMEN'S YEAR.

NATIONAL WOMEN'S COUNCIL OF IRELAND (NWCI). A coalition of older women's groups of the 1960s and **radical feminists** of the 1970s that formed the Council for the Status of Women in the 1970s. It adopted its present name in 1995 and has around 125 group-members. As the official representative of Irishwomen, NWCI is consulted by government, has ex officio seats on many boards and commissions, and also lobbies for its own agenda. It is considered the most representative of women's groups and has come to accept more radical stances on **rape**, **lesbian** rights, and **reproductive freedom**.

NATIONAL WOMEN'S HALL OF FAME. An institution that recognizes US women in all fields of accomplishment. Seneca Falls, New York, residents created the hall of fame in 1969 and by 2002 close to 200 women had been inducted, including many **woman suffrage movement** leaders and several **second wave feminists** such as **Betty Friedan** and **Gloria Steinem**. In addition to the Hall, the museum has exhibition galleries, a research library, and education programs.

NATIONAL WOMEN'S HEALTH NETWORK (NWHN). A feminist health care advocacy group, founded in 1975 as a coalition for the entire **women's health movement** in the United States. The NWHN provides information to its 11,000 individual and 300 organizational members and monitors proposed legislation and government regulations affecting women's health. It also serves as a watchdog over the medical profession to expose unsafe and unnecessary medical practices.

NATIONAL WOMEN'S POLITICAL CAUCUS (NWPC). A multipartisan feminist group formed in 1971 to increase the number of women in elected and appointed office in the US government and as delegates at national party conventions. To advance this goal, the Caucus conducts campaign training schools for potential female candidates and recommends qualified women for presidential appointments. Since 1985 the group has presented annual Good Guy Awards to men who actively support their mission, and, beginning in 1987, the EMMAs (Exceptional Merit Media Awards) have gone to journalists for reports on women's issues. The NWPC has over 200 local chapters in 45 states, a lobbying headquarters in Washington, D.C., and a political action committee. It publishes a newsletter, *The Women's Political Times*.

NATIVE AMERICAN FEMINISM. *See* AMERICAN INDIAN FEMINISM.

NATURAL CHILDBIRTH. A type of prepared childbirth in which the woman and her support person are educated in techniques of relaxation, breathing, and concentration to use during labor. Although the approach does not exclude the use of medications and other procedures to facilitate a safe childbirth, there is an emphasis on the minimal use of drugs and high technology. The revival of interest in natural childbirth began in the 1950s and has been embraced by the feminist movement as a part of a woman-controlled **alternative birth movement**. Some feminists, after going through an unpleasant birthing experience, have accused the movement of overselling natural childbirth and making women feel like failures when they must resort to drugs and technology. *See also* MEDICALIZATION OF CHILDBIRTH.

NESTLÉ BOYCOTT. *See* "BOTTLE BABY DISEASE."

NETWORK OF EAST-WEST WOMEN (NEWW). A group established in 1991 in Washington, D.C. to coordinate women's activism in more than 30 nations in postcommunist Central and Eastern Europe. NEWW supports the formation of independent women's movements through an electronic communications network, feminist research and advocacy, and a fellowship program for legal, economic, and social policy development. It sponsored its first annual **gender** policy conference in 2001.

NETWORKING. The informal social interactions involving individuals or groups. Networks provide information and contacts vital for career advancement and placement. They may also provide support and social functions. Feminists have consciously formed networks to advance the movement's political agenda and to support women. *See also* OLD BOYS CLUB/AGELESS WOMAN CLUB.

NEW FEMINIST MOVEMENT. A term that refers to the resurgence of an organized women's movement in the 1960s. A conventional view of the history of feminism is that **first wave feminism** died in the 1920s and **second wave feminism** emerged in the 1960s. Today many women's historians point to the persistence of feminist activity throughout the 20th century and view the contemporary feminist movement as a part of one continuous movement of different organizations and varying levels of mass support and activity.

NEW FEMINISTS (CANADA). *See* TORONTO WOMEN'S LIBERATION MOVEMENT.

NEW FRENCH FEMINISTS. A term used to identify the contemporary French feminists—Julia Kristéva, Luce Irigaray, Hélène Cixous, and Monique Wittig—who began publishing around 1960, several of them in the semiotic-**Marxist** journal *Tel Quel*. Although there are several conflicting factions within the **Mouvement pour la Libération des Femmes (MLF)**, in general French feminists believe that Western thought has been based on a systematic repression of women's experiences. Most French feminists assert the claim that there is an "**essential**" female nature and that it makes sense to begin there as a point from which to deconstruct Western notions of language, philosophy, psychoanalysis, and society. The diversity of positions within this movement can be seen in the anthology *New French Feminisms*, edited by Elaine Marks and Isabelle de Courtivron (1980).

NEW MAN. A 1980s term describing a feminist ideal male. He is portrayed as a caring, sensitive type who shares feelings, housework, and **child care**. These men have been influenced by feminist ideas and hold a nontraditional view of masculinity. Feminists do not view this archetype as widespread and suggest he may be a creation of the media. In the 1990s the New Lad, a beer-drinking, football-watching resident of a messy bachelor pad, appeared in the media.

NEW WOMAN LITERATURE. A term used to describe the literature written by young feminists who emerged in the 1890s in both Great Britain and America. Representative of these authors is the South African **Olive Schreiner** (1855-1920) and the British writers Mary Cholmondely (1859-1925) and Mona Caird (1858-1932), all of whom wrote novels that exposed the **misogyny** and xenophobia that propped up the British empire. These women were not advocates of women's rights or particularly involved in the **woman suffrage movement**, but instead were intent on challenging traditional Victorian ideas about marriage and femininity. The "new woman" was independent, self-reliant, and featured in a number of British and American novels. Other examples of such writers include Sarah Grand, **Charlotte Perkins Gilman**, Radclyffe Hall, and Rebecca West.

NEW YORK RADICAL FEMINISTS (NYRF). A group formed in 1969 by **Anne Koedt** and **Shulamith Firestone** as a city-wide mass-based organization that would avoid the ideological and organizational rigidities of the **Feminists** and the **Redstockings**. A three-stage process of **consciousness-raising** and feminist analysis within small brigades, followed by affiliation with the larger NYRF group, was devised to integrate new members. The founding Stanton-Anthony Brigade disbanded in 1970 after charges of **elitism**, and the three-stage structure was abandoned. The larger group continued until 1972 and in 1971 held the first **rape speak-out** and the first feminist conference on **prostitution**.

NEW YORK RADICAL WOMEN (NYRW). New York City's first **women's liberation** group, formed by **Shulamith Firestone** and Pam Allen in 1967. The group staged several widely noted demonstrations, including the **Miss America Pageant Protest** and the antiwar "Burial of Traditional Womanhood," published a journal, *Notes from the First and Second Years*, and attracted many prominent members such as **Kate Millett, Robin Morgan,** Ellen Willis, **Anne Koedt,** Kathie Sarachild, Ros Boxandell, and Patricia Mainardi. Deeply divided along **politico/feminist** lines, the group disbanded in 1969.

NINETEENTH AMENDMENT. An amendment to the US Constitution added in 1920 and stating "the right of the citizens of the United States to vote shall not be denied or abridged by the United States or by any State on account of sex." A **woman suffrage** amendment was first introduced in Congress in 1878 but was not passed until 1919.

NINE-TO-FIVE (9 TO 5, THE NATIONAL ASSOCIATION OF WORKING WOMEN). An organization of women office workers, founded in Boston in 1973 with members now in every state and over 200 cities. It seeks to assist employees with job problems: improved pay, race and **sex discrimination, sexual harassment,** health and safety conditions, advancement, and respect by one's peers and supervisors. 9 to 5 has actively supported state policies to protect video display terminal operators from health hazards. Their 20 chapters annually honor excellent supervisors and publicize examples of "heartless" behavior by those in positions of power. The group has an education fund that conducts research and has published *The 9 to 5 Guide to Combating Sexual Harassment: Candid Advice from 9 to 5* (1999).

NO-FAULT DIVORCE. A legal reform adopted in some form in all US states, 1969-1988, that allows dissolution of a marriage without proof of fault or grounds for divorce such as cruelty or adultery. The requirement is only a showing of irreconcilable differences or incompatibility. Although the impetus for these changes did not originate with the feminist movement, there was initial support because of the law's **gender-neutral** language, lack of assumptions about traditional **gender roles** in marriage, and potential to help **battered women** leave an abusive marriage. The impact of no-fault divorce, however, has contributed to the **feminization of poverty** in that the monetary awards to women have been less generous than under the former system. The courts may assume an economic equality between husbands and wives that has no basis, or mothers may accept lower **child support** in exchange for uncontested custody. No-fault divorce laws have been adopted widely throughout the world, with many of these same negative impacts. In Australia there is a movement to require the consent of both parties, so that divorce cannot be arbitrary. In China, which legalized no-fault divorce in 1980, and in other less-developed nations, the shortage of housing makes divorce very difficult. *See also* DISPLACED HOMEMAKER; MARRIAGE MOVEMENT.

NONSEXIST CHILDREN'S LITERATURE. Those reading materials for young people that do not reinforce traditional **gender roles**. Prohibited content includes: portrayal of men and women in stereotypical roles and jobs; a preponderance of male characters; passive behavior of female characters; and creative, problem-solving activities only by male protagonists. Under pressure from groups such as Feminists on Children's Media and independent nonprofit publishers of nonsexist children's books, both textbook and trade publishers have developed author guidelines that address this critique. The American Library Association's Association for Library Service to Children has also published bibliographies of nonsexist booklists and a list of folktales in which there are active heroines. *See also* FREE TO BE . . . YOU AND ME.

NONSEXIST LANGUAGE. Those inclusive words that do not discriminate against either sex. Examples of such language include "humanity" instead of "mankind," "s/he" instead of "he," "chair" instead of "chairman," and "supervisor" instead of "foreman" (and similar terms in other landuages). Communications studies have found that even when used in the generic sense, the words "he" and "man" do evoke thoughts of males. The plural pronoun "they" is the only generic pronoun that is genuinely nonsexist and does not exclude females. Over the past generation, publishers, businesses, educational institutions, governments, and religious bodies have adopted nonsexist language in their publications. The feminist movement is credited with having a greater impact on English language usage than any other movement in the past 400 years. This problem is less prevalent in those languages in which an article denotes the gender of a word. However, in France and other French-speaking countries and communities around the world, there has been a movement to "level" the language by providing a feminine form of professional titles that have been exclusively masculine. *See also* "YOU GUYS."

NONTRADITIONAL OCCUPATIONS, WOMEN IN. The entry of female workers into traditionally **male-dominated** skilled-craft jobs. With the Title VII of the **Civil Rights Act of 1964** mandate to employers to adopt sex-neutral hiring practices, there have been large increases in the numbers and percentages of women in blue-collar jobs but their occupational shares remain small. Women workers are especially attracted to these positions on the basis of higher pay, greater challenges, and variability of the tasks. Feminists are less concerned with moving women into nontraditional jobs than with challenging the wages for sex-segregated positions through adoption of **comparable worth**. "Nontraditional occupations" also implies that these jobs naturally belong to men.

NORPLANT. A long-term **contraceptive** method, marketed in the United States since 1991. A specially trained practitioner surgically implants six match-size capsules in a woman's arm for continuous slow release of a synthetic hormone. The implant remains effective for five years and may be surgically removed at any time. Feminists have generally been supportive of Norplant because it is safe and second only to tubal ligation in effectiveness, but recognize that not all women can afford the $600 lump-sum cost if uninsured. Its coercive use is also a concern as some states have considered incentives to poor women to elect the procedure and some judges have required Norplant use as a condition of probation for women convicted of child or substance abuse.

NORTON, CAROLINE SHERIDAN (1808-1877). An English author and activist in the **divorce** reform and **married women's property** rights movements. She was the victim of a violent marriage that ended in a separation, which denied her access to her children and her property. Norton wrote the long poem "The Mother," as well as *Caroline Norton's Defense: English Laws for Women in the Nineteenth Century* (1854) and other influential pamphlets on the legal status of women and the relation of men and women in England. However, she continued to believe in the natural superiority of men and the right of women to be protected.

NOW, ET AL. V. SCHEIDLER ET AL., 510 US 1215 (1994). A US Supreme Court decision granting feminists permission to charge **pro-life** militants under the Racketeer Influenced and Corrupt Organizations Act (RICO) for their campaign of violence and intimidation against **abortion** clinics. In 1998 a federal jury found Joseph Scheidler and his associates within the Pro-Life Action Network guilty. In 1999 a federal district court issued a permanent, nationwide injunction against the group, an action upheld by a federal court of appeals in 2001. The case established the principle that the right of free speech does not protect violent conduct and that women have the right to seek medical care free from **harassment**. The Supreme Court accepted the case on appeal to review the injunction (but not the finding involving free speech). In 2003 the Court ruled, 8-1, in *Scheidler v. National Organization for Women* that forcible blockages of clinics did not meet the definition of extortion under RICO because the defendents did not receive tangible money or property from the clinics. This decision nullified more than $250,000 in fines against the protesters. Feminists expressed fear that the decision could increase the need for **clinic protection** in defiance of the **Freedom of Access to Clinic Entrances Act** of 1994.

-O-

OCCUPATIONAL SEGREGATION. The employment patterns in the labor force whereby women and men are concentrated in different types of jobs. Female-typed jobs have lower pay and prestige than male-typed jobs, and there are fewer female-typed than male-typed jobs. **Equality feminists** believe that all jobs should be open to men and women on a nondiscriminatory basis. *See also* COMPARABLE WORTH; NONTRADITIONAL OCCUPATIONS, WOMEN IN; PINK-COLLAR GHETTO.

O'CONNOR, SANDRA DAY (1930-). The first woman to be appointed to the US Supreme Court. She formerly served in the Arizona State Senate, where she supported the **Equal Rights Amendment**, and on the Arizona Court of Appeals. Since joining the Court in 1981, O'Connor has generally supported the women's rights position in **gender discrimination** cases and several of her male colleagues moved toward that position after 1981, possibly because of her influence. She has also developed the "undue burden" test for review of state regulations on **abortion** that has been used by the Court since 1992. Under this test, no regulation may present a substantial obstacle to a woman's abortion decision.

OFFICE OF RESEARCH ON WOMEN'S HEALTH, NATIONAL INSTITUTES OF HEALTH. See WOMEN'S HEALTH INITIATIVE.

OLD BOYS CLUB/AGELESS WOMAN CLUB. Those informal social or professional friendships that are limited to individuals of the same sex. These provide significant **networking** functions involving access to information important for career advancement. Feminists once spoke of the "old boys club" with resentment because of its ability to exclude women. Now feminists use the second term, formerly the "old girls club," to refer to women in key positions who use their power to include other women.

OLDER BRANCH. See WOMEN'S RIGHTS MOVEMENT.

OLDER WOMEN'S LEAGUE (OWL). A US group founded in 1980 by Laurie Shields and Tish Sommers to address economic equality issues of particular importance to midlife and older women such as **pensions**, **social security**, and health **insurance**, and to improve the image and status of women. In the 2000s OWL had 58 local chapters and a lobbying headquarters in Washington, D.C. *See also* DISPLACED HOMEMAKER.

ONE-CHILD POLICY. A program introduced by the People's Republic of China in 1979. It restricts each urban married couple to one child unless both were only children. In rural areas a second child is allowed after an interval of several years. Feminists see both positive and negative impacts. The policy has had a positive impact on **family planning** and has permitted women to concentrate on their education and to play an expanded role in the workforce. But human rights violations have occurred, including forced **abortions**, female infanticide, and mass **sterilizations**. In 2002 China began to use a voluntary program in one-third of the country where couples who exceeded two children were fined.

OPERATION SAVE AMERICA (OSA). A US **pro-life** organization formed (as Operation Rescue) in 1986 and led by fundamentalist Protestant Randall Terry. The group assumed its current name under the leadership of Rev. Flip Benham in 1999. The group's followers frequently focus on one city and block access to all **abortion** clinics there to force clinic closings. Demonstrators are often arrested on charges of trespassing or disorderly conduct and are assessed heavy fines. Feminists have responded with local **clinic protection**, demands for federal and state laws to protect clinic access, such as the national **Freedom of Access to Clinic Entrances Act** (1994), and litigation charging the group with racketeering, extortion, and antitrust violations. *See also* NOW, ET AL. V. SCHEIDLER, ET AL.

OPPRESSIONS, INTERSTRUCTURING OF. A term used by feminists to denote the mutually reinforcing yet distinct effects of race, sex, and class oppression. **Audre Lorde**, **bell hooks**, Dorothy Solle, and Barbara Hilkert Andolsen are among those explicitly plumbing the interfacing dynamics and interlocking oppressions of race and class with **sexism** in Western societies. *See also* RACISM AND FEMINISM.

ORAL CONTRACEPTIVES. *See* BIRTH CONTROL PILL.

ORDINATION OF WOMEN. The investing of females with religious ministerial or priestly authority. By the end of the 20th century almost all mainline Protestant denominations and both Reform and Conservative Judaism accepted clergywomen. Only the Catholic Church, Orthodox Judaism, and some small, conservative Protestant groups continued to prohibit the ordination of women. The admission of women to the Catholic priesthood has attracted most attention from feminists (e.g., a button reading "Either Ordain Women or Stop Baptizing Them") but a "stained **glass ceiling**" that keeps women out of church leadership is also noted. While less researched, similar limitations exist on the role of women in other religions, including Buddhism, Hinduism, and Islam.

ORDINATION OF WOMEN, HISTORICAL EVIDENCE. The archaeological and inscriptional indications of the ministry of women in the early church. Evidence exists from the first century in catacomb frescoes, mosaics, and inscriptions that women served as bishops, priests, and deacons. Inscriptions also refer to women as leaders of synagogues. Such scholarship is used by feminists today to support demands for equality for women within organized religion.

ORGANISATION OF WOMEN OF AFRICAN AND ASIAN DESCENT (OWAAD). A group founded in Great Britain in 1978 by **women of color**, primarily black women, to challenge white domination of the feminist movement. The last annual OWAAD conference was held in 1982; thereafter, women of either Afro-Caribbean or Asian origin met together. Ethnic differences were the major factor in the demise of the OWAAD, but the **gay/straight split** and tensions between those interested in advancing women within Britain and those stressing **global feminism** played roles as well.

OSKA. A national information center for all Polish women's groups and projects, established in 1998 with Ford Foundation sponsorship. Oska's mission is to encourage women's participation in politics and promote **gender** equality and **networking**. It provides information on women's legal and policy issues, their economic status, media coverage, and public opinion.

"OTHER." See WOMAN AS OTHER.

OTTO-PETERS, LUISE (1819-1895). A feminist novelist, who is viewed as the founder of the German women's movement. Her *Kathinka* (1844) supported full equality for women, but by 1865 she had come to believe that a campaign for women's participation in politics would be premature. Under her leadership the General German Women's Association worked instead for marriage law reform.

OUR BODIES, OURSELVES. See BOSTON WOMEN'S HEALTH BOOK COLLECTIVE.

-P-

PAGLIA, CAMILLE (1947-). The US author of *Sexual Personae* (1990), *Sex, Art, and American Culture* (1992), and *Vamps and Tramps* (1994) and considered by many feminists to be a tool of right-wing **antifeminists** for her nontraditional attitudes. Paglia defends **pornography**, insists that **rape** is a type of sex, not violence, and champions motherhood as the most important role a woman can have. She sees a connection between art and violence, asserting that "There is no female Mozart because there is no female Jack the Ripper." Paglia sees herself as a feminist who is opposed to the current feminist establishment that she views as having degenerated into the dogma of **political correctness**. She also attacks the way feminists have waged war on romance and women as sexual partners, arguing that this sends a very negative message to young women who take pleasure in sex and **physical attractiveness**.

PALIMONY. The equivalent of spousal support and/or a property settlement received by an unmarried person after co-habiting with another. The relationship must be based on an expressed agreement or quasi-contract unless the contractual terms explicitly entail "immoral or illicit consideration of meretricious sexual services." "Palimony" is not a legal term and most case law was established in California. These claims are difficult to prove, and support rights and obligations depend on the duration of the relationship and the commingling of funds. *See also* MARVIN V. MARVIN.

PAN CHAO (ca. 45-116). The foremost woman scholar in China, trained in Han Confucianism and tutor to the Empress. She is famous for her *Nu Jie* (*Lessons for Women* [ca. 105]), a book of moral principles addressed to young women in which she advocates the education of girls and claims women are moral beings as are men and are capable of becoming wise.

PAN-AMERICAN ASSOCIATION FOR THE ADVANCEMENT OF WOMEN. A group formed at the Pan-American Women's Conference in Baltimore in 1922. Under the leadership of its first president **Carrie**

Chapman Catt, the Pan-American Association worked to build a strong network of national women's organizations that could pursue a broad women's rights agenda, including **woman suffrage**. One achievement was the creation in 1928 of an Inter-American Commission of Women (IACW) to investigate the status of women in the 21 American states. Critics have questioned the cultural bias and dominance of US leaders and note the creation of the International League of Iberian and Hispanic Women as an alternative to the IACW.

PANKHURSTS, THE. A family that produced England's premier women's rights activists beginning in the 1860s: Emmeline (1858-1928) and Richard Marsden (1835-1898) and their daughters Dame Christabel (1880-1958), Sylvia (1882-1960), and Adela (1885-1961). They were the founders in 1903 of the militant **Women's Social and Political Union** (WSPU). Their use of increasingly disruptive tactics to promote "votes for women" prompted an increasingly heavy-handed response from British authorities, including the **Cat and Mouse Act**. The Pankhursts abruptly terminated their orchestrated mayhem at the onset of World War I and committed their organization to war work, thus providing the government with a face-saving way to give women the vote in 1928 in recognition of their wartime patriotism. Richard Pankhurst had become active in the feminist movement by 1865 and, as a member of Parliament, drafted the **married women's property** bill and the **woman suffrage** bill. Both Christabel (in *Unshackled: The Story of How We Won the Vote* [1959]) and Sylvia (in *The Life of Emmeline Pankhurst: The Suffragette Struggle for Women's Citizenship* [1935]) wrote histories of that period.

PARAGRAPH 218. A part of the German criminal code of 1871 that made **abortion** illegal in that country. Reform of the code in 1974 by the Federal Republic had made it legal within the first trimester, but a ruling by the constitutional court forced a compromise law in 1976, whereby abortion became criminal except for medical, eugenic, criminological, or extraordinary social reasons. In the German Democratic Republic abortion had been legally available within the first trimester and funded by the state. The reunification agreement of 1989 mandated both a liberalization of the law and increased emphasis on the rights of the unborn. After several attempts at a compromise, a 1995 law made most abortion illegal but agreed that first-term abortions would not be prosecuted if preceded by mandatory counseling, which, after 1996, no longer must encourage the woman to carry to term. State funding of abortions for low-income women and exceptions for **rape** and a woman's health are provided.

PARDO BAZÁN, EMILIA (1851-1921). One of Spain's greatest novelists, a literary critic, and a life-long feminist. She had a philosophical interest in St. Francis of Assisi, partly because of the high regard in which he held women. She wrote on the subjection of women in Spain and on the life of the philosopher St. Catherine of Alexandria. In 1883 she caused a public furor with a series of articles defending, with reservations, the Naturalism of Émile Zola. She became the acknowledged leader of the new manner reflected in her two most famous works, *Los pazos de Ulloa* (*The House of Ulloa* [1886]), generally considered an example of gothic realism, and its sequel, *La madre naturaleza* (*Mother Nature* [1887]). In 1906 she became the first woman to chair the Literary Section of the Atheneum. Although she was the first woman appointed to a professorial chair at the University of Madrid (1916), her classes were boycotted by the male student body. She is considered a feminist forerunner for her support of women's rights in education and employment.

PARENTAL CONSENT/NOTIFICATION. A requirement of some US states that conditions a minor's right to **abortion** on notification or consent of at least one parent. Forty-two states have such laws, although they are enforced in only 32. The constitutionality of notification laws was upheld by the Supreme Court in *Bellotti v. Baird* (1979). Parental consent laws are permissible only if a judicial bypass is also available so that a young woman can go to court and get a judge's permission instead. Feminists oppose both barriers to **reproductive freedom**, particularly for women from abusive families. A majority of young women do involve parents in their abortion plans. And, although parental consent is required for most medical treatment of minors, exceptions are made in the case of treatment for drug abuse and sexually transmitted disease. In 1988 Rebecca Bell became the first minor in the United States known to have died because of a parental consent law. Told she would need her parents' permission for a legal abortion, she died from complications of an infection stemming from attempts to induce an illegal abortion.

PARENTAL LEAVE. *See* FAMILY LEAVE.

PARITÉ. *See* GENDER PARITY.

PARREN, KALLIROE (1861-1940). A Greek journalist and feminist. As editor after 1888 of her own *The Women's Newspaper*, Parren raised public awareness of women's rights. She founded several women's organizations, including the Union for the Emancipation of Women (1894), the Union of Greek Women (1896), and the Lyceum of Greek Women (1911). Her efforts also led to the passage of several women's rights laws and the establishment of many institutions to educate and aid women.

PARSONS, ELSIE CLEWS (1875-1941). A US writer, born into a prominent family in New York City, and one of the first repicipients of a Ph.D. in Sociology from Columbia University in 1898. A mother of four children, Parsons devoted her funds and time to the causes of feminism and pacifism, in addition to teaching graduate courses on the family and sex roles at Columbia from 1902-1905, which culminated in her first book, *The Family* (1906). Because she discussed trial marriage as an option in the book, her name was dropped from the social register and she was denounced in newspapers and from pulpits. She also published *Religious Chastity* (1913), *The Old-Fashioned Woman* (1913), *Fear and Conventionality* (1914), *Social Freedom* (1915), and *Social Rule* (1916). As an early anthropologist, she also published two studies based on her research in the American Southwest, *Pueblo Indian Religion* (1939) and *Tewa Tales* (1926). Her major feminist work, *Journal of a Feminist* (1994), was not published until after her death and used the device of a character named Cynthia writing about the experiences of Elsie. In the journal she argues for the liberation of women and free expression for all people. Her research on **gender** roles in Native American societies and gender-crossing also influenced her opinions. A contributor to Max Eastman's *Masses*, she also was involved with **Heterodoxy**, a feminist **network** in Greenwich village. Later she was one of the founders of the New School for Social Research in New York City.

PARTIAL-BIRTH ABORTIONS (PBA). A term used by the **pro-life movement** to describe a rarely used technique of late term **abortion** that opponents seek to prohibit in the United States. Medical personnel note that, while there is no procedure with this name, the proposed policy appears to encompass several techniques, principally that of dilation and extraction (D&X) in which the fetus is partially delivered and then destroyed. Because the fetus becomes viable between the 20th and 24th weeks, late term abortions are only performed when a woman's health or life is at risk or the fetus has life-ending abnormalities. Congressional bills to outlaw these procedures have been vetoed by the president (in 1996 and 1997) and similar state legislative policies have been rejected by the courts, most recently in *Stenberg v. Carhart* (2000), because the laws could prohibit abortions performed before viability and there is no protection for women whose health is endangered. In 2003 President George W. Bush signed another version, which was immediately challenged in court. There are no exact statistics concerning the number of D&Xs performed annually, the need for them, and when they occur. Many feel that the **pro-choice movement**, which has strongly opposed these policies, has lost the struggle for public support because of the horrific rhetoric used to describe the procedure.

PARTON, SARA PAYSON WILLIS (1811-1872). A US journalist and feminist. Writing a syndicated column under the pseudonym "Fanny Fern," Parton attacked the **double standard**, supported women's rights, and challenged the **patriarchy**. She was the highest paid journalist of her time even though she regularly complained of the poor status of women writers.

PATERSON, EMMA (1848-1886). An English **suffragist** and women's trade union leader. In 1872 she became the secretary of the Women's Suffrage Association; in 1874 she formed the Women's Protective and Provident League and began organizing women in different trades: bookbinding, dressmaking, millinery, and upholstery. She worked for the appointment of women factory inspectors but opposed **protective labor laws** because of their potential to jeopardize women's employment. Beginning in 1876 she edited the monthly *Women's Union Journal*, which covered **woman suffrage**, educational and legal rights, and **dress reform**.

PATRIA POTESTAD. A concept from Roman law, literally "power of the father." The principle is found in the civil code of many European and Latin American countries, where the husband/father is viewed as the household head with all powers of parental guardianship and authority. Women's rights advocates, particularly in Latin America, have sought legal reforms that would grant mothers a role in their children's guardianship.

PATRIARCHY. The rule by men as a group over women. The Latin *pater* refers to the social role of a father, not to the biological father, so that a father may be a celibate man (as in the Roman Catholic priesthood). Patriarchal societies exclude women from the exercise of citizens' political responsibilities, although some may have titular women (e.g., Queen Victoria). Patriarchal societies are hierarchical in that, at a minimum, they are a two-class society. A critique of the patriarchy is at the root of most **feminist political theory**. Although there is disagreement among feminists concerning the universality of patriarchy, the term provides a common understanding of the subordinate role of women and **male dominance**. *See also* MATRIARCHY.

PAUL, ALICE (1885-1977). A Quaker social worker, lawyer, and early leader of the movement for women's equal rights. Deeply influenced by her work with the militant English **suffragettes**, Paul introduced protest marches into the US **woman suffrage movement** through her group, the Congressional Union, which broke with the **National American Woman Suffrage Association** over tactical issues. Alice Paul formed the **National Woman's Party** (NWP) in 1913 and in 1920 she and the NWP commissioned the **portrait monument** to be presented to Congress as a commemoration of the **Nineteenth Amendment**. Paul wrote the first version of the **Equal Rights Amendment** in 1923.

PAY EQUITY. *See* COMPARABLE WORTH.

PC. *See* POLITICALLY CORRECT.

PEARCE, DIANA. *See* "FEMINIZATION OF POVERTY."

PEDESTAL. *See* "UP FROM THE PEDESTAL."

PELLETIER, MADELEINE (1874-1939). A French physician, **suffragette**, and founder of the journal *La Suffragiste* (1908). Pelletier's flamboyant **cross-dressing**, militant tactics, and sexual liberalism marginalized her within the French **woman suffrage movement** and the socialist and communist parties. She later turned to anarchism and a campaign for **birth control** and **abortion**. In 1939 she was arrested for performing illegal abortions and imprisoned in a mental asylum.

PENIS ENVY. *See* FREUD, SIGMUND; HORNEY, KAREN.

PENSION AND INSURANCE EQUITY. A feminist demand that women be able to buy the same benefits for the same amount as men in most types of policies. Pension plans related to employment once either demanded a higher contribution from women or paid lower benefits on the grounds that women lived longer than men. The US Supreme Court ruled in *Los Angeles Department of Water and Power v. Manhart* (1978) and *Arizona Governing Committee v. Norris* (1983) that this is prohibited under the **Civil Rights Act of 1964, Title VII**. Insurance companies in most states are allowed to charge men and women different rates for automobile as well as life and health insurance not related to employment. Women pay less than men for car and private life insurance policies and more for private health insurance because of the costs of pregnancy. Feminists now focus on **contraceptive equity** and discrimination against women with **breast cancer** and **domestic violence survivors** in both private and group health insurance.

PERFORMANCE ART. A recent variation on dramatic performance in which a single performer or a small troupe perform a satirical, outrageous, or controversial statement on some current social or political topic through art, dance, or music or the intersection of several media. Feminist performance art focuses on **body politics** and emerged with the **second wave** in the 1960s. Examples include the work of Karen Finley, one of the NEA Four, who was denied funding by the National Endowment for the Arts because her performances were deemed obscene. Finley's one-woman show, "Shut Up and Love Me," included writhing naked on the floor, covered only with honey. Another performance featured her naked body smeared with chocolate and yams while she painted with her breast milk. Finley's most recent performance is entitled "The Distribution of Empathy," an ironic look at the 9/11 disaster. *See also* GUERRILLA GIRLS.

PERÓN, EVA MARIA DUARTE DE (1919-1952). The wife of Argentine President Juan Domingo Perón and considered by many to be an early Argentine feminist. She galvanized popular support, especially among women and workers, for Peronism and her husband during his first term, 1946-52. Known as Evita, she was the first wife to accompany an Argentine political candidate on his electoral campaign. In 1947 her public support for **woman suffrage** aided its passage through Congress. Two years later she created the Peronist Women's (or Feminist) Party. Although without a formal government portfolio, she acted as the de facto minister of health and labor. In 1948 she established, with government funds, the Eva Perón Foundation, a social welfare agency dedicated to working-class housing, education, employment, and health care. A cult developed around her after her death at age 33.

"PERSONAL IS THE POLITICAL." A **consciousness-raising** motto that argues that women's private experiences are based in the sociopolitical system. This is viewed as a necessary belief for the **empowerment** of women in a common experience. Other feminists see this as **essentialism** that ignores class differences between and within groups of women.

PERSONAL RESPONSIBILITY AND WORK OPPORTUNITY RECONCILIATION ACT OF 1996 (PRWORA). *See* TEMPORARY ASSISTANCE TO NEEDY FAMILIES (TANF).

PERSONAL-DEVELOPMENT FEMINISM. The strand of the movement that focuses on surviving addiction, **codependency**, and abuse and maintaining **self-esteem**. Growing out of a concern with child abuse, violence, and **pornography**, this recovery movement, critics charge, can contribute to women perceiving themselves as "victims" rather than **empowered** "survivors." *See also* VICTIMIZATION OF WOMEN.

PERSONS CASE OF 1929. A major victory of the **first wave feminist** movement in Canada. Five **woman suffrage** leaders petitioned the federal Senate for an interpretation of the word "persons" in a law. Although the Supreme Court's initial ruling in 1928 was that women were not included, the Judicial Committee of the Privy Council in England reversed that decision in 1929 and permitted qualified women to be appointed to the Senate. The case is viewed as recognizing the "legal personhood" of Canadian women and is celebrated on October 18 with Persons Day, an occasion for the presentation of the Governor General's Awards to five persons who have advanced the equality of women.

PETHICK-LAWRENCE, EMMELINE (1867-1954). An English social worker, **suffragette**, pacifist, and member of the **Women's Social and Political Union**. In 1907 she founded the newspaper *Votes for Women* to advocate for the civil and political rights of women. She was active internationally in the Women's International League for Peace and Freedom, the Women's Peace Congress, and the **Women's Freedom League**. In 1918 she ran unsuccessfully for the House of Commons as a Labour candidate in the first election open to women.

PHALLOCENTRISM. A general feminist critique of the privileging of the male sex (symbolized by the erect phallus) in politics, literature, culture, and society in general. Within the realm of culture, phallocentrism is manifested in the exclusive valuing and study of male authors. More narrowly, the term also suggests the tendency to conceive of sexuality from a male perspective. Since the penis (phallus) plays a central role both in erotic pleasure and in **reproduction** in the male, it may be erroneously assumed that vaginal penetration has parallel importance in the female. Feminists have noted that such phallocentrism may lead to disregard of clitoral stimulation and its importance for sexual pleasure in the female. *See also* "MYTH OF THE VAGINAL ORGASM."

PHALLOGOCENTRIC. A term coined by the **New French feminists** to denote the tyranny of the Symbolic Order, the **patriarchy**, to stabilize, organize, and rationalize all systems of language, thought, and culture around one meaning (represented by the phallus, the symbol of the father's power over all aspects of culture). The term is very similar in its meaning to the earlier concept of **androcentrism**, or the masculine bias within Western scholarship. Feminists note that histories, ethnographies, social science, and literature are largely written by men, who focus on topics based on their socialization as males in Western societies. Androcentrism—like **phallogocentrism**—may also be seen as an instrument to enforce the ideology of patriarchy by excluding the points of view, and experiences, of women.

PHAN BOI CHAU (1867-1940). Vietnamese intellectual, reformer, and author of several works on the status of women. The best known of these, *Van De Phu Nu* (*The Women's Question*, 1929), not only attacked traditional attitudes and marriages but also encouraged women to become active within movements for their own liberation. He voiced these ideas earlier in a 1926 speech to the opening session of the Women's Labor Study Association.

PHYLLIS SCHLAFLY REPORT. *See* SCHLAFLY, PHYLLIS.

PHYSICAL ATTRACTIVENESS. A subjective quality which is determined by comparing an individual's appearance to the prevailing standard of attractiveness as set by social convention. Attractive people are seen to be happier, kinder, more socially competent, and more successful than less attractive people. Feminists have noted that there is also a **gender** bias in that physical attractiveness is emphasized more in females than in males. Males place greater emphasis on physical attractiveness than do females when picking a mate. However, attractiveness is also a liability for women in professional positions. Attractive women are often seen as not as capable of handling a job, and they are more readily the victims of **sexual harassment**. Feminists have raised a number of issues related to physical attractiveness, including **eating disorders** and commercial exploitation. *See also* FAT OPPRESSION.

PICTURE BRIDES. *See* MAIL-ORDER BRIDES.

PILL, THE. *See* BIRTH CONTROL PILL.

PINK-COLLAR GHETTO. Those female-dominated segregated positions in the sales, clerical, and service sectors. Pink-collar positions have lower status, pay, and opportunites for advancement than blue-collar, male-typed positions, even though women in these positions often have more years of education than their male counterparts. Feminists have offered **comparable worth** as a solution, but critics charge that the movement has been more active on breaking the **glass ceiling** than on addressing the more common problem of the "sticky floor" faced by pink-collar women. *See also* OCCUPATIONAL SEGREGATION.

PIZAN, CHRISTINE DE (1364-1430). A French poet and the first professional woman writer. In her most famous work, *The Book of the City* *of Women* (completed 1405), she steps out of a **patriarchal** frame of reference and the tradition of Aristotelian **antifeminism** to construct a reality in which women emerge as powerful and authoritative in all areas of human endeavor. It is modelled partly after Augustine's *City of God* and is a response to the popular **misogynist** works of the time. Pizan presents philosophical arguments against the oppression of women, maintaining that it is contrary to the goal of improving society as a whole.

PIZZEY, ERIN (1939-). The British founder of the first **women's battery shelter** in Chiswick, London, in 1971. Her *Scream Quietly or the Neighbours Will Hear* (1974) brought wide attention to the problem of **domestic violence** and its prevalence among all classes. She has been recognized for her popular novels and other writings with the Nancy Astor Journalism Award in 1983 and the San Valentino d'Oro Literature Prize in 1994.

PLAMÍNKOVÁ, FRANTIŠKA F. (1875-1942). A Czech suffrage leader, feminist, and nationalist politician. She founded the first Czech feminist group, the Women's Club of Prague, in 1901 and the Committee for Women's Suffrage in 1905. As a local council member and national legislator, Plamínková supported women's access to the professions, **woman suffrage**, and the nomination of women to public office. She served as the first head of the Czech Council of Women in 1923.

PLANNED PARENTHOOD. A social reform group committed to voluntary family planning and access to **contraceptive** methods, including **abortion**. The Planned Parenthood Federation of America (PPFA) was originally founded by **Margaret Sanger** in 1921 as the American Birth Control League and adopted its present name in 1942. The PPFA is organized in all states and more than 250 cities, operates about 875 clinics, and recently has begun to directly provide abortion services. The International Planned Parenthood Federation has affiliates in more than 180 nations and concentrates on limiting population growth in developing nations. *See also* GLOBAL GAG RULE.

PLATFORM FOR ACTION (PFA). The final document of the UN Fourth World Congress on Women, held in Beijing in 1995 and popularly known as the "agenda for women's **empowerment**." Twelve areas were addressed: **violence against women,** armed conflict, human rights, poverty, the economy, institutional mechanisms, education and training, health, the media, women in power and decisionmaking, the environment, and the girl child. A conservative coalition of some Catholic and some Muslim delegations, led by the Vatican, united against the women's rights position on issues of sexuality, sexual orientation, and **abortion.**

PLATH, SYLVIA (1932-1963). A US poet and author of the autobiographical coming-of-age novel *The Bell Jar* (1961). Her suicide at age 30, after learning of her husband poet Ted Hughes' affair with another woman, established her as a feminist icon and martyr. For three decades feminists blamed Hughes for her suicide and for losing or destroying two of her journals. She is viewed as a woman trapped in the home in the absence of a supportive feminist movement. However, her view of the nature of women as incomplete without a man and only fulfilled through childbirth was very much rooted in the **feminine mystique** of her era.

PLURALISTIC ACTION GROUPS FOR EQUAL RIGHTS OF MEN AND WOMEN (PAG). An organization established in 1970 in several Flemish towns in Belgium and modeled on the Dutch **radical feminist** group **Man-Woman-Society.** The PAG campaigned for **equal pay, marital property,** and greater political participation by women; it formed **women's centers** and **consciousness-raising** groups and published a newsletter. By the end of the 1970s the PAG had become less active as its members joined the women's committees of political parties.

POLISH WOMEN'S LEAGUE/LIGA KOBIET POLSKICH (LK). The Communist Party women's group established in 1945. It was viewed by the public as a way to control women in the state's interest in its focus on women workers. After the fall of communism in 1989, the LK became the Democratic Union of Women, a coalition of all women's groups. It continues to be ineffective in advocating for women because of its past history.

POLITICAL LESBIANISM. A conscious adoption of a homosexual orientation in response to peer pressure or personal feminist ideology. Here lesbianism is viewed as primarily a political, not a sexual, choice, and **lesbians** are hailed as model feminists. Although the pressure within **radical feminism** to adopt a lesbian orientation has declined since the early 1970s, this period caused a major **gay/straight split** in the movement as heterosexual women became defensive about their own sexual preferences and roles in the movement and older lesbians expressed distrust of these "instant lesbians" as potential sex partners. These fears appeared to be confirmed in the 1990s as the media were filled with stories of lesbians who now identified as heterosexuals (dubbed "hasbians"). *See also* BISEXUALITY; LAVENDER MENACE; WOMAN-IDENTIFIED WOMAN.

POLITICALLY CORRECT (PC). A term originally used within the US feminist movement to refer to acceptable behaviors and opinions. Deviations by movement participants from these official doctrines were subject to sanctions and even expulsion. In the 1990s the term was appropriated by political conservatives to discredit feminists as well as others who challenged the status quo and attempted to make society more inclusive. In particular, university policies to diversify the curriculum and to enact codes of unacceptable behavior toward women, gays, and racial and religious minorities have drawn charges of "political correctness." *See also* ANTIOCH COLLEGE SEXUAL CONSENT CODE; HATE CRIMES.

POLITICO/FEMINIST SPLIT. A division within the US **women's liberation movement**, 1967-69, over its relationship with the larger New Left political movement. **Politicos** viewed women's liberation as a key branch of the Left. Feminists supported an independent movement on the grounds that both capitalism and male supremacy oppressed women; that being so, women's issues would inevitably be peripheral within that **male-dominated** movement. By 1969 the feminist tendency prevailed as the movement broke away from the Left.

POLITICOS. Those who wish feminism to remain a part of the New Left rather than to become an independent women's movement. They believe that women's oppression is rooted in capitalism, racism and/or imperialism and that only a new revolutionary political order can liberate women. **Liberal feminist** reforms are opposed on the grounds that reform may prevent or retard revolution. *See also* POLITICO/FEMINIST SPLIT.

POLITIQUE ET PSYCHANALYSE. A small French feminist political theory group best known as Psych et Po, founded in 1968 by psychoanalyst Antoinette Fouqué and including prominent theorists **Hélène Cixous, Luce Irigaray,** and **Julia Kristéva.** The group's entrepreneurialism and appropriation of the generic term **"mouvement pour la libération des femmes" (MLF)** was widely resented by other French feminists. Psych et Po conversely considered the rest of the movement bourgeois and insufficiently attendant to its own Lacanian intellectualism and psychosexual linguistic analysis. It did not use "feminist" because of that term's association with reform and egalitarianism and even called itself **"antifeminist."** Psych et po was active in the 1981 election, but no longer exists. Antoinette Fouque, however, is still visible and important in representing feminism through service in the European Parliament.

POPE JOAN. A legendary or real woman who disguised herself as a man and became Pope John VIII, 853-855. Her sex was discovered when she gave birth in the middle of a religious procession through Rome and was immediately dragged and stoned to death. The Catholic Church accepted her existence until 1601, when she was declared a mythical figure by Pope Clement VIII in the wake of the Protestant Reformation. Modern scholarship has been unable to resolve her existance.

PORNOGRAPHY, FEMINIST DEBATE ON. A divisive issue emerging within the feminist movement in the late 1970s and 1980s concerning responses to the depiction of sexual activity. Antipornography feminists and their group Women Against Pornography, formed in 1979, argue that **violence against women** is caused by pornography that depicts pain, **dominance,** and violence. Writer **Andrea Dworkin** and lawyer **Catharine MacKinnon** have written a model ordinance that allows a woman to file a **sex discrimination** suit against the makers and distributors of pornography. Feminists opposed to this antipornography movement formed the Feminist AntiCensorship Taskforce (FACT) in 1984. FACT members generally support the right to free speech and press but are more concerned with the dangers of a **patriarchal** legal system's power to prohibit feminist writings and with preserving women's newly acknowledged sexuality and right to sexual expression. Anticensorship feminists tend to be drawn from the **radical, socialist,** and **liberal** traditions of feminism. **Cultural feminists,**

especially **lesbian separatists,** are more often allied with the antipornography faction. *See also* MINNEAPOLIS PORNOGRAPHY ORDINANCE; REGINA V. BUTLER.

PORTRAIT MONUMENT. The statue of **Susan B. Anthony, Elizabeth Cady Stanton,** and **Lucretia Mott** that was presented to Congress in 1921 by the **National Woman's Party** to honor the adoption of **woman suffrage.** The statue came to be called "three ladies in a bathtub" because the sculptor left the base unfinished as a symbol of the unfinished work of the women's movement. It originally stood in the rotunda of the Capitol but was removed shortly after its dedication to the crypt, a storage closet in the basement. In 1997 the statue was moved back to the rotunda after 78 women's groups, noting that all 11 statues there were of men, lobbied and raised the money for its return.

POST-ABORTION STRESS SYNDROME (PASS). A medical condition experienced by some women after having an **abortion.** Although most women are relieved and never have regrets, 1 percent, according to a recent study, have a grief or guilt reaction that becomes severe. PASS is not recognized as a diagnosis by either the American Psychiatric Association or the American Psychological Association and is seen by feminists as an invention of the **pro-life movement** to appear more concerned with women's health.

POSTFEMINIST. A term used by the US media after the defeat of the **Equal Rights Amendment** to describe the more conservative environment of the 1980s and the supposed demise and disintegration of the women's movement. It is argued that **gender** equality has been achieved, and feminism has become an anachronism, irrelevant to and even reviled by women, especially within the younger generation. In fact, the term was first used in 1919 at the height of the **woman suffrage movement.** Feminists believe that postfeminism is impossible so long as the **patriarchy** still exists. The term is sometimes viewed as **antifeminism** in disguise; others see it as a new stage of feminism that is dismissive of some feminist issues but still interested in others. In academic feminist theory, the term is linked with **postmodernism, poststructuralism,** and **multicultural** analysis.

POSTMODERNISM. A contemporary intellectual movement modified and adapted by feminist theory, which rejects traditional assumptions about truth and reality and emphasizes instead the plurality, diversity, and multiplicity of women as distinct from men, who are thought to be unitary and rational. It focuses on expressing the unexpressed through new language (scratching, jotting, scribbling). One faction of feminists is committed to the notion of **poststructural** analyses, including **deconstructionism**. The purpose of the movement is to unveil the layers of meaning society has attached to certain **misogynist** beliefs in an effort to reveal the inner core of meanings and make evident their inconsistencies. Some postmodern feminists have an active emancipatory agenda of social reform. Prominent authors, principally **New French Feminists**, include **Simone de Beauvoir, Hélène Cixous, Luce Irigaray**, and **Julia Kristéva**.

POSTPARTUM DEPRESSION (PPD). A condition experienced by some women after giving birth, ranging from a few days of sadness to a long period of depression or postpartum psychosis (PPP). This most severe form of PPD occurs in only one to three cases in a thousand births and can result in suicide or infanticide. The case of Andrea Yates, the Houston mother who drowned her five children in 2001, raised public awareness of PPP and allowed feminist groups to call attention to the shortcomings of a medical system that cuts corners for the mentally ill and devotes little money to research on PPP.

POSTSTRUCTURALIST FEMINIST CRITICISM. Based on the theories of **deconstruction** and using the writings of **Jacques Derrida**, Paul de Man, and **Michel Foucault**, among others, to claim a radical decentering of the subject and understanding of history. Most of the **New French Feminists—Julia Kristéva, Hélène Cixous**, and **Lucy Irigaray**—would be considered poststructuralist in their visions and philosophical orientations. All of them to some extent believe in an **essential** female nature, but only as a starting point from which they then go on to deconstruct all intellectual and social traditions—psychoanalysis, philosophy, language, and **patriarchal** culture. Denise Riley's *'Am I That Name?' Feminism and the Category of 'Women' in History* (1988) is an example of a poststructural feminist history that dissects the arbitrary notion of "women" in the history of the feminist movement.

POWER FEMINISM. A tradition advocated by **Naomi Wolf** in *Fire with Fire* (1993) in reaction against the cult of **victimization of women** that she believed was dominating the feminist movement in the 1980s and early 1990s. Power feminism emphasizes female strength, ability, and power directed toward positive action and social change. It draws a distinction between hating men and hating **sexism**; it presents itself as pro-men but also tolerant about other women's decisions concerning their own appearance and sexuality. Both men and women are acknowledged as aggressive, self-interested, competitive, individualistic beings interested in money and success. The basis for a women's movement lies in the shared pleasures and strengths of being female rather than common vulnerability, pain, or a constructed fantasy of **sisterhood**. Critics argue that power feminism is possible only for women who already have some power and that it excludes the poor and many non-Western women.

PREGNANCY DISCRIMINATION ACT (PDA). A law enacted by the US Congress in 1978 which amended Title VII of the **Civil Rights Act of 1964**. Its passage was driven by two Supreme Court decisions that mobilized the feminist movement to appeal to Congress. In *Geduldig v. Aiello* (1974) and *General Electric Co. v. Gilbert* (1976), the Court ruled that employee benefits policies that excluded pregnancy as a temporary disability did not involve the use of a sex classification in that the policy was based on pregnancy and "non-pregnant persons" also included women. The PDA defined the Civil Right Act's prohibition against **sex discrimination** to include discrimination based on pregnancy, childbirth, or related medical conditions and required that women affected by these conditions be treated the same as other persons who are not pregnant but similar in their ability or inability to work. This mandate extended to "all employment-related purposes, including receipt of fringe benefit programs."

PREMENSTRUAL SYNDROME (PMS). A variety of symptoms that occur in some women in the days before the onset of menstruation. It includes, but is not limited to, nervous tension, irritability, weight gain, edema, bloating, headache, food cravings, fatigue, and depression. British researcher Katherine Dalton is credited with much of the early research on the relationship between a woman's **menstrual cycle and behavior**; her research on PMS has been used as a successful **insanity plea defense** argument in a murder trial. In 1994 the American Psychiatric Association recommended that severe PMS be included in its manual of **mental illnesses** as Premenstrual Dysphoric Disorder

(PMDD). Some feminists believed this classification would ensure serious treatment of PMS by physicians; others feared child custody or mental competency hearings could be affected by the diagnosis.

PRESIDENT'S COMMISSION ON THE STATUS OF WOMEN (PCSW). A body established in 1961 by US President John F. Kennedy to defuse demands for the **Equal Rights Amendment**. Eleanor Roosevelt was appointed as honorary chair and Esther Peterson, head of the **Women's Bureau**, was chosen as executive vice-chair. The first government body ever to study the status of US women released its report *American Women* in 1963. Among its 24 recommendations were: **equal pay**, equal employment opportunities, paid **maternity leave**, **marital property**, **day care**, and a litigation campaign against **sex discrimination** using the Fifth and **Fourteenth Amendments**. The mere existence of the commission is credited with reviving interest in women's issues; more than 64,000 copies of the report were sold in less than a year.

PRIVACY. A US constitutional doctrine deriving from the First, Third, Fourth, Fifth, and Ninth Amendments, as well as the Due Process and **Equal Protection** Clauses of the Fourteenth Amendment that was first noted in *Griswold v. Connecticut* (1965). The Supreme Court has not recognized a comprehensive constitutional right of privacy. Instead, it has preferred to identify "zones of privacy" on a case-by-case basis. In terms of the **Fourteenth Amendment**, the right to privacy has come to mean a right to engage in certain highly personal activities, such as freedom of choice in marital, sexual and **reproductive** matters. In *Lawrence v. Texas* (2003) the Court ruled that a right to privacy prevents states from prosecuting **lesbians** and gay men for consensual sexual relations. *See also* ROE V. WADE.

PROBLEM PREGNANCY COUNSELING. A service for women who have become pregnant at a time when the pregnancy is perceived as a problem. Problem pregnancy counselors help their clients identify all options available to them, including marriage, becoming **single parents**, adoption, and **abortion**. Each woman is assisted to make her own decision according to her own wants, needs, and circumstances. *See also* FAKE CLINICS.

"PROBLEM THAT HAS NO NAME, THE." The widespread feelings of profound female dissatisfaction identified by **Betty Friedan** in *The Feminine Mystique* (1963). This discontent did not stem from problems with children, husband, or home but was rooted in the traditional role of women as housewives. Friedan suggested that there was no medical diagnosis for these frequent complaints of unhappiness because such would have challenged existing standards of feminine normality, adjustment, fulfillment, and maturity.

PRO-CHOICE MOVEMENT. A coalition organized for the purpose of maintaining a pregnant woman's right to choose among all possible options: having and keeping her baby, adoption, or **abortion**. Efforts include public education, personal counseling, social action, litigation, and lobbying for legislation in many areas. These include maintaining a woman's right to choose abortion and establishing rights to medical care and adequate financial support for those who choose to deliver and keep their babies. The name signals that this is not a "pro-abortion" movement but one about alternatives and options, freely chosen. Since the 1980s these goals have been among the top priorities of the feminist movements in Western nations. *See also* NARAL PRO CHOICE AMERICA; PLANNED PARENTHOOD; REPRODUCTIVE FREEDOM.

PRO-FAMILY MOVEMENT. A group coalition formed by US social conservatives in 1977 to coordinate support of laws reflecting traditional morality and opposition to the **Equal Rights Amendment, abortion, day care, comparable worth**, and **homosexuality**. The movement was announced by **Phyllis Schlafly** at the National Women's Conference, but the label is primarily used to describe the generic **antifeminist movement**. *See also* MORAL MAJORITY.

PROGRESSIVE WOMEN'S ASSOCIATION. A Pakistani women's group, begun in 1994 to work against **honor killings** and **stove deaths**. In its first year it monitored 1,600 cases of stove deaths, only 60 of which were prosecuted; two convictions resulted. Because many victims cannot use the legal system or the police because husbands have bribed both institutions, the group tries to educate and find employment for **survivors** who are primarily young women between the ages of 16 and 20.

PRO-LIFE FEMINISM. *See* FEMINISTS FOR LIFE.

PRO-LIFE MOVEMENT. A movement that seeks to make **abortion** illegal and places **fetal rights** above those of the pregnant woman. It encourages adoption as the solution for unwanted pregnancies and uses personal counseling, social action, litigation, and the legislative process to prevent abortion. *See also* FAKE CLINICS; NATIONAL RIGHT TO LIFE COMMITTEE; OPERATION SAVE AMERICA.

PROMISE KEEPERS (PK). A **pro-family** evangelical **men's movement** begun in 1990 by Bill McCartney, the head football coach at the University of Colorado. Within a decade the PK had attracted more than 3.5 million US men to male-only conferences in stadiums and arenas and had reached 100,000 men at events outside the United States. The organization is strongly criticized by the **new feminist movement** for its belief in a God-ordained **patriarchy** and its opposition to **abortion** and **lesbianism**. The PK movement stresses the importance of being loving and responsible fathers and husbands in their leadership role.

PROSTITUTION. A crime traditionally defined as a female offering her body for intercourse with men, usually for money. More recently, some courts have interpreted the term in a **gender neutral** fashion to include conduct of any person who engages in sexual activity as a business. **First wave feminists** were critical of laws such as the **Contagious Diseases Acts** and the **Mann Act** as repressive and reflecting a **double standard**. **Second wave feminists** were initially split as to whether prostitution could involve free choice or was always economic exploitation of women desperate for money. A minority of women engaged in sex work, particularly in Europe where prostitution is often decriminalized or licensed, have organized to promote their right to choose this business and to lobby for pro-prostitution public policy. While sometimes sympathetic with this perspective, feminists today are more likely to support punishment of clients and pimps and to organize against **sex tours** and other types of **international traffic in women**. This focus recognizes that far more women in less-developed nations are being forced by poverty or gang violence into prostitution under much worse conditions in systems that offer little legal or health protection. *See also* CALL OFF YOUR OLD TIRED ETHICS (COYOTE).

PROTECTIVE LABOR LAWS. The late 19th and early 20th century laws enacted in a number of US states to protect women working in factories from hardships such as long work days, low pay, and heavy lifting. Initially these laws were invalidated under federal constitutional doctrines which exalted personal liberties and freedom to contract over state legislative efforts to regulate the workplace. However, in 1908 the Supreme Court in *Mueller v. Oregon* upheld one of these protective laws, citing women's physical weakness, economic dependence, and special role in **reproduction**. Although initially supported by **social feminists**, protective labor legislation is now viewed as having negatively affected the job opportunities that would become available for women. For example, in *Goesaert v. Cleary* (1948) the Court upheld a Michigan law that prohibited the licensing of women as bartenders unless related to male bar owners. Protective labor legislation increased **occupational segregation** and stratification in the labor market. Enforcement of Title VII of the **Civil Rights Act of 1964** eventually led to the general invalidation of sex-specific state protective labor laws.

PRO-WOMAN LINE. A feminist argument, developed by the **Redstockings**, that rejects **gender role** socialization or women's inherent nature as an explanation of women's behavior. Instead of being "brainwashed" or "programmed" into accepting a subordinate status, women consciously acquiesce because they recognize the dangers of noncompliance. Women are thus not responsible for their own oppression; men need to change their behavior, not women. Other feminists charge that this view glorifies **victimization** and actually rationalizes the status quo in that women's behavior is seen as a rational response to the culture.

PSYCH ET PO. *See* POLITIQUE ET PSYCHANALYSE.

PSYCHOANALYTIC FEMINIST CRITICISM. The work of a wide-ranging and often disparate group of critics who seek to redefine in feminist terms the basic issues enunciated by **Sigmund Freud** over a century ago. Those issues center on the nature of **gender** as a process of sexual maturation, the role of the parents in the formation of gender, the "**anatomy is destiny**" credo, and the transition a girl makes from identification with her mother to her father or to the **patriarchy**. Contemporary psychoanalytic critics have sought to rethink such Freudian concepts as "the oedipus complex," "penis envy," and "infantile sexuality," rather than merely reject them. The major theorists who have attempted to recast the **masculinism** of Freud's theories have been **Karen Horney** and Clara Thompson, and more recently **Dorothy Dinnerstein, Nancy Chodorow, Carol Gilligan,** and Jane Gallop. Perhaps the most widely known text is **Juliet Mitchell's** *Psychoanalysis and Feminism* (1974), which argues that patriarchy is no longer crucial for the construction of society because society no longer depends on men exchanging women.

PUBLIC-PRIVATE DICHOTOMY. *See* DOMESTIC SPHERE.

PURDAH. The practice within Muslim and Hindu society removing women from public view with concealing clothing and high walls, curtains, and screens in private homes. Feminists feel this is oppressive, but others argue that women gain greater respect by not being judged by **physical attractiveness.** Since the emergence of the contemporary women's movement, the tradition has almost disappeared from Hindu practice and is only practiced to greater or lesser degrees in Islam. *See also* BURQA; CAMPAIGN TO STOP GENDER APARTHEID IN AFGHANISTAN.

-Q-

QUEEN BEE SYNDROME. The situation, described by psychologists Graham Staines, Carol Tavris, and Toby Jayaratne, in which a woman who has risen to the top in a **male-dominated** profession is unconcerned about the plight of other women and may even deny that feminist issues have any substance. Such women are seen as preferring to occupy a position of exclusive female achievement in a world of men. It has been suggested that, with the advance of feminist ideas, the "syndrome" has been less frequently observed.

QUERELLE DES FEMMES (THE WOMEN'S QUESTION). A debate on the nature of women begun in France in the early 15th century as a reaction to the blatant **misogyny** expressed in *The Romance of the Rose*, a 13th century poem that was revised at the beginning of the 15th century by Jean de Meun. The argument raged on in the literary circles of Europe for at least three centuries and centered on the belief in the inherent intellectual and moral equality of women and men versus the age-old and commonly held belief in women's **essential** deficiency. *See also* PIZAN, CHRISTINE DE.

QUESTIONS FÉMINISTES. A French **women's studies** journal begun in 1977 by a **radical feminist collective**. In 1981 it underwent a name change (to *Nouvelles Questions Féministes*) and a reorganization that rejected **Marxist** and neo-feminist intolerance of men and heterosexuality. It remains France's sole women's studies journal and is currently edited by Christine Delphy.

QURRAT AL-'AYN (1815-1851). An Iranian leader of the heretical Babism (later Baha'ism) movement, a religion that supported a higher status for women and limits on polygyny and **violence against women**. She appeared unveiled in 1844 at a time when women had first begun to question Islamic dress. She spoke in public, was a battlefield participant in Babi revolts, and died a martyr.

-R-

RACISM AND FEMINISM. The recognition by feminists that the systematic devaluation and oppression based on racial and sexual differences (along with **classism**) are simultaneous and interlocking forms of exploitation, subjecting **women of color** to double jeopardy. Authors such as **bell hooks**, **Audre Lorde**, and Barbara Hilkert Andolsen have challenged white feminists to address the racism that has corrupted middle-class white women's movements around the world in the **first** and **second waves**. This has prompted Anglo-Saxon feminists to examine and seek theoretical and practical ways to combat their own racism, and to forge genuinely collaborative alliances with black, Latina, Aboriginal, and other feminists dedicated to race and **gender** justice. *See also* OPPRESSIONS, INTERSTRUCTURING OF.

RADICAL FEMINISM. A dynamic contemporary tradition generated by the **women's liberation movement** of the 1960s. It is informed by the ideals and politics of the New Left and emphasizes the importance of personal feelings, experiences, and relationships. Women's experiences of oppression are an especially significant impetus in the formation of radical feminist ideals and politics. Radical feminists argue that **gender**

is a system of **male dominance**, and that women's biology is a root cause of **patriarchy**. Women's liberation, therefore, requires female control over their own sexuality. In terms of theory, radical feminists seek to understand gender as a system of male domination; their political goal is to end it. Although most local radical feminist groups had ceased to exist by the mid-1970s, the impact of radical feminist theory is still felt in **global feminism** and the debates over **reproductive freedom, pornography,** and **prostitution**.

RADICALESBIANS. *See* LAVENDER MENACE.

RAICHO, HIRATSUKA. *See* BLUESTOCKING SOCIETY; ICHIKAWA, FUSAE.

RAMABAI, PANDITA (1858-1922). A Sanskrit scholar and prominent feminist activist in India. She founded a group of women's organizations, lectured in India and abroad on women, and wrote *Women's Religious Law* (1882) and *The High Caste Hindu Woman* (1887), both of which supported women's rights. She founded girls' schools, orphanages, and widows' homes. In 1889 she was one of the delegates to the Indian National Congress.

RANKIN, JEANNETTE (1880-1973). The first woman member of the US House of Representatives, elected in 1916 from the state of Montana. She had been very active in the **woman suffrage movement** and had her greatest impact as the leader of the floor debate on the **Nineteenth Amendment**. She was defeated in her race for the Senate in 1918 but returned to the House in 1941. She is the only member of Congress to have voted against US entry into both world wars and was the sole vote against World War II. Between congressional terms, she lobbied for the **National Consumers League** and the Women's International League for Peace and Freedom. As a life-long pacifist, she led the Jeannette Rankin Brigade of the Women's Strike for Peace to the Capitol in Washington, D.C., in 1968 to protest the Vietnam War.

RANSOME-KUTI, FUNMILAYO (1900-1978). The leading supporter of **woman suffrage** in Nigeria. In 1932 she founded a local ladies' club of elite women to perform charitable work, but in the 1940s she began to work across ethnic and class lines for the vote and women's rights through the Nigerian Women's Union (1949). In 1953 she organized a conference that became the Federation of Nigerian Women's Societies. With independence in 1960, suffrage was granted in all parts of the nation except in the Islamic Northern Region. Ransome-Kuti continued to work for universal enfranchisement until it was granted in 1976.

RAP GROUP. A method used by participants in the **women's liberation** branch of the **new feminist movement** to analyze the political meaning of personal experiences. Women regularly meet in a small group to share personal problems and feelings as women and to gain insight into the commonalities of these experiences.

RAPE. The use of coercion or violence to force a person to engage in sexual activity against her or his will. Under English common law, rape was narrowly defined as penile penetration of a woman's vagina by force and against her will. In the early 1970s the **new feminist movement** organized around the issue of rape by holding **speak-outs**, founding **rape crisis centers**, and seeking reforms of rape laws. In most US jurisdictions today, rape laws are **gender neutral** and in some areas the term "sexual assault" is used to encompass different offenses from "unwanted touching" to acts of intercourse (oral, anal, or vaginal) with penetration by an "object." Feminists have succeeded in redefining the nature of rape from an act of sex to an act of violence. Police and court procedures in investigating and prosecuting rape have also undergone major changes: special sexual offense investigative and prosecution units have been established; rules of evidence regarding corroboration and consent have been altered; greater protection is afforded the victim in terms of public testimony and questions about prior sexual history. Health care and social service professionals too have revised their treatment of rape victims to conform with physical evidentiary standards and new mental health knowledge of posttraumatic stress disorder that is the aftermath of rape. Because these changes have been most effective in prosecuting rapes by strangers ("real rape"), feminists have begun to define rape as a crime of sexual coercion that occurs between spouses, acquaintances, dates, and strangers. Sexual violence has also emerged as a global issue as many nations have adopted similar laws as well as new laws to permit rape victims to find out if their assailants are infected with **AIDS**, to stiffen penalties for sexual offenses, and to establish special registers for sex offenders. In developing nations these protections are less available to women. Because of the association of rape with loss of family honor and the difficulty women face in proving rape under these legal systems, rapes are less likely to be reported or prosecuted. In 1998 the treaty creating the **International Criminal Court** defined rape as a war crime. *See also* DATE RAPE; MARITAL RAPE; STATUTORY RAPE.

RAPE CRISIS CENTER. A feminist **self-help** institution that offers advice and support to the victims of sexual assault by providing persons to accompany victims to hospitals, police stations, and the courts. Typically such centers provide some combination of crisis counseling (with a 24-hour hotline), legal advocacy, medical care, and evidence-gathering services. The first rape crisis centers were established in 1972 and now almost all large US cities and other world cities have these special services for **rape** victims.

RATHBONE, ELEANOR (1872-1946). An Englishwoman selected as the first president of the National Union of Societies for Equal Citizenship (formerly the **National Union of Women's Suffrage Societies**) in 1919. She was elected to Parliament in 1929 as an Independent Member for the Combined English Universities. During her tenure, Rathbone pressed for equal rights, family allowances, and relief for women in gender-repressive societies across the empire, particularly in India.

REAL (REALISTIC, EQUAL, ACTIVE FOR LIFE) WOMEN OF CANADA. An organization of conservative Canadian women, formed in 1982 as an alternative women's movement. Adopting the "**pro-family**" label of their US counterparts, REAL Women opposes all **abortions**, sex education, **contraception**, **day-care** subsidies, **no-fault divorce**, **comparable worth**, **affirmative action**, and **homosexuality**. Although REAL Women supports equal opportunities for women in education, employment, and **pensions**, it is more concerned with policies that permit women to remain in the home.

RECLAIM THE NIGHT. *See* TAKE BACK THE NIGHT.

REDSTOCKINGS. A New York-based **radical feminist** group founded by **Shulamith Firestone** and writer Ellen Willis in 1969. Although it functioned for less than two years, the group became nationally known when it disrupted state legislative hearings on **abortion** law reform to demand repeal. It is also credited with: developing the theory of **con-**

sciousness-raising; voicing the **pro-woman line**; and inventing the **speak-out**. Its circulation of the "Redstockings Manifesto" (1969) and other literature helped to spread the messages of feminism. It was briefly reconstituted in 1975 in an attempt to revive radical feminism.

REFORM FEMINISM. *See* LIBERAL FEMINISM.

REFRAMING. A technique to shift the meaning of thoughts, behaviors, feelings, or situations that allows the reframer to think differently (hopefully, more positively) about these. This technique can be useful and therapeutic, but feminists note that women are more often expected to reframe situations to make them work more quickly and more smoothly than men. For example, if a man is questioning a woman she might resent this and label it a cross-examination. Reframing might have this woman change the label to requests for information.

REGINA V. BUTLER. A ruling by the Canadian Supreme Court in 1992 that permitted the criminalization of **pornography** when there is harm to women's **self-esteem**, physical safety, and pursuit of equality. The court thus defined obscenity as that which degrades women rather than offends a moral standard. The **Women's Legal Education and Action Fund** (LEAF), which intervened in the case, and most other Canadian women's groups supported the decision. The following guidelines were established: violence, child nudity, and bondage are pornographic; adult erotica is not. In the post-Butler era, however, most heterosexual materials have freely circulated and feminist, **lesbian**, and gay erotica have been suppressed by the Canadian government.

RELIGIOUS COALITION FOR REPRODUCTIVE CHOICE (RCRC). A **pro-choice** coalition of over 40 Christian, Jewish, and other religious organizations representing 18 faith traditions in the United States. It formed in 1973 to counter the role of the Catholic Church in the **pro-life movement** and to provide a moral argument for **reproductive freedom**. The coalition now has 22 affiliates in 19 states as well as individual members, including many prominent theologians and religious leaders within its Clergy for Choice network.

REPRESENTATION, FEMINIST THEORIES OF. A view based on the poststructuralist emphasis on the contextual rather than a fixed relationship between sign and signified. Feminist theories of representation analyze the politics of textual representations of **gender**. Most radically, feminist theorists would argue that all textual representations of women are **pornographic** as language is **phallogocentric** and necessarily objectifies **woman as other**.

REPRESENTATION OF THE PEOPLE (EQUAL FRANCHISE) ACT OF 1928. The law that gave British women equal voting rights with men. The act received little opposition after its introduction in March and became law on July 2, 10 years after the franchise had been extended to women over 30. **Woman suffrage** groups had actively worked to remove this age restriction and were aided by the election of eight female members of Parliament in 1923.

REPRODUCTION. The traditional primary role of women. Feminists distinguish between "biological reproduction," or procreation, and "reproduction of the labor force." Because biological reproduction requires both sexes, the societal attitude that it is the principal role of women is a social construction limiting women's roles and behavior. In **patriarchal** capitalist societies, reproduction of the labor force is assigned to women ("mothers"), who are rewarded with subsistence but not wages. If childbearers and childrearers were given wages, the labor cost to capitalists for commodities production would be greatly raised. Feminists' campaigns for **wages for housework** are based on this undercompensated labor. In some societies, "reproduction of culture" is also women's role. Women may be seen as innately gifted with the capacity for fine craftwork, better able than men to create beautiful and valued material objects. The Western cultural tradition, however, tends to see men as gifted with the capacity to create material objects and women with the capacity to reproduce organisms and the food and clothing necessary for their nurture.

REPRODUCTION OF MOTHERING. *See* CHODOROW, NANCY.

REPRODUCTIVE FREEDOM. A term encompassing a woman's right to control her own fertility, to choose not to become a mother and the right to become one. This includes access to sex education, birth control and **family planning**, **abortion**, and voluntary sterilization.

REPRODUCTIVE TECHNOLOGIES (RT). A term encompassing various technological interventions into conception, pregnancy, and childbirth. These include methods that enhance the probability of conception through fertility drugs, allow conception of children by means other than intercourse as in artificial insemination, in vitro fertilization, **surrogacy**, and, in the future, **ectogenesis**. Radical feminists once viewed these advances as a means to free women from their own biology, and some **liberal feminists** still support a woman's right to choose these methods. Other feminists view them as the latest examples of male control over women's bodies and argue that these technologies are exploitative, costly, often ineffective and unsafe, and present a high risk of multiple births. The purpose of RT is not to cure infertility but instead may encourage women to keep trying each new technology in search of a baby, thereby reinforcing **reproduction** as their primary role. *See also* AMNIOCENTESIS.

REPUBLICAN MOTHER. A concept that emerged in the aftermath of the American Revolution and during the French Revolution "Reign of Terror." It was argued that the best contribution that a woman could make to the republican cause was to instill republican values in her children by educating them at home herself and **breastfeeding** them herself (rather than using a wet nurse, as was fashionable at the time). In addition, a republican mother was required to unquestioningly support her spouse in the performance of his civic duties. Although the concept did not include a political role for women, it did legitimate the charitable work of women and the further education of women to facilitate this new role. The ideology of the republican mother informs a number of the proposals that **Mary Wollstonecraft** makes in her *Vindication of the Rights of Woman* (1792).

REVERSE DISCRIMINATION. A term that refers to allegations of discrimination brought by employees or other individuals, such as US white men, who have not been designated under **affirmative action** programs as preferred for employment opportunities. The US Supreme Court considers each charge of reverse discrimination on its own merits and has generally accepted the principle of **gender** or racial preference as a way of redressing past discrimination. In *Johnson v. Transportation Agency of Santa Clara County* (1987) the Court rejected the complaint of a man who was denied the supervisory position given to a woman, despite his longer work experience and a slightly higher score on an oral interview. Because of the gender imbalance in the agency workforce (no woman held any of the 238 skilled positions), the Court ruled that the **Civil Rights Act of 1964, Title VII** allows some discretion to end discrimination.

REVOLUTIONARY ASSOCIATION OF THE WOMEN OF AFGHANISTAN (RAWA). The oldest and most radical Afghan women's political organization, established in 1977 in Kabul to fight for women's rights and equality. It was the only Afghan women's group to oppose the Soviet invasion. It was also the only group, male or female, to organize a resistance to the Taliban. Using the **burqa**, they secretly photographed beatings and executions and posted the pictures on their website. They educated girls and women in underground schools, ran clinics, and published a magazine. Members kept their identities secret because the Taliban had sworn to kill them and Meena, the founder of RAWA, was assassinated in Pakistan in 1987. Other Afghan women's groups still avoid them because of their secular Western ideas about women's role in society. A RAWA member participated in the 2001 meetings in Bonn to negotiate peace in Afghanistan.

RICH, ADRIENNE (1929-). A contemporary American feminist poet and theorist and more recently one of the most prominent spokespersons for **lesbian feminism**. In her early books of poetry she reflects her Radcliffe education, which exclusively focused on studying male poets. Her own experience with motherhood produced the more radical later works, "When We Dead Awaken: Writing as Re-Vision" (1972) and *Of Woman Born* (1976), the latter a portrait of motherhood compiled through literary, anthropological, political, and medical documents. Her book of poetry, *Diving into the Wreck*, won the National Book Award in 1974, while her *Twenty-one Love Poems* (1976) is a sonnet cycle about **lesbian** love. In her *It Is the Lesbian in Us* (1976) Rich wrote, "Even before I wholly knew I was a lesbian, it was the lesbian in me who pursued that elusive configuration. And I believe it is the lesbian in every woman who is compelled by female energy, who gravitates toward strong women, who seeks a literature that will express that energy and strength. It is the lesbian in us who drives us to feel imaginatively, render in language, grasp, the full connection between woman and woman."

RIGHT TO LIFE. *See* NATIONAL RIGHT TO LIFE COMMITTEE (NRLC).

RÍOS CARDENAS, MARIA. A Mexican journalist and founder of the feminist journal *Mujer* (1926-29) in Mexico City. She urged women to join together in one national federation of women to gain equal legal rights to combat **street harassment**, physical assault, and **rape**, and to support children and unmarried mothers. Under her leadership the first Congress of Women Workers and Peasants was held in 1931 in Mexico City and attracted some 600 delegates, most of whom were professional women. Ríos Cardenas led two more national congresses of women workers, and each failed to create a single unified feminist group. Thereafter, communist women took over the leadership of the women's movement in Mexico.

RIOT GRRRLS MOVEMENT. A feminist movement in North America and Western Europe, comprised primarily of young women, ages 14-25, who use their sexiness, **assertiveness**, and loudness to debunk the notions of women as dumb, inferior, or bad. Riot Grrrls use their bodies as art, wear sexually revealing clothes, and use punk rock to convey their message. The movement emerged in the early 1990s around female groups such as the United States' Bikini Kill and Hole and Britain's Huggy Bear and Spice Girls. The movement, burned by media coverage, retreated into on-line zines and chat rooms in the late 1990s, but has become visible again in the **Lilith Fair** and **Ladyfest** concerts. *See also* GIRL POWER.

ROBINSON, MARY (1944-). The first female president of Ireland, 1990-1997, and the UN High Commissioner for Human Rights, 1997-2002. As a lawyer and throughout her political career, Robinson took on **gender** equality issues. A self-labeled feminist, she supported the decriminalization of **homosexuality** and the **ordination of women** as Catholic priests.

ROE V. WADE, 410 US 113 (1973). A US Supreme Court decision that overturned a Texas statute that criminalized **abortion** except when necessary to save the life of the mother. The Court determined that the statute at issue violated the **Fourteenth Amendment's** Due Process Clause in that it unnecessarily infringed on a woman's right to **privacy**. With abortion rights now included within the meaning of the Fourteenth Amendment, the state could only act to restrict abortions if necessary to promote a compelling state interest. Such a compelling interest could be found only in two situations: where a restriction was necessary to protect the health or safety of the mother; and where the fetus was viable. Because abortion performed under a doctor's care was as safe as or safer than a completed pregnancy, the majority opinion determined that there could be no significant restriction on a woman's right to choose abortion during the first trimester. During the second trimester, there was increased risk to the health of a pregnant woman, presenting a compelling state interest in establishing further medical regulations on abortions performed during that stage. With respect to the state's compelling interest in the existence of the fetus, that would exist only when the fetus became viable, typically at the beginning of the third trimester. Thus, after the time of viability, the state could prohibit abortions except where necessary to protect the health or life of the mother. The lawyer (Sarah Weddington) who argued the case before the Court has been active in the feminist-led movement to preserve the opinion's liberal guidelines. Most Court decisions on abortion since *Roe* have weakened **reproductive freedom** by narrowing access, allowing more state regulations, and breaking with the trimester framework. *Webster v. Reproductive Health Services* (1989) and *Planned Parenthood v. Casey* (1992) alerted the **pro-choice movement** that recriminalization of abortion was possible, particularly with the retirement of supportive members of the Court. *See also* HYDE AMENDMENT; MCCORVEY, NORMA; O'CONNOR, SANDRA DAY; PARTIAL-BIRTH ABORTION.

ROHYPNOL. *See* DATE RAPE DRUG.

ROLE MODEL. A person to whom another, usually younger, person can look for inspiration and guidance by example. Feminists have decried the limited and stereotypical role models available to girls in textbooks, **television**, films, and (often) their neighborhoods and local institutions. Because women are socialized from an early age to accept certain roles and reject others as "inappropriate," a lack of female role models is a barrier to pursuit of professional and **nontraditional occupations**. *See also* MENTORING; OLD BOYS CLUB/AGELESS WOMAN CLUB.

ROMANCE NOVELS. A genre descended from sentimental and gothic novels. The contemporary romance novel, also known popularly as "supermarket gothic" or "Harlequin romances," has been criticized by feminists for perpetuating regressive fantasies about the "knight in shining armor" or the "happily-ever-after marriage." Recent variations on Harlequins depict young female heroines who enter the job market and triumph professionally as well as personally. Late capitalist versions of the romance script depict women who successfully consume goods and achieve celebrity in their own rights. In the novels of Judith Krantz, for instance, women are rewarded, not punished, for their consumption and their successful marketing of their own beauty.

ROSENBERG, ROSALIND. *See* EQUAL EMPLOYMENT OPPORTUNITY COMMISSION V. SEARS, ROEBUCK & CO.

ROSIE THE RIVETER. A World War II era song and media image promoting women's employment in undermanned US defense industries. "Rosie" has come to symbolize for feminists the entry of women into heavy industrial jobs traditionally restricted to men and the demonstrated ability of women to perform these duties. After the end of the war, women were encouraged to return to the home. Although most women were pushed out of these nontraditional jobs, they remained in the paid labor force in jobs predominantly held by women.

ROUDY, YVETTE (1929-). A French politician, writer, and feminist. She translated **Betty Friedan**'s *The Feminine Mystique* (1963), which brought her into closer association with French feminist groups. She was a co-founder of the **Mouvement Démocratique et Féminin**, a small group of noncommunist feminists of the left. In 1979 she was elected to the European Parliament, and in 1981 she became the first head of the **Ministère des Droits de la Femme**, where she served until 1986. In 1996 she recruited five liberal and five conservative women who issued the "Manifesto of the Ten," calling for more women in elected office and ultimately a policy of **gender parity**.

ROY, RAJA RAMMOHAN (1772-1833). A pioneer Bengali advocate for women's rights in India through the reform of Hinduism. Roy supported women's education and property rights and opposed polygamy. In 1818 and 1820 he published pamphlets on **suttee**, which was criminalized in 1829.

ROYAL COMMISSION ON THE STATUS OF WOMEN IN CANADA (RCSW). A body established by Prime Minister Lester B. Pearson on February 16, 1967, at the request of the anglophone women's coalition, the Committee for the Equality of Women (CEW), and its Quebec counterpart, the **Fédération des Femmes du Québec** (FFQ). In December 1970 its moderate report was tabled in the House of Commons. Even so, during the period of its writing, most Canadian women's organizations developed a feminist perspective, and by 1979 one-third of its reforms had been implemented, including the creation of a federal Advisory Council on the Status of Women on May 31, 1973. In 2002 the National Coalition of Provincial and Territorial Advisory Councils on the Status of Women called for the creation of a new royal commission to study Canadian women's equality.

RU 486 (MIFEPRISTONE). An abortifacient pill available since 1988 in France, but not until 2000 in the United States. It is highly safe and effective in inducing termination of pregnancy during the first 12 weeks when used with another drug. Threatened by a boycott of all their products by the **pro-life movement**, US drug companies delayed seeking government approval for the marketing of the drug. Because of its many promising applications in the treatment of other conditions, the drug is welcomed in the medical community. Feminists sought its availability in the United States as an alternative to the surgical procedures that have made **abortion clinics** the target of antiabortion activists. Early studies indicate that the drug is less commonly used due to its greater discomfort and the three doctor's appointments required.

RUKEYSER, MURIEL (1913-1980). A New York writer, considered to be one of the major feminist poets of the 20th century. Rukeyser published 18 collections of poetry. One of her poems, "The Poem as Mask," contained a line ("No more masks") that was adopted as a feminist slogan. Rukeyser's poetry uses traditional images associated with women, childbirth, fertility, transcendence, and female mythic figures, and transforms these symbols into powerful representations of women's strength. Although she was never formally allied with the feminist movement, she understood the centrality of race and **gender** in life.

RUSS, JOANNA (1937-). A contemporary American **lesbian feminist** author, best known for *The Female Man* (1975) and the theoretical work *How to Suppress Women's Writing* (1983). Russ claims that she writes "realism disguised as fantasy," or **feminist science fiction**, and is credited with bringing **lesbian** and feminist issues into that genre. Her novels and short story "When It Changed" present a world where men no longer exist, having been exterminated by the superior women who have finally found the ultimate solution to the **gender** dilemma. Russ has expressed a concern that feminism is becoming watered down in order to appeal to middle-class white professional women. Her most recent writings have been critical essays such as *What Are We Fighting For: Sex, Race, Class, and the Future of Feminism* (1998).

RUTH. The Moabite daughter-in-law of Naomi in the book that bears her name in the Old Testament. She is usually seen as a model of faithfulness because she refuses to leave her mother-in-law after both are widowed, stating "whither thou goest, I will go . . . thy people will be my people." Some feminists believe that the account shows a desire to suppress the independence of women. In particular this story of loyalty between two women has been used to deny a married woman the right to establish her own legal domicile apart from her husband without risking a charge of desertion.

-S-

EL-SAADAWI, NAWAL (1931-). An Egyptian writer, feminist, and psychiatrist, whose explicit 1972 book *al-Mar'ah wa al-Jins* (*Women and Sex*) cost her her job at the Ministry of Health and caused a controversy comparable to that of **Qasim Amin's** *Tahrir al-Mar'a* (1899). In denouncing the practice of **clitoridectomy** and other forms of sexual and commercial exploitation of women's bodies, el-Saadawi politicized the topic of sexuality in Arab society. As the author of 40 books on Arab women, as well as several novels, autobiographies, and short fiction collections, she has received national and international awards. She also served as the first president of the **Arab Women's Solidarity Association.** In 2001 she was accused in a private lawsuit of defaming Islam by urging women not to cover their heads. The suit, aimed at annulling her marriage on the grounds that Islam prohibits marriage to heretics, was closely watched by human rights activists and was rejected by a family court.

EL-SA'ID, 'AMINAH (1914-1995). An Egyptian journalist and advocate of women's rights. She was the editor of *Hawa* (Eve), a women's weekly magazine with the largest foreign readership of any Arabic publication. One of the first female graduates of Cairo University, El-Sa'id was a frequent lecturer on Arab women at international conferences.

SALEM WITCH TRIALS (1692-1693). The proceedings in Salem, Massachusetts, where 26 people were convicted and 19 (including 16 women) were executed by hanging as witches. Fifty more people confessed to being witches. The men involved were victims of guilt by association. The women were primarily poor widows with no male protector within the society. They were generally accused of crimes against their appropriate female roles: of not loving their families, preying on children, adultery, inspiring fear in men for their lack of deference, or rebellion against an authority figure (usually a magistrate). One woman had been married three times and "would not be **dominated**" by her husbands; another was accused of dressing provocatively. Many women who displayed psychological, emotional, or behavioral deviance were labeled a witch throughout the 15th to 17th centuries in Europe as well, where as many as 85,000 women may have been executed.

SAMENESS. A neutral legal standard that prohibits **sex discrimination** by requiring that like individuals be treated the same. **Difference feminists** argue that this involves an unstated male norm (i.e., "same" means "the same as men") which often results in inequities growing out of women's differences such as pregnancy. *See also* GENDER-NEUTRAL LAW.

SAME-SEX MARRIAGES. The legal recognition of marriages between two persons of the same sex. Although only the Netherlands, Belgium, and two Canadian provinces currently recognize same-sex marriages, a number of national, state, and local governments have given same-sex **domestic partnerships** some of the same rights and privileges given to heterosexual couples. Vermont passed a law in 2000 that treats same-sex civil unions the same as heterosexual marriages. However, the US Congress passed the Defense of Marriage Act in 1996 to allow states to refuse to recognize any other state's law that legalizes same-sex marriages. By 2003, 37 states had passed this legislation. The feminist movement supports such marriages and has hailed the decision of the *New York Times* in 2002 to include gay and

lesbian committment ceremonies along with the engagement and wedding stories of heterosexual couples.

SAMPSON, DEBORAH GANNETT (1760-1827). The only known woman to serve in the US Revolutionary War. Sampson, who wore men's clothing for greater freedom, used a male name and enlisted for the salary. Her sex was discovered when she was hospitalized for battle wounds. She received an honorable discharge and a pension from Massachusetts. However, her Baptist church expelled her. After the war, Sampson appeared in theaters on the East Coast in uniform. *See also* WOMEN IN COMBAT.

SANDER, HELKE (1937-). A German filmmaker and feminist activist. As a student, she founded the Berlin Action Council for Women's Liberation and presented its program for practical assistance to women at the conference of the Socialist German Students' Federation (SDS) in 1968. This speech, which stated that women are only accepted when they adapt to male norms, is viewed as the beginning of the German **new feminist movement**. She also founded the women's group Brot und Rosen (Bread and Roses, 1972) and the journal *Frauen und Film* (*Women and Film*, 1974). Her films include: *Redupers* (1977); *Der Subjektive Faktor* (*The Subjective Factor*, 1981), which focuses on the history of the new women's movement; and *The Germans and Their Men* (1989), which suggests that without equal rights German women are not equally responsible for the crimes of the nation.

SANGER, MARGARET (1879-1966). A US pioneer in sex education and "**birth control**," a term that she originated. Her interest began as a child, when she observed her mother's health weaken with many pregnancies. She began her work with poverty-stricken immigrants on New York's Lower East Side. In 1916 she opened the first birth control clinic in the United States. She founded the American Birth Control League (later, the **Planned Parenthood** Federation of America), organized the first world population conference, and served as the first president of the International Planned Parenthood Federation.

SAPPHO (ca. 610-580 B. C.). A celebrated Greek poet and the earliest known female writer in Western literature. She was at the center of an intimate circle or school of young women on the Island of Lesbos who studied music and poetry and worshipped Aphrodite. Her poetry, which survives only in fragments, is characterized by simplicity, passion, and lyric beauty. Because some of the love poems were dedicated to favorites among her female companions, the word "**lesbian**" has acquired its current meaning of female homosexual. Her poetry was widely admired in antiquity, and she herself was known as "The Poetess" and "The Tenth Muse."

SATI. *See* **SUTTEE.**

SCHLAFLY, PHYLLIS (1924-). An American **antifeminist** and conservative spokesperson, lawyer, and author. She was the founder of the Stop ERA movement in 1972 and the **Eagle Forum** in 1975. Since 1967 she has published the monthly newsletter, *The Phyllis Schlafly Report*. She also has a daily radio show and a syndicated column. She has long been a conservative activist within the US Republican Party. Schlafly came to public prominence as the leading opponent of the **Equal Rights Amendment** and is widely credited with preventing its ratification. Among her 20 books are: *The Power of the Positive Woman* (1977); *Pornography's Victims* (1987); and *Feminist Fantasies* (2002).

SCHREINER, OLIVE (1855-1920). A South African feminist and writer, best known as the author of *The Story of an African Farm* (1883). A socialist, pacifist, and antiimperialist, Schreiner also published a wide-ranging history of women's subjugation entitled *Woman and Labour* (1911). Born into a family of missionaries, Schreiner spent her youth traveling across Africa and witnessing injustices and discrimination. Later she served as vice-president of the Women's Enfranchisement League in South Africa, but resigned when it refused to fight for the "colored" woman's right to vote. When she spoke before a meeting of the Women's Political Union in 1914, she demanded "a society in which all women of all races on earth should equally find their place." Perhaps her most provocative contribution to feminism can be found in her essay "Sex-Parasitism" (in *Woman and Labour*), in which she compares the modern unemployed female to a large insect that feeds off the body of its mate.

SCHROEDER, PATRICIA (1940-). A feminist leader within the US House of Representatives, 1973-1997. The Colorado Democrat and Harvard-educated lawyer co-chaired the **Congressional Caucus for**

Women's Issues for 10 years. She was a leading advocate for the **Freedom of Access to Clinic Entrances Act**, the **Family and Medical Leave Act**, the **Violence Against Women Act**, and the right of women in the military to fly combat missions. She is remembered for her quick wit ("I have a brain and a uterus and I use both") and for her unsuccessful presidential bid in 1988.

SCHWARZER, ALICE (1942-). A German activist, writer, and publisher. In 1971 she organized the first public protest against Germany's **abortion** law, by arranging for the magazine *Stern* to publish names and photographs of 374 women who admitted to having had abortions. Since 1977 she has edited the bimonthly magazine *EMMA*, where she has addressed issues ranging from the theory of sexuality to household politics. She is the author of several books, including *So Fing Es An! Die Nue Frauenbewegung* (*That's How It Started! The New Women's Movement*, 1983).

SCHWIMMER, ROSIKA (1877-1948). A Hungarian journalist, feminist, and **woman suffrage** leader. While in her early 20s, she founded the first women's trade union group, the Council of Women, the Hungarian Feminist Association, and edited a pacifist feminist journal. She became prominent in the **International Woman Suffrage Alliance**, but withdrew in favor of peace work during World War I. In 1918 she became the world's first woman ambassador (to Switzerland). She emigrated to the United States after the communist takeover and continued her advocacy for women by proposing in 1935 that an international women's archives be established.

SCIENCE, FEMINIST CRITIQUE OF. The assessment of conventional scientific research by feminist scientists, who have identified bias in the scientific questions asked, the choice of experimental subjects, the data acquisition process, and the methods of drawing conclusions and postulating theories based on research results. For example, a standard explanation of human **reproduction** once was based on **sex role stereotypes** that featured an active sperm coming in contact with a passive egg, while in fact both are active in the process of fertilization.

SCOTT, ROSE (1847-1925). An Australian feminist and **woman suffrage** leader. Founder of the Womanhood Suffrage League in 1891, Scott also worked for **protective labor laws**, raising the age of consent, and other **moral reforms**. She rejected proposals of marriage on the grounds that life should not be wasted on the admiration of one man.

SEARS CASE. *See* EQUAL EMPLOYMENT OPPORTUNITY COMMISSION V. SEARS, ROEBUCK & CO.

SECOND SEX. *See* BEAUVOIR, SIMONE DE.

SECOND SHIFT. *See* DOUBLE SHIFT.

SECOND TIER. A term coined by Sheila Tobias to describe college students, a disproportionate number of whom are women, who choose not to pursue studies in science, engineering, or mathematics despite considerable demonstrated aptitude and interest. Students in the second tier are often discouraged by the way that science is taught and not by the pursuit of science itself. Sheila Widnall explains this leakage from the educational pipeline and failure to advance in science careers as a function of response to educational and career pressures, self-perception, and the perceptions of teachers and **mentors**, which differ significantly between women and men. *See also* MATH ANXIETY.

SECOND WAVE FEMINISM. The worldwide revival of an organized **women's rights movement**, beginning in the late 1960s in the United States and Western Europe within movements for international peace, racial equality, student power, and socialist politics. Most regions of the Third World also have autonomous groups organized around women's rights issues; **women's liberation groups** are still primarily found only in Western democracies. Second wave feminists, now in late middle age or older, are still active and continue to control most movement institutions. *See also* FIRST WAVE FEMINISM; THIRD WAVE FEMINISM.

SELF-DEFENSE (LEGAL DEFENSE). *See* BATTERED WOMAN SYNDROME; INSANITY PLEAS (DEFENSE).

SELF-DEFENSE TRAINING. An early form of antirape action adopted by local **women's liberation** groups. Because **rape** victims were often blamed for failing to defend themselves, courses in judo, karate, and street-fighting techniques were offered at **women's centers**. By learning to trust her body, a woman could gain self-confidence and self-reliance and reduce the sense of vulnerability and helplessness that comes with dependence on a man for protection. Use of these tactics contributed to the initial militant image of the **new feminist movement**.

SELF-ESTEEM. The way in which a person perceives personal worth. A person with low self-esteem is assumed to be more anxious and more willing to respond to pressures to assume a role. Psychologists believe that girls may not utilize all their abilities due to traditional **gender role** expectations, and therefore, are less likely to develop an independent sense of self-worth. Instead they depend on others' opinions of them and define themselves in terms of their relationships with others, especially their **physical attractiveness** to men. The **new feminist movement** has linked low self-esteem with **eating disorders, math anxiety,** and commitment to abusive relationships among girls and women. With the publication of *Revolution from Within: A Book of Self-Esteem* (1992) by **Gloria Steinem**, the term "self-esteem" came into popular use by feminists. *See also* SECOND TIER.

SELF-HELP. A feminist strategy for **empowering** women to act together for change in their own lives. Self-help groups have been organized for victims of **rape** and **domestic violence** and in the areas of family law, **self-defense**, and health care. Participants in such groups learn to effect changes in the present system and to create woman-controlled **alternative institutions**.

SELF-HELP HEALTH MOVEMENT. A network composed of feminist health centers and local groups that diagnose and treat simple gynecological problems. Common services include: pelvic exams, Pap smears, **abortions**, pregnancy tests, **menstrual extraction,** and the treatment of vaginal infections and syphilis. In 1983 women began performing alternative insemination with the common turkey baster as a service to single and **lesbian** women often denied access to that procedure. The goal is to demystify medical procedures and to **empower** women by involving them in their own health care. After peaking at almost 50 centers in the mid-1970s, there are now only a few women-controlled health centers in the United States due to the rise of **abortion clinic violence** in the 1980s and the attendant costs of security and insurance, as well as regulatory battles over clinic licensing and the definition of medical services and providers.

SELF-MUTILATION. A set of actions also referred to as the "deliberate self-harm syndrome." Self-mutilation covers a wide range of behaviors, from making shallow cuts on the skin (called cutting) to eye removal. Estimated to affect 0.77 percent of the population, self-mutilation occurs much more frequently among women and also includes people driven to burn themselves or break their own bones. Self-mutilation also tends to occur in people who have had **eating disorders**, particularly bulimia or anorexia. Research has shown that cutters tend to engage in the activity as a means of diverting attention from some deeper psychic trauma, such as childhood sexual abuse. The cycle of cutting includes a state of mounting anxiety or anger followed by the need to cut, which is done alone and in private. After the cutting there is generally a period of relief until the cycle builds again. Feminists have been concerned with the fact that **adolescent girls**, at most risk for developing cutting behaviors, have not received education or counseling to prevent the syndrome. Sources on the topic include Armando R., Favazza, *Bodies under Siege: Self-Mutilation in Culture and Society* (1996).

SENECA FALLS CONVENTION. The first Woman's Rights Convention in the United States, held in Seneca Falls, New York, in July 1848. It is often used to mark the "official" beginning of the US **woman suffrage movement**. Under the leadership of **Lucretia Mott** and **Elizabeth Cady Stanton,** the convention of more than 300 attendees approved a Declaration of Sentiments modeled on the Declaration of Independence. It was signed by 68 women and 32 men. The Declaration stated that all women and men are created equal and contained 12 resolutions, one of which called for the vote for women. The suffrage resolution was the only one that did not receive unanimous approval.

SENECA WOMEN'S PEACE ENCAMPMENT. *See* GREENHAM COMMON WOMEN'S PEACE CAMP.

SEPARATE SPHERE. *See* DOMESTIC SPHERE.

SEPARATISM. A feminist strategy ranging from male exclusion from the women's movement to withdrawal of women into an all-female community and **counter-culture** in order to learn to trust and value other women. Some women see the withdrawal as temporary, until integration with **gender** equality is possible. For others, permanent separatism from the **patriarchal** world and the creation of women's communities is the core goal. **Lesbianism** is affirmed and heterosexuality is viewed as an institution that favors men and obstructs women's relationships with each other. Early separatist movement groups include the **Feminists** and the **Furies**. Prominent theorists of separatism are Charlotte Bunch, Sonia Johnson, Jill Johnston, and **Adrienne Rich**.

SETTLEMENT HOUSE MOVEMENT. A movement that began with Toynbee Hall in London, England, in which concerned persons, usually of above-average means, lived among the poor to improve their conditions. The movement came to the United States in the 1880s and involved teaching **self-help** skills to the urban poor, largely immigrants. Hull House in Chicago, founded by **Jane Addams** in 1889, served 19 different nationalities. Staff lived in the settlement houses where they provided **child care** for working women, facilitated cultural enrichment programs, and became involved in direct political action toward reform, including improving neighborhood conditions, industrial safety laws, and child labor laws. Many **social feminists** came out of this movement, which was unique for having a female majority in leadership and staff until the end of World War II. Feminists have taken pride in the accomplishments of these female settlement workers, but have also been critical of their nativism and **racism**.

SEX DISCRIMINATION. *See* GENDER DISCRIMINATION.

SEX OBJECT. The idea that women exist to please and be acquired by men. This perspective is often used in **advertising** to attract male viewers. Feminists believe that this encourages women to perceive their bodies as inadequate and fosters damaging **sex role stereotypes**.

SEX ROLE. *See* GENDER ROLE.

SEX ROLE SOCIALIZATION. The process of learning the culturally prescribed behavioral expectations relevant to our gendered roles in society. Theories of **gender** socialization differ in the extent to which they view such processes to be rooted in inherent biological processes, psychological processes related to cognitive development, or social (e.g., parental and cultural) processes. While most feminists agree that gender roles are culturally mapped, they differ concerning the relative importance of cognitive development, imitation, and social learning.

SEX ROLE STEREOTYPES. The exaggerated beliefs about appropriate behaviors and traits that relate to **gender roles**. Such stereotypes affect how we see ourselves and others, so that we identify different traits as "naturally" occurring in females or males, rather than viewing "traits" (e.g., "masculinity" or "femininity") as culturally prescribed. Feminists note how stereotypes are used to explain, for example, why women are fulfilled through mothering and caring, while men are rewarded by fighting and working.

SEX SELECTION. *See* AMNIOCENTESIS.

SEX TOURS. The vacations, booked through travel agencies, in which foreign men are brought in for sex with poor Third World, often Asian, girls and women who also engage in **prostitution** near US military bases. Feminists in North America and Western Europe have organized against this **international traffic in women** and, under this pressure, the sex-tour business has been curtailed. Although a 1994 US law prohibits travel with the intent to engage in a sexual act with a minor, no law bans arranging for prostitution in a foreign country. The law does make tour operators more careful not to be linked with a client's underage prostitutes.

SEXISM. The assumption that men are superior to women, and thus, deserve power over them. The term was coined by feminists working in the **civil rights movement** of the 1960s to draw parallels between racism and the negative **sex role stereotypes** employed against women. It is frequently used to explain **sex discrimination**. Sexist attitudes result in behaviors such as **sexual harassment, street harassment**, and unfair hiring practices. Feminists charge that sexism not only permeates individual attitudes and behaviors, but is also embedded in the major institutions of society.

SEXIST LANGUAGE. Language (phrases or words) that ignores or objectifies and demeans women. Sexist language is any use of language that reduces the respect due to women as persons. One example is language that assumes words denoting maleness also include women. Communication and linguistic research has shown such assumptions to be false. Other examples include naming women by their body parts or calling women by animal names or names that ridicule women's sexuality. Any language use that assumes male experience is normative for all humans is sexist. *See also* NONSEXIST LANGUAGE.

SEXUAL ASSAULT. *See* RAPE.

SEXUAL CASTE SYSTEM. The view of **radical feminists** that societies not only have a class system but also classes cross-cut by castes, one of which is based on sex. According to this analysis, the **dominant male caste** oppresses women in the manner of the dominant economic class over its subordinates.

SEXUAL DIVISION OF LABOR. *See* GENDER STRATIFICATION.

SEXUAL HARASSMENT. The abuse of or discrimination against a person, usually a woman, because of his or her sex. This behavior may involve verbal abuse, unwanted touching or pushing, seeking to exchange sexual favors for career opportunities, or any unwelcome sexual advances tied to rewards or performance in employment or other situations in which the abuser is in a position of power over another. The action is considered harassment when submission to the conduct is a term or condition of employment or used as a basis for employment decisions (quid pro quo). In *Meritor Savings Bank v. Vinson* (1986), the US Supreme Court rejected the claim that only sexual harassment that results in an economic loss is covered under the **Civil Rights Act of 1964**. Harassment may also exist when the action interferes with an individual's work performance or creates a pervasive, intimidating, and **hostile environment**. In *Harris v. Forklift Systems* (1993) the Court unanimously agreed that there need not be evidence of extreme psychological harm to prove sexual harassment. In *Oncale v. Sundowner Offshore Services, Inc.* (1998) the Court also declared same-sex harassment illegal. The charge is still difficult to prove due to the challenge it presents to the acceptability of behavior between men and women. This is reflected in the controversies surrounding **Anita Hill** and **Paula Jones**. In 2002 the European Union Parliament voted to require all member states to enact laws to prohibit workplace harassment.

SEXUAL POLITICS. A term used to suggest the use of overt or covert sexuality in the workplace. A woman who relies on her **physical at-**

tractiveness or who flirts in a suggestive manner is said to be using sexual politics in order to advance her position. A man who insinuates that his power within a company can profit a woman is said to be using sexual politics in the workplace.

SEXUAL POLITICS (BOOK). *See* MILLETT, KATE.

"SEXUAL POLITICS OF SICKNESS." A phrase coined by Barbara Ehrenreich and Deirdre English in *Complaints and Disorders: The Sexual Politics of Sickness* (1973). They explored the notion of sickness having both a **gender** and a class. They concluded that the medical system is a powerful instrument of social control that enforces **gender roles**.

SEXUAL REVOLUTION. An event made possible by the advent of the **birth control pill**'s availability during the 1960s, when sexual relations between unmarried partners did not have to result in pregnancy. Hence, the "sexual revolution" is said to have begun when women had the same sexual freedoms as men. No longer in fear that any act of sexual intercourse would produce a pregnancy, women were free to engage in what Erica Jong called "the zipless fuck," or sex without forethought or consequences. Feminist author Barbara Ehrenreich and her co-authors (in *Remaking Love: The Feminization of Sex* [1986]) have argued that the sexual revolution had little effect on the beliefs and behaviors of heterosexual men. It was primarily an opportunity to assert **female sexuality** rights. The sexual revolution cooled considerably in the early 1980s with the **AIDS** epidemic and the increase in a variety of sexually transmitted diseases.

SEXUAL SLAVERY. *See* INTERNATIONAL TRAFFIC IN WOMEN.

SEXUAL VIOLENCE. *See* VIOLENCE AGAINST WOMEN.

SEXUALITY. *See* FEMALE SEXUALITY.

SHAFIK, DORIA (1908-1975). A French-educated Egyptian feminist who, after being denied a post at the University of Cairo, turned to building a women's movement. In 1945 she founded the magazine *Bint al-Nil* (Daughters of the Nile); in 1949 she formed Ittihad Bint al-Nil, a women's union that was successful in getting **woman suffrage** and women's rights on the political agenda and which became a political party in 1952. In 1951 she led 1,500 women into parliament to demand the vote, followed by a variety of other marches, debates, and publications. Full suffrage was achieved in 1956. Shafik's vocal liberalism led to her house arrest in 1957 under President Gamal Abdel Nasser and her effective removal from political life.

SHAH NAWAZ, JAHANARA (1896-1979). A prominent **woman suffrage** leader and advocate for Islamic women's rights in British India through the All-India Muslim Women's Conference. Because of her loyalty to the Muslim minority in India, Shah Nawaz found it impossible after 1935 to work with Indian women's organizations and became active in the movement for an independent Pakistan. After partition in 1947, she was one of two female members of the first Constituent Assembly of Pakistan.

SHAKESPEARE, FEMINIST CRITICISM OF. A break with the early 18th and 19th century criticism of Shakespeare by women (among them Elizabeth Montagu and **Anna Jameson**) that tended to focus on an examination of his female characters, treating them as if they were actual people whose lives could be further explored. A book by Mary Cowden Clarke, for example, was entitled *The Girlhood of Shakespeare's Heroines* (1851-1852). With the publication of **Virginia Woolf's** *A Room of One's Own* (1929), a new era of feminist criticism of Shakespeare began to emerge. Woolf writes in that book of her imaginary creation, Shakespeare's sister, just as talented as her brother, but frustrated in her literary attempts and finally dying pregnant and abandoned. Since the 1980s **feminist literary critics** have focused on the limited and stereotypical presentation of Shakespeare's female characters: Lady Macbeth and the *"cherchez la femme"* mode of blaming active women for their involvement in political intrigue; Ophelia and the "love-crazed" suicide; Hamlet's mother Gertrude and the incestuous, lustful caricature of a sexually aggressive mother; and Desdemona as Othello's wife, another sexually aggressive deviant who desires a black man and is punished by him for her lasciviousness. Most recently feminist authors have attempted to rewrite Shakespeare's plots from a woman's point of view, hence Jane Smiley's rewrite of *King Lear*, *A Thousand Acres* (1991).

SHALIT, WENDY (1975-). A US journalist who is viewed by feminists as a **faux feminist**. As an undergraduate at Williams College, Shalit published an article in the *Reader's Digest* supporting a single-sex bathroom in her dormitory. Her *A Return to Modesty* (1999) argued that the **sexual revolution** is linked to **eating disorders** and **date rape**. She calls for a return to Victorian-era **gender roles**; modest dress and behavior will protect women by masking their vulnerability.

SHA'RAWI, HUDA (1879-1947). The founder of the **Egyptian Feminist Union** and convenor of Arab feminist conferences in 1938 and 1944. At the latter meeting, the Arab Feminist Union was formed, with Sha'rawi as president. Sha'rawi, who had a large inheritance, substantially financed these organizations. Her dramatic gesture of publicly unveiling at the Cairo train station upon returning from an international feminist meeting began a radical activist phase of the movement.

SHARI'A. A form of Islamic law that is very **gender** biased and threatens women's rights, particularly in criminal cases. Even though punishments such as beheadings and stonings may be unconstitutional under national law, religious Shari'a courts are imposing them in regions controlled by fundamentalists. This is most common in Nigeria, Pakistan, Iran, Sudan, Saudi Arabia, and Somalia. The **global feminist** movement has widely publicized several cases and pressured the United Nations and the nation involved to recognize women's human rights.

SHEKHINAH. A Talmudic concept of God's feminized and nurturing presence in the world. The passivity of the concept has linked it with the feminine face of God. Some **Jewish feminists** use the term generally to denote a female divinity, coequal with a masculine God.

SHELTER MOVEMENT. *See* WOMEN'S BATTERY SHELTER.

SHEPPARD, KATE (1848-1934). A **woman suffrage** organizer and strategist in New Zealand, the first country (in 1893) to enfranchise all women over the age of 21. The Women's Suffrage Campaign grew out of the **temperance movement** and utilized nationwide petition drives, one of which obtained the signatures of a quarter of all adult women. Her leaflet *Ten Reasons Why the Women of New Zealand Should Vote* drew a wide audience.

SHEPPARD-TOWNER MATERNITY ACT OF 1921. A US program that established grants to the states to provide health care for mothers and children of all classes through public health centers and prenatal clinics. The first and perhaps greatest achievement of the post-suffrage coalition, the **Women's Joint Congressional Committee**, the program was attacked by conservatives and the American Medical Association as "socialized medicine" and was allowed to expire in 1929.

SHIELDS, LAURIE. *See* DISPLACED HOMEMAKER.

SHIKIBU, MURASAKI (ca. 970-ca. 1040). A Japanese novelist who secretly learned Chinese when this was forbidden to women and wrote the epic novel *Genji Monogatari* (*The Tale of Genji*, ca. 1011). In this, Shikibu questions women's place in Shinto and in Buddhism. The main character is a woman who struggles with the unhappiness of a woman's destiny in a male-oriented society and seeks to be self-determining. Many of the concerns in the book are **existentialist** from a notably feminine perspective: intentionality, freedom, objectification, and existence.

SIGNS. One of the first US feminist academic journals to publish serious and academically respected scholarship. Begun in 1975 by the University of Chicago Press and first edited by Catharine R. Stimpson, *Signs* continues to be the premier academic journal in **women's studies**, even though in the mid-1990s, it announced that it was shifting to a less academic and more accessible format to promote feminist debate inside and outside the academy. It is credited with helping to legitimize interdisciplinary women's studies as a field of academic research.

SIMPSON VERDICT. The jury decision in the 1995 criminal trial of black US football star O. J. Simpson that found him not guilty of the murder of his ex-wife Nicole Brown and her friend Ron Goldman, despite extensive evidence that he was responsible. Simpson had a history of **domestic violence**, and the feminist movement used the case to build awareness of the pervasiveness of the problem. In the wake of the decision that was overwhelmingly supported by black women, feminists acknowledged the past injustices experienced by persons of color in the legal system. In a 1997 civil suit brought by the family of Ron Goldman, a jury found Simpson liable for Goldman's death and the battering of his ex-wife and awarded $8.5 million in compensatory damages to the Goldman family and $25 million in punitive damages to be split between Goldman's father and the estate of Nicole Brown. Although the standard of proof is somewhat lower in a civil case, the jury finding here is comparable to a murder conviction in a criminal case.

SINGLE MOTHERS. *See* SINGLE-PARENT FAMILY.

SINGLE-PARENT FAMILY. Families headed by a single parent who does not reside with, or is not married to, the children's other parent. A near-majority of single-parent families are headed by women who have incomes below the poverty line. Feminists have been supportive of single mothers and the difficulty these women face in supporting their families. *See also* "FEMINIZATION OF POVERTY"; TEMPORARY ASSISTANCE TO NEEDY FAMILIES.

SINGLE-SEX EDUCATION. The schooling of male and female students in separate institutions. Single-sex education remains important in private and church-related schools in the West, as well as in traditional Islamic societies. In developed nations, girls in single-sex settings are more likely to take classes in math, science, and information technology; boys are more likely to study the fine arts and foreign languages. Sex-segregated public education was the usual practice in the United States until the 19th century when coeducation was introduced. Feminists have praised the earlier female seminaries and colleges for providing women with access to higher education. Today US women's college graduates are more likely to have majored in nontraditional fields and to earn the doctorate. Feminist organizations have generally opposed public single-sex education at all levels as a violation of **Title IX**. The US Supreme Court partially agreed in *Mississippi University for Women v. Hogan* (1982) when it ordered that school to admit a man to its nursing program. The Court, however, did not order that all programs be opened to men; a woman-only program in nursing, they argued, only served to maintain the stereotypical image of nursing as a female occupation. Research is inconclusive on single-sex education and often all-female institutions receive fewer resources within an artificial environment. *See also* UNITED STATES V. VIRGINIA.

SISTERHOOD. A concept stressing female friendship, solidarity, and support, analogous to the term "brotherhood" for male relationships.

Feminists believe that women should establish close ties and bonds with other women in recognition that men should not play an exclusive role in women's lives, that women are worth relating to, and that all women share interests. This term is controversial within feminism because of its implied equality and connection of all women in a movement that has a history of excluding **women of color**, poor women, **lesbians**, and **women with disabilities**.

SISTERHOOD IS GLOBAL INSTITUTE (SIGI). The first international feminist think-tank, formed to support and promote women's rights at all levels of society in all nations. The group grew out of the 1984 Global Feminist Strategy Meeting, organized to celebrate the publication of **Robin Morgan's** *Sisterhood Is Global* (1984). The SIGI has 1,300 group and individual members in 70 countries. Its headquarters rotates every five years and has been in Montréal since 2000.

SISTERHOOD IS POWERFUL. The title of an important collection of early feminist essays (1970), edited by **Robin Morgan**. The volume codified the **radical feminist** position and the term has passed into general parlance to mean that the united actions of women can effect powerful changes in society.

SISTERS IN CRIME (SinC). An organization formed in 1987 to promote the work of women mystery writers. The 3,300 members are writers, editors, and bookstore owners who are concerned that mysteries written by women are not reviewed as often or promoted on the same basis as those of male mystery writers. *See also* FEMALE DETECTIVE FICTION.

SISTERS IN ISLAM (SIS). A Malaysian women's advocacy group committed to promoting women's rights within the framework of Islam. Founded in 1987, the group notes that women actively participated in public life during the time of Muhummad and Islam raised the status of women. They charge that Islamic practices today that subordinate women stem from male control over the interpretation of the Koran. The group was a major force in adoption of the 1994 Domestic Violence Act.

SIX POINT GROUP. A British feminist group established in 1921 by Lady Rhondda to seek equal rights for women. The group, composed of upper-middle-class and professional women, rejected **social feminism** and social welfare reforms as not being feminist. Even so, the group's objectives included **equal pay**, widow's and mother's pensions, equal employment opportunity in government service, child abuse laws, and equality in child guardianship. It remained active after World War II, but disbanded in 1980 after becoming a group existing to honor aging **suffragists**.

SIXTEEN DAYS OF ACTIVISM AGAINST GENDER VIOLENCE CAMPAIGN. A project begun in 1991 by the Center for Women's Global Leadership (CWGL) to eliminate all forms of violence against women. The events, coordinated by the CWGL, run from November 25 (International Day Against Violence Toward Women) to December 10 (International Human Rights Day) and involve more than 800 women's groups in over 90 countries in demonstrations, vigils, arts events, and lectures.

SKEFFINGTON, HANNA SHEEHY (1877-1946). An Irish nationalist, feminist, and suffragette. She was a co-founder and head of the militant Irish Women's Franchise League. Skeffington spent time in prison in 1909 for smashing windows in Dublin Castle and, as a result, lost her college lectureship. She also was falsely imprisoned on charges of assaulting a policeman in 1913. She and her husband adopted Sheehy-Skeffington as a common surname upon their marriage, a practice that became popular with new feminists of the 1960s.

SLUT. A perjorative for a female who is sexually promiscuous. **Third wave feminists** have begun to reclaim the term, defining it as just a girl with a healthy libido who finds pleasure on an equal basis with young men. **Naomi Wolf's** *Promiscuities: The Secret Struggle for Womanhood* (1997) adopts this position, as does Leora Tanenbaum in *Slut!: Growing Up Female with a Bad Reputation* (1999).

SMEAL, ELEANOR (1939-). A US women's rights leader. Smeal served three terms as president of the **National Organization for Women (NOW)**, 1977-1982 and 1985-1987. During that time she more than doubled the size of NOW, publicized the **wage gap**, led a national campaign for ratification of the **Equal Rights Amendment**, and brought over 100,000 women back into the streets in 1986 for the first national **abortion** rights march. She was one of the first to recognize the **gender gap** and wrote about it in *How and Why Women Will Elect the Next President* (1984). She is the co-founder and current leader of the **Feminist Majority Foundation**.

SOCIAL CONSTRUCTION OF GENDER. An argument, differing markedly from those of reductionists and **biological determinists**, that roots **gender** distinctions in social and cultural circumstances and interactions. It is a cultural assumption, not a biological given, that there are two genders, and cultures differ markedly in how these categories are encoded.

SOCIAL FEMINISM. The dominant tradition of US and Canadian feminism during the first half of the 20th century, in competition with **equality feminism**. Social feminists viewed the sexes as having fundamentally different physiological and social roles, and therefore, supported **protective labor laws** for women and opposed the **Equal Rights Amendment**. *See also* WOMEN'S JOINT CONGRESSIONAL COMMITTEE.

SOCIAL GOSPEL MOVEMENT, WOMEN AND. A late 19th to early 20th century movement that sought to relate the Christian message to the problems of labor, economics, and politics. Although the participation of women in this movement has been largely ignored by scholars, the role of **social feminist** women such as Vida Scudder, Beatrice Webb, and **Frances Willard** is beginning to be explored.

SOCIAL PURITY MOVEMENT. *See* MORAL REFORM FEMINISM.

SOCIAL SECURITY ACT OF 1935. The major piece of US post-Depression social **welfare** legislation that established the first federal means-tested assistance program to women and their children, Aid to Families with Dependent Children, and the current system of social **insurance** benefits for retirement, disability, and survivors. Although the latter reflected the social reality of the time in which it was passed, the legislation does not reflect the current changing work and childbearing habits of women in its preferential treatment given to women with children in stable marriages who were supported by their husbands. The act is also inequitable in its treatment of elderly women. Benefit payment levels reflect women's contributions to the program throughout their working lives, yet discrimination, child-rearing responsibilities, and the failure to recognize housework as legitimate employment preclude women from contributing significant amounts to their own retirement funds. Often they receive less in retirement benefits. Under feminist pressure, some of these inequities have been corrected.

SOCIALIST FEMINISM. A tradition of **feminist political theory** that seeks to synthesize **radical feminism** and **Marxism** in response to the dominance of **liberal feminism**. Both **sexism** and **classism** are used to explain women's oppression; feminist insights into **male dominance** and the Marxist critique of capitalism are incorporated by contemporary socialist feminists. In contrast to the liberal emphasis on individual rights, there is attention to social relations and the larger community within this tradition. With the fall of Eastern European communism in the late 1980s and the election of more conservative governments in North America and Western Europe in that same period, socialist feminism became less credible. It is possible that the rise of a capitalist global economy exploitative of women will revive this tradition in the 21st century.

SOCIALIST WOMEN'S INTERNATIONAL. A group formed in 1907 by **Clara Zetkin** at the International Socialist Women's Conference, held in conjunction with the Second International. At its founding, it urged that socialist parties work for universal **woman suffrage** and later endorsed **equal pay** and maternity insurance. After World War I, Austrian Socialist Adelheid Popp built the group into a major movement of more than 900,000 women.

SOCIÉTÉ FRATERNELLE DES PATRIOTES DE L'UN ET L'AUTRE SEXE/THE FRATERNAL SOCIETY OF PATRIOTS OF BOTH SEXES. A French Revolutionary club, formed in 1793, to which women were admitted as full members and as officers. Its membership included the Dutchwoman, Etta Palm d'Aelders, who advocated political liberty and equality for both sexes. Another member and advocate of equal rights for women, Théroigne de Méricourt, unsuccessfully attempted to establish a political society and a women's militia company. She urged female participation in patriotic societies dedicated to ferreting out enemies of the revolution and to performing benevolent works on behalf of women, especially the poor. Still another member of the Société, Pauline Léon, petitioned the National Assembly for the right of women to bear arms. Léon was also a leader with the actress Claire Lacombe of the Club des Citoyennes Républicaines Révolutionnaires (Club of Republican Revolutionary Women Citizens), a radical group associated with those who supported *sans culottes* demands for wage and price controls. Other women's revolutionary clubs included the Club des Femmes de Dijon and the Breteuil Soeurs de la Constitution. All women's clubs and associations were outlawed on October 30, 1793.

SOCIETY FOR THE PROTECTION OF UNBORN CHILDREN (SPUC). A British **pro-life** group formed in 1967 after passage of the Abortion Act and drawing members from many religions. The SPUC uses public education, often through church sermons, more often than direct contacts with Parliament. The group has a large membership, is well-funded, and has drawn favorable media attention for its exposé of **abortion** abuses. The publication of *Babies for Burning* (1974) was especially effective, although critics charged that accounts were highly sensationalized. The SPUC has ties with the Conservative and Unionist Party and is an affiliate of the International Right to Life Federation.

SOCIOBIOLOGY. A theory of human nature, drawn from studies on animal and insect populations, that suggests that **gender** differences in behavior are rooted in genetically evolved strategies that promote **reproduction** of the species. Accordingly, underneath the differing behaviors associated with being male and being female (e.g., promiscuity and aggression in males; domesticity in women) lie genetically based universals. Most feminists reject this theory as another form of **biological determinism**. A few feminist scholars, however, have presented alternative theories of evolution and hormonal differences that do not accept the male norm but instead legitimate women's culture and values. No theory based on sociobiology is well-supported by evidence; explanations of human behavior are probably not rooted in biology.

SOMMERS, TISH. *See* DISPLACED HOMEMAKER.

SOPHIA (PSEUDONYM). The author of *Woman Not Inferior to Man* (1739) that criticized male philosophers who argued for women's inferiority. The tract rejected the view of men as having superior reason and women as being more driven by the passions. The arguments made by males in favor of men are biased, the author stated, because they are motivated by self-interest, not logic or reason. The writer believed that rationality should be the criterion for evaluation, not the sex of the presenter of the argument. Sophia is now presented as the spirit of wisdom and a primordial source of power within Christian **feminist spirituality.**

SOULEY-DARQUÉ, MARGUERITE. The woman credited with teaching the first **women's studies** course in Paris in 1902 at the College Libre des Sciences Sociales. The course was cross-disciplinary and combined philosophical, sociological, and historical approaches to understanding the nature, experience, and perceptions of women. Souley-Darqué sought to demonstrate that women's social inferiority could be explained as a response to past environmental conditions that industrial capitalism made obsolete.

SOUTHALL BLACK SISTERS (SBS). An Asian and Afro-Caribbean women's group formed in London in 1979 to combat **domestic violence.** Working with Justice for Women to support women who have fought back against or killed their violent male partners, SBS has been successful in winning the release or lower sentences for several of these women. The group has also become active on issues of relevance to new immigrants such as homelessness, police and racial harassment, health issues, immigration problems, and concerns about their children.

SPARE RIB. The best-known of the British **new feminist** periodicals, founded in 1972 by a **collective** of women formerly with the alternative press. The nationally circulated monthly magazine, at its height, had 32,000 readers and served as a central focus for all parts of the British women's movement. In 1993 it ceased publication.

SPEAK-OUT. The open discussion through public testimony of personal experiences that women had never previously told to anyone except perhaps a few close friends or family members. Feminist forums on topics such as **abortion, rape, sexual harassment, domestic violence,** and incest attempt to raise public awareness and to mobilize support for legal changes.

SPENDER, DALE (1943-). A British researcher, writer, and feminist theorist of linguistics. Spender's book, *Man-Made Language* (1980), has set the terms of discussion for feminist communication scholars. When women's meanings are not encoded into the language used in public discourse, such as dictionary definitions and public speech, the language that dominates the culture is language made by men. Subsequently Spender has shown the effect of **male dominance** of publication on women's writing. Her work increases the visibility of women writers and also brings insight into the cultural constraints on women built into the English language. *See also* GENDER AND COMMUNICATION.

SPORTS AND GENDER. An examination of women athletes from a feminist perspective. The medical community for more than a century used women's **reproductive** capacity to limit their participation in physical exercise. Women in sports were viewed as unfeminine. A revolution in women's sports occurred in the 1970s with the passage of **Title IX, Education Amendment of 1972** in the United States and the emergence of feminist athletes such as Billie Jean King and Martina Navratilova. The rapid growth in female participation in sports at all levels of the education system and in an expanding number of Olympic events has led to a **gender-neutral** definition of the athlete.

SPOUSAL RAPE. *See* MARITAL RAPE.

SPOUSE ABUSE. *See* DOMESTIC VIOLENCE.

STALKING. A universal pattern of harassing behavior that terrorizes the victim, usually a woman. Although the practice is not illegal in all societies, laws making stalking a criminal offense exist in all US states as a deterrent to **domestic violence**, and Japan adopted an antistalking law in 2000. Cyberstalking through electronic communication is prohibited in 45 US states. Ninety percent of women who are murdered by their husbands or boyfriends had previously been stalked. Feminists support these laws but also express concern that they may be ineffective because of vague language and the extensive record of stalking required for conviction and imprisonment. In 2000 a Michigan stalking law was voided as being so broad as to apply to journalists, tele-marketers, and door-to-door sales personnel.

STANDPOINT THEORY. A feminist critique of traditional scholarship and its claim of neutrality. The view here is that this research involves a nonobjective interpretation of women's lives and renders the experience of women invisible. Standpoint theory suggests that since all research (and knowledge) is produced from a particular standpoint (or social location) and "**dominant**" (male) standpoints prevail, other perspectives remain hidden. Women's views are less partial and incomplete because their views are shaped by unique experiences within a **patriarchal** society. Standpoint theory assumes that those who gain most from positions of power and privilege (and who sustain systems that ensure them) are least equipped to see the bias, while those most marginalized (e.g., women) see it most clearly.

STANTON, ELIZABETH CADY (1815-1902). A 19th century US feminist and **abolitionist**. Believed to be the first woman to appear as a witness at a congressional hearing, Stanton gave testimony in 1869 in support of **woman suffrage**. With **Lucretia Mott**, she was one of the organizers of the **Seneca Falls Convention** and wrote the Declaration of Sentiments adopted there. After the Fifteenth Amendment failed to extend the right to vote to women, she and **Susan B. Anthony** founded the **National Woman Suffrage Association** and she served as president, 1869-1890. At her request in 1878, the first constitutional amendment to enfranchise women was introduced in Congress. Stanton also opposed the secondary position of women within Christian doctrine and published *The Woman's Bible* (1892 and 1895) as a corrective.

STATE COMMISSIONS ON THE STATUS OF WOMEN (SCSW). The organizations created, 1963-1967, in every state in the United States, patterned on the **President's Commission on the Status of Women** and mandated to collect data on women and to suggest changes in discriminatory laws and policies in the states. Linked through the **Citizens' Advisory Council on the Status of Women** within the **Women's Bureau**, the state commissions became the core of a national network for women's rights. It was at their third national conference that around two dozen delegates, thwarted in efforts to present a resolution demanding that the **Equal Employment Opportunity Commission** enforce the sex provision of Title VII of the **Civil Rights Act of 1964**, formed the **National Organization for Women**. In 1970 the National Association of Commissions for Women (NACW) was formed as a private organization that also includes city and county commissions. The NACW includes 270 commissions; only five states do not have active commissions.

STATE FEMINISM. The perspective that government institutions and officials can promote feminism and help the women's movement to attain its goals. The model for state feminism is the Nordic countries, especially Sweden, where governments adopted and implemented policies to advance women without extensive feminist organization or pressure. State programs for gender equality were also developed by communist nations such as the then Soviet Union and the People's Republic of China in the absence of an independent women's movement. Initially Western **radical feminists** rejected engagement with a **patriarchal** state. Women in repressive non-Western countries also avoided politics out of fear. The **femocrats** of Australia and New Zealand within women's policy bureaucracies demonstrated the benefits of cooperation between women's movements and governments. By 1992, 153 nations had at least one (and usually several) offices for women's programs, and 36 countries had a Minister of Women's Affairs.

STATUS OF WOMEN CANADA (SWC). A federal government agency that promotes **gender** equality and women's participation in society. Created in 1971 as an office within the Privy Council and gaining department status in 1976, the SWC manages the Women's Programme that supports feminist women's organizations in Canada.

STATUTORY RAPE. Any sexual intercourse with a female below the "age of consent." This age has varied from age 7 to 18 years within the United States. In some states, the victim must be below the age of puberty for the offense to be charged; some states require the perpetrator to be a specified number of years older than the victim. In *Michael M. v. Superior Court* (1981) the US Supreme Court upheld a California law that punished only adult males for intercourse with a female child but not underage or adult females who engaged in sexual intercourse with underage boys. This case exemplifies those relatively few instances where the Court has upheld sex-based classifications because a majority of the justices believe that the classification reasonably advances a significant state interest, in this case preventing teen pregnancy.

STEFAN, VERENA (1947-). A German **women's studies** teacher, feminist activist, and author of the highly successful book *Häutungen* (*Shedding*, 1975). This book, an account of a young woman's developing consciousness during the rise of the German **new feminist movement** in the early 1970s, has become a feminist classic. Her

Wortgetreu ich Traume (*Literally Dreaming*, 1987) is a collection of eight stories about women living together in rural settings, independent of men. Stefan was a co-founder of Brot und Rosen (Bread and Roses) in 1972 and has translated the work of **Adrienne Rich** and **Monique Wittig**. She emigrated to Canada in 2000 and currently offers creative writing workshops on "Girls as Literary Heroines."

STEINEM, GLORIA (1934-). A journalist, editor, and prominent US feminist spokesperson. Steinem was one of the founders of *Ms.* magazine, the **National Women's Political Caucus**, and Voters for Choice. She is a popular lecturer on women's topics and the author of *Outrageous Acts and Everyday Rebellions* (1983), *Revolution from Within: A Book of Self-Esteem* (1992), and *Moving Beyond Words* (1994). In the mid-1970s Steinem was attacked by the **Redstockings** for having once been affiliated with a Central Intelligence Agency-funded student group and with using *Ms.* to supplant **radical feminism** with **liberal feminism**. Although the **trashing** of Steinem eventually discredited the Redstockings, radical feminists have never been comfortable with the liberal mainstream *Ms.* or with the media's choice of the formerly unknown Steinem as a movement spokesperson. She surprised many when she married for the first time in 2000.

STEM CELL RESEARCH. A type of scientific investigation that involves the harvesting of embryonic cells, called stem cells, that are formed soon after conception and have the ability to become many types of cells. Researchers hope that this will lead to effective treatments for many diseases, including **breast cancer**, osteoporosis, and other common women's diseases, and may also permit the creation of organs for transplants. The debate over the ethics of this type of research, as well as all research involving cloning and fetal tissue, has spilled over into the US **abortion** controversy. Scientists generally favor a ban on all **reproductive** human cloning (asexually creating a child who is a genetic duplicate of another organism) but support embryonic cloning, where scientists create embryos in order to extract stem cells for use in medical research. The **pro-life movement** views embryos as human life and the extraction of stem cells as the destruction of life. Feminists have either supported the ban on reproductive human cloning or remained neutral in an attempt to allow antiabortion politicians to support embryonic cloning.

STERILIZATION ABUSE. The term for making people (mostly women) infertile against their will or without their informed consent often as a condition for receiving **welfare** or holding a job believed to be potentially harmful to a fetus. This problem is especially pronounced among mentally disabled, institutionalized, and poor women and **women of color**. In 1979, responding to pressure from the **women's rights movement**, the US government issued strict regulations on surgical sterilization. The marketing of the long-term **birth control** device **Norplant** has also raised fears among feminists that a woman's right to refuse **contraception** may be endangered. Both men and women in developing nations such as China and India have been involuntarily sterilized as part of a population control program and sterilization abuse has been reported in Eastern Europe since the fall of communism.

STEWART, MARIA W. (1803-1879). An early 19th century US orator, **abolitionist**, and feminist. She was the first woman, in 1832, to address a mixed **gender** audience on racial (political) issues and was probably the first black American to lecture in defense of women's rights. Religious, militant, and outspoken, her speeches used arguments drawn from religious sources and were published in a collection of her works in 1835.

STÖCKER, HELENE (1869-1943). A leader in the radical wing of the first German women's movement and an outspoken advocate of the sexual emancipation of women. In 1904 she founded the Federation for the Protection of Mothers and Sexual Reform; its manifesto demanded sexual freedom (including free love as a positive alternative to conventional marriage), the end of the compulsory recognition of marriages by church and registry, and the loosening of **divorce** laws. Her views were far more radical than those held by the Federation of German Women's Associations.

STONE, LUCY (1818-1893). A founder of the **American Woman Suffrage Association** in 1869, as well as an early lecturer on **abolition** and women's rights. In her marriage to Henry Blackwell in 1855, she omitted the word "obey" from her vows and together they pledged to establish an egalitarian relationship. Stone may have been the first woman to retain her birthname, a practice which gave rise to the **Lucy Stone League**. Her husband and her daughter, **Alice Stone Blackwell**, were also active in the women's movement. In 1870 she and her husband founded the pro-suffrage *Woman's Journal,* which they or their daughter owned and edited until 1917. The *Journal* continued to promote the **woman suffrage** cause under new ownership until 1931.

STOP ERA. *See* EAGLE FORUM; SCHLAFLY, PHYLLIS.

STOPES, MARIE CHARLOTTE CARMICHAEL (1880-1958). A pioneer English advocate of sex education and **birth control** and founder of the first birth control clinic in Britain in 1921. Coming out of an unhappy first marriage to an impotent man, Stopes had little knowledge of **contraception** until her meeting with **Margaret Sanger** in 1915. In 1918 she published a famous marriage manual, *Married Love: A New Contribution to the Solution of Sex Difficulties,* in which she promoted sexual enjoyment for women, and a guide to contraception, *Wise Parenthood.*

STORNI, ALFONSINA (1892-1938). An Argentine poet, considered the most prominent feminist writer of her time in Latin America and the first woman to frequent the literary gatherings of Buenos Aires. Her first book, *La Inquietud del Rosal (The Disquietude of the Rosebud,* 1916), was controversial because it was considered improper for single women to write openly of love and relationships. Her later poetry centered on her rejection of **sex role stereotypes**. She was an enemy of social conventions and a supporter of **woman suffrage** and women's rights. She saw her femininity as an individual and social problem and was among the first feminists to fight **male dominance**.

STOVE DEATH/CHOOLA. A term referring to the dousing of young Pakistani wives in kerosene and setting them aflame. This is primarily done by husbands or in-laws because of mother-in-law disputes, the wish to take a second wife, or the failure to bear a son within a year of the marriage. Human rights advocates estimate that three attacks of this type occur daily and most are fatal because there are no burn centers in Pakistan. The government rarely prosecutes because officials often take bribes to certify that suicide or an exploding stove was the cause of death.

STOWE, EMILY HOWARD (1831-1903). The first woman physician in Canada and founder in 1876 of the first **woman suffrage** society, the

Toronto Women's Literary Club (later, in 1883, the Toronto Women's Suffrage Association). Stowe and her group also worked for women's educational opportunities and in 1889 formed the first national suffrage group, the Dominion Women's Enfranchisement Association (later, the Canadian Suffrage Association).

STREET HARASSMENT. The abusive, mostly sex-related, language or action directed by male strangers toward women in public places. Such behavior is believed to be especially embedded in the culture of certain occupations, such as truck driver and construction worker, and young women, **women of color**, and (perceived) **lesbians** are particularly vulnerable. Existing laws on **sexual assault** ("touching"), "fighting words," intentional infliction of emotional distress, and invasion of **privacy** offer no effective remedies. A state law or city ordinance to make such harassment a misdemeanor, punishable by a fine, may be in violation of constitutional or other protections of free speech. Since 1999 the Street Harassment Project, a New York City woman-only activist group, has staged street theater and distributed sets of cards to build public awaremenss of the problem. *See also* HATE CRIMES.

STRUCTURELESSNESS. *See* TYRANNY OF STRUCTURELESSNESS.

SUFFRAGETTE. A term used to describe **woman suffrage** supporters who adopted militant tactics in contrast to those who used legal and conventional methods. The term was first used to describe members of the **Women's Social and Political Union**, who then used the label as the name of one of their newspapers.

SUFFRAGIST. A term generally applied to those who supported the movement to enfranchise women. In Britain it was used to differentiate between those who used legal and conventional methods, such as members of the **National Union of Women's Suffrage Societies**, and the militant **suffragettes**.

SUMMERSKILL, EDITH (1901-1980). A British politician, physician, and active member of the Labour Party who won a seat in Parliament in 1934. A long-time champion of women's causes, she successfully proposed legislation on property rights and financial equality for **married women**. She also worked to make less painful childbirth procedures available to women, but opposed **oral contraceptives** on the grounds that their side effects had not been thoroughly investigated.

SUPERHEROINES. A group of female comic book, motion picture, and television characters that exhibit superhuman powers. One of the first was Wonder Woman, introduced in 1941, in *All Star Comics*. An **Amazon**, she fought for equal rights for women and provided a **role model** for girls in a male comic book world. Wonder Woman appeared in books and on television and was on the cover of the first issue of *Ms*. Other superheroines followed but were often only a sidekick of the superhero. An exception was US television's *Xena: Warrior Princess*, who fought to protect women, children, and the poor. Xena became a feminist and **lesbian** icon in the 1990s.

SUPERWOMAN SYNDROME. A pattern of high achievement by women in both the world of paid labor and in the home as wife and mother. Once viewed as the embodiment of feminism's promise that women can "have it all," these "supermoms" are increasingly seen as stressed-out victims of society's excessive expectations.

SURROGACY. The process by which a woman carries and bears a child, usually conceived through **artificial insemination** or **in vitro fertilization**, for another woman and contractually relinquishes all parental rights to the child commonly in exchange for a cash payment. By the early 1990s private arrangements and around 20 agencies had been involved in over 4,000 births. It is referred to as "womb renting" by some feminists who consider surrogacy a form of oppression of low-income women. Other feminists support a woman's right to make this choice and see surrogacy as a relatively low-tech woman-controlled solution to infertility. State law varies widely in the United States. Only three states require enforcement of surrogacy contracts; others regulate paid contracts, prohibit contracts, or ban the process entirely. Surrogacy has been banned in Australia, and in Germany a US surrogacy agency was barred from operating after public protest. The demand for babies in wealthier nations has led to an international traffic and reportedly the establishment of "gestation houses" in Sri Lanka and Guatemala, where poor women either agree to bear a child for Western couples or produce a baby for trafficking. In Sri Lanka these "baby factories" appear to be run by the government or, at a minimum, the export of babies to

Switzerland and Australia meets with no interference. *See also* IN RE BABY M.

SURVIVOR. *See* VICTIMIZATION OF WOMEN.

SUTTEE. The custom, in Hindu India, of a wife immolating herself on the funeral pyre of her deceased husband. The custom is said to derive from the demand that a bride be a virgin, so that a widow will be unlikely to remarry and may be destitute; to avoid such a fate, the despairing woman was encouraged to depart life with her husband. The practice was criminalized in cities under British rule in 1829 and outlawed nationally in 1987 after a well-publicized incident of suttee by a young widow. The government of India has recently been more active in enforcement under pressure from contemporary Indian women's groups, but temple tributes to women who committed suttee still attract crowds.

SUU KYI, AUNG SAN (1945-). A Myanmar politician and recipient of the Nobel Peace Prize in 1991. As co-founder and leader of the National League for Democracy, she has been an activist for human rights and democracy in Myanmar (formerly Burma), a military dictatorship. Her period as a political prisoner under house arrest, 1989-1995, was widely publicized and monitored by the **global feminist** movement. After her release, afraid to leave her country for fear that she would not be able to return, Suu Kyi sent a videotaped speech on women's rights to the Nongovernmental Organizations Forum on Women in Beijing. She was again subjected to house arrest, 2000-2002, and in 2003 was detained by the government after a confrontation between her supporters and the military.

SWEATSHOP. A workplace in the early stages of the Industrial Revolution, characterized by unfair wages, long hours, and dangerous working conditions. In the United States, the **Women's Trade Union League** worked to improve conditions for women and children and were successful in securing the passage of new labor standards legislation in 1937. During the 1980s sweatshops returned to many advanced industrial democracies with the rise of global competition, increased immigration, and weaker labor unions. Sweatshops have also proliferated in poorer nations as multinational corporations seek cheap female labor and less attention from government and human rights groups. Agricultural workers worldwide are also subjected to sweatshop conditions. Feminists have organized demonstrations and boycotts against products, particularly clothing and food, produced under conditions that violate wage, child labor, health, and safety laws. *See also* MAQUILADORA.

SWISS ASSOCIATION FOR WOMEN'S RIGHTS/ SCHWEIZ-ERISCHER VERBAND FÜR FRAUENRECHTE (SVF). A group formed in 1909 as the Swiss Association for Woman Suffrage. As a suffrage movement the association did not participate in demonstrations, including the first (and only large) one, the March on Bern in 1969. Instead it pursued a campaign of national public education and local chapter activities. The current name was adopted in 1971 after suffrage was won. The SVF helped to organize an initiative campaign for an **equal rights amendment**, which passed in a 1981 referendum. The group has also been active in **International Women's Year** activities and in supporting the Plan of Action.

-T-

TAHRIR AL-MAR'A. *See* AMIN, QASIM.

TAILHOOK ASSAULT. An incident at the 1991 convention of the aviation group, the Tailhook Association. Several dozen women were molested by their drunken US naval and marine aviator colleagues. When Navy Lt. Paula Coughlin later complained that the Navy had failed to investigate properly, a number of male officers were forced to resign or were denied promotions. Since then, issues of **sexual harassment** in the military have been a frequent topic in the media, congressional investigations, and feminist publications. In 2003 the US Air Force Academy was forced to investigate reports of at least 56 **sexual assaults** over the past decade. Women cadets reporting them have been disciplined or even forced to withdraw from the college.

TAKAYAMA, SHIGERI (1899-1977). A Japanese feminist and founder of the League for Defense of Women's Rights, which demanded a role in government for women in Imperial Japan. Takayama worked for pensions for the war widows of World War II. Beginning in 1952, she became active in and later led Chifuren, a women's civil rights group of more than six million members. Takayama was a member of the upper house of the Diet, 1965-1971.

TAKE BACK THE NIGHT. An annual demonstration held first in Germany in 1973 and now in cities around the world to draw attention to the problem of violent **pornography** and **violence against women**. As the name implies, the action addresses the inability of women to freely move as freely within the city as do men. The rallies and marches are organized in local communities and are especially popular on US college campuses.

TAKE OUR DAUGHTERS TO WORK DAY. An event begun on April 28, 1993, as an annual US public education action designed to introduce girls, ages 9 to 15, to a positive workplace environment. The campaign, sponsored by the **Ms. Foundation for Women**, was a response to research showing that in **adolescence**, girls suffer a loss in ambition and **self-esteem**. It was originally recommended that male classmates receive special sensitivity training on **gender** issues in their regular classrooms on that day. In 2003 a new program, "Take Our Daughters and Sons to Work," was introduced to encourage both boys and girls to participate fully in family, work, and community. The event continues to occur in April on a regular school day.

TALAQ. An Islamic law that gives a man the right to verbally **divorce** his wife by stating "I divorce thee" three times. A woman has no similar right and, in some interpretations, no right to divorce unless written into the marriage contract. Although the majority of Muslims oppose *talaq*, some Islamic countries retain the practice in legal codes. Feminists in these countries oppose the provision as do nonfundamentalist Islamic theologians.

TANAKA, MITSU. The leader of the *uman ribu* (**women's liberation**) **movement** in Japan during the 1960s. Her group engaged in protest, published a newsletter, and received much media attention. Her manifesto *Benjo Kara no Kaiho* (*Liberation from Toilets*) charged that men treated women as a place to release bodily fluids. Tanaka founded the first **women's center** in Japan in 1972.

THE DICTIONARY • 315

TANG JUNYING. The founder of the Chinese Suffragette Society after the revolution of 1911 had established a republic. She modeled her group on the **Women's Social and Political Union** and once led members in a violent three-day takeover of the national legislature, which called in troops to restore order. In 1913 a militarist government took power and arrested Tang Junying, who may have been executed. Laws were passed prohibiting women from joining political groups and all **woman suffrage** groups were suppressed.

TANNEN, DEBORAH (1945-). *See* GENDER AND COMMUNICATION.

TELEVISION, IMAGE OF WOMEN IN. A topic that the **National Organization for Women (NOW)** has for the past several years adresssed in a "Watch Out, Listen Up!" report on the presentation of women on primetime television. It has listed among its most offensive programming the "male-centric sitcoms," with stereotypical depictions of women as nagging housewives, sexually exploited young women, or frustrated and love-starved career women. Women are consistently outnumbered and outranked by male stars, while professional wrestling shows that feature women manage to offend by presenting the women as Vegas-style showgirls in a regressive, insulting comedy routine. Most alarming is the presentation of **domestic violence** against women on television, tending to normalize the behavior for its viewers. NOW readers rated *"Cagney and Lacey"* as their all-time favorite television show, followed by *"ER," "Ellen,"* and *"Golden Girls."*

TEMPERANCE MOVEMENT. A campaign, primarily led by women after the 1850s, to promote moderation or complete abstinence in the consumption of alcohol. The first local temperance society was formed in the United States in 1808, and by 1833 there were 6,000 groups there. The movement emerged in Ireland in 1829 and in Scotland, England, Norway, and Sweden in 1836-1837. By 1851 there was a loosely coordinated movement of temperance groups, including Canada, India, Australia, New Zealand, Japan, South America, other nations in Europe, and parts of Africa. The **Woman's Christian Temperance Union (WCTU)**, formed in 1874 under the leadership of **Francis Elizabeth Willard**, through its World WCTU coordinated women's efforts around the world to change the status of women and achieve **woman suffrage**. With the formation of the US Prohibition

Party in 1882 and particularly with the passage in 1919 of the Eighteenth Amendment that banned the production, sale, and consumption of alcohol, **suffragists** in the United States encountered negative impacts from this alliance and began to separate the two movements. In Canada and other nations, however, the two issues remained linked, as the temperance movement continued as an important member of the suffrage coalition. *See also* BRITISH WOMEN'S TEMPERANCE ASSOCIATION.

TEMPORARY ASSISTANCE TO NEEDY FAMILIES (TANF). A US program of cash assistance to the poor that replaced Aid to Families with Dependent Children as a part of the Personal Responsibility and Work Opportunity Reconciliation Act (PRWORA) of 1996. That law ended welfare as an entitlement and replaced it with grants given to the states to run a program that requires TANF recipients to work within two years of entering the program, limits their lifetime participation to five years, and allows states to refuse to give additional TANF payments with an increase in family size. Feminists view the PRWORA as compromising the sexual **privacy** and vocational and **reproductive** choices of low-income women, who must disclose the paternity of their children and live with parents or other adults if underage. This policy, feminists charge, suggests that mothering has no value nor is it work, despite the fact that mothers in two-parent families are exempt from the work requirement. Although some feminists continue to focus on women's equality as waged workers, others suggest that a caregiver's allowance should be established. A cash grant for caregiving would increase equality between men and women and between all women. Currently middle-class marrried women who choose to work in the home are honored and respected.

TENDER YEARS DOCTRINE. The invalidated presumption that custody should be granted to the caregiving parent (usually the mother) during the child's early years. Rooted in traditional **gender roles**, this solution was viewed as uniformly in the "best interests of the child." Since 1983, every US state has adopted a **gender-neutral** doctrine and most allow **joint custody**.

TERRELL, MARY CHURCH (1863-1954). An African American civil rights activist and co-founder of the **National Association of Colored Women** in 1896. She addressed the **National American Woman Suf-**

frage Association convention with **Susan B. Anthony** in 1898. Her attempts to integrate the **woman suffrage movement** failed, however, and black **suffragists** worked within their own groups after 1900.

THATCHER, MARGARET (1925-). The first female prime minister of Great Britain. During her service, 1979-1990, this "Iron Lady" was known for her determination, resolve, and strength. Her **androgynous** leadership style reshaped British women's attitudes toward power and has been linked with the election of an historic number of female members of Parliament in 1997. Much to the dismay of feminists, she was hostile to social welfare policies and pursued an aggressive military policy in the Falkland Islands dispute with Argentina. Although she supported **abortion** rights, she was indifferent to most parts of the feminist agenda and personally sought to restore Victorian family values. She resigned after a challenge to her leadership and was made a life peer in 1992.

"THELMA AND LOUISE." The quintessential contemporary female "buddy" film. The 1991 motion picture portrays dreams, desires, and frustrations in the everyday life of women, trapped like Thelma, in a confining marriage. After a sexually threatening encounter with a demeaning truck driver, the two women revenge themselves and hit the road. Women turn the **female gaze** on a grinning Brad Pitt as Thelma takes carnal delight in him. Susan Sarandon (Louise) had to insist that the film conclude with the joint suicidal deaths of both its heroines. It was chosen by members of the **National Organization for Women** as the "best" movie about the lives of women and girls.

THESMOPHORIAZUSAE, OR A WOMEN'S FESTIVAL. Another play written by Aristophanes in 392 B.C., shortly after he wrote **Lysistrata**. The action concerns the decision of Athenian women to punish the famous tragedian Euripides for the **misogyny** in his dramas. They take him into custody and decide to punish him during the festival of the Thesmophoria, at which women alone may be present. Euripides disguises his brother-in-law Mnesilochus as a woman who tries to plead the case for Euripides. When he fails and is unmasked, Euripides takes the stage and impersonates various famous mythological and literary characters (Menelaus looking for his wife Helen; Echo helping Andromache; Persues releasing Andromache from her chains, etc.) Aristophanes's play appears to parody Euripides's works in order to absolve him of the charge of misogyny. Like his **Ecclesiazusae,** Aristophanes makes light of the political aspirations of Athenian women, mocking their concerns and consigning them to their proper sphere, the home.

THIRD WAVE FEMINISM. A resurgent involvement of young women, 15-30, in feminist activism. This generation of women, principally in the Anglophone democracies, came of age in the 1980s and sees feminism as alive in a new **postmodernist** form. They consciously seek to include **women of color** and poor women and to use direct action in order to spread feminism through the media. They charge that **second wave feminists** left many unsolved problems and an image of women as victims. The third wave values equal rights but not at the expense of their sexuality. Their agenda appears in *Manifesta: Young Women, Feminism, and the Future* (2000) and on the Web pages of the 3rd WWWave and the Third Wave Foundation, a project-oriented organization originally formed in 1992 as the Women's Action Coalition (WAC).

THOMAS, CLARENCE. *See* HILL, ANITA.

THOMAS, MARTHA CAREY (1857-1935). An American educator, feminist, and advocate for women's equal educational opportunities. She was the first foreigner and the first woman to earn a doctorate from the University of Zurich. She served as president of Bryn Mawr College, 1894-1922, and attempted to make it the equal of the Ivy League men's colleges. Her support for women's entry into the professions was reflected in her comment that "our (Bryn Mawr) failures only marry." She was also active in the **woman suffrage movement** and served as president of the National College Women's Equal Suffrage League, 1908-1917.

300 GROUP. A British multi-partisan organization to promote more women in elected office, politics, and public life from the local level to the European Parliament. The group was formed in 1980 by Lesley Abdela after her parliamentary election to increase the number of women in the House of Commons. Three hundred represents around half of House seats and signaled a goal of **gender parity** at a time (1979) when only 19 of 635 seats were held by women. The 300 Group provides campaign training and works on women's public appointments.

"THREE LADIES IN A BATHTUB." *See* PORTRAIT MONUMENT.

THREE MARIAS, THE. The three Portuguese women (Maria Isabel Barreño, Maria Fatima Velho da Costa, and Maria Teresa Horta) known for their collection of essays, stories, and poems, *New Portuguese Letters* (1972). The book was the result of their many meetings and discussions concerning controversial issues common to them as women and writers. They based their work on a seventeenth century Portuguese classic, *Letters of a Portuguese Nun* (1669). Upon publication their book was banned because of its feminist content and erotic passages, and the three women were arrested. Their case provoked outrage internationally (especially from women's groups), and charges were dropped in 1974 when a new revolutionary government assumed control. The work was released and is now recognized for its literary value.

TITLE VII. *See* CIVIL RIGHTS ACT OF 1964.

TITLE IX, EDUCATION AMENDMENTS OF 1972. A US law that prohibits educational programs or activities receiving federal financial assistance from excluding, denying benefits to, or discriminating against any person based on that person's sex. Title IX also prohibits discrimination against employees as well as students. In 1984 the Supreme Court issued an opinion, *Grove City College v. Bell,* which briefly narrowed the application of Title IX to only that program receiving federal money until Congress overturned the ruling by legislation. The impact of Title IX has been extensive: vocational and physical education classes have been integrated; **gender-neutral** career counseling is required; women's athletic programs have been expanded; **single-sex education** is much rarer; and **sexual harassment** of students by teachers or other students is covered. It still remains one of the most violated civil rights laws due to little enforcement, 1972-1992, and the continuing controversy over athletic opportunity. The rule of "proportionality," which requires that the proportion of a school's female athletes must equal that of female enrollment, is strongly opposed by those who support a "reasonable variance." In 2002 Congress renamed Title IX in honor of its advocate, the late Congresswoman Patsy Mink of Hawaii.

TOKEN WOMAN. The only female who holds a position of power, especially in the corporate world, and, therefore, must represent her entire sex. Her presence is presented as evidence that the organization does not engage in **gender discrimination**. When women constitute less than 15 percent of a group's membership, all are considered tokens and are not viewed by others as individuals. Feminists argue that only after women exceed that level is a "critical mass" achieved, and women can "act for" other women effectively within that group. Otherwise, women are marginalized.

TORONTO WOMEN'S LIBERATION MOVEMENT (TWLM). One of the first **younger branch** organizations, formed in 1968 by the University of Toronto's Women's Caucus of the peace group, the Student Union for Peace Action. The group was active on the issue of **abortion**, and in 1969 it took over a campus building for use as a **day care** center and also staged a protest against the scanty attire worn in the Miss Winter Bikini Contest. That same year **radical** and **lesbian feminists**, objecting to the lack of attention to sexuality and **Marxist** class analysis, left to form the New Feminists. In 1970 another faction interested in Third-World issues broke away and formed the Leila Khaled Collective.

TRADE UNIONS. *See* KNIGHTS OF LABOR, WOMEN; WOMEN'S TRADE UNION LEAGUE (WTUL).

TRAFFIC IN WOMEN. *See* INTERNATIONAL TRAFFIC IN WOMEN.

TRANSCENDENTAL FEMINISM. *See* FULLER, MARGARET.

TRANSGENDERISM. The condition of seeking to transform the **gender** of one's birth through clothing **(cross-dressing)** or living in a condition that deliberately obscures the two genders. Highly contested explanations have been offered for the desire to transform one's gender, with the most controversial currently being offered by Northwestern University Psychology Professor J. Michael Bailey, *The Man Who Would Be Queen* (2002). Bailey asserts that men who seek sex-change surgery are either "extremely gay" or suffering from sexual fetishism. His notoriety and condemnation by the lesbian, gay, bisexual, and transgendered community has elicited support for his findings by the National Association for Research and Therapy of Homosexuality, a group that is committed to "curing" gays. Feminists have condemned Bailey's research because it pathologizes transgendered people. *See also* TRANSSEXUALISM.

TRANSNATIONAL FEMINISM. *See* GLOBAL FEMINISM.

TRANSSEXUALISM. The wish, often present from early childhood, to have the body of the other sex because it seems more congruent with personal experience of **gender**. The process may involve a series of procedures, medical and psychological, to change anatomy, **sex role**, and gender identity to that of the opposite sex. Feminists are concerned about those cases of wished-for or actual surgical transsexual change that are motivated by **sex role stereotypes** or homophobia. In particular they fear that persons, especially children, who do not conform to conventional sex-role behavior will be viewed as potential transsexuals. *See also* TRANSGENDERISM.

TRASHING. A form of character assassination leveled against feminists by other feminists in which a woman's personality, ideology, or commitment to the movement is questioned. These attacks were particularly common within **radical feminist** groups, 1969-71, and were directed against women who rose to prominence because of a special talent such as writing or oral communication skills. In a movement committed to nonhierarchical consensual governance, such visibility was viewed as **elitist** and was strongly sanctioned. Trashing was responsible for the destruction of parts of the early **women's liberation movement** and continues to be used as a shorthand term for vicious internal disputes.

TRISTÁN, FLORA (1803-1844). A French socialist and author of various feminist tracts, including "Women's Emancipation, or The Pariah's Testament," in which she termed women "the proletariat of the proletariat." She called for equal education and professional training, the right to free choice of a husband, **divorce** and remarriage, and the rights of unwed mothers to respect and equality. Influenced by Fourier, Robert Owen, Chartism, and extensive travels in England, she proposed a Socialist International organization in 1843. Tristán believed that a society could measure its progress according to the status of its women and workers.

TROKOSI. A word in the Ewe language meaning "slaves of the gods" and a religious tradition in parts of West Africa (particularly Ghana) where families give virgin girls and women to priests to atone for the sin of an ancestor. The *trokosi* become the sex slave of the priest and also work in the fields and markets. An international movement to outlaw the practice and free the slaves has been supported and publicized by feminists.

TROPHY WIFE. A derisive term describing the second wife of a successful man. Such women are usually much younger and more attractive than the first wife and often have an interesting career of their own. These women are supposedly symbols that men in their 50s and 60s are still competitive in the bedroom as well as the boardroom. See also "BOY-TOY."

TRUBNIKOVA, MARIIA (1835-1897). The founder of the Russian **social feminist** movement of the 1860s. Inspired by her correspondence with prominent European feminists such as **Jenny d'Hericourt**, she started the first Russian salon for women. She and her friends established **self-help** institutions to serve poor and working-class women, including housing, schools, a **child care** center, cafeterias, and trades workshops. With the formation of a women's publishing cooperative in 1863 and her successful campaign for women's university courses in 1878, Trubnikova also provided educated women with opportunities for economic advancement.

TRUE LOVE WAITS (TLW). A national abstinence movement to help US teens and college students save sex for marriage. Since TLW's formation in 1993, more than 2.4 million youth have signed pledge cards to remain chaste. Feminists have dismissed the group as a part of the religious right's attack on sex education and the sexual agency of the young. A 2003 study found that 6 out of 10 college students taking the pledge broke the vow. Of the 40 percent who abstained from intercourse, 55 percent had oral sex.

TRUTH, SOJOURNER (c. 1797-1883). A US evangelist, **abolitionist**, former slave, reformer, and women's rights activist. In 1850 Truth discovered the new women's rights movement at a conference in Worcester, Massachusetts. Her impassioned **"Ain't I a Woman?"** speech at an 1851 women's rights convention in Akron, Ohio, challenged **"cult of domesticity"** stereotypes about feminine frailty. She was one of the most prominent advocates of **woman suffrage** for black women as a member of the **American Equal Rights Association.**

TSVETAYEVA, MARINA IVANOVNA (1892-1941). A Russian whose work forms the cornerstone of modern feminist poetry in the former Soviet Union. Born in Moscow, she emigrated to Western Europe in 1922 and returned in 1939 to the Soviet Union, where she committed suicide two years later. Tsvetayeva's works did not receive wide recognition during her life because of the extreme individuality of her style and her open opposition to the regime. Among her themes were the special place of women in the world and human passions; her work makes abundant use of materials from Russian folklore, as well as of heroic figures from the Western literary tradition. Her writing is notable for its use of **nonsexist language** and its rejection of **sex roles** and **gender** limitations. Her first collection of poems, *Evening Album*, was published in 1910.

TYRANNY OF STRUCTURELESSNESS. A phrase used by political scientist Jo Freeman to describe feminist commitment to a nonhierarchical egalitarian form of organization that often limited the effectiveness and longevity of the group. Small feminist groups of the late 1960s and early 1970s, based on consensus decision-making and rotation of all group tasks, found it more difficult to adopt goals and develop strategies for their advancement. Even here, a (less accountable and less democratic) leadership structure did emerge, based on friendship ties and time commitment.

-U-

UK MEN'S MOVEMENT. A British **backlash** group, formed in 1994 to oppose women's bureaucracies and programs, including **women's studies**. It has merged with the **fathers' rights movement** group Dads After Divorce and has attempted to overwhelm the Equal Opportunity

Commission with **reverse discrimination** complaints. Its pamphlet "Discrimination Against Men in the UK" argues that men are discriminated against in education, family law, employment, taxation, government representation, and the media. At least one search engine refuses to provide links to their homepage on the grounds that the content is offensive to women and inappropriate.

UKRAINIAN WOMEN'S UNION/SOIUZ UKRAINOK. An organization formed in 1921 to represent all Ukrainian women and seek their cultural, economic, and political advancement. By the 1930s its mass membership (peasant-dominated) approached 100,000. The union set up **child care** centers, offered vocational and domestic arts training courses, and established cooperatives for the sale of women's crafts. The union also linked Ukrainian women with international feminism as an affiliate of the **International Council of Women**, the **International Woman Suffrage Alliance**, and the Women's International League for Peace and Freedom. In the post-Soviet era the union adopted a new charter in 1991. It remains a traditional women's group working to advance the status of women in a newly independent Ukraine.

UKRAINKA, LESYA (1871-1913). A leading Ukrainian feminist writer and the first to turn people's attention to questions of women's rights and **woman suffrage** in Ukraine. Among her better-known works are the poems *On the Wings of Songs* (1893); the plays *The Blue Rose* (1896) and *Cassandra* (1908); and the novel *The Forest Song* (1912). The Theater of Russian Drama and numerous libraries, schools, and collective farms are named for her.

UNDUE BURDEN. *See* O'CONNOR, SANDRA DAY.

UNION FÉMININE CIVIQUE ET SOCIALE (UFCS)/WOMEN'S CIVIC AND SOCIAL UNION. The Catholic wing of the French feminist movement during the suffrage era. Formed in 1925 after the Pope endorsed **woman suffrage**, the UFCS today is similar to the United States **League of Women Voters** in its nonpartisanship and dedication to training women for citizenship. It was a founding member of the **European Women's Lobby**.

UNION FRANÇAISE POUR LE SUFFRAGE DES FEMMES (UFSF)/FRENCH UNION FOR WOMEN'S SUFFRAGE. The largest **woman suffrage** group in France, 1909-1940. Under the leadership of Cécile Braunschwicg, the UFSF provided a moderate alternative to **Hubertine Auclert** and her militant Suffrage des femmes and represented France in the **International Woman Suffrage Alliance**. Because of a widespread fear by socialists and left-wing republicans (who were most likely to sponsor a woman suffrage bill) that women would vote as their priests told them, and thus, strengthen the conservative parties, French women were not enfranchised until 1944.

UNION OF GREEK WOMEN/ENOSIS GYNAIKON ELLADAS (EGE). A **socialist feminist** organization, formed in 1976, in close association with the Panhellenic Socialist Movement political party. The EGE has won many reforms, including the Family Law of 1983. Greece established a General Secretariat for Sex Equality in 1985, with Equality Bureaus in every local government to implement **gender** equity policies.

UNION OF HEBREW WOMEN FOR EQUAL RIGHTS. An Israeli women's organization formed in 1919 to obtain suffrage and contest elections. In 1920 14 women were elected as delegates to the Jewish Representative Assembly (the forerunner of the Knesset) and in 1925 the assembly ratified the principle of **woman suffrage**. The Union of Hebrew Women ran its own list of female candidates in five national elections, published a feminist magazine called *Woman* and a legal handbook for women, and established domestic relations legal aid services for women. By the end of the 1930s Israeli feminism was supplanted by the crisis of the Holocaust, the World War, and the Arab challenge.

UNISEX. The facilities, materials, and styles of appearance appropriate for both sexes. For feminists, the marketing of such items as clothing, haircuts, toys, and children's books to both sexes is viewed positively as a way to break down rigid and restrictive **gender roles**. **Antifeminists** oppose such trends as violating natural differences between the sexes, bringing a boring "sameness" to society, and threatening the physical safety of women with sex-integrated public facilities (e.g., unisex toilets).

UNITED NATIONS COMMISSION ON THE STATUS OF WOMEN. An international body, established in 1946 to prepare recommendations and reports on promoting women's rights in the political, economic, civil, social, and educational fields and now a part of the UN Division for the Advancement of Women. The commission is composed of 45 delegates who represent and speak for governments. The commission was responsible for many of the activities of the **International Women's Year** (1975) and the UN Decade for Women (1975-1985). It also drafted the Convention on the Political Rights of Women (adopted 1953) and the **Convention on the Elimination of All Forms of Discrimination Against Women** (adopted 1979).

UNITED NATIONS DECADE FOR WOMEN. See INTERNATIONAL WOMEN'S YEAR.

UNITED NATIONS DEVELOPMENT FUND FOR WOMEN (UNIFEM). A program created in 1976 to provide financial and technical assistance to programs and strategies that promote women's rights. UNIFEM was created at the request of women's groups attending the First World Conference on Women in Mexico City in 1975. Today the fund is active in over 100 countries to ensure human rights, end **violence against women**, and increase women's economic security, particularly that of poor women affected by globalization.

UNITED NATIONS INTERNATIONAL WOMEN'S YEAR. See INTERNATIONAL WOMEN'S YEAR.

UNITED STATES V. ANTHONY, 24 FED. CAS. 829 (1873). A US case in which **Susan B. Anthony** challenged the denial of voting rights to women. She had voted in an 1872 New York election and was indicted for "knowingly voting without having a lawful right to vote." The court examined the language of the newly ratified **Fourteenth Amendment** and Fifteenth Amendment and held that the State of New York could limit the voting franchise to the male sex. It determined that the right or privilege of voting was not a right of national citizenship under the United States Constitution. Although Anthony was fined $100 for voting illegally, she never paid the fine and no further action was taken. The case signaled that a constitutional amendment would be needed for the national enfranchisement of women.

UNITED STATES V. VIRGINIA, ET AL. 116 S. CT. 2264 (1996). A US case in which the state-supported Virginia Military Institute (VMI) was ordered to admit women. The VMI, whose mission was to produce "citizen soldiers" through a very adversarial system, was the sole single-sex public college in the state. Under court order to either admit women or provide an equal alternative, Virginia established a new program at a private all-female college. The Supreme Court decided that this program did not provide an equal opportunity for women. Although the legality of all **single-sex education** was not addressed, The Citadel in South Carolina had been forced to admit Shannon Faulkner, its first woman, in a very similar case in 1994. Feminists had supported the admission of women to both institutions, but also feared that the decisions may raise questions about the future of private women's colleges and voluntary all-girl public schools. There was also some chagrin when Faulkner, the sole female at the Citadel, withdrew in her first week as a cadet because of extreme stress.

UNWAGED LABOR. *See* WAGES FOR HOUSEWORK.

"UP FROM THE PEDESTAL." A phrase popularized during the 1970s to convey the attempt to free women from the infantilization of traditionally protective attitudes toward women. Treating women as idealized objects on a pedestal actually serves to keep women in their place—the home—and further hinders women's advancement as equals in the job market.

-V-

VAGINA MONOLOGUES. A performance piece written and originally performed in 1999 by Eve Ensler about women's attitudes toward and experiences with their vaginas. In a series of short monologues, Ensler examines **rape** in Bosnia, shame, **lesbianism**, orgasm, childbirth, and related topics. Translated into 26 languages and performed in 31 other countries, the *Vagina Monologues* has also been performed on college campuses in conjunction with V-Day on February 14. V-Day is also a nonprofit organization that channels profits from the performance to victims of **domestic violence** and battered **women's shelters** in the United States, Canada, Africa, Asia, Afghanistan, and the Middle East. V-Day has raised over $14 million in its first five years of activity.

VAGINAL ORGASM. *See* "MYTH OF THE VAGINAL ORGASM."

VAN GRIPPENBERG, ALEXANDRA (1859-1913). A Finnish feminist and charter member of the Finnish Women's Association in 1884. She worked for a broad range of women's issues in addition to **woman suffrage**, which was won in 1906. As a member of the Finnish Diet in 1909, Van Grippenberg opposed **protective labor laws** in favor of absolute equality for women. In 1912 she founded the Finnish National Council of Women but died shortly after being elected its first president.

VAN SCHURMAN, ANNA MARIA (1607-1678). A Dutch philologist who wrote extensively on philosophy and religion. In her *Whether a Maid May Be a Scholar?* (1641; translated into English 1659), she uses syllogisms to prove her theory that single women should receive scholarly education. She also asserted that education for women was suitable but need not affect traditional social roles.

V-DAY. *See* VAGINA MONOLOGUES.

VETERAN FEMINISTS OF AMERICA (VFA). A US organization founded in 1992 by **second wave feminists** to document their history, inspire young feminists, and revive the movement today. Patterned on the model of the Veterans of Foreign Wars, the group holds reunions and conferences and has a newsletter and website. Observers have noted a rift between VFA members and **third wave feminists**, with the former viewing young feminists as undermobilized, self-centered, and unappreciative of the accomplishments of the previous generation.

VETERAN'S PREFERENCE. A policy adopted by many US employers that grants special advantages in hiring to those having previously served in the armed services. Feminists note that these policies have the effect of reducing employment opportunities for women, who until 1967 could not fill more than 2 percent of armed forces positions. In an **Equal Protection** challenge to a state law that granted a permanent preference in civil service jobs to veterans, the US Supreme Court ruled in *Personnel Administrator of Massachusetts v. Feeney* (1979) that there was no evidence of intent to discriminate against women. Mere evidence of an adverse impact on women was insufficient to establish a constitutional violation.

THE DICTIONARY • 329

VIAGRA. A prescription drug for male impotence, introduced in 1998. Its inclusion in many group health **insurance** plans aided the campaign for **contraceptive equity**. **Backlash** critics suggested that if one-third of all men are impotent, feminism is responsible or, alternatively, feminists, in search of sexual pleasure, are forcing men to take a potentially dangerous drug. The new drug's popularity brought calls for a female version, although some noted that a woman's absence of arousal or orgasm has no impact on intercourse or **reproduction**.

VICTIM BLAMING. *See* "BLAMING THE VICTIM."

VICTIMIZATION OF WOMEN. A feminist critique of the vulnerability of women to abuse, violence, and oppression. The portrayal of women as weak and victimized, particularly in sexual relations, has proven effective in creating a **feminist consciousness**. Other feminists, however, believe that the movement should make women feel strong and prefer the term "survivor" (e.g., "rape survivor") not "victim." Katie Roiphe, in her book on **date rape** (*The Morning After*, 1993), has accused feminists of teaching young women to fear all interpersonal relations with men.

VINDICATION OF THE RIGHTS OF WOMAN. *See* WOLLSTONECRAFT, MARY.

VIOLENCE AGAINST WOMEN. A term encompassing **rape**, violent **pornography**, **domestic violence**, incest, and crimes against **prostitutes**. Internationally, feminists have spoken out against the cultural practices of **female genital mutilation**, female infanticide, **suttee**, and **honor killings**. Other global issues include selling women into **sexual slavery** as prostitutes and war crimes against women in Bosnia. A 2002 study by the World Health Organization found that 70 percent of women murdered worldwide were killed by their male companions, and as many as one-third of girls are forced into their first sexual encounter. *See also* CLOTHESLINE PROJECT.

VIOLENCE AGAINST WOMEN ACT (VAWA). A US law passed in 1994 as part of an omnibus crime bill. The act adopted a multipronged approach to the problem, including changes in the criminal justice system, a national **domestic violence** hotline, protections for battered immigrant spouses, and more funding for battered **women's shelters**. In

2000 the US Supreme Court struck down the provision in the VAWA that permitted victims of domestic violence and **rape** to file a civil suit in federal court against their attackers for monetary damages. In a 5-4 decision the court ruled that Congress lacked the power to legislate in this area.

VIRGIN MARY. *See* MARY OF NAZARETH, FEMINIST INTERPRETATIONS; VIRGIN OF GUADALUPE.

VIRGIN OF GUADALUPE. On December 9, 1531, the Mexican peasant Juan Diego saw a vision of a beautiful, dark-skinned woman who addressed him as "my son," and declared herself to be the **Virgin Mary**, the mother of Jesus Christ. She instructed him to tell the local bishop to have a church built in her name on the spot where the Aztec goddess Tonatzin, earth goddess and mother of the gods and protectress of humanity, had been worshipped. The popularity of the Virgin of Guadalupe served to wipe out the residue of Aztec and Mayan religions, which had practiced human sacrifice. Her worship as a face of the divine, and a woman of color, has also served to spread Christianity throughout the Hispanic and Latin American societies, and most recently she has been celebrated by the Hispanic feminist Sandra Cisernos, "Guadalupe: The Sex Goddess," (*Ms.* 7/8 [1996], 43). *See also* ISIS.

VIRGINIA MILITARY INSTITUTE. *See* UNITED STATES V. VIRGINIA.

VOICES FROM THE PIPELINE. *See* SECOND TIER.

VOLUNTARY ASSOCIATIONS. *See* CLUB WOMAN'S MOVEMENT.

VOLUNTEERISM. The **unwaged labor** of individuals to alter society, usually through participation in groups. In a controversial early position paper, the **National Organization for Women (NOW)** urged women to refrain from volunteer work because it contributes to women's low **self-esteem** in that it confers little status and is society's alternative for those who have no employment choice. Other feminists argue that, although volunteerism has been gendered by society, it has historically been essential to the advancement of women's status.

VON MEYSENBERG, MALWIDA (1816-1903). An early feminist who was dedicated to women's equality in the new German state. She believed that women needed to be self-supporting, have equal access to education, and participate in shaping society. Von Meysenberg remained single after turning down a proposal of marriage in order to attend the women's college in Hamburg. In the 1850s she was a leader in implementing elementary school coeducation and in secondary education for girls.

VOTES FOR WOMEN! An English suffrage newspaper, 1907-1918, and a 1906 play by Elizabeth Robins, who novelized it as *The Convert* (1907). The newspaper was the official publication of the **Women's Social and Political Union** until 1912 and served as a fund-raiser and a tool of recruitment. It ceased publication with the achievement of partial **woman suffrage** in 1918. The suffrage propaganda drama (and novel) defended militant tactics and presented **suffragettes** in a positive manner to a wide audience.

-W-

WAGE GAP. The disparity existing between salaries earned by men and women. These pay differentials exist on all continents and are even larger in developing countries. They were formerly justified by the concept of the **family wage** for the male breadwinner and women's preference for lower-paying jobs that were more compatible with family life. In the United States in 2003, the wage gap between full-time, non-seasonal male and female employees was 81 cents for women for every dollar received by men, a slight gain due to men's falling wages. This gap is larger than those in Australia and many Western European nations. The **Equal Pay Act of 1963** and Title VII of the **Civil Rights Act of 1964** have had less impact because of **occupational segregation**; men and women hold different jobs. These gap figures undercount the real disparities since only about half of all employed women work full-time over 12 months, and a disproportionate number of working women lack fringe benefits such as health care and **pensions**. *See also* COMPARABLE WORTH; EQUAL EMPLOYMENT OPPORTUNITY COMMISSION V. SEARS, ROEBUCK & CO.; PINK-COLLAR GHETTO.

WAGES FOR HOUSEWORK. A feminist demand derived from **Charlotte Perkins Gilman's** analysis of the economic value of childrearing, food preparation, and cleaning. US women's rights groups have recommended that homemakers receive **Social Security** coverage in their own names, based on their **domestic labor**, not as a dependent of a male wage earner. This would require that the cash value of unpaid housework be calculated and perhaps even be included in the Gross Domestic Product (GDP). Such a policy would lessen the vulnerability and dependency of homemakers. Although these changes in the Social Security system have not been adopted, married women have been given additional rights to participate in their former husbands' retirement benefits and to establish their own Individual Retirement Accounts. The International Wages for Housework Campaign, a London-based network of women in developing and industrialized countries, has been working since 1972 to pay wages gained from reductions in defense spending. The United Nations has estimated that women spend two-thirds of their working hours on unpaid work and that if this work were counted in the GDP, it would add $11 trillion to the world economy.

WALKER, ALICE (1944-). A contemporary African American novelist, poet, and essayist, best known for her novel *The Color Purple* (1982), which won the Pulitzer Prize and the National Book Award. In addition to five collections of poetry, Walker has also published other novels, *The Third Life of Grange Copeland* (1970), *In Love and Trouble* (1973), *Meridian* (1976), and *Possessing the Secret of Joy* (1992)—all of which celebrate the many survival skills black women have developed, not the least of which is the power of a **matrilineage**, which Walker describes in *In Search of Our Mothers' Gardens* (1983). Her most recent book has exposed the practice of **female genital mutilation (FGM)** as a cultural practice in Africa: *Warrior Marks* (1996). Walker and Pratibha Parmar traveled throughout Africa in order to document the lives of individual women whose bodies were mutilated in order to conform to their village's dictates.

WALKING MARRIAGE. A contemporary form of legal marriage in which the couple chooses not to live together in order to preserve personal freedom and independence. Some Chinese urban residents, particularly women raised as single children, do not want to be crowded by a spouse or the **one child** permitted to couples there. Marriage, however, is required to get an apartment. A version of a "walking marriage" was adopted by writer Woody Allen and actress Mia Farrow and philosophers Jean-Paul Sartre and **Simone de Beauvoir**, who did not formally marry but were longtime companions. *See also* COMMUTER MARRIAGE.

WAL-MART CASE, THE. *See* EQUAL PAY ACT OF 1963.

WARD, MARY AUGUSTA (MRS. HUMPHREY) (1851-1920). A popular British author and the most prominent **antisuffragist**. Although she supported women's entry to Oxford and a role for women in local government, she opposed **woman suffrage** on the grounds that colonial and foreign policy issues were outside the realm of a woman's experience. In 1889 Ward collected the signatures of over 1,300 distinguished women in support of her manifesto, "Appeal against the Extension of the Parliamentary Franchise to Women." In 1908 she joined the Women's National AntiSuffrage League (later the National League for Opposing Women's Suffrage, 1910-1918) and began the *AntiSuffrage Review*.

WATKINS, GLORIA. *See* HOOKS, BELL.

WEDDINGTON, SARAH. *See* ROE V. WADE.

WELFARE. *See* TEMPORARY ASSISTANCE TO NEEDY FAMILIES.

WELLS-BARNETT, IDA BELL (1862-1931). An African American journalist and civil rights activist, best known for her antilynching campaign. In 1913 she began to work for **woman suffrage**, forming Illinois' first black female suffrage group, the Alpha Suffrage Club of Chicago, and helping to integrate that movement by refusing to march last in suffrage parades.

WHEELER, ANNA (1785-1848). An English utopian and utilitarian, nicknamed the "Goddess of Reason," who thought that the happiness of women counted equally and was not subsumed under that of men. In response to James Mill's article endorsing **coverture**, she and William Thompson wrote *The Appeal of One Half of the Human Race against the Pretensions of the Other Half* (1825), which argued that a social system is not utilitarian if it only considers the happiness of half of its members. They concluded that the interests of neither single women nor wives are covered by their male relatives' interests and that the social dependence of women, especially in marriages where the contracts are the moral equivalent of slavery contracts, demeans women and corrupts men. The *Appeal* was one of the most important feminist tracts of the early 19th century and is considered a forerunner of the writings of **John Stuart Mill.**

WHITE RIBBON CAMPAIGN. *See* MONTRÉAL MASSACRE.

WHITE SLAVERY. *See* MANN ACT.

WHITEHEAD, MARY BETH. *See* IN RE BABY M.

WICCA. A resurrected Anglo-Saxon word now used for a religion, popular among some feminists. Although "wicca" originally meant a male witch, it now refers to a **goddess** or cosmic female principle identified with the earth, vegetation and (re)generation. The religion is based on **witches** persecuted in the 15th through 17th centuries who were devotees of an ancient Germanic nature religion. Like Goddess Religion, Wicca is a contemporary religion fulfilling the spiritual needs of some who reject the **patriarchal** themes and figures of Judeo-Christian religions. Wicca emphasizes egalitarian relations between persons and between humans and the earth. Its devotees organize in local small groups and worship on the date of a new or full moon and during eight seasonal festivals. There are an estimated 200,000 initiated Wiccans in the United States and increasingly members are encountering opposition as they seek to serve as state prison chaplains or to open public meetings with a prayer. *See also* FEMINIST SPIRITUALITY.

WICKEDARY. A gynocentric "metapatriarchal dictionary" by **Mary Daly** and Jane Caputi (*Webster's First Intergalactic Wickedary of the English Language*, 1987). It creates new words and exposes **sexist** assumptions in old words by playing with etymological and metaphorical meanings in order to subvert **patriarchy** through language. In addition to coining new words and satirically playing with words in order to show their patriarchal bias, they also outline a strategy for feminists who would attack patriarchal language: expose "elementary terms and phrases: mummies, dummies, antibiotics, and reversals"; "BeLaughing:

Nixing, Hexing, and X-ing"; "Spinning beyond the Compass: Regaining the Sense of Direction"; and "Jumping off the doomsday clock." Such phrases suggest both the playfulness and anger in this book, written, according to Daly, as an attack on "the academented fraternities of Bearded Brother No-it-alls."

WIFE ABUSE. *See* DOMESTIC VIOLENCE.

WIFE RAPE. *See* MARITAL RAPE.

WILD WOMAN MOVEMENT. A term coined by Clarissa Pinkola Estes and popularized by her 1992 book *Women Who Run with the Wolves*. The wild woman, analogous to Robert Bly's wild man, represents the woman who attacks society's strictures and rebels against the conformities imposed on her to behave in an acceptable and nonthreatening way. The book on which the movement is based consists of folktales, myths, and Jungian analysis about women who assert their **sexuality** and unique feminine ways of knowledge against the deadening influences of **male-dominated** society. Estes retells traditional stories with the wild woman twist; when she meditates on the meaning of the Little Match Girl, she writes that the girl wasted her art and was destroyed because she failed to "unresign herself and come out kicking ass. When Wild Woman is cornered, she does not surrender, she comes ahead, claws out and fighting." Estes asserts a clear distinction between men and women, based on her **essentialist** Jungian understanding.

WILLARD, EMMA HART (1787-1870). The founder of the Troy Female Seminary (1821), the first US women's college, and of a women's college in Athens, Greece. After leaving the seminary in 1838, she worked for laws to improve women's education. She is credited with educating a generation of **first wave feminists**, including **Elizabeth Cady Stanton**, a graduate of her seminary.

WILLARD, FRANCES ELIZABETH (1839-1898). A US educator, social reformer, and founder of the **Woman's Christian Temperance Union (WCTU)** in 1874. The first mass organization of women devoted to social reform, the WCTU viewed alcohol and alcoholism as the causes of poverty and women's subjugation. Willard served as president of the WCTU from 1879 until her death. Under her leadership, the group endorsed **woman suffrage**, linking the vote to the adoption of prohibition. The involvement of over 200,000 traditional, religious women in the suffrage movement gave the cause a mass base for the first time. Willard also served as president of the Evanston College for Ladies and later as dean of Northwestern University's Woman's College. As a social reformer, she worked for **protective labor laws**, prison reform, early childhood education, raising the age of consent, and **rape** and **prostitution** law reform.

WISH LIST. *See* EMILY'S LIST.

WITCH HUNTS. *See* SALEM WITCH TRIALS.

WITCHCRAFT. The magic employed for malevolent purposes, a form of personal revolt practiced largely by women in virtually every society. Although men and women were both originally involved in covens, women became the focus of **witch hunts** after the publication in 1486 of *Malleus Maleficarum* (*The Hammer of Witches*), commissioned by Pope Innocent VIII. It associated witchcraft with women, particularly elderly and poor women. Just as witchcraft allowed women to rebel against **male-dominated** societies, the witch hunt and active persecution allowed society to punish such rebellion. Although rare, a 2002 study by the World Health Organization reported that 500 older women are accused of witchcraft and killed annually in Tanzania. *See also* SALEM WITCH TRIALS (1692).

WITTIG, MONIQUE (1935-). A contemporary French novelist and theorist, author of the **lesbian** epic *Les Guérillères* (1969), the novel *Le Corps Lesbien* (1973), and *The Straight Mind and Other Essays* (1992). Wittig is suspicious of oppositional thinking that defines woman as the opposite of man, as well as mythical-idealist formulations of *féminité*: She claims that women must define themselves as a class, "which is to say that the category 'woman,' as well as 'man,' is a political and economic category, not an eternal one. Our first task is thoroughly to dissociate 'women' (the class within which we fight) and 'woman,' the myth. For 'woman' does not exist for us; it is only an imaginary formation, while 'women' is the product of a social relationship." Wittig has taught French and Italian at the University of Arizona since 1990.

WOLF, NAOMI (1962-). A US author who, over a decade, has written four best-selling books on cutting-edge feminist topics: *The Beauty*

Myth (1991); *Fire with Fire: The New Female Power* (1993); *Promiscuities: The Secret Struggle for Womanhood* (1997); and *Misconceptions: Truth, Lies, and the Unexpected Journey to Motherhood* (2001). She was briefly employed in 2000 to advise Al Gore on his presidential bid, designing his widely touted "alpha male" look. Wolf is widely read and admired by young women of the **third wave**. *See also* POWER FEMINISM.

WOLLSTONECRAFT, MARY (1759-1797). An English feminist and author, widely considered the founder of the modern feminist movement. Author of *Mary, a Fiction* (1788), *A Vindication of the Rights of Man* (1790), *A Vindication of the Rights of Woman* (1792), and *The Wrongs of Woman, or Maria* (1798), Wollstonecraft was a mistress, wife, and mother; her lover's infidelity drove her to attempt suicide twice. She later married William Godwin (1797) and died shortly after the birth of her second daughter, Mary, later to become Mary Shelley, author of *Frankenstein* (1819). Wollstonecraft's rich and varied experiences provided the material for her novels, while her novels provided the gothic and melodramatic impetus for her prose works, particularly *A Vindication of the Rights of Woman*. Her writings brilliantly exposed the **double standard** between men and women in contemporary society. According to Wollstonecraft, this disparity encouraged in men the fullest exercise of their powers of rational autonomy and the development of moral virtue, while imposing social, political, and economic constraints on the development in women of both reason and virtue. Wollstonecraft argued for changes in education which would enable women to become as autonomous as she thought men were. She proposed a theory of human nature, claiming that all humans have reason, and that women and the lower classes are believed to have less only because of the wrongful practices and neglect of **patriarchal** society. She also argued against Jean Jacques Rousseau, who claimed that women should be dependent on men and not utilize their intelligence. Instead, Wollstonecraft supported education for women so that they could better educate their children at home. *See* REPUBLICAN MOTHER.

WOMAN AND RUSSIA/ZHENSHCHINA I ROSSIIA. The first feminist samizdat in the Soviet Union, circulated in 1979 in Leningrad and edited by Marina Oulianova and **Tatiana Mamonova**. The issue discussed conditions in maternity hospitals, **abortion** clinics, and **child**

care centers; **rape**; alcoholism; and the **double shift**. Over time the collective split along political and religious lines, pitting secular feminists who still revered Leninist revolutionary ideals against Russian Orthodox Christian feminists who rejected **Marxism** and started their own *Mariia* journal and club. In response to the appearance of this samizdat, the Soviet KGB questioned, searched, arrested, and exiled several authors. Concurrently, the official Soviet press began to examine many of these same women's issues. Five more issues were produced after the leaders' exile. These essays attracted the attention of Western feminists who translated, published, and circulated them in at least 11 languages and 22 countries.

WOMAN AS OTHER. A concept developed in **Simone de Beauvoir's** *Second Sex* (1963). According to this view, woman is defined by man as everything he is not. If he is culture, she is nature. If he is rational, she is emotional. If he is the mind, she is the body. This endless series of binary oppositions serves to valorize male characteristics and values and objectify and subjugate women in a series of inferior postures. By defining the woman as inherently "other than" man, **male-dominated** culture is able to define women, keep them in inferior postures, and cause them to view themselves as less than man.

WOMAN SUFFRAGE (CASE LAW). *See* CHORLTON V. LINGS; MINOR V. HAPPERSET; UNITED STATES V. ANTHONY.

WOMAN SUFFRAGE MOVEMENT. The organized national and international efforts of the 19th and 20th centuries to extend the franchise to female citizens. Woman suffrage has been achieved at different times in different countries and under different circumstances, but feminism's first campaign universally has been for the vote. Only in Finland was universal suffrage extended to men and women at the same time. New Zealand in 1893 was the first country to adopt woman suffrage; Bahrain in 2002 is the most recent addition to the rank of full suffrage nations. Only a small number of nations, primarily traditional Islamic societies, have not acted to enfranchise women. The suffrage campaigns in the United States and Great Britain are the best documented, perhaps due to their length, size, and central roles in coordinating the **International Woman Suffrage Alliance** and the **International Council of Women**. Historians have also been attracted to the contrasting tactics of the more conventional **National American**

Woman Suffrage Association and the National Union of Women's Suffrage Societies and the militant National Woman's Party and the Women's Social and Political Union.

WOMAN SYMBOL. The shorthand notation in medicine and science consisting of an ankh (ansate cross) and circle to represent the female sex. Feminists have traced its origins to Egyptian, Roman, and Greek symbols for the planet Venus, life, and Aphrodite, the **goddess** of love, beauty, and **sexuality**. In 1968 **Robin Morgan** inserted a clenched fist within the circle to represent **radical feminism**. The equality symbol is more commonly seen there today as a symbol of women's equality.

WOMANCHURCH. A Christian feminist movement to combat the discriminatory actions of institutional religion. The term stems from a 1983 gathering of 1,400 Catholic women from the Americas who declared themselves WomanChurch and vowed never again to be slaves to **patriarchy**. Members feel that Christianity marginalizes women with male-centered language, monopoly of ritual by men, and scriptural interpretations. The movement for the **ordination of women** in the Catholic and Anglican Churches has allied with WomanChurch. **Feminist theologians** associated with this movement include Rosemary Radford Ruether, Elizabeth Schüssler Fiorenza, and Carol P. Christ.

"WOMAN-IDENTIFIED WOMAN, THE." A 1970 **Radicalesbian** position paper by **Rita Mae Brown** in which **lesbianism** is defined as a political choice (in contrast to a sexual alternative) required by feminism. Many heterosexual women felt the paper also suggested that straight women were male-identified, collaborating with the enemy, and untrustworthy. *See also* GAY/STRAIGHT SPLIT; LAVENDER MENACE; LESBIAN FEMINISM; POLITICAL LESBIANISM.

WOMANIST. A synonym for **African American feminism** that uses black women's experience as its foundational source and was popularized by **Alice Walker**. Attention is drawn to the need to encompass race and class, as well as **gender**, in the movement to transform systems of oppression. Womanists challenge other feminists to acknowledge, deeply integrate, and respond to the reality of differences between and among women. Emphasis is placed on knowledge of black women's history, experiential understanding of the lives of contemporary black women, and ongoing dialogue.

WOMAN'S BIBLE, THE. A two-volume collection of essays and commentaries on the Bible, published in 1892 and 1895 by a committee of academic and church women, chaired by **Elizabeth Cady Stanton.** Stanton, who did most of the writing, sought a critical study of biblical texts which are used to degrade and subject women in order to demonstrate that it is not divine will that humiliates women, but human desire for **domination.** She argued for the concept of an **androgynous** God. The book was a best-seller, although never a major work of theology. The 1896 convention of the **National American Woman Suffrage Association,** fearing a setback to their cause, passed a resolution, 53-41, disassociating itself from the work despite a plea from **Susan B. Anthony** on free expression grounds to reject the motion.

WOMAN'S CHRISTIAN TEMPERANCE UNION (WCTU). A US **temperance movement** group, founded in 1874 to oppose the consumption of alcohol. Under the leadership of **Frances Elizabeth Willard,** 1879-1898, the WCTU became the largest US women's group of the 19th century and an important supporter of **woman suffrage** and other social reforms. Women were attracted to the WCTU by promises of being protected in the home through their exercise of the vote. In 1884 their World's WCTU (WWCTU) became the first international women's organization. The WWCTU organized temperance groups around the world and by 1920 had more than 40 national affiliates representing over one million women. Many suffrage leaders, both in and outside the United States, were first associated with the temperance movement. The membership of the WCTU peaked in 1920 and fell to 40,000 by the early 1990s. It continues to appeal to young mothers concerned with drug and alcohol abuse among children and teenagers.

WOMAN'S JOURNAL, THE. *See* STONE, LUCY.

WOMEN AGAINST PORNOGRAPHY (WAP). *See* PORNOGRAPHY, FEMINIST DEBATE ON.

WOMEN AND ECONOMICS. *See* GILMAN, CHARLOTTE PERKINS.

WOMEN FOR DEMOCRACY/MUJERES POR LA DEMOCRACIA (MUDE). A Peruvian **women in development** organization that provides credit and technical assistance to peasant women for their business projects. It is allied with the Peruvian human rights and feminist movements and with the struggle for democracy.

WOMEN FOR DIGNITY AND LIFE/MUJERES POR LA DIGNIDAD Y LA VIDA (LAS DIGNAS). The largest women's group in El Salvador, established in 1990 after the end of the war. Las Dignas is primarily engaged in **grass-roots** projects in literacy, job training, community development, and **domestic violence**. It operates 11 health clinics in rural areas, where it trains midwives, educates on sex and **reproduction**, and provides maternity care.

WOMEN FOR WOMEN. One of the most important feminist groups in Bangladesh. Established in 1973 by professional women as an autonomous research center, the group does public education to advance the status of women and publishes its own research as well as some overlooked women writers. It has recently developed programs for the victims of **acid attacks**.

WOMEN IN BLACK. A women's movement for peace and human rights, which began in Jerusalem in 1988 to protest the Israeli occupation of land gained in the Six-Day War in 1967. Modeled upon the **mothers' movements** in Latin America, the women demonstrated each Friday at major intersections, dressed in black and holding signs in Hebrew, Arabic, and English. Women in Black quickly spread to 39 other cities in Israel and by 2003 had groups in 142 cities and 30 nations around the world. Many of the vigils address other international human rights problems. Although the movement has no constitution or recognized spokesperson, Women in Black has twice been nominated for the Nobel Peace Prize, and the Belgrade group was awarded the Millennium Peace Prize for Women by the **United Nations Development Fund for Women** in 2001.

WOMEN IN COMBAT. The participation of females in national warfare. Until modern times, except for tales of the **Amazons** and women such as **Deborah Sampson** who disguised themselves as men, women were excluded from combat within national military forces. Women combatants have often participated, not always by choice, in revolutionary movements for national liberation. Italy until 1999 was the only NATO member to exclude women from its active-duty armed forces. In some countries the role of women in the military has been a topic of great debate; in others, women's role has not been discussed. Even though Israel has long had compulsory military service for women, they continue to be exempt from combat. The United States has pioneered in the integration of women into the military, and in 2003 about 15 percent of uniformed US service personnel were female. Laws barring women from combat have been repealed, although each service can establish restrictions. Women cannot serve on Navy submarines nor may they join units whose primary mission is ground combat. When opponents of the **Equal Rights Amendment** used the spector of women in combat as an argument against ratification, the **National Organization for Women** responded that equal rights require equal responsibilities, including participation in the nation's defense and registering for the draft. Feminists in the United States, Australia, and Canada have supported greater opportunities for women who choose this career. US feminists have also raised issues of **sexual harassment** in the military and the higher dismissal rates of **lesbians**.

WOMEN IN DEVELOPMENT. *See* DEVELOPMENT, WOMEN IN.

WOMEN IN NIGERIA (WIN). The first feminist organization in Nigeria, formed in 1982 by university-educated professional women to appeal across religious, class, and ethnic lines. It currently has chapters in 24 of the 36 Nigerian states. Even though the members are elite, they are antiestablishment and are viewed by some Muslims as Western, radical, and non- or antiIslamic. When the group in the 1990s rejected membership in the official council of women's organizations, the government refused to register WIN as a legal entity and threatened to jail some of its leaders. WIN has been active against child marriage and in **grass-roots** projects on adult education, housing, and business.

WOMEN LIVING UNDER MUSLIM LAWS (WLUML). An international network to support all women controlled by the laws and customs of Islam. The group was formed in response to incidents during 1984 and 1985, including the arrest of three Algerian feminists who were jailed without trial for discussing laws unfavorable to women with other women. The WLUML attempts to link local feminist groups with international groups.

WOMEN OF COLOR. *See* COLOR, WOMEN OF.

WOMEN OF RUSSIA (WOR). A women's electoral coalition, formed by three women's organizations in 1993 to contest legislative elections in post-Soviet Russia. The WOR rejected feminist appeals in favor of social programs and the election of more women to public office. Without the quotas for **gender parity** that had reserved one-third of the seats for women, female representation fell to barely 5 percent in the 1990 election. In the 1993 election the WOR received 8 percent of the party list votes and 21 seats in the Duma. The bloc was able to achieve several policy goals for women, families, and children, including the adoption of a new family code. With the proliferation of political parties, the WOR won no seats in the 1995 and 1999 elections and women-only electoral coalitions are no longer viable in Russia.

WOMEN ON WAVES (WOW). A group founded in 1999 by Dutch physician Rebecca Gomperts to provide offshore **abortion** services to women living in nations where abortion is illegal. The plan is to dock their ship and provide **family planning** information; if an abortion is requested, the ship sails into international waters to perform the procedure. In June 2001, the ship docked in Dublin for eight days but was unable to perform any of the 300 requested abortions because of the Dutch government's failure to certify the ship. WOW is authorized to provide **RU 486** on board and can place its mobile unit on a truck to go into war zones and refugee camps. On June 26, 2003, WOW performed its first abortion with RU-486 in international waters off the coast of Poland.

WOMEN WITH DISABILITIES. A group that experiences discrimination based on both **gender** and physical or mental characteristics. Women with disabilities violate the social ideal of perfection and are particularly likely to be perceived as passive and helpless. They often are subject to **sterilization abuse** and **sexual assault**. Feminist groups have tried to make their activities accessible, engaged in **consciousness-raising** around the issue, and formed disability caucuses.

WOMEN WORKERS' COUNCIL (WWC). *See* NA'AMAT/PIONEER WOMEN.

WOMEN'S ACTION COALITION (WAC). *See* THIRD WAVE FEMINISM.

WOMEN'S ACTION COMMITTEE (WAC). An Australian **women's liberation movement** group established in 1970. Its three founders had gained notoriety in 1969 by chaining themselves to the doors of the Arbitration Committee to demand (successfully) a ruling on **equal pay**. The WAC chose **consciousness-raising** over formal organization and engaged in **zap actions** against targets such as men-only bars and **beauty pageants**.

WOMEN'S ACTION GROUP (WAG). A Zimbabwe women's rights group formed in 1983 in response to an indiscriminate street sweep against **prostitution** that netted many other working women, including teachers and nurses. The WAG was founded by an interracial urban group of middle-class women from Zimbabwe, the United States, Australia, and the United Kingdom. Currently the members are primarily black rural and shantytown residents. WAG focuses on health care, **AIDS**, **violence against women**, legal literacy, and counseling. It produces a magazine, radio show, **self-help** workshops and actively lobbies for women's landownership rights.

WOMEN'S AWAKENING/NAHZAT-E BANOVAN. A period in Iranian history, 1936-1941, in which Reza Shah Pahlavi attempted to transform the status of women. Employment and educational opportunities for women improved, marriage law was reformed, and the state enforced unveiling. But male guardianship was not challenged, and **woman suffrage** was not addressed. Despite this, a male **backlash** against female office workers began in 1941, and in 1943 unveiled women were attacked in Tehran. The era ended with the forced abdication of the shah, but Iranian women began to demand **gender** equality and the vote. A Women's Party was formed in 1944.

WOMEN'S BATTERY SHELTER. A British term referring to housing available to women and their children when women have been abused by the men in their lives. Services include shelter, food, counseling, legal advice, and eventual return to the community. The women's battery shelter movement began in the early 1970s. Charging **sex discrimination**, a US **fathers' rights** group filed a 2003 lawsuit against 10 California shelters for denying a bed to a man. See also BATTERED WOMAN SYNDROME.

WOMEN'S BUREAU, DEPARTMENT OF LABOR. A US government agency, established in 1920 to serve the interests of working women in industry. Although the bureau always supported, in principle, equal employment policies, it defended **protective labor laws** for women until 1956 and did not endorse the **Equal Rights Amendment** until 1970. Through much of its history, the agency held the view that mothers and wives should only work out of economic necessity. The bureau, beginning in 1961 with its major role in the establishment of the **President's Commission on the Status of Women**, has moved into the mainstream of the **women's rights movement** and has served as a forum, advocacy agency, and data-gathering resource for women's issues. **Antifeminists** have supported its elimination, arguing that the government should be committed to jobs for all Americans, not just women. Efforts by the George W. Bush administration in 2002 to reduce the bureau's funding were quickly withdrawn in the wake of mobilized women's groups.

WOMEN'S BUREAU COALITION. See SOCIAL FEMINISM.

WOMEN'S CAMPAIGN FUND (WCF). The first of the women's political action committees (PACs), formed in 1974, to provide campaign money and other resources to **pro-choice** women candidates seeking national, state, and local elective offices in the United States. Republican, Democratic, and Independent party members are eligible, and over 2,000 campaigns have been supported by the WCF.

WOMEN'S CENTER. A meeting place and information center for local feminist movement activists. These institutions have been formed throughout the world. Typical activities include: classes on **women's history, self-defense,** legal rights, and **assertiveness**; a community calendar of women's events; referrals to female professionals and women-run businesses; a job bank; a feminist resource library; **consciousness-raising** groups; a magazine or newsletter; and targeted services to victims of **rape** and **domestic violence** and to **displaced homemakers**. These centers often begin as **grass-roots**, volunteer-run enterprises, funded by donations and minimal program fees, but evolve into complex social service organizations supported by a myriad of government and private foundation grants.

WOMEN'S CLUB MOVEMENT. See CLUB WOMAN'S MOVEMENT.

WOMEN'S COMMUNITY/ZHINOCHA HROMADA. A Ukrainian women's group, organized in 1992. The group works to advance the status of women, particularly in public office, by holding seminars, training courses, and conferences. Before the 1994 elections, it held the Ukrainian Congress of Women's Organizations, which resulted in the formation of the Women's Council of Ukraine, an election bloc of 10 women's organizations that nominated over 50 candidates.

WOMEN'S DEMOCRATIC UNION (WDU). See BULGARIAN WOMEN, THE COMMITTEE OF.

WOMEN'S EDUCATIONAL EQUITY ACT (WEEA). A bill passed by the US Congress in 1974 as a part of the larger Special Education Projects Spending Act. The WEEA program receives money for developing curriculum and guidance materials and funding projects that support the goal of sex equity in education of **Title IX, Education Amendments of 1972**. The program came under attack during the early years of the Reagan administration as a stronghold of feminists. Congress refused to abolish the program, however, and in 1984 rewrote the WEEA authorization to prevent future presidents from ignoring legislative intent. Even so, George W. Bush (unsuccessfully) attempted in 2002 to abolish the WEEA, which has funded more than 750 programs despite a budget that has never exceeded $3 million annually.

WOMEN'S ELECTORAL LOBBY (WEL). An Australian women's rights group established in 1972. WEL combines the broad feminist policy agenda of the **National Organization for Women** and the interest of the **National Women's Political Caucus** in women's elective and appointive public office. Like these two groups, it has national officers, annual conventions, and local chapters. It is not associated with a political party but is closer in its views to the Labor Party even though leftists see WEL as conservative and middle class. The Australian Federation of Women Voters disbanded in 1982 after transferring its mission to WEL. The **Women's Action Committee** and WEL have overlapping memberships and cooperate on some projects.

WOMEN'S ENVIRONMENTAL AND DEVELOPMENT ORGANIZATION (WEDO). An international organization founded in 1990 to seek greater influence for women within the United Nations system by analyzing and monitoring UN documents' impact on women. The group sponsors independent meetings such as the 1991 World Women's Congress for a Healthy Planet and has organized women's caucuses at all UN conferences affecting women. In 2000 WEDO began the 50/50 Campaign for **gender parity** in public office. More than 150 groups in 45 nations have joined this project as partners.

WOMEN'S EQUALITY DAY. The anniversary (August 26) of the passage of the **Nineteenth Amendment** extending voting rights to US women. Although the day is not an official national holiday, American presidents often issue proclamations marking the day and feminist groups plan major rallies on that date.

WOMEN'S EQUITY ACTION LEAGUE (WEAL). A US group founded in Ohio in 1968 by lawyer Dr. Elizabeth Boyer in protest against the support of legalized **abortion** by the **National Organization for Women**. In the opinion of Boyer, such a radical goal would serve to discredit the newly revitalized feminist movement. WEAL sought to attract the participation of professional women in a more respectable and moderate arm of the **new feminist movement** by concentrating on educational equity and economic issues affecting women. The group disbanded in 1989.

WOMEN'S FRANCHISE UNION. The **woman suffrage** group in Sri Lanka, organized in 1927 by Evadne de Silva, the wife of George E. de Silva, a national hero, statesman, and advocate of universal suffrage. After suffrage was won in 1931, the union helped elect the first woman to the state council in 1932 and helped to form other women's groups, including the All-Ceylon Women's Conference.

WOMEN'S FREEDOM LEAGUE (WFL). The smallest of the three primary English **woman suffrage** groups, formed in 1907 out of a split in the **Women's Social and Political Union**. Some members challenged the autocratic leadership of the **Pankhursts** and the dominance of wealthy women over the group. The WFL used militant but nonviolent tactics. Even so, their demonstrations and tax resistance were met with prison sentences. Their own newspaper, the *Vote*, supported many other feminist issues, which extended their organizational life to 1961.

WOMEN'S FREEDOM NETWORK (WFN). A US group established in 1993 as an alternative to both **fringe feminism** and the traditionalism of **antifeminism**. The WFN supports full equality for women and men as individuals but rejects different standards for either sex. Cathy Young's *Ceasefire: Why Women and Men Must Join Forces to Achieve True Equality* (1999) presents this position in fuller detail. The group's leadership includes several prominent academic women such as Jean Elshtain, Christina Hoff Sommers, and Jeane Kirkpatrick. Feminists view the WFN as **faux feminist** because of its funding from well-known conservative foundations.

WOMEN'S HEALTH INITIATIVE. A $625 million study, begun under the sponsorship of the US National Institutes of Health (NIH) in 1993, of major diseases (cancer, heart disease, and osteoporosis) in postmenopausal women. A permanent Office of Research on Women's Health within the NIH has also been established. Women's rights advocates charge that past studies of diseases that occur in both sexes have excluded women from clinical trials and that diseases that only affect women are ignored by researchers. Critics note that even this study does not address the dearth of medical research on women of childbearing years due to researchers' fears of causing birth defects through drug trials. Designed as a 15-year program, the Women's Health Initiative discontinued its **estrogen replacement therapy** drug trial in 2002 because of the adverse effects encountered.

WOMEN'S HEALTH MOVEMENT. A US feminist challenge to **patriarchal male dominance** of the medical profession. The first feminist health conference was held in 1971, and in 1975 a coalition group, the **National Women's Health Network**, was formed to coordinate this new movement. Issues of particular interest are: **reproduction**, including childbirth, **reproductive technology**, and **abortion**; drug safety; medical **self-help** and self-knowledge; unnecessary surgery, such as Cesarean births, radical mastectomies, and hysterectomies; **fetal protection policies**; and **sterilization abuse**.

WOMEN'S HISTORY MONTH. A period (March) set aside each year in the United States to focus on the effort to reconstruct the female past. At least three US states require women's history in their elementary and high schools. In Canada the event is observed in October to coincide with Persons Day, which commemorates the **Persons Case of 1929**. Although historians agree that women have rarely been written into history, there is less agreement on the proper approach to addressing this omission. Much attention has been given to women's achievements, the movement for women's legal and political rights, and the changing economic role of women. More recently women's historians have documented the female experience as distinct from that of men and have focused on the family and women's domestic role.

WOMEN'S INTERNATIONAL TERRORIST CONSPIRACY FROM HELL (WITCH). The **politico** wing of the **New York Radical Women**, founded by (among others) **Robin Morgan** in 1968 to stage **zap actions**. These included the hexing of the New York Stock Exchange, the release of live white mice at a bridal fair in Madison Square Garden, and a hairy legs demonstration. Covens in other cities emerged with their own guerrilla theater targets and new names to fit the WITCH acronym. These highly visible tactics led to both new recruits and ridicule for the feminist movement. Some feminists also deplored the tactics as too derivative of New Left male counter-cultural politics.

WOMEN'S JOINT CONGRESSIONAL COMMITTEE (WJCC). A post-suffrage US coalition of 14 women's rights groups, formed in 1920 to coordinate lobbying efforts. Members included the **American Association of University Women**, the **League of Women Voters**, the **National Consumers League**, the **National Federation of Business and Professional Women's Clubs**, and the **Women's Trade Union League**. Their **social feminist** agenda supported education, health care, peace, and **protective labor laws**. The WJCC remained effective only through the early 1930s, when it became apparent that women did not constitute a cohesive and participatory voting bloc. *See also* SHEPPARD-TOWNER MATERNITY ACT OF 1921.

WOMEN'S LEAGUE FOR SOCIAL ACTION/LIGUE FEMININE D'ACTION SOCIALE. The first feminist organization in Haiti. Formed in 1934, this group of elite women focused on education, woman suffrage, and **married women's** rights. In 1950 married women were given the vote (with their husbands' permission) and full suffrage was extended in 1957. Many members of the league were victims of the Duvalier regimes, 1957-1986, and the league was silenced during this period.

WOMEN'S LEGAL EDUCATION AND ACTION FUND (LEAF). A Canadian litigation group, established in 1985 to use **Canadian Charter** provisions for women. LEAF has participated in over 140 cases, including those dealing with **domestic violence, employment discrimination, sexual harassment, reproductive freedom,** and **family leave.** Currently LEAF is challenging a 1996 law that eliminated maternity benefits for part-time workers, arguing that this constitutes unlawful **gender discrimination** because 70 percent of part-time workers are women.

WOMEN'S LIBERATION MOVEMENT (WLM). One of the two major strands in the early history of the **contemporary feminist movement** in the United States. The WLM, also called the radical, revolutionary, or younger branch, was based in numerous local groups spontaneously created as early as 1967 in cities by women formerly active in New Left groups or the African American **civil rights movement.** These local groups were small, informal, nonhierarchical **networks** committed to a radical vision of a new society. Well-publicized **zap actions,** protests, and **speak-outs** were utilized as were **consciousness-raising** and **self-help** projects. These groups were often short-lived, having fallen victim to a **tyranny of structurelessness.** *See also* BATTERED WORD SYNDROME; WOMEN'S RIGHTS MOVEMENT.

WOMEN'S MUSEUM: AN INSTUTUTE FOR THE FUTURE. A Dallas institution, opened in 2000, to document women's role in US life and history. Although initially welcomed by the feminist movement, there are now complaints that dependence on corporate sponsorship of exhibits has meant that certain topics like **female sexuality** and **sexism** have not been included, resulting in a nonfeminist approach that consciously avoids **male bashing.** There are hopes that the three planned women's museums in San Francisco, New York, and Washington, D.C. will avoid some of these pitfalls when each opens by 2006.

WOMEN'S NATIONAL COALITION OF SOUTH AFRICA (WNC). A coalition of 70 South African women's groups, founded in 1992 by the African National Congress (ANC) Women's League, to ensure the inclusion of women's rights in the new national constitution. The groups encompassed the entire political spectrum, including the white Conservative and National Parties and the ANC and Inkatha Freedom Movement. The coalition attempted to survey every woman in the country on a Women's Charter for the new document. Topics addressed included property and contract rights, **reproductive freedom, comparable worth, domestic violence,** and **sexual assault.** The charter was submitted to the state president on August 9, 1994, which has been designated as South Africa's National Women's Day, a public holiday. The WNC remains in operation and coordinates the **World March of Women.**

WOMEN'S NATIONAL COMMISSION (WNC). An official (but independent) British advisory board, established in 1969, to ensure that the views of women's organizations are included in government. The commission, by law, is composed of long-established and large national groups. In practice, this eliminates virtually all **new feminist** groups; member-organizations are primarily women's sections of trade unions and political parties. The WNC studies women's issues and presents position papers.

WOMEN'S ORGANIZATION OF IRAN (WOI). A group formed in 1966 by the government in the tradition of the High Council of Women's Organizations of Iran, which led the movement for **woman suffrage,** achieved in 1963. The WOI provided educational and vocational training for women under the guise of modernization, not women's rights. It worked for positive changes in the legal status of women after gaining the support of the shah and the religious authorities. The WOI was the only women's organization permitted in Iran, making any **grass-roots** women's movement impossible. By 1978 the WOI claimed 400 branches and 51 affiliated groups, active in **child care,** literacy, and **family planning.** After the revolution in 1979, many of these changes were reversed, programs were dropped, and the WOI was labeled "a den of corruption" by the new government.

WOMEN'S POLICY NETWORKS. A term used to describe feminist strategies within government. The concept refers to a group of expert or interested groups and individuals, public and private, forming around a policy area. These may include women's groups; the media; experts in government, academe, private sector think-tanks, and professional associations; elected and appointed governmental officials; and public bureaucracies. From the perspective of the feminist movement, membership in such a policy system offers information on new government programs and regulations, policy shifts, and effective strategies. *See also* FEMOCRAT.

WOMEN'S RIGHTS MOVEMENT. One of the two major strands in the early history of the **contemporary feminist movement** in the United States. This sector, also called the reform or older branch, began with the founding of the **National Organization for Women** in 1966 and grew rapidly as many other groups were formed. As a primary proponent of **liberal feminism**, this branch has concentrated on eliminating **sex discrimination** through the traditional channels of legislative and judicial reforms and has operated through formal, hierarchical, and national organization structures. *See also* WOMEN'S LIBERATION MOVEMENT.

WOMEN'S RIGHTS NATIONAL HISTORICAL PARK. A part of the US National Historic Park System that commemorates the **Seneca Falls Convention** of 1848. It includes the home of **Elizabeth Cady Stanton**, the Hunt House where the idea of the convention was conceived, the M'Clintock House where the **Declaration of Sentiments** was drafted, and the restored remains of the Wesleyan Chapel, where the convention met. It was dedicated in 1979 and became a part of the national park system in 1980.

WOMEN'S ROOM, THE. *See* FRENCH, MARILYN.

WOMEN'S SHELTER. *See* WOMEN'S BATTERY SHELTER.

WOMEN'S SOCIAL AND POLITICAL UNION (WSPU). The militant British suffrage organization founded in 1903 by Emmeline and Christabel **Pankhurst**, among others. The WSPU was an all-female group that sought broad equality for women. From 1905 to 1914 these **suffragettes** engaged in violent and aggressive tactics that led to arrests, prison terms, wide public attention for **woman suffrage**, and the emergence of **antisuffragism**. The WSPU suspended its campaign during World War I and changed its name to the Women's Party in 1917 in advance of the limited suffrage bill of 1918.

WOMEN'S STRIKE FOR EQUALITY. A nationwide demonstration, the largest ever for women's rights up to that time, held on August 26, 1970, to commemorate the 50th anniversary of US **woman suffrage**. Women's Strike Day was the idea of **Betty Friedan** and the **National Organization for Women** and was organized by local feminist groups in virtually every major city and some smaller ones in the United States and in several European cities as well. Newspapers and television, in covering the marches, pickets, rallies, and **zap actions** that marked the day's events, brought the public its first real awareness of the **new feminist movement**. The strike proved pivotal for the **women's rights movement**; many new participants were attracted into active membership as a result of the media coverage.

WOMEN'S STUDIES. An area of research and teaching, often interdisciplinary in nature, which began to develop in the 1960s. It typically includes not only the study of women but also brings a critical feminist perspective to the study of all disciplines. Most American and European universities offer these courses and approximately 650 **women's** or **gender studies** programs exist in US institutions. Conservatives and **antifeminists** have criticized these curricular developments, charging that women's studies courses are biased exercises in **male bashing** and, at a minimum, encourage illiteracy in the standard canons of Western civilization. *See also* FEMINOLOGY.

WOMEN'S TRADE UNION LEAGUE (WTUL). A US organization of female reformers and women in labor formed in 1903 by Progressives and labor officials to help women organize within trade unions, improve workplace conditions for women through **protective labor laws**, and promote feminism and **woman suffrage**. **Settlement House** workers Lillian Wald and **Jane Addams** were among the founders, but no trade union women served as WTUL president until 1921. Although the league was active in virtually every strike of women workers, by 1913 it had become primarily a social **welfare** group devoted to public advocacy and lobbying for legislation through the **Women's Joint Congressional Committee**. By the late 1920s the League had ceased most efforts to unionize women, and in 1950 it closed its small Washington, D.C., office.

WOMEN'S UNION OF RUSSIA (WUR). A group formed in 1990 by former leaders of the **Committee of Soviet Women**. The WUR was the largest member of the **Women of Russia** electoral coalition and serves as advisor to the president of the Russian Federation and to the Duma on women's issues. Because of its roots in the Soviet system, the WUR has been distrusted by other women activists, particularly feminists. Even so, the group protested when **maternity leave** went unpaid, **day care** was dismantled, and women's representation in elected office declined sharply. Although the WUR does not embrace the feminist label, it has grown closer to the positions of Russia's independent feminist movements and cooperates with them.

WOODHULL, VICTORIA CLAFLIN (1838-1927). An outspoken feminist advocate of **woman suffrage** and free love, and the first woman to run for president of the United States, in 1872 on the Equal Rights Party ticket. Woodhull and her sister Tennessee Celeste Claflin variously worked as spiritualist physicians, stockbrokers in their own firm near Wall Street in New York City, and publishers of *Woodhull and Claflin's Weekly*. She prepared testimony on women's rights, arguing that the recently passed **Fourteenth Amendment** and Fifteenth Amendment to the Constitution guaranteed the vote to women as members of races, and delivered her statement on January 11, 1871, before the House Judiciary Committee. This brought her to the attention of **Elizabeth Cady Stanton**, who befriended her, only to be castigated by other members of the **National Woman's Suffrage Association** for associating with a notorious lower-class Free Lover. Despite the suffrage movement's **classist** rejection of her, the **new feminist movement** has given her more attention as a feminist pioneer of her day.

WOOLF, ADELINE VIRGINIA (1882-1941). A British novelist, essayist, critic, letter writer, diarist, and pamphleteer who influenced both the Modernist and feminist movements of the 20th century. Her critical essays in *The Common Reader* (1925) celebrate the canon of English literature while also introducing literary works by women. Woolf's *A Room of One's Own* (1929), and *Three Guineas* (1938) have greatly influenced contemporary feminisms, the former having been especially important in modeling methods of **feminist literary criticism** and recovery of women's texts, while she is credited with coining the phrase "**equal pay for equal work**" in her *Three Guineas*. These two feminist essays argue, respectively, that women need intellectual and economic freedom if they are to be artists and that the **patriarchal** structures of **sexism**, fascism, and **classism**, which permeate public and private lives, lead inevitably to war.

WORK-FAMILY CONFLICT. The incompatibility between employment and domestic role demands. This may result in role overload and stress. Such conflict may be reduced by delegation of household activities to paid staff or other household members and by flexible and "family-friendly" organizational practices, such as **day care** and **flexitime**.

WORKING-CLASS FEMINISM. A movement of wage-earning women for **gender** equality and more equitable distribution of wealth and access to resources, often channeled through participation in labor unions, a socialist party, or neighborhood organizations. The problems of the suburban middle-class wife and mother, initially articulated by **second wave feminists**, have little meaning for these women. Caught on the "sticky floor" of the **pink-collar ghetto**, working-class feminists are also less affected by the **glass ceiling**.

WORLD MARCH OF WOMEN. A global feminist movement to eradicate poverty and **violence against women**. The first march in 2000 was coordinated by the *Fédération des Femmes du Québec (FFQ)* and was held at the UN headquarters in New York on October 17, the International Day for the Eradication of Poverty, and was preceded and accompanied by a variety of local actions around the world. In 2001 the World March collected more than 5 million signatures from 5,200 groups and 161 nations and territories on a petition to the UN secretary general demanding an end to global **gender** injustice.

WORLD PLAN OF ACTION FOR WOMEN. *See* INTERNATIONAL WOMEN'S YEAR.

WRIGHT, FRANCES (1795-1852). A Scottish-born American journalist and lecturer on controversial topics such as **abolition**, **divorce**, **birth control**, women's education, equality in marriage and economics, and authoritarian religions. "Fanny Wrightism" came to be a demeaning term indicating an amoral and heretical woman. Her travelogue of her visit to America, *Views of Society and Manner in America* (1821), noted the oppression of women here, as in Europe. In 1825 she founded the utopian community of Nashoba, Tennessee, where slaves could work to buy their freedom.

-X-

X CASE. A 1992 legal dispute involving a 14-year-old pregnant **rape** victim in Ireland. A High Court had issued an injunction that prevented "Miss X" from traveling to England for an **abortion**. The Supreme Court lifted the injunction in March and found abortion was legal if a woman's health was endangered by her threatened suicide. In November 1992 Irish voters established the right to obtain abortion information and the right to travel for an abortion. The case renewed interest in the **reproductive freedom** of Irish women. Irish feminists called Ireland "a police state" because the government only discovered the situation when the girl's parents contacted the police to see if DNA testing of the **fetal tissue** would be admissible evidence in the trial of her rapist.

X-LINKAGE HYPOTHESIS. An attempt by some **sociobiologists** to explain the seemingly different abilities between boys and girls in several areas, including mathematics, visualization, and spatial reasoning, by associating these abilities with sex. There appears to be little valid scientific data to support this hypothesis, yet **gender** differences in these areas have been widely publicized as facts, possibly leading to lowered parental expectations for girls and correspondingly lower demonstrated abilities by girls. *See also* MATH ANXIETY.

-Y-

YATES, ANDREA. *See* POSTPARTUM DEPRESSION.

"YEAR OF THE WOMAN." A term applied to the US election of 1992 in which women candidates, female voters and contributors, and women's issues were central. Feminists, fearing that media predictions of a major breakthrough for women in elected office were setting unrealistic expectations, emphasized that no single year is the "year of the woman" and wondered if women would only receive "one year." Even so, women's representation in the US Senate tripled to six members (of 100) and women gained 19 seats in the House of Representatives.

YEWWU YEWWI ASSOCIATION. A Senegalese feminist organization whose name means "raise **consciousness** for liberation." The group is based in Dakar and draws its membership primarily from Islamic students and intellectuals. Muslims, however, accuse the group of deliberately baiting their fundamentalist co-religionists.

"YOU GUYS." A common American English phrase that emerged in an era of **nonsexist language** to refer to a group or pairs that include or may be entirely composed of females. This is viewed as just one example of the return to noninclusive language in the popular press, even when style manuals require nonsexist terms. Although some argue that the term is now a **gender-neutral** term, feminists note that the generic use of "he" and "man" has declined after decades of their criticism. They argue that calling women "guys" also marginalizes femaleness and should be challenged.

YOUNG FEMINIST SUMMIT. A series of three-day conferences sponsored by the **National Organization for Women (NOW)**, 1991-1997, to appeal to high school and college age women by focusing on issues vital to younger women such as **sexual harassment** and **violence against women**. Around 1,200 women attended the last two conferences held in the Washington, D.C. area.

YOUNGER BRANCH. See WOMEN'S LIBERATION MOVEMENT.

YOURCENAR, MARGUERITE (1903-1987). A French-American novelist, poet, and in 1980 the first woman to be elected to the Académie Française since its formation in 1635. At her inaugural, she ignored the academy's past neglect of women writers; she previously had stated that feminism held no interest for her. Yourcenar supported the equality of women but viewed all movements with suspicion. She translated some of **Virginia Woolf**'s books but refused to be published by England's Virago Press because they only publish women. **Feminist literary critics** are divided on her characterization of women. Some feel that she neglected women and even showed contempt. Others find her treatment balanced.

"YOU'VE COME A LONG WAY, BABY." An **advertising** slogan used, 1968-1996, by the Virginia Slims cigarette company to market a product aimed at women. The campaign utilized symbols of the feminist movement in a patronizing manner and recalled the 1920s campaign by tobacco companies to support a woman's right to smoke in public. Over time the phrase has become associated with attempts to convince women that they have made such great progress that further changes in women's role and status are no longer needed. The slogan was replaced in 1996 by "It's a *woman* thing." US tobacco companies continue to donate millions of dollars to feminist projects to elect women and to provide critical services. This poses a dilemma for the groups which are sensitive to the health hazards of the product for women.

-Z-

ZAP ACTION. A form of ad hoc feminist protest designed to deal with a specific issue or a single event through the use of dramatic and often symbolic tactics. One such action was staged on Halloween 1968 by women dressed as **witches** who cast a hex upon the New York Stock Exchange, a symbol of **male-dominated** capitalism.

ZENG BAOSUN (1893-1978). A Chinese feminist who was a pioneer in modern education for women. University-educated in England and a convert to Christianity, Zeng Baosun was a nationalist who opposed communism and the Japanese invasion. She was elected to the National Assembly in 1948, but moved to Taiwan in 1951. There she became a leading spokesperson for women's rights and served as Taiwan's representative on the **United Nations Commission on the Status of Women**.

ŽENSKI POKRET/WOMEN'S MOVEMENT. A Serbian organization formed in 1919 as the Society for the Enlightenment of Woman and the Defense of Her Rights. Although unsuccessful in getting women's political and civil rights included in the new constitution, Ženski Pokret published a journal and founded orphanages, maternity centers, and employment bureaus for women. They offered home economics and literacy classes in the villages and sponsored lectures and recreation for working women.

ZETKIN, CLARA (1857-1933). A leading theoretician of the German Social Democratic Party and self-proclaimed feminist who argued in *The Question of Women Workers and Women at the Present Time* (1889) that socialism and feminism were inextricably intertwined. Founder and leader of the **Socialist Women's International** and editor of the women's newspaper *Equality*, she contended that women's subordination was the consequence of property relations determined by economic conditions. A critic of the feminist **Lily Braun**, Zetkin opposed the socialization of housework and **child care** and saw **contraception** as an "easy out." She believed that women should have an equal role in production and equal aspirations with men, while simultaneously functioning as wives and mothers to the highest degree. She is also credited with the establishment of **International Women's Day**.

ZHENOTDEL. The Women's Department of the Russian Communist Party, formed by Lenin in 1919. As the women's branch of the government, it handled all "women's issues" such as literacy, abolition of **prostitution**, and workplace reform. The Zhenotdel focused on women primarily as workers and mothers but also existed to recruit and socialize women into the new political system. Stalin abolished the organization in 1930 and declared that women's equality had been achieved. This was untrue, but observers have suggested that there were no more resources for women's social programs nor was there further need for socialization with governmental control now complete.

ZHENSOVETY. The local women's organizations created in Russia by Nikita Khrushchev in 1958 and revived by Mikhail Gorbachev in the 1980s. Because their agendas were set by the government and the Communist Party, the groups were the official women's movement of that era. By the late 1980s there were almost 250,000 zhensovety in the Soviet republics and some have continued to operate in the post-Soviet era and lend support to the **Women of Russia** movement.

Bibliography

Compiling a bibliography for a volume like this is always a daunting task. In the first place, the sheer volume of material is overwhelming, and, while the editors know that some material is of more importance than others, there is simply no provision for such nuances in this sort of listing. With those caveats in mind, it is necessary to state at the outset that the scholarly study of feminism as an ideology has burgeoned in the eight years since we last compiled a bibliography on the topic.

In the 1970s a number of pioneering works were published, and there is no question that those early works still bear scrutiny and deserve attention. As such, we have made the decision to keep the most important works published in the early days of feminist scholarship. Not particularly theoretical, these early works simply attempt to map an emerging field. During the 1980s, however, the field begins to come into its own, and one sees works that assume a new theoretical and critical stance toward the issue of feminism. The French Feminists begin to be translated into English, and feminism has an impact on such diverse fields as psychoanalysis, economics, politics, history, sociology, and literary studies.

During the 1990s, when we first assembled this bibliography, the field of feminism was under attack, both from the right and from the left. As the ideological stakes began to be understood, that is, as equal opportunity policies such as Title VII and Title IX in the United States, began to make an impact on salary and access issues for women, "backlash" studies began to emerge, and there was a number of hostile or defensive works written against or on feminism. In addition to the proliferation of the "backlash" studies another new field began to emerge: global feminism. As the world community has shrunk, so have women from all parts of the globe begun to share common stories and struggles. The growth of feminism in countries as beleaguered as Afghanistan and Nigeria attests to the growing globalization of feminism as a social, cultural, and political movement. The studies that we have included here reflect the early stages of the feminist movement within those countries.

Another change in feminist thinking is reflected in our revision of the earlier category "African American and Hispanic Feminism" to "Women of Color Feminism." This change is indicative of the current thinking on the subject by women of color themselves, who see themselves less as individual racial categories and more as a pan-racial group that shares commonalities of interest with all other women of color, both nationally and internationally.

Another addition to this bibliography is the inclusion of works on "Third Wave" feminism, another important recent development in the field. Although this is a growing field led by young feminists, there is already a fairly substantial body of works that the reader is advised to consult in order to grasp the different concerns and varying approaches of young feminists.

Also during the 1990s, the Internet began to assume a new prominence in the field, and the number of Internet sites devoted to feminism and feminist issues proliferated. We have included a listing of the primary Internet sites, with the warning that URL addresses frequently change and that the reader should be advised to search should such an address not operate.

Finally, the listing of reference materials—as well as the increase in the number of journals devoted to feminist approaches to a wide variety of topics is also of particular note to anyone interested in the field. In addition to this dictionary, the sheer increase in the number of other dictionaries, guides, and overviews of the field suggest that feminism as a movement is being widely discussed as well as critiqued. We would like to think that the days of unthinking or misinformed attacks on feminism would be corrected by a study of this and other reference guides that attempt to elucidate and inform readers of all issues related to feminism.

I. Reference Material
(Bibliographies, Encyclopedias, Dictionaries, and Almanacs)

Amico, Eleanor B. (ed.) (1998). *Reader's Guide to Women's Studies.* Chicago: Fitzroy Dearborn.

Andermahr, Sonya, Terry Lovell, and Carol Wolkowitz (1997). *A Glossary of Feminist Theory.* New York: Oxford University Press.

Bachmann, Donna G., and Sherry Piland (1978). *Women Artists: An Historical Contemporary and Feminist Bibliography.* Metuchen, NJ: Scarecrow Press.

Baer, Judith A. (ed.) (2002). *Historical and Multicultural Encyclopedia of Women's Reproductive Rights in the United States.* Westport, CT: Greenwood.

Boles, Janet K., and Diane Long Hoeveler. (1996). *The Historical Dictionary of Feminism*. Metuchen, NJ: Scarecrow Press. Also published as *From the Goddess to the Glass Ceiling: A Dictionary of Feminism*. Lanham, MD: Madison Books.
Bourne, Paula et al. (eds.) (1994). *Feminism and Education: A Canadian Perspective, Volume 2*. Toronto: Centre for Women's Studies in Education.
Broude, Norma, and Mary D. Garrard (eds.) (1994). *The Power of Feminist Art: The American Movement of the 1970s, History and Impact*. New York: Abrams.
Carson, Anne (1986). *Feminist Spirituality and the Feminine Divine: An Annotated Bibliography*. Trumansburg, NY: Crossing Press.
―――――. (1992). *Goddesses and Wise Women: The Literature of Feminist Spirituality, 1980-1992: An Annotated Bibliography*. Freedom, CA: Crossing Press.
Code, Lorraine (ed.) (2000). *Encyclopedia of Feminist Theories*. New York: Routledge.
Crawford, Elizabeth (1999). *The Women's Suffrage Movement: A Reference Guide*. New York: St. Martin's Press.
De Coste, F. C., K. M. Munro, and Lillian MacPherson. (1991). *Feminist Legal Literature: A Selective Annotated Bibliography*. New York: Garland.
Dixon, Penelope (1991). *Mothers and Mothering: An Annotated Feminist Bibliography*. New York: Garland.
Driel, Joan, Ellen Broidy, and Susan Searing (1985). *Women's Legal Rights in the United States: A Selective Bibliography*. Chicago: American Library Association.
Eigler, Friederide, and Susanne Cord (eds.) (1997). *The Feminist Encyclopedia of German Literature*. Westport, CT: Greenwood.
Evans, Mary (2001). *Feminism: Critical Concepts in Literary and Cultural Studies*. New York: Routledge.
Feinberg, Renee (1986). *The Equal Rights Amendment: An Annotated Bibliography of the Issues, 1976-1985*. Westport, CT: Greenwood.
Frost, Wendy, and Michele Valiquette (1986). *Feminist Literary Criticism: A Bibliography of Journal Articles, 1975-1981*. New York: Garland.
Gager, Nancy (1975). *Women's Rights Almanac*. New York: Harper and Row.
Gamble, Sarah (ed.) (2000). *The Routledge Critical Dictionary of Feminism and PostFeminism*. New York: Routledge.
Gelfand, Elissa D., and Virginia Thorndike Hules (1985). *French Feminist Criticism: Women, Language, and Literature: An Annotated Bibliography*. New York: Garland.
Godard, Barbara (1987). *Bibliography of Feminist Criticism*. Toronto: ECW Press.
Greenberg, Hazel (1976). *The Equal Rights Amendment. A Bibliographical Study*. Westport, CT: Greenwood Press.
Greenberg, Judith et al. (1998). *Women and the Law*. New York: Foundation Press.

Hannam, June, Mitzi Auchterlonie, and Katherine Holden (2000). *International Encyclopedia of Women's Suffrage*. Santa Barbara, CA: ABC-CLIO.
Harlan, Judith (1998). *Feminism: A Reference Handbook*. Santa Barbara, CA: ABC-CLIO.
Holland, Frances Schmid (1996). *Feminist Jurisprudence: Emerging from Plato's Cave—a Research Guide*. Lanham, MD: Scarecrow.
Humm, Maggie (1987). *An Annotated Critical Bibliography of Feminist Criticism*. Boston: G. K. Hall.
———. (1995). *The Dictionary of Feminist Theory*. Columbus: Ohio State University Press.
Isherwood, Lisa, and Dorothea McEwan (eds.) (1996). *An A to Z of Feminist Theology*. Sheffield, UK: Sheffield Academic Press.
Jagger, Alison M., and Iris Marion Young (eds.) (1998). *A Companion to Feminist Philosophy*. Malden, MA: Blackwell.
Kester-Shelton, Pamela (1996). *Feminist Writers*. Detroit: St. James Press.
Kinnard, Cynthia D. (1986). *Antifeminism in American Thought: An Annotated Bibliography*. Boston: G. K. Hall.
Kolin, Philip C. (1991). *Shakespeare and Feminist Criticism: An Annotated Bibliography and Commentary*. New York: Garland.
Kowaleski-Wallace, Elizabeth (ed.) (1997). *Encyclopedia of Feminist Literary Theory*. New York: Garland.
Kramarae, Cheris, and Dale Spencer (eds.) (2000). *Routledge International Encyclopedia of Women's Studies*. New York: Routledge.
Kramarae, Cheris, and Paula Treichler (1985). *A Feminist Dictionary*. London: Pandora Press.
Krichmar, Albert (1972). *The Women's Rights Movement in the United States, 1848-1970: A Bibliography and Sourcebook*. Metuchen, NJ: Scarecrow Press.
Mankiller, Wilma, Gwendolyn Mink, Marysa Navarro, Barbara Smith, and Gloria Steinem (eds.) (1998). *The Reader's Companion to US Women's History*. Boston: Houghton Mifflin.
McPhee, Carol, and Ann Fitzgerald (1979). *Feminist Quotations: Voices of Rebels, Reformers, and Visionaries*. New York: Crowell.
Miller, Cheryl (ed.) (1997). *Beyond Beijing: The International Women's Movenemt: The Handbook*. Chicago: Beyondmedia.
Myers, JoAnne (2003). *Historical Dictionary of the Lesbian Liberation Movement*. Lanham, MD: Scarecrow Press.
Noonan, Norma Corigliano, and Carol Nechemias (eds.) (2001). *Encyclopedia of Russian Women's Movements*. Westport, CT: Greenwood.
Nordquist, Joan (1994). *Ecofeminist Theory: A Bibliography*. Santa Cruz, CA: Reference and Research Services.
———. (1992). *The Feminist Movement: A Bibliography*. Santa Cruz, CA: Reference and Research Services.

———. (1996). *Feminism and Postmodern Theory: A Bibliography*. Santa Cruz, CA: Reference and Research Services.
———. (1996). *Feminism Worldwide: A Bibliography*. Santa Cruz, CA: Reference and Research Services.
Perez, Janet, and Maureen Ihrie (eds.) (2002). *The Feminist Encyclopedia of Spanish Literature*. Westport, CT: Greenwood.
Piland, Sherry (1994). *Women Artists: An Historical, Contemporary, and Feminist Bibliography, 2nd ed.* Metuchen, NJ: Scarecrow.
Russell, Letty M., and Shannon J. Clarkson (eds.) (1996). *Dictionary of Feminist Theologies*. Louisville, KY: Westminster/John Knox.
Russell, Rinaldina (ed.) (1997). *The Feminist Encyclopedia of Italian Literature*. Westport, CT: Greenwood.
Sakelliou Schultz, Liana (1994). *Feminist Criticism of American Women Poets: an Annotated Bibliography, 1975-1993*. New York: Garland.
Sartori, Eva Martin (ed.) (1999). *The Feminist Encyclopedia of French Literature*. Westport, CT: Greenwood.
Scanlon, Jennifer (ed.) (1999). *Significant Contemporary American Feminists: A Biographical Sourcebook*. Westport, CT: Greenwood.
Schultz, Jeffrey D., and Laura van Assendelft (eds.) (1999). *Encyclopedia of Women in American Politics*. Phoenix: Oryx.
Sellen, Betty-Carol, and Patricia A. Young (1987). *Feminists, Pornography and the Law: An Annotated Bibliography of Conflict, 1970-1986*. Hamden, CT: Library Professional Publications.
Slavin, Sarah (ed.) (1995). *US Women's Interest Groups: Institutional Profiles*. Westport, CT: Greenwood.
Steadman, Susan M. (1991). *Dramatic Revisions: An Annotated Bibliography of Feminism and Theatre, 1972-1988*. Chicago: American Library Association.
Taylor, Betty W. et al. (1999). *Feminist Jurisprudence, Women and the Law: Critical Essays, Research Agenda, and Bibliography*. Littleton, CO: F. B. Rothman.
Tierney, Helen (ed.) (1999). *Women's Studies Encyclopedia*. Rev. and expanded ed. Westport, CT: Greenwood.
Tuttle, Lisa (1986). *Encyclopedia of Feminism*. New York: Facts on File Publications.
Watson, G. Llewellyn (1990). *Feminism and Women's Issues: An Annotated Bibliography and Research Guide*. New York: Garland.
Williamson, Jane (1979). *New Feminist Scholarship: A Guide to Bibliographies*. Old Westbury, NY: Feminist Press.
Wright, Elizabeth (ed.) (1992). *Feminism and Psychoanalysis: A Critical Dictionary*. New York: Blackwell.

II. Feminist Journals

Affilia: Journal of Women and Social Work. Thousand Oaks, CA: Sage, 1986. Quarterly.
Agenda: Empowering Women for Gender Equity. Kwa Zulu Natal, South Africa, 1987. Quarterly.
Ahfad Journal: Women and Change. Omdurman, Sudan: Ahfad University for Women, 1984. Biannual.
Arise: A Women's Developmental Magazine. Kampala, Uganda: Action for Development, 1990. Quarterly.
Asian Journal of Women's Studies. Seoul, South Korea: Asian Center for Women's Studies, Ewha Woman's University, 1995. Quarterly.
Asian Women. Seoul, South Korea: Research Institute for Asian Women, Sookmyung Women's University, 1995. Biannual.
Atlantis. Halifax, Nova Scotia: Institute for the Study of Women, Mount Saint Vincent University, 1975. Biannual.
Australian Feminist Studies. Adelaide, South Australia: Research Center for Women's Studies, University of Adelaide, 1985. Triannual.
Berkeley Women's Law Journal. Berkeley: University of California Press, 1986. Annual.
CAFRA News/Novedades Cafra. Tunapuna, Trinidad, and Tobago: Caribbean Association for Feminist Research and Action, 1987. Biannual.
Canadian Journal of Women and the Law. North York, Ontario: University of Toronto Press, 1985. Biannual.
Canadian Woman Studies/Les Cahiers de la Femme. North York, Ontario: York University, 1978. Quarterly.
Columbia Journal of Gender and Law. New York: Columbia University School of Law, 1991. Biannual.
Critical Matrix: The Princeton Journal of Women, Gender, and Culture. Princeton, NJ: Program in the Study of Women & Gender, Princeton University, 1985. Biannual.
differences: A Journal of Feminist Cultural Studies. Bloomington: Indiana University Press, 1989. Triannual.
European Journal of Women's Studies. London: Sage, 1994. Quarterly.
f/m feminist magazine. Dublin: Women's Education Research & Resource Centre, University College, 1997. Biannual.
Feminism & Psychology: An International Journal. London: Sage, 1991. Quarterly.
Feminist Economics. Philadelphia: Taylor & Francis, 1995. Triannual.
Feminist Europa. Review of Books. Heidelberg: German Foundation for Gender Studies, 1998. Biannual.
Feminist Legal Studies. The Hague: Kluwer Law, 1993. Triannual.
Feminist Review. Houndmills, Basingstoke, England: Palgrave, 1979. Triannual.

Feminist Studies. College Park: University of Maryland, 1972. Triannual.
Feminist Teacher. Eau Claire: University of Wisconsin-Eau Claire, 1984. Triannual.
Feminist Theory. London: Sage, 2000. Triannual.
Friends of Women Newsletter. Bangkok, Thailand: Friends of Women Foundation, 1992. Annual.
Frontiers: A Journal of Women Studies. Lincoln: University of Nebraska Press, 1975. Triannual.
Gender & Development. Basingstoke, England: Taylor & Francis, 1993. Triannual.
Gender and Education. Basingstoke, England: Taylor & Francis, 1989. Quarterly.
Gender & History. Oxford: Blackwell, 1989. Triannual.
Gender & Society. Thousand Oaks, CA: Sage, 1987. Bimonthly.
Gender Issues. Piscataway, NJ: Rutgers University, 1980. Quarterly.
Harvard Women's Law Journal. Cambridge, MA: Harvard Law School, 1978. Annual.
Hecate: A Women's Interdisciplinary Journal. Brisbane, Queensland, Australia: 1975. Biannual.
Hypatia. Bloomington: Indiana University Press, 1986. Quarterly.
Indian Journal of Gender Studies. New Delhi, India: Sage, 1994. Biannual.
International Feminist Journal of Politics. Basingstoke, England: Taylor & Francis, 1999. Triannual.
Irish Journal of Feminist Studies. Cork: Cork Univesity Press, 1996. Biannual.
Isis International Women in Action. Quezon City: 1984. Quarterly.
Journal of Feminist Studies in Religion. Williston, VT: Society of Biblical Literature, 1985. Biannual.
Journal of Gender Studies. Basingstoke, England: Taylor & Francis, 1991. Triannual.
Journal of Women and Religion. Berkeley, CA: Center for Women & Religion, Graduate Theological Union, 1981. Annual.
Journal of Women's History. Bloomington: Indiana University Press, 1989. Quarterly.
Lila: Asia Pacific Women's Studies Journal. Manila, Philipines: Institute of Women's Studies, St. Scholastica's College, 1992. Annual.
Lilith Magazine. Denville, NJ: 1976. Quarterly.
Manushi: A Journal About Women and Society. Delhi, India: 1978/79. Bimonthly.
Media Report to Women. Colton's Point, MD: Communication Research Associates, 1972. Quarterly.
Meridians. Middletown, CT: Wesleyan University Press, 2000. Biannual.
Minerva: Quarterly Report on Women and the Military. Pasadena, MD: Minerva Center, 1983. Quarterly.
Ms. Magazine. Arlington, VA: Liberty Media for Women, 1972. Quarterly.
NWSA Journal. Bloomington: Indiana University Press, 1988. Triannual.
Nashim: A Journal of Jewish Women's Studies and Gender Issues. Jerusalem: Schechter Institute of Jewish Studies, 1998. Annual or Biannual.

Nora: Nordic Journal of Women's Studies. Oslo: Taylor & Francis, 1993. Triannual.
n.paradoxa: international feminist art journal. London: 1998. Biannual.
Off Our Backs. Washington, DC: 1970. Bimonthly.
Pakistan Journal of Women's Studies/Alam-E-Niswan. Karachi: 1994. Biannual.
Psychology of Women Quarterly. Maiden, MA: Blackwell, 1976. Quarterly.
Resources for Feminist Research/Documentation sur la Recherche Feministe. Toronto, Ontario: University of Toronto, 1979. Quarterly.
SAFERE: Southern African Feminist Review. Harare, Zimbabwe: SAPPHO, 1995. Biannual.
Sex Roles: A Journal of Research. Norwell, MA: Kluwer Academic, 1975. Monthly.
Signs: Journal of Women in Culture and Society. Chicago: University of Chicago Press, 1975. Quarterly.
Sister Namibia. Windhoek, Namibia: 1989. Bimonthly.
Social Politics: International Studies in Gender, State & Society. Oxford: Oxford University Press, 1994. Triannual.
Speak Out/Tauri/Khulumani. Harare, Zimbabwe: 1987. Quarterly.
13th Moon: A Feminist Literary Magazine. Albany: English Department, State University of New York-Albany, 1973. Annual.
Trouble and Strife: A Radical Feminist Magazine. London: 1982. Biannual.
Tulsa Studies in Women's Literature. Tulsa, OK: University of Tulsa, 1982. Biannual.
US-Japan Women's Journal. Riverside: Josai Center, University of California-Riverside, 1991. Biannual.
Wisconsin Women's Law Journal. Madison: University of Wisconsin Law School, 1985. Biannual.
Woman and Earth (Zhenshchina/Zemlia). New York: 1979. Annual.
Women: A Cultural Review. Basingstoke, England: Taylor & Francis, 1990. Triannual.
Women & Environments International Magazine. Toronto, Ontario: Institute for Women's Studies & Gender Studies, University of Toronto, 1976. Quarterly.
Women & Language. Fairfax, VA: Communication Department, George Mason University, 1975. Biannual.
Women & Performance: A Journal of Feminist Theory. New York: New York University/Tisch School of the Arts, 1983. Biannual.
Women & Politics. Binghamton, NY: Haworth, 1980. Quarterly.
Women-Church: An Australian Journal of Feminist Studies in Religion. Sydney, Australia, 1987. Biannual.
Women's History Review. Wallingford, England: Triangle Journals, 1992. Quarterly.
Women's International Network News (WIN News). Lexington, MA: 1975. Quarterly.

Women's Review of Books. Wellesley, MA: Wellesley College Center for Research on Women, 1983. Eleven issues yearly.
Women's Rights Law Reporter. Newark, NJ: 1970. Triannual.
Women's Studies: An Interdisciplinary Journal. Philadelphia: Taylor & Francis, 1972. Bimonthly.
Women's Studies in Communication. Fort Collins: Department of Speech Communication, Colorado State University, 1977. Biannual.
Women's Studies International Forum. Amsterdam, Netherlands: Elsevier Science, 1978. Bimonthly.
Women's Studies Journal. Dunedin, New Zealand: University of Otago Press, 1984. Biannual.
Women's Studies Quarterly. New York: Feminist Press at the City University of New York, 1981. Biannual.
Women's Studies Review. Galway: U.C.G. Women's Studies Centre, National University of Ireland, 1993. Annual.
Women'Space. Almonte, Ontario: 1995. Quarterly.
Yale Journal of Law and Feminism. New Haven, CT: Yale University, 1989. Biannual.

III. Feminist Web Sites

American Civil Liberties Union Women's Rights Project:
 www.aclu.org/issues/women/hmwo.html
Center for American Women and Politics: *www.cawp.rutgers.edu*
Concerned Women for America: *www.cwfa.org*
Eagle Forum: *www.eagleforum.org*
EMILY's List: *www.emilyslist.org*
European Women's Lobby: *www.womenlobby.org*
Feminist.com: *www.feminist.com*
Feminist Majority Foundation: *www.feminist.org*
Feminists for Life: *www.feministsforlife.org*
Global Fund for Women: *www.globalfundforwomen.org*
Global Reproductive Health Forum: Women of Color Web Group:
 www.hsph.harvard.edu/grhf/WoC/index.html
Independent Women's Forum: *www.iwf.org*
Institute for Women's Policy Research: *www.iwpr.org*
League of Women Voters: *www.lwv.org*
Making Face, Making Soul: Chicana Feminists: *www.chicanas.com*
Muslim Women's League: *www.mwlusa.org*
National Abortion and Reproductive Rights Action League: *www.naral.org*
National Council of Women's Organizations: *www.womensorganizations.org*
National Organization for Women: *www.now.org*
National Women's Political Caucus: *www.nwpc.org*

Network of East-West Women: *www.neww.org*
Planned Parenthood Federation of America: *www.plannedparenthood.org*
Revolutionary Feminist Internationalists: *www.socialism.com*
Third Wave Foundation: *www.thirdwavefoundation.org*
Third WWWave: *www.io.com/~wwwave*
United Nations Development Fund for Women: *www.unifem.undp.org*
Veteran Feminists of America: *www.cometo/VFA*
Wider Opportunities for Women: *www.wowonline.org*
WISH List: *www.thewishlist.org*
Women for Women International: *www.womenforwomen.org*
Women Leaders Online/Women Organizing for Change: *www.wlo.org*
Women on the Road for Afghanistan: *www.worfa.org*
Women's eNews: *www.womensenews.org*
Women's Studies Online Resources: *www.umbc.edu/wmst/*
Women's Work: *www.womenswork.org*

IV. Feminism—General

Beauvoir, Simone de (1953). *The Second Sex*. New York: Vintage Books.
Bell, Diane, and Renate Klein (eds.) (1996). *Radically Speaking: Feminism Reclaimed*. New York: Zed Books.
Berkovitch, Nitza (1999). *From Motherhood to Citizenship: Women's Rights and International Organizations*. Baltimore: Johns Hopkins University Press.
Brooks, Ann (1997). *Postfeminisms: Feminism, Cultural Theory, and Cultural Forms*. New York: Routledge.
Browne, Alice (1987). *The Eighteenth Century Feminist Mind*. Detroit: Wayne State University Press.
Crow, Barbara A. (ed.) (2000). *Radical Feminism: A Documentary Reader*. New York: New York University Press.
Donovan, Josephine (1985). *Feminist Theory: The Intellectual Traditions of American Feminism*. New York: Ungar.
DuPlessis, Rachel Blau, and Ann Snitow (eds.) (1998). *The Feminist Memoir Project: Voices from Women's Liberation*. New York: Three Rivers Press.
Eisenstein, Hester (1983). *Contemporary Feminist Thought*. Boston: G. K. Hall.
_____, and Alice Jardine (1980). *The Future of Difference*. Boston: G. K. Hall.
Elshtain, Jean Bethke (1990). *Power Trips and Other Journeys: Essays in Feminism as Civic Discourse*. Madison: University of Wisconsin Press.
Evans, Judith (1995). *Feminist Theory Today: An Introduction to Second Wave Feminism*. Thousand Oaks, CA: Sage.
Feder, Ellen K. et al. (eds.) (1996). *Derrida and Feminism: Recasting the Question of Woman*. New York: Routledge.

Fox-Genovese, Elizabeth (1991). *Feminism without Illusions.* Chapel Hill: University of North Carolina Press.
Friedan, Betty (1974). *The Feminine Mystique.* New York: Dell.
Gergen, Mary McCannen (ed.) (1989). *Feminist Thought and the Structure of Knowledge.* New York: New York University Press.
Gornick, Vivian, and Barbara K. Moran (eds.) (1971). *Woman in Sexist Society.* New York: Basic Books.
Grant, Judith (1993). *Fundamental Feminism: Contesting the Core Concepts of Feminism.* New York: Routledge.
Grimshaw, Patricia et al. (2001). *Women's Rights and Human Rights: International Historical Perspectives.* New York: Palgrave.
Hawksworth, Mary E. (1990). *Beyond Oppression: Feminist Theory and Political Strategy.* New York: Continuum.
Herrmann, Anne C., and Abigail J. Stewart (eds.) (1994). *Theorizing Feminism: Parallel Trends in the Humanities and Social Sciences.* Boulder, CO: Westview Press.
Hesse-Biber, Sharlene et al. (eds.) (1999). *Feminist Approaches to Theory and Methodology: An Interdisciplinary Reader.* New York: Oxford University Press.
Hirsh, Marianne, and Evelyn Fox Keller (eds.) (1990*). Conflicts in Feminism.* New York: Routledge.
hooks, bell (1984). *Feminist Theory: From Margin to Center.* Boston: South End Press.
Humm, Maggie (ed.) (1992). *Modern Feminisms: Political, Literary, Cultural.* New York: Columbia University Press.
Jaggar, Alison M., and Paula Rothenberg Struhl (1993). *Feminist Frameworks: Alternative Theoretical Accounts of the Relations between Women and Men.* New York: McGraw-Hill.
Janeway, Elizabeth (1971). *Man's World, Woman's Place.* New York: William Morrow Press.
Jones, Kathleen B., and Anna G. Jonasdottir (1988). *The Political Interests of Gender: Developing Theory and Research with a Feminist Face.* London: Sage.
Kauffman, Linda S. (1993). *American Feminist Thought at Century's End: A Reader.* Cambridge, MA: Blackwell.
Keohane, Nannerl O., Michelle Zimbalist Rosaldo, and Barbara Charlesworth Gelpi (1982). *Feminist Theory: A Critique of Ideology.* Chicago: University of Chicago Press.
Kimball, Meredith M. (1995). *Feminist Visions of Gender Similarities and Differences.* New York: Haworth.
Laslett, Barbara et al. (eds.) (1996). *History and Theory: Feminist Research, Debates, Contestations.* Chicago: University of Chicago Press.
Lay, Mary M. et al. (eds.) (2002). *Encompassing Gender: Integrating International Studies and Women's Studies.* Old Westbury, NY: Feminist Press.

Messer-Davidow, Ellen (2002). *Disciplining Feminism: From Social Activism to Academic Discourse.* Durham, NC: Duke University Press.

Miles, Angela (1996). *Integrative Feminisms: Building Global Visions.* New York: Routledge.

Millett, Kate (1970). *Sexual Politics.* Garden City, NY: Doubleday.

Morgan, Robin (1970). *Sisterhood Is Powerful: An Anthology of Writings from the Women's Liberation Movement.* New York: Vintage Books.

Nelson, Hilde Lindemann (ed.) (1996). *Feminism and Families.* New York: Routledge.

Nicholson, Linda (ed.) (1996). *The Second Wave: A Reader in Feminist Theory.* New York: Routledge.

Oakley, Ann (1984). *Taking It Like a Woman.* London: Jonathan Cape.

O'Barr, Jean F., and Mary Wyer (1992). *Engaging Feminism: Students Speak Up and Speak Out.* Charlottesville: University Press of Virginia.

Pilcher, Jane (1998). *Women of their Times: Generation, Gender Issues, and Feminism.* Burlington, VT: Ashgate.

Richards, Janet Radcliffe (1980). *The Skeptical Feminist.* London: Routledge and Kegan Paul.

Rivers, Caryl (1991). *More Joy Than Rage: Crossing Generations with the New Feminism.* Hanover, NH: University Press of New England.

Rowbotham, Sheila (1972). *Women, Resistance and Revolution.* New York: Pantheon Books.

_____. (1983). *Dreams and Dilemmas.* London: Virago Press.

Scott, Joan Wallach (ed.) (1996). *Feminism and History.* New York: Oxford University Press.

Steinem, Gloria (1983). *Outrageous Acts and Everyday Rebellions.* New York: Holt, Rinehart and Winston.

Thompson, Denise (2001). *Radical Feminism Today.* Thousand Oaks, CA: Sage.

Thompson, Mary Lou (ed.) (1970). *Voices of the New Feminism.* Boston: Beacon Press.

Walker, Barbara G. (1987). *The Skeptical Feminist: Discovering the Virgin, Mother, and Crone.* San Francisco: Harper and Row.

Whelehan, Imelda (1995). *Modern Feminist Thought: From the Second Wave to Postmodernism.* New York: New York University Press.

V. Women of Color Feminism

Bhavnani. Kum-Kum (ed.) (2000). *Feminism and "Race."* New York: Oxford University Press.

Bobo, Jacqueline (2001). *Black Feminist Cultural Criticism.* Malden, MA: Blackwell.

Caraway, Nancie (1991). *Segregated Sisterhood: Racism and the Politics of American Feminism.* Knoxville: University of Tennessee Press.

Christian, Barbara (1985). *Black Feminist Criticism: Perspectives on Black Women Writers.* New York: Teachers College Press.
Cole, Johnnetta B. (1986). *All American Women: Lines that Divide, Ties that Bind.* New York: Free Press.
_____, and Beverly Guy-Sheftall (2003). *Gender Talk: The Struggle for Women's Equality in African American Communities.* New York: Random House.
Collins, Patricia Hill (1999). *Black Feminist Thought: Knowledge, Consciousness, and the Politics of Empowerment.* New York: Routledge.
Cornwell, Anita (1983). *Black Lesbian in White America.* Tallahassee, FL: Naiad.
Davis, Angela (1981). *Women, Race, and Class.* New York: Random House.
Donaldson, Laura E. (1992). *Decolonizing Feminisms: Race, Gender, and Empire-Building.* Chapel Hill: University of North Carolina Press.
Garcia, Alma M., and Mario T. Garcia (eds.) (1997). *Chicana Feminist Thought: The Basic Historical Writings.* New York: Routledge.
Giddings, Paula (1984). *When and Where I Enter: The Impact of Black Women on Race and Sex in America.* New York: Morrow Press.
Hoeveler, Diane Long, and Janet K. Boles (eds.) (2001). *Women of Color: Defining the Issues, Hearing the Voices.* Westport, CT: Greenwood.
hooks, bell (1981). *Ain't I a Woman: Black Women and Feminism.* Boston: South End Press.
_____. (1989). *Talking Back: Thinking Feminist. Thinking Black.* Boston: South End Press.
_____. (1990). *Yearning: Race, Gender, and Cultural Politics.* Boston: South End Press.
Hull, Gloria T., Patricia Dell Scott, and Barbara Smith (eds.) (1982). *But Some of Us Are Brave.* Old Westbury, NY: Feminist Press.
James, Stanlie M., and Abana P. A. Busia (eds.) (1993). *Theorizing Black Feminisms: The Visionary Pragmatism of Black Women.* New York: Routledge.
Latina Feminist Group (2001). *Telling to Live: Latina Feminist Testimonios.* Durham, NC: Duke University Press.
Shah, Sonia (ed.) (1997). *Dragon Ladies: Asian American Feminists Breathe Fire.* Boston: South End Press.
Smith, Valerie (1998). *Not Just Race, Not Just Gender: Black Feminist Readings.* New York: Routledge.
Solomon, Irvin D. (1989). *Feminism and Black Activism in Contemporary America: An Ideological Assessment.* Westport, CT: Greenwood.
Twine, Frances Winddance, and Kathleen M. Blee (2001). *Feminism and Antiracism: International Struggles for Justice.* New York: New York University Press.
White, E. Frances (2001). *Dark Continent of Our Bodies: Black Feminism and the Politics of Respectability.* Philadelphia: Temple University Press.
Williams, Patricia J. (1991). *The Alchemy of Race and Rights.* Cambridge, MA: Harvard University Press.

Wing, Adrien K. (ed.) (1996). *Critical Race Feminism: A Reader.* New York: New York University Press.

VI. Global Feminism

Ali, Suki et al. (2000). *Global Feminist Politics: Identities in a Changing World.* New York: Routledge.
Anderson, Bonnie S. (2000). *Joyous Greetings: The First International Women's Movement, 1830-1860.* New York: Oxford University Press.
Bassnett, Susan (1986). *Feminist Experiences: The Women's Movement in Four Cultures.* Boston: Allen and Unwin.
Basu, Amrita (1995). *The Challenge of Local Feminisms: Women's Movements in Global Perspective.* Boulder, CO: Westview Press.
Bayes, Jane H., and Neyereh T. (eds.) (2001). *Globalization, Gender, and Religion: The Politics of Implementing Women's Rights in Catholic and Muslim Contexts.* New York: Palgrave.
Benería, Lourdes. *Gender, Development, and Globalization: Economics as If People Mattered.* New York: Routledge.
Bouvard, Marguerite Guzman (1996). *Women Reshaping Human Rights: How Extraordinary Activists Are Changing the World.* Wilmington, DE: Scholarly Resources.
Bulbeck, Chilla (1998). *Re-Orienting Western Feminisms: Women's Diversity in a "Post-Colonial" World.* New York: Cambridge University Press.
Daley, Caroline, and Melanie Nolan (eds.) (1994). *Suffrage and Beyond: International Feminist Perspectives.* New York: New York University Press.
D'Itri, Patricia Ward (1999). *Cross Currents in the International Women's Movement.* Bowling Green, OH: Bowling Green State University Popular Press.
Duran, Jane. (2001). *Worlds of Knowing: Global Feminist Epistemologies.* New York: Routledge.
Eschle, Catherine (2001). *Global Democracy, Social Movements, and Feminism.* Boulder, CO: Westview Press.
Kelly, Rita Mae et al. (2001). *Gender, Globalization, and Democratization.* Lanham, MD: Rowman and Littlefield.
Lycklama a Nijeholt, Geertje et al. (eds.) (1998). *Women's Movements and Public Policy in Europe, Latin America, and the Caribbean.* New York: Garland.
Moghadam, Valentine M. (ed.) (1993). *Identity Politics and Women: Cultural Reassertions and Feminisms in International Perspective.* Boulder, CO: Westview Press.
Mohanty, Chandra Talpade, Ann Russo, and Lourdes Torres (eds.) (1991). *Third World Women and the Politics of Feminism.* Bloomington: Indiana University Press.
Morgan, Robin (ed.) (1996). *Sisterhood Is Global: The International Women's Movement Anthology.* Old Westbury, NY: Feminist Press.

Naples, Nancy A., and Manisha Desai (eds.) (2002). *Women's Activism and Globalization: Linking Local Struggles and Global Politics.* New York: Routledge.
Nelson, Barbara J., and Najma Chowdhury (eds.) (1994). *Women and Politics Worldwide.* New Haven, CT: Yale University Press.
Peters, Julie, and Andrea Wolper (eds.) *Women's Rights: An International Feminist Perspective.* New York: Routledge.
Pettman, Jan Jindy. (1996). *Worldly Women: A Feminist International Politics.* New York: Routledge.
Rai, Shirin M., and Geraldine Lievsley (eds.) (1996). *Women and the State: International Perspectives.* London: Taylor and Francis.
Robinson, Fiona (1999). *Globalizing Care: Ethics, Feminist Theory, and International Relations.* Boulder, CO: Westview Press.
Roscheleau, Dianne et al. (eds.) *Feminist Political Ecology: Global Issues and Local Experience.* New York: Routledge.
Rowbotham, Shelia, and Stephanie Linkogle (2001). *Women Resist Globalisation: Mobilising for Livelihood and Rights.* New York: Palgrave.
Rupp, Leila J. (1998). *Worlds of Women: The Makings of an International Women's Movement.* Princeton, NJ: Princeton University Press.
Russell, Diana, and Roberta A. Harmes (eds.) (2001). *Femicide in Global Perspective.* New York: Teachers College Press.
Schachar, Ayelet (2001). *Multicultural Jurisdictions: Cultural Differences and Women's Rights.* New York: Cambridge University Press.
Smith, Bonnie G. (ed.) (2000). *Global Feminisms since 1945: A Survey of Issues and Controversies.* New York: Routledge.
Stienstra, Deborah (1994). *Women's Movements and International Organizations.* New York: St. Martin's Press.
Walter, Lynn (2001). *Women's Rights: A Global View.* Westport, CT: Greenwood.
West, Lois A. (ed.) *Feminist Nationalism.* New York: Routledge.
Whitworth, Sandra (1994). *Feminism and International Relations: Towards a Political Economy of Gender in Interstate and Non-Governmental Institutions.* New York: St. Martin's Press.
Wing, Adrien Katherine (ed.) (2000). *Global Critical Race Feminism: An International Reader.* New York: New York University Press.

VII. Ecofeminism

Adams, Carol Jo (ed.) (1992). *Ecofeminism and the Sacred.* New York: Continuum.
Biehl, Janet (1990). *Rethinking Ecofeminist Politics.* Boston: South End Press.
Bigwood, Carol (1993). *Earth Muse: Feminism, Nature, and Art.* Philadelphia: Temple University Press.
Cuomo, Chris J. (1997). *Feminism and Ecological Communities: An Ethic of Flourishing.* New York: Routledge.

Diamond, Irene, and Helen Wilcox (eds.) (1990). *Reweaving the World: The Emergence of Ecofeminism.* San Francisco: Sierra Club.
Eaton, Heather, and Lois Ann Lorentzen. (2003). *Ecofeminism and Globalization.* Lanham, MD.: Rowman and Littlefield.
Gaard, Greta (ed.) (1993). *Ecofeminism: Women, Animals, and Nature.* Philadelphia: Temple University Press.
_____. (1997). *Ecological Politics: Ecofeminists and the Greens.* Philadelphia: Temple University Press.
_____, and Patrick D. Murphy (1998). *Ecofeminist Literary Criticism: Theory, Interpretation, Pedagogy.* Urbana: University of Illinois Press.
Griffin, Susan (1978). *Woman and Nature: The Roaring Inside Her.* New York: Harper and Row.
Mellor, Mary (1997). *Feminism and Ecology.* New York: New York University Press.
Miess, Marea, and Vandana Shiva (1993). *Ecofeminism.* Halifax, NS: Zed Books.
Murphy, Patrick D. (1995). *Literature, Nature, and Other: Ecofeminist Critiques.* Albany: State University of New York Press.
Plumwood, Val (1993). *Feminism and the Mastery of Nature.* New York: Routledge.
Ruether, Rosemary Radford (1992). *Gaia and God: An Ecofeminist Theology of Earth Healing.* San Francisco: Harper San Francisco.
Salleh, Ariel (1997). *Ecofeminism as Politics: Nature, Marx, and the Postmodern.* New York: St. Martin's Press.
Seager, Joni (1993). *Earth Follies: Coming to Feminist Terms with the Global Environmental Crisis.* New York: Routledge.
Sturgeon, Noel (1997). *Ecofeminist Natures: Race, Gender, Feminist Theory and Political Action.* New York: Routledge.
Warren, Karen J. (ed.) (1996). *Ecological Feminist Philosophies.* Bloomington: Indiana University Press.
_____. (ed.) (1997). *Ecofeminism.* Bloomington: Indiana University Press.
_____. (2000). *Ecofeminist Philosophy: A Western Perspective on What It Is and Why It Matters.* Lanham, MD: Rowman and Littlefield.

VIII. Liberal Feminism

Baehr, Amy. (2003). *Varieties of Feminist Liberalism.* Lanham, MD.: Rowman and Littlefield.
Berg, Barbara (1979). *The Remembered Gate: Origins of American Feminism.* New York: Oxford University Press.
Bird, Caroline, and Sara Well Briller (1969). *Born Female: The High Cost of Keeping Women Down.* New York: Pocket Books.
Eisenstein, Zillah (1984). *Feminism and Sexual Equality: Crisis in Liberal America.* New York: Monthly Review Press.

———. (1986). *The Radical Future of Liberal Feminism*. Boston: Northeastern University Press.
Elshtain, Jean Bethke (1981). *Public Man, Private Woman*. Princeton, NJ: Princeton University Press.
McElroy, Wendy (1982). *Freedom, Feminism, and the State: An Overview of Individualist Feminism*. Washington, DC: Cato Institute.
———. (ed.) (2002). *Liberty for Women: Freedom and Feminism in the Twenty First Century*. Chicago: Ivan Dee.
Pateman, Carole (1979). *The Problem of Political Obligation: A Critique of Liberal Theory*. Berkeley: University of California Press.
Phillips, Anne (1993). *Democracy and Difference*. University Park, PA: Penn State Press.
———. (ed.) (1990). *Feminism and Equality*. New York: New York University Press.
Rossi, Alice S. (ed.) (1970). *Essays on Sex Equality. John Stuart Mill and Harriet Taylor Mill*. Chicago: University of Chicago Press.
Sabrosky, Judith A. (1979). *From Rationality to Liberation: The Evolution of Feminist Ideology*. Westport, CT: Greenwood.
Salper, Roberta (1972). *Female Liberation; History and Current Politics*. New York: Knopf.
Stetson, Dorothy McBride (ed.) (2002). *Abortion Politics, Women's Movements, and the Democratic State: A Comparative Study of State Feminism*. New York: New York University Press.
Taylor, Joan Kennedy (1992). *Reclaiming the Mainstream: Individualist Feminism Rediscovered*. Buffalo, NY: Prometheus Books.
Teske, Robin L., and Mary Ann Tetreault (eds.) (2000). *Conscious Acts and the Politics of Social Change: Feminist Approaches to Social Movements, Community and Power*. New York: Columbia University Press.
Wollstonecraft, Mary (1983). *A Mary Wollstonecraft Reader*. New York: New American Library.

IX. Marxist Feminism

Assiter, Alison (1993). *Althusser and Feminism*. Boulder, CO: Westview Press.
Bannerji, Himani (1995). *Thinking Through: Essays on Feminism, Marxism, and AntiRacism*. London: The Women's Press.
Barrett, Michele (1980). *Women's Oppression Today: Problems in Marxist Feminist Analysis*. London: Verso.
Bebel, August (1971). *Woman under Socialism*. New York: Schocken Books.
Bell, Susan Groag, and Karen M. Offen (eds.) (1983). *Women, the Family, and Freedom: The Debate in Documents*. Stanford, CA: Stanford University Press.

Dunayevskaya, Raya (1982). *Rosa Luxemburg, Women's Liberation, and Marx's Philosophy of Revolution*. Atlantic Highlands, NJ: Humanities Press.
Eastman, Crystal (1978). *On Women and Revolution*. New York: Oxford University Press.
Engels, Friedrich (rpt. 1972). *The Origin of the Family, Private Property, and the State*. New York: International.
Foreman, Ann (1977). *Femininity as Alienation: Women and the Family in Marxism and Psychoanalysis*. London: Pluto Press.
Guettel, Charnie (1974). *Marxism and Feminism*. Toronto: Women's Educational Press.
Hamilton, Roberta (1978). *The Liberation of Women. A Study of Patriarchy and Capitalism*. London: Allen and Unwin.
Holt, Alix (ed.) (1977). *Selected Writings of Alexandra Kollontai*. Westport, CT: Hill.
Kuhn, Annette, and Ann Marie Wolpe (eds.) (1978). *Feminism and Materialism: Women and Modes of Production*. Boston: Routledge and Kegan Paul.
Lenin, Vladimir Ilich (1975). *The Emancipation of Women: From the Writings of V. I. Lenin*. New York: International Press.
Saffiote, Heleieth I. B. (1978). *Women in Class Society*. New York: Monthly Review Press.
Sargent, Lydia (ed.) (1981). *Women and Revolution: A Discussion of the Unhappy Marriage of Marxism and Feminism*. Boston: South End Press.
Vogel, Lise (1983). *Marxism and the Oppression of Women: Towards a Unitary Theory*. New Brunswick, NJ: Rutgers University Press.

X. Postmodern Feminist Thought

Agger, Ben (1993). *Gender, Culture, and Power: Toward a Feminist Postmodern Critical Theory*. Westport, CT: Praeger.
Ahmed, Sara (1998). *Differences that Matter: Feminist Theory and Postmodernism*. New York: Cambridge University Press.
Buker, Eloise A. (1999). *Talking Feminist Politics: Conversations on Law, Science, and the Postmodern*. Lanham, MD: Rowman and Littlefield.
Diamond, Irene, and Lee Quinby (eds.) (1988). *Feminism and Foucault: Reflections on Resistance*. Boston: Northeastern University Press.
Felski, Rita (2000). *Doing Time: Feminist Theory and Postmodern Culture. Doing Time: Feminist Theory and Postmodern Culture*. New York: New York University Press.
Irigaray, Luce (1985). *This Sex Which Is Not One*. Ithaca, NY: Cornell University Press.
Kristéva, Julia (1982). *Desire in Language*. New York: Columbia University Press.
_____. (1982). *Powers of Horror*. New York: Columbia University Press.

———. (1984). *Revolution in Poetic Languages*. New York: Columbia University Press.
Mitchell, Juliet, and Jacqueline Rose (eds.) (1982). *Feminine Sexuality: Jacques Lacan and the Ecole Freudienne*. New York: Norton.
Moi, Toril (ed.) (1987). *French Feminist Thought: A Reader*. New York: Blackwell.
Tristan, Anne, and Annie de Pisan (1977). *Histoires du M.L.F.* Paris: Calmann-Lévy.
Van Lenning, Alkeline van et al. (eds.) (1997). *Feminist Utopias in a Postmodern Era*. Tilburg, Netherlands: Tilburg University Press.
Zalewski, Marysia (2000). *Feminism after Postmodernism: Theorizing through Practice*. New York: Routledge.

XI. Radical Feminism

A. Reproduction

Arditti, Rita, Renate Duelli Klein, and Shelley Minden (eds.) (1984). *Test-Tube Women: What Future for Motherhood?* London: Pandora Press.
Atwood, Margaret (1985). *The Handmaid's Tale*. New York: Fawcett Crest Books.
Corea, Genea (1985). *The Mother Machine: Reproductive Technologies from Artificial Insemination to Artificial Wombs*. New York: Harper and Row.
Dworkin, Andrea (2002). *Heartbreak: The Political Memoir of a Feminist Militant*. New York: Basic Books.
Eisenstein, Zillah R. (1988). *The Female Body and the Law*. Berkeley: University of California Press.
Firestone, Shulamith (1971). *The Dialectic of Sex: The Case for Feminist Revolution*. New York: Bantam Books.
Kennedy, Angela (ed.) (1997). *Swimming against the Tide: Feminist Dissent on the Issue of Abortion*. Dublin: Open Air Press.
O'Brien, Mary (1981). *The Politics of Reproduction*. Boston: Routledge and Kegan Paul.
Piercy, Marge (1976). *Woman on the Edge of Time*. New York: Fawcett Crest Books.

B. Mothering

Chesler, Phyllis (1988). *Sacred Bond: The Legacy of Baby M*. New York: Times Books.
Dornbusch, Sanford M., and Myra H. Strober (1988). *Feminism, Children, and the New Families*. New York: Guilford Press.
Koven, Seth, and Sonya Michel (1993). *Mothers of a New World: Maternalist Politics and the Origins of Welfare States*. New York: Routledge.

Oakley, Ann (1974). *Woman's Work: The Housewife, Past and Present.* New York: Pantheon Books.
Rich, Adrienne (1976). *Of Woman Born: Motherhood as Experience and Institution.* New York: Norton.
Trebilcot, Joyce (ed.) (1984). *Mothering: Essays in Feminist Theory.* Totowa, NJ: Rowman and Allanheld.

C. Gender and Sexuality

Barry, Kathleen (1979). *Female Sexual Slavery.* Englewood Cliffs, NJ: Prentice-Hall.
Boston Women's Health Book Collective (1992). *The New Our Bodies, Ourselves.* New York: Simon and Schuster.
Brownmiller, Susan (1975). *Against Our Will: Men, Women and Rape.* New York: Simon and Schuster.
Clark, Lorenne, and Debra Lewis (1977). *Rape: The Price of Coercive Sexuality.* Toronto: Women's Educational Press.
Coveney, Lal, Margaret Jackson, Sheila Jeffreys, Leslie Kay, and Pat Mahoney (eds.) (1984). *The Sexuality Papers: Male Sexuality and the Social Control of Women.* London: Hutchinson.
Daly, Mary (1978). *Gyn/Ecology: The Metaethics of Radical Feminism.* Boston: Beacon Press.
Dinshaw, Carolyn (1999). *Getting Medieval: Sexualities and Communities, Pre and Post-Modern.* Durham, NC: Duke University Press.
Dworkin, Andrea (1974). *Woman Hating: A Radical Look at Sexuality.* New York: E. P. Dutton.
_____. (1981). *Our Blood: Prophecies and Discourses on Sexual Politics.* New York: G. P. Putnam.
Fausto-Sterling, Anne (2000). *Sexing the Body: Gender Politics and the Construction of Sexuality.* New York: Basic Books.
Frankfort, Ellen (1973). *Vaginal Politics.* New York: Bantam Books.
Gilman, Sander L. (1985). *Difference and Pathology: Stereotypes of Sexuality, Race, and Madness.* Ithaca, NY: Cornell University Press.
Ginsburg, Faye D. Tsing, and Anna Lowenhaupt (1990). *Uncertain Terms: Negotiating Gender in American Culture.* Boston: Beacon Press.
Gordon, Linda (1977). *Woman's Body, Woman's Right: A Social History of Birth Control in America.* New York: Penguin Books.
Griffin, Susan (1979). *Rape: The Power of Consciousness.* San Francisco: Harper and Row.
Jackson, Stevi, and Sue Scott (eds.) (1996). *Feminism and Sexuality: A Reader.* New York: Columbia University Press.
Jeffrays, Sheila (1985). *The Spinster and Her Enemies: Feminism and Sexuality, 1880-1930.* Boston: Pandora Press.

Johnston, Carolyn (1992). *Sexual Power: Feminism and the Family in America.* Tuscaloosa: University of Alabama Press.
Karmen, Paula (2000). *Her Way: Young Women Remake the Sexual Revolution.* New York: New York University Press.
LeMoncheck, Linda (1997). *Loose Women, Lecherous Men: A Feminist Philosophy of Sex.* New York: Oxford University Press.
Parker, Richard G. et al. (eds.) (2000). *Framing the Sexual Subject: The Politics of Gender, Sexuality and Power.* Berkeley: University of California Press.
Pateman, Carole (1988). *The Sexual Contract.* Stanford, CA: Stanford University Press.
Tessier, Linda J. (1997). *Dancing after the Whirlwind: Feminist Reflection on Sex, Denial, and Spiritual Transformation.* Boston: Beacon Press.

D. Pornography

Berger, Ronald J., Patricia Searles, and Charles E. Cottle (1991). *Feminism and Pornography.* Westport, CT: Praeger.
Caught Looking, Inc. (1988). *Caught Looking: Feminism, Pornography and Censorship.* Seattle: Real Comet Press.
Chancer, Lynn S. (1998). *Reconcilable Differences: Confronting Beauty, Pornography, and the Future of Feminism.* Berkeley: University of California Press.
Cornell, Drucilla (ed.) (2000). *Feminism and Pornography.* New York: Oxford University Press.
Dworkin, Andrea (1981). *Pornography: Men Possessing Women.* New York: Perigee Books.
Griffin, Susan (1981). *Pornography and Silence.* New York: Harper and Row.
Kipnis, Laura (1999). *Bound and Gagged: Pornography and the Politics of Fantasy in America.* Durham, NC: Duke University Press.
Lederer, Laura (ed.) (1980). *Take Back the Night: Women on Pornography.* New York: William Morrow Press.
Leidholdt, Dorchen, and Janice G. Raymond (1990). *The Sexual Liberals and the Attack on Feminism.* New York: Pergamon Press.
MacKinnon, Catharine A. (1993). *Only Words.* Cambridge, MA: Harvard University Press.
Mielke, Arthur J. (1994). *Christians, Feminists, and the Culture of Pornography.* Lanham, MD: University Press of America.
Russell, Diana E. H. (ed.) (1993). *Making Violence Sexy: Feminist Views on Pornography.* New York: Teachers College Press.
Soble, Alan (1986). *Pornography: Marxism, Feminism and the Future of Sexuality.* New Haven, CT: Yale University Press.

E. Lesbianism

Atkinson, Ti-Grace (1974). *Amazon Odyssey*. New York: Links Press.
Birkby, Phyllis, et al. (eds.) (1973). *Amazon Expedition: A Lesbian-Feminist Anthology*. Washington, DC: Times Change Press.
Butler, Judith (1993). *Bodies that Matter*. New York: Routledge.
Calhoun, Cheshire (2000). *Feminism, the Family, and the Politics of the Closet: Lesbian and Gay Displacement*. New York: Oxford University Press.
Campbell, Jan (1997). *Arguing with the Phallus: Feminist, Queer, and Postcolonial Theory: A Psychoanalytic Contribution*. New York: Zed Books.
Case, Sue-Ellen (1996). *Split Britches: Lesbian Practice/Feminist Performance*. New York: Routledge.
Ditzinger, Celia, and Rachel Perkins (1993). *Changing Our Minds: Lesbian Feminism and Psychology*. New York: New York University Press.
Dunne, Gillian A. (1996). *Lesbian Lifestyles: Women's Work and the Politics of Sexuality*. Toronto: University of Toronto Press.
Green, Sarah F. (1996). *Urban Amazons: Lesbian Feminism and Beyond in the Gender, Sexuality, and Identity Battles of London*. New York: St. Martin's.
Grier, Barbara, and Colette Reid (eds.) (1976). *The Lavender Herring: Lesbian Essays from "The Ladder."* Baltimore: Diana Press.
Harne, Lynne, and Elaine Miller (eds.) (1996). *All the Rage: Reasserting Radical Lesbian Feminism*. New York: Teachers College Press.
Harris, Laura, and Elizabeth Crocker (eds.) (1997). *Femme: Feminists, Lesbians, and Bad Girls*. New York: Routledge.
Heller, Dana (ed.) (1997). *Cross-Purposes: Lesbians, Feminists, and the Limits of Alliance*. Bloomington: Indiana University Press.
Johnston, Jill (1974). *Lesbian Nation: The Feminist Solution*. New York: Simon and Schuster.
Mohin, Lilian (1996). *An Intimacy of Equals: Lesbian Feminist Ethics*. New York: Harrington Park Press.
Myron, Nancy, and Charlotte Bunch (eds.) (1975). *Lesbianism and the Women's Movement*. Baltimore: Diana Press.
Phelan, Shane (1989). *Identity Politics. Lesbian Feminism and the Limits of Community*. Philadelphia: Temple University Press.
Stein, Arlene (1997). *Sex and Sensibility: Lesbianism, Feminism, and Generational Change*. Berkeley: University of California Press.
Vicinus, Martha (ed.) (1996). *Lesbian Subjects: A Feminist Studies Reader*. Bloomington: Indiana University Press.
Weed, Elizabeth, and Naomi Schor (eds.) (1997). *Feminism Meets Queer Theory*. Bloomington: Indiana University Press.

XII. Socialist Feminism

Boxer, Marilyn J., and Jean H. Quataert (eds.) (1978). *Socialist Women European Socialist Feminism in the Nineteenth and Early Twentieth Centuries*. New York: Elsevier North-Holland.
Delphy, Christine (1984). *Close to Home: A Materialist Analysis of Women's Oppression*. Amherst: University of Massachusetts Press.
Eisenstein, Zillah (ed.) (1979). *Capitalist Patriarchy and the Case for Socialist Feminism*. New York: Monthly Review Press.
Ferguson, Ann (1991). *Sexual Democracy: Women, Oppression, and Revolution*. Boulder, CO: Westview Press.
Hansen, Karen V., and Ilene J. Philipson (eds.) (1990). *Women, Class, and the Feminist Imagination: A Socialist-Feminist Reader*. Philadelphia: Temple University Press.
Martin, Gloria (1978). *Socialist Feminism: The First Decade, 1966-1976*. Seattle, WA: Freedom Socialist Publications.
Meyer, Alfred G. (1985). *The Feminism and Socialism of Lily Braun*. Bloomington: Indiana University Press.
Miller, Sally M. (1981). *Flawed Liberation: Socialism and Feminism*. Westport, CT: Greenwood.
Mitchell, Juliet (1971). *Woman's Estate*. New York: Pantheon Books.
Nicholson, Linda J. (1986). *Gender and History: The Limits of Social Theory in the Age of the Family*. New York: Columbia University Press.
Phillips, Anne (1983). *Hidden Hands: Women and Economic Policies*. London: Pluto Press.
Rowbotham, Sheila, Lynne Segal, and Hilary Wainwright (1979). *Beyond the Fragments: Feminism and the Making of Socialism*. London: Merlin Press.
Slaughter, Jane, and Robert Kern (eds.) (1981). *European Women on the Left: Socialism, Feminism, and the Problems Faced by Political Women*. Westport, CT: Greenwood.
Taylor, Barbara (1983). *Eve and the New Jerusalem: Socialism and Feminism in the Nineteenth Century*. New York: Pantheon Books.
Weinbaum, Batya (1978). *The Curious Courtship of Women's Liberation and Socialism*. Boston: South End Press.

XIII. Feminist/Women's Movement

Andrews, Maggie (1997). *The Acceptable Face of Feminism: The Women's Institute as a Social Movement*. New York: New York University Press.
Banks, Olive (1981). *Faces of Feminism: A Study of Feminism as a Social Movement*. New York: St. Martin's Press.
_____. (1987). *Becoming a Feminist: The Social Origins of "First Wave" Feminism*. Athens: University of Georgia Press.

Black, Naomi (1989). *Social Feminism*. Ithaca, NY: Cornell University Press.
Bolt, Christine (1993). *The Women's Movements in the United States and Britain from the 1790s to the 1920s*. New York: Harvester Wheatsheaf.
Bouchier, David (1984). *The Feminist Challenge: The Movement for Women's Liberation in Britain and the USA*. New York: Schocken Books.
Brown, Brenda Lee (ed.) (1996). *Bringing It Home: Women Talk about Feminism in Their Lives.* Vancouver, BC: Arsenal Pulp Press.
Charles, Nickie (2000). *Feminism, the State, and Social Policy*. New York: St. Martin's Press.
Cooper, Davina (1995). *Power in Struggle: Feminism, Sexuality and the State*. New York: New York University Press.
Dahlerup, Drude (ed.) (1986). *The New Women's Movement: Feminism and Political Power in Europe and the USA*. Beverly Hills, CA: Sage.
Eisenstein, Hester (1991). *Gender Shock: Practicing Feminism on Two Continents*. Boston: Beacon Press.
Evans, Richard J. (1977). *The Feminists: Women's Emancipation Movements in Europe, America, and Australia, 1840-1920*. New York: Barnes and Noble.
Gelb, Joyce (1989). *Feminism and Politics*. Berkeley: University of California Press.
Gleadle, Kathryn (1995). *The Early Feminists: Radical Unitarians and the Energence of the Women's Rights Movements, 1831-51*. New York: St. Martin's Press.
Griffin, Gabriele (ed.) (1995). *Feminist Activism in the 1990's*. London: Taylor and Francis.
Hollis, Patricia (1979). *Women in Public: The Women's Movement, 1850-1900*. London: Allen and Unwin.
Kamm, Josephine (1966). *Rapiers and Battle-axes. The Women's Movement and Its Aftermath*. London: Allen and Unwin.
Katzenstein, Mary Fainsod, and Carol McClurg Mueller (eds.) (1987). *The Women's Movements of the United States and Western Europe: Consciousness, Political Opportunity, and Public Policy*. Philadelphia: Temple University Press.
Kuzmack, Linda Gordon (1990). *Woman's Cause: The Jewish Woman's Movement in England and the United States, 1881-1933*. Columbus: Ohio State University Press.
Liddington, Jill, and Jill Norris (1978). *One Hand Tied Behind Us. The Rise of the Women's Suffrage Movement*. London: Virago.
Lovenduski, Joni (ed.) (2000). *Feminism and Politics*. Burlington, VT: Ashgate.
Lunardini, Christine A. (1995). *Women's Rights*. Phoenix, AZ: Oryx Press.
Marshall, Susan E. (1997). *Splintered Sisterhood: Gender and Class in the Campaign against Woman Suffrage*. Madison: University of Wisconsin Press.
McQuiston, Liz (1997). *Suffragettes to She-Devils: Women's Liberation and Beyond*. New York: Phaidon.

Meyer, Donald B. (1987). *Sex and Power: The Rise of Women in America, Russia, Sweden and Italy*. Middletown, CT: Wesleyan University Press.

Miles, Angela, and Geraldine Finn (eds.) (2002). *Feminism: From Pressure to Politics*. New Delhi, India: Rawat.

Misciagno, Patricia S. (1997). *Rethinking Feminist Identification: The Case for DeFacto Feminism*. Westport, CT: Greenwood.

Moghadam, Valentine M. (ed.) (1993). *Identity Politics and Women: Cultural Reassertions and Feminisms in International Perspective*. Boulder, CO: Westview Press.

Naples, Nancy (ed.) (1998). *Community, Activism and Feminist Politics: Organizing Across Race, Class and Gender*. New York: Routledge.

Randall, Jane (1984). *The Origins of Modern Feminism: Women in Britain, France and the United States*. New York: Schocken Books.

―――. (1987). *Equal or Different: Women's Politics, 1800-1914*. New York: Basil Blackwell.

Rendel, Margherita (1997). *Whose Human Rights?* Stoke on Trent, UK: Trentham Books.

Richardson, Laurel et al. (1997). *Feminist Frontiers IV*. New York: McGraw Hill.

Robinson, Victoria, and Diane Richardson (eds.) (1997). *Introducing Women's Studies: Feminist Theory and Practice*. New York: New York University Press.

Rogers, Mary F. (ed.) (1997). *Contemporary Feminist Theory: A Text/Reader*. New York: McGraw-Hill.

Rowbotham, Sheila (1989). *The Past Is before Us: Feminism in Action since the 1960s*. London: Pandora.

―――. (1992). *Women in Movement: Feminism and Social Action*. New York: Routledge.

Rubinstein, David (1986). *Before the Suffragettes: Women's Emancipation in the 1890s*. New York: St. Martin's Press.

Russ, Joanna (1997). *What Are We Fighting For? Sex, Race, Class, and the Future of Feminism*. New York: St. Martin's Press.

Scharf, Lois, and Joan M. Jensen (1983). *Decades of Discontent: The Women's Movement, 1920-1940*. Westport, CT: Greenwood Press.

Stetson, Dorothy McBride, and Amy Mazur (eds.) (1995). *Comparative State Feminism*. Thousand Oaks, CA: Sage.

Tax, Meredith (1980). *The Rising of the Women: Feminist Solidarity and Class Conflict, 1880-1917*. New York: Monthly Review Press.

Thom, Mary (1997). *Inside MS: 25 Years of the Magazine and the Feminist Movement*. New York: Henry Holt.

Thomis, Malcolm I., and Jennifer Grimmett (1982). *Women in Protest, 1800-1850*. New York: St. Martin's Press.

Thonnessen, Werner (1973). *The Emancipation of Women: The Rise and Decline of the Women's Movement in Social Democracy, 1863-1933*. Bristol, England: Pluto Press.

Threlfall, Monica (ed.) (1996). *Mapping the Women's Movement: Feminist Politics and Social Transformation in the North.* New York: Verso.
Tobias, Sheila (1997). *Faces of Feminism: An Activist's Reflections on the Women's Movement.* Boulder, CO: Westview Press.
West, Guida, and Rhoda Lois Blumberg (eds.) (1990). *Women and Social Protest.* New York: Oxford University Press.
Yates, Gayle Graham (1975). *What Women Want. The Ideas of the Movement.* Cambridge, MA: Harvard University Press.
Young, Stacey (1997). *Changing the Wor(l)d: Discourse, Politics, and the Feminist Movement.* New York: Routledge.

A. Asia/Mideast/Africa

Abu-Lughod, Lila (ed.) (1998). *Remaking Women: Feminism and Modernity in the Middle East.* Princeton, NJ: Princeton University Press.
Afray, Janet (1996). *The Iranian Constitutional Revolution, 1906-1911: Grassroots Democracy, Social Democracy, and the Origins of Feminism.* New York: Columbia University Press.
Ali, Azrh Ashgar (2000). *The Energence of Feminism among Indian Muslim Women, 1920-1947.* New York: Oxford University Press.
Amin, Qasim (2000). *The Liberation of Women and the New Woman: Two Documents in the History of Egyptian Feminism.* Cairo, Egypt: The American University in Cairo Press.
Andors, Phyllis (1983). *The Unfinished Liberation of Chinese Women, 1949-1980.* Bloomington: Indiana University Press.
Badran, Margot (1995). *Feminists, Islam, and Nation: Gender and the Making of Modern Egypt.* Princeton, NJ: Princeton University Press.
Baig, Tara Ali (1976). *India's Woman Power.* New Delhi, India: S. Chand and Co.
Bamdad, Badrol-Moluk (1977). *From Darkness into Light: Women's Emancipation in Iran.* Hicksville, NY: Exposition Press.
Buckley, Sandra (ed.) (1996). *Broken Silence: Voices of Japanese Feminism.* Berkeley: University of California Press.
Calman, Leslie J. (1992). *Toward Empowerment: Women and Movement Politics in India.* Boulder, CO: Westview Press.
Condon, Jane (1985). *A Half Step Behind: Japanese Women of the '80s.* New York: Dodd, Mead.
Croll, Elizabeth J. (1978). *Feminism and Socialism in China.* Boston: Routledge and Kegan Paul.
Ezeigbo, T. Akachi (1996). *Gender Issues in Nigeria: A Feminine Perspective.* Lagos, Nigeria: University of Lagos Press.
Fan, Hong (1997). *Footbinding, Feminism, and Freedom: The Liberation of Women's Bodies in Modern China.* Portland, OR: L. Cass.

Fox, Diana, and Naima Ali Hasci (eds.) (1999). *The Challenges of Women's Activism and Human Rights in Africa.* Lewiston, NY: Edwin Mellen Press.

Fujimara-Fanselow, Kumiko, and Atsuko Kameds (eds.) (1995). *Japanese Women: New Feminist Perspectives on the Past, Present, and Future.* Old Westbury, NY: Feminist Press.

Jayawardena, Kumari (1986). *Feminism and Nationalism in the Third World.* Atlantic Highlands, NJ: Zed Books.

Judd, Ellen R. (2002). *The Chinese Women's Movement between State and Market.* Stanford, CA: Stanford University Press.

Kibwana, Kivutha (ed.) (2000). *Law and the Quest for Gender Equality in Kenya.* Nairobi: Claripress.

Mackie, Vera. *Feminism in Modern Japan: Citizenship, Embodiment and Sexuality.* Cambridge: Cambridge University Press, 2003.

Mehta, Sunita (ed.) (2002). *Women for Afghan Women: Shattering Myths and Claiming the Future.* New York: Palgrave.

Mernissi, Fatima (1991). *The Veil and the Male Elite: A Feminist Interpretation of Women's Rights in Islam.* Reading, MA: Addison-Wesley.

Mikell, Gwendolyn (ed.) (1997). *African Feminism: The Politics of Survival in Sub-Saharan Africa.* Philadelphia: University of Pennsylvania Press.

Misra, Kalapana, and Melanie Rich (eds). (2003). *Jewish Feminism in Israel: Some Contemporary Perspectives.* Lebanon, NH: University Press of New England.

Moghissi, Haideh (1994). *Populism and Feminism in Iran: Women's Struggle in a Male-Defined Revolutionary Movement.* New York: St. Martin's Press.

Moore, Erin P. (1999). *Gender, Law, and Resistance in India.* Tucson: University of Arizona Press.

Nelson, Cynthia (1996). *Doria Shafik: Egyptian Feminist: A Woman Apart.* Gainesville: University Press of Florida.

Premalatha, P. N. (2002). *Nationalism and Women's Movement in South India, 1917-1947.* New Delhi, India: Gyan Books.

Sievers, Sharon L. (1983). *Flowers in the Salt: The Beginnings of Feminist Consciousness in Modern Japan.* Stanford, CA: Stanford University Press.

Wesoky, Sharon R. (2002). *Chinese Feminism Faces Globalization.* New York: Routledge.

Wierenga, Saskia (2002). *Sexual Politics in Indonesia.* New York: Palgrave.

Young, Marilyn Blatt (1973). *Women in China: Studies in Social Change and Feminism.* Ann Arbor: Center for Chinese Studies, University of Michigan.

B. Australia/New Zealand

Bulbeck, Chilla (1997). *Living Feminism: The Impact of the Women's Movement on Three Generations of Australian Women.* New York: Cambridge University Press.

DuPlessis, Rosemary, and Lynne Alice (eds.) (1998). *Feminist Thought in AOTEAROA/New Zealand: Differences and Connections*. New York: Oxford University Press.
Eveline, Joan, and Lorraine Hayden (eds.) (1999). *Carrying the Banner: Women, Leadership, and Activism in Australia*. Nedlands, W.A.: University of Western Australia Press.
Grimshaw, Patricia (1972). *Women's Suffrage in New Zealand*. Wellington, New Zealand: Oxford University Press.
Hughes, Kate Pritchard (ed.) (1994). *Contemporary Australian Feminism*. Melbourne: Longman Cheshire.
Lake, Marilyn (1999). *Getting Equal: The History of Australian Feminism*. St. Leonards, NSW: Allen and Unwin.

C. Europe/Great Britain

Ackelsberg, Martha A. (1991). *Free Women of Spain: Anarchism and the Struggle for Emancipation of Women*. Bloomington: Indiana University Press.
Alberti, Johanna (1989). *Beyond Suffrage: Feminists in War and Peace. 1914-1928*. New York: St. Martin's Press.
Allen, Ann Taylor (1991). *Feminism and Motherhood in Germany, 1800-1914*. New Brunswick, NJ: Rutgers University Press.
Anderson, Harriet (1992). *Utopian Feminism: Women's Movements in Fin-de-Siècle Vienna*. New Haven, CT: Yale University Press.
Banaszak, Lee Ann, Karen Beckwith, and Dieter Rucht (eds.) (2003). *Women's Movements Facing the Reconfigured State*. New York: Cambridge University Press.
Bidelman, Patrick Kay (1987). *Pariahs Stand Up!: The Founding of the Liberal Feminist Movement in France, 1858-1889*. Westport, CT: Greenwood.
Birnbaum, Lucia Chiavola (1986). *Liberazione della donna: Feminism in Italy*. Middletown, CT: Wesleyan University Press.
———. (1993). *Black Madonnas: Feminism, Religion, and Politics in Italy*. Boston: Northeastern University Press.
Blackburn, Helen (1971). *Women's Suffrage: A Record of the Women's Suffrage Movement in the British Isles*. New York: Kraus Reprint Co.
Bouten, Jacob (1975). *Mary Wollstonecraft and the Beginnings of Female Emancipation in France and England*. Philadelphia: Porcupine Press.
Breitensach, Esther (ed.) (2001). *Women and Contemporary Scottish Politics: An Anthology*. Edinburgh, Scotland: Edinburgh University Press.
Brunt, Rosalind, and Caroline Brown (eds.) (1987). *Feminism, Culture and Politics*. London: Lawrence and Wishart.
Bull, Anna et al. (eds.) (2000). *Feminisms and Women's Movements in Contemporary Europe*. New York: St. Martin's Press.
Caine, Barbara (1997). *English Feminism, 1790-1980*. New York: Oxford University Press.

_____. (1992). *Victorian Feminists*. New York: Oxford University Press.
Duchen, Claire (1986). *Feminism in France: From May '68 to Mitterrand*. Boston: Routledge and Kegan Paul.
Duchen, Claire (ed. and trans.) (1987). *French Connections: Voices from the Women's Movement in France*. Amherst: University of Massachusetts Press.
Ellsworth, Edward W. (1979). *Liberators of the Female Mind: The Shirreff Sisters, Educational Reform, and the Women's Movement*. Westport, CT: Greenwood.
Evans, Richard J. (1976). *The Feminist Movement in Germany, 1894-1933*. Beverly Hills, CA: Sage.
_____. (1987). *Comrades and Sisters: Feminism, Socialism, and Pacifism in Europe, 1870-1945*. New York: St. Martin's Press.
Fauré, Christine (1991). *Democracy without Women: Feminism and the Rise of Liberal Individualism in France*. Bloomington: Indiana University Press.
Fayet-Scribe, Sylvie (1990). *Associations féminines et Catholicisme: XIXe-XXe siècle*. Paris: Editions Ouvrières.
Flam, Helena (ed.) (2001). *Pink, Purple, Green: Women's Religious, Environmental and Gay/Lesbian Movements in Central Europe Today*. New York: Columbia University Press.
Frevert, Ute (1989). *Women in German History: From Bourgeois Emancipation to Sexual Liberation*. New York: Berg.
Funk, Nanette, and Magda Mueller (eds.) (1993). *Gender Politics and Post-Communism: Reflections from Eastern Europe and the Former Soviet Union*. New York: Routledge.
Garner, Les (1984). *Stepping Stones to Women's Liberty: Feminist Ideas in the Women's Suffrage Movement, 1900-1918*. Rutherford, NJ: Fairleigh Dickinson University Press.
Gordon, Felicia, and Maire Cross (1996). *Early French Feminisms, 1830-1940: A Passion for Liberty*. Northampton, MA: Edward Elgar.
Harrison, Brian (1987). *Prudent Revolutionaries: Portraits of British Feminists Between the Wars*. New York: Clarendon Press.
Hause, Steven C., and A. Kenney (1984). *Women's Suffrage and Social Politics in the French Third Republic*. Princeton, NJ: Princeton University Press.
Hellman, Judith Adler (1987). *Journeys among Women: Feminism in Five Italian Cities*. New York: Oxford University Press.
Herminghouse, Patricia, and Magola Mueller (eds.) (2001). *German Feminist Writings*. New York: Continuum.
Holcombe, Lee (1983). *Wives and Property: Reform of the Married Women's Property Law in Nineteenth-Century England*. Toronto: University of Toronto Press.
Hollis, Patricia (1979). *Women in Public, 1850-1900: Documents of the Victorian Women's Movement*. Boston: Allen and Unwin.
Holton, Sandra Stanley (1986). *Feminism and Democracy: Women's Suffrage and Reform Politics in Britain, 1900-1918*. New York: Cambridge University Press.

Hume, Leslie Parker (1982). *The National Union of Women's Suffrage Societies, 1897-1914.* New York: Garland.
Kaplan, Gisela (1992). *Contemporary Western European Feminism.* New York: New York University Press.
Kaplan, Marion A. (1979). *The Jewish Feminist Movement in Germany: The Campaigns of the Judischer Frauenbund, 1904-1938.* Westport, CT: Greenwood.
Kent, Susan (1987). *Sex and Suffrage in Britain, 1860-1914.* Princeton, NJ: Princeton University Press.
Lacey, Candida Ann (1987). *Barbara Leigh Smith Bodichon and the Langham Place Group.* New York: Routledge and Kegan Paul.
Leneman, Leah (1991). *A Guid Cause: The Women's Suffrage Movement in Scotland.* Aberdeen, Scotland: Aberdeen University Press.
Levine, Philippa (1987). *Victorian Feminism, 1850-1900.* Tallahassee: Florida State University Press.
Lovenduski, Joni (1986). *Women and European Politics: Contemporary Feminism and Public Policy.* Amherst: University of Massachusetts Press.
_____, and Vicky Randall (1993). *Contemporary Feminist Politics: Women and Power in Britain.* Oxford: Oxford University Press.
Mirza, Heidi Safia (ed.) (1997). *Black British Feminism: A Reader.* New York: Routledge.
Morgan, David (1975). *Suffragists and Liberals. The Politics of Woman Suffrage in England.* Oxford: Blackwell.
Moses, Claire Goldberg (1984). *French Feminism in the Nineteenth Century.* Albany: State University of New York Press.
Offen, Karen M. (2000). *European Feminisms, 1700-1950: A Political History.* Stanford, CA: Stanford University Press.
Prelinger, Catherine M. (1987). *Charity, Challenge and Change: Religious Dimensions of the Mid-Nineteenth Century Women's Movement in Germany.* Westport, CT: Greenwood.
Pugh, Martin (1992). *Women and the Women's Movement in Britain, 1914-1959.* Houndmills, Basingstoke, England: Macmillan Education.
Quataert, Jean H. (1979). *Reluctant Feminists in German Social Democracy, 1885-1917.* Princeton, NJ: Princeton University Press.
Renne, Tanya (ed.) (1997). *Ana's Land: Sisterhood in Eastern Europe.* Boulder, CO: Westview Press.
Rodgers, Katherine M. (1987). *Feminism in Eighteenth-Century England.* Urbana: University of Illinois Press.
Rosen, Andrew (1974). *Rise Up Women! The Militant Campaign of the Women's Social and Political Union, 1903-1914.* London: Routledge and Kegan Paul.
Rover, Constance (1967). *Women's Suffrage and Party Politics in Britain, 1866-1914.* London: Routledge and Kegan Paul.
Sanford, Jutta Schroers (1978). *The Origins of German Feminism: German Women, 1789-1870.* Ann Arbor, MI: University Microfilms International.

Shanley, Mary Lyndon (1989). *Feminism, Marriage, and the Law in Victorian England, 1850-1895*. Princeton, NJ: Princeton University Press.
Sneeringer, Julia (2002). *Winning Women's Votes: Propaganda and Politics in Weimar Germany*. Chapel Hill: University of North Carolina Press.
Stetson, Dorothy M. (1982). *A Woman's Issue: The Politics of Family Law Reformism in England*. Westport, CT: Greenwood.
Stetson, Dorothy M. (1987). *Women's Rights in France*. Westport,CT: Greenwood.
Walker, Linda (1999). *The Women's Movement in Britain, 1790-1945*. New York: Routledge.
Wilson, Elizabeth (1986). *Hidden Agendas: Theory, Politics, and Experience in the Women's Movement*. New York: Tavistock Publications.
Wolchik, Sharon L., and Alfred G. Meyer (eds.) (1985). *Women, State, and Party in Eastern Europe*. Durham, NC: Duke University Press.

D. Latin America

Alvarez, Sonia F. (1990). *Engendering Democracy in Brazil: Women's Movements in Transition Politics*. Princeton, NJ: Princeton University Press.
Andreas, Carol (1985). *When Women Rebel: The Rise of Popular Feminism in Peru*. Westport, CT: Hill.
Baldez, Lisa (2002). *Why Women Protest: Women's Movements in Chile*. New York: Cambridge University Press.
Carlson, MariFran (1988). *Feminismo! The Woman's Movement in Argentina from Its Beginnings to Eva Perón*. Chicago: Academy Chicago.
Dandarati, Annie G. (1996). *The Women's Movement and Transitions to Democracy in Chile*. New York: P. Lang.
Fitzsimmons, Tracy (2000). *Beyond the Barricades: Women, Civil Society, and Participation after Democratization in Latin America*. New York: Garland.
Hahner, June Edith (1990). *Emancipating the Female Sex: The Struggle for Women's Rights in Brazil*. Durham, NC: Duke University Press.
Isbester, Katherine (2001). *Still Fighting: The Nicaraguan Women's Movement, 1977-2000*. Pittsburgh: University of Pittsburgh Press.
Jaquette, Jane S. (ed.) (1994). *The Women's Movement in Latin America: Feminism and the Transition to Democracy*. Boulder, CO: Westview Press.
Lavrin, Asuncion (1995). *Women, Feminism, and Social Change in Argentina, 1890-1940*. Lincoln: University of Nebraska Press.
Macias, Anna (1987). *Against All Odds: The Feminist Movement in Mexico to 1940*. Westport, CT: Greenwood.
Miller, Francesca (1991). *Latin American Women and the Search for Social Justice*. Hanover, NH: University Press of New England.
Morton, Ward (1962). *Woman Suffrage in Mexico*. Gainesville: University of Florida Press.

Randall, Margaret (1992). *Gathering Rage: The Failure of Twentieth-Century Revolutions to Develop a Feminist Agenda.* New York: Monthly Review Press.

———. (1994). *Sandino's Daughters Revisited: Feminism in Nicaragua.* New Brunswick, NJ: Rutgers University Press.

Stephens, Lynn (1997). *Women and Social Movements in Latin America: Power from Below.* Austin: University of Texas Press.

Stob, Barbara, and Nena Terrell (1988). *Confronting the Crisis in Latin America: Women Organizing for Change.* Santiago, Chile: Isis International and Development Alternatives with Women for a New Era.

Stoner, K. Lynn (1991). *From the House to the Streets: The Cuban Women's Movement for Legal Reform, 1898-1940.* Durham, NC: Duke University Press.

Tooley, Michelle (1997). *Voices of the Voiceless: Women, Justice, and Human Rights in Guatemala.* Scottsdale, PA: Herald Press.

E. Russia/Soviet Union

Ashwin, Sarah. (ed.) (2000*).* *Gender, State and Society in Soviet and Post-Soviet Russia.* New York: Routledge.

Bohachevsky-Chomiak, Martha (1988). *Feminists Despite Themselves: Women in Ukrainian Community Life, 1884-1939.* Edmonton, Alberta: Canadian Institute of Ukrainian Studies. Toronto: University of Toronto Press.

Clements, Barbara Evans (1979). *Bolshevik Feminist: The Life of Aleksandra Kollontai.* Bloomington: Indiana University Press.

Edmondson, Linda Harriet (1984). *Feminism in Russia, 1900-1917.* Stanford, CA: Stanford University Press.

Heitlinger, Alena (1979). *Sex Inequality in the Soviet Union and Czechoslovakia.* London: Macmillan.

Holland, Barbara (ed.) (1985). *Soviet Sisterhood.* Bloomington: Indiana University Press.

Jancar, Barbara Wolfe (1978). *Women under Communism.* Baltimore: Johns Hopkins University Press.

Johanson, Christine (1987). *Women's Struggle for Higher Education in Russia, 1855-1900.* Montreal: McGill-Queen's University Press.

Mamonova, Tatyana (ed.) (1984). *Women and Russia: Feminist Writings from the Soviet Union.* Boston: Beacon Press.

Racioppi, Linda, and Katherine O'Sullivan See. (1997). *Women's Activism in Contemporary Russia.* Philadelphia: Temple University Press.

Sperling, Valerie. (1999). *Organizing Women in Contemporary Russia: Engendering Transition.* New York: Cambridge University Press.

Stites, Richard (1978). *The Women's Liberation Movement in Russia.* Princeton, NJ: Princeton University Press.

F. United States/Canada

Adamson, Nancy (1988). *Feminist Organizing for Change: The Contemporary Women's Movement in Canada.* New York: Oxford University Press.
Armstrong, Elizabeth (2002). *The Retreat of Organization: US Feminism Reconceptualized.* Albany: State University of New York Press.
Bacchi, Carol (1983). *Liberation Deferred? The Ideas of the English-Canadian Suffragists, 1877-1918.* Toronto: University of Toronto Press.
Backhouse, Constance, and David H. Flaherty (eds.) (1992). *Challenging Times: The Women's Movement in Canada and the United States.* Buffalo, NY: McGill-Queen's University Press.
Bacon, Margaret Hope (1986). *Mothers of Feminism: Quaker Women in America.* San Francisco: Harper and Row.
Becker, Susan D. (1981). *The Origins of the Equal Rights Amendment: American Feminism between the Wars.* Westport, CT: Greenwood.
Beckwith, Karen (1986). *American Women and Political Participation: The Impacts of Work, Generation, and Feminism.* Westport, CT: Greenwood.
Beeton, Beverly (1986). *Women Vote in the West: The Woman Suffrage Movement, 1869-1896.* New York: Garland.
Berkeley, Kathleen C. (1999). *The Women's Liberation Movement in America.* Westport, CT: Greenwood.
Berry, Mary Frances (1986). *Why ERA Failed: Politics, Women's Rights and the Amendment Process of the Constitution.* Bloomington: Indiana University Press.
Boles, Janet K. (1979). *The Politics of the Equal Rights Amendment.* New York: Longman.
_____. (ed.) (1991). *American Feminism: New Issues for a Mature Movement.* Newbury Park, CA: Sage.
Bookman, Ann, and Sandra Morgen (1988). *Women and the Politics of Empowerment.* Philadelphia: Temple University Press.
Boydston, Jeanne et al. (1988). *The Limits of Sisterhood: The Beecher Sisters on Women's Rights and Woman's Sphere.* Chapel Hill: University of North Carolina Press.
Buechler, Steven M. (1990). *Women's Movements in the United States: Woman Suffrage, Equal Rights, and Beyond.* New Brunswick, NJ: Rutgers University Press.
Carden, Maren Lockwood (1974). *The New Feminist Movement.* New York: Russell Sage Foundation.
Carty, Linda (ed.) (1993). *And Still We Rise: Feminist Political Mobilization in Contemporary Canada.* Toronto: Women's Press.
Castro, Ginette (1990). *American Feminism: A Contemporary History.* New York: New York University Press.

Chafe, William Henry (1977). *Women and Equality: Changing Patterns in American Culture.* New York: Oxford University Press.

Cleverdon, Catherine Lyle (1950). *The Woman Suffrage Movement in Canada.* Toronto: University of Toronto Press.

Cohen, Marcia (1988). *The Sisterhood: The True Story of the Women Who Changed the World.* New York: Simon and Schuster.

Costain, Anne N. (1992). *Inviting Women's Rebellion: A Political Process Interpretation of the Women's Movement.* Baltimore: Johns Hopkins University Press.

Cummings, Bernice, and Victoria Schuck (eds.) (1979). *Women Organizing: An Anthology.* Metuchen, NJ: Scarecrow Press.

Davis, Flora (1991). *Moving the Mountain: The Women's Movement in America Since 1960.* New York: Simon and Schuster.

DuBois, Ellen Carol (1978). *Feminism and Suffrage: The Emergence of an Independent Women's Movement in America, 1848-1869.* Ithaca, NY: Cornell University Press.

Echols, Alice (1989). *Daring to Be Bad: Radical Feminism in America, 1967-1975.* Minneapolis: University of Minnesota Press.

Evans, Sara M. (1979). *Personal Politics: The Roots of Women's Liberation in the Civil Rights Movement and the New Left.* New York: Knopf.

_____. (2003). *Tidal Wave: How Women Changed America at Century's End.* New York: Free Press.

Faludi, Susan (1991). *Backlash: The Undeclared War against American Women.* New York: Crown.

Fishman, Sylvia Barack (1993). *A Breath of Life: Feminism in the American Jewish Community.* New York: Free Press.

Flexner, Eleanor (1974). *Century of Struggle. The Woman's Rights Movement in the United States.* New York: Atheneum.

Forster, Margaret (1985). *Significant Sisters: The Grassroots of Active Feminism, 1839-1939.* New York: Knopf.

Freeman, Jo (1975). *The Politics of Women's Liberation: A Case Study of an Emerging Social Movement and Its Relation to the Political Process.* New York: McKay.

Friedan, Betty (1976). *It Changed My Life: Writings on the Women's Movement.* New York: Random House.

_____. (1981). *The Second Stage.* New York: Summit Books.

Friedl, Bettina (ed.) (1987). *On to Victory: Propaganda Plays of the Women's Suffrage Movement.* Boston: Northeastern University Press.

Fritz, Leah (1979). *Dreamers and Dealers: An Intimate Appraisal of the Women's Movement.* Boston: Beacon Press.

Gelb, Joyce, and Marian Leaf Palley (1987). *Women and Public Policies.* Rev. and expanded ed. Princeton, NJ: Princeton University Press.

Gingras, Francois-Pierre (ed.) (1995). *Gender and Politics in Contemporary Canada.* New York: Oxford University Press.

Green, Elna C. (1997). *Southern Strategies: Southern Women and the Woman Suffrage Question.* Chapel Hill: University of North Carolina Press.
Grimes, Alan P. (1967). *The Puritan Ethic and Woman Suffrage.* New York: Oxford University Press.
Harrison, Cynthia Ellen (1988). *On Account of Sex: The Politics of Women's Issues, 1945-1968.* Berkeley: University of California Press.
Hartmann, Susan M. (1998). *The Other Feminists: Activists in the Liberal Establishment.* New Haven, CT: Yale University Press.
Hawkes, Ellen (1986). *Feminism on Trial: The Ginny Foat Case and Its Meaning for the Future of the Women's Movement.* New York: Morrow Press.
Hersh, Blanche Glassman (1978). *The Slavery of Sex: Feminist-Abolitionists in America.* Urbana: University of Illinois Press.
Howell, Sharon (1990). *Reflections of Ourselves: The Mass Media and the Women's Movement, 1963 to the Present.* New York: Lang.
Kraditor, Aileen (1965). *The Ideas of the Woman Suffrage Movement, 1890-1920.* New York: Columbia University Press.
Lemons, Stanley J. (1973). *The Woman Citizen: Social Feminism in the 1920s.* Urbana: University of Illinois Press.
Linkugel, Wil A., and Anna Howard Shaw (1991). *Anna Howard Shaw: Suffrage Orator and Social Reformer.* Westport, CT: Greenwood.
Luker, Kristin (1984). *Abortion and the Politics of Motherhood.* Berkeley: University of California Press.
Lunardini, Christine A. (1986). *From Equal Suffrage to Equal Rights: Alice Paul and the National Woman's Party, 1910-1928.* New York: New York University Press.
Madsen, Carol Cornwall (ed.) (1997). *Battle for the Ballot: Essays on Woman Suffrage in Utah, 1870-1896.* Logan: Utah State University Press.
Mansbridge, Jane J. (1986). *Why We Lost the ERA.* Chicago: University of Chicago Press.
Mathews, Donald G., and Jane Sherron Dehart (1990). *Sex, Gender, and the Politics of ERA: A State and the Nation.* New York: Oxford University Press.
Melder, Keith E. (1977). *Beginnings of Sisterhood. The American Woman's Rights Movement, 1800-1850.* New York: Schocken Books.
Morgan, David (1972). *Suffragists and Democrats: The Politics of Woman Suffrage in America.* East Lansing: Michigan State University Press.
Morgan, Robin (1978). *Going Too Far: The Personal Chronicle of a Feminist.* New York: Vintage Books.
Newton, Janice (1995). *The Feminist Challenge to the Canadian Left, 1900-1918.* Montreal: McGill-Queen's University Press.
O'Neill, William L. (1989). *Feminism in America: A History.* New Brunswick, NJ: Transaction Books.
Riddel-Dixon, Elizabeth M. (2001). *Canada and the Beijing Conference on Women: Governmental Politics and NGO Participation.* Vancouver: University of British Columbia Press.

Rivers, Caryl (1991). *More Joy than Rage: Crossing Generations with the New Feminism.* Hanover, NH: University Press of New England.
Rossi, Alice S. (1982). *Feminists in Politics: A Panel Analysis of the First National Women's Conference.* New York: Academic Press.
Rowland, R. (ed.) (1984). *Women Who Do and Women Who Don't (Join the Feminist Movement).* London: Routledge and Kegan Paul.
Rupp, Leila J., and Verta A. Taylor (1987). *Survival in the Doldrums: The American Women's Rights Movement, 1945 to the 1960s.* New York: Oxford University Press.
Ryan, Barbara (1992). *Feminism and the Women's Movement: Dynamics of Change in Social Movement, Ideology, and Activism.* New York: Routledge.
Sangster, Joan (1988). *Dreams of Equality: Women on the Canadian Left, 1920-1950.* Toronto: McClelland and Stewart.
Schramm, Sarah Slavin (1979). *Plow Women Rather than Reapers: An Intellectual History of Feminism in the United States.* Metuchen, NJ: Scarecrow Press.
Shanley, Mary Lyndon (1988). *Women's Rights, Feminism, and Politics in the United States.* Washington, DC: American Political Science Association.
Simon, Rita James (1991). *Women's Movements in America: Their Successes, Disappointments, and Aspirations.* New York: Praeger.
Sochen, June (1971). *The New Feminism in Twentieth-Century America.* Lexington, MA: Heath.
———. (1972). *The New Woman. Feminism in Greenwich Village, 1910-1920.* New York: Quadrangle.
———. (1973). *Movers and Shakers: American Women Thinkers and Activists, 1900-1970.* New York: Quadrangle/New York Times Book Co.
Staggenborg, Suzanne (1991). *The Pro-Choice Movement: Organization and Activism in the Abortion Conflict.* New York: Oxford University Press.
Steiner, Gilbert Y. (1985). *Constitutional Inequality: The Political Fortunes of the Equal Rights Amendment.* Washington, DC: Brookings Institution.
Stewart, Debra W. (1980). *The Women's Movement in Community Politics in the US.* New York: Pergamon Press.
Taymor, Betty (2000). *Running against the Wind: The Struggle of Women in Massachusetts Politics.* Boston: Northeastern University Press.
VanBurkleo, Sandra F. (2001). *Belonging to the World: Women's Rights and American Constitutional Culture.* New York: Oxford University Press.
Vickers, Jill, Christine Appelle, and Pauline Rangin (1993). *Politics as If Women Mattered: A Political Analysis of the Action Committee on the Status of Women.* Toronto: University of Toronto Press.
Wandersee, Winifred D. (1988). *On the Move: American Women in the 1970s.* Boston: Twayne.
Wheeler, Marjorie Spruill (1993). *New Women of the New South: The Leaders of the Woman Suffrage Movement in the Southern States.* New York: Oxford University Press.

Wheeler, Marjorie Spruill (ed.) (1995). *Votes for Women!: The Woman Suffrage Movement in Tennessee, The South, and the Nation*. Knoxville: University of Tennessee Press.
Whittier, Nancy (1995). *Feminist Generations: The Persistence of the Radical Women's Movement*. Philadelphia: Temple University Press.
Wolbrecht, Christina (2000). *The Politics of Women's Rights: Parties, Positions, and Change*. Princeton, NJ: Princeton University Press.
Yellin, Jean Fagan (1989). *Women and Sisters: The Antislavery Feminists in American Culture*. New Haven, CT: Yale University Press.
Young, Lisa (2001). *Feminist and Party Politics*. Ann Arbor: University of Michigan Press.

G. Men and Feminism/The Men's Movement

Bly, Robert (1990). *Iron John*. Reading, MA: Addison-Wesley.
Boone, Joseph A., and Michael Gadden (eds.) (1990). *Engendering Men: The Question of Male Feminist Criticism*. New York: Routledge.
Digby, Tom (ed.) (1998). *Men Doing Feminism*. New York: Routledge.
Farrell, Warren (1974). *The Liberated Man*. New York: Random House.
_____. (1986). *Why Men Are the Way They Are: The Male-Female Dynamic*. New York: McGraw-Hill.
_____. (1993). *The Myth of Male Power: Why Men Are the Disposable Sex*. New York: Simon and Schuster.
Goldrick-Jones, Amanda (2002). *Men Who Believe in Feminism*. Westport, CT: Praeger.
Hagen, Kay Leigh (1992). *Women Respond to the Men's Movement*. San Francisco: Pandora.
Jardine, Alice, and Paul Smith (eds.) (1987). *Men in Feminism*. New York: Routledge.
Jesser, Clinton J. (1996). *Fierce and Tender Men: Sociological Aspects of the Men's Movement*. Westport, CT: Praeger.
John, Angela V., and Claire Eustance (eds.) (1997). *The Men's Share?: Masculinities, Male Support, and Women's Suffrage in Britain, 1890-1920*. New York: Routledge.
Keen, Sam (1991). *Fire in the Belly: On Being a Man*. New York: Bantam.
Kimmel, Michael S. (ed.) (1995). *The Politics of Manhood: Profeminist Men Respond to the Mythopoetic Men's Movement (and Mythopoetic Leaders Answer)*. Philadelphia: Temple University Press.
May, Larry, and Robert A. Strikwerda (eds.) (1992). *Rethinking Masculinity: Philosophical Explorations in Light of Feminism*. Totowa, NJ: Rowman and Littlefield.
Messner, Michael A. (1997). *Politics of Masculinities: Men in Movements*. Thousand Oaks, CA: Sage.

Porter, David (ed.) (1993). *Between Men and Feminism*. New York: Routledge.
Rowan, John (1987). *The Horned God: Feminism and Men as Wounding and Healing*. New York: Routledge.
Seidler, Victor J. (1991). *Recreating Sexual Politics: Men, Feminism, and Politics*. New York: Routledge.
_____. (ed.) (1991). *Achilles Heel Reader: Men, Sexual Politics, and Socialism*. New York: Routledge.
Symonds, Richard (1999). *Inside the Citadel: Men and the Emancipation of Women*. New York: St. Martin's Press.

H. AntiFeminism

Abbott, Pamela, and Clare Wallace (1993). *The Family and the New Right*. Boulder, CO: Westview Press.
Amneus, Daniel (1979). *Back to Patriarchy*. New Rochelle, NY: Arlington House.
Bachetta, Paol, and Margaret Power (eds.) (2002). *Right-Wing Women: From Conservatives to Extremists Around the World*. New York: Routledge.
Burack, Cynthia, and Jyl J. Josephson. (2003). *Fundamental Differences: Feminists Talk Back to Social Conservatives*. Lanham, MD.: Rowman and Littlefield.
Conover, Pamela Johnston, and Virginia Gray (1983). *Feminism and the New Right: Conflict over the American Family*. New York: Praeger.
Davidson, Nicholas (1988). *The Failure of Feminism*. Buffalo, NY: Prometheus Books.
Decter, Midge (1972). *The New Chastity and Other Arguments against Women's Liberation*. New York: Coward, McCann and Geoghegan.
Dworkin, Andrea (1983). *Right-Wing Women*. New York: Coward, McCann and Geoghegan.
Fox-Genovese, Elizabeth (1996). *'Feminism Is Not the Story of My Life': How Today's Feminist Elite Has Lost Touch with the Real Concerns of Women*. New York: Nan A. Talese.
Graglia, F. Carolyn (1998). *Domestic Tranquility: A Brief against Feminism*. Dallas, TX: Spence.
Hammer, Rhonda (2001). *Antifeminism and Family Terrorism: A Critical Feminist Perspective*. Lanham, MD: Rowman and Littlefield.
Harrison, Brian (1978). *Separate Spheres: The Opposition to Women's Suffrage in Britain*. London: Helm.
Hewlett, Sylvia Ann (1986). *A Lesser Life: The Myth of Women's Liberation in America*. New York: Morrow Press.
Howard, Angela, and Sasha Ranae Adams Tarrant (eds.) (2000). *AntiFeminism in America, a Reader: A Collection of Readings from the Literature of the Opponents to US Feminism*. New York: Garland.
_____. (eds.) (1997). *Opposition to the Women's Movement in the United States, 1848-1929*. New York: Garland.

Hudson, Kenneth (1968.) *Men and Women: Feminism and AntiFeminism Today.* Newton Abbot, England: David and Charles.
Klatch, Rebecca G. (1987). *Women of the New Right.* Philadelphia: Temple University Press.
Klein, Ellen R. (1995). *Feminism under Fire.* Amherst, NY: Prometheus Books.
LaHaye, Beverly (1993). *The Desires of a Woman's Heart: Encouragement for Women When Traditional Values Are Challenged.* Wheaton, IL: Tyndale House.
Marshall, Susan E. (1997). *Splinterd Sisterhood: Gender and Class in the Campaign against Woman Suffrage.* Madison: University of Wisconsin Press.
Mason, Mary Ann (1988). *The Equality Trap.* New York: Simon and Schuster.
Schlafly, Phyllis (1978). *The Power of the Positive Woman.* New York: Jove Publications.
————. (2003). *Feminist Fantasies.* Dallas, TX: Spence.
Sommers, Christina Hoff (1994). *Who Stole Feminism?* New York: Simon and Schuster.

I. Third Wave Feminism

Baumgardner, Jennifer, and Amy Richards (2000). *Manifesta: Young Women, Feminism, and the Future.* New York: Farrar, Straus and Giroux.
Denfield, Rene (1995). *The New Victorians: A Young Woman's Challenge to the Old Feminist Order.* New York: Warner Books.
Dicker, Rory, and Alison Piepmeier (eds.) (2003). *Catching a Wave: Reclaiming Feminism for the 21st Century.* Boston: Northeastern University Press.
Edut, Ophira (ed.) (1998). *Adios Barabie: Young Women Write about Body Image and Identity.* Seattle: Seal Press.
Findlen, Barbara (ed.) (2001). *Listen Up: Voices from the Next Feminist Generation.* revised ed. Seattle: Seal Press.
Hernandez, Daisy, and Bushra Rehmon (eds.) (2002). *Colonize This!: Young Women of Color on Today's Feminism.* Seattle: Seal Press.
Heywood, Leslie, and Jennifer Drake (eds.) (1997). *Third Wave Agenda: Being Feminist, Doing Feminism.* Minneapolis: University of Minnesota Press.
Kamen, Paula (1991). *Feminist Fatale: Voices from the "Twentysomething" Generation Explore the Future of the Women's Movement.* New York: Fine.
Mitchell, Allyson, Lisa Bryn Rundle, and Lana Karaian (eds.) (2001). *Turbo Chicks: Talking Young Feminisms.* Toronto: Sumach Press.
Trioli, Virginia (1996). *Generation F: Sex, Power, and the Young Feminist.* Melbourne, Australia: Minerva.
Walker, Rebecca (ed.) (1995). *To Be Real: Telling the Truth and Changing the Face of Feminism.* New York: Anchor Books.
Walter, Natasha (1998). *The New Feminism.* London: Little, Brown.

———. (ed.) 2000). *On the Move: Feminism for a New Generation*. London: Virago.
Wolf, Naomi (1993). *Fire with Fire*. New York: Random House.

XIV. Anthropology and Sociology

Abbott, Pamela, and Claire Wallace (1996). *An Introduction to Sociology: Feminist Perspectives*. New York: Routledge.
Adams, Carol J., and Josephine Donovan (eds.) (1995). *Animals and Women: Feminist Theoretical Explorations*. Durham, NC: Duke University Press.
Banet-Weiser, Sarah (1999). *The Most Beautiful Girls in the World: Beauty Pageants and National Identity*. Berkeley: University of California Press.
Benokraitis, Nijole, and Joe R. Feagin (1995). *Modern Sexism: Blatant, Subtle, and Covert Discrimination*, 2nd ed. Englewood Cliffs, NJ: Prentice Hall.
Buss, David M., and Neil M. Malamuth (eds.) (1996). *Sex, Power, Conflict: Evolutionary and Feminist Perspectives*. New York: Oxford University Press.
Carbert, Louise I. (1995). *Agrarian Feminism: The Politics of Ontario Farm Women*. Toronto: University of Toronto Press.
Cavanagh, Kate, and Viviene E. Cree (1995). *Working with Men: The Thin End of the Feminist Wedge*. New York: Routledge.
Cole, Sally, and Lynne Phillips (eds.) (1995). *Ethnographic Feminisms: Essays in Anthropology*. Ottawa: Carleton University Press.
Corrin, Chris (ed.) (1996). *Women in a Violent World: Feminist Analyses and Resistance across "Europe."* Edinburgh, Scotland: Edinburgh University Press.
Daly, Kathleen, and Lisa Maher (eds.) (1998). *Criminology at the Crossroads: Feminist Readings in Crime and Justice*. New York: Oxford University Press.
Daniels, Cynthia R. (ed.) (1997). *Feminists Negotiate the State: The Politics of Domestic Violence*. Lanham, MD: University Press of America.
Denton, Barbara (2001). *Dealing: Women in the Drug Economy*. Sydney, Australia: University of New South Wales Press.
Dobash, Emerson et al. (1995). *Gender and Crime*. Cardiff: University of Wales Press.
Doyal, Lesley et al. (eds.) (1994). *AIDS: Setting a Feminist Agenda*. Bristol, England: Taylor and Francis.
Dube, Leela (2001). *Anthropological Explorations in Gender: Intersecting Fields*. Thousand Oaks, CA: Sage.
Elliot, Faith Robertson (1996). *Gender, Family and Society*. New York: St. Martin's Press.
Ellis, Kathryn, and Hartley Dean (eds.) (2000). *Social Policy and the Body: Transitions in Corporeal Discourse*. New York: St. Martin's Press.
Etienne, Mona, and Eleanor Leacock (eds.) (1980). *Women and Colonialization*. New York: Praeger.

Feinman, Ilene Rose (2000). *Citizenship Rites: Feminist Soldiers and Feminist AntiMilitarists.* New York: New York University Press.
Gero, Joan M., and Margaret W. Conkey (eds.) (1991). *Engendering Archaeology.* Oxford: Basil Blackwell.
Gimlin, Debra L. (2002). *Body Work: Beauty and Self-Image in American Culture.* Berkeley: University of California Press.
Goddard, Victoria (ed.) (2000). *Gender, Agency, and Change: Anthropological Perspectives.* New York: Routledge.
Gottfried, Heide (ed.) (1996). *Feminism and Social Change: Bridging Theory and Practice.* Urbana: University of Illinois Press.
Gowaty, Patricia Adair (ed.) (1996). *Feminism and Evolutionary Biology: Boundaries, Intersections, and Frontiers.* New York: Chapman and Hall.
Hanson, Mary Ellen (1995). *Go! Fight! Win!: Cheerleading in American Culture.* Bowling Green, OH: Bowling Green University Popular Press.
Hooyman, Nancy R., and Judith Gonyes (1995). *Feminist Perspectives on Family Care: Policies for Gender Justice.* Thousand Oaks, CA: Sage Press.
Kaplan, E. Ann (1996). *Looking for the Other: Feminism and the Imperial Gaze.* New York: Routledge.
Laslett, Barbara, and Barrie Thorne (eds.) (1997). *Feminist Sociology: Life Histories of a Movement.* New Brunswick, NJ: Rutgers University Press.
Luxton, Meg (ed.) (1997). *Feminism and Families: Critical Policies and Changing Practices.* Halifax, Nova Scotia: Fernwood.
McKie, Linda, and Kathryn Backett-Milburn (eds.) (2001). *Constructing Gendered Bodies: Explorations in Sociology.* New York: St Martin's Press.
Miller, Jody (2001). *One of the Guys: Girls, Gangs, and Gender.* New York: Routledge.
Myers, Kristen A. et al. (eds.) (1997). *Feminist Foundations: Toward Transforming Sociology.* Thousand Oaks, CA: Sage.
Naffine, Ngaire (1996). *Feminism and Criminology.* Malden, MA: Polity Press.
Oakley, Ann (1974). *The Sociology of Housework.* New York: Pantheon Books.
———. (1981). *Subject Women.* New York: Pantheon Books.
Pearsall, Marilyn (1997). *The Other within Us: Feminist Explorations of Women and Aging.* Boulder, CO: Westview Press.
Peterson, Susan Louise (1998). *The Changing Meaning of Feminism: Life Cycle and Career Implications from a Sociological Perspective.* San Francisco: International Scholars Press.
Presser, Harriet B., and Gita Sen (eds.) (2000). *Women's Empowerment and Demographic Processes: Moving beyond Cairo.* New York: Oxford University Press.
Simonds, Wendy (1996). *Abortion at Work: Ideology and Practice in a Feminist Clinic.* New Brunswick, NJ: Rutgers University Press.
Stanley, Liz (1990). *Feminist Praxis: Research, Theory, and Epistemology in Feminist Sociology.* New York: Routledge.

Waller, Marguerite, and Jennifer Rycenga (eds.) (2000). *Frontline Feminisms: Women, War, and Resistance.* New York: Garland.
Walters, Suzanna Danuta (1995). *Material Girls: Making Sense of Feminist Cultural Theory.* Berkeley: University of California Press.
Weiss, Penny A., and Marilyn Friedman (eds.) (1995). *Feminism and Community.* Philadelphia: Temple University Press.
Wiber, Melanie (1997). *Erect Men/Undulating Women: The Visual Imagery of Gender, Race and Progress in Reconstructive Illustrations of Human Evolution.* Waterloo, Ontario: Wilfrid Laurier University Press.
Wolff, Diane L. (ed.) (1996). *Feminist Dilemmas in Fieldwork.* Boulder, CO: Westview Press.
Zalk, Sue Rosenberg, and Janice Gordon-Kelter (1992). *Revolutions in Knowledge: Feminism in the Social Sciences.* Boulder, CO: Westview Press.

XV. Arts, Architecture, and Aesthetics

Aston, Elaine (1999). *A Handbook of Feminist Theatre Practice.* New York: Routledge.
Battersby, Christine (1989). *Gender and Genius: Towards a Feminist Aesthetics.* Bloomington: Indiana University Press.
Broude, Norma (1991). *Impressionism: A Feminist Reading.* New York: Rizzoli.
_____, and Mary D. Garrard (eds.) (1982). *Feminism and Art History: Questioning the Litany.* New York: Harper and Row.
_____. (eds.) (1992). *The Expanding Discourse: Feminism and Art History.* New York: Icon Editions.
_____. (eds.) (1994). *The Power of Feminist Art: The American Movement of the 1970s, History and Impact.* New York: H. N. Abrams.
Brunsdon, Charlotte (2000). *The Feminist, the Housewife, and the Soap Opera.* New York: Oxford University Press.
Carson, Fiona, and Claire Pajaczkowska (2001). *Feminist Visual Culture.* New York: Routledge.
Case, Sue-Ellen (1988). *Feminism and Theatre.* New York: Routledge.
Cherry, Deborah (2000). *Beyond the Frame: Feminism and Visual Culture.* New York: Routledge.
Coleman, Debra et al. (eds.) (1996). *Architecture and Feminism: Yale Publications on Architecture.* Princeton, NJ: Princeton Architectural Press.
Cook, Susan C., and Judy S. Tsou (eds.) (1994). *Cecilia Reclaimed: Feminist Perspectives on Gender and Music.* Urbana: University of Illinois Press.
Creed, Barbara (1993). *The Monstrous-Feminine: Film, Feminism, Psychoanalysis.* New York: Routledge.
Deepwell, Katy (1999). *New Feminist Art Criticism.* Manchester, UK: Manchester University Press.

Doane, Mary Ann (1991). *Femmes Fatales: Feminism, Film Theory, Psychoanalysis.* New York: Routledge.
⎯⎯⎯⎯, Patricia Mellencamp, and Linda Williams (eds.) (1984). *Re-vision: Essays in Feminist Film Criticism.* Frederick, MD: University Publications of America.
Dolan, Jill (1988). *The Feminist Spectator as Critic.* Ann Arbor, MI: UMI Research Press.
Ecker, Gisela (ed.) (1985). *Feminist Aesthetics.* London: The Women's Press.
Erens, Patricia (ed.) (1990). *Issues in Feminist Film Criticism.* Bloomington: Indiana University Press.
Friedan, Sandra, et al. (1993). *Gender and German Cinema: Feminist Interventions.* New York: St. Martin's Press.
Gentile, Mary C. (1985). *Film Feminisms: Theory and Practice.* Westport, CT: Greenwood.
Goodman, Lizbeth (1993). *Contemporary Feminist Theatres.* New York: Routledge.
⎯⎯⎯⎯. (1996). *Feminist Stages: Interviews with Women in Contemporary British Theatre.* Amsterdam, Netherlands: Harwood Academic Publishers.
Haskell, Molly (1997). *Holding My Own in No Man's Land: Women and Men, Film, and Feminists.* New York: Oxford University Press.
Hayden, Dolores (1982). *The Grand Domestic Revolution: Feminist Designs for American Homes, Neighborhoods and Cities.* Cambridge, MA: MIT Press.
Hein, Hilde, and Carolyn Korsmeyer (eds.) (1993). *Aesthetics in Feminist Perspective.* Bloomington: Indiana University Press.
Humm, Maggie (1997). *Feminism and Film.* Bloomington: Indiana University Press.
Krauss, Rosalind E. (1999). *Bachelors: Essays on Nine Women "Bachelors" who Challenged Masculinist Aesthetics.* Cambridge, MA: MIT Press.
Kuhn, Annette (1993). *Women's Pictures: Feminism and Cinema.* New York: Routledge.
Lane, Christina (2000). *Feminist Hollywood: From Born in Flames to Point Break.* Detroit: Wayne State University Press.
Lippard, Lucy R. (1995). *The Pink Glass Swan: Selected Essays on Feminist Art.* New York: New Press.
MacArthur, Sally (2001). *Feminist Aesthetics in Music.* Westport, CT: Greenwood.
Manning, Susan A. (1993). *Ecstasy and the Demon: Feminism and Nationalism in the Dances of Mary Wigman.* Berkeley: University of California Press.
Martin, Carol (ed.) (1996). *A Sourcebook on Feminist Theatre and Performance: On and beyond the Stage.* New York: Routledge.
Mascia-Lees, Frances E., and Patricia Sharpe (2000). *Taking a Stand in a Postfeminist World: Toward an Engaged Cultural Criticism.* Albany: State University of New York Press.
Mayne, Judith (1990). *The Woman at the Keyhole: Feminism and Women's Cinema.* Bloomington: Indiana University Press.

McCormick, Richard W. (1991). *Politics of the Self: Feminism and the Postmodern in West German Literature and Film*. Princeton, NJ: Princeton University Press.

Mellencamp, Patricia (1990). *Indiscretions: Avant-Garde Film, Video, and Feminism*. Bloomington: Indiana University Press.

———. (1995). *A Fine Romance: Five Ages of Film Feminism*. Philadelphia: Temple University Press.

Moore, Catriona (ed.) (1994). *Dissonance: Feminism and the Arts, 1970-1990*. St. Leonards, NSW: Allen and Unwin.

Neumaier, Diane (ed.) (1995). *Reframings: New American Feminist Photographies*. Philadelphia: Temple University Press.

Paglia, Camille (1990). *Sexual Personae: Art and Decadence from Nefertiti to Emily Dickinson*. New Haven, CT: Yale University Press.

Parker, Rozsika, and Griselda Pollack (eds.) (1987). *Framing Feminism: Art and the Women's Movement, 1970-1985*. New York: Routledge.

Penley, Constance (1989). *The Future of an Illusion: Film, Feminism, and Psychoanalysis*. Minneapolis: University of Minnesota Press.

———. (ed.) (1988). *Feminism and Film Theory*. New York: Routledge.

———, et al. (eds.) (1990). *Close Encounters: Film, Feminism, and Science Fiction*. Minneapolis: University of Minnesota Press.

Phelan, Peggy, and Helena Reckitt (2001). *Art and Feminism*. New York: Phaidon.

Piteropaolo, Laura, and Ada Testaferri (eds.) (1995). *Feminisms in the Cinema*. Bloomington: Indiana University Press.

Pollack, Griselda (1988). *Vision and Difference: Femininity, Feminism, and Histories of Art*. New York: Routledge.

Raven, Ariene (1988). *Crossing Over: Feminism and Art of Social Concern*. Ann Arbor, MI: UMI Research Press.

Rich, B. Ruby (1998). *Chick Flicks: Theories and Memories of the Feminist Film Movement*. Durham, NC: Duke University Press.

Robin, Diana, and Ira Jaffe (eds.) (1999). *Redirecting the Gaze: Gender, Theory and Cinema in the Third World*. Albany: State University of New York Press.

Rosenberg, Jan (1983). *Women's Reflections: The Feminist Film Movement*. Ann Arbor, MI: UMI Research Press.

Rothschild, Joan (ed.) (1999). *Design and Feminism: Re-Visioning Spaces, Places and Everyday Things*. New Brunswick, NJ: Rutgers University Press.

Schor, Mira (1997). *Wet: On Painting, Feminism, and Art Culture*. Durham, NC: Duke University Press.

Slide, Anthony (1996). *The Silent Feminists: America's First Women Directors*. Lanham, MD: Scarecrow.

Thornham, Sue (ed.) (1999). *Feminist Film Theory: A Classical Reader*. New York: New York University Press.

———. (1997). *Passionate Detachments: An Introduction to Feminist Film Theory*. New York: St. Martin's Press.

Topliss, Helen (1996). *Modernism and Feminism: Australian Women Artists, 1900-1940*. Roseville East, NSW: Craftsman House.
Waldman, Diane, and Janet Walker (eds.) (1999). *Feminism and Documentary*. Minneapolis: University of Minnesota Press.
Wolff, Janet (1995). *Resident Alien: Feminist Cultural Criticism*. New Haven, CT: Yale University Press.

XVI. Communication

Ayim, Maryann Neely (1997). *The Moral Parameters of Good Talk: A Feminist Analysis*. Waterloo, Ontario: Wilfrid Laurier University Press.
Blumenthal, Dannielle (1997). *Women and Soap Opera: A Cultural Feminist Perspective*. Westport, CT: Praeger.
Bradley, Patricia (2003). *Mass Media and the Shaping of American Feminism, 1963-1975*. Oxford, MS: University of Mississippi Press.
Brunsdon, Charlotte et al. (eds.) (1997). *Feminist Television Criticism: A Reader*. New York: Oxford University Press.
Cameron, Deborah (1998). *The Feminist Critique of Language: A Reader*, 2nd ed. New York: Routledge.
Campbell, Karlyn Kohrs (1989). *Man Cannot Speak for Her*. New York: Praeger.
Christie, Christine (2001). *Gender and Language: Towards a Feminist Pragmatics*. Edinburgh, Scotland: Edinburgh University Press.
Ferguson, Marjorie (1985). *Forever Feminine: Women's Magazines and the Cult of Femininity*. Brookfield, VT: Gower.
Foss, Karen A. et al. (1999). *Feminist Rhetorical Theories*. Thousand Oaks, CA: Sage.
Gibbon, Margaret (1999). *Feminist Perspectives on Language*. New York: Longman.
Houston, Marsha, and Olga Idriss Davis (2002). *Centering Ourselves: African American Feminist and Womanist Studies of Discourse*. Cresskill, NJ: Hampton Press.
Howell, Sharon (1990). *Reflections of Ourselves: the Mass Media and The Women's Movement, 1963 to the Present*. New York: Lang.
Kramerae, Cheris (1981). *Women and Men Speaking: Frameworks for Analysis*. Rowley, MA: Newbury House.
Lakoff, Robin Tolmach. (1975). *Language and Women's Place*. New York: Harper and Row.
Miller, Casey, and Kate Swift (1977). *Words and Women: New Language in New Times*. Garden City, NY: Doubleday.
_____. (1988). *The Handbook of Nonsexist Writing*, 2nd ed. New York: Harper and Row.
Penfield, Joyce (1987). *Women and Language in Transition*. Albany: State University of New York Press.

Rapping, Elayne (1994). *Mediations: Forays into the Culture and Gender Wars.* Boston: South End Press.
Simpson, Megan (2000). *Poetic Epistemologies: Gender and Knowing in Women's Language Oriented Writing.* New York: State University of New York Press.
Spender, Dale (1980). *Man Made Language.* London: Routledge and Kegan Paul.
Tannen, Deborah. (1994). *Talking from 9 to 5: How Women's and Men's Conversational Styles Affect Who Gets Heard, Who Gets Credit, and What Gets Done at Work.* New York: Morrow Press.
_____. (1990). *You Just Don't Understand: Men and Women in Conversation.* New York: Morrow Press.
Thorne, Barrie, and Nancy Henley (eds.) (1975). *Language and Sex: Difference and Dominance.* Rowley, MA: Newbury House.
Valdivia, Angharad N. (ed.) (1995). *Feminism, Multiculturalism, and the Media: Global Diversities.* Thousand Oaks, CA: Sage.
Van Zoonen, Liesbet (1994). *Feminist Media Studies.* Thousand Oaks, CA: Sage.
Yeo, Eileen James (1998). *Radical Femininity: Women's Self-Representation in the Public Sphere.* Manchester, UK: Manchester University Press.

XVII. Economics/Labor Movement

Albeda, Randy (1997). *Economics and Feminism: Disturbances in the Field.* New York: Twayne.
Balser, Diane (1987). *Sisterhood and Solidarity: Feminism and Labor in Modern Times.* Boston: South End Press.
Blum, Linda (1991). *Between Feminism and Labor: The Significance of the Comparable Worth Movement.* Berkeley: University of California Press.
Briskin, Linda, and Patricia McDermott (eds.) (1993). *Women Challenging Unions: Feminism, Democracy, and Militancy.* Toronto: University of Toronto Press.
Catrerall, Miriam et al. (eds.) (2000). *Marketing Feminism: Current Issues and Research.* New York: Routledge.
Chhachhi, Amrita, and Renee Pittin (eds.) (1996). *Confronting State, Capital, and Patriarchy: Women Organizing in the Process of Industrialization.* New York: St. Martin's Press.
Cuneo, Carl J. (1990). *Pay Equity: The Labour-Feminist Challenge.* New York: Oxford University Press.
Dimand, Mary Ann et al. (eds.) (1996). *Women of Value: Feminist Essays on the History of Economics.* Brookfield, VT: E. Elgar.
Dye, Nancy Shrom (1980). *As Equals and as Sisters: Feminism, the Labor Movement, and the Women's Trade Union League of New York.* Columbia: University of Missouri Press.
Ferber, Marianne, and Julie A. Nelson (eds.) (1993). *Beyond Economic Man: Feminist Theory and Economics.* Chicago: University of Chicago Press.

Fudge, Judy, and Patricia McDermott (eds.) (1991). *Just Wages: A Feminist Assessment of Pay Equity.* Toronto: University of Toronto Press.
Gabin, Nancy F. (1990). *Feminism in the Labor Movement: Women and the United Auto Workers, 1935-1975.* Ithaca, NY: Cornell University Press.
Gibson-Graham, J. K. (1996). *The End of Capitalism (As We Knew It): A Feminist Critique of Political Economy.* Cambridge, MA: Blackwell.
Gilman, Charlotte Perkins (1966). *Women and Economics.* New York: Harper and Row.
_____. (rpt. 1972). *The Home, Its Work and Influence.* Urbana: University of Illinois Press.
Hill, Mary A. (1980). *Charlotte Perkins Gilman: The Making of a Radical Feminist, 1860-1896.* Philadelphia: Temple University Press.
Jordan, Ellen (1999). *The Women's Movement and Women's Employment in Nineteenth Century Britain.* New York: Routledge.
Kuiper, Edith et al. (eds.) (1995). *Out of the Margin: Feminist Economics Today.* New York: Routledge.
Marchand, Marianne H., and Jane Parpart (eds.) (1994). *Feminism/ Postmodernism/ Development.* New York: Routledge.
Nelson, Julie A. (1994). *Feminism, Objectivity, and Economics.* New York: Routledge.
Olson, Paulette, and Zohren Emami (2002). *Engendering Economics: Conversations with Women Economists in the United States.* New York: Routledge.
Pujol, Michele A. (1992). *Feminism and AntiFeminism in Early Economic Thought.* Brookfield, VT: Elgar.
Sperling, Liz, and Mairead Owen (eds.) (2000). *Women and Work: The Age of Post-Feminism?* Burlington, VT: Ashgate.
Still, Judith (1998). *Feminine Economies: Thinking against the Marketplace.* Manchester, UK: Manchester University Press.
Triece, Mary (2001). *Protest and Popular Culture: Women in the US Labor Movement, 1894-1917.* Boulder, CO: Westview Press.
Venkatesh, Allandi (1985). *The Significance of the Women's Movement to Marketing: A Life Style Analysis.* New York: Praeger.
Whittock, Margaret (2000). *Feminising the Masculine?: Women in Non-Traditional Employment.* Burlington, VT: Ashgate.

XVIII. History

Alexander, Sally (1995). *Becoming a Woman: And Other Essays in 19th and 20th Century Feminist History.* New York: New York University Press.
Anderson, Bonnie S., and Judith P. Zinsser (1988). *A History of Their Own: Women in Europe from PreHistory to the Present.* New York: Harper and Row.

Aptheker, Bettina (1982). *Woman's Legacy: Essays on Race, Sex, and Class in American History*. Amherst: University of Massachusetts Press.
Banaszak, Lee Ann (1996). *Why Movements Succeed or Fail: Opportunity, Culture, and the Struggle for Woman Suffrage*. Princeton, NJ: Princeton University Press.
Bauer, Carol, and Lawrence Ritt (1979). *Free and Ennobled: Source Readings in the Development of Victorian Feminism*. New York: Pergamon Press.
Blair, Karen J. (1980). *The Clubwoman as Feminist: True Womanhood Redefined, 1868-1914*. New York: Holmes and Meier.
Blocker, Jack S. Jr. (1984). *Give to the Winds Thy Fears: Women's Temperance Crusade, 1873-1874*. Westport, CT: Greenwood.
Bolt, Christine (1995). *Feminist Ferment: "The Woman Question" in the USA and Britain*. London: UCL Press.
Bordin, Ruth (1981). *Woman and Temperance: The Quest for Power and Liberty, 1873-1900*. Philadelphia: Temple University Press.
Chesler, Phyllis et al. (eds.) (1995). *Feminist Foremothers in Women's Studies, Psychology, and Mental Health*. New York: Haworth.
Clark, Elizabeth A. (1971). *Religion, Rights and Difference: The Origins of American Feminism, 1848-1860*. Madison, WI: Institute for Legal Studies.
Cott, Nancy F. (1987). *The Grounding of Modern Feminism*. New Haven, CT: Yale University Press.
Dinkin, Robert J. (1995). *Before Equal Suffrage: Women in Partisan Politics from Colonial Times to 1920*. Westport, CT: Greenwood.
Domosh, Mona, and Joni Seager (2001). *Putting Women in Place: Feminist Geographers Make Sense of the World*. New York: Guilford Press.
Douglas, R. M. (1998). *Feminist Freikorps: The British Voluntary Women Polics, 1914-1940*. Westport, CT: Praeger.
DuBois, Ellen Carol (1981). *Elizabeth Cady Stanton, Susan B. Anthony: Correspondence, Writings, Speeches*. New York: Schocken Books.
_____. (ed.) (1998). *Woman Suffrage and Women's Rights*. New York: New York University Press.
Early, Frances H. (1997). *A World without War: How US Feminists and Pacifists Resisted World War I*. Syracuse: Syracuse University Press.
Epstein, Barbara Leslie (1981). *The Politics of Domesticity: Women, Evangelism and Temperance in Nineteenth-Century America*. Middletown, CT: Wesleyan University Press.
Eustance, Claire et al. (eds.) (2000). *A Suffrage Reader: Charting Directions in British Suffrage History*. Leicester: Leicester University Press.
Fletcher, Sheila (1980). *Feminists and Bureaucrats: A Study in the Development of Girls' Education in the Nineteenth Century*. New York: Cambridge University Press.
Freedman, Estelle B. (2002). *No Turning Back: The History of Feminism and the Future of Women*. New York: Ballantine.

Freudi, Ann, and Michael Hume (eds.) (1997). *Abortion Law and Reformers: Pioneers of Change.* London: Birth Control Trust.
Giele, Janet Zollinger (1995). *Two Paths to Women's Equality: Temperance, Suffrage, and the Origins of Modern Feminism.* New York: Twayne.
Graham, Sarah Hunter (1996). *Women Suffrage and the New Democracy.* New Haven, CT: Yale University Press.
Grimké, Sarah (1970). *Letters on the Equality of the Sexes and the Condition of Woman.* New York: Franklin.
Groenwegen, Peter (ed.) (1994). *Feminism and Political Economy in Victorian England.* Brookfield, VT: E. Elgar.
Heeney, Brian (1988). *The Women's Movement in the Church of England, 1850-1930.* New York: Clarendon Press.
Herstein, Sheila R. (1985). *A Mid-Victorian Feminist: Barbara Leigh Smith Bodichon.* New Haven, CT: Yale University Press.
Hoffert, Sylvia D. (1995). *When Hens Crow: The Women's Rights Movements in Antebellum America.* Bloomington: Indiana University Press.
Holton, Sandra Stanley (1996). *Suffrage Days: Stories from the Women's Suffrage Movement.* New York: Routledge.
Howard, Angela, and Sasha Ranae Adams Tarrant (eds.) (1998). *Reaction to the Modern Women's Movement, 1963 to the Present.* New York: Garland.
_____. (eds.) (1998). *Redefining the New Woman, 1920-1963.* New York: Garland.
Hu, Ying (2000). *Tales of Translation: Composing the New Woman in China, 1899-1918.* Stanford, CA: Stanford University Press.
Hunt, Karen (1996). *Equivocal Feminists: The Social Democratic Federation and the Woman Question, 1884-1911.* New York: Cambridge University Press.
Jordan, Ellen (1999). *The Women's Movement and Women's Employment in Nineteenth Century Britain.* New York: Routledge.
Keetley, Dawn, and Joh Pettigrew (eds.) (1997). *A Documentary History of American Feminism, Volume I: Beginnings to 1900.* Lanham, MD: Rowman and Littlefield.
Kerber, Linda K. et al. (eds.) (1995) *US History as Women's History: New Feminist Essays.* Chapel Hill: University of North Carolina Press.
Kraditor, Aileen S. (1968). *Up from the Pedestal: Selected Writings in the History of American Feminism.* Chicago: Quadrangle Books.
Leach, William (1980). *True Love and Perfect Union: The Feminist Reform of Sex and Society.* New York: Basic Books.
LeGates, Marlene (2001). *In Their Time: A History of Feminism in Western Society.* New York: Routledge.
Lerner, Gerda (1979). *The Majority Finds Its Past: Placing Women in History.* New York: Oxford University Press.
_____. (1986). *The Creation of Patriarchy.* New York: Oxford University Press.

_____. (1993). *The Creation of Feminist Consciousness: From the Middle Ages to Eighteen-Seventy.* New York: Oxford University Press.

_____. (1997). *The Grimke Sisters from South Carolina: Pioneers for Women's Rights and Abolition.* New York: Oxford University Press.

_____. (1998). *The Feminist Thought of Sarah Grimke.* New York: Oxford University Press.

Levine, Philippa (1994). *Victorian Feminism, 1850-1900.* Tallahassee: University Press of Florida.

Long, Jane et al. (eds.) (1997). *Forging Identities: Bodies, Gender, and Feminist History.* Nelands, Western Australia: University of Western Australia Press.

Lumsden, Linda J. (1997). *Rampant Women: Suffragists and the Right of Assembly.* Knoxville: University of Tennessee Press.

Magarey, Susan (2002). *Passions of the First Wave Feminists.* Sydney, Australia: New South Wales University Press.

Marilley, Suzanne M. (1996). *Woman Suffrage and the Origins of Liberal Feminism in the United States, 1820-1920.* Cambridge, MA: Harvard University Press.

Martin, Wendy (1972). *The American Sisterhood: Writings of the Feminist Movement from Colonial Times to the Present.* New York: Harper and Row.

Martineau, Harriet, and Gayle G. Yates (1985). *Harriet Martineau on Women.* New Brunswick, NJ: Rutgers University Press.

McFadden, Margaret H. (1999). *Golden Cables of Sympathy: The Transatlantic Sources of Nineteenth Century Feminism.* Lexington: University Press of Kentucky.

Moses, Claire Goldberg, and Heide Hartmann (eds.) (1995). *US Women in Struggle: A Feminist Studies Anthology.* Urbana: University of Illinois Press.

Norquay, Glenda (ed.) (1995). *Voices and Votes: A Literary Anthology of the Women's Suffrage Campaign.* Manchester, UK: Manchester University Press.

Papachristou, Judith (1976). *Women Together: A History in Documents of the Women's Movement in the United States.* New York: Knopf.

Paulson, Ross E. (1997). *Liberty, Equality, and Justice: Civil Rights, Women's Rights, and the Regulation of Business, 1865-1932.* Durham, NC: Duke University Press.

Roberts, Marie Mulvey, and Tamae Miztua (eds.) (1995). *Controversies in the History of British Feminism.* New York: Routledge.

Rodnitzky, Jerome L. (1999). *Feminist Phoenix: the Rise and Fall of a Feminist Counterculture.* Westport, CT: Praeger.

Romero, Patricia W. (1987). *Sylvia Pankhurst: Portrait of a Radical.* New Haven, CT: Yale University Press.

Rosenberg, Rosalind (1982). *Beyond Separate Spheres: Intellectual Roots of Modern Feminism.* New Haven, CT: Yale University Press.

Rossi, Alice (ed.) (1973). *The Feminist Papers: From Adams to de Beauvoir.* New York: Columbia University Press.

Scharf, Lois (1980). *To Work and to Wed: Female Employment, Feminism, and the Great Depression.* Westport, CT: Greenwood.
Schneir, Miriam (1972). *Feminism: The Essential Historical Writings.* New York: Random House.
_____. (ed.) (1994). *Feminism in Our Time: The Essential Historical Writings, World War II to the Present.* New York: Vintage Books.
Scott, Joan Wallach (1988). *Gender and the Politics of History.* New York: Columbia University Press.
_____. (1996). *Only Paradoxes to Offer: French Feminists and the Rights of Man.* Cambridge, MA: Harvard University Press.
Showalter, Elaine (2001). *Inventing Herself: Claiming a Feminist Intellectual Heritage.* New York: Scribner.
Smith, Paul (1996). *Feminism and the Third Republic: Women's Political and Civil Rights in France.* New York: Oxford University Press.
Stafford, William (2002). *English Feminists and Their Opponents in the 1790s: Unsex'd and Proper Females.* Manchester, UK: Manchester University Press.
Sterba, James P. (1998). *Social and Political Philosophy: Classical Western Texts in Feminist and Multicultural Perspectives.* Belmont, CA: Wadsworth.
Ware, Susan (1981). *Beyond Suffrage: Women in the New Deal.* Cambridge, MA: Harvard University Press.
_____. (1987). *Partner and I: Molly Dewson, Feminism, and New Deal Politics.* New Haven, CT: Yale University Press.
Weatherford, Doris (1998). *A History of the American Suffragist Movement.* Santa Barbara, CA: ABC-CLIO.
Weigand, Kate (2001). *Red Feminism: American Communism and the Making of Women's Liberation.* Baltimore: Johns Hopkins University Press.
Wheeler, Marjorie Spruill (ed.) (1996). *One Woman One Vote: Rediscovering the Woman Suffrage Movement.* Troutdale, OR: New Sage Press.
Yellin, Carol Lynn, Janann Sherman, and Ilene Jones-Cornwell (1998). *The Perfect 36: Tennessee Delivers Woman Suffrage.* Oak Ridge, TN: Iris Press.

XIX. Law/Feminist Jurisprudence

Agnes, Flavia (1999). *Law and Gender Inequality: The Politics of Women's Rights in India.* New York: Oxford University Press.
Askin, Kelly Dawn (1997). *War Crimes against Women: Prosecution in International War Crimes Tribunals.* Cambridge, MA: Kluwer Law International.
Baer, Judith A. (1999). *Our Lives before the Law: Constructing a Feminist Jurisprudence.* Princeton, NJ: Princeton University Press.
Bartlett, Katharine T., and Rosanne Kennedy (eds.) (1991). *Feminist Legal Theory: Readings in Law and Gender.* Boulder, CO: Westview Press.
Beveridge, Fiona et al. (eds.) (2000). *Making Women Count: Integrating Gender into Law and Policy-Making.* Burlington, VT: Ashgate.

Bottomley, Anne, and Joanne Conaghan (eds.) (1993). *Feminist Theory and Legal Strategy*. Cambridge, MA: Blackwell.
_____. (ed.) (1996). *Feminist Perspectives on the Foundational Subjects of Law*. London: Cavendish.
Boyd, Susan B. (ed.) (1997). *Challenging the Public/Private Divide: Feminism, Law, and Public Policy*. Toronto: University of Toronto Press.
Bridgeman, Jo. (1998). *Feminist Perspectives on Law: Law's Engagement with the Female Body*. London: Sweet and Maxwell.
Chamallas, Martha (1998). *Introduction to Feminist Legal Theory*. Gaithersburg, MD: Aspen Law and Business.
Charlesworth, Hilary, and Christine Chinkin (2000). *The Boundaries of International Law: A Feminist Analysis*. Manchester, UK: Manchester University Press.
Cossman, Brenda et al. (1996). *Bad Attitudes on Trial: Pornography, Feminism, and the Butler Decision*. Toronto: University of Toronto Press.
Cushman, Clare (ed.) (2001). *Supreme Court Decisions and Women's Rights: Milestones to Equality*. Washington, DC: CQ Press.
Dahl, Tove Stang (1988). *Women's Law: An Introduction to Feminist Jurisprudence*. New York: Oxford University Press.
Dobrowolsky, Alexandra Z. (2000). *The Politics of Pragmatism: Women, Representation, and Constitutionalism in Canada*. New York: Oxford University Press.
Dowd, Nancy E. (ed.) (2003). *Feminist Legal Theory: An AntiEssentialist Reader*. New York: New York University Press.
Fineman, Martha Albertson, and Mary Sweet Thomadsen (eds.) (1991). *At the Boundaries of Law: Feminism and Legal Theory*. New York: Routledge.
_____, and Isabelle Karpin (eds.) (1995). *Mothers in Law: Feminist Theory and the Legal Regulation of Motherhood*. New York: Columbia University Press.
_____, and Martha T. McCluskey (eds.) (1997). *Feminism, Media, and the Law*. New York: Oxford University Press.
Francis, Leslie (ed.) (1996). *Date Rape: Feminism, Philosophy, and the Law*. University Park, PA: Penn State Press.
Frost-Knappman, Elizabeth, and Kathryn Cullen-DuPont (1996). *Women's Rights on Trial: 101 Historic American Trials from Anne Hutchinson to Roe V. Wade to Virginia Military Institute*. Detroit: Gale.
Frug, Mary Joe (1992). *Postmodern Legal Feminism*. New York: Routledge.
Goldstein, Leslie Friedman (1992). *Feminist Jurisprudence: The Difference Debate*. Lanham, MD: Rowman and Littlefield.
Hoff, Joan (1992). *Law, Gender, and Injustice: A Legal History of US Women*. New York: New York University Press.
Hull, N. E. H., and Peter Charles Hoffer (2001). *Roe V. Wade: The Abortion Rights Controversy in American History*. Lawrence: University Press of Kansas.

Jamieson, Beth Kiyoko (2001). *Real Choices: Feminism, Freedom, and the Limits of Law.* University Park, PA: Penn State Press.
Kapur, Ratna, and Brenda Cossman (1996). *Subversive Sites: Feminist Engagements with Law in India.* Thousand Oaks, CA: Sage.
Kingdom, Elizabeth (1990). *What's Wrong with Rights?: Problems for Feminist Politics of Law.* Edinburgh, Scotland: Edinburgh University Press.
Lee, Ellie (1998). *Abortion Law and Politics Today.* New York: St. Martin's.
Levit, Nancy (1998). *The Gender Line: Men, Women, and the Law.* New York: New York University Press.
MacKinnon, Catharine A. (1987). *Feminism Unmodified: Discourses of Life and Law.* Cambridge, MA: Harvard University Press.
Maschke, Karen J. (ed.) (1997). *Feminist Legal Theories.* New York: Garland.
McColgan, Aileen (2000). *Women under the Law: The False Promise of Human Rights.* Harlow, UK: Longman.
McGlynn, Clare (ed.) (1998). *Legal Feminisms: Theory and Practice.* Brookfield, VT: Ashgate.
Miller, Susan L. (ed.) (1998). *Crime Control and Women: Feminist Implications of Criminal Justice Policy.* Thousand Oaks, CA: Sage.
Minow, Martha (1990). *Making All the Difference: Inclusion, Exclusion, and American Law.* Ithaca, NY: Cornell University Press.
Morris, Anne, and Susan Nott (1995). *All My Worldly Goods: A Feminist Perspective on the Legal Regulation of Wealth.* Brookfield, VT: Dartmouth.
Naffine, Ngaire (1990). *Law and the Sexes: Explorations in Feminist Jurisprudence.* Boston: Allen and Unwin.
_____, and Rosemary J. Owens (eds.) (1997). *Sexing the Subject of Law.* Sydney, Australia: Sweet and Maxwell.
Nelson, Robert L., and William P. Bridges (1999). *Legalizing Gender Inequality: Courts, Markets, and Unequal Pay for Women in the United States.* New York: Cambridge University Press.
O'Donnell, Anne Morris Therese (1999). *Feminist Perspectives on Employment Law.* London: Cavendish.
Olsen, Frances E. (ed.) (1995). *Feminist Legal Theory Volume I: Foundations and Outlooks.* New York: New York University Press.
Olsen, Frances E. (ed.) (1995). *Feminist Legal Theory Volume II: Positioning Feminist Theory within the Law.* New York: New York University Press.
Packer, Corrine A. A. (1996). *The Right to Reproductive Choice: A Study in International Law.* Abo, Finland: Abo Akademi University.
Rhode, Deborah L. (1989). *Justice and Gender: Sex Discrimination and the Law.* Cambridge, MA: Harvard University Press.
Richards, David A. J. (1998). *Women, Gays, and the Constitution: The Grounds for Feminism and Gay Rights in Culture and Law.* Chicago: University of Chicago Press.
Saguy, Abigail C. (2003). *What Is Sexual Harassment?: From Capitol Hill to the Sorbonne.* Berkeley: University of California Press.

Samuels, Suzanne Uttaro (1995). *Fetal Rights, Women's Rights: Gender Equality in the Workplace.* Madison: University of Wisconsin Press.
Schneider, Elizabeth M. (2000). *Battered Women and Feminist Lawmaking.* New Haven, CT: Yale University Press.
Seymour, John (2000). *Childbirth and the Law.* New York: Oxford University Press.
Simon, Rita James (1998). *Abortion: Statutes, Policies, and Public Attitudes the World Over.* Westport, CT: Praeger.
Smart, Carol (1989). *Feminism and the Power of Law.* New York: Routledge.
Smith, Patricia (ed.) (1993). *Feminist Jurisprudence.* New York: Oxford University Press.
Stetson, Dorothy M. (1997). *Women's Rights in the USA: Policy Debates and Gender Roles.* New York: Garland.
Thornton, Margaret (ed.) (1995). *Public and Private: Feminist Legal Debates.* New York: Oxford University Press.
Toubia, Nahid (2000). *Female Genital Mutilation: A Human Rights Analysis: A Practical Guide to Worldwide Laws and Practices.* New York: Zed Books.
Traina, Christina L. H. (1999). *Feminist Ethics and Natural Law: The End of the Anathemas.* Washington, DC: Georgetown University Press.
Weisberg, D. Kelly (ed.) (1996). *Applications of Feminist Legal Theory to Women's Lives: Sex, Violence, Work, and Reproduction.* Philadelphia: Temple University Press.
_____. (ed.) (1993). *Feminist Legal Theory: Foundations.* Philadelphia: Temple University Press.

XX. Literature

Alberghene, Janice M. et al. (eds.) (1998). *Little Women and the Feminist Imagination: Criticism, Controversy, Personal Essays.* New York: Garland.
Allan, Tuzyline Jita (1995). *Womanist and Feminist Aesthetics: A Comparative Review.* Athens: Ohio University Press.
Ardis, Ann L. (1990). *New Women, New Novels: Feminism and Early Modernism.* New Brunswick, NJ: Rutgers University Press.
Atkinson, Clarissa W. (1983). *Mystic and Pilgrim: The Book and the World of Margery Kempe.* Ithaca, NY: Cornell University Press.
Barr, Marleen S. (1987). *Alien to Femininity: Speculative Fiction and Feminist Theory.* Westport, CT: Greenwood.
_____. (1992). *Feminist Fabulation: Space/Postmodern Fiction.* Iowa City: University of Iowa Press.
Basham, Diana (1992). *The Trial of Woman: Feminism and the Occult Sciences in Victorian Literature and Society.* New York: New York University Press.
Benstock, Shari, Suzanne Ferriss, and Susanne Woods (2002). *A Handbook of Literary Feminisms.* New York: Oxford University Press.

Berkman, Joyce Avrech (1979). *Olive Schreiner: Feminism on the Frontier*. St. Albans, VT: Eden Press Women's Publications.
Bloomberg, Kristin M. Mapel (2001). *Tracing Arachne's Web: Myth and Feminist Fiction*. Gainesville: University Press of Florida.
Bowlby, Rachel (1997). *Feminist Destinations and Further Essays on Virginia Woolf*. Edinburgh, Scotland: Edinburgh University Press.
Bristow, Joseph, and Trev Lynn Broughton (eds.) (1997). *The Infernal Desires of Angela Carter: Fiction, Femininity, Feminism*. London: Longman.
Brown, Janet (1979). *Feminist Drama: Definition and Critical Analysis*. Metuchen, NJ: Scarecrow Press.
Brown, Nathaniel (1979). *Sexuality and Feminism in Shelley*. Cambridge, MA: Harvard University Press.
Browne, Alice (1987). *The Eighteenth Century Feminist Mind*. Detroit: Wayne State University Press.
Burke, Sally (1996). *American Feminist Playwrights: A Critical History*. New York: Twayne.
Burwell, Jennifer (1997). *Notes on Nowhere: Feminism, Utopian Logic, and Social Transformation*. Minneapolis: University of Minnesota Press.
Chedgzoy, Kate (2001). *Shakespeare, Feminism and Gender*. New York: Palgrave.
Clark, Veve A., et al. (1993). *Revising the Word and the World: Essays in Feminist Literary Criticism*. Chicago: University of Chicago Press.
Cocalis, Susan L. (1986). *German Feminist Poems from the Middle Ages to the Present: A Bilingual Anthology*. Old Westbury, NY: Feminist Press at the City University of New York.
Conboy, Katie et al. (eds.) (1997). *Writing on the Body: Female Embodiment and Feminist Theory*. New York: Columbia University Press.
Cooke, Miriam (2000). *Women Claim Islam: Creating Islamic Feminism through Literature*. New York: Routledge.
Cosslett, Tess et al. (eds.) (2000). *Feminism and Autobiography: Texts, Theories, Methods*. New York: Routledge.
Cunningham, Gail (1978). *The New Woman and the Victorian Novel*. New York: Barnes and Noble.
Diamond, Elin (1997). *Unmaking Mimesis: Essays on Feminism and Theater*. New York: Routledge.
Donovan, Josephine (1999). *Women and the Rise of the Novel, 1405-1726*. New York: St. Martin's Press.
Donovan, Kathleen M. (1998). *Feminist Readings of Native American Literature: Coming to Voice*. Tucson: University of Arizona Press.
Fay, Elizabeth A. (1998). *A Feminist Introduction to Romanticism*. Oxford: Blackwell.
Felski, Rita (1989). *Beyond Feminist Aesthetics: Feminist Literature and Social Changes*. Cambridge, MA: Harvard University Press.
Ferguson, Margaret, and Jennifer Wicke (1994). *Feminism and Postmodernism*. Durham, NC: Duke University Press.

Ferguson, Moira (1985). *First Feminists: British Women Writers, 1578-1799*. Bloomington: Indiana University Press.
Fernando, Lloyd (1977). *"New Women" in the Late Victorian Novel*. University Park, PA: Penn State Press.
Fleischman, Fritz (1982). *American Novelists Revisited: Essays in Feminist Criticism*. Boston: G. K. Hall.
Foster, Shirley, and Judy Simons (1995). *What Katy Read: Feminist Re-Reading of "Classic" Stories for Girls*. London: MacMillan.
Fuller, Margaret (rpt. 1971). *Woman in the Nineteenth Century*. New York: Norton.
Ghosh, Bishnupriya, and Brinda Bose (eds.) (1997). *Interventions: Feminist Dialogues on Third World Women's Literature and Film*. New York: Garland.
Glenn, Susan A. (2000). *Female Spectacle: The Theatrical Roots of Modern Feminism*. Cambridge, MA: Harvard University Press.
Hall, Donald (1996). *Fixing Patriarchy: Feminism and Mid-Victorian Male Novelists*. New York: New York University Press.
Harman, Barbara, and Susan Meyer (eds.) (1999). *The New Nineteenth Century: Feminist Readings of Underread Victorian Fiction*. New York: Garland.
Higonnet, Margaret R., and Joan Templeton (eds.) (1995). *Reconfigured Spheres: Feminist Explorations of Literary Space*. Amherst: University of Massachusetts Press.
Hirsch, Marianne (1989). *The Mother/Daughter Plot: Narrative, Psychoanalysis, Feminism*. Bloomington: Indiana University Press.
Hoeveler, Diane Long (1998). *Gothic Feminism: The Professionalization of Gender from Charlotte Smith to the Brontës*. University Park, PA: Penn State Press.
_____. (1990). *Romantic Androgyny: The Women Within*. University Park, PA: Penn State Press.
Hogeland, Lisa Maria (1998). *Feminism and Its Fictions: The Consciousness-Raising Novel and the Women's Liberation Movement*. Philadelphia: University of Pennsylvania Press.
Hohne, Karen, and Helen Wussow (eds.) (1994). *A Dialogue of Voices: Feminist Literary Theory and Bakhtin*. Minneapolis: University of Minnesota Press.
Howard, Jean E., and Phyllis Rackin (1997). *Engendering a Nation: A Feminist Account of Shakespeare's English Histories*. New York: Routledge.
Howells, Carol Ann, and Lynette Hunter (1991). *Narrative Strategies in Canadian Literature: Feminism and Postcolonialism*. Philadelphia: Open University Press.
Humm, Maggie (1995). *Practising Feminist Criticism: An Introduction*. Hempstead, UK: Harvester Wheatsheaf.
Innes, Catherine Lynette (1993). *Woman and Nation in Irish Literature and Society, 1880-1935*. Athens: University of Georgia Press.
Irons, Glenwood (ed.) (1995). *Feminism in Women's Detective Fiction*. Toronto: University of Toronto Press.

Joannou, Maroula (1995). *Ladies, Please Don't Smash These Windows: Women's Writing, Feminist Consciousness, and Social Change, 1918-1938*. Providence, RI: Berg.

Johnson, Barbara (1998). *The Feminist Difference: Literature, Psychoanalysis, Race, and Gender*. Cambridge, MA: Harvard University Press.

Johnston, Judith (1997). *Anna Jameson: Victorian Feminist, Woman of Letters*. Brookfield, VT: Ashgate.

Jones, Anny Brooksband, and Catherine Davies (eds.) (1996). *Latin American Women's Writing: Feminist Readings in Theory and Crisis*. New York: Oxford University Press.

Jones, Libby Falk, and Sarah Webster Goodwin (1990). *Feminism, Utopia, and Narrative*. Knoxville: University of Tennessee Press.

Jordan, Constance (1990). *Renaissance Feminism: Literary Texts and Political Models*. Ithaca, NY: Cornell University Press.

Kaplan, Carla (1996). *The Erotics of Talk: Women's Writing and Feminist Paradigms*. New York: Oxford University Press.

Kitch, Sally (2000). *Higher Ground: From Utopianism to Realism in American Feminist Thought and Theory*. Chicago: University of Chicago Press.

Krishnaswamy, Revathi (1998). *Effeminism: The Economy of Colonial Desire*. Ann Arbor: University of Michigan Press.

Lambert, Ellen Zetzel (1995). *The Face of Love: Feminism and the Beauty Question*. Boston: Beacon Press.

Lara, Maria Pia (1998). *Moral Textures: Feminist Narratives in the Public Sphere*. Berkeley: University of California Press.

Lefanu, Sarah (1988). *Feminism and Science Fiction*. Bloomington: Indiana University Press.

―――. (1988). *In the Chinks of the World Machine: Feminism and Science Fiction*. London: Women's Press.

Little, Judy (1983). *Comedy and the Woman Writer: Woolf, Spark, and Feminism*. Lincoln: University of Nebraska Press.

Markey, Janice (1985). *A New Tradition?: The Poetry of Sylvia Plath, Anne Sexton, and Adrienne Rich, a Study of Feminism and Poetry*. New York: Lang.

Meese, Elizabeth (1986). *Crossing the Double-Cross: The Practice of Feminist Criticism*. Chapel Hill: University of North Carolina Press.

Meijer, Maaike (ed.) (1998). *The Defiant Muse: Dutch and Flemish Feminist Poetry from the Middle Ages to the Present: A Bilingual Anthology*. Old Westbury, NY: Feminist Press.

Mezei, Kathy (ed.) (1996). *Ambiguous Discourse: Feminist Narratology and British Women Writers*. Chapel Hill: University of North Carolina Press.

Miller, Jane Eldridge (1997). *Rebel Women: Feminism, Modernism, and the Edwardian Novel*. Chicago: University of Chicago Press.

Mills, Sara (1995). *Feminist Stylistics*. New York: Routledge.

Moi, Toril (1985). *Sexual/Textual Politics: Feminist Literary Theory*. New York: Methuen.

Novotny, Marianne (ed.) (1999). *Transforming Shakespeare: Contemporary Women's Re-Visions in Literature and Performance.* New York: St. Martin's Press.
Pearce, Lynne (1997). *Feminism and the Politics of Reading.* New York: St. Martin's Press.
Perreault, Jeanne (1995). *Writing Selves: Contemporary Feminist Autobiography.* Minneapolis: University of Minnesota Press.
Perry, Ruth (1986). *The Celebrated Mary Astell: An Early English Feminist.* Chicago: University of Chicago Press.
Quinsey, Katherine M. (ed.) (1996). *Broken Boundaries: Women and Feminism in Restoration Drama,.* Lexington: University of Kentucky Press.
Reddy, Maureen T. (1988). *Sisters in Crime: Feminism and the Crime Novel.* New York: Continuum.
Rich, Adrienne (1980). *On Lies, Secrets and Silence: Selected Prose, 1966-1978.* London: Virago.
Richards, Constance S. (2000). *On the Winds and Waves of Imagination: Transnational Feminism and Literature.* New York: Garland.
Richards, Earl Jeffrey, et al. (1992). *Reinterpreting Christine De Pizan.* Athens: University of Georgia Press.
Robbins, Ruth (2000). *Literary Feminisms.* New York: St. Martin's Press.
Roller, Judi M. (1986). *The Politics of the Feminist Novel.* Westport, CT: Greenwood.
Rosinsky, Natalie M. (1984). *Feminist Futures—Contemporary Women's Speculative Fiction.* Ann Arbor, MI: UMI Research Press.
Russ, Joanna (1995). *To Write Like a Woman: Essays in Feminism and Science Fiction.* Bloomington: Indiana University Press.
Salmonson, Jessica Amanda (1989). *What Did Miss Darrington See?: An Anthology of Feminist Supernatural Fiction.* Old Westbury, NY: Feminist Press.
Salvaggio, Ruth (1999). *The Sounds of Feminist Theory.* Albany: State University of New York Press.
Schroeder, Patricia R. (1996). *The Feminist Possibilities of Dramatic Realism.* Madison, NJ: Farleigh Dickinson University Press.
Showalter, Elaine (1971). *Women's Liberation and Literature.* New York: Harcourt.
Stanton, Domna C. (1986). *French Feminist Poems from the Middle Ages to the Present: A Bilingual Anthology.* Old Westbury, NY: Feminist Press.
Threadgold, Terry (1997). *Feminist Poetics: Poiesis, Performance, Histories.* New York: Routledge.
Traub, Valerie et al. (eds.) (1996). *Feminist Readings of Early Modern Culture: Emerging Subjects.* New York: Cambridge University Press.
Trites, Roberta Seelinger (1997). *Waking Sleeping Beauty: The Feminist Voices in Children's Novels.* Iowa City: University of Iowa Press.
Vollendorf, Lisa (ed.) (2001). *Recovering Spain's Feminist Tradition.* New York: Modern Language Association of America.

Wagner, Geoffrey Atheling (1972). *Five for Freedom: A Study of Feminism in Fiction.* London: Allen and Unwin.
Warhol, Robyn R., and Diane Price Herndl (eds.) (1997). *Feminisms: An Anthology of Literary Theory and Criticism.* New Brunswick, NJ: Rutgers University Press.
Wilson, Anna (2001). *Persuasive Fictions: Feminist Narrative and Critical Myth.* Lewisburg, PA: Bucknell University Press.
Woolf, Virginia (1929). *A Room of One's Own.* London: The Women's Press.
_____. (1938). *Three Guineas.* London: The Women's Press.
_____. (rpt. 1979). *Women and Writing.* London: The Women's Press.
Yegenoglu, Meyda (1998). *Colonial Fantasies: Towards a Feminist Reading of Orientalism.* New York: Cambridge University Press.
Zehava, Irene, (ed.) (1996). *Feminism 3: The Third Generation in Fiction.* Boulder, CO: Westview Press.

XXI. Mythology

Bachofen, Jacob J. (rpt. 1967). *Myth, Religion, and Mother Right.* Princeton, NJ: Princeton University Press.
Berger, Pamela (1985). *The Goddess Obscured: Transformation of the Grain Protectress from Goddess to Saint.* Boston: Beacon Press.
Bolen, Jean Shinoda (1984). *Goddesses in Every Woman.* San Francisco: Harper and Row.
Dexter, Mirian Robbins (1990). *Whence the Goddess: A Sourcebook.* Elmsford, NY: Pergamon.
Gadon, Elinor W. (1989). *The Once and Future Goddess: A Sweeping Visual Chronicle of the Sacred Female and Her Reemergence in the Cultural Mythology of Our Time.* San Francisco: Harper and Row.
Gimbutas, Marija (1982). *The Goddesses and Gods of Old Europe: 6500-3500 BC.* Berkeley: University of California Press.
Goodison, Lucy, and Christine Morris (eds.) (1999). *Ancient Goddesses: The Myths and the Evidence.* Madison: University of Wisconsin Press.
Goodrich, Norma Lorre (1989). *Priestesses.* New York: Harper Collins.
Johnson, Buffie (1988). *Lady of the Beasts: Ancient Images of the Goddess and Her Sacred Animals.* San Francisco: Harper and Row.
Kinsley, David (1989). *The Goddess' Mirror: Visions of the Divine from East and West.* Albany: State University of New York Press.
Larrington, Carolyne (ed.) (1992). *The Feminist Companion to Mythology.* London: Pandora Press.
Lefkowitz, Mary R. (1986). *Women in Greek Myth.* Baltimore: Johns Hopkins University Press.
Orenstein, Gloria (1990). *The Reflowering of the Goddess.* Elmsford, NY: Pergamon.

Pomeroy, Sarah B. (1975). *Goddesses, Whores, Wives, and Slaves: Women in Classical Antiquity.* New York: Schocken Books.
_____. (1984). *Women in Hellenistic Egypt: From Alexander to Cleopatra.* New York: Schocken Books.
Slater, P. E. (1968). *The Glory of Hera: Greek Mythology and the Greek Family.* Boston: Beacon.
Woolger, Jennifer Barker, and Roger J. Woolger (1989). *The Goddess Within: A Guide to the Eternal Myths That Shape Women's Lives.* New York: Fawcett.

XXII. Pedagogy and Research

Anderson, Mary et al. (eds.) (1997). *Doing Feminism: Teaching and Research in the Academy.* East Lansing: Michigan State University Press.
Arnot, Madeleine (2002). *Reproducing Gender?: Essays on Educational Theory and Feminist Politics.* New York: Routledge.
Barton, Angela Calabrese (1998). *Feminist Science Education.* New York: Teachers College Press.
Bloom, Leslie Rebecca (1998). *Under the Sign of Hope: Feminist Methodology and Narrative Interpretation.* Albany: State University of New York Press.
Brock-Utne, Brigit (1985). *Educating for Peace: A Feminist Perspective.* New York: Pergamon.
Campbell, JoAnn (ed.) (1996). *Toward a Feminist Rhetoric: The Writing of Gertrude Buck.* Pittsburgh: University of Pittsburgh Press.
Clark, Veve et al. (eds.) (1995). *Antifeminism in the Academy.* New York: Routledge.
Coffey, Amanda, and Sara Delamont (eds.) (2000). *Feminism and the Classroom Teacher: Research, Praxis, and Pedagogy.* New York: Routledge.
Cohee, Gail E. et al. (eds.) (1998). *The Feminist Teacher Anthology: Pedagogies and Classroom Strategies.* New York: Teachers College Press.
Felman, Jyl Lynn (2001). *Never a Dull Moment: Teaching, and the Art of Performance: Feminism Takes Center Stage.* New York: Routledge.
Fischer, Berenice M. (2001). *No Angel in the Classroom: Teaching through Feminist Discourse.* Lanham, MD: Rowman and Littlefield.
Giroux, Henry A. (ed.) (1991). *Postmodernism, Feminism and Cultural Politics: Redrawing Educational Boundaries.* Albany: State University of New York Press.
Goldstein, Lisa (1997). *Teaching with Love: A Feminist Approach to Early Childhood Education.* New York: Peter Lang.
Gore, Jennifer M. (1992). *The Struggle for Pedagogies: Critical and Feminist Discourses as Regimes of Truth.* New York: Routledge.
Gumport, Patricia J. (2002). *Academic Pathfinders: Knowledge Creation and Feminist Scholarship.* Westport, CT: Greenwood.

BIBLIOGRAPHY • 421

Harper, Helen J. (1998). *Dangerous Desires: High School Girls and Feminist Writing Practices.* New York: Peter Lang.
Henry, Mary E. (1996). *Parent-School Collaboration: Feminist Organizational Structures and School Leadership.* Albany: State University of New York Press.
Holland, Janet et al. (eds.) (1995). *Debates and Issues in Feminist Research and Pedagogy: A Reader.* Oxon, UK: Open University Press.
Jipson, Janice et al. (eds.) (1995). *Repositioning Feminism and Education: Perspectives on Educating for Social Change.* Westport, CT: Bergin and Garvey.
Jones, John Paul III et al. (1997). *Thresholds in Feminist Geography: Difference, Methodology, and Representation.* Lanham, MD: Rowman and Littlefield.
Kelly, David H. (ed.) (1996). *International Feminist Perspectives on Educational Reform: The Work of Gail Paradise Kelly.* New York: Garland.
Kenway, Jane (1998). *Answering Back: Girls, Boys, and Feminism in Schools.* New York: Routledge.
Kirsch, Gesa E. (1999). *Ethical Dilemmas in Feminist Research: The Politics of Location, Interpretation, and Publication.* New York: University of New York Press.
Kramarae, Cheris, and Dale Spender (1992). *The Knowledge Explosion: Generations of Feminist Scholarship.* New York: Teachers College Press.
Lather, Patricia Ann (1991). *Getting Smart: Feminist Research and Pedagogy within the Postmodern.* New York: Routledge.
Laurentis, Teresa de (ed.) (1986). *Feminist Studies. Critical Studies.* Bloomington: Indiana University Press.
Looser, Devoney, and E. Ann Kaplan (eds.) (1997). *Generations: Academic Feminists in Dialogue.* Minneapolis: University of Minnesota Press.
Luke, Carmen (ed.) (1996). *Feminisms and Pedagogies of Everyday Life.* Albany: State University of New York Press.
Luke, Carmen, and Jennifer Gore (eds.) (1992). *Feminisms and Critical Pedagogy.* New York: Routledge.
Maher, Frances A., and Mary Kay Thompson Tetreault (2001). *The Feminist Classroom: Dynamics of Gender, Race, and Privilege.* Lanham, MD: Rowman and Littlefield.
Mayberry, Maralee, Banu Subramaniam, and Lisa H. Weasel (2001). *Feminist Science Studies: A New Generation.* New York: Routledge.
―――, and Ellen CronanRose (eds.) (1999). *Meeting the Challenge: Innovative Feminist Pedagogies in Action.* New York: Routledge.
McManus, Barbara F. (1997). *Classics and Feminism: Gendering the Classics.* New York: Twayne.
McWilliam, Erica (1994). *In Broken Images: Feminist Tales for a Different Teacher Education.* New York: Teachers College Press.
Middleton, Sue (1993). *Educating Feminists: Life Histories and Pedagogy.* New York: Teachers College Press.

Morley, Louise, and Val Walsh (eds.) (1995). *Feminist Academics: Creative Agents for Change.* Bristol, England: Taylor and Francis.

Myers, Lena Wright (2002). *A Broken Silence: Voices of African American Women in the Academy.* Westport, CT: Bergin and Garvey.

Naples, Nancy A., and Karen Bojar (eds.) (2002). *Teaching Feminist Activism: Strategies from the Field.* New York: Routledge.

Neilsen, Lorri (1998). *Knowing Her Place: Research Literacies and Feminist Occasions.* San Francisco: Caddo Gap.

Ng, Roxana et al. (eds.) (1995). *AntiRacism, Feminism, and Critical Approaches to Education.* Westport, CT: Bergin and Garvey.

Oram, Alison (1996). *Women Teachers and Feminist Politics, 1900-1939.* Manchester, UK: Manchester University Press.

Peck, Elizabeth G., and JoAnna Stephens Mink (eds.) (1997). *Common Ground: Feminist Collaboration in the Academy.* Albany: State University of New York Press.

Peterson, Spike V. (ed.) (1992). *Gendered States: Feminist Revisions of International Relations Theory.* Boulder, CO: Lynne Rienner.

Reinharz, Shulamith (1992). *Feminist Methods in Social Research.* New York: Oxford University Press.

Rensenbrink, Carla Washburne (2001). *All in Our Places: Feminist Challenges in Elementary School Classrooms.* Lanham, MD: Rowman and Littlefield.

Ropers-Huilman, Becky (1998). *Feminist Teaching in Theory and Practice: Situating Power and Knowledge in Post-Structural Classrooms.* New York: Teachers College Press.

Sanchey-Casal, Susan (2002). *Twenty-First Century Feminist Classrooms: Pedagogies of Identity and Difference.* New York: St. Martin's Press.

Spender, Dale (ed.) (1981). *Men's Studies Modified: The Impact of Feminism on the Academic Disciplines.* New York: Pergamon.

Stanley, Liz (ed.) (1997). *Knowing Feminisms: On Academic Borders, Territories, and Tribes.* Thousand Oaks, CA: Sage.

_____, and Sue Wise (1993). *Breaking Out: Feminist Consciousness and Feminist Research,* 2nd ed. London: Routledge and Kegan Paul.

Stanton, Domna, and Abigail J. Stewart (eds.) (1995). *Feminisms in the Academy.* Ann Arbor: University of Michigan Press.

Stone, Lynda (ed.) (1993). *The Education Feminism Reader: Developments in a Field of Study.* New York: Routledge.

Tsolidis, Georgina (2001). *Schooling, Diaspora, and Gender: Being Feminist and Being Different.* Oxon, UK: Open University Press.

Weiler, Kathleen (1988). *Women Teaching for Change: Gender, Class and Power.* Westport, CT: Bergin and Garvey.

XXIII. Philosophy

Akkerman, Tjitske, and Siep Stuurman (1998). *Perspectives on Feminist Thought in European History: From the Middle Ages to the Present.* New York: Routledge.
Allen, Anita. (2003). *Why Privacy Isn't Everything: Feminist Reflections on Personal Accountability.* Lanham, MD.: Rowman and Littlefield.
Antony, Louise M., and Charlotte Witt (eds.) (2002). *A Mind of One's Own: Feminist Essays on Reason and Objectivity.* Boulder, CO: Westview Press.
Bar On, Bat-Ami, and Ann Ferguson (eds.) (1998). *Daring to be Good: Essays in Feminist Ethico-Politics.* New York: Routledge.
Battersby, Christine (1998). *The Phenomenal Woman: Feminist Metaphysics and the Patterns of Identity.* New York: Routledge.
Benhabib, Seyla et al. (1995). *Feminist Contentions: A Philosophical Exchange.* New York: Routledge.
Bianchi, Emanuela (ed.) (1999). *Is Feminist Philosophy Philosophy?* Evanston, IL: Northwestern University Press.
Buchan, Morag (1999). *Women in Plato's Political Theory.* New York: Routledge.
Burt, Sandra, and Lorraine Cole (eds.) (1995). *Changing Methods: Feminists Transforming Practice.* Peterborough, Ontario: Broadview Press.
Card, Claudia (1991). *Feminist Ethics.* Lawrence: University Press of Kansas.
Cole, Eve Browning, and Susan Coultrap-McQuin (1992). *Explorations in Feminist Ethics: Theory and Practice.* Bloomington: Indiana University Press.
Coole, Diana (1988). *Women in Political Theory: From Ancient Misogyny to Contempory Feminism.* Boulder, CO: Lynne Rienner.
Crysdale, Cynthia S. W. (ed.) (1994). *Lonergan and Feminism.* Toronto: University of Toronto Press.
Daly, Mary (1984). *Pure Lust: Elemental Feminist Philosophy.* Boston: Beacon Press.
Deutscher, Penelope (1997). *Unstable Tendencies: Feminism, Deconstruction, and the History of Philosophy.* New York: Routledge.
_____. (1997). *Yielding Gender: Feminism, Deconstruction, and the History of Philosophy.* New York: Routledge.
DiQuinzio, Patrice, and Iris Marion Young (eds.) (1997). *Feminist Ethics and Social Policy.* Bloomington: Indiana State University.
Donovan, Josephine, and Carol J. Adams (eds.) (1996). *Beyond Animal Rights: A Feminist Caring Ethic for the Treatment of Animals.* New York: Continuum.
Duran, Jane (1998). *Philosophies of Science/Feminist Theories.* Boulder, CO: Westview Press.
Farley, Margaret A. (1997). *Just Love: Sexual Ethics and Social Change.* New York: Continuum.
Frazer, Elizabeth, Jennifer Hornsby, and Sabina Lovibond (1992). *Ethics: A Feminist Reader.* Cambridge, MA: Blackwell.

Freeland, Cynthia A. (ed.) (1998). *Feminist Interpretations of Aristotle*. University Park, PA: Penn State Press.
Fricker, Miranda, and Jennifer Hornsby (eds.) (2000). *The Cambridge Companion to Feminism in Philosophy*. New York: Routledge.
Garry, Ann, and Marilyn Pearsall (1996). *Women, Knowledge and Reality: Explorations in Feminist Philosophy*. New York: Routledge.
Gatens, Moira (ed.) (1998). *Feminist Ethics*. Brookfield, VT: Ashgate.
Gauthier, Jeffrey A. (1997). *Hegel and Feminist Social Criticism: Justice, Recognition, and the Feminine*. Albany: State University of New York Press.
Gould, Carol C. (1984). *Beyond Domination: New Perspectives on Women and Philosophy*. Totowa, NJ: Rowman and Littlefield.
_____, and Marx W. Wartofsky (1976). *Women and Philosophy: Toward a Theory of Liberation*. New York: Putnam.
Grimshaw, Jean (1986). *Philosophy and Feminist Thinking*. Minneapolis: University of Minnesota Press.
Harding, Sandra, and Merrill Hintikka (1983). *Discovering Reality: Feminist Perspectives on Epistemology, Metaphysics, Methodology, and Philosophy of Science*. Boston: Reidel.
Held, Virginia (1993). *Feminist Morality: Transforming Culture, Society, and Politics*. Chicago: University of Chicago Press.
Holland, Nancy J. (ed.) (1997). *Feminist Interpretations of Jacques Derrida*. University Park, PA: Penn State Press.
Jaggar, Alison M. (ed.) (1994). *Living with Contradictions: Controversies in Feminist Social Ethics*. Boulder, CO: Westview Press.
Jakobsen, Janet R. (1997). *Working Alliances and the Politics of Difference: Diversity and Feminist Ethics*. Bloomington: Indiana University Press.
Kennedy, Ellen, and Susan Mendus (eds.) (1987). *Women in Western Political Philosophy: Kant to Nietzsche*. New York: St. Martin's Press.
Koehn, Daryl (1998). *Rethinking Feminist Ethics: Care, Trust and Empathy*. New York: Routledge.
Kourany, Janet A. et al. (eds.) (1998). *Feminist Philosophies: Problems, Theories, and Applications*. Upper Saddle River, NJ: Prentice Hall.
_____. (ed.) (1998). *Philosophy in a Feminist Voice: Critiques and Reconstructions*. Princeton, NJ: Princeton University Press.
Leon, Celine, and Sylvia Walsh (eds.) (1997). *Feminist Interpretations of Soren Kierkegaard*. University Park, PA: Penn State Press.
Lloyd, Genevieve (ed.) (2002). *Feminism and History of Philosophy*. New York: Oxford University Press.
Mahowald, Mary (ed.) (1978). *Philosophy of Woman: Classical to Current Concepts*. Indianapolis, IN: Hackett.
Mills, Patricia Jagentowicz (ed.) (1996). *Feminist Interpretations of G. W. F. Hegel*. University Park, PA: Penn State Press.

Narayan, Uma, and Sandra Harding (eds.) (2000). *Decentering the Center: Philosophy for a Multicultural, Postcolonial, and Feminist World.* Bloomington: Indiana University Press.
Nicol, Iain G. (1992). *Schleiermacher and Feminism: Sources, Evaluations, and Responses.* Lewiston, NY: Mellen Press.
Noddings, Nel (1984). *Caring: A Feminine Approach to Ethics and Moral Education.* Berkeley: University of California Press.
Nye, Andrea (1995). *Feminism and Philosophy: At the Border.* New York: Twayne.
Okin, Susan (1980). *Women in Western Political Thought.* London: Virago.
Oliver, Kelly, and Marilyn Pearsall (eds.) (1998). *Feminist Interpretations of Friedrich Nietzsche.* University Park, PA: Penn State Press.
Porter, Elisabeth (1999). *Feminist Perspectives on Ethics.* New York: Longman.
Schildrick, Margrit (1997). *Leaky Bodies and Boundaries: Feminism, Postmodernism, and (Bio)Ethics.* New York: Routledge.
Schott, Robin May. (2003). *Discovering Feminist Philosophy.* Lanham, MD: Rowman and Littlefield.
_____. (ed.) (1997). *Feminist Interpretations of Immanuel Kant.* University Park, PA: Penn State Press.
Sharpley-Whiting, T. Denean (1997). *Frantz Fanon: Conflicts and Feminisms.* Lanham, MD: Rowman and Littlefield.
Simons, Margaret A. (ed.) (1995). *Feminist Interpretations of Simone de Beauvoir.* University Park, PA: Penn State Press.
_____. (2000). *Beauvoir and the Second Sex: Feminism, Race, and the Origins of Existentialism.* Lanham, MD: Rowman and Littlefield.
Sterba, James P. (ed.) (1999). *Ethics: Classical Western Texts in Feminist Multicultural Perspectives.* New York: Oxford University Press.
Tanesini, Alessandra (1999). *An Introduction to Feminist Epistemologies.* Malden, MA: Blackwell.
Tong, Rosemarie (1996). *Feminist Approaches to Bioethics: Theoretical Reflections and Practical Applications.* Boulder, CO: Westview Press.
Walker, Margaret Urban (1998). *Moral Understandings: A Feminist Study in Ethics.* New York: Routledge.
Ward, Julie K. (ed.) (1996). *Feminism and Ancient Philosophy.* New York: Routledge.
Weiss, Penny A. (1994). *Gendered Community: Rousseau, Sex, and Politics.* New York: New York University Press.
Wendell, Susan (1996). *The Rejected Body: Feminist Philosophical Reflections on Disability.* New York: Routledge.

XXIV. Psychoanalytic Feminism

Barr, Marleen S., and Richard Feldstein (1989). *Discontented Discourses: Femi-*

nism/ *Textual Intervention / Psychoanalysis*. Urbana: University of Illinois Press.
Bernheimer, Charles, and Claire Kahane (eds.) (1985). *In Dora's Case: Freud - Hysteria - Feminism*. New York: Columbia University Press.
Buhle, Mari Jo (1998). *Feminism and Its Discontents: A Century of Struggle with Psychoanalysis*. Cambridge, MA: Harvard University Press.
Burack, Cynthia (1994). *The Problem of the Passions: Feminism, Psychoanalysis and Social Theory*. New York: New York University Press.
Chodorow, Nancy (1978). *The Reproduction of Mothering: Psychoanalysis and the Sociology of Gender*. Berkeley: University of California Press.
Deutsch, Helene (1944). *The Psychology of Women: A Psychoanalytic Interpretation*. New York: Grune and Stratton.
Dinnerstein, Dorothy (1977). *The Mermaid and the Minotaur: Sexual Arrangements and Human Malaise*. New York: Harper Colophon Books.
DuBois, Page (1988). *Sowing the Body: Psychoanalysis and Ancient Representations of Women*. Chicago: University of Chicago Press.
Elliot, Patricia (1991). *From Mastery to Analysis: Theories of Gender in Psychoanalytic Feminism*. Ithaca, NY: Cornell University Press.
Enns, Carolyn Zerbe (1997). *Feminist Theories and Feminist Psychotherapies: Origins, Themes, and Variations*. New York: Haworth.
Flax, Jane (1993). *Disputed Subjects: Essays on Psychoanalysis, Politics, and Philosophy*. New York: Routledge.
Freud, Sigmund (rpt. 1963). *Dora: An Analysis of a Case of Hysteria*. New York: Collier Books.
Gallop, Jane (1982). *The Daughter's Seduction: Feminism and Psychoanalysis*. Ithaca, NY: Cornell University Press.
Kurzweil, Edith (1994). *Freudians and Feminists*. Boulder, CO: Westview Press.
Lawrence, Marilyn (1999). *Psychotherapy with Women: Feminist Perspectives*. New York: Routledge.
Mitchell, Juliet (1974). *Psychoanalysis and Feminism*. New York: Vintage Books.
Mitchell, Juliet, and Jacqueline Rose (eds.) (1982). *Feminine Sexuality, Jacques Lacan à l'École Freudienne*. London: Routledge and Kegan Paul.
Rudnytsky, Peter L., and Andrew M. Gordon (eds.) (2000). *Psychoanalyses/ Feminisms*. Albany: State University of New York Press.
Seu, I. Bruna, and M. Colleen Heenan (eds.) (1998). *Feminism and Psychotherapy: Reflections on Contemporary Theories and Practices*. Thousand Oaks, CA: Sage.
Smith, J. C., and Carla Perstman (1996). *The Castration of Oedipus: Feminism, Psychoanalysis, and the Will to Power*. New York: New York University Press.
Smith, Joseph H., and Afaf M. Mahfouz (eds.) (1994). *Psychoanalysis, Feminism, and the Future of Gender*. Baltimore: Johns Hopkins University Press.

XXV. Psychology

Babcock, Marguerite, and Christine McKay (eds.) (1995). *Challenging Codependency: Feminist Critiques.* Toronto: University of Toronto Press.
Baker Miller, J. (1978), *Toward a New Psychology of Women,* Boston: Beacon Press.
Balbus, Isaac D. (1998). *Emotional Rescue: The Theory and Practice of a Feminist Father.* New York: Routledge.
Belenky, Mary Field (1986). *Women's Ways of Knowing: The Development of Self, Voice, and Mind.* New York: Basic Books.
Brabeck, Mary M. (ed.) (2000). *Practicing Feminist Ethics in Psychology.* Washington, DC: American Psychological Association.
Burman, Erica (ed.) (1998). *Deconstructing Feminist Psychology.* Thousand Oaks, CA: Sage.
Carter, Pam (1995). *Feminism, Breasts, and Breast Feeding.* New York: St. Martin's Press.
Chesler, Phyllis (1972). *Women and Madness.* Garden City, NY: Doubleday.
Collins, Lynn H. (2002). *Charting a New Course for Feminist Psychology.* Westport, CT: Praeger.
Contratto, Susan, and Janice M. Gutfreund (eds.) (1996). *A Feminist Clinicians's Guide to the Memory Debate.* New York: Harrington Park.
Fischer, Jerilyn, and Ellen S. Silber (eds.) (1998). *Analyzing the Different Voice: Feminist Psychological Theory and Literary Texts.* Lanham, MD: Rowman and Littlefield.
Gilligan, Carol (1982). *In a Different Voice: Psychological Theory and Women's Development.* Cambridge, MA: Harvard University Press.
Hite, Shere (1981). *The Hite Report on Female Sexuality.* New York: Corgi.
_____. (1981). *The Hite Report on Male Sexuality.* New York: Knopf.
_____. (1995). *The Hite Report on the Family: Growing Up under Patriarchy.* New York: Grove Press.
Horney, Karen (1973). *Feminine Psychology.* New York: Norton.
Lamb, Sharon (ed.) (1999). *New Versions of Victims: Feminists Struggle with the Concept.* New York: New York University Press.
Mariechild, Diane (1986). *Mother Wit: A Feminist Guide to Psychic Development.* Trumansburg, NY: Crossing Press.
Miller, Patricia H., and Ellin Kofsky Scholnick (eds.) (2000). *Toward a Feminist Developmental Psychology.* New York: Routledge.
Schacht, Stephen, and Doris W. Ewing (eds.) (1998). *Feminism and Men: Reconstructing Gender Relations.* New York: New York University Press.
Unger, Rhoda Kesler, and Mary Crawford (1992). *Women and Gender: A Feminist Psychology.* New York: McGraw-Hill.
Ward, Colleen A. (1995). *Attitudes toward Rape: Feminist and Psychological Perspectives.* Thousand Oaks, CA: Sage.

Wilkinson, Sue (1986). *Feminist Social Psychology: Developing Theory and Practice.* Philadelphia: Open University Press.
_____, and Celia Kitzinger (1995). *Feminism and Discourse: Psychological Perspectives.* Thousand Oaks, CA: Sage.
_____ (ed.) (1996). *Feminist Social Psychologies: International Perspectives.* New York: Open University Press.
_____, and Celia Kitzinger (eds.) (1996). *Representing the Other: A Feminism and Psychology Reader.* Thousand Oaks, CA: Sage.
Worell, Judith, and Norine G. Johnson (1997). *Shaping the Future of Feminist Psychology: Education, Research, and Practice.* Washington, DC: APA Press.

XXVI. Religion

Antonelli, Judith S. (1995). *In the Image of God: A Feminist Commentary on the Torah.* Northvale, NJ: Jason Aronson.
Ashe, Kaye (1997). *The Feminization of the Church?* Kansas City, MO: Sheed & Ward.
Atkinson, Clarissa W., Constance Buchanan, and Margaret R. Miles (1985). *Immaculate and Powerful: The Female in Sacred Image and Social Reality.* Boston: Beacon Press.
Bayes, Jane H., and Nayereh Tohidid (eds.) (2001). *Globalization, Gender, and Religion: The Politics of Implementing Women's Rights in Catholic and Muslim Contexts.* New York: Palgrave.
Behnke, Donna A. (1982). *Religious Issues in Nineteenth Century Feminism.* Troy, NY: Whitston Co.
Braude, Ann (2001). *Radical Spirits: Spiritualism and Women's Rights in Nineteenth Century America.* Bloomington: Indiana University Press.
Brenner, Athalya (ed.) (1996). *A Feminist Companion to the Hebrew Bible in the New Testament.* Sheffield, UK: Sheffield Academic Press.
Brown, Mary Crist (2000). *Free to Believe: Liberating Images of God for Women.* Cleveland, OH: Pilgrim Press.
Cady, Susan, Marian Ronan, and Hal Taussig (1986). *Sophia: The Future of Feminist Spirituality.* San Francisco: Harper and Row.
Carmody, Denise Lardner (1995). *Christian Feminist Theology: A Constructive Interpretation.* Cambridge, MA: Blackwell.
Carr, Anne, and Mary Stewart von Leeuwen (eds.) (1996). *Religion, Feminism and the Family.* Louisville, KY: Westminster/John Knox Press.
Carson, Anne (1992). *Goddesses and Wise Women: The Literature of Feminist Spirituality, 1980-1992: An Annotated Bibliography.* Freedom, CA: Crossing Press.
Chittister, Joan D. (1998). *Heart of Flesh: A Feminist Spirituality for Women and Men.* Grand Rapids, MI: William B. Eerdmans.

Chopp, Rebecca, and Shelia Greeve Davaney (eds.) (1997). *Horizons in Feminist Theology: Identity, Tradition, and Norms.* Minneapolis, MN: Fortress Press.
Christ, Carol P. (1980). *Diving Deep and Surfacing: Women Writers on Spiritual Quest.* Boston: Beacon Press.
_____. (1987). *Laughter of Aphrodite: Reflections on a Journey to the Goddess.* San Francisco: Harper and Row.
_____. (1997). *Rebirth of the Goddess: Finding Meaning in Feminist Spirituality.* Reading, MA: Addison-Wesley.
Collins, Adela Yarbro (ed.) (1985). *Feminist Perspectives on Biblical Scholarship.* Chico, CA: Scholars Press.
Curran, Charles E. et al. (eds.) (1996). *Feminist Ethics and the Catholic Moral Tradition.* New York: Paulist Press.
Daly, Mary (1973). *Beyond God the Father: Toward a Philosophy of Women's Liberation.* Boston: Beacon Press.
Darr, Katheryn Pfisterer (1991). *Far More Precious than Jewels: Perspectives on Biblical Women, Gender and the Biblical Tradition.* Louisville, KY: Westminster/John Knox Press.
Davis, Philip G. (1998). *Goddess Unmasked: The Rise of Neopagan Feminist Spirituality.* Dallas, TX: Spence.
Devlin-Glass, Frances, and Lyn McCredden (eds.) (2001). *Feminist Poetics of the Sacred: Creative Suspicions.* New York: Oxford University Press.
Dixon, Joy (2001). *Divine Feminine: Theosophy and Feminism in England.* Baltimore: Johns Hopkins University Press.
Donaldson, Laura, and Kwok Pui-Lan (eds.) (2001). *Postcolonialism, Feminism, and Religious Discourse.* New York: Routledge.
Eller, Cynthia (1995). *Living in the Lap of the Goddess: The Feminist Spirituality Movement in America.* Boston: Beacon.
Erickson, Victoria Lee (1993). *Where Silence Speaks: Feminism, Social Theory, and Religion.* Minneapolis, MN: Fortress Press.
Feld, Merle (1999). *A Spiritual Life: A Jewish Feminist Journey.* Albany: State University of New York Press.
Ferraro, Barbara, Patricia Hussey, and Jane O'Reilly (1990). *No Turning Back: Two Nuns' Battle with the Vatican over Women's Right to Choose.* New York: Poseidon Press.
Field-Bibb, Jacqueline (1991). *Women towards Priesthood.* New York: Cambridge University Press.
Fiorenza, Elisabeth Schussler (1996). *The Power of Naming: A Concilium Reader in Liberation Theology.* New York: Orbis.
_____. (1998). *Sharing Her Word: Feminist Biblical Interpretation in Context.* Boston: Beacon Press.
Fischer, Kathleen R. (1988). *Women at the Well: Feminist Perspectives on Spiritual Direction.* New York: Paulist Press.
Flinders, Carol Lee (1998). *At the Root of This Longing: Reconciling a Spiritual Hunger and a Feminist Thirst.* San Francisco: Harper San Francisco.

Frascati-Lochhead, Marta (1998). *Kenosis and Feminist Theology: The Challenge of Gianni Vattimo.* Albany: State University of New York Press.
Goldenberg, Naomi R. (1979). *Changing of the Gods: Feminism and the End of Traditional Religions.* Boston: Beacon Press.
Goldstein, Elyse (1998). *Revisions: Seeing Torah through a Feminist Lens.* Woodstock, VT: Jewish Lights.
Graff, Ann O'Hara (ed.) (1995). *In the Embrace of God: Feminist Approaches to Theological Anthropology.* New York: Orbis.
Greene-McCreight, Kathryn (2000). *Feminist Reconstructions of Christian Doctrine: Narrative Analysis and Appraisal.* New York: Oxford University Press.
Grey, Mary, and Elisabeth Green (eds.) (1994). *Ecofeminism and Theology.* Kampen, Netherlands: Kok Pharos Publishing House.
Grob, Leonard, Riffot Hassan, and Haim Gordon (eds.) (1991). *Women's and Men's Liberation: Testimonies of Spirit.* Westport, CT: Greenwood.
Gross, Rita M. (1993). *Buddhism after Patriarchy: A Feminist History, Analysis, and Reconstruction of Buddhism.* Albany: State University of New York Press.
_____, and Rosemary Radford Ruether (2001). *Religious Feminism and the Future of the Planet: A Christian-Buddhist Conversation.* New York: Continuum.
Haddad, Yvonne Yazbeck, and John L. Esposito (eds.) (2001). *Daughters of Abraham: Feminist Thought in Judaism, Christianity and Islam.* Gainesville: University Press of Florida.
Hegy, Pierre (ed.) (1997). *Feminist Voices in Spirituality.* Lewiston, NY: Mellen Press.
Heine, Susanne (1988). *Christianity and the Goddesses: Systematic Criticism of a Feminist Theology.* London: SCM Press.
Hewitt, Marsha Aileen (1995). *Critical Theory of Religion: A Feminist Analysis.* Minneapolis, MN: Fortress Press.
Hiltebeitel, Alf, and Kathleen M. Erndl (eds.) (2000). *Is the Goddess a Feminist?: The Politics of South Asian Goddesses.* Sheffield, UK: Sheffield Academic Press.
Hurtado, Larry W. (1990). *Goddesses in Religions and Modern Debate.* Atlanta, GA: Scholars Press.
Isherwood, Lisa (ed.) (2000). *The Good News of the Body: Sexual Theology and Feminism.* New York: New York University Press.
Johnson, Elizabeth A. (1998). *Friends of God and Prophets: A Feminist Theological Reading of the Communion of Saints.* New York: Continuum.
Jung, Patricia Beattie et al. (eds.) (2001). *Good Sex: Feminist Perspectives from the World's Religions.* New Brunswick, NJ: Rutgers University Press.
Juschka, Darlene M. (2001). *Feminism in the Study of Religion: A Reader.* New York: Continuum.
Kassian, Mary A. (1992). *The Feminist Gospel: The Movement to Unite Feminism with the Church.* Wheaton, IL: Crossway Books.

Kellenbach, Katharine von (1994). *AntiJudaism in Feminist Religious Writings.* Atlanta, GA: Scholars Press.
Keller, Catherine (1996). *Apocalypse Now and Then: A Feminist Guide to the End of the World.* Boston: Beacon Press.
Laffey, Alice L. (1988). *An Introduction to the Old Testament: A Feminist Perspective.* Philadelphia: Fortress.
Loades, Ann (2001). *Feminist Theology: Voices from the Past.* Malden, MA: Blackwell.
MacKinnon, Mary Heather, and Moni McIntyre (eds.) (1995). *Readings in Ecology and Feminist Theology.* Kansas City, MO: Sheed & Ward.
Manning, Christel (1999). *God Gave Us the Right: Conservative Catholic, Evangelical Protestant, and Orthodox Jewish Women Grapple with Feminism.* New Brunswick, NJ: Rutgers University Press.
Merrim, Stephanie (1991). *Feminist Perspectives on Sor Juana Ines de la Cruz.* Detroit: Wayne State University.
Nason-Clark, Nancy, and Mary Jo Neitz (2001). *Feminist Narratives and the Sociology of Religion.* Walnut Creek, CA: AltaMira.
Neuger, Christine Cozad (ed.) (1996). *The Arts of Ministry: Feminist-Womanist Approaches.* Louisville, KY: Westminster/John Knox Press.
Newman, Barbara (1995). *From Virile Woman to Womanchrist: Studies in Medieval Religion and Literature.* Philadelphia: University of Pennsylvania Press.
Newsom, Carol A., and Sharon H. Ringe (eds.). (1992). *The Women's Bible Commentary.* Louisville, KY: Westminster/John Knox Press.
Orr, Elaine Neil (1987). *Tillie Olsen and a Feminist Spiritual Vision.* Jackson: University Press of Mississippi.
Ostriker, Alicia (1993). *Feminist Revision and the Bible.* Cambridge, MA: Blackwell.
Paper, Jordan (1997). *Through the Earth Darkly: Female Spirituality in Comparative Perspective.* New York: Continuum.
Parsons, Susan Frank (1996). *Feminism and Christian Ethics.* New York: Cambridge University Press.
Patrick, Anne E. (1996). *Liberating Conscience: Feminist Explorations in Catholic Moral Theology.* New York: Continuum.
Plaskow, Judith, (1990). *Standing Again at Sinai: Judaism from a Feminist Perspective.* New York: Harper and Row.
Plaskow, Judith and Carol P. Christ (1989). *Weaving the Visions: New Patterns in Feminist Spirituality.* San Francisco: Harper and Row.
Porterfield, Amanda (1989). *Feminine Spirituality in America: From Sarah Edwards to Martha Graham.* Philadelphia: Temple University Press.
Price, Robert M. (1997). *The Widow Traditions in Luke-Acts: A Feminist Critical Scrutiny.* Atlanta, GA: Scholars Press.
Purkiss, Diane (1996). *The Witch in History: Early Modern and Twentieth Century Representations.* New York: Routledge.

Ramshaw, Gail (1998). *Under the Tree of Life: The Religion of a Feminist Christian*. New York: Continuum.

Reimer, Ivoni Richter (1995). *Women in the Acts of the Apostles: A Feminist Liberation Perspective*. Minneapolis, MN: Fortress Press.

Ruether, Rosemary (1985). *Womanguides: Readings toward a Feminist Theology*. Boston: Beacon Press.

Russell, Letty M. (ed.) (1985). *Feminist Interpretation of the Bible*. Philadelphia: Westminster Press.

Salomonsen, Jone (2001). *Enchanted Feminism: Ritual Constructions of Gender, Agency, and Diversity in a Community of Witches*. New York: Routledge.

Schaup, Susanne (1997). *Sophia: Aspects of the Divine Feminine Past and Present*. York Beach, ME: Nicolas-Hays.

Schneider, Laurel C. (1998). *Re-Imagining the Divine: Confronting the Backlash against Feminist Theology*. Cleveland, OH: Pilgrim Press.

Schneiders, Sandra Marie (1991). *Beyond Patching: Faith and Feminism in the Catholic Church*. New York: Paulist Press.

_____. (2000). *With Oil in Their Lamps: Faith, Feminism and the Future*. New York: Paulist Press.

Schottroff, Luise et al. (1998). *Feminist Interpretation: The Bible in Women's Perspective*. Minneapolis, MN: Fortress Press.

_____. (1995). *Lydia's Impatient Sisters: A Feminist Social History of Early Christianity*. Louisville, KY: Westminster/John Knox Press.

Selvidge, Marla J. (1996). *Notorious Voices: Feminist Biblical Interpretation, 1550-1920*. New York: Continuum.

Sharma, Arvind, and Katherine K. Young (eds.) (1999). *Feminism and World Religions*. New York: New York University Press.

Sisters, Servants of the Immaculate Heart of Mary (1997). *Building Sisterhood: A Feminist History of the Sisters, Servants of the Immaculate Heart of Mary*. Syracuse: Syracuse University Press.

Smith, Elizabeth J. (1999). *Bearing Fruit in Due Season: Feminist Hermeneutics and the Bible in Worship*. Collegeville, MN: Liturgical Press.

Solberg, Mary M. (1997). *Compelling Knowledge: A Feminist Proposal for an Epistemology of the Cross*. Albany: State University of New York Press.

Soskice, Janet Martin (ed.) (2001). *Feminism and Theology*. Cambridge, MA: University of Cambridge Press.

Spretnak, Charlene (1982). *The Politics of Women's Spirituality: Essays on the Rise of Spiritual Power within the Feminist Movement*. Garden City, NY: Anchor Books.

Steichen, Donna (1991). *Ungodly Rage: The Hidden Face of Catholic Feminism*. San Francisco: Ignatius Press.

Trible, Phyllis (1984). *Texts of Terror: Literary-Feminist Readings of Biblical Narratives. Overtures to Biblical Theology*. Minneapolis, MN: Fortress Press.

_____, et al. (1995). *Feminist Approaches to the Bible: Symposium at the Smithsonian Institute*. Washington, DC: Biblical Archaeological Society.

Tumber, Catherine (2002). *American Feminism and the Birth of New Age Spirituality: Searching for the Higher Self, 1875-1915*. Lanham, MD.: Rowman and Littlefield.
VanDyke, Annette (1992). *The Search for a Woman-Centered Spirituality*. New York: New York University Press.
Wainwright, Elaine M. (1998). *Shall We Look for Another?: A Feminist Reading of the Matthean Jesus*. New York: Orbis.
Walsh, Mary-Paula (1999). *Feminism and Christian Tradition: An Annotated Bibliography and Critical Introduction to the Literature*. Westport, CT: Greenwood.
Washington, Harold C. et al. (eds.) (1999). *Escaping Eden: New Feminist Perspectives on the Bible*. New York: New York University Press.
Wolowelshy, Joel B. (1997). *Women, Jewish Law and Modernity: New Opportunities in a Post-Feminist Age*. Hoboken, NJ: KTAV.
Wren, Brian (1990). *What Language Shall I Borrow? God Talk in Worship: A Male Response to Feminist Theology*. New York: Crossroad.
Yamani, Mai (ed.) (1996). *Feminism and Islam: Legal and Literary Perspectives*. New York: New York University Press.

XXVII. Science/Medicine

Banks, Amanda Carson (2000). *Birth Chairs, Midwives and Medicine*. Jackson: University Press of Mississippi.
Bleier, Ruth (1984). *Science and Gender: A Critique of Biology and Its Theories on Women*. New York: Teachers College Press.
_____. (ed.) (1986). *Feminist Approaches to Science*. New York: Teachers College Press.
Boehmer, Ulrike (2000). *The Personal and the Political: Women's Activism in Response to the Breast Cancer and AIDS Epidemics*. New York: State University of New York Press.
Candib, Lucy M. (1995). *Medicine and the Family: A Feminist Perspective*. New York: BasicBooks.
Creager, Angela N.H. et al. (eds.) (2002). *Feminism in Twentieth Century Science, Technology and Medicine*. Chicago: University of Chicago Press.
Daniels, Cynthia (1993). *At Women's Expense: State Power and the Politics of Fetal Rights*. Cambridge, MA: Harvard University Press.
Donnison, Jean (1977). *Midwives and Medical Men. A History of Inter-Professional Rivalries and Women's Rights*. London: Heinemann.
Ehrenreich, Barbara, and Deirdre English (1973). *Witches, Midwives, and Nurses: A History of Women Healers*. Old Westbury, NY: Feminist Press.
Everts, Saskia Irene (1998). *Gender and Technology: Empowering Women, Engendering Development*. New York: Zed Books.

Fausto-Sterling, Anne (1985). *Myths of Gender: Biological Theories about Men and Women*. New York: Basic Books.
Fennema, Elizabeth, and Gilah C. Leder (eds.) (1990). *Mathematics and Gender*. New York: Teachers College Press.
Gulati, S. C., and Rama Patnaik (1996). *Women's Status and Reproductive Health Rights*. New Delhi, India: Har-Anand.
Harding, Jan (ed.) (1986). *Perspectives on Gender and Science*. New York: Falmer Press.
Harding, Sandra (1986). *The Science Question in Feminism*. Ithaca, NY: Cornell University Press.
_____. (1998). *Is Science Multicultural?: Postcolonialisms, Feminisms, and Epistemologies*. Bloomington: Indiana University Press.
Hardon, Anita, and Elizabeth Hayes (eds.) (1997). *Reproductive Rights in Practice: A Feminist Report on Quality of Care*. New York: Zed Books.
Harvey, Joy (1997). *"Almost a Man of Genius": Clemence Royer, Feminism, and Nineteenth Century Science*. New Brunswick, NJ: Rutgers University Press.
Henderson, Metta Lou (2002). *American Women Pharmacists: Contributions to the Profession*. New York: Pharmaceutical Products Press.
Hillyer, Barbara (1993). *Feminism and Disability*. Norman: University of Oklahoma.
Holmes, Bequaert, and Laura M. Purdy (1992). *Feminist Perspectives in Medical Ethics*. Bloomington: Indiana University Press.
Keller, Evelyn Fox (1984). *Reflections on Gender and Science*. New Haven, CT: Yale University Press.
Keller, Evelyn Fox, and Helen E. Longino (eds.) (1996). *Feminism and Science*. New York: Oxford University Press.
Lublin, Nancy (1997). *Pandora's Box: Feminism Confronts Reproductive Technology*. Lanham, MD: Rowman and Littlefield.
Marchessault, Janine, and Kim Sawchuck (eds.) (2000). *Wild Science: Reading Feminism, Medicine, and the Media*. New York: Routledge.
Marks, Lara (2001). *Sexual Chemistry: A History of the Contraceptive*. New Haven, CT: Yale University Press.
Mayberry, Maralee et al. (eds.) (2001). *Feminist Science Studies: A New Generation*. New York: Routledge.
Muff, Janet (1982). *Socialization, Sexism, and Stereotyping: Women's Issues in Nursing*. St. Louis, MO: Mosby.
Nadeau, Robert L. (1996). *S/He Brain: Science, Sexual Politics, and the Feminist Movement*. Westport, CT: Praeger.
Riska, Elianne (2001). *Medical Careers and Feminist Agendas: American, Scandinavian, and Russian Women Physicians*. New York: Aldine de Gruyter.
Rose, Hilary (1994). *Love, Power, and Knowledge: Towards a Feminist Transformation of the Sciences*. Bloomington: Indiana University Press.
Rose, Steven, Leon Kamin, and R. C. Lewontin (1984). *Not in Our Genes: Biology, Ideology and Human Nature*. Harmondsworth, England: Pelican.

Rosser, Sue Vilhauer (1985). *Teaching Science and Health from a Feminist Perspective.* New York: Pergamon Press.
_____. (1990). *Female Friendly Science: Applying Women's Studies Methods and Theories to Attract Students.* New York: Pergamon Press.
_____. (ed.) (1988). *Feminism within the Science and Health Care Professions.* New York: Teachers College Press.
Rothschild, Joan (1986). *Teaching Technology from a Feminist Perspective.* New York: Pergamon.
Ruzek, Sheryl Burt (1978). *The Women's Health Movement: Feminist Alternatives to Medical Control.* New York: Praeger.
Sazers, Janet (1982). *Biological Politics: Feminist and AntiFeminist Perspectives.* Totowa, NJ: Rowman and Allanheld.
Schiebinger, Londa L. (1999). *Has Feminism Changed Science?* Cambridge, MA: Harvard University Press.
Schneider, Beth E., and Nancy E. Stoller (eds.) (1995). *Women Resisting AIDS: Feminist Strategies of Empowerment.* Philadelphia: Temple University Press.
Sherwin, Susan (1992). *No Longer Patient: Feminist Ethics and Health Care.* Philadelphia: Temple University Press.
Shiva, Vandan, and Ingunn Moser (eds.) (1995). *Biopolitics: A Feminist and Ecological Reader on Biotechnology.* New York: Zed Books.
Tobias, Sheila (1990). *They're Not Dumb, They're Different: Stalking the Second Tier.* Tucson, AZ: Research Corporation.
Tuana, Nancy (1989). *Feminism and Science.* Bloomington: Indiana University Press.
Wear, Delese (1997). *Privilege in the Medical Academy: A Feminist Examines Gender, Race, and Power.* New York: Teachers College Press.
Wolmark, Jenny (ed.) (1999). *Cybersexualities: A Reader on Feminist Theory, Cyborgs, and Cyberspace.* Edinburgh, Scotland: Edinburgh University Press.
Wyer, Mare et al. (eds.) (2001). *Women, Science, and Technology: A Reader in Feminist Science Studies.* New York: Routledge.

XXVIII. Social Work and Feminist Therapy

Bricker-Jenkins, Mary, and Nancy Hooyman (1983). *Not for Women Only: Social Work Practice for a Feminist Future.* Silver Spring, MD: National Association of Social Workers.
Bricker-Jenkins, Mary, Nancy R. Hooyman, and Naomi Gottlieb (1991). *Feminist Social Work Practice in Clinical Settings.* Newbury Park, CA: Sage.
Burstow, Bonnie (1992). *Radical Feminist Therapy.* Thousand Oaks, CA: Sage.
Cavanaugh, Kate, and Viviene E. Cree (eds.) (1996). *Working with Men: Feminism and Social Work.* New York: Routledge.
Chaplin, Jocelyn (1999). *Feminist Counseling in Action.* Thousand Oaks, CA: Sage Press.

Davis, Allen F. (1967). *Spearheads for Reform. The Social Settlements and the Progressive Movement 1890-1914*. New York: Oxford University Press.
_____. (1973). *American Heroine: The Life and Legend of Jane Addams*. New York: Oxford University Press.
Gottlieb, Naomi (ed.) (1980). *Alternative Social Services for Women*. New York: Columbia University Press.
Hill, Marcia, and Esther D. Rothblum (eds.) (1996). *Classism and Feminist Therapy: Counting Costs*. New York: Harrington Park.
_____. (1998). *Feminist Therapy as a Political Act*. New York: Haworth.
Hogan, Susan (1997). *Feminist Approaches to Art Therapy*. New York: Routledge.
Masi, Dale A. (1981). *Organizing for Women: Issues, Strategies, and Services*. Lexington, MA: Lexington Books.
McLellan, Betty (1995). *Beyond Psychopression: A Feminist Alternative Therapy*. Victoria: Spinifex.
Miller, Dorothy C. (1990). *Women and Social Welfare: A Feminist Analysis*. New York: Praeger.
Pascall, Gillian (1986). *Social Policy: A Feminist Analysis*. New York: Tavistock Publications.
Saulnier, Christine Flynn (1996). *Feminist Theories and Social Work: Approaches and Applications*. New York: Haworth Press.
Valentich, Mary, and James Gripton (1985). *Feminist Perspectives on Social Work and Human Sexuality*. New York: Haworth Press.
Van Den Bergh, Nan, and Lynn B. Cooper (1986). *Feminist Visions for Social Work*. Silver Spring, MD: National Association of Social Workers.
Weingarten, Kathy, and Michele Bograd (eds.) (1996). *Reflections on Feminist Family Therapy Training*. New York: Haworth. West, Guida (1981). *The National Welfare Rights Movement: The Social Protest of Poor Women*. New York: Praeger.

About the Authors

JANET K. BOLES (Ph.D., University of Texas at Austin), Professor of Political Science, Marquette University. She teaches courses on women in American politics and the politics of race, ethnicity, and gender and has published extensively on the feminist movement, women in politics and elected office, and women and public policy. She is the author of *The Politics of the Equal Rights Amendment* (1979), editor of *American Feminism: New Issues for a Mature Movement* (1991) and *The Egalitarian City* (1986), and co-editor of *Women of Color: Defining the Issues, Hearing the Voices* (2001). She is a past president of the American Political Science Association Organized Section on Women and Politics Research and has served on the editorial or advisory boards for *Women and Politics*, the *Women's Studies Encyclopedia*, *Ms.*, the *American Journal of Political Science*, and the University of Nebraska Press Book Series on Women and Politics. Her current research on the impact of local elected women on public policy and the use of policy networks by women's groups has received several awards.

DIANE LONG HOEVELER (Ph.D., University of Illinois-Urbana), Professor of English, Marquette University, teaches courses on the Female Gothic, Romanticism and Race and Gender, Women's Literature, and Literature and Psychology. She is author of *Romantic Androgyny: The Women Within* (1990), *Gothic Feminism: The Professionalization of Gender from Charlotte Smith to the Brontës* (1998), co-author with Lisa Jadwin of *Charlotte Brontë* (1997), co-editor with Larry Peer of *Comparative Romanticisms* (1998) and *Romanticism and Its Other Discourses* (2005), co-editor with Beth Lau of *Approaches to Teaching Jane Eyre* (1993), co-editor with Tamar Heller of *Approaches to Teaching Gothic Fiction* (2003), co-editor with Janet Boles of *Women of Color* (2001), co-editor with Jeffrey Cass of *Doing Orientalisms: Theories and Practices* (2005), co-editor with Donna Schuster of *Written on the Bodily Text: Women and Creativity Across Cultures* (2005), editor of a special issue on Romantic Drama (*European Romantic Review* 2003), and editor of *Wuthering Heights* (Houghton Mifflin). She is past president of the International Conference on Romanticism (2001-2003) and serves on the editorial boards of four scholarly journals. She has been coordinator of Marquette University's Women's Studies program since 1993.